The Harrowsmith Reader
Volume II

Edited by James Lawrence

The Second Anthology from
Canada's National Award
Winning Magazine of
Country Life and
Alternatives to Bigness

A permanent reference edition
with material selected from
Issues Number Thirteen to
Number Twenty-Five

Camden House Publishing Ltd.

ISBN 0-920656-10-2 (Softcover)
ISBN 0-920656-11-0 (Hardcover)

Trade distribution by Firefly Books, Toronto, Ontario

Printed in Canada for
Camden House Publishing Ltd.
Queen Victoria Road
Camden East, Ontario
K0K 1J0

Cover Illustration by Roger Hill

The Harrowsmith Reader Volume II

Editor
James Lawrence

Associate Editors
Jennifer Bennett, Frank B. Edwards
Elinor Campbell Lawrence, Thomas Pawlick

Copy Editors
Alice O'Connell, Susan Cross, Joanna Dean
Pamela Cross, Dorrie Matthews, David Archibald

Design & Layout
Pamela McDonald, Lynn Dumbleton, Jennifer Ferguson

Typesetting
Johanna Troyer

General Manager
John R. Page

Contributors
Bob Anderson, Frank Appleton, Donalda Badone, Paul Bailey
Donna Barnett, Marlene Anne Bumgarner, John Bianchi
Larry Bracegirdle, Aili Förbom Brown, Jack Chiang, Harold Clark
Lisl Dennis, Frank A. Edwards, John Foster, Dr. William Friend
Richard Garrett, Larry Dale Gordon, Katherine Gifford, Ian Grainge
Ted Grant, Bart Hall-Beyer, Marian E. Harbard, Peter Hutchinson
Des Kennedy, Gerry Kenney, Edi Klopfenstein, Gerry Kopelow
Stephen Krasemann, Ulrich Kretschmar, David Ladd, Whitney L. Lane
Mickey Lammers, William Lammers, Drew Langsner, Louise Langsner
Andris Leimanis, Wayne Lennox, Elizabeth A. Long, Helen Mason
Tim Matson, Don McCallum, C.D. McKeen, Patricia Mestern
Pat Michener, Ted Michener, Bill Milliken, Merilyn Mohr, Rudy Muller
Alice Nangeroni, William Nunnelley, Maureen Paxton
Graham Pilsworth, Stephen Pitt, Kathleen Poff, Mike Poole
Matthew Radz, Catharine Reed, R.R. Sallows, Al Satterwhite
A.F. Sherf, Terry Shoffner, J. Peter Shinnick, Hal Smith, Ernie Sparks
David Square, David Stone, Ted Streshinsky, Al Sugerman
George Thomas, Martha Tobe, Dr. Stephen Tobe, Rene Tunney
Dr. Philip Warman, Geoff Wells, Mike Wells, Stephanie Wells
Elizabeth White, Robert G. White, J.D. Wilson, Horst Wolfe
Don Woodcock

Cohorts
Linda Abrams, Elaine Alkenbrack, Annette Baillargeon
Dianne Bartlett, Sandra Chalk, John H. Colville, Diane Dowling
Cheryl Empey, Gordon Flagler, Elizabeth Gardiner, Ruth Geddes
Margaret Hewitt, Carole Johnson, Mary Ann Lee, Ellen Maclean
Belle Micks, Brian Parker, Magret Paudyn, Pamela Richmond
Leslie Schültz, Wayne Skinner, Glenda Smith, Jim Thomson
Susan Woodend, Diane Young

Contents

Introductions

Never having been provoked to give a deeper answer, we have, for the past four years, described the birthplace of *Harrowsmith* as the kitchen table of an eastern Ontario farmhouse in 1976. People seemed cheered by the notion of a national magazine rising out of such circumstances, but the venerable table has been written and talked about to the point of becoming infamous among the editorial staff; mentioning it here breaks a personal resolution, as well as a promise to the copy editors, to burn, cast in bronze or otherwise file away all thought of the table and never write about it again.

Having recently been prodded by an interviewer to recount the history and philosophy upon which the magazine, and this book, are founded, I have found myself sitting at the unmentionable table, giving some late-night thought to retracing the mental pathway that stretches back from the actual physical genesis of *Harrowsmith*.

If memory of the actual moment of conception remains blurred, we can, at least, track things back to a student hotel/apartment in the Colombian town of Pasto sometime late in 1970. This particular residence served as home and flophouse for a number of Peace Corps, CUSO and Dutch-sponsored volunteers. It was the place where we occasionally indulged in a monthly hot shower and a two-night binge at the local movie houses, whose tastes ran mostly to spaghetti westerns with occasional relief provided by flawed copies of not-so-very-old American and British films.

Elinor and I were working at the time with the country's land reform agency in a mountain valley two and a half hours to the east, providing agricultural advice to 32 Sibundoy Indian families who, with government assistance, had recently bought their land back from the Catholic church. We lived in a village with sporadic electrical power (6 P.M. to 11 P.M. on the best of days), equally untrustworthy water supply (usually augmented by twice-daily bucket expeditions to the stream) and a doorless, seatless privy. We cooked over a one-burner kerosene stove, read by candlelight, bathed in a dishpan and tried to dispel the high altitude Andean cold with a barrel stove of our own (inept) design.

In addition to the bemusement of using an ancient toilet with a navy blue butterfly etched in the bottom of the porcelain bowl, the forays into town provided an exposure to fresh reading matter, and we can recall with some clarity the evening when we first encountered *The Whole Earth Catalog*. Oblivious to the volunteer party in progress, we sat reading descriptions of windmills, seed catalogues, air-

tight stoves and Aladdin lamps. Transfixed, we read until dawn, drinking resinous Chilean wine, ignoring the flea population of the mattress below and coming to a new awareness of alternative technology and communications.

We came to agonize over the lack of appropriate tools and information in Colombia, but worked, with mixed success, at opening up access to breeding stock, seeds, reforestation stock and professional advice for the farm families in the valley. Returning to Canada to settle on a farm of our own, we were surprised to discover that good information and alternative technology were only slightly less difficult to come by than in the mountains of South America.

Reading every alternative publication which we managed to find, we found a general lack of the kind of detailed information we were seeking and a very specific lack of anything with more than a cursory nod toward Canadian readers. Well aware of our own needs, and with the assumption that there must be many more like us throughout the country, we eventually came forth with *Harrowsmith*.

In the four years covered by this anthology and its earlier companion volume, we have seen the magazine move first into an abandoned bank building, then into a more spacious 100-year-old farmhouse. Paid circulation has grown to 150,000, and, using the standard magazine industry calculation of 3.2 readers per copy, our total readership is roughly one-half million people.

Clearly, a communications void had existed, and, just as clearly, the desire to achieve greater independence — in energy, food supply and one's day-to-day way of life — continues as strong as in the heady days of the Whole Earth movement a decade ago. However, as the articles in the collection show, we have come to realize the complexity involved in reaching anything approaching personal self-sufficiency.

Moving to the country does not automatically simplify one's life, as the first chapter of this book amply illustrates; buying an aerogenerator does not automatically cut one's ties to the power grid; ordering a carton of seed by mail does not automatically fill the freezer or root cellar.

We would like to think that the articles in this volume will help preserve the excitement of discovering that there are attractive, intelligent alternatives to the conventional ways of thinking and doing things, while at the same time tempering that enthusiasm with enough pragmatism and hard-learned information to help translate ideas and ideals into sustained realities.

—JL

Camden House, a former farmhouse which is now the home of Harrowsmith.

Scott Nearing, Architect Of The Good Life

"This yen for the wilderness, for adventure, this yen to break out of the ordinary is common to every generation...."

By Hal Smith with photography by Richard Garrett

In the paradoxical way that those who gladly follow schedules seem not to be bound by them, Scott Nearing rises every day at 4:30 A.M. and begins work on his latest manuscript. A homesteading, Maine ex-professor of economics, perhaps the oldest revolutionary in North America, he has written a book or pamphlet every year since 1908 and in his "Future Writing" notebook, which he has carried in his pocket since 1932, he has 14 more books to go.

In two or three hours he and his wife have breakfast: no bacon, eggs, toast and coffee — just apples, sunflower seeds and black molasses drink. Hardly the breakfast of champions? The proof is, as they say, in the pudding: Though he is 94, Nearing can quickly count the number of times he has visited a doctor in the last 40 years.

After breakfast the grunt work begins. It takes 12 cords of wood to get through the New England winter and Nearing fells the trees, cuts and splits them by hand — he doesn't like to wet-nurse fuming machines, he says, hence no chain saw. The artificial pond behind the century-old clapboard farmhouse

often needs attention, though Nearing has already lugged 14,000 wheelbarrows of dirt to create it. It took him 18 years.

Then there's the new house.

It is much like the old one on the Nearings' first homestead in Vermont, where they lived in a roomy, two-storey, native stone home of his own design until skiers, vacationers and developers began to crowd in. Though they'd spent 20 years there, building more than a dozen stone buildings and working a 4,200-bucket maple sugarbush (with seven miles of tubing running downhill to the evaporator), they sold out and started over again — when Scott was 70 years old.

He and his wife, Helen, cleared the building site of the dense forest, including stumps, none of which were pulled or dynamited. The Nearings took months to chop them out and, though there was ample standing firewood, they salvaged what they could for the chunk stove in the kitchen. The rocks from the excavation were sorted into five piles: cornerstones, wall stones, chimney stones, granite and

A man who was living today's ideas yesterday: Scott Nearing, 94, hand cultivating his 15,000-square-foot vegetable garden.

brick. The topsoil and sod were hauled to the numbered — Nearing is scrupulously organized — compost piles next to the garden, which supplies roughly 80 per cent of what the two of them need.

Every precisely-placed plant in the vegetable garden (roughly 150' by 100') seen against the carpetlike background of the black-grey earth is a photographic specimen of its kind. No weeds, not a stray blade of grass intrudes. The order and symmetry have cursed the Nearings by attracting frequent visits by garden clubs.

NOTORIOUS PAST

The four-foot wall enclosing the garden is built of fieldstones gleaned from the rest of the homestead, 100 acres of timberland on Cape Rosier, with a view of a cove opening into Penobscot Bay and then into the ocean. Spruce and hemlock stipple the clear,

crisp sky, the air smelling of the sea and the rich, black earth Nearing turns by pushing a hand cultivator.

Helen, 74, is tending mint, growing along the outside of the garden wall which, counting the first seven years for gathering stones, took them 14 years to build, 60 feet for seven summers. She stops, looking down the two-mile jeep road toward the sound of a vehicle. A pickup pulls lazily up the driveway.

"Hello!" she calls. "Helloooo!"

The driver, pretending not to hear, points from side to side, his passenger rubbernecking in each direction as the truck makes a U-turn in front of the house, and then slowly disappears in its own dust.

"Tourists," Helen sighs.

It's been like that for several years, publicity and admirers poking their way back into Scott Nearing's austere life after he decided to quit the headlines and dropped out 50 years ago. In 1928, by the time he was 45, he had become notorious. He had been blacklisted and booted out of several university teaching positions, beginning in 1910 when his first dismissal

People brought up in a money economy are taught to believe in the importance of getting and keeping money. Time and again folk told us, "You can't afford to make syrup. You won't make any money that way."

One year a neighbour, Harold Field, kept a careful record of the labour he put in during the syrup season and of the sale price of his product, and figured that he got only 67 cents an hour for his time. In view of these figures, the next year he did not tap out because sugaring paid less than wage labour. But, during that syrup season he found no chance to work for wages, so he didn't even make the 67 cents an hour.

Our attitude was quite different. We kept careful cost figures, but we never used them to determine whether we should or should not make syrup. We tapped our trees as each sap season came along. Our figures showed us what the syrup had cost. When the season was over and the syrup on hand, we wrote to various correspondents in California and Florida, told them what our syrup had cost, and exchanged our product for equal value of their citrus, walnuts, olive oil or raisins. As a result of these transactions, we laid in a supply of items at no cash outlay, which we could not ourselves produce.

We also sold our syrup and sugar on the open market. In selling anything, we tried to determine exact costs and set our prices not in terms of what the traffic would bear but in terms of the costs — figuring our own time at going day wages.
— Living The Good Life

started an historic battle over academic freedom: He had been working vigorously to keep children under 14 out of factories, but powerful interests in the state legislature, who profited from child labour, compelled state university trustees to fire him. Later, when he led the pacifists' fight against World War I, the federal raid on his home was the first of the war.

When he was accused of sedition, ostensibly for writing a pamphlet encouraging draft resistance, his trial making daily front-page news, he used the occasion to read his "seditious" book aloud to the jury and the press. He was acquitted. Eventually he would be barred from England for denouncing British empire-building, and drummed out of the Communist Party for "correcting" Marx.

Through his 25-year career as a "pacifist revolutionary" — the phrase seems quaint now — he gave as many as 400 lectures a year, debated Bertrand Russell, Clarence Darrow and Paul Douglas, and was defeated by Fiorello LaGuardia in a congressional race. Nearing never walked away from a fight, taking on all challengers. But by the time the Depression arrived, he had lost two tough split decisions: his academic career was destroyed and he was a radical out of step with the Established Left. When he and Helen decided to drop out and begin homesteading, he was still very much his own man.

"I never decided to do what some of my associates did — live out of a garbage can in various parts of Manhattan," he says.

"I had a feeling, which I still hold, that in a militant situation the decisions should not be made by older people but by younger people. It was a sort of extension of the Indian principle: first a student, then a householder, then a sage. I think this is sound. When I was 45 I dropped out of all political activity, not because I wanted to drop out of it, but because I knew perfectly well — from watching Sam Gompers and Eugene Debs and others who continued to work politically in their 70's and 80's — that a man that old is not as vigorous and as vital as he was when he was in his 20's, 30's and 40's. And I said I would never stick around in a position of authority in the left-wing movement as these other people had done when my period of maximum usefulness was past. So at about 45 I resigned all my committees and party connections and I've never been active in politics since.

"Another factor behind the decision to drop out was that what had been an alternative to teaching, namely free-lance lecturing and writing, which had gone very well through the period of muckraking on down through the early 30's — this period came to an end. It had been possible when there were 5,000 socialist locals in the U.S. to go to almost any city, ask where the socialist local was, find a literature committee, a lecture hall or forum or other things going on. This period came to an end. And people like me, talking on the left, had less and less opportunity to talk.

"Of course the third element entering the picture was that the Depression of 1928-38 came along at the same time. So these various factors made it essential to find an alternative way of earning a livelihood. We decided to set up a self-contained homestead society rather than to try to fit into a market economy. We had to have a place to live, clothing and food. We got all those things by producing them ourselves or substituting something for them."

He was 50, she 30 when they took to the wild Vermont hills and started a new life. While Nearing has hardly remained silent for four decades, he had slipped into relative obscurity until another generation began discovering health foods and organic gardening, women's rights, educational reform, radicalism, homesteading, vegetarianism, ecology and black liberation. Only Nearing had written more than 50 volumes on those trendy issues decades ago: his black lib book was published in 1929, his homesteading books in 1950 and 1954, his women's rights book in 1912.

So naturally, by the late sixties, Nearing was again a public figure. He had, as a *New York Times* headline said of him, "lived today's ideas yesterday." The Nearings' privately printed book, *Living The Good Life,* an account of their homesteading experience, had sold less than 5,000 copies in 15 years. But with the help of Pearl Buck, a former neighbour in Vermont, it was re-issued by Shocken Books, and promptly sold 50,000 copies. *Newsweek* called it "an underground bible," Ashley Montagu termed it "a

An inspiration for two generations of "back-to-the-landers," the Nearings have achieved an enviable balance between intellectual pursuits and what they call "bread labour."

new kind of Walden,'' and soon the interviewers from the *Wall Street Journal* to *Mother Earth News* went in search of the man who rebelled, dropped out and pioneered a life style decades before the new peasants were born.

Mike Wallace vied with the *Today Show* for permission to film at Forest Farm, and Nearing appeared with David Frost and other talkies. On another TV occasion he showed Dinah Shore how to split a log. Publishers, who for years had been uninterested in his books, sat up and took notice. Harper & Row bought Nearing's autobiography, *The Making of a Radical*, surrendering any right to edit it.

BURNING THE BONDS

Nearing insisted on that, probably because he is genuinely suspicious of publishers. Prior to World War I, Macmillan had published six of his books but when the war broke out — and Nearing's antiwar activities attracted publicity — his publishers dumped him. Fearing such a notorious figure would hurt textbook sales, Macmillan remaindered all his books.

Eventually, when no one would touch his stuff, he simply started his own publishing operation, the Social Science Institute, under whose imprimatur *Living The Good Life* first appeared. The institute consists entirely of three part-time workers (the Nearings and a distant secretary), a file cabinet, the hand-hewn table in the Nearing kitchen and a garage on the farm called the "book barn." Distribution, the high hurdle that trips up almost all such operations, is slow, simple and, for a man of patience, effective: Nearing hawks his titles in the classified pages of the counter-culture.

Sales barely creep along, but then the Nearings aren't in it for the money. When asked if independent publishing has been a success, Scott thought the question was funny. "Well," he chuckles, "we're surviving, we pay our bills." In fact, all his life he had paid his dues while dodging even the appearance of "getting something for nothing." He once rejected a sizeable inheritance, and sold their Vermont homestead for perhaps 25 per cent of its market value. During the thirties he discovered that he owned bonds worth $60,000. He contemplated his bank account for a few days, then burned the bonds.

"If I am rich and you are poor," he says, "both of us are corrupted by the inequality."

When scandalized friends tell him how much good he could have done with all the money he has refused to accept — by, say, funding a "worthy cause" — Nearing recalls his 10 years as a trustee of the Garland Fund, founded to promote left-wing causes. That decade of decisions totally soured him on private philanthropy.

"It may help an individual get through an emergency, but subsidies to institutions make the subsidized satisfied with handouts, and they'll be back for more before the ink is dry on the cheque. There isn't anything more corrupting than guaranteed, lasting comfort."

Helen and Scott Nearing at work on their new stone house.

Each day was divided into two main blocks of time — four morning hours and four afternoon hours. At breakfast time on weekdays we first looked at the weather, then asked, "How shall we arrange the day?"

Suppose the morning was assigned for bread labour (such as gardening, wood-cutting, sugarmaking, construction and repairs). We then agreed upon the tasks each should take on. If one's bread labour was performed in the morning, the afternoon automatically became personally directed. One might read, sit in the sun, walk in the woods, play music, go to town. We earned four hours of leisure by our four hours of labour.

—Living The Good Life

If Nearing's view of work and money rings ironic it is because he believes in self-reliance and honest work every bit as much as does the stereotypical capitalist he has been denouncing all his life.

But ideology is hardly the only reason for Nearing's lean life style. After being in the thick of history, warring with some of the best minds of the century, he has learned how to thrive on hard work and long-term challenge, as much because he enjoys it as for the fact that he was born in Pennsylvania, read Thoreau and lives in New England. He has very nearly broken down the distinction between work and play, a feat which would make any flower child salivate. When he is working in the garden, you'd never guess his winter menu depended on it. Small-scale farming is a demanding, serious business and every mistake hurts, but Nearing seems as happy at it as the hobbying weekend tulip tender. Whether he is chopping wood, building a house, whatever, he delights in finding out just how efficiently and skillfully he can do the job. If, in the beginning, it was his steel-willed guts which made him disavow "easy living," as he calls it, being a self-starter is no problem now. It all comes naturally because he has set up a semi-private world in which he rarely does anything he doesn't like.

COMPOST POLITICS

And who can say his self-inflicted quasi-poverty is eccentric? "My economic balance sheet shows not a penny of debt, a very low overhead and a small cash balance." Financial security in old age could very well have put him in the retirement resorts of Florida, helpless like a beached whale, waiting to suffocate. He's got to be outdoors, hefting an axe, breathing hard, seeing what he can make of the land.

Royalties, though, from the new books are going to be sizeable and even now he is planning how to give them — and the old house as well — to the nonprofit Social Science Institute, which just might become the first school with a Ph.D. teaching the politics of compost piles.

If this professor scorned by the colleges manages to pull off one last coup — by starting his own college — there will be no shortage of students. To alienated, idealistic youth — weaned on tales of cow-

boys, outlaws and pioneers — Nearing is a genuinely heroic figure. Every spring and summer scores of shaggy youths clutching one of his books make uninvited pilgrimages to Forest Farm looking for advice and encouragement. Traffic and mail has become so heavy that he has had to print a form letter asking would-be visitors to respect his need for privacy.

But when visitors and interviewers do show up, there aren't any problems of protocol; visitors aren't entertained, they are simply allowed to tag along or pitch in.

"Good afternoon," Helen says, greeting one guest in the front yard, "I'm so glad you didn't come all dressed up. The *Wall Street Journal* man came in his old clothes, too. It was awfully cute of him. We thought maybe he'd be here in a suit and bowler hat."

(Helen was little more than half his age, with a promising future as a violinist, when she met Nearing. Her father, a banker and one of seven Democrats in Ridgefield, N.J., had invited Nearing to town to lecture. Her father's courage paled next to Nearing's. She was impressed.)

"Scotto, Scotto," she calls.

He has just awakened from his one-hour midday nap and takes his guest into the garden, amiably answering questions as he works. In spite of his baggy pants and *Jets* basketball sneakers, he bears a striking resemblance to U.S. Supreme Court Justice William O. Douglas.

If he values his dwindling privacy, why does he go on television or give interviews?

Above, *a new wall takes shape, showing the slipform method of stone building that the Nearings have popularized.* **Right,** *the new home nearing completion.*

"I'm a teacher," he says, "and as a teacher I like to pass on what I know." In fact he takes his teaching seriously enough to have made a five-month world tour, speaking mainly to students in Japan and India, where his political and economic views have been translated and are still discussed.

Even though he lives with neither telephone ("people talk a lot but don't say much") nor television, he hardly feels isolated. He subscribes to more than 30 magazines and newspapers, and borrows library books by mail. Thus armed, he writes a regular column called "Current Events" for *Monthly Review,* an "old left" journal.

"In the last five years," he says, "there's been a very definite change in the number of young people who are dissatisfied with the established situation. They're looking for something different, not only reformistically, but revolutionarily different.

"Every new generation will produce a certain number of people who, in the old days, ran away and went to sea. Today they leave the city and try to find a living on the land. They're adventurous, but dissatisfied, they're unsettled, their roots aren't down anywhere and the land has a certain appeal, like the wilderness once had. Daniel Boone said he was never lost in the woods, though there were times when he didn't know for weeks exactly where he was. This yen for the wilderness, for adventure, this yen to

> **T**he main dish for supper was really a large salad, enough to provide at least one overflowing bowl per person. This salad was fruit or vegetable, depending on the garden resources. In a big wooden bowl we emulsified lemon or lime juice with rose-hip juice and olive oil, and into that cut peppers, celery, onion, radish, parsley, tomatoes, cucumbers, lettuce — whatever was growing in the garden at the time. Sometimes we shredded raw beet, carrot, squash, celery root, turnip and made a compete salad, with celery, nuts and raisins, lemon and oil. In winter, white or red cabbage was the bulk item instead of lettuce. To this we added cut up apples, nuts, oranges or grapefruit and celery. In summer we could add raw young peas, tips of asparagus or fresh raw corn.
>
> All of our meals were eaten at a wooden plank table, in wooden bowls, the same bowl right through the meal. This practically eliminated the dish-washing problem. With no sauces, no frying and the like, there were few dishes to wash and pans to scrub.
>
> — **Living The Good Life**

break out of the ordinary is common to part of every young generation. They go to war, or to Europe for an education, or they may go out on the land, which is what they're doing at the moment. And those of them who succeed will stay there.

"Now we're experiencing the fruiting of this experiment of ours. A great many people are becoming interested, not because of what we've been saying but because they're facing situations similar to what we faced in the twenties and thirties. At that time it was still possible for young people to look forward to some kind of self-respecting career. But now we're in a period where there are a lot of young people looking for jobs. Not only looking for a particular job, but *any* job. Meanwhile the central cities are deteriorating and becoming ugly and repulsive. The newer generation feels that very strongly; the older generation is accustomed to it. In the old days we didn't have smog, now we do. So the city becomes more and more invidious at the same time it offers less and less opportunity."

For beginners, however, homesteading is no easy alternative to city living unless they can learn from veterans like Nearing. In the solar greenhouse he built, for example, he proudly displays Chinese lettuce seedlings which will mature and thrive during the coming winter. He says that his technique, learned on one of his early trips to China, enables him to pick fresh, greenhouse lettuce in sub-zero weather. The design for the spillway by which his pond flows into a brook is also Chinese, and Nearing drains the pond in the summer to control mosquitoes.

On a knoll north of the house and garden is the open-faced cedar woodshed where, after 30 minutes, a reporter one-third Nearing's age had trouble manning his end of a two-man bow saw. Nearing hadn't even worked up a sweat. The shed's location on the edge of the woods protects it from winter storms and makes it easy to haul wood over snow: Nearing simply loads up a toboggan and guides it down the gentle slope to the house.

"It almost pulls itself," he says.

On the way back from the woodshed is the Rugosa rose garden, the main source of the Nearings' vitamin C. The rose hips, or Rugosa fruit, have 25 times more vitamin C than citrus juices and provide everything from tea and soup to salad ingredients.

Southeast of the house, just before the forest closes in on the meadow, is a quarter-acre patch of hybrid blueberries and raspberries, the homestead's only cash crop, covered with Japanese fishnetting to protect it from birds.

"Birds can wipe you out in a day," Nearing says, adding that the patch yields over 1,000 quarts, with the fruit reaching a peak size of nearly an inch. Next to the berry patch is a hand-built, 4,500-gallon water tank made of native stone. It is used for irrigation and filled early each season from the ice-cold spring which gravity-feeds the house. Nearing's guest was about to suggest that the tank was big enough to pass for a swimming pool and it was an awfully hot day and . . . then the dinner bell began clanging from the house.

The back door opened into the kitchen, smelling of sweet burning hardwood and drying herbs hung from the hand-hewn ceiling beams. The table was set with wooden bowls and a single wooden spoon for each diner. The menu consisted of cooked French endive, a tasty salad of mint, carrots, greens and cottage cheese, asparagus and a very exotic gelatin Helen calls "seaweed pudding," named for its heady prime ingredient. While Helen served, Scott was busy making the beverage: he chopped up some wheat grass (a garden cover crop), dumped it into a blender with some icy spring water and some pineapple juice. In a few seconds he had a pastel green brew looking very much like lime soda pop. He strained it and poured his guest a glass. While Helen's "pudding" was, well, interesting, the grass juice was fantastic, the ambrosia of the gods.

"I got the idea from King Nebuchadnezzar in the Bible," Nearing said. " 'He was driven from among men, and ate grass like an ox, and his body was wet with the dew of Heaven till his hair grew as long as eagles' feathers, and his nails like birds' claws.' "

Dinner conversation naturally turned to health and health foods. Not so long ago a 70-ish self-styled health expert, who took literally scores of vitamin and food supplement pills every day, dropped dead on a talk show after bragging how long he'd live if he weren't killed by a "sugar-crazed" cabdriver. Nearing doesn't touch pills of any sort.

"Sunshine, fresh air and clean water are health basics," Nearing says. "If you can find a market where you can get clean, fresh, unprocessed, unpoisoned food, then you've made another big step. It's increasingly possible to get such food in the U.S. Of course we emphasize raw, whole, unprocessed food, as directly as possible from the source. No drugs, no stimulants, no condiments, no sugar, no salt, no spices."

In keeping with their pacifism, there's never any meat or fish on the Nearings' table and, with the ex-

ception of cottage cheese, there aren't any dairy products or eggs either. (Helen was mildly horrified when her guest unwittingly enquired where he could buy live Maine lobsters to take home to his boiling pot.) Scott admires wild animals more than "docile, dish-fed" house pets and says he would no more domesticate an animal than enslave a man.

"Animal husbandry involves building and maintaining outbuildings, mending fences, chasing strays and cutting or buying hay. And, while draft animals work occasionally, they eat regularly, many eating more than they produce. I don't intend to become an agrarian chambermaid, feeding, tending and cleaning up after them."

If for no other reason, Nearing can't keep stock or pets because they would restrict his travels, one of his regular winter activities. Over the years he has been to all the mainland states several times each, lecturing and pamphleteering, and he has trekked all over the world, including the Iron Curtain countries.

THE COMING "TURNABOUT"

Obviously he is unsympathetic to violence as a tactic, which even among the young now seems passé. If so, what are the prospects for his life's goal — a non-violent revolution via the ballot, a "complete turnabout" of the system?

"One of the most interesting revolutions that has

Scott Nearing, proponent of vegetarian self-sufficiency: "I don't intend to become an agrarian chambermaid (to livestock), feeding, tending and cleaning up after them."

occurred in the U.S. during my lifetime is a complete turning away from the idea that you ought to pay a worker as little as possible.

"When I was young there was a business in Pittsburgh that paid 90 cents a day. The director of the firm was called 'Ninety-Cent Oliver.' Henry Ford came along a little later. He was paying his workers $1.50 a day and he proposed to make a car that cost $600. He figured out that it would take a worker, if he had a family, a long, long time before he could ever afford to buy a car.

"So Henry Ford did two things. He said: First I'm going to pay a minimum wage of $5 a day — I'm going up from $1.50 to $5. Second I'll loan you the money to buy the car and you'll pay me back over a certain period of time, and, in the meantime, you'll be driving to and from work in the car.

"Now this introduced what is now called the mass market. Henry Ford sold his Model T's by the millions because wages were raised and consumer credit was established. It was a complete turnabout from the days of Ninety-Cent Oliver.

"Today we say, in order to be self-respecting, we've got to have X dollars a week. This is the mini-

Above, *the year-round solar greenhouse that keeps salad greens and other vegetables on the Nearings' table even in the deep of Maine's cold winters. Sunlight that warms dark soil and stone walls is sufficient to keep hardy crops alive and healthy.* **Left,** *Scott Nearing thinning baby carrots.*

mum wage. If you pay less than that, you can't sell typewriters, bicycles, automobiles and TV's. Increasingly our economy is maintained by selling these rather expensive consumer goods. Therefore we pay the worker enough so he can afford to buy them."

Helen interjected. "If I've followed you this far," she said, "you're saying there could be an economic rather than a political revolution that — "

"No," Scott said, "I'm saying that this was one of the most impressive revolutions I've seen. Revolution means a complete turnabout."

So, then, he thinks a radical change is feasible in the U.S. without violence?

"Of course."

If his hopes for the future sound optimistic, his view of his own destiny is, more or less, incredible. Nearing has been interested in Oriental religions and the occult, particularly reincarnation, for about five decades. His belief, that, in some form, he will live forever is more than an article of faith, the kind of crutch the aged need to sleep and keep nightmares at bay. No, Nearing has stood on his own feet all his life, without regard for his personal safety or security. It is his belief that there is always a tomorrow which also allows him to live as if there weren't. That is why, at 94, he is in the midst of settling into a new house.

"The old place was never insulated," he says. "Besides, a man has got to keep busy."

Sometimes an Impossible Notion

Why some homesteaders fail

Illustrations by Graham Pilsworth

Intent on simplifying his life and "making the earth say beans instead of grass," Henry David Thoreau took to the woods on July 4, 1845. Living in a one-room cabin he built with his own hands, Thoreau spent the best years of his life on the shores of Walden Pond, practising his philosophy of "plain living and high thinking."

His noble experiment, of course, helped spawn a back-to-the-land movement a century later, but what is often forgotten is that Thoreau only lasted two years and two months at Walden Pond. "I left the woods," he later wrote, "for as good a reason as I went there. Perhaps it seemed to me that I had several more lives to live and could not spare any more time for that one."

Henry David Thoreau left the cabin in the woods with his philosophy intact, but more than one hundred years later there are those who return from the country disillusioned and feeling they have failed. We suspect that the great majority of those who attempt the great urban-rural transition today succeed — although in ways they could not have predicted before undertaking the move — because they are better prepared and more realistic than the first wave of back-to-the-landers in the 1960s.

Still, those who fail interest us. Their experiences, if we knew more about them, could be highly informative — especially to anyone now contemplating a move to the country. Hoping to shed some light on the possible pitfalls of a homesteading life, we asked a number of Harrowsmith contributors to answer the question: Why do (some) homesteaders fail?

These writers, of course, have a built-in bias: they have proved to themselves that success as "homesteaders" — although most would reject this title — is possible. Nevertheless, they have seen the comings and goings of others who didn't make it on the land and, in the articles that follow, offer their best advice on how not to repeat the most common mistakes. In reading these pieces, some would-be homesteaders may find their dreams shaken, may find themselves thinking twice about what they intend to do. If this is the case, this special section will have served its purpose admirably.

By Mike Wells

Jerry was predestined to fail in his venture into rural living. His age (early 20s), background (metropolitan Chicago), and diet regimen (strict vegetarian) were but a few of his shortfalls. There was also the matter of adequate funds. And a wife back in Chicago who doted on convenience food and the joys of urban life. Jerry, on the other hand, had a commitment. But unfortunately, that's all he had; and a desire or commitment, no matter how pervasive, is not enough to cope with the realities of "back-to-the-landing."

We met him through correspondence via a mutual friend. He'd write telling of his map search of the entire U.S. Northwest and his evaluation of the desirability of our area. We'd reply, warning him of the potential pitfalls: of inclement weathers and short growing seasons, of the scarcity of available land other than six-figure ranches.

Undaunted, he arrived here one June day in a pick-up/camper with $2,000 in the bank. We fixed him up with a place to camp for a few days until he got his bearings, and introduced him to the real estate agents in the area. There was, of course, nothing to be had for a down payment of a thousand or so. As a matter of fact, there was little to be had at any price. A month later we began to get restive. His few days of orientation stretched into weeks as he scoured the area and ate away at his depleting resources. When he rolled his pickup one day on a back country road, looking for a non-existent piece of property, we spent the following two days jacking his camper back into shape.

"Enough, Jerry. We've had it. You've got to move on."

He did. His next letter said that he was living in a trailer park a couple of counties over and had a job as a house painter. His wife had joined him, but she hated the trailer and she hated the town and she

hated the people and she hated the land. His final communiqué was from Chicago, telling us that he was back at his old job.

Though Jerry might not be typical of those inspired by the dream of a slower-paced life style, of growing one's own, of communing with nature, he is an example of some who harbour a dream so engrossing as to preclude attention to rural reality.

Chuck and Diane moved to our remote environs a couple of years ago out of one of the suburban bedrooms of Los Angeles. And they brought it all with them. Everything but the smog. The first time we called on them at their 20-acre farmette, we left in a state of shock. We had been at their place many times during years when it was occupied by other friends who were renting. It was an older farmhouse, and our earlier friends had retained in it the warmth and feeling of eras gone by. But with the later visit, the assault upon our optics of rooms full of plastic swag lamps and vinyl couches and leatherette chairs made us feel as though we had never left the city.

"What are you planning on doing here, Chuck?" I asked.

"Earthworms," Chuck replied. "I'm going to make it on earthworms."

When I made discreet enquiry as to where he intended to market them, he waved this and other questions aside. "I've got that all figured out," he said.

Shortly thereafter, he went to work as a menial at the mill. When the mill closed, he went to work as a menial on the railroad. When the railroad closed, he fled back to Los Angeles, leaving sturdy wife Diane to take care of things. She did. She divorced him.

"How was the City?" we asked Dan, when he returned from a short trip to San Francisco to take care of some unfinished business.

"Those burgers sure tasted good," he replied.

Some subtle prescience within us noted this as the beginning of the end. The end of a partnership, and very nearly the termination of a close friendship of many years.

Dan and Betty had come here to our 160 two months before our own arrival on the scene. His teaching contract had not been renewed, but I had to stick out the city grind until the end of the fiscal year, to reap the last year's profit sharing. We were equal partners, such an arrangement having been agreed upon years before. Whoever found that place in the country first would give the other the option of buying in.

Oh, the joys of planning during those last months in the city. There would be, eventually, a hand-hewn log sauna on the ledge below the big spring, and a barn, modest, but certainly of gambrel roof, and a pit solar greenhouse on the south slope, and so on, ad infinitum.

Then, Something Happened. In the two-month interim between their arrival and ours, they had changed. At first, so happy to have nested here, we thought we were to blame. We with our city ways versus them, after two rural months, the seasoned homesteaders. Though in years past, Dan and I had worked beautifully together, each knowing when the other needed a tool or nail or lift, such rapport vanished.

There were occasional good times, still. Evenings over a shared jug of cheap red, with Dan and me flailing at our guitars, autoharps and banjoes in maudlin renditions of Dylan or traditional folk, and stumbling through the verses of San Francisco Bay Blues, but by the morrow, the mutuality of work and interests had again waned.

By summer's end, Dan and Betty had decided to return to the urban southland. The many nights spent in the glow of our single Aladdin lamp, totting up who owed what to whom, dealt the final blow to our visions of fellow farming. Our friendship survives, but we doubt that it could have weathered a few more months like that disjunctive summer.

Having asked ourselves "What Happened?" many times through the years, we can only relate the divisions and problems to those which we have encountered on numerous occasions in the past, when we have taken friends to remote areas. Generally, they have been unable to cope with the rugged environs. To put it more succinctly, when they got away from their familiars, they sometimes freaked. Like the guy who brought a charger on a trip deep into Baja California in the event his battery ran down. The nearest AC plug was 200 miles away. (This cretin also took along a pearl-handled .38 for protection against the natives.)

In retrospect, why did Jerry fail, Chuck and Diane divorce and Dan and Betty return to the comforting blanket of smog and the delights of Big Macs? Jerry, despite a driving desire, was totally naïve in his approach. His inadequate funds, unsympathetic mate, and preconceived constriction to a geographic area were but a few of his problems. His advocacy of strict vegetarianism didn't help either. In his insistence on raw foods only, he'd as soon have ingested a soyburger as a pork chop. Just where he was going to get his raw greens in an environment that boasts a growing season which, in some years, may only run for 60 to 70 days never entered his mind. I have no quarrel with the vegetarian diet. In fact, with the continually rising cost of animal protein, we, by necessity, are verging on a quasi-vegetarianism ourselves, but fish and fowl still constitute a large part of our nourishment. Soybeans? Great. Problem is, they won't grow here, nor will rice. Man cannot live by lettuce alone.

Chuck (of the earthworms) had more than a plenitude of support. Diane was way beyond your everyday average earth-mother. She tended the flocks. She became an expert horse-person so she could make some income riding range for neighbouring ranchers. She put in the garden and raised the crops. She rebuilt the derelict bridge across the creek. All the while Chuck dreamed of earthworms. And while he relaxed over a pre-prandial drink after a "hard day" on the railroad, she did the chores. The meals, too, were, of course, her responsibility. He was, in a nutshell, a lazy, no-good slob. Whatever impelled him from his snug place in suburbia to our valley, we'll never know. Certainly not the earning of earthworm dollars. That requires work, and work was his least favourite endeavour.

Diane, on the other hand, is still in the country, having sold out and relocated in another rural area where her talents as a bookkeeper might enjoy some recompense. She and her son took their horses and milk pails with them, so we assume they are still determined ruralites.

ONE HAPPY ENDING

There was another couple. They were mature, with a background in the upwardly mobile life style of contemporary urban living. Seven years ago they decided to make a commitment to country living, and the Devil and the creditors take the hindmost. Being of moderate means, they totted the balance sheets and found that they could, in the pre-inflation early '70s, get by on $250 a month. But one year into country life their income from a second mortgage dissolved into a legal imbroglio involving fraud, grand theft and maybe even petty larceny. Overnight, a $10,000 piece of paper became worthless.

When their cherished $250 disappeared into a legal jungle from which there was no extrication, the couple was bereft, and destitute, their dreams shattered. The 80-mile view offered little solace, and though the two gurgling uphill springs submitted no monthly bills, it was small compensation for the loss.

The man's saintly, bromidial, late New England aunt would have claimed it "a blessing in disguise." At that time the pair had short shrift for either Babbitts or bromides, but she might have been right. The enforced penury and consequent shrinkage of savings left them but two alternatives: return to the rat-race, or make it in the country no matter what. They could not go to work. Not in a county where the only jobs available were tree murder or truck-jockeying the corpses to the mill.

So the writing that they had been dilettanting around with became a more serious enterprise. Occasional acceptances and cheques slowed the plummeting trend of the bank balance. For additional funds he turned his hobbies of knifemaking and smoking cheese into profitmaking ventures. The couple stayed.

So this is a story with several failures and one happy ending. The couple was Joanie (Jeanette MacDonald) and me (Nelson Eddy) and we're still here, despite the problems. True, our income still qualifies us for the sub-poverty bracket, but it wins hands-down over a fat income back there somewhere, with the concomitant inhalation of asbestos fibres on the freeways. If my lungs succumb to carcinoma, I want it to be my pipe smoke that did it, not some anonymous brake lining.

Some succeed in the rural renaissance; others don't. For those who have enjoyed success, the following will be ancient history. To those in transition, it may stimulate or depress. For those still trapped, it would be well to ponder before telling the boss what he can do with your job.

Upon removing to the country, first comes the "culture shock." Though some learned PhD probably coined the term, it is a reality which must be faced. There are no more nearby friends asking you over for a drink and stimulating conversation. No more convenience food. The nearest movie is (in our case) 90 miles distant. In learning to live and fraternize with people who have tilled and farmed and ranched the land for generations, you'll find they don't take kindly to your book-learned wholistic gardening or new-fangled solar assists. They've been using cheap energy for decades and don't want to hear what Soleri or the Nearings are doing with the elements they take for granted. But if he says, "Damn, you know what my last gas bill was?" talk softly and he just might listen a bit.

TALENTS UNLEASHED

Remember Jerry? Just commitment isn't enough. Adequate financial responsibility is mandatory. No matter how devoted to the land, you can't live there if you can't make the mortgage payments.

Remember Diane? She is a more than competent bookkeeper, but in these parts there was no need for her talent and she had to move on. Remember her ex-husband, Chuck? He had no resources in a resourceless area.

I recall a cartoon showing a guy with a whole yard of spread-out equipment. He was lying on his back under a pickup with a wrench in one hand, remarking to another party: "Mechanic, welder, electrician, carpenter, agronomist, labourer, ditch digger. I wonder why they call us 'farmers'?" That says it all. One of the most rewarding experiences of back-to-the-landing can be the unleashing of latent talents which were sublimated in the city. Often, a person who didn't know, back there, the difference between a clevis pin and a pinion finds him or herself out there installing a new rear axle on the rig because the other one was broken by grossly overloading the truck to bring in a load of gravel for the new greenhouse. Not everyone, however, has what it takes to learn to cope, and to those I would suggest they come well-funded in order to hire the services they will certainly need.

Jumping from a sheared axle to culture, I come to the matter of cultural deprivation. This is not to be confused with culture shock which is likely to come early on. If one survives the latter and feels "home free," he'd be well advised to watch for the delayed effects of the cultural deprivation syndrome. This usually manifests itself when you find yourself and your partner saying big words to one another. Not in a spirit of contest, for who gives a damn about interlocutory polemics? But the practice keeps the old larynx and cerebrum in shape, and in the deepest of winters, might urge such debates as who composed Brahms' First or who wrote *Ulysses*, Homer or Joyce?

Dedication is perhaps the operative noun. Dedication sufficient to cope with the inevitable adversity. Bobbie Burns said it in his oft misquoted: "The best laid schemes o' mice an' men/ Gang aft a-gley."

To go back to the land in these times probably requires as much or more dedication than that of our forebears. They had little choice. The land was there to be settled and tamed. It was the only thing to do if one chose to be a countryman. They grubbed and worked the land from its raw and sometimes spiteful virginity into viable farms and ranches. Even when they broke their butts in so doing, most of them persevered. If they hadn't, a lot of us wouldn't be around today debating the hows and wherefores. Those of us who choose to emulate them would do well to follow the best of their example: determination and perseverence.

Thoreau's admonition to "simplify, simplify" is as valid today as when it was written. What he neglected to add was that it isn't easy. But what of real worth is?

Can You Make It?

Seven questions for would-be homesteaders

By Gerry Kenney

Ralph Edwards started homesteading in the British Columbia interior when he was 22 years old. He was a self-taught, textbook pioneer, having immersed himself in agricultural books for four years. When he rode and walked the 55 miles from Bella Coola to his 160-acre homestead in the wilderness, he thought he was ready.

For the next 10 years, Ralph hacked out his farm from the towering Douglas firs and built his house, barn and other assorted buildings — alone. He constructed a raft so that he could float in cattle and horses across seven miles of lake. The motive power was Ralph at the oars of a rowboat. He brought in farm machinery piece by piece, throwing away the wooden parts which were easier to reproduce at the far end than to tote in. His sawmill, home-built of course, was run by moosehide belting soaked in bear grease. Wheel bearings were made from scorched birch.

Then one day, Ralph met a girl who lived 40 miles away. Courting Ethel wasn't easy. It required an 80-mile round trip on foot and by water. But that didn't stand in the young man's way. In 1923, Ethel became his wife and Ralph was no longer alone on the homestead.

For the next 32 years, the two of them farmed The Birches, as Ralph had dubbed his oasis in the wilderness, having three children along the way. In order to ease their isolated situation a bit, Ralph got his pilot's licence and bought a second-hand float plane — when he was 62. Now they could get some of their surplus farm produce to customers down the valley.

Ralph and Ethel did not fail as homesteaders.

Jocko and Marilyn (not their real names) also became homesteaders. They, too, were in their early 20s when they decided to take the plunge — on New Year's Eve, at a party. Together with their St. Bernard and three exotic cats, they moved into a rented farmhouse. Quiltmaking and taking in boarders would support them. Jocko and Marilyn put an ad in the newspaper for someone, preferably a couple, to share their homesteading with them.

In early March, Jocko started his seeds for the garden. Not just the tomatoes, green peppers, celery and all those things that everyone starts early, but all his seeds — his corn, his peas, snap beans, soybeans, Swiss chard, spinach — everything. The seedlings were all in little Styrofoam cups on the floor of a special room bathed in watts and watts of light. Jocko hovered over his spindly charges several times a day spraying them with a fine emulsion from an atomizer. The idea, as he explained to me, was to get a head start on the short Canadian growing season. When he would transplant his corn to the garden in May, it would already be a foot or two high, he prophesied. Only one type of plant was missing from the starting room — root crops. Jocko would not eat a root crop. That would kill the plant. Only fruit, leaves, seeds and stalks would grace their table.

Jocko and Marilyn decided they would need horses, so they arranged to buy two unbroken stallions. It seems that these were less expensive than the broken ones. They built a corral from pieces of wood held together with strong butcher's cord to contain their wild horses. The quiltmaking and tak-

ing-in-boarders business wasn't too good. Marilyn became pregnant.

Jocko and Marilyn didn't make it as homesteaders.

BLUEPRINT FOR FAILURE

Philippe Arreteau directs a soft technology research centre in southern France. In the summer of 1972, he gathered together a group of people interested in country living, provided them with a rural setting, work spaces, information and some soft technology methods to put into practice. By the end of his experiment, he concluded that the majority of the people who had been attracted to his research centre were not up to making a go of country living. He put his finger on four factors that contributed to this inability to adapt to a homesteading type of life: lack of physical stamina, lack of disciplined work habits, an underdeveloped sense of reality and insufficient manual dexterity or skills. In my contacts with various homesteaders, I have found these same four factors plus three more to be of prime importance in determining if one succeeds or fails in homesteading. Anyone pondering his or her possibilities of homestead success would be wise to consider these general areas

and the specifics that each encompasses. Anyone in whom all seven are — or can be — positively developed can almost certainly count on making a go of it. There is no score on this quiz — but if you can't foresee yourself measuring up to a majority of the obvious demands, all-out homesteading may not be for you.

STRONG DESIRE FOR THE HOME-STEADING LIFE

It is one thing to know that your job in the city is getting on your nerves and that you want out. But it is quite another thing to know that you want to be a homesteader. Many would-be homesteaders are fleeing something they dislike rather than embracing something they like. Homesteading appears attractive because living in the country seems so much more pleasant, easy and uncomplicated. Pleasant, yes. Easy and uncomplicated? I'm not so sure.

In fact, many back-to-the-landers know very little about homesteading and so can't have a strong desire for it. Instead what is often present is a strong desire for escape from one's present situation. Much better to try it first in small doses with friends or acquaintances who are already living in a rural way than to jump with both feet into an unknown field.

SENSE OF REALITY

Many back-to-the-landers come to the country with a grossly distorted sense of economic reality. A couple who became our friends arrived in this area with their six children and no more developed plans to support themselves than to plant apple trees and to harvest the fruit. That's fine as a long range plan, but what do you do in the meantime?

Bob and Marie did not lack most of the qualities necessary for successful homesteading. But an intense desire to get out of a distasteful urban situation seriously distorted their sense of reality, and led to their unsuccessful homesteading experience.

Too, the siren call of free power from the sun and the wind is luring a number of would-be homesteaders into the country with unrealistic dreams. The power is there, but it is far from free. Anyone moving to the country on the premise that everything, including energy, is there for the taking had better do the calculations beforehand. To rely completely on solar or wind power alone demands that you have some money in the bank or else have very modest power requirements — say, a pair of 60-watt lightbulbs.

SETTING GOALS

Developing a set of short- and long-range goals is essential in any undertaking of this scope. The long-range goals may be easier to put on paper, but don't count on achieving them in a year. Personal satisfaction should come from knowing that you are making progress toward the end goals, but it is important to know that the intermediate steps are not always satisfying in themselves.

Beekeeping is extremely fascinating work, but there comes a time at the end of the season when hour after hour of extracting honey becomes somewhat less than stimulating. Maple syrup season is one of the most beautiful times of the year, but washing 1,500 sap buckets and spiles, when it's all over, takes a bit of dedication. I love splitting wood, but there are times in the spring when, sweating and inhaling blackflies, I wish the woodshed were full. There are goals associated with each one of these activities — a good honey crop, gallons of syrup, a winter's wood supply — which in turn are all steps in achieving our overall goal of independence in the country.

WORK DISCIPLINE & ORGANIZATION

There are always a hundred jobs to be done around a homestead. Some are indoor jobs, some are outside work; some are 10-minute tasks, others will take several days; some are one-person jobs, a few require several sets of willing hands. Organization and priority-setting have to be applied to the accomplishment of all this, otherwise it is too easy to waste time. If you *plan* to do nothing for a couple of hours, that may be fine, but if you do nothing because you are disorganized, that's waste. Personal discipline in work habits is essential in homesteading. There is no boss to crack the whip.

PHYSICAL STAMINA

This refers not so much to brute strength as the ability to put in hour after hour of physical labour.

Old Arthur Lacombe sold his farm a few years

back to a couple of boys from the city. The other day, the 300-foot water pipe which is buried between the house and the barn became plugged and the boys were looking for a backhoe operator to come and dig it up so they could find the trouble. Old Arthur confided to me that he just couldn't understand why two healthy young lads would waste more time trying to find a backhoe than it would take to dig up the pipe by hand. Why, he used to dig it in half a day, he said, and take care of other chores besides. To get water to the house in the first place, Arthur and two friends had dug a 2,500-foot trench, four feet deep, in two days.

Few are the city dwellers today who have the stamina to keep up with the old-time farmers. Machinery is now available to do many of the jobs that used to be done by hand, but there is still a great deal of homestead work that requires physical stamina. Fortunately, stamina can be built up with lots of physical labour in a country environment — assuming one doesn't give up first.

MANUAL SKILLS, RESOURCEFULNESS

The farmers around here seem to thrive on problems. They don't seem to know that some of them are supposed to be impossible to solve. *"Pas de problème"* is their normal reaction to a difficult situation.

When you become a homesteader, it's usually on a "pre-owned" farm and sometimes they have been pre-owned for a hundred years or more. So the problems are numerous and of a maddening variety. This is where the new homesteader sometimes comes to ruin. He may start paying someone else to solve the problems and soon find his bank balance running low. Or he may try to solve them himself only to discover that he doesn't have the necessary skills or self-confidence. On the other hand, he may find that he has skills and resourcefulness that he never knew about because he never had to use them before. A long history of city dwelling and office jobs doesn't usually make for well-developed resourcefulness. But it may be there just the same, waiting to be challenged.

INDIVIDUALISM

The successful homesteaders that I have known all had a strong individualistic streak. They could make it on their own. They may have shared in cooperative ventures, but they were first of all successful on their own individual merits. Any venture they participated in benefited from a concrete contribution.

One of the first acts of many new homesteaders is to put an ad in the paper seeking someone to share their experience with them. This is done even before they have figured out what it is they want to share, as if the very act of sharing in itself has magical qualities that make one plus one equal five. It is true that a shared venture can often be more efficient than separate individual efforts, but only when the individual contributions have intrinsic value in themselves.

"Why do some homesteaders fail?" Perhaps it's not so much a question of failing as of learning. What many learn is that they weren't really homesteaders in the first place. And that's progress, not failure.

Hedda & Silas

"Be careful when you choose your hardships"

By Louise Langsner

Hedda and Silas are homesteaders' homesteaders. They were early drop-outs, leaving the San Francisco Bay area — sporadic art school, radical politics, Ban-the-Bomb demonstrations — on a Harley-Davidson headed for New York City in 1966. After a brief stint on the Lower East Side they migrated north with other back-to-the-land people to a commune in upstate New York. But West was home, so our friends went on the road (the Harley traded in on an untrustworthy pickup truck) toward the Southwest, where a boom of fledgling communities was taking place.

Passing by Colorado's Red Rockers and Drop City, Silas and Hedda made camp among the communes of northern New Mexico until they located a place of their own. Or the next best thing. The owners of a large tract of land gave them permission to homestead, with no financial obligation and no written agreement, for as long as they wished.

The new home was truly in the boonies — 20-odd miles from the nearest "town" (a store), past two ghost towns at the end of 18 miles of dusty dirt track. Camp was moved. The pickup promptly died. And Hedda and Silas dug in.

Painstaking work yielded a tiny one-room house of stone and adobe, a bountiful garden (irrigated with well water pumped by a windmill hauled in by a friend from South Dakota), storybook chickens and goats, and small fields of corn and millet.

During the next three years Silas and Hedda lost successive gardens to August frosts and hail storms. A drought resulted in a forest fire which burned to the edges of their fields and necessitated evacuation of family and animals. The following spring, heavy rains flooded the house which had been built into a hill. On top of these tribulations, Silas and Hedda were plagued by a growing disaffection between them and the land owners. It was time to move.

A modest gift from Silas' father made possible the purchase of 40 acres of beautiful but rocky and densely-wooded land in the Ozark Mountains. Silas made a preliminary trip to build a temporary, dirt-floored dwelling and to have a road bulldozed in. He then returned to New Mexico and rented a truck large enough to hold all their gear plus horse, goats, dogs, chickens and geese and to pull the now-defunct truck. They were off!

Though Silas and Hedda were old hands by this time, arriving at the new homestead in late fall was difficult, especially since the new road could not accommodate the rental truck. Their goods had to be stowed away on the state road and hauled in by horse or when friends with working vehicles came to visit. The horse was also the means by which Silas made his monthly 30-mile round trip into town for animal feed and supplies. Letters from Hedda tell the story of the settling in:

"Our garden is poor this year. No manure. Did you have manure on your place, or have to truck it in? This coming year we'll have our own so the garden should do better. Also the bugs are awful here! 'Specially in the cabbage family and the squashes and our old friends, the Mexican bean beetle. Organic remedies seemed to fail so I'm hand picking the beasts. Hate it! Sows had eight babies. They are all fat and healthy. Love them. We sold two so far. Shall keep one maybe and eat two ourselves.

"We dug a lovely spring near where the path goes down to the garden. Good thing, too, because the branch dried out. We've had quite a drought. I've canned about 30 quarts of blackberries, some poke and wild spinach but practically no garden vegetables. It's depressing . . . ."

"We like our area," Silas adds. "It's probably one of the best for growing outside of California. If we had our choice, we'd live in New Mexico just 'cause we like the space even though it's not especially good for homesteading. Here it is hot and wet but your garden sure grows. We like snakes!" (We had asked how they dealt with the problem.) "Been busy blasting, digging, chopping and pulling stumps in the new half-acre garden. Got two-thirds done already."

HEAVY MORALS

After one year in Arkansas, Hedda wrote:

"Good thing that you wrote us! I was just sort of starting to wonder if maybe your mule kicked you into an early grave. Glad it isn't so. Also glad about your group ownership decision." (We too had decided on individual ownership of land.) We saw it work really well once in Missouri. The group was called the 'Brothers of Levi' and it was very moralistic. (No pants or short skirts on women. No make-up. No flirting. Also lots of clothes, even on babies.) Very religious and very regimented. It also had a patriarch who made most major decisions.

"In a way I envy you guys for having met lots of people, or at least some that you really like." (Our local community is full of wonderful folks.) "Except for a very few we haven't come close to anybody here. Morals are heavy. Some of the homesteaders who are Jesus Freaks and go to church every Sunday find they like lots of the locals. Personally, I prefer the Chicanos to the local folk. They consider mushrooms 'repulsive' and some won't eat squirrel because the Bible says it's 'unclean.' I wish there were some old people left who liked the old ways. Folks here think what grandmother did was weird rather than interesting or useful.

"We had a wonderful Indian summer and I really started liking the place without reservations. I'd been missing New Mexico very much and most painfully all this year. I still do but it's become a background feeling. I was shocked at myself because I usually adjust easily to any place and don't mope over past places. Do you think it's because I'm getting old? San Francisco seems like a peculiar dream of long ago . . . .

"Si went apple-picking in Missouri for about six or seven weeks and earned $800. Most of it has been spent on insulation, tin and hay for the animals. Did you have to buy hay? Here it was $1.25 a bale, not even alfalfa, just grasses."

DILEMMAS

Homesteaders who can pare their budget to the barest minimum and learn to live on the thinnest shoestring still need to solve the income problem. One can economize and avoid a mortgage by buying cheap land, but it may mean buying animal feeds and building supplies as well as a long wait before the land is in good enough heart (or even clear) to offer a means of support. On the other hand, land which is more valuable for farming is generally priced beyond its capabilities of earning through crops (especially raised by beginning farmers). A dilemma.

"Just re-read your Xmas letter. You mentioned beans and sorghum for cash crops. Will you have to spray and use commercial fertilizer?" (No.) "I've read that sorghum is a very demanding crop, leaving the soil poor. You should try to get a green manure crop on it right after. I know all about the money situation. We are hoping that apple picking for six to eight weeks a year by Si will see us through the rest of the year. Of course, much depends on the weather and the economic situation, but growing for market has those risks, too. I'm not preaching, but just for me I can't ever see us using chemical fertilizer and sprays even if we were given them free.

"The new people around here aren't into doing much except raising vegetables this coming summer for market — not organically of course. Last year they all screamed about poisoning the environment and organic gardening; this year their depleted

purses are screaming louder. The rationale is: just once won't hurt. There is no other income available, et cetera. Personally, I prefer to be surrounded by Birchers than liberals."

This letter goes on to describe a visit to the free clinic: wading out in hip-deep snow, hitching 50 miles to be there at 9:00 a.m. . . . and waiting until 5:00 p.m. to be seen, then a botched examination room scene in which Hedda ends up socking the doctor. She muses, "I wonder if the mental cool of middle age will balance over physical decrepitude? Love, your aged friend, Hedda."

Some days on the homestead are idyllic and restful, but Silas and Hedda tend to keep active.

"We've been busy fencing our new one-acre garden and planting the old one and now planting and grubbing the new one. Si just finished sprout chopping on some of the pasture we cleared for the horse. Sure would like to have all five acres cleared — everything takes so long. We got manure on the pasture. The County Agriculture Board didn't approve us for their pasture improvement programme because we don't use their bloody 'fertilizer.' I bet they get a kickback from the manufacturer. Can't see why it should bother them if we use lime, manure and rock phosphate instead. The whole world is going down the drain and everybody thinks like in 1700: 'If you ruin it here you can always go west.' "

APPLE PIE! HIPPIE HORROR!

Sometimes homesteaders run into problems that they thought had been left behind in the cities.

"It's been a peculiar summer — not exactly my

idea of rural peace and leisure. First, the local big-wig wished to defoliate Bald Mountain (many newcomers live there). So there were petitions and threats and counter-threats and paranoia and people leaving and rumours and lies. Finally the spraying was called off, and the big-wig mentioned that he'd have all the hippies busted for pot. Time passes. The Rainbow Tribe had their annual gathering in Arkansas and about 20 of them camped near here. Local horror! Morals! God! Apple pie! Hippie horror! They are too far out. Ruining the reputation of good God-fearing hippies. Sure we all mess around, smoke and cuss, but we are land owners; they are drifters.

"Time passes. A cop car drives up to the food co-op distribution centre. One's a heavy and one's a groovy. As far as I am concerned, the handwriting is on the wall. The local hippies think no doubt the cops are only interested in the Rainbow people, until some of their own get busted for growing hemp. Twenty cops drive up with warrants for only one couple, stumble into a marijuana patch and end up arresting seven people. Bail is $5,000 each. They all spend a week or two in jail, put up their land and now await trial. They still think the sheriff and his 19 friends were only doing their duty, despite the fact that a week before, a local man was arrested for the same thing and got off with a $50 fine. It has helped to keep a detached attitude.

"I've canned 430 quarts and am totally out of canning jars. Now I'm drying green peppers, okra, zucchini, chilies, apples, pears and string beans. Soon persimmons and walnuts. The year has been wonderful for fruit.

"Oh, also, the community suffered from staph and lice. Our children both caught the staph and I took them to a doctor. Thirty-one dollars for the visit and antibiotics. Luckily, I'm picking tomatoes twice a week at $2.00 an hour, so am keeping up with myself.

"We need it because Si went apple picking in Missouri where he made a decent amount last year but (a) it's been raining a lot so the picking is bad and (b) 22 local hippies all went to the same place because Si made money there last year, so the place was overcrowded. He'll try Michigan next year.

"Si and I will go tree planting soon. Going with a crew of six and are waiting for the contract now. It will be in southern Arkansas and I'm really looking forward to it. For once we've got a running truck and Si built a camper on the back so we'll save money on rent by living out. We'll be a little cold and cramped . . . .

"Life has its little peculiarities. If someone had told me last year that I'd be camping out all winter in southern Arkansas I'd not have believed it. Yet, here we are.

TENT FEVER

"We have a contract with the Government to plant trees in the National Forest. Left two weeks before Xmas, pitched a huge circus tent and set up housekeeping. A friend is minding our place and the kids. Someone else brought two kids along. Si and I sleep in the camper. The other couple sleeps in a van, so only two men sleep in the tent. That's good because it leaks terribly and it also floods. We are almost ankle-deep in mud.

"This job pays well when you work. Si and I could easily make $50 a day each without much practice. But we haven't planted a single tree for three weeks now because you can't plant when the ground is frozen and snow is flying. It's a wonder that we haven't killed each other yet. Sitting in a leaky tent with the wind blowing and the water freezing isn't exactly conducive to harmony. Luckily, we all like to eat, so some time is spent inventing new dishes. Once we were snowed in and ran out of such essentials as eggs, powdered milk, tobacco, coffee, et cetera. It took some inventive cooking to get through. We buy lots of secondhand books to read. For entertainment we have two dogs and a cat. One man brought a Colt pistol, so I'm learning to shoot.

"We found an owl sitting in a tree and a hawk and some crows yelling at him. It was a horned owl and he glared at us. He was pretty cool and let us come to within two feet before he hissed."

There is more. Hedda, back on their own land, shares with us the sight of a full, silver moon rising through the trees, gathering wild strawberries, the birth of puppies, daffodils in spring, the dignity of a hawk . . . .

"Our house is like a zoo. The kids have a pet crawdad, a hognose snake and a black rat snake. Also occasional lizards and turtles. Four blue jays have fallen into our potbelly stove so far. We take them out, wash them off and let them fly. We hope they will learn to stay away from the stove pipe.

"Had a grand garden this year except for potatoes. There are 800 quarts of this and that canned and I took up drying again just because I couldn't find any more jars. Fruit this year was great! Also mushrooms galore.

"We've got a beaver busy building — he's just about doubled the size of the swimming hole and raised the water level almost two feet. We did a sweat bath yesterday and leaped into the water. A little cold but it felt great! Our sweat lodge is just a wickiup made out of saplings with tarps draped tightly all over and a pit in the middle for the hot rocks."

The more fascinating question for me is why some homesteaders succeed, rather than why some fail. After all, this country life just isn't for everyone, and if a would-be homesteader discovers that he or she would be a happier, more productive person living another way, is that a failure? Or, as Wendell Berry advises, "Be careful when you choose your hardships."

What continually amazes me about our friends Hedda and Silas is that through all the hardships, there is never a word of complaint — no whining about life being hard — and no hint of discouragement. Instead, there is ever-fresh wonder about the animals and plants that live with them, and a strong sense of belonging to their small piece of earth.

An understanding of their success, in my eyes, has to do with honesty. Hedda and Silas quite simply and totally are what they are — homesteading is their life and the best way they know to live. Honesty may well be a good beginning for those contemplating a homestead life. Maybe exactly where you are living now is the most honest place to start homesteading, if that is where you are happy.

Back From the Farm

Homesteading as a test of wits — and marriages

By Kathleen Poff

The Killaloe General Store, I suppose, would be a fertile stomping ground for a pop sociologist studying what he would probably refer to as the Neo-Homesteading Movement. Located in an area noted for its concentration of back-to-the-landers, the store is a perfect spot to keep track of the ebb and flow of local life, as well as to meet the newcomers.

Ed and Donna, just arrived from Toronto, came in last week, eager to meet some of the people in their new community. After our second cup of tea they explained that they'd owned their land since 1971, but had forced themselves to be patient in making a break with city life.

"We wanted to avoid the mistake most people make," Ed said confidently. "You know, coming to the country with city debts. We know what we're getting into, and we're prepared."

A friend I was with laughed, a touch nastily I thought, and said, "Everybody comes prepared. Tell me all about it in a year or so."

Sarcastic or not, my friend had a point. She's been living here now for five years and she's watched homesteaders come and go. Whether they stay or not seems to have little to do with their cash reserves or their state of preparedness. It all comes down to something else.

The new couple probably went away thinking that my friend had meant, "Wait until your goat gets mastitis," or, "You'll know what it's all about when you find yourself freezing to death some January night when your green elm won't burn."

Not many householders get done in so easily or painlessly. Failure, when it comes, manifests itself in ways you don't read about in the "good news" country magazines.

I recently spent some hours with another Killaloe veteran, attempting to find a theme common to those we knew who gave up and went back to wherever they came from. To answer any question about why some homesteaders fail, we quickly realized, one has to put a working definition on the word "homesteader." It isn't easy.

We finally broke down and turned to the dictionary. The word, it turns out, comes from the Homestead Acts passed during the 19th century in Canada and the United States. Individuals could acquire title to a quarter section (160 acres) if they lived on the land and worked it long enough. The law was designed to encourage settlers to go West by promising them that their homesteads — the house and buildings — could never be sold for default of taxes.

We discarded that one, because I seemed to remember a history course in which we talked about a high rise apartment building in downtown Dallas that is still exempt from property taxes because it is built on land owned by the same family that settled there under the protection of the Homestead Act. These people, one supposes, are entitled to call themselves homesteaders.

This confused the conversation for a bit, until my companion said thoughtfully, "It has to do with owning and working the land."

This seemed vague enough to suit our needs, but then we attempted to apply the definition to all the people we knew and thought of as "homesteaders." Most of them didn't qualify. Some owned the land, but didn't work it. Others worked the land, but didn't own it.

Our new definition excluded the glassblower and the weaver who do little actual farming, but who, by virtue of their crafts, are self-reliant in a rural setting.

In coming to this definition, we suddenly realized that we had bumped into one of the main causes of failure: people who think of themselves as homesteaders all buy the same dream and expect it to work for them. With a modest piece of land and very little money, they somehow had come to believe they could do as the true homesteaders did a hundred years ago — carve out a new life, raising their own food and living simply off the land.

It's something I should have realized a long time ago, because it is a dream I once bought without question, only to find it wasn't intended for me.

The first dream is a 100-acre homestead, with the added-on reality of seven years of mortgage payments left to make. The barnyard is full of pigs and chickens and goats, the garden bulging with corn

and beans and potatoes. To make this dream possible, Dennis commutes 15 miles daily to his job as a newspaper editor — it pays the mortgage — and I manage the small farm operation that provides most of the year's food. We cut what wood we can, but buy most of our feed because, with Dennis' full-time job and two small children at home, neither of us has

time to do more. The dream begins to fray around the edges.

Money becomes tight because country jobs don't pay very well. I'm bored and tired of being alone most of the time. Dennis is resentful because he hates the job and is tired of being away from home most of the time.

We finally trade that dream in, not fleeing back to the city, but trying something better tailored to our personal needs. We now have a small, wood-heated house on an acre of land, enough to grow a winter's produce. No mortgages, no full-time jobs, no farm animals.

Dennis is a woodworker now, and I, a freelance writer. Together we earn enough money to meet our needs; a few days' work in the fall can be traded for some fresh pork or range-fed poultry. We are both raising the children now; each of us is helping support the household with work we enjoy.

Friends ask: "Why did you give up your dream of self-sufficiency?" My answer is, "We didn't." I finally understand exactly what my own dreams are.

Looking around, I see that I was not alone with that mistake.

Linda bought her farm, a few miles away from ours, to escape — to escape meaningless jobs, pollution, alienation and a city life style that had grown repugnant to her. She knew without a doubt what she didn't want.

But she made the same mistake of assuming that the stereotyped alternative was the only alternative; that if the city wasn't the answer, then a farm was. It turned out that farming bored her. She didn't do very well at it, but at least she was ready to admit it to herself. She's in Vancouver now, learning a craft and finding that full-time agriculture isn't the only alternative to conventional jobs and urban life.

FATAL FLAWS

For couples, the collapse of a homesteading dream is often more difficult. In thinking back about the people we knew who failed at homesteading, we concluded that the downfall was almost inevitably tied — in case after case — to a breakdown of personal relationships.

If you hear something like, "Neil and Barbara's place is up for sale," around Killaloe, the immediate response is: "I didn't know they were splitting up."

Why?

We can tick the reasons off effortlessly: isolation, cabin fever, too much intimacy. Whatever personal problems might have existed in the city are brought out in sharp relief by the clear light and clean air of the country.

Bill and Sandra came to the country with a common dream: a bucolic farmstead where they would work together in harmony and peace to raise their own food and their children.

Perhaps back in Toronto there had been faint rumblings of discontent. Sandra was housebound, tied to the children and glued to the floor wax. But here, in the free and open spaces, all that would be sorted out.

A year on the farm and the floor never has to be waxed, but somebody is obliged to sweep up the wood chips. And the children step on the cabbage plants while she's weeding and fall into the mash when she's feeding the pigs.

"I can't possibly roof the granary and look after two kids at the same time," Bill says firmly.

And somehow Sandra is in the chicken coop whitewashing the walls while the children play happily in the shavings under the ladder.

They worked that one out, and they're both still here. There's a schedule pinned to the mirror above the sink now and their names can be found alternating under the chore headings: Dishes, Cooking, Wood.

That schedule is a tip-off. When it appears suddenly in a friend's kitchen, experienced homesteaders know there is a change in the wind. Either the farm will be up for sale within months or there will be a profound and permanent change in the roles of that relationship.

Isolation helps bring it all to a head. The arguments and disagreements that in the city were relieved when one person rushed off to a movie or a bar to cool out now tend to hang in the air for days. There are precious few places to rush off to, especially when it's 20 degrees below zero and the truck won't start.

But when the goals are the same, usually things can be worked out. Too often the move to the country comes when both people are looking for a change, but not necessarily the same one.

Janice and Jim left the city together two years ago. He was thrilled to get away from his job as a high school teacher and to have the freedom he'd been dreaming of for a long time. Janice, on the other hand, is looking fiercely and steadily for some kind of paying work she can enjoy. She is 32, the kids are in school and she is ready to move on and out in a direction Jim has abandoned. No schedules or compromises have worked; they were moving in different directions when they left the city. The move to the country has just served to emphasize their differences.

THOSE WHO STAY

People who stay find ways to let their dreams evolve. Some adapt a former profession to their newer surroundings, others learn skills they never would have considered before. When subsistence farming fails, they turn to other professions. When boredom begins to set in, they find new creative outlets — organizing theatre groups, getting involved in local politics, taking courses in music and art and languages.

Those who stay seem to have a strong, overriding commitment to something special, while those who leave invariably seem lost when asked what they really wanted to accomplish.

Bob and Lucy returned to the city because they wanted to earn enough money, quickly, to buy their own piece of land. They didn't feel they could do it here.

On the other hand, Ish and Kathy have managed, under the same circumstances, to get money together for their homestead without ever leaving the area. Their commitments — to an alternate school, to farm animals, to a way of life they believe in — is so strong they allow nothing to stand between them and their goals. They think they can succeed, and they probably will.

Looking back over the roster of local "homesteaders" who have stayed with it for five, six or even 10 years, we find they all have strong commitments — even though the commitments may have changed since they first arrived. Those who came just because it seemed like the thing to do have mostly gone home.

The Not-So-Simple Life

Lessons from the Sloughs of Despond: You can make it work

By Katherine Gifford

Without sounding smug or slipping into the role of the pedantic guru of Homesteading 109, this is a difficult subject to talk about.

First off, there is the problem of semantics; we want to be sure we're all talking about the same thing, so definitions are necessary. For the sake of discussion, let us take "homesteading" to mean a drastic change in way of life, involving a change of setting, presumably from urban or suburban to rural. (This could be anywhere from a few miles out of town, to the fringes of a rural village to the isolation of a Rocky Mountain valley or a coastal island.) Also presumed is some degree of self-sufficiency and a significant change in occupations for the homesteaders, with a resulting change in family income.

Then there is the definition of "failure." Is ceasing to homestead ever a real failure? Or is it simply a recognition that such a life is not for you, no matter how wonderful the idealization may have seemed?

Real failure in homesteading is, I think, rare. While Tom and Susan really love the homesteading life, while they are motivated by all sorts of high ideals and good intentions, despite the fact that they seem to have the necessary skills and abilities, they just cannot continue.

It may be poor health or, more likely, lack of money that finally causes them to leave. Employment is impossible to find, the sock where your savings lived is totally flat, chickens and children need to be fed, the roof leaks, taxes are overdue. Quitting seems to be the only way out. Accompanying this may be a breakdown of relationships between a man and woman, whether husband and wife or partners in an adventure. When homesteading reality doesn't match up with expectations, personal relationships of all sorts can be strained.

Having said all this, I would much rather talk about insurance for success. Living on the north shore of Masset Inlet, about midway up British Columbia's coast, we are very isolated, with the nearest anything eight miles away by boat. We don't, to be truthful, have much firsthand experience with other people's failures or homesteading horror stories. We can speak with authority only about our own nine years of living in the bush, of the steps we took to ensure, as nearly as possible, that *we* could succeed. We have had our Sloughs of Despond, our near misses, and we have the benefit of hindsight in talking about the turning points and the things that really count.

DIJON WHAT?

The first, if not the most important, consideration in planning any homesteading move is the degree of isolation you really want — just how far you need to "get away from it all."

If all you are seeking is clean air, quiet, a place to garden and raise some small livestock with a healthy degree of elbow room between neighbours, put away that map of the Yukon Territory. Too many would-be homesteaders look so far afield for land that they ignore the belts of marginal land that lie waiting within commuting distance of most North American urban areas.

Of course, the closer you stay to what passes for "civilization," the larger money must loom in your plans. The farther out you go, the more important will be your own personal skills and abilities to adapt. Every familiar amenity that you abandon multiplies the problems you will have to consider. It also multiplies the possible rewards of this way of life.

If you have no close neighbours, you won't have

anyone peering over your fences or shoulders, criticizing the things you may do, allowing their children, livestock or machinery to intrude upon your peace and living space. Neither will you have a helping hand on the other end of a heavy, dirty job, a friendly face sitting above a tractor ready to pull your stuck car out of the ditch. Nor will there be help in feeding your animals if you suddenly need to have your appendix out. Nor advice on when to plant potatoes, how to hatch chicks or make pickles, split roof shakes or dry firewood.

The farther you move from town, the less chances of entertainment other than that you can provide for yourselves. If you adore live theatre, can't live without a weekly trip to the cinema or consider Saturday night wasted without a disco or dinner out, don't put too many miles between yourself and the source of these diversions.

Consider supermarkets, shopping centres, health food stores and salvage yards. The farther "out" you go, the less possibility you have of taking advantage of what they have to offer. And — despite what you may think now — you can't really appreciate what they do have to offer until you've coped with weekly or monthly visits to a small country store that carries one kind of soap, one kind of tea, and no Sales. Where they stock steel nails, you want galvanized. Where you've waited two weeks to get a needed pipe fitting, their entire stock is the wrong size. Where everything costs more than it did in the supermarket and where no one ever heard of Feta cheese or green chilies or Dijon mustard.

On the other side of the coin is the friendliness and real concern of people running a small rural store. Unlike a bored teenage check-out clerk at the supermarket, you will find merchants who are interested in you, and, like you, are just trying to get along. They will order almost anything for you, as long as you want a case of it. They will save things for you, like a block of your favourite cheese, a package of suet or sturdy cartons for your child's pet crow. All this sorts out your priorities and opinions. You find one soap is as good as another, you discover what you can do without and what your ingenuity can produce out of not-quite-the-right things.

NON-ELECTRIC HOMES

In your planning, consider that far out in the country, where the land is cheapest, there is often no communication system available. Our only contact with The World is a Citizen's Band radio, which depends on friends remembering to turn their sets on at 9 P.M. Not having a telephone can be, and generally is, a real blessing. But if you need to reach other people, and can't, there can be trouble. Available solutions can be expensive and are only as good as whoever is listening on the other end. And all require some form of electricity.

Which brings up another unavoidable item in your planning. Can you get along without electricity? Are you sure you can — or that you really want to? If there is any doubt in your mind, it is asking for failure to move beyond the reach of power lines.

Most of us are willing to sacrifice the electric carving knives and can survive well enough without a Cuisinart, but are you certain you want to do without a washing machine? Without a freezer? Can you be happy and comfortable without electric lights? Without a stereo system? A steam iron? Hot water heater? Hair dryer or television? Certainly a generator can and does run things with little trouble, but gasoline and diesel fuel cost money and did you move out into the peaceful countryside to listen to the constant rumble and clatter of a generator?

There are ways around the power issue: Make your own with wind or water (can you afford to?), learn to do without (possible but not realistic for most families), or make limited use of a small generator. We heat and cook with wood, and use a 5 kw gas generator that runs electrical things when we need them. Often it stays silent for weeks at a time. Even with a generator, it means relearning many of your ways of doing things; before you cut that board with your Skil saw, you have to pull the rope on the generator. After nine years, we still sometimes forget. The end of the power lines is something to consider.

The other key element, if you have children or plan to, is the availability of public schools. In some places there are none, in other sparsely settled areas children may have to ride buses for long hours and distances. Kids have natural desires to be with the crowd, and friends may be few and far between. Parents may feel they are running a jitney service getting youngsters back and forth from extra-curricular activities and sports.

We, personally, have concluded that it is difficult to move into homesteading with teenaged children. It's your adventure, not theirs. They balk. Either do it before the kids are 10 years old, or after they are on their own. Before 10 years, children seem to adjust to anything as long as they have lots of parenting; once in their teens, the kids may consider you nuts.

We have one child, a daughter of 19, who has done all her schooling from Grade 4 on, by correspondence, through the Provincial Department of Education.

All of us think it was a marvelous experience and feel she has a better basic education than that offered in many modern schools. But it certainly wasn't easy for any of us, particularly in the first years, and it won't work for every child or parent. It is time-consuming and you haven't lived until you've tried to teach a mandatory French course when you have no French yourself. Again, the rewards can be great — on the same scale with the amount of involvement required.

ON YOUR OWN

It is obvious that we have chosen a spot that is sort of the end of the beyond, a place where there are no roads, where civilization is us. Here, abilities count for more than money. All normal homesteading considerations are multiplied tenfold, chances of failure are infinitely greater and the rewards are incalculable. You are on your own.

Planning a one or two year "homesteading experience" is one thing, but if you intend to stay, you must consider maturity, both physical and mental, both yours and that of your partner or family.

Age is, I think, a definite factor. You need to be young enough to stand up to the very real physical demands of bush life, and old enough to have the necessary experience for handling unusual situations. And in homesteading, most situations are unusual.

You can't do anything about your age, but the thirties are about right. You know yourself fairly well — though not nearly as well as you will after five years of living by your own wits — know what you want and why, and have acquired enough experience that you should succeed if you really want to.

You'd better like, as well as love, your partner in this sort of adventure. You are going to be spending a great deal of time together and you are going to rely on each other more than you can ever imagine. Under these circumstances, you need a good friend and companion as well as a lover. You need a cushion of abiding affection and respect the day you lay a water line, or rush to get the hay in before the rain storm hits, or try to paddle a loaded canoe into an uphill wind.

You need to consider your weaknesses as well as your strengths, both of you. Are you terrified, or even uneasy, about being alone? Can you cope with bugs? Mice? Spiders and bats? How about bears? If someone comes all unstuck at the sight of dead animals or of blood, can you really plan to raise your own meat?

Even quirks like requiring three cups of coffee and an hour of vertical motion to become human in the morning need to be considered. (If you are beyond the power lines, who is going to build the fire in that black monster of a kitchen stove, so necessary for the production of those cups of coffee?) You need to be able to work long and hard toward a goal; you have to take your gratification in small doses in homesteading. These things can be forgotten or ignored in suburbia or a high-rise apartment, but when all the distractions and easy escape routes are taken away, small things can assume monumental proportions.

Recognize the abilities of everyone involved. Who does the best long-range planning? Who is the self-starter? Who has a strong back? Who can't really be counted on for hard physical work? Who can and will feed chickens, weed gardens, shovel snow, build fires, haul ashes, can peas, build a house, dig a privy, balance a cheque book, make Christmas presents? Do these balance out, or all end up with one person?

A decided asset is one person who is unflappable in emergencies. Someone who will cope, without shrieking, with a cow that comes home with a torn udder; who matter-of-factly carries wood when the tractor won't start or the snow is too deep; who would, if the roof caught fire, know what to do and do it without panic; who would not come apart if the Premier or a local drunk dropped in for tea and a chat.

Too, it is a plus if everyone concerned has a lively sense of the ridiculous, for if you can't see humour in many homesteading situations, they will become intolerable.

FREEDOM AT A PRICE

Perhaps the biggest consideration in planning, as well as succeeding in a homesteading adventure, is plain old filthy Money. It is essential, no matter where you plan to live, no matter how simple your life, no matter how good you are at bartering. Land isn't cheap anywhere, and it becomes less so by the day. We have all read of people who set out with only

a rifle, axe, some sacks of flour and sugar, a tin of tea and a change of socks. This sounds more like Survival in the Bush than homesteading.

You will have to decide early and fairly permanently on the degree of self-sufficiency in which you hope to indulge. While a purist may brag that he cuts all of his wood by hand with a bucksaw, chances are that he is heating a cabin and not a five-room house. All too many of these purists seem to pack up one day and head for home, complaining of the drudgery and boredom of rural life.

We would be the last to sneer at the fellow who comes to the country with a Noah's Ark load of tools and labour-saving devices. If he knows how to use them, every piece of equipment can add to his chances of success. The family with a good chain saw, a log splitter, and airtight stoves will have time for reading, writing, cabinetry, weaving, walks through the woods, beachcombing — the pleasures they came to the country for in the first place. It all depends on your goals.

One thing that must figure prominently in your homesteading finances is property taxes. They have a way of rising alarmingly — just as your income decreases — and they are generally high enough to begin with. This tax elevation was our greatest problem in nine years, and very nearly our nemesis. After managing to come up with the annual taxes on our wilderness acreage for several years, suddenly we were faced with a tax statement that almost equalled our annual income. A new provincial government apparently felt that private ownership of land was not a Good Thing.

It took a lot of time, and a great deal of work, plus another change in government, but the final solution was to give our land to the Province, with a lease back of a fraction of the acreage. Now all the land we owned is set aside as "greenbelt," for the protection of wildlife and its habitat. And we are still here.

The other aspect of the Money Question is income. Homesteaders and other self-sufficient country-dweller types can get along with very little, but you must have *some*. The farther "out" you go, perhaps the less you need. We have no hydro bills, no phone bills, no water, gas or sewage bills, no fire insurance premiums, no licence, gas, or insurance for car or truck, no shopping sprees . . . but there are some or all of these things in less remote spots, and something has to replace these services. A water system, radiophone, composting toilet, generator or a boat all cost money. Your income, however limited, can be from proceeds of the sale of your city home, proceeds of savings or investment, from a part-time job, sale of products of whatever creative skills you may possess, or from special "in demand" abilities that can be pursued from a country location.

In your planning, give much thought to possibilities for income, even though for the first year or so you are going to be too busy to pursue them. Also, as your homesteading life progresses, new and better ideas for income may occur to you. Always plan for a "cushion" for emergencies; a sum of money that lives, untouchable and not figuring in month-to-month calculations, in the bank, savings account, bonds, or a can buried in the backyard. It is a great

stress-reliever to know that reserve is at your back, between you and the wall.

Somewhere along the line you need to think over your motivation in choosing a rural homesteading life. Is it to get a simpler, more basic way of living? Well, homesteading life is far from simple. It is just that the multiplying complications are varied enough to be endlessly fascinating. Most important, far more of the frustrating problems that plague any life are, in the boonies, of your own making and for your own solution. It isn't the landlord's problem, or the Transit Authority's mess to clean up; it's yours, and solving those problems is one of the satisfactions of this life.

THE POSSIBLE DREAM

Do you want to homestead to test and prove your personal abilities? Do you want to provide for your own family with the strength of your back and skill of your mind and hands? Fine. Go to it. It's a perfectly good reason. Do you view it as a salvation in a world gone mad? You may well be right. Do you hope to forge closer ties and deeper relationships with your family? Well, homesteading will at least allow you to know each other very very well, for better or worse. And you certainly come to know your children when you are with them all the time. Do you hope to get closer to nature, the basic and beautiful turn of the seasons, the harmony of wind and weather, the incredible variety and beauty of the wild things that share your piece of the world? Emphatically, you will — and we have found this to be the greatest reward of all.

Certainly there are drawbacks to homesteading,

and all of them are possible reasons for failure. There is nothing easy about it. Homesteading is hard work, much of it dirty, messy and unpleasant. A garden that provides most of your food is a real job, not always to be tended when, if and as you feel like it. The same holds true for poultry and livestock. Mucking out stalls runs low in entertainment value. Cutting wood loses its amusing qualities in a hurry. Lots of things have to be done when you are cold and wet, hot and dirty, or just plain feeling rotten. There are an incredible number of things that can go wrong, and most seem to do so at once.

And then one day you realize that your kids are downright nice, grown-up, responsible people, friends instead of adversaries. And the garden you cursed mightily for so long has produced enormous quantities of everything you planted, and even the weeds are high quality. All the hens are laying, of the family of five half-grown chicks three are pullets, you have found the nest by the creek where the ducks are laying daily, all the machinery is working properly because you personally have fixed it, the woodpile is in good winter health, and you feel rightly that your homesteading is a success.

When you reach this stage, then you, too, will think back on what led to this success, to the things that staved off failure; the deep and abiding interest in this way of life, the skills and abilities that brought you to the venture, and those learned by practice and experience.

Above all, it takes a real desire to succeed, a commitment to make this new life work, no matter what. Although no success is permanent and no failure forever, nothing truly rewarding or successful is gained otherwise.

Hand-Hewn Homes On $5,000 (Or Less)

"Warm, dry, light, spacious . . . and paid for"

By Des Kennedy with photography by Paul Bailey

"We may fight like cats and dogs amongst ourselves," advises an old-timer with a spirited glint in her eye, "but just let someone from off-island try telling us what to do and he'll have all of us to deal with!"

The Strait of Georgia, lying between the mountainous bulk of Vancouver Island and the British Columbia mainland, is dotted with small islands, isolated and heavily wooded, that have developed people as remarkable for their self sufficiency as for their loyalty and clannishness. Once used as seasonal foraging grounds by the indigenous peoples, the islands were homesteaded in the latter part of the 19th century by European settlers.

Old photographs now treasured by third and fourth generation descendants of the pioneers show sturdy-looking fellows astride the beams of newly raised barns, or standing with double-bitted axes and cross-cut saws on the prone trunks of just-felled forest giants; the women stand smiling in long dresses, although they clearly were no strangers to heavy labour either. These were a tenacious and vigorous people, and the ones who stayed to put down roots in the acidic forest soil or along the sheltered coves developed a distinctive island culture.

Over the past century, new settler groups and individuals drifted to these Pacific rain forest islands. Some, like the Japanese labourers brought to Canada to build the logging railways, or the mainlanders who came to establish small truck gardens or oyster operations, left their transitory marks. Others were absorbed into the concentrated complexities of a community bounded by water and rife with independence.

The isolation has been broken during the last decade, however, with radical changes in traditional living patterns. Improved access, speculative land development and a surge of new freedom-seekers have cracked the established order of things. Refugees from the cities, who fanned out all across the rural British Columbia landscape beginning in the late sixties, landed on the shores of the Gulf Islands to start from the earth up as others had done before

them. Though itself one of the forces to overturn "the old ways," this wave of immigrants is entirely consonant with the traditional island values of independence and self sufficiency in a way that the mobile homes and vacation lots will never be.

The half-dozen homes glimpsed in these photographs are owner-built and hand-hewn — a localized small verse in the growing canticle of the woodbutcher's art. These are among dozens in the small community of Denman Island, each as different, one from the other, as the homes shown here. Surrounded by vegetable gardens, new orchards and tentative clearings, they are harmonious with the turn of the century clapboard farmhouses, weathered barns and split rail fences.

Unhampered by building codes and inspectors (with only the wood nymphs to look on), with sometimes limited skill and the unbounded panache of fresh freedom, the new islanders flung themselves into woodcraft. A rare synthesis of aesthetics, the renegade spirit and the practical values of warmth,

Every lamp in this owner-built Denman Island home was lit to show the expanses of recycled windows.

durability, comfort and convenience occurred. Strong on aesthetics, by all means, but aesthetics to be savoured in a building that is, as architect Rex Roberts advises, warm, dry, light, quiet, clean, useful, spacious, pleasant and paid for.

The coastal zone is a treasure-trove of debt-free building materials—beach stone, driftwood logs, salvaged timbers and recycled doors and windows. But even in this abundance, there is none that can compare in versatility and beauty with *Thuja plicata* — the Great Western Red Cedar. Stands of huge tapering cedars once clothed the coast, maturing in about 800 years, bulging to fluted 20-foot diameter trunks and towering 200 feet above the forest floor. Though the old giants have long since disappeared from the area, these Denman houses pay homage to the excellence of cedar. All are roofed in cedar shakes or shingles which should shed the rains for 35 winters or more. These shakes and shingles are common

Top left, *the author's own hand-hewn house, displaying some intricate angles accomplished by an amateur man-and-wife building team. Kennedy says the home "grew right out of the surrounding forest" — it was built with hand-split cedar shakes, milled cedar siding and has a hewn beam skeleton.* **Bottom left,** *inside the Kennedy's octagonal country kitchen — a masterful blend of salvaged oak floors, recycled doors and windows. Cedar cabinets and bench were built of lumber produced on a simple chain saw mill.* **Above,** *using poles cut and peeled on their own property, along with creosote-pressure-treated logs reclaimed from the sea, these builders created a house with Japanese architectural influences.*

enough nowadays, but splitting them by hand is the prerequisite of only the most determined do-it-yourselfers. Searching the deep woods for old dead cedars, cutting blocks from their trunks, then bolts from the blocks, hauling these home, splitting out shakes with a froe and hardwood maul and then finally nailing them on the roof in overlapping layers is, notwithstanding the chain saw and pickup truck, a rite of passage in a centuries-old veneration of cedar. And those roofs! The straightness of shakes doesn't preclude a roof line as gracefully swooping as the trees from which it came.

Beneath the roofs are cedar boards for exterior siding, solid-piece countertops milled with an Alaska Mill chain saw attachment, window casings, milled and hand-hewn beams and posts, scorched and brushed boards for interior panelling, and handmade doors. Weathered to silvery grey by rain and sun or oiled smooth to bright red-gold swirls of grain, cedar is a principal delight of the Denman hand-built house.

Partner to cedar in the rain forest land of giants is the Douglas fir (*Pseudotsuga menziesii*), second only to the California redwood in sheer awesome size. "Discovered" in 1829 by the noted Scottish botanist, David Douglas, it has been the backbone of the coastal logging industry ever since. While not as perfect for log cabins as the Lodgepole Pine of the province's drier interior, young firs have provided several islanders with snug log houses, and many more with sturdy, inexpensive house frames, rafters, floor joists and hewn beams. Used as posts and beams, these stout logs permit the owner-builder to span large spaces, allowing interior walls to be put where they're wanted, not just where they're needed to hold something else up.

From the water's edge come driftwood logs, their smooth skins bleached and polished by saltwater and sun, their shapes twisted so that somewhere in the miles-long tangle lies the perfect piece for each architectural whim — arches, extravagant centre poles, spiral staircases.

From other shores come flat, smooth, slate-grey sandstones for pathways, foundations, porches, chimneys, flooring and facing. In a wet land where everything wooden sooner or later rots away, the gritty semi-permanence of stone has its charm.

Scavenging — or as we now say, recycling — materials no longer needed by the disposable society is a venerable tradition with owner-builders going well back beyond Thoreau dragging his precious barn boards through the Walden Pond thickets. By happy circumstance, Vancouver and Victoria were in a tearing-out-the-old-and-putting-in-the-new phase

just as the discards were needed on the islands. Old bricks, leaded glass doors and windows, fancy hardware, cast-iron tubs and many of the things since reclassified as "antique" were given a second life in these Denman homes, showing their charms again like an irrepressible old flirt. As one of these builders says, "I wasn't much at design, but I was a great collector, so I just amassed this pile of stuff and let it dictate where it wanted to go."

With all of these vital ingredients at hand, and lumber mills not far off to supply the rest, all that was left was to begin.

Fashioned from local materials, these houses rest gracefully in their various surroundings. There is no great dichotomy between interior and exterior; rather, they flow into one another, through alcoves and courtyards, with the possibility that the cedar tree just beyond the window is an offspring of the tree from which the window casement is fashioned. Aesthetics are not slathered on like so much veneer. These homes aren't skeletons draped with disguising skins. What you see is what they're made of.

Openness is the common interior feature. The space in which food is prepared flows into where it is eaten and into the living space. In short, the old country kitchen. Cozy places where you can keep an eye on a pie in the wood stove while the neighbours are in for coffee, or where big gatherings can feel relaxed and children can scuttle about. There are private places too, alcoves or rooms set at removed angles, for bathing, sleeping, study, craftwork or meditation. But there are no corridors and few doors that don't open to the outside.

All these homes are heated with radiant wood heaters — in itself a great inducement to avoid too many inside walls, and a challenge to design public and private spaces around a single heater whereby all can be warm enough and none too warm.

Similarly, in an area more noted for dank overcast than for gleaming sunshine, the luminous environment becomes an object of some serious study. More than mere decoration, those leaded windows and doors are located to throw light into particular activity spots: the first warm rays of the morning sun slanting into the breakfast alcove, or late afternoon light suffusing areas for preparing food or for reading, and skylights to brighten spaces by day and let the moon and stars shine in by night. Many of the walls and ceilings are finished in white plaster (not an indigenous material, but a perfect complement to rich, oiled wood) which has 95 per cent reflectance. Rain forest dwellers like to make the most of whatever light they can get.

Not one of these places sprang from a blueprint. A few preliminary sketches, perhaps a balsa wood model and a healthy dose of optimism launched most of them.

One of the homes pictured here cost slightly more than $5,000, including plumbing and wiring. The others were all built for less than that amount. Common sense, a keenness for the nonconventional and a desire to create a personalized space in har-

mony with the surroundings dictated an approach to building that was labour intensive and low on capital requirements. The results are startling from more than an economic viewpoint. These homes fairly exude warmth and friendliness. Parents and other visitors who, in the early days were more than a little dubious about the whole undertaking, are now inclined to stay longer, to stretch out before the fire and wax eloquent on the glories of getting out of the rat race, of not being crippled with a mortgage, and other related topics. Life, for the moment, is every bit as sweet as the fantasies of it were during the months of work.

The $5,000 home is still a possibility — across the continent in Maine, the Shelter Institute is teaching people to build wood homes that have the same architectural bloodlines as these structures. Post and beam construction, using local materials, including rough-sawn lumber from small nearby mills, with all labour supplied by the owners and their friends and neighbours make it possible in a time when most new houses cannot be had for eight or 10 times the price.

Here, however, the building phase illustrated by these homes is already winding down. Quality recycled goods are at a premium, island land prices have soared over the past 10 years, speculative development of vacation lots has increased, the long arm of building codes grows ever longer and ferry service has improved. The pace of life, still light years away from the metropolis, speeds up.

The old island life style, of which these homesteads are perhaps a last manifestation, evolves into something else. Soon enough these buildings, too, like the farmhouses and barns before them, and the longhouses before them, will crumble back into the moist earth, and the cedars and firs and other living things will grow from them.

Poor Man's Architecture

Stackwall construction — putting a new home well within economic reach of the owner-builder

By David Square

"Throw me the end of that mason's line." The order comes from a black-bearded, heavy-set workman whose overalls are so encrusted with mortar as to suggest that he may be building a monument of himself up on the scaffold.

A tall, thin-hipped fellow in a conspicuously clean red plaid shirt and neatly pressed jeans turns to his partner, who is heaving shovel loads of sand into a cement mixer.

"Sheila," he asks as quietly as he can, considering the din of construction which surrounds him, "what the hell is a mason's line?"

A cry goes out for more logs and a tall graceful girl with the exquisite hands of a concert pianist, and a short muscular man with the white, corn-fed teeth of the Midwestern United States step forward carrying a two-foot log between them. The tall girl holds one end of the log above her head while her shorter partner bunches his muscles and, placing one hand on the lower end of the piece of poplar, shot puts it onto the scaffolding. They repeat this procedure many times as others working above them lay the logs into a thick bed of mortar.

Despite this unlikely crew, the wall rises rapidly, and, during a coffee break, Drs. Allen Lansdown and Arthur Sparling sit on a pile of poplar logs and watch with satisfaction. For them this peculiar scene on the campus of the University of Manitoba represents a sweet victory over a government bureaucracy which, in the spring of 1974, had branded them as architectural heretics.

At that time, at the request of the Manitoba Housing and Renewal Corporation, the two engineers had just completed a study of housing in the northern part of the province where MHRC had invested heavily in conventional, two-by-four frame dwellings.

Lansdown and Sparling confirmed what the government had suspected but was reluctant to admit — the boxy frame houses were woefully unsuited to a northern climate, terrain and life style. These "transplanted California bungalows," as the two engineers referred to them, were found to have two-by-four wall studs that were in various states of decay — some completely rotten only five years after construction.

One of the causes was overcrowding in the home, generating an above-average moisture content in the air which penetrated the walls through ripped or torn vapour barriers. In many cases, the plastic film had been torn down before the houses were completed, while in others it was ripped when punctures were made in the flimsy plasterboard interior walls.

After weathering 40 prairie winters, this stackwall home near Gimli, Manitoba, remains sound, snug and paid for.

In either case, the core of the walls provided an ideal environment for rot-causing fungi.

Other problems included inadequate insulation — two-by-four stud walls only accommodate four inches of fibreglass for a maximum R (insulating) value of 14, well below the R20 minimum now demanded in the north by government building codes. High cost was also cited as a drawback to frame construction in northern areas, because of material shipping charges and the expense of flying carpenters and masons into remote communities which do not have skilled labourers. The end result in too many cases, the study concluded, was little more than plywood boxes whose flimsy nature manifested itself within a year of construction as hollow-core doors fell off hinges, windows cracked, foundations shifted and paint peeled.

After listening to this sobering report, a special MHRC committee asked Lansdown and Sparling to suggest an alternative to conventional wood framing for northern housing.

"Gentlemen," said Dr. Lansdown, addressing the committee, "my colleague and I have already considered an alternative. It's a form of log construction we call the stackwall system."

After digesting the details of stackwall construction, the housing committee adjourned to discuss the proposal amongst themselves. Their unanimous decision was not long in coming: "Drs. Lansdown and Sparling must be crazy."

But the two engineers were not to be put off so easily. For one thing, they had confidence in the stackwall system. It fit all the criteria in their proposal: it was cheap, utilizing available building materials, not expensive British Columbia plywood; it was simple to construct — they called it "Poor Man's Architecture" —and would allow members of a remote community to plan and build their own homes, saving money and gaining confidence in themselves; and it was attractive from an energy conservation viewpoint: the houses would be easy to heat in the worst northern winters. Moreover, the log and concrete walls were almost indestructible.

The inspiration for all of this came, simply enough, from Dr. Sparling's father-in-law, who lives in a 1,500-square-foot stackwall home built near Gimli, Manitoba, in 1937. The walls consist of eight-inch pieces of log, stacked firewood fashion and embedded in mortar, and after 40 winters remain attractive and in sound condition.

There are several other similar structures in the Gimli area, built in the late '30s, perhaps in response

to the economic situation. Along the Ottawa River Valley between Quebec and Ontario there are a number of stackwall barns and houses built some 200 years ago. Curiously, the origin of the technique remains mysteriously obscure. In Siberia and the northern areas of Greece, stackwall structures estimated to be 1,000 years old are still standing. Yet no one is quite certain where it all began.

INDIGENOUS MATERIALS

Convinced that stackwall — also variously referred to as cordwood, log-butt and log-end construction — was an idea worth reviving, Lansdown and Sparling continued to haggle with the Manitoba Housing and Renewal Corporation. They eventually persuaded it to provide funds for a one-year pilot project to build several stackwall structures for northern Indian bands.

The scrawny poplar and spruce trees indigenous to many northern areas are wholly unsuitable for traditional horizontal log construction, but Sparling and Lansdown found them perfectly acceptable for the stackwall method. They built a prototype, using 12-inch logs and then another with a modified design, using 24-inch logs with a space left in the wall to be filled with insulation. Many of the original objections to the project were quelled when the walls of this structure, built on the Manitoba campus, were rated at R24, double the R12 found in most existing Canadian homes.

From that point, the project rapidly gained momentum. Sparling and Lansdown formed the Northern Housing Committee with themselves as co-chairmen and the Engineering Building of the University as headquarters. The next phase of the project was the construction of a stackwall building at Wabowden, Manitoba, a small Métis community 575 miles north of Winnipeg.

The design was started in the spring of 1975, the construction team began laying the logs in June, and a few weeks later the walls were up. The Northern Housing Committee group acted as consultants and instructors, showing the workers how to prepare the foundation, cut the logs to equal length, mix the mortar in wheelbarrows, and build the walls in straight lines.

Rob Patterson, one of the research associates who worked on the Wabowden project, says the people were quick to learn the stackwall system even though many had no previous building experience.

Every aspect of an NHC stackwall house, from foundation to window and door frames, has been designed with ease of construction in mind. The foundation is a trench dug to clay level (six to 14 inches) and filled with two-inch crushed rock to form a bevelled berm or platform about six inches above ground level. Next, two layers of railway ties, set at right angles to each other, are laid over the berm. The final step is to set the centre floor beam on adjustable jackposts which can be lowered to prevent the middle of the floor from "bulging up" as the heavy outside walls gradually settle over a period of years.

Top, *once the foundation of railroad ties is laid, corners go up and walls are filled in, layer by layer.* **Bottom,** *eight-by-eight rough sawn lumber is used for lintels over doors and windows.*

"A two-foot-thick wall can weigh up to a ton per linear foot," says Prof. Sparling.

Although concrete beams may be substituted for railway ties, the latter are recommended because they are generally available in the most remote communities. Prof. Sparling says the ties for the Wabowden building were purchased for almost nothing from the nearby Hudson's Bay railway. He does not expect any problem with rotting since the ties are heavily creosoted and the gravel berm on which they sit keeps them dry and well-ventilated.

Once the foundation is laid, a bed of mortar is spread evenly over the ties and the first row of logs is tamped lightly into the wet mixture. Almost any kind of wood from poplar to oak is acceptable, although the so-called softwoods like pine and poplar are better insulators. The rough bark of poplar gives a superior mortar bond: The bumps act like the corrugations on reinforcing steel. A mason's line clipped to each corner of the building serves as a guide to keep the walls straight and level as they go up. A 16- to 18-inch gap is left between the strips of mortar, and this is filled with some form of insulation, either fibreglass or wood chips treated with lime to deter insects. Door and window frames are built on-site of rough-cut lumber usually purchased from a local sawmill, as is the lumber for the roof trusses and roof sheathing. Only the glass for windows and the asphalt shingles for the roof need be purchased from an outside source. The NHC has been experimenting with jack pine, which can be split into shakes with a froe for roofing the same way cedar is used in British Columbia. Prof. Lansdown says jack pine shakes will outlast cedar, but the most durable are those split from oak trees. "A roof of oak shakes may last a century compared to 10 or 15 years for asphalt shingles and 50 to 60 years for cedar, and a little longer for jack pine."

Lansdown says the original stackwall design has slowly evolved into a more sophisticated structure. "We've learned from our mistakes. For our first house, we used green poplar logs which shrank as they dried. This left cracks in the walls which accommodated the winter winds. Now we insist on well-seasoned logs."

A further modification is in the corner detailing. Originally, the corners were constructed of overlapping round logs. This made it difficult to establish a square corner and, consequently, a square building. To overcome this problem, eight-by-eight inch rough-sawn timbers were substituted for the round logs, not only making the building easier to construct, but giving it a neat, professional appearance. Another change was to increase the thickness of the walls from 12 inches in the original building to 24 inches or more in ensuing buildings.

Inside one of the prototype buildings on the University of Manitoba campus, it is warm, cozy and virtually soundproof because of the thick walls. The test house at the University was built directly behind the main bus stop, yet the screech of brakes and rumble of diesel engines is a distant echo inside the building.

Student John Markowsky lived in the house for a winter and found it easy to heat, even in minus 30 degree Centigrade temperatures if there was no wind.

His one complaint was that on blustery days the wind cut through the uncaulked cracks in the walls. Dr. Lansdown says this problem has been largely overcome by building with well-seasoned logs that shrink very little after the house is completed. However, he says that even the driest logs will swell slightly after touching the wet mortar and then, about a year later, contract to their original size. Considering this, Lansdown says caulking remains an *essential* step in stackwall construction and the price of the caulking compound is included in the construction cost of the completed building. The present practice is to caulk the building about one year after completion, using any of the numerous commercial grouting materials on the market. This procedure sounds simple enough, but to caulk even a small stackwall structure is a tedious, time-consuming job.

SINKING FAST

Another criticism Sparling and Lansdown encountered was in the foundation department, although in this case the builder, not the method, was at fault. The incident is worth mentioning because it provides good advice for any person considering a stackwall structure: Don't cut corners when dealing with walls which may weigh one ton per linear foot. The case in question involved a man who built a stackwall garage near St. Adolphe, Manitoba. One day soon after the building had been completed, he phoned Dr. Lansdown to complain that his building was sinking into the ground at an alarming rate. Lansdown drove out to the building site and, after a close inspection of the foundation, discovered that the rock-filled trench supporting the building was only half the recommended width. "People won't believe us when we tell them loads spread laterally, as well as straight down," says Lansdown. In this case, the builder had substituted an 18-inch trench for the 36-inch-wide trench recommended for the height and weight of his building.

As a result, the prodigious weight of the walls slowly forced the crushed rock in a lateral or outward direction and, as it flattened, the building sank.

A final problem encountered by one stackwall builder is of a less technical nature. In this case, after taking a building course through the University of Manitoba, he started to build a stackwall house on a piece of land he owned in Michigan. Halfway through the project, he was stopped by the State of Michigan building authorities who demanded technical data to prove the house met local building codes.

Dr. Lansdown explains there are five points which a dwelling must meet before it is accepted under a building code: 1) durability 2) fire resistance 3) moisture movement 4) insulation 5) structural safety. According to recent studies conducted at the University of Manitoba, a stackwall structure greatly exceeds the requirements in all these categories, especially fire resistance and moisture movement. Tests indicate that the walls are virtually unburnable, and

the moisture movement through the logs is exceptional. In response to a plea for help from the builder in Michigan, Lansdown sent a copy of his data to the Michigan authorities and, to his knowledge, construction has now resumed.

Similar problems may arise in Canada, especially if a person applies for mortgage money to build a stackwall home. The technique has not yet been accepted under the national building code, even though the federal government has reportedly financed stackwall projects in at least one province. Drs. Lansdown and Sparling are willing to help people if they encounter difficulties with the Central Mortgage and Housing Corporation, but their best advice is to take out a small bank loan and build the house with "private" money.

But these problems seem to be the exception, not the norm for stackwall builders. For the most part, they seem satisfied with the technique. A family from Richer, Manitoba, whose uninsured frame dwelling had been destroyed by fire, found they simply could not afford to build a new "California bungalow." They heard about the stackwall system from a sympathetic neighbour and contacted the Northern Housing Committee for details. Beginning work on their stackwall house in the spring of 1976, they built only on weekends and were ready to move in by November. The entire 700-square-foot home including doors, windows and roofing cost only $1,600. They borrowed the money on a small bank loan, and will soon own the home outright — a feeling that the owners of mortgage-encumbered conventional dwellings may never enjoy.

The stackwall system has even encroached on the sacred ground of big tree country and the traditional log builder: A man near Banff, Alberta who found full-size logs too heavy a building material is planning to build his home using the stackwall system.

Allen Lansdown estimates that there are at least 150 stackwall buildings now under construction in Canada and the United States. Recent stackwall building courses at the University of Manitoba attracted participants from all parts of the continent, and Sparling and Lansdown are heartened by the ease with which non-carpenters learn the method. The thin fellow with the too-clean jeans — a New York City civil rights attorney — quickly found himself cutting logs, slinging mortar and thoroughly enjoying a relatively frustration-free construction method.

Among those who have taken the NHC building courses, the majority have been people from rural areas interested in constructing year-round homes, while others planned to use the technique on barns, greenhouses, cottages and, in one case, a winery.

Unlike almost any other North American construction technique, the resurrected stackwall method demands little in the way of tools or cash. Anyone with the will, say Allen Lansdown and Art Sparling, can build his own stackwall home.

Stackwall Basics

Northern Housing Committee

Would-be stackwall builders will find a detailed, no-frills explanation of the technique — from laying the foundation to splitting roof shakes to heating with wood or solar energy — in *Stackwall: How to Build It*, a 94-page manual from the University of Manitoba.

Anyone even mildly ingenious will quickly master the technique and perhaps refine it to suit individual tastes, but the Manitoba manual offers a number of guidelines for success:

1. To determine the amount of cordwood that will be required, determine the number of square feet of interior wall surface area and multiply by .015 to give the number of cords needed. (For example, a rectangular single-storey house measuring 30 by 40 feet with eight-foot-high walls would have 1,120 square feet of interior walls. It would require 16.8 cords of wood.)

Almost any type of tree will supply adequate wood for a stackwall house, but the low density species (such as poplar, cedar, tamarack and pine) offer the best insulating value.

2. All logs must be well-seasoned before construction begins. Trees cut in the fall should be ready for building the following summer, but this will vary according to the species of tree, the local climate and how the logs are dried. (Optimally, they should be stacked up off the ground to allow free circulation of air, but with a simple roof or covering to protect them from rain and snow.)

A convenient length for the logs is eight feet, four inches, which will yield four 24-inch building logs once rough ends are cut off and the thickness of saw cuts is taken into consideration.

Squared corner timbers should be 30 inches long and cut from eight-by-eight or six-by-six railroad ties.

3. Once well-dried and cut into desired lengths, the logs and timbers should be dipped in a preservative solution of copper sulphate (bluestone) and water for five minutes. This may be done in a 45-gallon drum, where 56 pounds of the chemical are dissolved in 40 gallons of water.

4. Do not remove the bark from the logs — it will help form a better bond with the mortar. The copper sulphate will act as a pesticide and fungicide.

5. It is not necessary to have log pieces that are all of the same diameter. Drs. Sparling and Lansdown say that using random-sized logs is much simpler and gives a pleasing final appearance.

6. Build the corners first and fill the walls in afterwards. Use a bubble level at all times in constructing the corners to assure that they are plumb and square. Run a string line between outside corners

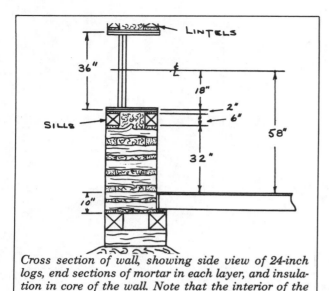

Cross section of wall, showing side view of 24-inch logs, end sections of mortar in each layer, and insulation in core of the wall. Note that the interior of the wall, right, is inset to allow support of floor beams.

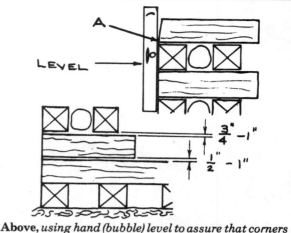

Above, *using hand (bubble) level to assure that corners are straight and plumb. Out-of-kilter corners will throw the entire house out of balance.* **Below,** *detail of railroad tie corner, showing one-inch layer of mortar between timbers.*

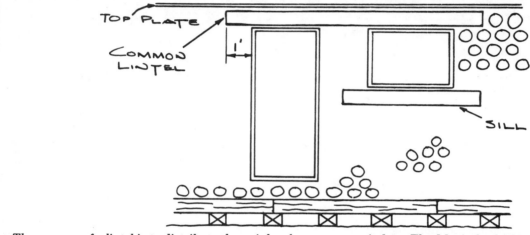

The purpose of a lintel is to distribute the weight of a wall above a window or door. It should extend from six inches to a foot beyond each side of the opening below, or a common lintel can serve both a door and an adjacent window. The Manitoba builders use six-by-six rough sawn timbers studded with nails protruding an inch and a half to form a bond with the mortar.

using a mortar clip (available at hardware stores), and adjust each log as it is laid to be sure the outside wall is vertical. (This will result in the interior wall being slightly less even, but you must decide whether appearance is more important inside or out. Many builders decide to plaster or panel interior walls to further seal air leaks.)

7. Mortar can be mixed by hand, but better results will be had using a mechanical mixer. A recommended formula is:

    6 parts sand
    2 parts Portland Cement
    1 part lime

8. Logs — each 24 inches in length — are laid in layers, completing a full course across the wall before advancing to the next layer.

Lay three or four inches of mortar in a strip along the inside and outside edges of each layer of logs. This will leave a space approximately 18 inches wide in the centre of the wall. Set each log of the next layer into the mortar, adjust its face and level it. (See diagram.) Pack insulation into the cavities and continue, cleaning up excess mortar as you go.

9. Wall logs should never touch each other — at least one-half inch of mortar should separate each piece. Do not stack logs one atop the next, but stagger the layers — this will prevent one layer of insulation from being directly above another layer which would allow future settling.

10. Insulation may be fibre material, or, as the Northern Housing Committee recommends, sawdust mixed with dry lime to deter insects and fungal growth. This type of insulation is inexpensive, but must be tamped carefully at each stage to prevent later settling.

11. Mist new walls each night during the construction period to allow the mortar to cure slowly.

12. Plan to caulk around each log when the inevitable cracks appear surrounding each piece of wood. This can be done with a putty knife or caulking gun.

Copies of *Stackwall: How to Build It* by the Northern Housing Committee are available for $12.50 by mail order from:
University of Manitoba
417 Engineering Building
Winnipeg, Manitoba

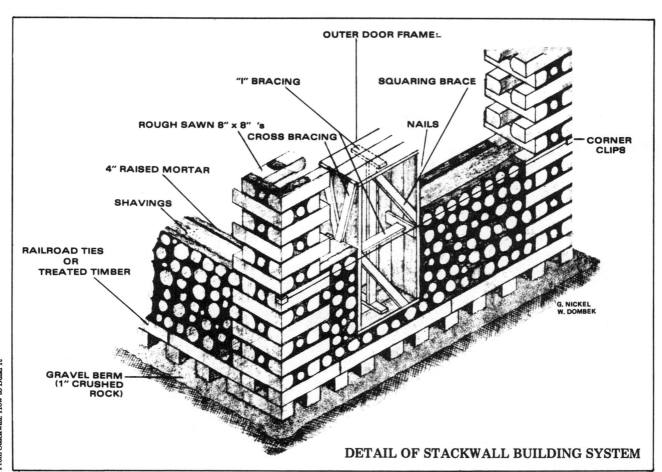

OUTER DOOR FRAME

"I" BRACING

SQUARING BRACE

ROUGH SAWN 8" x 8" 's

NAILS

CROSS BRACING

4" RAISED MORTAR

CORNER CLIPS

SHAVINGS

RAILROAD TIES OR TREATED TIMBER

G. NICKEL
W. DOMBEK

GRAVEL BERM (1" CRUSHED ROCK)

DETAIL OF STACKWALL BUILDING SYSTEM

Solar Ms. Adventures

Self-taught retrofitting: success despite everything

Article and photography by Alice Nangeroni

The moment I first glimpsed its graceful lines a decade ago, I was charmed by the simple beauty of the Nova Scotia farmhouse that was to become my rural retreat and, eventually, my permanent home. Typical of mid-19th-century frame architecture in this southwestern region of the province, the white storey-and-a-half clapboard stood beside a quiet lane in the open countryside. Just beyond, a bay glinted in the sun, promising fine swimming and virtually selling me on the house before I even entered it.

Inside, its eight rooms were small and a bit damp. The indoor plumbing consisted of a hand pump. A kerosene lamp with a mercury reflector mounted on an iron bracket provided the lighting, and Queen Victoria's severe gaze kept watch over things from a huge gilt and plaster frame. As a summer residence, the house proved itself worthy enough, after being partially restored and given a bathroom and electric baseboard heating panels (this was in the heyday of cheap electricity) in the main rooms on the first floor. To grace the house with the friendly glow of wood heat, I found a century-old Excelsior parlour stove which fitted the surroundings perfectly.

Unfortunately, the stove, like the house itself, was hardly airtight, and when I started plans to move in permanently, it became clear that an additional source of heat would be needed to make the place habitable in winter.

The easiest and most obvious choices — adding more electric baseboard units or installing an oil furnace — were becoming less and less easy and obvious in view of the price of energy, especially here in the Maritimes. Having become an avid reader of articles and books on alternative energy, I wanted as much as possible to avoid future dependence on non-renewable fuels. I considered wood, but realized that an expensive new chimney would have to be built (the old one had rotted through to the cellar and I had used a multi-elbowed insulating pipe for the Excelsior). Wood seemed impractical in the long run, as I had no ready access to a fuel supply and felt misgivings about being able to deliver the constant attention that responsible wood burning demands.

While wind is an abundant power source along Nova Scotia's coastline, I found the technology of harnessing it for home use formidable. At the same time, I discovered that I was able to follow

Following an existing roofline, the new addition provided both solar collection and a new sunroom.

the solar literature and diagrams. Indeed, even to my relatively non-technical mind (I left an administrative position at a university to move to Nova Scotia), the solar ideas seemed quite simple. Solar heat had a very personal appeal as well, because I love the sun, dislike wind and am slightly afraid of fire.

The choice was easy and it was solar. Between this decision and the actual completion of the solar conversion, there were reverses, moments of doubt and some high skepticism from friends and onlookers. One neighbour in particular watched the proceedings with growing doubt, and his opinion seemed important to me. In the 10 years I had owned the farmhouse, I had grown to depend on this man's advice on all things pragmatic: when to set plants out into the garden, how to keep the house in running order. Backed as it was by a lifetime of on-the-land experience and intimate knowledge of local lore, his advice had always been sound, and I could hardly imagine succeeding in country life without it.

But as he viewed the new work in progress, he finally delivered a verdict that threw a heavy pall over my enthusiasm.

"Shingle it over ... that solar thing will never work, so you might as well put a real roof on 'er right now," he pronounced with a finality that left me shaken and quite alone in nurturing the vision of clean, pure, quiet and automatic solar heat.

Despite the sting of his prediction, I was not about to retreat at this point, and my resolve was bolstered by the conviction that this time the refugee from the city knew something the neighbour did not.

Wherever and whenever the sun shines, even on lightly overcast days, some solar heat can be trapped. With the plethora of solar articles, how-to books and government publications that have appeared recently, it is relatively simple for the layman to locate information on climate, temperature and radiation in specific regions of North America, as well as guidelines for estimating the heating needs of houses in those regions.

In my case, I found that the provincial Energy Council supplies such information, but since it is still of a very general nature, I had to search further for data on my own local conditions. Here, local means a very small area — 20 miles away there may be five inches of snow covering the ground when there is none outside my window. Inland, a July day may be unbearably hot while our weather is comfortably right.

In our Maritime climate, area weather is greatly influenced by distant ocean currents and the two bays around the three-mile-wide strip of land where I live. My planning was based on a composite of sunshine and heating needs data for Portland, Maine, radiation data for the entire province of Nova Scotia and my own rather spotty records of temperature and sunshine.

When I became aware recently that our radio station, CKDY in Digby, has kept records for the federal government's Atmospheric Environment Service for the past 10 years, a check revealed that their data confirmed my impression — in the summer we need slightly more heat than Portland but slightly less heat is required here in the winter. Averaged over eight years, the temperatures for our coldest three months were 28 degrees F in December, 21 degrees F in January and 23 degrees F in February. For the two warmest months, July and August, the average was a cool 64 degrees F.

Local data on sunshine was spotty, but we seem to get slightly less winter sun than the province as a whole. Locally, the least recorded sun for January was two days, and in a sample year, 1976, sun was reported on only one out of four days during the three winter months.

By March of the sample year, however, the records indicated at least some sun on 21 days of the month. Much of our winter is overcast, most of it windy with the 1976 records showing wind on two out of three days, the strongest a Groundhog Day gale with gusts up to 119 miles per hour. The most common southwesterly wind is warm and usually brings with it rain, rather than snow.

From my reading, I knew that in most northern building situations, solar cannot provide all the heat a dwelling needs, the range falling somewhere between 50 and 66 per cent of the annual requirements. My aim was to reduce drastically the reliance on the existing electric heaters for the 800 square feet of space they heated and to supply warmth for the remaining unheated 600 square feet of space and to the cellar housing the water pump, pipes and tank.

Matching what I wanted and needed against what the weather might allow, I opted for a warm-air system because I had read such installations produce useable heat faster and at lower collector temperatures than water systems. Also, a hot air system appeared easier to install.

The warm air from the collector would have to be circulated through the house, extra heat would have to be stored for use at night or on cloudy days, and I needed a collector to trap the sun's energy. Since the size of the collector is in direct proportion to the amount of heat it produces, it would have to be as large as possible.

Where to put it and how to add it on are questions anyone refitting a solar system to an old house must answer. A collector should face south and the tables in one reference book showed that at this latitude it should be pitched at a 55-degree angle.

CONSTRAINTS

My house has the traditional square roof sloping at a 45-degree angle and facing northwest and southeast, both unsuitable exposures. However, one side of a roof covering a wing at the back, a pantry-shed I had previously converted into a screened porch, faces south-southwest. A stand of spruce trees off to one side gives some protection against the wind. Because the wing is not visible from the road, the appearance of its exterior has no effect on the old charm I had been so carefully preserving. It would have made a perfect location for the collector, but the useable roof area measured only about 100 square feet, and I wanted at least 400 square feet. While the porch had been a favourite spot for summer living with its sweeping and uninterrupted view of the bay and the far shore, it was too cold to use most of the year. It was also beginning to rot from the constant exposure to the weather and needed repairs, insulation and new windows. But the wing's structure was basically sound, and once I realized it could be easily expanded to carry a collector of adequate size, I decided that building on what was already there was the best course to follow.

Using the less than ideal pitch of the existing roof would increase the efficiency of solar collection in the mid-seasons (spring and fall) but reduce it in midwinter. The rock foundation of the porch was a possible heat storage area, but because it was shallower than needed, combined with the less than perfect roof pitch, it would cut the efficiency of the system by about 10 per cent. Using it, however, also meant a considerable savings in the cost of the actual construction, an important consideration since I could only afford an installation with a price tag competitive with a more conventional heating system such as an oil furnace or additional electric heaters.

Solar skills are in short supply in Nova Scotia. I knew of no technical or professional resources here, and I was on my own. I kept on reading and working out plans, drawings and cost estimates. Learning about thermostats, air pressure and rock densities proved slow going until I located a family actually building a sun-heated house.

Theirs was a far more ambitious project than my own, but it finally offered a chance to see what I had been reading about. These informal consultants agreed to look over my house and plans, proposing a few modifications and suggesting the appropriate solar materials and suppliers. After returning to their native Ontario, they answered a few written or telephoned questions. My technical knowledge was non-existent and my practical experience had been limited to replacing a fuse and building a shelf; I might have managed without their help, but less well.

There are several ways to trap and use solar power. The installation I had chosen was a forced air circulation system with rock storage. The collector is made of sheet metal roofing, painted black and mounted on inch-thick wooden strips nailed to the roof sheathing. Anchored by wooden battens, caulked and screwed down, the fibreglass glazing was mounted on a second set of strips directly above those holding the metal roof above the sheathing.

A blower forces the air through the collector and across the hot metal roofing, down a duct into the storage bed from where it is drawn through another duct back to the collector. A differential thermostat turns the blower "on" when the collected air is warmer than the stored air and "off" when the stored air is warmer than the air in the collector.

Simply put, the metal roofing collector was painted black because a dark colour best absorbs heat; the clear fibreglass covering traps the solar warmth against the roofing. Air blown through the collector picks up warmth from the black metal; the

more surface it touches the more heat it absorbs. If there is some turbulence in the air, heat collection increases, and the corrugated metal roofing supplies both a more absorbing surface and roughness for turbulence than would a flat plate. To prevent heat leakage, the collector must be well-insulated underneath.

In summer, when it gets very hot, the collector should be opened to allow a sufficient flow of outside air to avoid heat damage, and one way to do this is by placing bimetallic plugs along its top and bottom. The plugs open automatically when the temperature inside the collector reaches a certain level and shut when it cools, because the metals used expand at different temperatures and act like a spring. This same principle is used to control the draft in an "automatic" wood heater.

The heat drawn off the roof in my system is either blown directly into the house, when needed, or pushed through a rock storage container, where reserves of energy can be held for later use.

CONCESSIONS

Because electric blowers are used to control the flow of air through the collector and into the house, my design could be classified as a rudimentary active solar heating system, but I found passive design ideas very useful in thinking about the space created in expanding the old porch wing. A passive system uses no external power to operate, either making direct use of in-streaming solar radiation or storing it in a dense, heat-holding mass (such as floor or wall) that is struck by sunlight. I planned to install large double-glazed windows at the end of the wing to let in morning and midday sun for direct heat and to warm the thick concrete slab floor. The expanded wing would be heavily insulated to retain as much solar energy as possible.

The final fillip of my solar plan called for heating water by placing a tank in the storage pit. My water comes from an old stone well and it is very cold. While the air passing through the storage bed would not be warm enough to bring it to bathing temperatures, I had hoped this pre-heating scheme would cut down the energy consumption of the existing electric hot water tank. The water tank in the storage bed would require a pipe from the pressure tank to bring in the cold water from the well and another pipe leading to the electrically heated water tank.

To translate my plan into a functioning solar heating system required carpentry as well as electrical and plumbing skills. The local workmen had no knowledge at all of solar technology, little equipment, few power tools and their experience was confined to wooden structures. In view of these limitations, the construction plans were made as simple as possible with many compromises along the way.

The air flow pattern through the collector is horizontal instead of vertical as in most solar systems, but doing it that way eliminated the need for special ducts to get air in and out of the collector with the two pairs of end roof rafters used to accomplish this.

Unsophisticated but economical and effective, the author's solar collector surface consists of metal roofing sheets nailed in place and painted black.

Cold air enters at the bottom of one pair of rafters, flows up and across the collector to the other pair of rafters and leaves through a hole at the top. Air crosses the collector between the sets of wooden strips above the sheathing. Placed horizontally, the strips provided footholds for the collector building crew whose only equipment for roof work consisted of two wooden ladders.

Initially, the plan called for aluminum roofing but, after testing a piece underfoot, I found it bent too easily and substituted galvanized material, a slightly less efficient collector but better able to withstand the pressure of work boots. In most solar systems the fibreglass covering is usually placed vertically to allow easy water runoff. I had planned to do it that way but the fibreglass glazing cannot be walked on and, since there was no way to elevate the workmen above the roof, I had it placed horizontally, like shingles, but from the top down with the crew backing down the roof as they caulked and battened each strip.

The design adjustments made necessary because of the crew's solar inexperience were anticipated in time to be manageable but the unforeseen problems which developed once construction began proved more difficult to solve. The builder used boards for sheathing instead of the requested plywood and the consequent shrinking resulted in a multitude of air leaks. Many were plugged but a few still remain. The caulking compound on the cover also shrank and separated. A different compound had to be applied and recaulking is still required from time to time. Because the question of which way to face the vapour barrier in the insulation underneath the sheathing is yet to be resolved, some was placed one way, some the other. When I discussed this with the building inspector, he just shook his head in confusion and said bleakly: "You've got me there. I don't know anything about this solar stuff, so it's whatever you say . . . ."

As it turned out, sometimes what I said didn't come across with perfect clarity. With the construction well along the way, I devoted one entire weekend to building a model of the collector out of old boards, a piece of metal and plastic film in an effort to better demonstrate how the system was supposed to work. This proved rather more helpful than earlier, oral, step-by-step directions, but in some cases I lost, or nearly lost, the fight to turn my solar vision into reality.

The cement slab for the added wing was poured without the planned insulation. The duct bringing the cold air from the storage bed to the collector was to be laid in the slab, and this was remembered only at the absolute last minute. The hot water tank idea had to be abandoned altogether because when the storage bed was being completed neither the water tank nor a plumber was available.

SOLAR LOGIC

I did anticipate some construction problems but none quite as monumental as this . . . and I had missed what was obviously an indication of things about to go awry: "You take care of the solar part, I don't know anything about that, and I'll take care of the building part — that's what I know," the builder had told me. This was the kind of frankness I like, but things didn't quite click because solar construction requires non-traditional, somewhat experimental and innovative use of techniques and materials. I knew what the end result should be but not how to get there. The builder knew the materials and methods required for frame house construction, but it was soon apparent solar has a logic quite different from that of a traditional wood structure.

Things worked best when problems were tackled as challenges, not just tasks. When I found that warm air was being wasted at night as it drifted from the rock storage back into the then cold collector, I asked the electrician what could be done. "Oh, I'll put in a furnace damper," he suggested. It seemed a sensible idea, but once in place the damper opened and closed at irregular intervals without a discernible pattern, often blocking the warm air as it tried to leave the collector. The controls were made more sensitive, then less sensitive. Nothing helped. Instead of giving up right there, the electrician tried a damper from an automatic clothes dryer and this inspired improvisation worked splendidly.

What seemed like endless adjustments were needed to set the speed of the air flow through the collector. We had no way of gauging the air flow and we didn't know what the best blower speed ought to be. We tried a variety of speeds, testing each by comparing the feel of the warm and cold ducts and by watching smoke blown from a cigarette being drawn into the storage bed through the trap door.

We wanted the air to flow rapidly enough to move as much of the collected heat as possible in from the panel, yet slowly enough to create useable temperatures in the storage rocks. We knew the rocks blocked the air flow to some extent, and the smoke showed us when the blower was too slow to draw air. The temperature of the ducts told us when the air was moving too fast, carrying the collected heat right through storage and back into the collector.

The differential thermostat came with full instructions for wiring but little information about the precise placement of the sensors. Like the proper blower speed, this required many trials and errors before we found locations which didn't turn the blower "on" until the collector was hot and turned it "off" before it had a chance to cool the storage air.

The new room required a vent at its peak to be opened in hot weather. Without much enthusiasm, I had planned to climb a ladder every time the vent cover had to be opened or shut but one member of the work crew came up with the idea of using a screen-door hinge with a long rope for a "handle," making it possible to operate the cover from the floor.

The plugs which vent the collector itself needed to be adjusted to open at about 180 degrees F, and I couldn't find anyone to tell me how to accomplish this when they arrived.

I finally called the distributor and his advice was succinct: "Bake them!" He also explained how to move the metal-strip adjustment. After heating the plugs in a slow oven all afternoon I was sure the adjustments were slightly imperfect, but all 20 plugs open on very hot days and close when it is cool.

Finding the proper materials was almost as chal-

lenging as the construction. Many were just not available in Nova Scotia and three items had to be ordered from the United States — the fibreglass for the collector (Kalwall's Sun-Lite; cost $292 U.S.), the differential thermostat (a Delta made by Heliotrope General; cost $38 U.S.) and the bi-metallic collector vent plugs (Temp Vents also from Kalwall; cost $95 U.S.). Fortunately, solar hardware is now becoming more readily available in Canada (see Sources).

LONG HAUL

Everything had to be ordered well in advance of construction because, in addition to the time it took for the items to arrive from the various distributors, they had to be shepherded through the Customs maze and trucked home from the import centre. Freight, the exchange on the dollar, import duty and taxes nearly doubled my total cost for these items to $671.39. Characteristically the authorities paid no heed at all to my argument that as energy-saving devices unavailable in Canada the imports should be duty-free and tax exempt.

Other materials that I had expected to be easily available were not — metal roofing was hard to find and had to be ordered. To get it in time I had to settle for standard lengths and join them because the longer strips, which would have made better collector air channels, required a special order and a much longer delivery time. The day the collector cover was put down and battened, no washers were available in town and we went ahead without them, lessening its stability in high winds.

Getting rocks for the storage bed turned out to be such a ridiculously arduous chore that construction came to a complete halt for the better part of a week. It was ironic. Here in a land of rocky fields and rugged coastline I envisioned clean, round stones golf-to-baseball-size hauled from the nearby shores of the Bay of Fundy. The rounded granite pebbles scoured by seawater and fragrant with the scents of the ocean, were not, however, as easy to acquire as I had thought.

Making the arrangements for hauling, I discovered that it was illegal. I searched out a gravel dealer who was willing to make a special effort to get good gravel, but it looked so flat I feared it would pack too densely to allow good air flow. The gravel was also very dirty and since no one could figure out a way to clean it, I was back on the beach.

The Nova Scotia Department of Lands and Forests granted me permission to use all the rocks I wanted as long as they were "removed by hand only." A dozen tons of rocks by hand. The job I had expected a bulldozer and a gravel truck to do in half a day turned into days and days of collecting, loading and delivering in a pickup truck, trip, after trip, after trip, after trip for a crew of three to five persons, including two friends enlisted for this backbreaking detail when they stopped for a visit one evening.

But then something rather wonderful happened. As parts of the system were completed and began to function, interest in and understanding of the project perked right up. Construction became easier.

The collector was first "on-line," and it generated heat immediately. A knothole in the sheathing below

Covering the collector with flexible fibreglass, local workmen put finishing touches on their first solar project.

the collector was large enough to poke a finger through to touch the metal roofing inside the collector. Everyone, the work crew, the skeptical neighbour and I would do this time after time. Heat was leaking out through the cracks in the sheathing, but now no time was lost in placing insulation on the underside of the roof.

The collector circulation system was next to be finished. I stuck a thermometer down into the rocks and whoever looked at it would call out the reading to the rest of us. Now and then someone would snatch a rock from the storage bed to hold it and feel its warmth. "Hot enough for cooking dulse," we concurred one sunny afternoon.

The last part to be finished was the house air circulation system of ducts, blowers and vents and when it was ready to go I placed thermometers in various vents. Now that all the work was completed, suddenly there was no one left to call out: "What's it reading now?"

Checking the thermometers, it still surprises me how much heat the sun can deliver. It can be freezing and windy outside yet the collector will pump out air at 104 degrees F as long as the sun shines. Even when it's hidden behind light clouds, the sun can often heat the collector air enough for it to be useful. At worst, sun power produces sufficient heat for the cellar. At best, on a midsummer afternoon, the heat has to be wasted by venting it back outside.

It is impossible to estimate how a largely improvised system like this compares with a more conventional solar installation, especially since I didn't live in the house in winter before the solar retrofit.

The cost of my system, excluding the construction of the expanded porch wing itself, was slightly less than it would have cost to install a furnace, new chimney and heat distribution system — $4,065.42 compared with $5,000. The collector, at $2,584.10 was two-thirds of the total cost. The solar installation was quite a bit more expensive than adding more electric baseboard heaters but now that it is in place it costs almost nothing to operate while the prices of electricity and oil continue to soar.

The only operating expense is for the one-half kilowatt per hour used by the blower. Cost comparisons, however, seem an inadequate measure of a solar system's value. It is far better to consider how much and what kind of heat the installation supplies.

The system does provide all the necessary heat for summer's cool mornings and evenings, and it does what no other heat has done — it keeps the house comfortably dry. Spring and fall it provides all the heat needed on a sunny day and stores enough for 12 to 30 hours depending on how and where it is used. For the mid-season month of October, my heating records show: all solar, 15 days; some solar, 11 days; no solar, 5 days. In winter, whenever there is sun, I use the heat directly as it is collected, leaving little for storage.

When the outside temperature is at the freezing point, there is enough heat for the whole house as long as the sun is out. If the temperature outside is

14 degrees F, about as cold as daytime temperatures get here, I heat only the upstairs while the sun shines. With overcast skies, even when there is light rain or snow, the collector is still capable of producing air that is up to 59 degrees F warmer than the outside air — not warm enough for the house, yet adequate for the cellar where only minimal heat is needed.

The new room created by expanding the old porch wing to carry the solar collector is about 12 feet by 20 feet, the rest of the wing taken up by the storage bed. The only heat in this new room is passive solar and does not come from the house air circulation system. The large windows plus radiant heat from the warm collector duct (left uninsulated for this purpose) keep it warm enough for daytime use two-thirds of the year. In winter, this heat plus occasional warmth from the storage bed which forms part of the floor keep the addition warm enough for use as a plant room.

Nearly half, about 48 per cent, of our heating needs here are in the three months of December, January and February. While I get very little hot air then from the collector, I do get a fair supply of low-grade heat for the cool parts of the house, and I estimate that the solar system produces about 20 per cent of my overall winter heating needs. The rest of the year the system is adequate for most of my heating and I estimate the annual average of the heat it supplies to be about 50 per cent of my total need.

The author's century-old Maritime farmhouse before and after entering the solar age. A small wing on the back was extended with a collector built into the new roof system.

It would not be an exaggeration to say that I am less handy than the average homeowner, but I managed to create a solar space-heating system that works. Had I been able to do the relatively simple carpentry and plumbing tasks required, my costs would have been almost 40 per cent less. As it is, the heat from this collector represents an annual saving of about $600, at our current base rate of 6.66 cents per kilowatt hour of electricity. So far there have been no maintenance costs and, if this continues, I will have recovered my investment in five to six years, depending on how rapidly electric rates increase.

The major maintenance cost I anticipate would be for the collector covering. I tried to have the fibreglass installed twice as securely as recommended by the manufacturer, but I would prefer if it were never tested with another Groundhog Day wind.

There are some non-monetary operating expenses because, in an effort to keep my system as simple as possible, I used the minimum number of automatic devices and that means work for me.

The differential thermostat, for example, turns the collector blower "on" when the collected air is warmer than the air in storage but it cannot decide whether this air is actually worth collecting. It is up to me to decide, and I turn the system "off" if that decision is no. The second blower, feeding the main house circulation system from the rock storage, comes "on" if its thermostat registers an appropriate drop in the house temperature, but it also cannot tell whether the solar heat is hot enough to use. I make that decision as well, and if the solar heat is colder than what I want, I turn it "off" and switch on the backup electric heaters.

The upstairs duct from the top of the collector and independent of the house circulation system is strictly manual. I open it when I want heat upstairs and shut it when none is required. All these decisions could be automated but that would add to the costs.

Not only that, the necessary equipment is unavailable locally and installation would be complicated.

I don't find the solar operating chores onerous or boring. Adjustments are usually necessary in late winter afternoons, prime times for visitors. I have yet to encounter a guest who doesn't at least once peer through the direct duct into the top of the collector, check a thermometer or touch a hot rock. As one caller told me one cold, damp day: "You know this is the first time I have ever felt comfortable in this house."

I had already discovered the truth in this statement myself.

Sources

THE HARROWSMITH SOURCEBOOK
Edited by James Lawrence
Camden House Publishing
Camden East, Ontario K0K 1J0
Solar energy equipment and expertise are available in Canada from coast to coast, but may be difficult to find. An extensive listing of manufacturers, suppliers and designers, together with a consumer's overview to solar hardware is available in this volume.

SOLAR ENERGY CATALOGUE NO. 2
Edited by Michael Glover
Can. Government Publishing Centre
Supply and Services Canada
Hull, Quebec K1A 0S9
Another excellent directory for solar information, products and expertise.

CONSUMER HANDBOOK OF SOLAR ENERGY
(For United States and Canada)
By John H. Keyes
Morgan and Morgan
145 Palisade Street
Dobbs Ferry, New York 10522
General and valuable consumer information on buying solar products and evaluating solar claims.

THE PASSIVE SOLAR ENERGY BOOK
By Edward Mazria
Rodale Press
Emmaus, Pennsylvania
In the field of passive design, this reference is extremely valuable.

THE SUN CATALOG
Solar Usage Now, Inc.
Box 306
Bascom, Ohio 44806
This fascinating solar hardware catalogue for U.S. residents is updated each year.

Moving Into The Sun

Solar metamorphosis for a drafty old farmhouse

By Elizabeth White

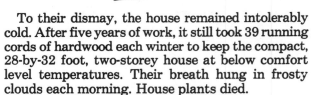

When our neighbours Geoff and Stephanie Wells bought their farm in Scotstown, Quebec, six years ago, they hadn't planned on spending their first winter trapped in the kitchen, bundled in overcoats and huddling next to the wood stove. But their charming old farmhouse, perched a windy 1,300 feet above sea level on an east-facing slope of the Salmon River Valley overlooking Mount Megantic, was an almost classic study in heat loss.

Btu's leaked from it like smoke through a sieve: through the uninsulated roof, the badly-fitted door, the sawdust-filled walls and broken storm windows. The basement wood furnace wasn't operable and the temperature of the flooring at ground level was often sub-zero.

Gamely, the two of them set about plugging holes. They insulated the roof with R20 fibreglass, repaired the storm windows and replaced the door. Wall by wall, they removed plaster and lath, replacing the original sawdust with R12 fibreglass. The old wood furnace in the basement was restored to working order as a supplement to the wood stove, and attempts were made to insulate the perimeter of the dry stone wall foundation with sawdust, branches and plastic.

To their dismay, the house remained intolerably cold. After five years of work, it still took 39 running cords of hardwood each winter to keep the compact, 28-by-32 foot, two-storey house at below comfort level temperatures. Their breath hung in frosty clouds each morning. House plants died.

A desperate attempt to shut out the cold from the basement by stuffing fibreglass between the floor joists only resulted in freezing the cellar plumbing pipes, trapping them beneath the fibreglass where even the meagre warmth the upstairs floors *did* hold couldn't reach. Cold blasts of air spouted into the living room through the single, large floor register above the furnace, while the furnace's heat fled up the new, insulated chimney. To put it mildly, Geoff and Stephanie were disheartened.

The core of the problem, they concluded, was the basement. The cracks and crevices between the aged foundation's stones defied all efforts at insulation in a windy region with a winter mean of less than 634 hours of sunshine and more than 5,136.4 annual degree-days below 64 degrees F. The solution was inescapable. They needed a new foundation; either that, or abandon the house.

They met the problem head-on. Besides being thermally inadequate, the house was too near the

Photos by Geoff and Stephanie Wells

road and sat in a hilltop depression which cut off a magnificent view across the valley. They decided not only to replace the foundation, but to move the whole house to a better site, shifting its axis 90 degrees to face south, and adding a 10-foot extension to the foundation along the south wall over which to build a greenhouse. The greenhouse, they decided, could be employed for winter food production and would include a rock storage area to retain excess heat, which could be used to supplement the furnace.

Once the decision was made, however, it was time to face the realities of costs and attendant complications.

The resolution to move entailed budgeting for a new septic system and new water supply, both needed anyway as the present septic system consisted of a four-inch pipe running into a ditch, and the water supply was insufficient for both house and barn. They guessed that $10,000 would cover the cost of the work, found a local contractor who specialized in house moving and foundation work, and proceeded to pour the footings. These they located about 150 feet to the southwest, on a gravel knoll (which contained such a rich deposit of iron pyrites that Geoff was tempted to abandon the house-moving endeavour at the outset and take up prospecting instead).

This was where we came into the picture. (I design energy-efficient homes.) My companion and I were leaning on a split rail fence one mellow August evening, enjoying the measured grazing of the cows and listening to the woodcocks preparing for dusk when Geoff and Stephanie drove into the yard.

"The form-work man is coming tomorrow, and I thought I'd better check my plans with you people before he arrives," Geoff announced.

"Oh," we sighed, groaning inwardly at the prospect of another last-minute consultation. "Well, let's see them." He picked up a twig and scratched a rectangle in the dirt. Like many farmers, Geoff suffered from a deep-seated aversion to blueprints.

After a hasty explanation of what they hoped to accomplish, we deserted the scratched-dirt plans for the greater practicality of paper and pencil and the kitchen table.

Several hours and many cups of coffee later, we had some solutions. Stephanie's concern was that the new site and changed orientation would make access to the barn more difficult and, unless some provision were made for a mudroom, the kitchen would remain a jumble of boots and children's wet snowsuits for six months of the year. Geoff wanted to be able to back a trailer, loaded with firewood, into

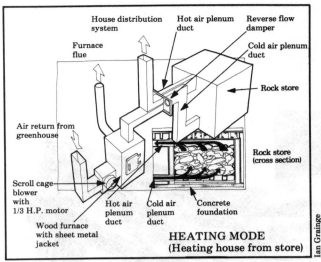

Air return from greenhouse

Furnace flue

House distribution system

Hot air plenum duct

Reverse flow damper

Cold air plenum duct

Rock store

Rock store (cross section)

Scroll cage blower with 1/3 H.P. motor

Hot air plenum duct

Cold air plenum duct

Concrete foundation

Wood furnace with sheet metal jacket

HEATING MODE
(Heating house from store)

Ian Grainge

Rather than attempting to damp down the wood fire to prolong the burn, this design lets the fire roar — but traps excess heat in the cellar rock storage vault. For this 2,400-square-foot house, the rock storage space is 800 cubic feet, insulated with six inches of fibreglass and filled with large pieces of rock.

the basement and to bring in equipment for repairs. The answer was a set of eight-foot double doors in the east wall of the basement, which would form the main entrance to the house, putting mudroom functions in the basement and giving access to a work area. The doors would be plywood sandwiches, with styrofoam inside to insulate. The stairway to the main level was put in the southeast end of the greenhouse extension, one end of it running down to the basement, giving light to the mudroom area.

On the main level, a deck was added on the east side, facing the view, with access through a new door in the dining area. For ease of construction and to cut down on summer overheating, the greenhouse had vertical glazing with a two-foot overhang on the eave. Part of the wall between dining room and greenhouse was removed so that the latter could double in function as living area. The rock storage was located in the southwest end of the extension, enabling the rocks to be placed with a loader after the house had been moved — thus avoiding the usual problem with retrofits: how to get the rocks into the basement.

Next, we tackled the heating system. The trick was to move the heat before it went up the flue and move it rapidly enough so that the furnace wouldn't turn cherry red. It then had to be transferred into storage before the house became a sauna. Once in storage, it could be distributed as required — if necessary, many hours after the furnace had gone out.

We came up with a plan which had two basic operating functions: storing heat and distributing heat. The system planned could be used to perform five separate functions: 1) store heat from the furnace; 2) store heat from the greenhouse; 3) store heat from the furnace and greenhouse simultaneously; 4) distribute heat to the house from the store, and 5) cool the house from the store.

Because the system had to be cheap, the old furnace was retained and manual rather than automatic

controls specified. A sheet metal jacket was designed to surround the furnace and to connect to the rock heat storage by ducts. A blower mounted on the jacket would circulate air taken from the top of the sun room/greenhouse down to the furnace, around the heated jacket and on into the rock storage.

We designed a manual reverse-flow damper to enable the same fan to power the distribution loop to the house. (See diagram.) The budget for the ductwork, we knew, could be kept in bounds by a craftsman of our acquaintance who can produce the impossible out of sheet metal (and frequently has to when working with us). We had a cheap supply of thermopane for the greenhouse and grants were available from the Canadian Home Insulation Programme and the Quebec Bureau des Economies d'Energie Programme d'Isolation des Maisons for the purchase of insulation materials, which would help cover the cost of the extremely expensive extruded polystyrene foam required for exterior insulation of the new foundation. When Geoff and Stephanie finally left in the early hours of the morning, we were almost convinced the metamorphosis could be accomplished for close to $10,000.

The form-work man arrived as promised at 8:30 the following morning, and in three hours he and Geoff erected the plywood forms, framed in the door opening and the slots required for the house-moving operation, and placed three horizontal bars of three-eighth-inch reinforcing steel around the upper perimeter of the foundation. At 1:00 P.M., the first ready-mix truck arrived. The concrete pouring took two hours and forms were removed the following day. The cost of the new foundation, including excavation, insulation and floor slab, was just under $3,200. The following weeks were spent installing the new water line and septic system; Geoff and Stephanie managed to do this for about $1,200 by employing a multiple-pit system for the leach field, which is legal in Quebec. They eliminated the need for a well pump by taking the water supply from a spring-fed stream about 20 feet above the house site, using gravity to obtain pressure.

On September 4th, Geoff was in the middle of pouring the basement floor, up to his ankles in wet concrete, shovelling as fast as possible to keep up with the driver and within the ready-mix drying time allowance of 10 minutes per yard, when the house-moving crew drove into the yard. Instant panic! At $500 per day he couldn't afford to keep those boys sitting around, but Hydro Quebec had not yet been told to disconnect the power and the concrete was setting in interesting mounds on the basement floor. Miraculously, a Hydro truck appeared on the horizon and Geoff rushed off to flag it down.

After some grumbling, the crew was persuaded to oblige and threw the main breaker at the transformer. When Geoff returned to the basement, he was amazed to discover the ready-mix driver kneeling on a couple of boards trowelling a finish in a most professional manner. With some basic instruction from the driver, who evidently thought Geoff needed all the help he could get, and the aid of a couple of rapidly rounded-up friends, a passable job was done on the floor. Meanwhile, the house movers started work.

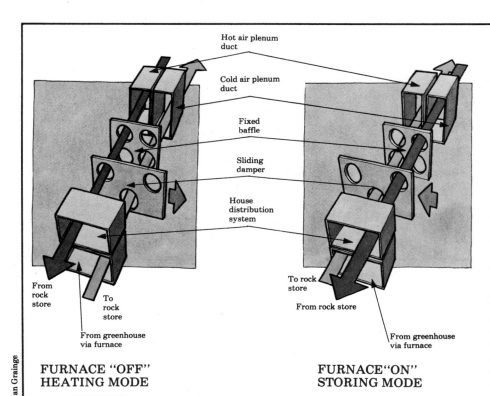

Hot air plenum duct

Cold air plenum duct

Fixed baffle

Sliding damper

House distribution system

From rock store

To rock store

From greenhouse via furnace

FURNACE "OFF"
HEATING MODE

To rock store

From rock store

From greenhouse via furnace

FURNACE "ON"
STORING MODE

Ian Grainge

Exploded view of the air control damper box invented to control the home's combination wood/solar heating system. In the heating mode, **left,** *warm air is drawn from the top of the rock storage and cool air drains from the house into the bottom of the vault. A natural convection current is thus set up. In the storing mode, hot air from the furnace is blown down through the rocks, heating them for future use.*

They began by prying loose some stones in the old foundation, which enabled them to winch two steel I-beams under the house. Geoff disconnected the water and sewer lines and the house was jacked up. A building is normally moved in three stages. First, the I-beams are placed and the building winched off the old foundation. Then the I-beams are hitched to a truck at one end and a special type of rear axle at the other, and the building is driven to the new location. Last, reversing the procedure, the house is winched onto the new foundation and the I-beams removed through slots in the foundation walls. This can be done with such skill that a good foreman will boast that a glass of water set on the dining table at the beginning of the operation will still be full when the job is finished.

In this case, since the new foundation was close by and the terrain rough and sloping, the foreman decided to winch the house the full distance, sliding it onto hardwood rollers on six-by-six-inch wooden cribbing, periodically jacking up the house to raise it to its new level and swinging it in an arc to achieve the 90-degree shift in axis. The move took three and a half days for five men, one at each of the four sets of cribwork to reset the rollers and move the six-by-six cribbing, and one on the winch. For some unfathomable reason, the original builders, when framing the house, had neglected to nail the joists to the studs, which were spaced in random fashion along the eight-by-eight-inch sills. During the move, both north and south walls of the house, not to mention the roof, hung precariously from a few dozen nails.

Everyone heaved a sigh of relief when the house was set in its final resting place and new beams installed under the floor joists. The total cost of the move was only $1,265, thanks to the contractor who donated some time.

The next phase of the project was construction of the rock store, for $700. It was framed in two-by-

sixes, insulated with fibreglass on the sides and top and extruded polystyrene foam on the bottom. The cold air plenum at the base was made from cement blocks, spaced to permit even airflow through the rocks. As soon as the stone was in the bin, Geoff and Stephanie began framing the greenhouse addition. By the time cold weather set in, it was closed and insulated. On sunny days it warmed beautifully to a temperature of about 90 degrees F and maintained itself around 65 degrees on overcast days, so they went ahead and replaced the wall between greenhouse and living room with posts and beam. Much to their delight, the dreaded cold drafts which usually heralded the beginning of winter failed to materialize. The ductwork had not yet been installed, so the old furnace was sitting in its original location happily belching heat up the chimney as usual. But this year, with the furnace supplying only radiant heat, the basement was warm and the children could play on the living room floor without fear of frostbite. One memorable sunny day in December, with 45 mile per hour winds howling outside, the temperature in the greenhouse was 85 degrees F.

By the end of January, the sheet metal work was complete and the heating system was finished. The ductwork cost $500, which brought the grand total for the job to $11,047 — not too far off the original budget of $10,000. Geoff and Stephanie still have to finish the interior of the greenhouse and build insulating shutters for the windows. The siding is not yet on the addition and the deck has to be laid. But these are details. Geoff and Stephanie are inordinately enthusiastic about their transplanted house but warn other would-be house movers to get their dates straight with the contractor and make sure the utility companies are notified. The thermal performance of the house is far beyond their expectations and Geoff and Stephanie are convinced that no home, no matter how cold, is beyond hope.

High Stake Sweeps

*The return of wood heat
has brought with it new fire hazards
— and the rebirth of chimney sweeping skills*

By Matthew Radz with photography by William Nunnelly

It is the archetypal family station wagon — two kids and Labrador retriever in back — sagging along under the burden of a U-Haul piled dangerously high with fireplace-ready chunks of wood. A chain saw and gas can sit atop it all, and the family flagship seems to beg for someone to scrawl a sign on its tailgate: Cheap Energy or Bust!

It hardly takes an energy sociologist to document the spread of interest in burning wood — even the most casual of Sunday afternoon drivers cannot, today, fail to notice the signs: wood stoves for sale in every hardware store and shopping centre, crusty pickups plying the country roads heavily loaded with logs, freshly split firewood stacked in farm sheds, jamming carports, piled into garages or tossed in heaps by back doors.

Half a dozen years ago, North American wood stove makers, all 30 of them, made and sold about 75,000 units per year. At the end of 1979, it is estimated that the 600 firms now casting or assembling wood stoves had sold 750,000 wood burners. Add to this the countless numbers of ancient but serviceable stoves rescued from garbage dumps, barns, back alleys and attics and the statistics become staggering enough to make even the most cynical oilman pause for thought.

One media commentator explained it all away by calling the airtight wood burner the pet rock of the energy crunch, while more serious observers have compared it to a loaded revolver thrust into the hands of a public woefully ignorant of basic woodburning practices. While hundreds of thousands of families are now able to eliminate or decrease their monthly fuel bills, others have met with tragedy as a result of improper use of wood stoves.

The number of fires related to wood heat is "going up noticeably, even disturbingly so," says Gerald A. Pelletier, a fire protection engineer with the Ontario Fire Marshall's Office. During 1978, according to Pelletier, there were 288 chimney, flue and house fires attributed to wood burning, while in the first half of 1979, the total was already up to 363, with statistics covering only single-family, year-round dwellings.

Although the exact causes of all these fires is not known, a recent study by the Center for Fire Research in Washington, D.C. showed the three major causes of woodburning-related fires to be: poor maintenance (32 per cent), improper installation (21 per cent) and chimney sparks (11 per cent).

Numerous guides to the correct installation of wood stoves are now available (see Sources), and the addition of a spark-arresting screen at the top of the chimney is a simple matter. Maintenance of a woodburning system, on the other hand, is an on-going responsibility — and one that is all too often misunderstood or ignored.

Improper care and feeding of a wood stove most commonly manifests itself in a chimney fire, an occurrence as terrifying as it is hazardous. Uncleaned, a chimney or stovepipe may become lined with soot and creosote which can be ignited by high flue temperatures and then burn with a violent, skyward roar that has been compared with the sound of a jet lifting off or the approach of a runaway freight train.

Temperatures within the chimney can exceed 2,500 degrees Fahrenheit, leading to the possible destruction of metal pipes or the spread of the fire to nearby combustible materials. Even if the fire is extinguished or contained within the flue, it may have seriously damaged the chimney itself, weakening the metal, destroying the mortar or causing cracks in bricks, blocks or flue tiles. In fact, the only positive thing that can be said about chimney fires is that they are highly preventable with proper chimney care and cleaning.

Enter, or rather re-enter, the chimney sweep and his black bag of cleaning tricks. Sooty-faced, wearing a top hat and a cutaway coat, the modern sweep may appear to have been plucked from an Elizabethan London rooftop and he does, in fact, represent the revival of a centuries-old profession, albeit one with a mottled history.

In Olde England, children often as young as six were sold by their parents to apprentice with a master sweep. Distressing numbers of them, however, never lived to full adulthood. Virtual slaves, they were forced to crawl through the circuitous flue systems of medieval homes and commercial establishments, risking life and limb to clean the impossibly narrow smoke passages.

The use of these human scrub brushes became a running controversy in Parliament, with the House of Lords stubbornly refusing to institute reforms until a better method of cleaning chimneys was found. Untold numbers of the young sweeps died prematurely of tuberculosis ("consumption") or cancer of the scrotum. Known as "chimney sweepers' cancer," this disease has the distinction of being, in 1832, the first occupational health hazard documented by the medical profession.

Today's chimney sweep may be as different from the Dickensian stereotype as the modern airtight is from yesterday's bulky and inefficient smoke belcher, but his most important sweeping tool is very similar to the device that finally freed the chimney cleaning children. Introduced by an inventor named George Smart in 1805, the instrument consisted of a basine brush worked through the chimney by a series of interconnecting bamboo poles. Today the brushes are usually steel and the poles made of flexible fibreglass, but the usefulness of Smart's invention remains undiminished.

Norman Lenz has been practising the chimney sweep's

craft in Toronto for the past 40 years, after earning the right to wear the Lincolnesque top hat (symbol of the master sweep) by serving an eight-year apprenticeship of climbing roofs and scraping chimneys in his native Germany. Today Lenz wears a safety helmet and says he wouldn't be caught dead wearing a stovepipe hat on the job, but if anyone has claim to the title of dean of Canadian chimney sweeps, it is Lenz.

The president of Toronto Chimney Sweeps Ltd., Lenz has fought a long, still unsuccessful fight to give North American sweeps the kind of status that masters of the trade enjoy in Europe. "The chimney sweep in Europe performs a civic function as well as a private one," says Lenz. "He is able to detect and warn the householder about defects in the heating system.

"You have no idea of the kind of thing we find in chimneys — even in new houses. You get bricks tossed down there, two- and three-foot lengths of two-by-four, pieces of iron — all sorts of things, and they're all dangerous."

Lenz recalls that it was 18 years ago when most of Toronto's chimney sweeping firms were driven out of business by the offer of free and comprehensive home heat service adopted by the major oil companies. Once the service was introduced, the number of sweeping companies in that city quickly dwindled from 10 down to two, where it remained until two years ago. Today there are a dozen or more part-time chimney sweeps and five full-time firms operating in Toronto.

"Toronto could use 50 sweeps, and there's work for about 1,000 in the province. There is an industry in the making, but professionals are needed, not fly-by-night guys.

"In North America there are no regulations, no licensing standards, no apprenticeship programmes. Anyone with a set of brushes can be a sweep and I think many of the jokers that are starting out now should keep their hands off."

Lenz would like to see all sweeps licensed, and is in favour of enforced chimney cleaning. After a chimney fire lead to the death of four children in Toronto, he wrote a letter to the Toronto *Star:*

"This could happen to a lot more people, I want to tell you. I am a chimney sweep and I see a lot of places that are really dangerous and nothing is ever done about them. In Montreal they have a by-law which says chimneys have to be cleaned every year and I think Toronto should have the same thing. I am not complaining because (my) business is bad, do not think that, it's because the danger is bad."

"When you are a craftsman you create something you can see and be proud of," says Lenz. "A bricklayer can actually see his completed work. But for the chimney sweep there is nothing greater or more rewarding than when you get an emergency call and you can help. Money doesn't mean anything. You can help someone with your hands and your tools and that means everything."

Professional sweeps are encouraged to use gas masks to filter out carcinogenic carbon particles when working in dusty chimneys and fireplaces. Note flexible fibreglass sweeping rod, **top.**

VIEW FROM THE TOP

After the rain the slates of the roof were as slippery as a snake oil salesman's smile. I didn't want to be up there but it was an emergency. There was a house full of smoke down there. I dug in my soft-soled boots and made my way toward the stack with unusual care. You move slowly. It's almost like slow motion up there. There is no room for a false step and no time for a mistake. It's a bit like mountain-climbing, you never let go until the other foot or hand has a firm grip. You don't need anyone to remind you that a five-storey fall could splinter your legs like so much kindling. Suddenly, I was on my back sliding down the steep roof slope. Fast. I saw the sky flash by my eyes, felt a bump and flipped onto my stomach. Microseconds had passed but it seemed a year. It's eerie how lucid and calm your mind goes at times like that. I was sliding toward the edge ... faster, and head-first.

Most sweeps have had one or more close calls such as this, and most are lucky enough to survive to tell how it all ended when, as if by a miracle, they managed to get a grip on the very edge of the roof to dangle there until plucked off by helpful hands.

"Sure it's dangerous up there," says former sweep David O'Connell. "Some of these chimneys are really high and hard to get at. So you are on top of a chimney which can be 10 or more feet above the roof line, on top of a three-storey building. There is nothing you can attach a safety belt to and many chimneys that tall sway quite a bit at the top."

Lured by the possibility of financial independence, O'Connell and a partner bought a $1,200 chimney cleaning outfit, only to learn that stories about riches to be made in chimney sweeping ("Net $1,000 a week!" exclaimed one U.S. magazine) are perhaps a bit exaggerated. Operating in and around a medium-sized Canadian city, O'Connell and his partner found the woodburning community to have a reluctance to use the services of a professional sweep.

Most roof work, typified by the classic scam involving a smooth-talking con artist and the proverbial silver-haired widow, is difficult to check on, and this may be part of the reason that some stove users won't call a sweep, much less pay his fee, generally $35 to $40 for a complete scrape and clean job (with $10 less for each additional chimney at the same house).

O'Connell's brush with chimney sweeping left him horrified at the public's general disregard of basic woodburning safety. The most common hazard he encountered was an installation where the orientation of the stovepipe was literally upside-down, allowing creosote and condensed water to drip out at the joints, running down the pipe and sometimes onto the floor. (Part of this problem is tradition: Old-timers will tell you that the male end of a stovepipe always goes up, to prevent smoke leakage, but their knowledge generally falls short of the modern, efficient airtight and its prodigious ability to produce creosote along with the all-night burn times.)

"Many people burn wet, unseasoned wood," continues O'Connell, "and that compounds the problem of creosote buildup. You'd be surprised how few burners of wood are aware that wood should be aged before it becomes fuel.

"Another common hazard is the use of the type of thin stovepipe sold by most hardware stores. I have seen a horizontal run of this pipe along the length of a ceiling and suspended by wires. If there is a flue fire the wires could burn through and the whole pipe would crash down into the middle of the room."

Unlike Lenz, O'Connell believes that anyone with good balance and who is not terribly afraid of heights can clean a chimney. The increasing availability of chimney cleaning tools makes the task all the easier, and he says no one need spend the $1,200 for a complete chimney cleaning package just to keep the home fires burning safely. The commercial sweeping kits often include an industrial vacuum cleaner, an item totally unnecessary for amateur sweeps. A steel flue brush and a set of extension poles can usually be had for $60 to $75 (see Sources), and most other necessary items can be found around the typical home or workshop.

BLACK PERIL

Whether cleaning one's own chimney or relying on the services of a sweep, the burner of wood should be aware of what is being removed and why it cannot be allowed to accumulate in a flue.

Creosote is the bane of many contemporary wood heating systems, and it is produced in quantity by a slow-burning, smoldering fire — the very sort that makes for the six-to-16-hour burns of which many stove owners are so proud.

Creosote is the name of a specific chemical compound ($C_8H_{10}O_2$), which, in its commercially available form, is used to weatherproof railroad ties and other wood. It also occurs in chimneys used to vent wood smoke, but creosote from a sweep's viewpoint is a complex mixture of wood tar, soot and other by-products produced by the burning of wood.

It appears in three primary forms: a thin, watery fluid that consists of creosote and soot mixed with water which has condensed in the chimney; a dry, black, grey or brownish brittle crust found clinging to the inside of the flue or accumulating at elbows or in the bottom of the chimney, and a tar-like, thick, sticky layer which, in severe cases, can seriously clog a chimney. The sooty fluids and the tar-like layer are practically impossible to remove before they become pyrolized. These forms of creosote ignite only at extremely high temperatures. It is the brittle, pyrolized creosote which is the potential fuel for a flue fire.

Although relatively little research has been done on creosote formation, it is believed that three main factors determine the amount that is deposited at a given time or in a given chimney.

Smoke Density: Creosote builds up when thick smoke, sometimes known as *tar fog*, condenses on the walls of a cool flue. Dense smoke occurs when a fire is oxygen-starved or when green wood is burned.

Contrary to the popular notion that seasoned hardwood will not yield creosote, there is ample evidence to show that even the driest, hardest of woods can cause problems if improperly burned. An airtight stove kept constantly in a tightly dampered state burns wood very slowly, producing heavy smoke and large amounts of incompletely burned wastes — no matter what fuel is used.

Stack Temperature: A cold chimney serves as a distillation tube for warm tar fog, and a slow-burning fire is accompanied by lower flue temperatures, and a correspondingly high rate of creosote formation. Other factors that come into play are the type of chimney and its location. The newer, insulated metal flues are reported by many sweeps to be much less prone to creosoting problems, while masonry chimneys that run up an outside wall are among the worst. The ideal chimney, in most opinions, is one which is contained within the house and therefore much easier to keep warm.

Residence Time: This term refers to the period necessary for smoke to exit from the stove and chimney. In a slow-burning fire, smoke rises sluggishly up the chimney, providing increased exposure to cooling effects of the flue walls. Bends and elbows in the stovepipe and flue also serve to increase the residence time by creating turbulence and swirls of tar fog.

One environment in which creosote formation is kept to a minimum is the typical open fireplace. With an unhampered flow of air, the wood burns rapidly and completely, with nearly complete combustion of flammable particles in the smoke and wood gas. The chimney of such a fireplace should be checked at least once each year, but cleaning may only be necessary in alternating years.

At the other end of the spectrum we find the efficient airtight stove, which, if kept in a perpetual slow burn, may clog a flue with creosote in two weeks or less.

BURN HABITS

The stack temperature above a roaring fire may exceed 500 degrees F, and will cause any tar-like creosote deposits in the flue to pyrolize or dry into brittle flakes which usually fall harmlessly to the base of the chimney. Such a fire, unfortunately, is very fuel-inefficient and requires constant feeding to sustain.

A damped-down, smoldering burn uses appreciably less wood, and may be accompanied by flue temperatures of 125 degrees, with heavy distillation of creosote. At a compromise temperature of 212 degrees, creosote formation is kept within bounds while fuel efficiency remains respectable. (Flue thermometers are available for taking readings on smoke temperatures.)

Many airtight stove owners have formed a habit of letting the stove burn freely at least twice each day. This serves to pyrolize creosote deposits collected in the previous slow-burn cycle and appears to reduce the need for cleaning substantially. These two hot fires are usually scheduled for the morning (helping, at the same time, to take any lingering chill from the room) and in the evening or just before damping the stove down for the night. It is recommended that the fire be fuelled only with wood, and not aided by the addition of paper, trash or pine boughs.

This procedure must, of course, be started only with the assurance that the chimney is clean and sound. A flue already seriously laden with creosote

may simply go up in flame with the building of the first hot fire. Likewise, a weak or cracked chimney should be repaired or fixed before any fire — especially a very hot one — is lit.

Gerald Pelletier, of the Ontario Fire Marshall's Office, says that the majority of flue fires are caused by people who buy too-large wood stoves and then find they must operate them constantly with the dampers nearly closed. Dr. Jay Shelton, author of a new text entitled *Wood Heat Safety*, says that large, infrequent loading of wood also tends to produce more creosote than regular, smaller feedings.

"Most airtight stoves can be operated to yield as clean a burn as any other wood burner," says Shelton. "Typically, smoke-free clean burning requires small fuel loads — two to four logs at a time, or one-quarter to one-half load — and leaving the air inlet relatively wide open, especially during the first 10 to 30 minutes after each loading, when most of the smoke-generating pyrolysis reactions are occurring. Toward the end of each burning cycle, the air inlet can be turned down substantially without fear of smoke generation; charcoal (when pure carbon) cannot generate creosote-producing smoke. . . .

"Constant checking and fiddling, is, of course, impractical and unnecessary. The real and necessary sacrifice is more frequent refuelling of the wood heater — perhaps every one to three hours instead of every three to nine hours. If the long duration, large load, unattended burn is important, more frequent chimney cleaning will be required."

Shelton goes on to say that his own observations of a Jotul 602 stove indicate that fuel efficiency is relatively unaffected by the size and frequency of fuel loading. He also debunks the belief that "ultra-dry" wood is the safest to burn — stating that anything below 15 per cent moisture in fuelwood will lead to extremely hot, rapid combustion, with considerable smoke production and, usually, the necessity of damping down the stove to control the amount of heat produced. (Most wood stored in an outdoor environment, but protected from the rain, will stabilize at 20 to 30 per cent moisture — an ideal fuelwood condition. Firewood kept in a heated basement, however, may dry down to 6 or 10 per cent moisture, and thus may lead to unexpected creosoting problems.)

SWEEPING BASICS

Various folk methods of cleaning chimneys have evolved over the years, and range from sending the Christmas goose up the flue prior to beheading it, to pulling a small evergreen through the pipes. Other techniques involve drawing a burlap sack filled with sand up (or down) the flue, or rattling lengths of chain in the chimney to dislodge creosote and soot deposits (a tactic that may lead to cracked masonry or flue tiles).

None of the above can compare with the effectiveness — and ease — of using a modern steel chimney brush. A single, slow pass through the chimney with one of these bristling devices is usually sufficient to remove virtually all removable creosote.

Two types are commonly available, the first being a brush with eyelets at the top and bottom and designed to be pulled through the chimney on a rope or ropes. A one-man method using this type of brush involves hanging a weight from the lower eyelet and lowering the brush down through the chimney. This method is occasionally used by professional sweeps when faced with a restricted access chimney, in which the extension poles cannot be employed.

Most sweeps, however, prefer to work with a brush fitted to the end of a rod. This system allows one to work either from the rooftop or from inside the house, provided there is adequate clearance for entry of the rod. (The highly flexible fibreglass lets the extension rod angle rather sharply into and up a flue.)

Assuming that the brush is of the correct size for the chimney being cleaned (an eight-inch flue calls for an eight-inch metal brush; a larger size for the flexible plastic brushes is suggested), it is merely worked slowly through the chimney — either from top down or bottom up. As the brush progresses, it should be worked in short, up-and-down scrubbing strokes, with a pause at the end of the downward stroke to allow time for loosened debris to fall. Additional extension rods are screwed on as needed until the brush emerges from the top of the chimney or strikes the bottom.

The flex in the rods allows the brush to be worked around most slight angles and jogs in the flue, but in especially tortuous chimneys a plumber's snake may have to be employed. Most sweeps recommend steel brushes over the cheaper plastic versions and, although they generally work with .48-inch diameter fibreglass rods, the homeowner should be well-served with the less expensive .35-inch diameter rods.

Brushes — round, square and rectangular — can be ordered to fit most chimneys, but in the event that the exact size needed is not available, the next size smaller should be chosen. Steel brushes should not be used on some types of prefabricated steel chimneys because this will scratch the metal and invalidate the guarantee. In these cases, a flexible bristle or nylon brush should be used instead.

Steps should have been taken to assure that dislodged creosote, soot, ash and dust are kept from entering the house. If an open fireplace is being cleaned from the top, its damper should be shut tightly, and if this seems insufficient, a sheet or piece of paper can be taped over the mouth of the fireplace. A closed airtight stove will contain any clouds of dust, but if the stove has been disconnected for cleaning, the wall exit should be stuffed with paper to seal the flue from the interior of the house.

When cleaning from inside the house, it is important that downdrafts be avoided, or loosened soot will be drawn back into the house. Cleaning on a cool day usually assures an upward flow of air, but it may be necessary to open a first-floor window or two to create the proper flow of air. (To determine the direction of flow, hold a smoking piece of paper near the opening of the stove, fireplace or flue.)

A badly creosoted stovepipe, **top,** *with a typically heavy accumulation at the elbows, which creates turbulence in the flow of smoke. The cleaning of such pipes is best done outdoors,* **below.**

Having cleaned the chimney, one should next shovel out the fallen creosote and soot and bag it to go to the dump (it serves no useful purpose around farm or garden). Using a flashlight, the chimney should be inspected to assure that the walls are now clean; they need not be shining bright or spotless, but any obvious deposits of creosote should have been removed. In an especially dirty chimney, the falling creosote occasionally jams in the flue, creating a thick block of fallen waste. If you are unable to visually check the flue, insert a fire poker or other tool to assure yourself that the chimney is open.

To clean the stovepipe connecting stove to chimney, it is often best to take it down and move it outdoors to avoid creating a mess inside. If the pipe is properly screwed together at each joint, it may be possible to carry it out in one piece and clean it without totally disassembling the sections. When taking apart any stovepipe, it is wise to first make a small scratch at each joint, so that the pieces can be rejoined easily (used stovepipe sections can stubbornly refuse to be connected in a new order or alignment). The pipes can be cleaned with a sweep's brush or with a simple, long-handled wire brush available from hardware stores.

For the occasional cleaning of the stove or fireplace itself, a drop cloth should be spread to protect surrounding floor space, and any hint of a downdraft avoided. If the chimney is drawing air briskly, the inevitable dust that arises will be carried up and out the flue. Professional chimney sweeps make use of an industrial vacuum cleaner to clean stoves and fireplaces, as well as to filter dust from the air during the indoor cleaning process. The average home vacuum should not, however, be used for cleaning up heavy amounts of ash, as the fine particles can damage the motor bearings. Using a wire brush, scraper, flashlight, ash shovel and whisk broom, however, it is possible to do a completely acceptable job of cleaning any stove. Occasionally a fireplace will have an almost inaccessible smoke shelf or other space where creosote, ash and soot have accumulated, and an industrial vacuum (available at rental outlets) may have to be employed to complete the job. Dampers, too, must be a part of the cleaning routine to ensure that they are free of creosote deposits, and damper openings must be cleared of bits of mortar.

HOW OFTEN?

The frequency of such cleanings, of course, depends on the type of stove, the wood being burned and the habits of those who use the stove. It is generally recommended that the chimney and stovepipes be checked after two weeks of using a new stove. If no serious deposits are found, the stove can be used for another two to four weeks, and checked again until the owner has a feeling for how often a sweeping is necessary. The standard guideline states that any deposit of creosote more than one-quarter-inch thick should be cleaned.

The prime place to check is the point where the stovepipe enters the chimney flue. If the deposits are sticky and tar-like, the chimney cannot be cleaned without fouling one's brush. A hot fire should be

Sources

Chimney Cleaning Equipment:

AARAN CHIMNEY SWEEPS
206 Hodgson Drive
Newmarket, Ontario L3Y 1E2
Chimney cleaning services and equipment.

THE CHIMNEY BRUSH
R.R.1
Kinmount, Ontario K0M 2A0
Twenty-five sizes of wire chimney brushes.

SOOT AND CINDERS
Box 1861
Peterborough, Ont. K9J 7X7
(705) 742-2911
Steel and poly brushes, rods and brooms. Free catalogue and price list.

TOP HAT CHIMNEY SWEEPS
Box 3457H, Station C
Ottawa, Ontario K1Y 4J6
(613) 722-1226
Canadian distributor for Black Magic chimney supplies.

WOOD-FUEL TECHNOLOGY
Box 22
La Have, Nova Scotia B0R 1C0
(902) 543-2289
Steel brushes in custom-made sizes. Rods in ½m, 1m and 1½m lengths.

TOPPER CHIMNEY SERVICE
Box 1081
Kitchener, Ontario N2G 1Y0
(519) 745-8861
Steel and poly brushes and fibreglass rods.

WOOD 'N ENERGY PRODUCTS
Main Street
McDonald's Corners, Ont. K0G 1M0
(613) 278-2023
Steel and basine brushes in all standard sizes. Fibreglass or steel rods.

ENERGY ALTERNATIVES
2 Croft Street
Box 671
Amherst, Nova Scotia B4H 4B8
(902) 667-2790
Steel chimney brushes in all standard sizes. Twisted steel rods with flexible handles.

HEAT & SWEEP
Box 823
Beausejour, Manitoba R0E 0C0
Steel chimney brushes and accessories. Free catalogue.

POWRMATIC OF CANADA LTD.
1169 Caledonia Road
Toronto, Ontario M6A 2X1
(416) 781-9384
Wholesale dealer in steel and basine chimney brushes in 29 sizes. Seventy-five brush dealers across Canada. Write for location of nearest distributor.

IMPROVED CONSUMER PRODUCTS INC.
100 Towne Street
Attleboro Falls, Mass 02763
(617) 695-6841
Vacu-Stack, an "automatic chimney sweep" which also eliminates down-drafts and puff-backs and keeps rain, snow, leaves and birds out of the chimney. Will ship to Canada.

AUGUST WEST SYSTEMS INC.
Box 603W
Westport, Connecticut 06880
Equipment for chimney cleaning business. Send for free booklet.

BLACK MAGIC CHIMNEY SWEEPS INT'L. INC.
Box 977
Stowe, Vermont
Chimney sweeps catalogue $1.00. *Chimney Sweeping and Wood Stove Cleaning* booklet $1.50.

CHIMNEY CARE
Box 426
Cavendish, Vermont 05142
Chimney brushes and supplies.

KRISTIA ASSOCIATES
Box 1118
Portland, Maine 04104
Chimney brushes in all standard sizes. *The Chimney Brush* booklet $1.00.

Chimney Cleaning Courses:

TORONTO CHIMNEY SERVICE LIMITED
36 Rivalda Road
Weston, Ontario M9M 2M3
Chimney sweeping service and information seminars.

BLACK KNIGHT COMPANY
R.R.6
Kensington, P.E.I. C0B 1M0
Chimney sweep course, including private training, manual, tool access information, business advice.

TOWN & COUNTRY CHIMNEY SERVICE LTD.
Box 1305, Postal Station B
Mississauga, Ontario L4Y 4B6
Chimney cleaning services and courses.

Books:

WOOD HEAT SAFETY
By Jay W. Shelton

Garden Way Publishing
Charlotte, Vermont 05445
165 pages, (Paperback)
Jay Shelton is a former member of the Williams College department of physics, and he brings to the inexact science of burning wood a much-needed critical approach and the kind of hard information that is badly needed. *Wood Heat Safety* is the best book to date covering the all-important topics of stove, fireplace and chimney installation, as well as operation, maintenance and a great deal of information on the safe, efficient burning of firewood.

BE YOUR OWN CHIMNEY SWEEP
By Christopher Curtis & Donald Post
Garden Way Publishing
Charlotte, Vermont 05445
101 pages, (Paperback)
Clearly written and well-illustrated with step-by-step photographs, this book should give the average stove or fireplace owner the confidence to start sweeping his own chimneys.

Information:

CANADIAN CHIMNEY SWEEPS ASSOCIATION
Chimney Sweep Niagara
223 Scott Street
St. Catharines, Ontario L2N 1H6

built to pyrolize the creosote, turning it into dry flakes which are easily swept. If a hard, slag-like deposit is found, it is usually best left alone. It can be chiselled or hammered out, but only at the risk of damaging the chimney.

In the wake of a chimney fire, the flue should be swept and the entire system checked for the presence of leaks or cracks. This can be done visually and with the use of a smoke test, in which a wet blanket or burlap sack is used to seal the top of the chimney once a small but smoky fire has been built (using hay, green leaves, grass clippings or wet leaves). One person should be on the roof ready to apply and remove the wet cloth, and another below to watch the fire and check for smoke leaking out the chimney. While the flue is well filled with smoke, someone should inspect its entire length, looking for tell-tale wisps of escaping smoke.

If all of this boggles the mind, calling a professional sweep may be the answer (ignoring the chimney is not). A good sweep will do more than clean the chimney. He should be able to tell you if a stove and chimney are safely installed and should report on the condition of the chimney. He should be willing to explain what he's doing and may provide the would-be chimney sweep with the confidence to do the job himself.

To hire a sweep, ask for estimates from several professionals in the area — if they exist. Ask how much experience the sweep has had, if he carries insurance (a good sweep does) and if he guarantees that the job will be done without mess. A trail of soot across a rug is the footprint of a careless and/or incompetent sweep.

Orrin C. Kerr is bearded, long-haired and as tall and wide as a lot of chimneys. Burly is the word that springs to mind. "You'll find that each sweep has his own, slightly different method. Each sweep does things a little bit differently," he said, in extending an invitation to watch him work his black magic.

The overnight snow squall has left the roof icy, and Kerr is working inside a very handsome Kingston home with an enormous driveway and a stunning view of the sun shimmering off the waters of Lake Ontario directly across the quiet street.

Using a steel brush at the end of fibreglass rods, Kerr is ready to move on to the second of three fireplaces he will clean that afternoon. A business administration student, Kerr has been supplementing his income by working as a part-time sweep. At $35 for the first chimney and $10 less for each additional flue in the same dwelling, he made about $1,500 last year, but looks to a higher income in his second full year as a part-time sweep.

For one thing, he has built up a clientele for his services, a growing list of homeowners who now rely on him for regular cleaning and fire-safety advice. Also, what he calls his "direct advertising campaign" is starting to pay off.

He has taken out a Yellow Pages listing and he distributes an advertising brochure in neighbourhoods with a lot of chimneys on the roofs. To keep a seasonal business going year-round — the Kingston

A professional sweep often relies on an industrial vacuum, a useful tool but not essential for do-it-yourself cleaning.

family wanted their fireplaces clean and ready in time for Christmas festivities — Kerr offers special summer rates, $5 less per flue across the board.

He now removes the gas mask he has been wearing and, after greetings are exchanged, he remarks that the mask is one necessary item of the sweep's equipment which is missing from most start-your-own-sweeping-business kits. "The low capital outlay is what attracted me to do this in the first place. For $600 to $800 you can set yourself up in business," says Kerr who drove to the job in his station wagon. "The mask is important," he emphasizes, "because all that dust is carcinogenic, you know. You don't want to inhale too much of the stuff. Any industrial-type gas mask will do. You can get them for less than $5, but if I were just cleaning my own chimney a few times a year I wouldn't bother — just tie a piece of cheesecloth, or something like that, across your face to cover your nose and mouth."

CLEAN SWEEP

He now removes the three strips of masking tape which hold up a piece of shiny, light purple cloth covering the fireplace opening. Not only are there no soot marks on the greenish, deep-pile carpet, there's hardly a speck of dust on the drop sheet he has spread around the work area directly in front of the hearth. Kerr extracts the ribbed rubber hose from inside the fireplace and triggers the "off" switch on a very ordinary, very battered household vacuum. The whirr stops. "It works well enough," he notes, nodding his head at the Hoover. "Of course you can't use it to clean your house again . . . this one's really old, I think it will need a new motor soon."

The sweep surveys the work area and proudly indicates the foot-high mound of pyrolized creosote now covering the floor of the firebox. "That's the stuff that ignites in a flue fire," he says, handing me a pebble-sized piece. The chunk is very light, and all the tiny airholes make it appear almost greyish. The slightest finger pressure turns it into dust.

Kerr scoops the now defused fire hazard out of the fireplace and into a brown grocery bag that he places alongside his tool kit on the dropsheet. Beside it sits a 35-gallon, or more, stovepipe hat. It is enormous and is hand-fashioned of black leather. Folded neatly next to it is the black tailcoat, its brass buttons gleaming in the sunlight.

One last look.

Aha! There's a half-inch long sooty smudge on the whitewashed bricks above the fireplace opening. Kerr yanks off the blue welder's cap he has been wearing, crumples it into a ball and sticks it in the back pocket of his faded jeans. He takes off his leather work gloves, moistens the thumb and the index finger of his right hand and rubs the spot clean. He moves on to the next room where he safely navigates the bulky tool kit, the brushes swinging with each step, past the immaculate baby grand piano and the expensively fragile bric-a-brac.

He begins again. The dropsheet is spread over the hearth and the carpet next to it. This time the roll of tape stays in the tool box because this fireplace opening is narrow enough to enable him to use an extendible rod inserted through one end of the light purple cloth and secured in place to cover the fireplace opening.

He straps on the gas mask, flicks the "on" switch of the vacuum and repeats the task of working the flexible steel bristles up the chimney, adding extension rods as he goes along.

It's a routine and it goes along smoothly, without grunts and with no dust flying into the expensively-furnished room. There's time to chat and exchange bits of chimney-sweeping lore. The job itself is hardly romantic, yet its practitioners have nurtured through the ages a certain aura, an air of professional mystique.

"Traditionally the sweep is considered a creature of good luck," says Kerr. "In Germany, custom had it that if you touch the sweep's brushes good luck will rub off on you. In England and the Scandinavian countries, the luck is picked up by shaking the sweep's hand, or in the case of ladies, by kissing him . . . this is the part of the job I like best. Another Olde English custom is to invite a chimney sweep to the wedding to kiss the bride and to shake the groom's hand, ensuring a lucky marriage."

Not being superstitious, yet not wishing to take any unnecessary chances at the same time, I hold out my hand. We shake. As I leave, Kerr turns his back to return to his task and here's my opportunity: On the way to the door I sneak a quick feel of the steel bristles . . . just in case.

Windsteading Into the Eighties

Three families who live — and cope — with the most alternative of the alternative technologies

By Frank B. Edwards

The old ladies from Westmount sit on their elegant front verandah overlooking Lake Massawippi complaining of the muggy, midsummer heat, looking to the gathering clouds at the south end of the lake for relief. An isolated breeze stirs from somewhere on the water's surface and climbs the steep hillside toward the house, gently shaking the maple leaves in its path to life and sending a ripple through the summer people's Canadian flag.

"If it rains, this heat could break," suggests the larger of the matrons as she fans herself with a magazine. "Even a breeze would help. It's *soooo* humid."

"You're right dear. Yes, yes. Let's move inside where it's nicer." Struggling up, the second lady straightens her white skirt and heads slowly through the door to the darkened living room. Her friend follows closely behind as the breeze drops and the flag falls still once more.

The oppressive temperatures have brought the usually slow pace of North Hatley, Quebec, to a standstill. Summer residents from Montreal in their huge clapboard homes on the sides of the treed hillsides surrounding the lake stay on their porches or indoors out of the heat. There are few swimmers, as it is midweek and grandchildren will not arrive until the weekend. In the hazy humidity, indolence seems the most appropriate course of action.

Although some of the summer residents might seem oblivious to the fact, there are people in the area not on vacation. Ten miles away, across the Massawippi and over a ridge of hills, David Simms drives slowly along the winding laneway that leads through a freshly mowed hayfield to his log house. Parking the Saab in the front yard, he enters the house to change quickly into shorts and T-shirt, and plucks a cold ale from an old horizontal Kelvinator ice-cream freezer which dominates one wall of the kitchen.

Built over a period of two years from a pre-fabricated kit, the Simms' home is a world removed from the turn-of-the-century elegance of the summer residences. The log walls, in concert with floor boards of birch, maple and pine, give the kitchen an aura of 19th-century pioneer rusticity. A hulking McClary cookstove dominates the kitchen, and a Clivus Multrum composting toilet system provides the ultimate in ecological waste disposal.

The house site is quiet, well back from the gravel road and tucked behind a row of trees. Driving past, one can see only the shiny galvanized steel roof and, glinting in the sun, a three-bladed generator atop a 50-foot-high tower. From a distance, the owner-built home and wind machine make for a postcard scene, but today, sitting at the Simms' kitchen table, one cannot help but think about the languorous breeze which gives the wooden propellers a lazy turn once in a while but which generates not a watt of energy.

"We can go about 10 or 14 days," says Simms. "We spend some time looking at the weather, I suppose, but then we are playing the game in a chancy area." (The nearest provincial meteorological office shows the average annual wind speed for the area to be 8.4 miles per hour with a winter peak of 9.4 miles per hour in February and a low of 7.0 miles per hour in July. Many wind experts consider anything below

Lisl Dennis/Image Bank of Canada

10 miles per hour to be very poor wind, indeed.)

The Simms family, however, has lived on home-generated wind power for four years, in part because their entire household consumption of electricity averages but 100 kilowatt hours per month — less than the energy burned by a single room air conditioner used two and a half hours per day in one of the Lake Massawippi summer homes.

The Simms are what one observer refers to as "windsteaders," newcomers to the countryside bent on energy independence through the use of an aerogenerator. The technology they have adopted is a curious amalgam of the very new and the very old, with the latter serving as the backbone of most wind-powered households in North America today.

While solar energy surges forward, with improved technology, simple but successful passive (no moving parts) design advances and increasing public acceptance, wind power — in contrast — advances slowly, caught in its own technological doldrums. The major hardware breakthrough, predicted and hoped for by many, has failed to materialize; prices of equipment remain prohibitively high for many would-be purchasers; inconveniences, for the wind power users, have not been greatly lessened in the past decade.

LIFE OUTSIDE THE GRID

Of all the widespread owner-user alternative technologies, wind energy remains the most remote, the most demanding, the most alternative. And yet, there are those who have not been willing or able to wait for its blossoming, those who are attempting to

The so-called bicycle wheel, **above,** *is but one of dozens of exotic aerogenerator designs now vying for success.*

make the best of existing, off-the-shelf technology, determined to make it work.

The decision to power their home with wind was made easy for David and Linda Simms, natives of Sherbrooke, Quebec, who bought 100 acres of bush and pasture near Lake Massawippi in 1975. While many of their new neighbours were weekend or summer people, the Simms came to live year-round, making their livings in homestead fashion, as best they could.

The relative isolation of the area, which had first attracted them, proved to include a major challenge to their limited budget: Quebec Hydro wanted $1,200 to connect them to the provincial power grid. They would also be required, by law, to have a provincially licensed electrician wire their house, at a cost of about $1,500. A teacher by profession — he is currently augmenting the family income by teaching English to French-speaking students — Simms had proved his ability to handle tools in building the new home, and the decision was made to wire the house themselves and put up a wind machine.

They lived for three months without power, using kerosene lamps, carrying water and doing their laundry in town, while David installed an 1800-watt Jacobs generator bought in Vermont. Although the unit eventually proved too small, Simms was immediately hooked on wind power and hooked on the rebuilt Jacobs generators, holdovers from decades ago.

The 2800-watt reconditioned Jacobs that now runs their house feeds power into a bank of 16 two-volt batteries bought from the telephone company, and thence into a simple but effective electrical system. The wind-powered household has 17 light bulbs, ranging from 50 to 100 watts, a water pump, a refrigerator, a wringer washer and several small appliances, including an iron, vacuum cleaner and food blender.

Because the components of this autonomous system operate on 32-volt direct current (DC) power — long ago abandoned by the utilities for 120-volt alternating current (AC) — the Simms have had to rewind motors, scrounge antique-vintage appliances and adapt various modern devices to their maverick system.

Refrigeration, says Simms, was a particular problem that — in the form of a conventional upright kitchen unit — threatened to put a fatal drain on their wind energy production.

COLD INGENUITY

Designed to run in households with unlimited power to burn, the modern refrigerator is, in Simms' words, "a monument to inefficient energy use." Poorly insulated, it allows warmth in and cold out through thin walls, and it dumps valuable cold air onto the floor every time the door is opened.

The motor and compressor are sealed into the bottom, producing heat that is trapped under the unit while the coils that run down the back, draining warm air out of the box, radiate heat against the back wall of the refrigerator. It is, says Simms, little wonder that modern units run so much of the time, producing heat and using from 100 to 150 kilowatt hours a month.

Once Simms realized that the refrigerator was using most of their power, he set out to solve the problem by switching to an older, heavier ice-cream freezer of the kind still found in small variety stores. With five inches of cork insulation in its walls and heavy rubber lids that sit on top of the unit, the old horizontal Kelvinator was a steal at five dollars. To solve the heat radiation problem, Simms removed the motor and compressor and, after replacing the motor with one which would use 32-volt DC power, mounted them in the basement directly below the refrigerator. He ran copper tubes through the floor to carry the freon coolant from compressor to refrigerator box and ended up with an unusually efficient refrigeration system. By adjusting the thermostat, the old freezer became a refrigerator.

The tamed refrigerator is the cornerstone of the Simms' particular energy conservation pattern — they heat with wood and have eliminated all extraneous appliances — but the rebuilt Jacobs spinning high above the house is in the business end of the system.

Forty years ago, the Jacobs wind generator was perhaps the ultimate rural status symbol. In areas where power lines had not been strung, those who wanted the newfangled gadgetry of the fledgling electric era had to provide their own power and the Jacobs did the job admirably. It was not for the ordinary man though, selling in 1935 for the seemingly unattainable price of $3,000.

Frank B. Edwards

Now writing a book about small-scale wind systems, David Simms and his family have lived with wind energy for four years, running lights, water pump, appliances such as a vacuum, blender and iron, as well as an ice-cream freezer that was converted into an energy-efficient refrigerator.

Built simply and to last a lifetime, the Jacobs was virtually maintenance-free and provided a dependable 32 or 110 volts of direct current to those who could afford it. The simple construction had a direct-drive, shunt-wound DC generator coupled directly to the blades. Only 125 rpm was sufficient to produce electricity which flowed through wires to a battery storage bank where it was kept until required. A few refinements, such as a regulator to keep the power from flowing back to the generator once it reached the batteries, made it an attractive if slightly crude and simple method of producing electricity. With their three blade propellers turning in the wind, the Jacobs provided isolated farms with lights, radio and, if the owner had splurged on direct current accessories, even power for irons and vacuum cleaners.

The Jacobs' popularity, however, was short-lived. Between 1931 and 1956, tens of thousands of the units were produced for distribution across North America, but, as the utility companies extended their services across the countryside, the lure of 120-volt alternating current proved stronger than the less comfortable pioneer traditions of independence and self-sufficiency. The survival of the wind generator faltered in the face of the utilities' economies of scale and the attraction of a plethora of new electric consumer goods which ranged from stoves to can openers, juice squeezers and television sets, all produced to serve the new mass market on 120-volt AC.

Of the large number of Jacobs that were made, few survived their owners' purges of outdated technology. They were relegated to barns and garages or to the bottom of back-acre sloughs to rust and decay with Model-T trucks and Massey-Harris tractors of similar vintage. The same fate befell the equally durable Wincharger generators as pride and widespread acceptance of high voltage alternating current signalled the end of wind power's short-lived acceptance. By the 1950s the spinning of the generators' propellers was a symbol of rural backwardness and their production ceased. Once seen as the answer to farmers' energy requirements, they were viewed finally as a novel stopgap between the 19th century and the modern age.

"Especially on the prairies, there was an unfortunate association of wind power with the hard times of the '30s, and that is one reason why so many generators were abandoned," says Simms. "That, and the basic difficulties arising from the use of 32-volt DC."

Decades after thousands of families switched to the grid lines for power, Simms and a number of like-minded people have recently scoured the countryside looking for the wind relics. The one that now lights Simms' house came from a barn floor somewhere in Iowa, and he bought it from Roland Coulson, an Iowa wind machine dealer who specialized in finding old Jacobs, buying low and selling them just a bit higher, either reconditioned or as they had been found. Today there are few Jacobs left to uncover, and Simms says that Coulson regrets selling his stock so hastily. Both men swear that the Jacobs units were built to last a lifetime and usually do.

"When I repaired it, it was in quite doubtful looking condition. They really draw mice when left in a barn — they're excellent nesting spots — and this one was stuck together, full of nests and dung and rust."

The armature which holds the generator's induction coils was so gummed up that Simms needed a sledge hammer to loosen it; yet after cleaning it did not need to be rewound. He simply changed the bearings and brushes and replaced the propeller blades and the governor, which regulates the speed of the generator in high winds. Simms paid $1,900 for the generator and spent another $600 for the props and governor. A second-hand tower cost $400 and his storage bank of 16 two-volt batteries from a telephone exchange came to $320 for a total of about $3,200, compared to the $2,600 price tag Hydro was wearing back in 1976. Simms is quick to point out that it was a capital investment and he is free of bi-monthly hydro bills. In fact, his generator alone is now worth about $5,000 on the current market.

Through his own hard-earned success with wind power, Simms has influenced others to put in aerogenerators and has established a small cottage business rebuilding and selling Jacobs and Wincharger units. Having lived for a year in Newfoundland and toured the Maritime provinces, he is confident that it is on the windy East Coast — where energy is most expensive — that wind power will prove most useful.

"If we were in Prince Edward Island with our 2800-watt generator, we could run three houses like this. What I'm looking at essentially is to provide a home with minimal electrical service by using a rather small wind generator and smaller batteries so it is more cost effective. Right now in places like Newfoundland or P.E.I. where there is plenty of wind, I can visualize someone setting up a one-kilowatt (1000-watt) wind generator and running perfectly well what we're running here with a three-kilowatt unit and perhaps even having a surplus.

"I also think that what people must have in order to switch to wind power is absolute reliability — never running out of electricity. So you design the system to meet that requirement. And you can do it. All you have to do is play with your variables. The size of the generator, the wind speed, appliances, storage capacity . . . .

"We must design ways to conserve energy so people can get by with a smaller machine. If wind is going to make a dent in our energy usage, people have to be able to afford it. Not everyone can invest $6,000 or $10,000 in wind systems. I don't know what we can shoot for in terms of cost, but I'm sure in some windy areas cost can be quite minimal.

Simms says that low wind areas now demand a greater investment in hardware, but, as his own experience shows, wind power can work in very marginal wind areas, provided the users are willing to hone their talents for saving energy.

ENERGY-EFFICIENT UNIT

Critics of people like the Simms clearly take a certain amount of glee in the "hardships" they have brought upon themselves by adopting a not-quite-perfected technology. One such skeptic is Hans S. Classen, an information officer with the federal government's Department of Energy, Mines and Resources, who in 1977 published an analysis of wind energy's potential, concluding that it would solve few energy problems.

"For a single-family home using the common electrical appliances without electrical heating," he wrote in *Canadian Geographic*, "the cost of an installed wind-powered electrical system, in an area where the average wind speed is adequate, has been variously estimated at $20,000 to $60,000. To this there would have to be added the cost of maintenance and replacements."

Such estimates are the bane of wind power advocates as they assume the use of appliances which are both unnecessary and inefficient in their use of electricity. Simms, taking a common-sense approach to the technology, points out that a wind-powered household must also be an energy-efficient unit.

"If I were doing it again, I would try to design the house more around the wind system, building a second floor water tank, for example, so that we could run a gravity-fed water supply, pumping water to fill it only when the batteries were charged up. You have to be conservation-minded to get by in a low wind area like this, but you can do it. When there is no wind for a day or two, you start being really careful. You don't waste electricity. Wind power puts you more in touch with the house and what it takes to run it."

Although Simms is not completely sure of the velocity of the wind that finds its way up the face of

Acrophobia is no problem for Simms, making adjustments on a rebuilt Jacobs which is still the paragon of excellence among North American wind machines.

Frank B. Edwards

their small hill from day to day, he does know that the family has cut its energy usage to one-seventh or one-eighth of the Canadian average and that he has not had to use the gasoline back-up generator to restore power to the battery bank since he modified the refrigerator.

JES' PORE COUNTRY FOLK

A 40-minute drive through the backroads of Quebec's Eastern Townships will take anyone who shies from the admittedly spartan Simms' homestead to the small town of Holland, Vermont, and the home of a different breed of wind user. With the exception of the occasional American flag and Exxon station, there is not a great deal of visible difference between this part of New England and nearby Quebec. It is just as miserably hot on this particular day as it had been outside North Hatley where the Simms live. When the wind blows here, it

is part of the same weather system that turns David Simms' generator, and when it snows with a vengeance on the Simms' place in winter, one can be sure that Douglas and Mary Rossier are settling in for the same storm.

A retired farm implement dealer who moved to this 38-acre piece of woods and meadows after selling his business to a son, Doug Rossier is a tall, thin, sinewy man with a deliberate way of speaking and a good nature. His eyes appear steely behind his tinted glasses, but each time he makes a good point in the conversation, he flashes a self-conscious grin. He is a man with a sense of humour very clearly streaked with stubbornness.

The Rossiers' wind tower sits about 100 yards from the house, well away from the thick wall of trees which surround the building, and without keeping it in view, one is inclined to forget the energy frugality involved here. This could be the country house-of-the-month in *Shelter* magazine. A stretch of well-kept lawn lies to the south of the house, allowing the sun full access to the high windows that rise from the floor of the dining/living room at the top of its cathedral ceiling, while the other three sides are surrounded by spruce trees full of chattering blue jays. Inside the house, a red brick fireplace soars to the high ceiling, separating the dining area from the living room.

While the Simms' home is frontier-rustic, the Rossiers' does not present a picture of deprived windsteading. The floors are broadloomed wall-to-wall, the kitchen is a mixture of stainless steel, arborite and cushion flooring. Everything is new and glistening.

"Well what did you expect?" roars Doug, obviously enjoying the reaction he has seen countless times before. He slips into a well-rehearsed shuffling old-timer routine.

" 'lec-tri-ci-ty?" he stammers, shaking his head slowly from side to side, his shoulders stooped over. "No, we got no 'lectricity. We're jes' pore country folk trying to survive out here in the wilderness, doing the best we can. Can't get no newfangled things." He and his wife guffaw when it's over, and Mary explains the performance in her soft, kindly tone.

"I always get a kick out of how people view this house. Some people just seem so surprised to see that we're living in the 20th century."

First impressions are deceiving, however, and it soon becomes clear that the Rossiers have picked and chosen their comforts carefully. On first glance, some of the appliances and fixtures don't seem to fit into the capabilities of a wind-powered system. The house has what appear to be fluorescent lights, the dining room has a small television, the living room an impressive stereo and the sewing room an electric sewing machine.

Each of these, it turns out, is carefully matched to the power source and has been chosen at the expense of an electric refrigerator and water heater. Cooking and heating are done with wood, a plentiful resource in the area.

"Never use the fireplace, you know," says Rossier, flashing his smile. "It looks good and when we sell in the future that will be the thing that convinces the new owner to buy. But we never use it. Just too impractical."

Instead, the house is heated with a small Jøtul wood stove that sits virtually dwarfed beside the glass doors of the open fireplace, and on which food is cooked and wash water heated. The Rossiers view many appliances as "useless and wasteful in a lazy age," and they have spent a lot of thought and money in achieving the basic comforts of life in this retirement house.

Rossier is clearly happy to be free of power lines and telephone cables and is unlikely ever to bring them in while he and his wife live there.

"I don't like being beholden to people," he explains, "and when the phone company made it seem like they were doing me a favour by hooking us up, we decided that we didn't need them. We just write a lot of letters now."

His story about the power company is a familiar one among wind power users — it was going to charge him too much to connect the house to its line because of the distance from the main road, so he told them to forget it. He didn't need them either.

"Convenience," he reflects, carrying an armful of vegetables from the garden to the house, "costs too much anyway. If you have electricity you have to have all the gadgets that go with it. We don't feel controlled by gadgets, not like some people are. We're free — we've escaped Madison Avenue."

"INVERTER CRAZY"

Closer inspection of the Rossier household reveals an unusual mix — for a wind-powered house — of AC and DC appliances. Reduced to layman's terms, DC (direct current) is that produced by the aerogenerator — or other electrical generating device; it is energy which is storable in batteries, but it cannot be transmitted over long runs of wire efficiently. Alternating current, on the other hand, is not storable but is able to be transmitted by power utilities with relatively good efficiency.

The Rossiers have fitted three 12-volt light bulbs in each light fixture, hooked up in series to draw 32 volts, as produced by their own Jacobs unit. The television is a 12-volt recreational vehicle model plugged into a 32-volt outlet, but the stereo and sewing machine are standard 120-volt AC units. They, and a few other small appliances such as vacuum cleaner and water pump, are run on AC power produced from stored wind energy but changed in form by an inverter.

Inverters are perhaps the most contentious piece of equipment being discussed by wind-powered households at the moment because, while no one can seriously debate their usefulness in a 120-volt world, they are expensive, inefficient in their use of low voltage current and inclined to break down constantly.

The Rossiers now own a small General Electric rotary model inverter Doug bought from an ambulance outfitter. Designed to boost low automotive electrical voltage to 120-volt AC for operating medical equipment in ambulances, it is simply a small DC motor which turns a small generator, which in turn produces an alternating current of 120 volts. Although it is not particularly efficient — wasting about 40 per cent of the 32-volt current to produce

AC — it works without problem and only cost $350. Comparing it with his last solid state inverter (Rossier is now on his fourth inverter) which cost $2,800, weighed 300 pounds and broke down constantly, he says it is perfect for their needs.

"Sure it is less efficient than the fancy solid state inverters (which waste only about 25 per cent of the incoming current) but it works and the first three (all solid state) didn't.

"The others have too many safety and back-up devices. Under a heavy load, small wires burn out to protect the system but they drop — burning — onto expensive circuit boards causing more damage than you can imagine. My dealer finally decided that solid state inverters are too experimental. He just threw up his hands in despair and gave me my money back on the last one."

The importance of either type of inverter (the solid state units change low direct current voltage to alternating current through an oscillator before boosting it to 120 volts in a transformer) is that they produce a perfect sine wave, rather than a "square" wave, in the electricity that pulses through the wires. While some appliances will take any shape of electronic wave, stereo equipment requires the smooth flowing sine wave for distortion-free sound reproduction.

"We've spent a long time looking for a 12-volt record player, but they don't make them," explains Rossier. "With the inverter we now can run a normal stereo hi-fi. Mind you, the inverter uses a lot of power so we only listen for an hour a day at most but I like a bit of music in the evening."

Admitting that he went "inverter crazy," Rossier double-wired the house, putting both direct and alternating current plugs throughout the rooms. Although use of AC appliances is limited by the small inverter's 900-watt capacity, there is never a shortage of plugs for the vacuum cleaner on cleaning days or for any other equipment that the couple wants to use in the house. For added convenience, the inverter is a "load demand" model which operates automatically as soon as the AC appliance is plugged in.

The house is really a maze of 12-, 32- and 110-volt circuits, plugs and appliances. At the moment most of the lights are 32 volts, but as soon as he gets a 12-volt battery bank, Rossier plans to convert them all to 12 volts so that he can use recreational vehicle (RV) light bulbs which are much easier to buy than 32-volt bulbs.

"Right now people in stores don't listen. You go into a place to buy 32-volt bulbs and they think you mean watts and then they start telling you there's no such thing or they just look at you as if you're crazy."

When the 12-volt battery bank is in place it will take only 12 volts from the wind generator and redirect the excess 20 volts to the basement water heater through a regulator, rather than simply letting the extra power go to waste as is now the case.

TRACTOR HEAT

Proving that they are more practical than purist, the Rossiers do a weekly laundry by firing up their diesel tractor (which has a 110/220-volt generator with a 13,000-watt capacity) that will heat water and run their modern washer and dryer for $2.00 worth of diesel fuel a session. It also heats up the 50 gallons of water in their hot water tank so that laundry day is also bath day. With a few batts of home insulation wrapped around the hot water tank it keeps whatever water is leftover warm for two or three days before the couple has to rely on their daily pans of hot water on the upstairs Jøtul for washing.

So far the Rossiers have spent about $7,000 on their wind system, depending on new equipment for everything but the 2800-watt rebuilt Jacobs which cost $3,000. Their tower cost $1,000 installed, the tractor generator another $1,000, the inverter $350 and assorted cables and wires a total of $600. The battery storage bank consists of 20 golf cart batteries hooked up in five units of four batteries each (the batteries are rated at eight volts each so the system is 32 volts in total with ample storage capacity). They cost $50 each for a total of another $1,000.

For their investment, the Rossiers have a comfortable if slightly confusing arrangement, which gives them a fair amount of electricity — in the order of 200 or 300 kilowatt hours a month. Compared to the Simms' household, theirs is slightly more luxurious but is missing the important element of refrigeration.

At present, they have a modern upright refrigerator which stands unplugged in the cool basement. Although it can be close to 100 degrees F outside, the cellar remains a cool 55 degrees, and the appliance stands mute in silent testimony to its near uselessness, wearing a two-inch layer of Styrofoam slabs in an effort to increase its cooling efficiency.

Every few days, one of the Rossiers goes into nearby Holland to buy ice for this most inadequate refrigerator, storing some in the small 12-volt RV freezer for future use and putting the daily offering into the fridge-cum-icebox. In winter it's a slightly different story as they can freeze their own ice on the porch at night.

"When we first got here," Mary explains, "we used the fridge and a microwave oven plugged in to run off the inverter, but they used too much power. Besides the microwave wasn't very healthy."

"Just sitting on trays on the basement floor keeps much of the food cool," Doug adds "but we are eventually going to have to come up with something else. Perhaps a 12-volt camper-trailer fridge or some such thing. We'll have to see."

But other than refrigeration, or rather the lack of it, the two have run into few serious problems. Lightning struck their tower two years ago, damaging the propeller and sending an electric charge through the line which destroyed the regulator in the basement, but the problems have been more aggravating than serious. Doug has yet to replace the regulator and must disconnect the generator's tail vane manually to keep the unit from boiling the batteries over when they are fully charged. He must also flip a switch to keep the batteries from pumping juice back into the generator when it is not producing power. A new regulator is finally on the way after a long search for an appropriate model. It does, however, point up one of the problems of those who choose any wind power system, but especially those who use the obsolete 32-volt systems.

"Nothing is ever built for wind power people," says Rossier. "We are always left to improvise. We have to scrounge everything we need . . . . People would buy these if they didn't have to beg, but right now that's what you have to do to get equipment.

"For the technology to succeed, the dealers have got to go into the whole line of products. Right now for $6,000 they'll give you a system to produce 300 or 400 kilowatt hours a month but they can't sell you efficient appliances to go with it."

Having been a farm equipment dealer, Rossier knows all about the need for a big enough market to support large inventories, the problems of scattered customers and all the other curses of the small businessman. He doesn't have a bad word to say about North Wind Power Company, with whom he has dealt almost exclusively, but he does admit that, like everyone else, they too have problems.

"You look to the dealer for everything but they're still learning themselves. They have done marvelously to have stayed in business. They'll come over 100 miles for free warranty service. They're very good, very conscientious, but the industry has got to change if it is to survive."

OU EST L'HELICE?

The road from St. Adolphe de Dudswell to Joe Smillie's homestead is long and dusty. It climbs steep hills, plunges down others and winds every which way. If you miss the turn near the old abandoned church you'll end up in Ham Sud wondering just how you got there. There's not much use in stopping to ask directions because Joe and Sue Smillie have only lived in the area for three years and that's hardly long enough for anyone here to know who they are. Some of the locals do know "the place with the propeller," so if you have the word *hélice* at your command it's some help, but if you don't, then the only thing to do is to roam the back roads keeping one eye on the gas gauge and one out for the silhouette of another Jacobs.

If the Rossiers and Simms are off the main road, then the Smillies are off a road that's off the road off the main road, but that is why they moved here. Isolation and a superb view that extends for miles, all the way across the rolling countryside. On the distant horizon, the local lime plant distinguishes itself for quite a distance by pumping thick black clouds of bottom line bunker oil into the sky. It's a great way to find St. Adolphe but is no help at all if you're looking for the Smillies.

Joe Smillie has had a rough day and it's not just because of the heat. Decked out in a fresh T-shirt and shorts, he's barefooted and squeaky clean, his hair still wet from a bath he took in hopes of refreshing himself. His eyes are red and his whole body seems as droopy as his moustache. His wife had a baby a few days ago and his life is in an uproar. The daily trip to the hospital 33 miles away to visit her last night extended into travelling to Montreal to see a baseball game and the night has taken its toll. Today some old friends have stopped in for a few days' visit, his mother is here to take care of his two-year-old daughter, the new baby is due home any day, and he is trying to hold up his end of an organic fertilizer business.

Joe Smillie is a busy man despite the serene setting, and wind power, to him, is just an incidental technology he added to the house for convenience.

"I think you have to be a little nuts to get into wind energy because it's such a strange technology .... You've got watts, amperes, volts, inverters, regulators, sine waves. You're dealing with weird electricity. Everything in North America has been standardized to the point that people think they are dealing with a very simplified system and they don't realize how incredibly complex the whole workings are. With a wind generator you find out."

For two years, 32-year-old Smillie and his wife Sue, 28, lived without electricity on the brow of a hill in the house they had designed and built not to need electricity. But two years of reading by the light cast from kerosene lamps was enough, and last fall, with a second child on the way, they decided to bring in electricity.

"There's no question about it," says Smillie as he sits at his kitchen table looking through the expanse of glass that, on calmer days, lets his mind wander for miles, "if electricity is a convenience, living without it is an inconvenience .... No, it is nigh on impossible."

He slaps a large hand down on his kitchen table for emphasis and then pauses in mid-conversation shaking his head bemusedly.

"For some obscure reason which I really can't remember, we wanted to see if we could do without electricity. We tried really hard for two years and couldn't. We had to get a bit more convenient."

His story about Hydro Quebec sounds familiar. Because their house sat a quarter of a mile from the road, it would cost $2,800 to bring the lines in and another $1,000 to $1,500 to have the building wired by an electrician. Even when they haggled the hookup price down to $2,000 it was still clear that convenience bore a heavy price tag.

That's when Smillie made the acquaintance of David Simms one weekend at a biological agriculture conference. Simms offered them an 1800-watt rebuilt Jacobs generator for $2,000, a tempting offer indeed.

Since their arrival in the Eastern Townships from Ontario, Joe and Sue Smillie had come to accept the fact that the site of their home had no shortage of wind. They had had to build snowfence windbreaks around their garden to keep the vegetables from succumbing to the force of the winds that constantly sweep across the wide-open valley and up the face of the hill. They had planted trees to block the gusts that blew across the hill's crest and hit their pine house. The windward side of the house was designed as a wedge-shape to cut through the cold winter blasts.

They had built the house on the hill, far from the road, in order to capture the spectacular view it afforded, but it meant living in a natural wind tunnel. At the time, it seemed only sensible to take advantage of all that wind, so with $2,000 in the bank and few alternatives, they accepted Simms' offer and bought the Jacobs.

The romanticism of wind power soon faded, as Smillie found himself immersed in long-forgotten

Frank B. Edwards

"Like dropping a motor into a car in mid-air," was Joe Smillie's description of the installation difficulties in placing the rebuilt Jacobs generator atop a tower high above his new, energy-efficient home in Quebec.

high school physics formulae interrelating amperes, ohms, watts and volts, each affecting the others in strange antithetical and reciprocal ways. Without a great deal of money in the bank to pay others to install the hardware, Smillie also found himself taking on the roles of electrician, lineman and crew boss.

Having no illusions of himself as a welder, he traded some woodworking hours to a welder for building his 50-foot tower and then enlisted the help of Simms and some neighbours to help him erect it. Once the guy wires were pulled tight and fastened in place, he and Simms mounted the generator on top of the tower in an operation Smillie compares somewhat unfavourably to "dropping a motor into a car in mid-air."

About the most fascinating and challenging aspect of the entire operation was the acquisition of the battery bank. Because the 175-pound batteries are worth about $200 apiece new, Smillie decided to find a source of good used ones but encountered difficulties. Given the size of the market for used batteries, most scrap dealers quickly break them down in order to sell the lead back to battery manufacturers. A friend, however, tipped Smillie off to the availability of some used industrial batteries that Bell Telephone was removing from a telephone exchange. Although the two-volt batteries are made to last for 10 years or more, Bell scraps theirs every two years, selling them to salvage dealers at extremely low prices.

On the day a local dealer was to pick them up, Smillie boldly showed up ahead of schedule, backed his truck up to a loading platform and took delivery of a dozen batteries, paying less than a dollar a piece. The heist was successful, although Bell later tightened its battery scrapping procedures and raised the prices. Smillie had to look elsewhere to complete his 20-battery bank.

Such antics aside, however, installation of the generator was serious business, took time in planning and worrying and cost an additional $1,000 in equipment. For their $3,000, the Smillies got 25 light bulbs and a few outlets in their house.

While wind power skeptics would say it was too much money to spend for such a small return and wind aficionados would shudder in despair at such high-handed tactics, the Smillies are pleased with the final result, if not the initial hassles.

Most of the worries are past, and now Smillie's one abiding fear is of lightning. On top of a 2,000-foot hill, their tower is the highest point for miles around and it makes him nervous to think that it is separated from the house by only a few yards of wire. (Donald Mayer of Vermont's North Wind Power says that lightning need not be a fear for wind system owners, provided that all legs of the tower are properly grounded. Lightning suppressors would serve to protect most components, he says, pointing out that his own system has had "10 or 15" strikes of lightning with the only damage of consequence being to an anemometer.) But aside from that, he tends to treat the generator as casually as possible.

"At the moment I follow the rules of Chinese maintenance: If it works, I don't touch it.

"Now we have it, we're extremely happy with it. It's just great because we're not coming from a 220- or 120-volt entrance to wind power. We're coming from kerosene to wind power and that's important. I can see that some people leaving a totally modern electrically wired house and coming to a 32-volt system might experience some culture shock. But coming from kerosene, it really gives you a different view. We might not be prepared to do it all again, but we're happy now. To me it's lights. We've solved our other needs by house design basically and all we needed were lights."

One point which comes across clearly during a visit to the Smillie household is the importance of overall house design. Their home was planned to be comfortable without creature comforts such as electricity and as a result their electrical needs are few.

A spring 50 yards uphill from the house supplies them with a natural gravity-fed water system and the springhouse doubles as a refrigerator. The family cooks on a wood stove, which also provides heat and warm water. While it is fuelled with wood cut from the trees on the 100-acre farm, Smillie had the house

designed along solar lines so that he may eventually use solar collectors for heat or simply continue to make use of the natural warming and lighting effect of sunshine streaming in through the expansive south-facing kitchen windows.

So far the couple has avoided a flurry of appliance buying with the exception of a blender and an inverter. The inverter is actually an "N1625 Tester afterburner speed sensing switch" from a scrapped Voodoo jet fighter whose original use is still a mystery to its new owners. But, at $80 from a Boston scrapyard, it was too good a bargain to pass up, and the Smillies use it to adapt their slide projector and stereo to the Jacobs voltage.

The household might also be in line for a refrigerator or a washing machine, or both, for with two small children, Smillie predicts that Sue will find it a problem having to walk up to the springhouse for food and milk. Trips to the local village laundromat are also difficult in winter because it means a quarter-mile hike through cold winds and high drifts just to reach the car in its roadside garage.

But for the moment Smillie is just biding his time and burning his lights. More appliances mean either more money or more time innovating and scrounging around junkyards looking for suitable motors and gadgets to adapt to the 32-volt DC power supply. And for now he has neither the time nor the inclination.

"We could run many more appliances, but it's a question of finances. It costs money to rig up all these things because I'm not a boy electrician. I'm not really that handy. I don't go down to the basement when I'm finished my work to play with motors.

"I just want lights so I can read. I'm not interested in becoming a part of the wind power movement. I'm just a consumer."

Although he has attended a few wind power workshops, Smillie does not go out of his way looking for allies in the wind power field. He has just about given up on reading about the technology, abandoning his spec sheets in the hope that one day someone will come out with a book that explains it all to him in layman's terms.

"I won't go to wind power meetings and conventions unless it's really convenient. It's not one of my major interests. If these guys start talking about Savonius rotors vs. Darrieus rotors, I'll just walk away.

"Wind power to me is just lights."

INTO THE EIGHTIES

When one considers that the Smillies, Rossiers and Simms are relative success stories among contemporary wind-powered households, the rough state of the art becomes fairly clear. Providing a family is prepared to make radical changes in its energy pattern usage, current technology may be perfectly adequate and may be cost-competitive with utility charges when living far from the power lines.

The strongest argument against wind power in most cases is the fact that, if the family reduced its energy use radically *without* unplugging the utility, its hydro bills would become very low indeed. Most

Rebuilt 1800-watt Jacobs supplies the modest power needs of the Smillie family in their energy-efficient home.

Frank B. Edwards

households, paying an average of about $500 per year for electricity (in central Canada, not relying on electric heat) would find that by cutting consumption to the bare bone standards of the Smillies or Simms, or the modest level of the Rossiers, they would save 50 or perhaps 75 per cent of their annual outlay to the power company (even after accounting for the utility's moribund policy of charging diminishing amounts for increased residential consumption). Thus, if one could save $300 or $400 per year without spending the requisite thousands on a wind system, why bother with wind power at all?

The answer, of course, is in the future cost of electricity from the utility. At least for the moment, wind power makes solid economic sense only for those who have no other choice or who face high installation fees for rural power. That will change, of course, as rising petroleum prices escalate the cost of thermal power plants that burn fossil fuels or as governments allow the cost of nuclear development to soar.

At some point, the current price tag of $6,000 to $10,000 for a household wind system may sound cheap, granting — as it does — independence from the grid and the ability to pay for itself over a reasonable period of time, be it five years or 10.

Already the wind power industry is looking well into the future and preparing itself for the worst (our worst, their best), predicting the most popular model of wind machine will be the *utility interface* type.

While at current equipment prices and electrical rates, it is not yet practical, most industry forecasters predict that it will be the most popular form of household power production in coming years.

Michael Evans, editor and publisher of *Wind Power Digest*, is not as convinced as some, claiming, "it is not yet clear which will be most popular — synchronous machines or autonomous units. The U.S. government, however, seems convinced that grid interface (with synchronous machines) is the direction the technology will take."

Simply explained, the synchronous models are synchronized with power lines coming into a house so that when a wind is blowing and they are producing power, the household's needs are served by the wind. If demand for power exceeds the generator's production, then the deficit is made up through the line. If the wind machine is creating a surplus, then that flows into the line and back to the utility. The ebb and flow of the power between grid and house would all be recorded by a meter (or two) to be read by the utility at intervals to see who owes whom money.

The theory of this arrangement is attractive: Winds tend to be the strongest in the winter months, when peak demands for power exist. The doldrums in one geographical area could be countered by windy conditions occurring simultaneously elsewhere.

John Ramsey, founder of Prince Edward Island's Alternatech, a wind power consulting firm operating out of his Dunlite-powered rural home, says that synchronous generators could produce up to 300 to 400 kilowatt hours a month, giving the homeowner substantial savings over the course of the year, especially during windy periods when the machine would, literally, be turning a profit. Prince Edward Island is one of the few provinces and states that will now accept power from individual wind system owners, but Ramsey says problems remain to be ironed out.

"Right now it isn't economically important (to the wind system owner), but P.E.I. currently pays only one-half the going rate for power you might put into the grid. As rates go up, (a synchronous system) will become more attractive."

North Wind Power Company's Donald Mayer takes the scenario one step further, perhaps too far for those who have always looked at wind power as a giant step toward independence from the utilities.

"At $6,000 to $10,000 per system, the interface market is unlimited, unlike the number of remote outlets one can sell. Eventually, of course, there is a chance that utilities will own and lease wind machines to interested customers making them more readily available."

Mayer goes on to predict that those machines, in the right locations, will eventually be able to produce 500 to 600 kilowatt hours of power a month allowing families not only to supply a large part of their own electrical needs but also saving them the inconvenience of having to restrict their power consumption drastically.

The future for 32-volt DC systems is dim, to no one's surprise, least of all David Simms'. Because low voltages experience serious power drops during transmission along wires, in many ways the higher the voltage the better. For his money, however, Simms still prefers 32 volts.

"Because of the power drop, the 32-volt systems are an excellent compromise, but the lack of other equipment on the market is discouraging. Twenty-four volt is fairly practical because there is a lot of 24-volt equipment around from a variety of sources — the marine and aircraft industries, for example.

"Some new generators are 12-volt, but these are only really useful for small cabins because the voltage drops noticeably between the generator and the batteries. The appeal there is that recreational vehicle equipment can be run on 12 volts.

"Thirty-two volt systems are obsolete and I don't think anyone is pretending that they aren't . . . however they don't experience serious voltage drop and are low enough to be very safe and that's a big advantage. The 110 direct current is pretty dangerous stuff. With 32 you can virtually work on *hot* wire, but if it were 110 DC it would put you right on your head."

Thus, from a practical standpoint, 32-volt Jacobs-powered systems may not be as dead as some might first think. Certainly most people recognize their antiquity right from the start but they have their advantages. It is a tried and true design and, especially at the time that the Rossiers and Simms invested in it, it was more affordable than lesser known models that were as experimental as they were new. From that perspective, their investments were probably wise.

VOLTAGE CHAOS

Judging from the current trends toward 12-, 24-, 48- and 110-volt systems, the wind power industry is still far from reaching any consensus as to what the optimum voltage is and, until some standard is reached and suitable equipment is manufactured to match it, everyone who invests in a wind system is gambling that it is his particular type of current which will one day survive the others.

As *Wind Power Digest's* editor Michael Evans points out, "the greatest number of generators will be privately owned home models but most of the power will come from large, utility-owned generators." Referring to a 1975 U.S. government study which suggested that a major commercial push starting then would result in six or seven million privately owned wind machines by 1995, he predicts that, despite the vast number powering households, the largest amount of wind power in the U.S. would still come from a few thousand utility operated generators pumping megawatts (million watts) into the grids.

John Ramsey foresees about 10 per cent of Canada's energy needs being met by such large-scale projects in the next 10 years. "In fact," he adds, "there is no reason why isolated communities shouldn't buy their own generators for their own needs. But there are corporate and government roles and responsibilities to sort out before that happens."

No matter where the future of wind power lies, be it in millions of mass-produced private systems or thousands of large corporate installations, right now it is in a very early renaissance stage that has left those who have made the initial investment to fend for themselves. They must get by with whatever they can devise or discover that is suitable for use with their particular system. While Doug Rossier searches through RV catalogues for new refrigerators, Joe Smillie must keep an eye open for a discarded unit suitable for modification. Regardless of their approaches, they are both working alone.

Don Mayer agrees that lack of suitable equipment and appliances is "certainly a problem" but from his position as a dealer he can afford to be philosophical for the time being. "Ingenuity," he soothingly rationalizes, "is not a negative thing. It teaches people where energy is from, how it works . . . . People begin to realize that it does not just come from a plug in the wall."

Perhaps the industry will not standardize until it is in the hands of the conglomerates who can dictate their own standards as well as their own prices. That is one of the fears of *Wind Power Digest* editor Michael Evans.

"There is a danger," he warns, "that the aerospace industry will gobble up all the good companies, leaving the small ones to disappear or be swallowed up. There are very real parallels to this: It happened to the American aircraft industry after the war."

He suggests that while there could be a detrimental change of attitude as large-scale manufacturers replace small-time philosophy with mass production, the real problem could be with monopolies and price fixing, all at the consumer's expense. Standardization could have a high price.

For the moment though, wind power is attracting those who want it to solve their problems of isolation or to fulfill their dream of independence from the utilities.

Wind skeptics, such as Hans Classen of Energy Mines and Resources, view these individual acts as either insignificant or worthy of disdain. In an article questioning the potential of wind power development in Canada, Classen repeated the following story:

"Some years ago, before the People's Republic of China had been internationally recognized and before it had exploded its first atomic bomb, a story went around that a scientist had suggested how China could make its weight felt in the community of nations.

"His proposal was simple: Let all inhabitants of China climb onto two-metre platforms and, at a radio signal, jump off. The impact of 700 million bodies hitting the ground at the same instant would send a tremendous shock wave all over the surface of the globe, bringing down the Empire State Building, Big Ben and a Kremlin tower or two, and demonstrating to the world that China was a power to be reckoned with."

Classen admits that the story is "wholly apocryphal" but only after stating that "some of the calculations that are being advanced in support of wind energy are not entirely unlike this story."

There are people who think Classen is wrong. The next decade, both sides agree, should prove a turning point in the development of both small- and large-scale wind technology.

Sources

Several years ago an enterprising energy writer sought out the grand old man of North American wind power, M.L. Jacobs, whose Wind Electric aerogenerators remain the standard of excellence nearly 50 years after they were built. When asked about the chances of a great technological breakthrough, the invention that would extract vast amounts of energy from a modest-sized wind unit, Jacobs responded with this pithy prediction: A board nailed to a broomstick will do as well as anything else in a 20 mph wind.

Relatively few original Jacobs units remain undiscovered today, and those that become available tend to carry a price tag that commands respect. Although the occasional vintage wind plant does become available, the near future of wind energy will hinge on small companies manufacturing new units — either reproductions of the classics or completely new designs.

There are currently about 50 different wind generator models available from 20-odd manufacturers in North America. To date, no one has produced the sort of side-by-side, controlled condition testing that would make the choice among these easier for a would-be purchaser. Donald Marier, editor of *Alternative Sources of Energy* magazine, recently gathered specification and performance sheets from a great many manufacturers, but, with varying ground rules and test criteria, the information proved less useful than might have been hoped for.

Marier says that the most interesting thing which emerged was the similarity in efficiency among the units, perhaps a reinforcement of Jacobs' prediction. "The main thing to consider when buying a new wind plant," advises Marier, "is will it stay together?" He predicts that many of the wind firms existing today will be gone in five years, and the prospective buyer should meet the people he or she intends to deal with to get an idea of their economic stability and the level of service they can provide.

Of especial interest to many observers are two firms which are setting out to follow in the Jacobs tradition of quality. Their units are the Dakota Wind & Sun 4 kw, 140-volt model and the Aeropower SL 1500, 24-volt unit. Both utilize a superior, time-tested governor and blade control design initiated by Jacobs. Unlike the Jacobs, both incorporate solid-state electronic controls.

From this point, the approach differs. Dakota opts for the heavy, direct-drive Jacobs-type generator. Aeropower uses a smaller, geared-up alternator. Both companies make reliability and quality top priorities. Mario Agnello of Aeropower says that their machine will produce a peak of 2100 watts, although it is rated conservatively at 1500 watts.

According to tests, the unit will produce more power per month than the more expensive and highly respected Dunlite plant from Australia.

This can be accounted for by Aeropower's atten-

Pinson Cycloturbine

tion to the importance of low cut-in speed (it generates power in lower winds than the Dunlite) and a solid mid-range output. The art of wind machine design is maximizing the more prevalent wind speeds at a particular site and, for many North American institutions, Aeropower has produced a seemingly superior unit.

Dakota's approach can best be described as improving the already proved Jacobs. They've extracted more power by lengthening the armature, but they've kept the reliability, the slow speed efficiency, and they've added a three-year guarantee. The Dakota needs annual greasing (service requirements should play an important role in any wind plant purchase decision), and brushes must be replaced every three years as well. Both units can be owner-maintained, but the Aeropower, being lighter, would be easier to install.

There are, of course, many more choices, and the following list of current wind power sources indicates the diversity of the field today. Who will emerge as the paragon of quality and reliability remains to be seen, but one certainty exists: No one is likely to make enormous gains in efficiency. Greater output will cost considerably more; the energy available from the wind is proportional to the area swept by the blades. To cover a greater area requires a bigger, heavier rotor and entails greater sophistication, cost and risk.

AERO POWER SYSTEMS INC.
2398 Fourth Street
Berkeley, California 97410
(415) 848-2710

THE ALTERNATE CURRENT
Box 905
Boulder, Colorado
(303) 442-7193

ALTERNATECH ASSOCIATES LTD.
Emyvale, P.E.I. C0A 1V0
(902) 658-2537

AMERICAN WIND TURBINE
1016 East Airport Road
Stillwater, Oklahoma 74074
(405) 377-5333

**BEST ENERGY SYSTEMS FOR
TOMORROW INC.**
Route 1, Box 106
Necedah, Wisconsin 54646
(608) 565-7200

**CANADIAN ENERGY
CONVERSION INDUSTRIES**
2779 Lake City Way
Burnaby, B.C. V5A 2Z8
(604) 420-3030

CANUSA ENERGY CO.
R.R.2
Wainfleet, Ontario L0S 1V0
(416) 899-1888

CAREFUL ECO SYSTEMS
Box 1212
Whaletown, B.C. V0P 1Z0
(604) 886-7336

COULSON WIND ELECTRIC
RFD 1, Box 225
Polk City, Iowa 50226
(515) 984-6038

DAF INDAL
3570 Hawkestone Road
Mississauga, Ontario L5C 2V8
(416) 275-5300

DAKOTA WIND AND SUN
Box 1781
Aberdeen, South Dakota
(605) 229-0815

DUNLITE ELECTRICAL PRODUCTS
28 Orsmond Street
Hindmarsh, Australia 5007

DYNERGY CORPORATION
Box 428
1269 Union Avenue
Laconia, New Hampshire 03246
(603) 542-8313

Frank B. Edwards

ENERGY SYSTEMS
4874 Cherry Tree Lane
Sykesville, Maryland 21784
(301) 795-3828

ENERTECH CORPORATION
P.O. Box 420
Norwich, Vermont 05055
(802) 649-1145

FRIESEN INDUSTRIES
32032 South Fraser Way
Clearbrook, B.C.
(604) 859-7101

FUTURE RESOURCES AND ENERGY LTD.
Box 1358, Station B
Downsview, Ontario M3H 5W3
(416) 630-8343

GRUMMAN ENERGY SYSTEMS, INC.
4175 Veterans Memorial Highway
Ronkonkoma, New York 11779
(516) 737-3709

INDEPENDENT ENERGY SYSTEMS, INC.
6043 Sterrettania Road, Dept. H
Fairview, Pennsylvania 16415
(814) 833-3567

KEDCO
9016 Aviation Blvd.
Inglewood, California 90301
(213) 776-6636

MASSAWIPPI WIND ELECTRIC CO.
R.R.3
Ayer's Cliff, Quebec J0B 1C0

MILLVILLE WIND AND SOLAR
Box 32
Millville, California 96062
(916) 547-4302

NATURAL POWER, INC.
Francestown Turnpike
New Boston, New Hampshire 03031
(603) 487-5512

NORTH WIND POWER CO. INC.
Box 315
Warren, Vermont 05674

OAKRIDGE WINDPOWER
Route 1
Underwood, Maine 56586
(218) 826-6446

PINSON ENERGY CORPORATION
Box 7
Marston Mills, Massachusetts 02648
(617) 428-8535

SENCENBAUGH WIND ELECTRIC
Box 11174
Palo Alto, California 94306
(415) 964-1593

R.A. SIMERL INSTRUMENT
238 West Street
Annapolis, Maryland 21401
(301) 849-8667

THERMAX CORPORATION
Box 275
Hawkesbury, Ontario
(613) 632-8111

WADLER MANUFACTURING CO.
Rt. 2, Box 76
Galena, Kansas 66739
(316) 783-1355

WELLINGTON WIND POWER
Box 15
Wellington, Ontario K0K 3L0

WHIRLWIND POWER CO.
2458 W. 29th Avenue
Denver, Colorado 80211
(303) 477-6436

WINCO — DIV. OF DYNA TECHNOLOGY
7850 Metro Parkway
Minneapolis, Minnesota 55420
(612) 853-8400

WIND POWER SYSTEMS
Box 17323
San Olego, California 92117
(714) 452-7040

WIND TURBINE CO. OF CANADA LTD.
21 Howard Avenue
Elmira, Ontario N3B 2C9
(519) 669-5421

WINDWORKS
Box 44A, Rt. 3
Mukwonago, Wisconsin 53149
(414) 363-4408

ZEPHYR WIND DYNAMO
Box 241

Brunswick, Maine 04011
(207) 725-6534

Periodicals
WIND POWER DIGEST
Jester Press
54468 County Road 31
Bristol, Indiana 46507

ALTERNATIVE SOURCES OF
ENERGY MAGAZINE
Route 3, Box 90A
Milaca, Minnesota 56353

RAIN — JOURNAL OF
APPROPRIATE TECHNOLOGY
2270 N.W. Irving
Portland, Oregon 97210

Books
THE WILDERNESS HOME POWER
SYSTEM AND HOW TO DO IT
By Jim Cullen
Wilderness Home Power Co.
Box 732
Laytonville, California 95454

HARNESSING THE WIND
FOR HOME ENERGY
By Dermot McGuigan
Garden Way Publishing
Charlotte, Vermont 05445

SIMPLIFIED WIND POWER SYSTEMS
FOR EXPERIMENTERS
By Jack Park
Helion Inc.
P.O. Box 445
Brownsville, California 95919

THE HOMEBUILT, WIND-GENERATED
ELECTRICITY HANDBOOK
By Michael Hackleman
Earthmind
4844 Hirsch Road
Mariposa, California 95338

THE WIND BOOK
By Ian Hornby
Pollution Probe
53 Queen Street
Ottawa, Ontario

CATCH THE WIND
By Landt and Lisl Dennis
Four Winds Press
50 West 44th Street
New York, New York 10036

ELECTRIC POWER FROM THE WIND
By Henry Clews
Enertech
P.O. Box 420
Norwich, Vermont 05055

Return From (Energy) Oblivion

Getting airtight performance from an old or inexpensive stove

By Matthew Radz

Driving north out of Kingston toward the nation's capital, on Highway 15, you quickly pass the marshy eastern reaches of Lake Ontario, pass the benign-looking Joyceville Penitentiary, pass the sign for Woodburn Road but, having taken the left for Seeleys Bay, you cannot pass Reg Kumm's hulking barn — home, according to his seemingly outrageous claim, of The World's Largest Collection of Recycled Wood Stoves.

Inside, the 1,200 wood burners of every conceivable shape, vintage and price give credence to Kumm's assertion and stand as testament to his belief that some of today's best wood burners were made before anyone had heard of Scandinavian baffles, downdrafts or bimetallic thermostatic coils.

According to Kumm, a middle-aged man who recalls helping his blacksmith father repair cast-iron heaters four decades ago, the golden age of wood stove construction took place in the 1920s, when labour was cheap and any man was glad to have a job. When pressed, Kumm will admit that, yes, they can make a good stove today, but that the prices frighten off many buyers. "All this talk you hear about airtight stoves, I'll show you an airtight stove that was made in 1914," he says and leads the visitor past the old padlocks, the keys, the straw hats with striped bands, the pottery jugs, the sauerkraut crocks, the china, the silverware, a mid-1950's-model baby carriage with an antique doll sprawled insolently on its seat; past the books, the yellowed pages of old *Family Heralds* and the 100,000 other collected items which pack every nook and cranny of

the barn's 22,000 square feet of floor space; past the old dressers, the chests of drawers and the phalanxes of stoves, heaters and kitchen ranges, all restored, waiting for a second lifetime of service.

To the first-time visitor, the Bay Barn is overwhelming, a mind-boggling journey through the not-so-distant past and a surprising triumph of order over chaos. Everything has its place. The ashtrays are stacked inside other ashtrays, the silver is arranged in neat mounds and thousands of chairs, visible from the floor above, hover, legs dangling, suspended from the ceiling.

"Look at this," Kumm orders, bending his bulky frame down to caress the air inlets of an ornate round heater which towers nearly six feet above the floor and contributes to the sagging brought on by this avalanche of collectibles, cast iron and steel.

Sliding the draft controls back and forth, Kumm opines that the unit's air intake can be carefully controlled for a long efficient burn. The visitor resists the temptation to give the stove legs an approving kick.

Behind the barn, which is covered with what seems an acre of plastic that flaps in the breeze with an eerily dry sound, a hundred or more old stoves huddle together, each under its own blanket of heavy-duty white plastic. A Favorite Homesteader, a Dew Diamond, a squat but very ornate and rusty parlour heater made by the Connell Bros. of Woodstock, N.B., an Acme, a Wingham Classic and various Royals all await their turn in Kumm's repair shop in the basement of the huge barn.

Walking around the yard, the impression that this

Ernie Sparks

is some bent, smashed, rusted-out dream of an indiscriminate scavenger is fuelled by the sight of an enormous army surplus generator and a doorless, red VW bug with weeds growing where the seats used to be. Yet the same order prevails here, and Kumm makes it very clear that he is selling stoves that will burn wood, that will work, that aren't meant to be used as fern stands in someone's interior decorating scheme. There are, to start with, the stove parts.

"About 30 to 40 tons of them," by Kumm's reckoning. "But I don't really know because they are not all sorted out yet." The inventory includes stacks of grates several feet high, bottom assemblies pressed together with legs thrust skyward, handles, doors and parts for which the non-expert has no name.

WHAT'S RUST?

Kumm, who acquires his stock at auctions and on trips through Ontario with occasional forays into Quebec and the United States, suggests old stoves are best restored by a professional but offers some basic advice for those intent on finding and revitalizing a venerable wood burner. "Don't worry too much about rust on cast iron," says Kumm, who formerly worked for the Ontario Construction Safety Association. "What's rust? It's only F-E-O-Two, eh? It doesn't hurt, you can paint right over surface rust, but don't touch a stove if you know it has been sitting outside for a long time.

"Custom made parts can be cast to your order for about $4.00 a pound of iron . . . if you can find someone to do the job. Many foundries won't even talk to you if it's a small, custom job. If you buy a heater with missing or unusable parts, you have problems. Grates are a little easier to come by, since the original ones can be replaced by modifying a piece from another stove. Chipped or cracked firebrick inside can be rebuilt with castable firebrick. It's cheap, about 35 cents a pound, and it works something like concrete — you build a wooden frame inside the firebox and pour the mixture into it. Let it set and remove the frame. You usually need a mason to rebuild with firebricks."

Airtightness and fuel efficiency are only rarely found among the old stoves, and Kumm's business is based on the fact that his burners are ruggedly built with moulded-in beauty and nickel-polished character — and they are cheap, often selling for half the price of a new airtight.

BETTER THAN NEW

In answer to those who feel that Kumm and others like him are dealing in nostalgia is Dr. Marc H. Schneider, a professor of Wood Science and Technology at the University of New Brunswick whose special interest is domestic heating using wood fuel. His scientific credentials aside, Schneider is among those who feel that older stoves are underrated and too often by-passed for newer models.

When Schneider and his family bought a one-and-a-half-storey farmhouse near Fredericton six years ago, it had a wood stove already in place, ready to be stoked and put into daily use. It wasn't a thing of energy-efficient beauty, and the cracks between im-

perfect joints around the stove gave a clear view of flames flickering inside.

"The heater was made early in this century," says Schneider, "and is constructed of quality materials — sheet steel, cast iron, firebrick. We used it in its leaky condition almost continuously every winter for about six years before I became seriously interested in the technical aspects of space heating with wood.

"I came to realize that improvement in the stove's tightness and internal gas flow pattern could reduce our requirement for eight cords of wood each winter and lengthen the time between refuellings. I began to tinker with my stove."

Schneider says he began to study other old stoves and found that many did have adjustable air inlets designed to control the amount of air reaching the fire and thus the rate of burn. "Unfortunately," says Schneider, "in many old stoves little attention was paid to fitting various pieces together, and often, over a period of years, warping worsened an already poor fit. The result is that many old stoves — and many new ones of old design or careless assembly — have uncontrolled air entry through a myriad of leaks, rendering the adjustable air inlets nearly useless.

"Poorly controlled burning with fast gas passage and large amounts of excess air gives poor heat transfer efficiency in these leaky stoves and allows too much heated air from inside the house to go up the chimney."

In Schneider's case, the old rectangle box stove has a cast-iron front and top-loading door with sheet steel forming the rest of the box. There were air leaks all around the steel-to-iron joints, around the top and front doors and around the traditional circular lid set in the top.

"Ideally," says Schneider, "the way to improve the steel-to-iron bond would have been to remove all the joining bolts, put an asbestos gasket in the joint between steel and iron, place a pre-drilled strip of stout steel over the thinner stove steel at the joint and then tightly rebolt the assembly.

"I balked at this task because it would have required loosening rusted bolts in nearly inaccessible places." Instead, Schneider used a putty knife to apply stove cement to the seam all the way around the perimeter of the stove. The swinging loading door at the top sat on a flange and it had warped with age, making the fit uniformly sloppy with large air gaps in several places. Rather than attempt a major repair of this joint, Schneider decided to seal the door permanently and revert to using the front door to fuel the fire. He began by preparing a strip of asbestos tape to go around the top door where it met the flange and then placing this tape in a layer of wet stove cement that had been applied to the flange.

Schneider then covered the asbestos with another layer of cement and set the door back in place to squeeze out the excess cement. The purpose of the tape was to allow for the differential movement of the two bodies of metal without cracking the cement and breaking the seal. Protruding tape was trimmed with a knife and the excess stove cement was wiped

away with a moist rag before work on the front door began.

The front door had a protruding lip around its periphery and, because it too was warped by age, it made a poor fit with the outside of a similar lip extending from the door frame. To solve the problem, liberal amounts of cement were applied all around the inside of the lip with asbestos tape on top of the seal. Next, ordinary wax paper was placed around the door frame before the door was shut not quite as tightly as it would go. This seal reduced the gap between the door and the frame and made the route that air would have to travel to enter the stove through the remaining air gaps more circuitous. All this was done with the stove cold.

Schneider next kindled a small fire to speed the cement's curing-drying process. He points out that care must be taken to keep such a fire moderate, because if the water in the sealing compound boils, it will foam up and reduce the effectiveness of the seal.

The seals were dry within several hours, but Schneider found that the front door of the stove was stuck shut, held by cement which had worked its way around the wax paper. A few firm yet gentle taps with a wooden block pried the door open and the excess cement was carefully chipped off. Because the sealing compound and the tape both contain asbestos, caution is advised in order to avoid lung damage from inhaled asbestos dust. Schneider wore a mask to cut the tape and, when the job was complete, used a powerful vacuum for the cleanup operation.

BAFFLEMENT

Schneider then carried the rejuvenation one step further, adding a simple baffle plate to increase the efficiency of combustion. With the various door and body leaks now sealed, the fire would be fed primarily by air coming in the front door inlets, with a clearly defined path directly back to the chimney outlet at the rear of the stove. By adding a baffle which would protrude from the rear wall, below the flue opening, Schneider changed the route of exiting smoke and burning gases, forcing them to the front of the stove before they could escape. Using an oxygen-propane torch, Schneider cut a piece of 18-gauge sheet metal and bent it so that it would sit on the ledge of firebrick around the edge of the stove, leaving ample room above the baffle plate for the smoke to exit. This simple modification allowed for better heat transfer, as the hot gases remained in the stove longer, and for better combustion, brought about by the gas turbulence in the combustion zone.

Finally, the circular lid in the top of the stove was ground to effect a better fit all around, but it was left unsealed because the family found it convenient for cooking or adding small scraps of fuel to the fire.

"The old veteran was again ready for service," says Schneider. "An afternoon had been required to accomplish the entire refitting." Two winters after the session with the old stove, he is certain it was time and money — less than $10.00 — well spent.

"In the first full winter of operation we burned just six cords of wood, compared to an average of eight over each of the five winters prior to the modification. We had been using about 250 gallons of fuel oil in the furnace, and this dropped to 100 before

Dr. Marc Schneider's antique cast-iron and steel wood-burning stove was converted into an efficient, almost-air-tight heater by sealing joints with stove cement and asbestos tape and by improving the fit of the front door of the stove. The top-loading door was sealed permanently shut.

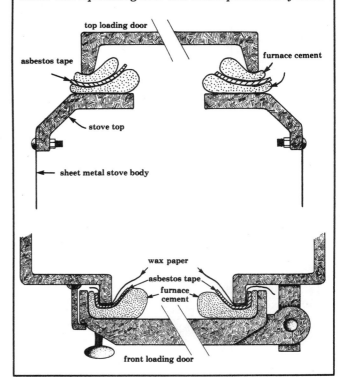

being replaced with a new unit which burns wood chips.

"The stove yields much more steady heat than before, and four feedings (morning, noon, suppertime and bedtime) rather than five per 24-hour period are required for high-power operation."

The addition of the baffle made very clear differences in the burn characteristics of the stove, says Schneider. "The top of the stove is now hottest near its front, whereas, before modification, it was hottest at the rear and the first length of stovepipe was equally hot. The flames now swirl in the area beneath the baffle, and just lick over the front of the baffle.

At high-power operation, the whole below-baffle volume not occupied by fuel is one turbulent flame. Previously, the flame was swept straight up the stovepipe, with less chance of mixing and good combustion. A well-fuelled fire at bedtime, 10:00 P.M., is often still going at 8:00 A.M., and in the few instances where it is not actively burning, many glowing coals are left. The stove now appears to be nearly as convenient and efficient as a modern airtight heater — I still must close the stovepipe damper to minimize the effects of leaks I did not completely seal."

The single drawback the modification created proves its effectiveness. Creosote builds up more quickly now in the Schneiders' "almost airtight," but the more frequent chimney clean-outs are a small price to pay for the considerable fuel savings and the greater comforts the rejuvenated box heater now offers.

SKINFLINT SPECIAL

In the hierarchy of wood stoves, the very bottom is permanently occupied by the cast-iron "reproduction" stoves that have been mass-produced in Taiwan, Hong Kong, Korea and North America over the past few years. Sold in hardware stores, discount marts and even, at times, in cut-rate drug stores, these stoves vary greatly in quality and price, but are uniformly notorious as inefficient burners of wood.

Yet even these least-desirable of stoves can be made better, according to Hazelton, British Columbia's Merve Fedrau, who took a nameless heater, described as "a versatile box stove made of sturdy cast iron" in the Sears catalogue, and modified it to become the sole source of heat for a small, poorly insulated dwelling in an area of British Columbia where winter nighttime temperatures often dip below —32 degrees F. Although the stove was purchased for $84.95 several years ago (it is still offered, but at $99.98), it now can be counted on for the 10-hour burns that are the pride of airtight stove owners.

"I wouldn't recommend a reproduction stove to heat a large house," says Fedrau, a part-time ambulance driver, furniture maker and devoted tinkerer, who boasts he made a hand-brake for his tricycle when he was four years old "and never looked back." Still, he says, "It's perfect for a place the size of ours, which is one floor with a sleeping loft above. I am quite impressed with the Sears stove but you have to keep in mind that some of these reproduction models are cast with poor quality iron . . . you have to be careful when you buy one." (Editor: Many wood stove experts feel that these mass-produced wood stoves, as a whole, are so poorly made as to render them unsafe. Hot fires can result in the cast-iron walls turning white and becoming weakened, and such stoves should not be used for serious heating purposes.)

"Our stove is very sturdy. We have even placed pots of ice water on it when it was hot, which is a definite no-no in woodburning circles, because the shock of such a sudden temperature difference can crack the body."

The technique employed by Fedrau to modify his reproduction stove is similar to that used on the New Brunswick box heater in that all the joints were sealed with stove cement. In most inexpensive reproduction stoves, the joints are not welded, allowing free passage of air; the lids, door and draft are not airtight and, when the fire is going well, air is sucked in through every crack. Closing the draft has little effect on the fire, especially when very dry wood is being used.

If the stove has been in use already, the iron must be cleaned before the cement is applied. Any heavy soot buildup has to be removed with water and a scrub brush, but soap should be avoided since it will cause a poor bond once the cement is applied. The next step is to seat the lids and the door by applying cement to one surface and grease to the other and then pressing the parts firmly together. Once the cement is dry, it will come free of the greased part but will adhere to the other surface. In seating the lids, the cement should be applied to the stove body with the grease smeared on the lids. Fedrau, who used both butter and bear grease, suggests that if butter and bears happen to be in short supply, lard or shortening can be substituted for the same effect.

He also advises that the cement must be completely dry before the parts are separated — a few taps with a block of wood may be necessary to break inadvertent bonds between parts of the stove. If the stove has an I-shaped piece supporting the lids, it, too, will have to be seated. Fedrau emphasizes that this piece must be pressed down as far as it will go or the lids will not align themselves properly and the top of the stove will be uneven.

If the stove is equipped with an ash clean-out door, it too will have to be fitted to prevent its acting as an entry point for air to be drawn up through the grates. Unless the draft regulator is excessively sloppy, it may be best not to tamper with it. Otherwise, the procedure is similar to seating the other parts of the stove: apply cement to the stationary part and grease the moving or sliding piece. Fedrau says to use a bolt to reassemble the regulator, even if a rivet was used as original equipment, as the bolt will allow adjustment for the best fit.

If starting with a brand-new stove, at least two or three fires should be burned in it before refitting, to prevent warping of the new points of alignment.

Fedrau says the entire conversion of a cheap reproduction stove can be done for about $2.00, or the price of a can of stove cement, which is composed of asbestos fibres and sodium silicate. (Avoid furnace cement unless the label specifically states that it may be used on stoves. Most furnace cement is intended for use in repairing heating ducts.)

Just how well a refitted department store stove or a reworked antique heater would compare in side-by-side laboratory comparisons with a good, new airtight wood burner is a question that remains to be answered. For those whose sense of parsimony is aroused by the thought of making the most out of a "hopeless" stove, however, it may be enough to know that energy efficiency need not be bought with money, but can be had for an investment of time and ingenuity.

Adventures in the New Horticulture

Home hydroponics is coming of age

By Dr. Stephen Tobe and Dr. William Friend

It was one of those wretched mornings in late February, with lake winds whipping the snow off my driveway only to reveal a glaze of fresh ice. While the radio weatherman was making dire predictions of more freezing rain and warning Toronto motorists about the abysmal winter driving conditions, I picked the last five fully vine-ripened tomatoes in my basement. Dozens more hung on the vines, oblivious to the storm and promising many harvests yet to come.

Here, the fluorescent lights were cheerful and the smell of growing plants and the warmth of the room seemed proof that my colleague, Steve Tobe, had introduced me to the perfect formula for endless summer. Seasons removed from the whirling snow outside, the pumps of my hydroponic unit cut in. I watched, through the tangle of green foliage, as the gravel bed slowly darkened with moisture and then I heard the nutrient solution trickling back into the reservoir under the gravel.

"No doubt about it," I thought, sampling a sweet, juicy *Starshot* tomato, "hydroponic gardening can change your whole outlook on winter."

It will come as no surprise to anyone who witnesses this near miracle of displaced summer that hydroponics made possible one of the Seven Wonders of the World. The Hanging Gardens of Babylon grew, some say, hydroponically, much as the jungle of suspended house plants at Steve's place grows today.

King Nebuchadnezzar II's amazing gardens thrilled travellers centuries before the term hydroponics was coined. Derived from two Greek words — *hydro* (water) and *ponos* (labour) — the system is essentially soilless horticulture. As practised by the man who invented the term "hydroponics" in 1929, the root system of a plant was suspended in a solution of water containing all of the known essential plant nutrients.

The usual modern practice is to grow the plant in an inert aggregate of gravel or vermiculite (puffed granules of mica ore) and to pump a nutrient solution through this several times a day at preset intervals of the light cycle. This aggregate serves to support the root system and — since the nutrient solution does not bathe the roots continuously — allows oxygen, necessary for plant growth, to reach the roots more easily.

The most important advantage of any type of greenhouse or indoor plant culture is its extension of gardening time and space. The growing season is not only prolonged indefinitely, but food gardening is brought into the domain of city apartments and Arctic homes.

Furthermore, hydroponics has some considerable advantages over soil growing systems — enough advantages that both Steve and I, who grow vegetables outdoors in summer, also keep our hydroponic gardens active year-round.

Hydroponic crop yields are very high in relation to the area of growing surface. I have done experiments with plants potted in soil and plants growing in the hydroponic unit, and the latter are incredibly more productive. In hydroponics, there are no weeds and therefore no cultivation. Depending on the nutrient medium you use, there are no necessary objectionable odours. Too, the nutrient solution can be adjusted for the benefit of particular plants, rather like being able to grow a group of vegetables in its own special plot of precisely chosen garden soil. This enhances flavour and nutritional value, qualities noticeably lacking in winter supermarket produce.

NO PESTICIDES

As the system can easily be kept clean, insect problems are kept to a minimum, and those that crop up can often be cured with a dusting of such botanical controls as rotenone and pyrethrum. By keeping a close watch on our units so that we can catch any outbreaks of disease early, we manage to keep our units pest-free — and that means no pesticides.

As members of the University of Toronto Department of Zoology, we are both wary of such chemicals. Recently Steve's lab assistant, having run out of the customary feed of sprouted grain for the laboratory population of African locusts, bought a head of supermarket lettuce. Soon, half the insects were dead, the result of systemic pesticides that no amount of washing would have removed from the vegetable. These chemicals are right in the cells of the plant.

We have also found that, using our homemade system, we are able to save money. We like vegetables, and so could easily spend five or 10 dollars a week during the winter on such items as English cucumbers at a dollar each and hothouse tomatoes for at least that price per pound. The only considerable expense, after constructing the unit, is electricity, and during the winter of 1978 that cost $2.50 to $3.00 a month for each of our units in Toronto.

There were more subtle advantages, too. Our eating habits changed, with all that fresh produce available daily. We were prompted to try new salads and adventurous recipes using our indoor herbs. And, of course, there is an immeasurable value in the sight of green growing things in winter. Steve's "warm" room is a meditation area, where a couch faces the inviting tangle of cucumbers, tomatoes, peppers and basil.

Proponents of organic gardening are often suspicious of hydroponic culture, citing the use of chemical fertilizers and growing conditions that, obviously, are not natural. Hydroponic systems are not for everyone, but the fact is that nutrient solutions comprised of fish emulsion, liquid seaweed and blood meal can be used if one wishes to be strictly organic.

Whether organic or not, whether grown in soil or hydroponically, all plants require proper light for healthy growth and highest yields. In addition to the proper nutrient solution, the plants need carbon dioxide and oxygen from the air, as well as proper temperature conditions and a good supporting medium,

Maureen Paxton

which is one that will allow adequate aeration for the roots, especially at the crown.

In a hydroponic system, all these needs must be satisfied manually or automatically, and they must be supplied within a closed system. The basic components of any hydroponic unit are: a container, the aggregate, the nutrient solution, the reservoir and lights. An automated system requires a small water pump and a timer to activate the lights and pumping system.

THE CONTAINER

Virtually any container which doesn't leak and won't rot can be used for a hydroponic garden. Hydroponic planters vary from plant pots or simple porch hangers to entire greenhouses. The most basic type of container that we have found practical is the common dishpan — ideal for the cautious neophyte or for those who wish to take advantage of south-facing windows that would not accommodate larger tanks. We have used these 11-by-13-inch Rubbermaid-type dishpans to grow a variety of vegetables including tomatoes, English cucumbers, green beans, lettuce and watercress.

In soil, tomato roots reach very deep, but because

Dr. Friend's hydroponic cellar garden in mid-winter — pro-digious amounts of tomatoes, peppers, lettuce, spinach, cu-cumbers and herbs in a minimum of space.

Stephen Tobe

all the plant's nutritional needs are met in the richly-fed aggregate, hydroponic root systems are small. I have grown a 10-foot-high tomato plant in such a container. Normally, a dishpan will hold one large plant (a tomato or cucumber or pepper) or two small ones (herbs or lettuce).

With this type of container, it is necessary to install a spout on the side of the pan near the bottom, or simply drill a hole and fit it with a cork or rub-ber stopper to provide drainage. The aggregate is flooded with nutrients once or twice a day and the solution is allowed to drain out after the appropriate time through the spout or drainage hole. With all the systems described in this article, the nutrient solu-tion will be poured on the aggregate either manually or by electric pump, and then the solution will drain back into the reservoir by itself, using gravity.

Although we still make limited use of such simple containers, we discovered, as we became increas-ingly involved with hydroponics, that the most con-venient containers are those which are large enough to house all our plants plus the reservoir of nutrient solution. In other words, the units are completely self-contained. As we still wanted our units to be relatively inexpensive, we set about designing our own.

To this end, we constructed tanks of ¾-inch ply-wood approximately two feet wide by four feet long by one foot deep. Each tank thus has a growing area of about eight square feet.

After nailing together the tank, we chose to line it with fibreglass. Two coats of fibreglass resin proved more than adequate and, to date, our tanks have shown no sign of deterioration (and no leaks) al-though they have been in almost continuous use for two years. Some, however, may consider fibreglass cloth and resin to be expensive, although they can be bought quite reasonably at specialty shops catering to boating/sailing enthusiasts. Those who don't wish to make the investment in the almost indestructible fibreglass tank can, instead, line the box with thick (at least six mil), construction-grade polyethylene sheeting and fasten it to the edge of the tank with

strapping. With this approach, it is advisable to paint the inside of the tank with asphalt paint before putting in the plastic so that condensation on the plastic will not rot the wood.

One great advantage of this type of tank over a smaller unit is that the nutrient reservoir is located right beneath the aggregate. For an eight-square-foot tank, a four- to five-inch-deep reservoir is all that is necessary, and will hold 15 to 20 gallons of nutri-ent solution. This space for the reservoir is easily created. Once the tank is built, obtain some three-inch PVC drainage pipe from a builders' supply; this will support the platform on which the aggregate will rest, but will not displace much of the nutrient solution. Cut the pipe into five-inch lengths and cut notches on the top and bottom of each piece to allow free circulation of the nutrient. One 10-foot length of PVC pipe will provide sufficient support for three tanks — in other words, eight five-inch lengths of PVC pipe are used to support eight square feet of aggregate. The platform upon which the aggregate will be placed is simply a piece of arborite or other plastic laminate cut to fit fairly snugly inside the tank and resting upon the lengths of PVC pipe. The platform must not fit tightly — the nutrient solu-tion must be able to drain from the aggregate over the edges of the platform into the reservoir.

At one edge of the arborite, a semicircle of 10-inch diameter is cut, and a piece of arborite 12 inches high and of appropriate length is bent to fit in the semi-circle. The pump will be placed in this enclosure.

THE AGGREGATE

The container must now be filled with the growing medium, or aggregate. The most commonly used ag-gregate is gravel, usually 3/8-inch size or finer, and well cleaned. Impurities on the gravel, such as clay or soil, can affect the pH of the medium quite dramati-cally, and also may contain minerals which will upset the nutrient balance. We have used gravel in both large and small containers successfully and consider it to be the cheapest and most reliable growing me-dium. The least expensive is available from a build-ing supplier and is often called "pea" gravel. How-ever, this gravel is usually "contaminated" with clay and must be washed until the water runs clear before being used as a hydroponic aggregate.

Commercially available hydroponic aggregates, which require no cleaning, consist of porous rock, and come in 25-pound bags under such trade names as *Heydite* and *Herculite*. Because they are prewashed and ready for use in the tanks, they are relatively expensive. Nonetheless, this porous aggregate appears to have two advantages. It retains water better than ordinary gravel and provides a greater surface area for root growth. We have had excellent results with both gravel and the porous rock and leave it to the reader to decide which aggregate to use.

The major problem with gravel as the growing me-dium is its weight. A large tank filled with gravel weighs several hundred pounds and is very difficult to move. If portability is desired, lighter materials for aggregates can be used. The two most commonly available materials are Vermiculite, an expanded mica, and Perlite, an expanded volcanic rock. We have used both of these materials successfully, although they have several disadvantages. They tend to retain salts on their surfaces and must be backwashed to remove these salts at regular intervals. Because of their lightness, plants may require external support, and because these materials retain excessive moisture due to their large surface area, algae and fungi tend to grow on them and insufficient oxygen may reach the plant roots, causing rot.

The water-retaining characteristics of Vermiculite and Perlite can, however, be used to advantage. We have obtained excellent results by combining one of these materials with gravel, thereby utilizing the best qualities of each. We make a sort of gravel sandwich in the large tank by placing a one-inch layer of gravel in the bottom, on the aggregate platform, covering this with a one- or two-inch layer of Vermiculite or Perlite, and then adding three or four additional inches of gravel. We now use this mixture routinely in our hydroponic tanks. The same system — with thinner layers — can be used in a dishpan, although it is easiest to use only one aggregate in these. If I use Vermiculite in a dishpan, I put a bit of gravel over the drainage hole so that the finer aggregate will not flow out.

NUTRIENT SOLUTIONS

Nutrient solutions are really a matter of personal taste — "organic" versus "inorganic." We have used both types successfully but have discontinued using the organic solutions because of the ripe odour they create (essence of dead fish, ripe seaweed and blood meal). We offer two nutrient formulations, but, at the risk of precipitating a controversy, must say that the so-called "organic/natural" mixture utilizes processed compounds and is probably no more organic than the straight salt mixture, the components of which can be mined directly from the ground, with little processing.

Plants cannot take up organic matter directly; they can only absorb inorganic molecules. Organic materials such as compost or manure must break down into various inorganic components before they can be taken up by the plant as nutrients — as far as the plant is concerned, there is no difference. Those who advocate purely organic practices, of course, claim that seaweed, fish emulsion and other "natural" fertilizers contain trace elements that are neither measurable nor completely understood yet. We leave the choice to you.

Inorganic Salt Mixture
11½ oz. (345 g) ammonium sulphate
8 oz. (240 g) ammonium phosphate
4 oz. (120 g) potassium chloride
3 oz. (90 g) calcium sulphate
5½ oz. (165 g) magnesium sulphate
Mix well and use 1 to 2 tsp. per gallon of water.

Organic Mixture
(from Institute for Local Self-Reliance)

1½ tsp. (18 ml) fish emulsion
1½ tsp. (18 ml) liquid seaweed
1 tsp. (12 ml) blood meal
1 gallon water

We have listed the inorganic mixture primarily so that the ingredients can be examined. It is very difficult for someone without access to chemicals to obtain the necessary individual salts, although some hydroponic greenhouses may be willing to sell small quantities. The organic mixture must be made by the gardener (sources are listed at end of this article).

We feel that the most practical answer for the individual who does not mind using a chemical fertilizer is a commercial hydroponic mixture. We have used the formulation sold as *City Green* with good results and recommend it. It is unnecessary to use trace elements as they are already present. All the salt mixtures are used at the rate of approximately one or two tablespoons (15 to 30 g) in four gallons (15 litres) of water. Exceeding this rate appreciably will upset the nutrient balance of the solution. As the water level in the reservoir drops because of evaporation and transpiration, add more water (*not* nutrient solution) —we usually add water once or twice a week, never letting the water level drop below about 80 per cent of the original volume. We usually check the pH of the nutrient solution every two weeks. This is simply a measure of the acidity or alkalinity of the solution and for most plants that we have grown, the ideal pH is around 6 to 6.5. If the pH drops much below this (that is, if the solution becomes more acidic), it indicates that microorganisms have been at work and the nutrient solution should be changed immediately. Plants grown at too acid a pH show flower drop and yellowing leaves. Litmus, or pH paper, can be obtained from many seed houses and garden supply shops.

We usually add nutrients once every three or four weeks. It is difficult to specify exactly how often nutrients should be added because this depends upon the number and type of plants being grown. The rate of nutrient addition is determined by experimentation. As a rough guide, one or two tablespoons of "inorganic" or "organic" mixture every three or four weeks should be ample for an eight-square-foot tank containing a full complement of actively growing plants.

As a final note, the nutrient solution should be changed regularly, about every four months. In the large tanks, the old solution must be siphoned off — not the most pleasant job in the world, but the slightly salty taste of the solution, should the siphoner get a mouthful, is not too objectionable. The aggregate is then washed off with five to 10 gallons of water, is siphoned off again, and new nutrient solution is introduced. This process cleans adhering salts off the aggregate. The same process must be followed with the dishpan containers, but siphoning will not be required.

FEEDING

Having the properly balanced nutrient solution sitting in a reservoir may be commendable, but it must get to the aggregate to do the plants any good. The cheapest method can be employed with the dishpans. The gardener simply pours the solution onto the aggregate twice a day (or three times if the plants wilt frequently), leaves the solution there for about 15 minutes, and then removes the stopper or opens the spout, allowing the solution to drain back into the reservoir. Such a manual system will, of course,

require that somebody be available at least twice a day to service the plants.

A slightly more convenient system, especially if more than one unit is in use, is made by connecting the reservoir to the hydroponic tank, or tanks, with tubing. We have used one-, two- and five-gallon plastic gasoline or oil containers as reservoirs connected to the spout of the hydroponic tank with flexible tubing. (These containers must *never* have been used for oil or gas — buy new ones.)

To flood the tank, simply raise the reservoir above the level of the hydroponic tank until the solution has flowed into the tank. Once again, leave the solution for 15 minutes and then return the reservoir to a position below the tank, repeating once or twice a day. A useful feature of this approach is that several containers may be connected to a single reservoir through flexible tubing and T-junctions. We have connected up to five dishpans to a single five-gallon reservoir with excellent results. Using this multiple setup, all tanks are watered at the same time with no additional labour. To leave this system for the occasional weekend, we simply place the nutrient reservoir at a level *slightly* higher than the tanks so that there is a small amount of nutrient at the bottom of the tanks. We would not recommend this procedure for more than a weekend, because of the danger of oxygen deprivation and root rot.

Because both of us desired more freedom from the daily maintenance of our hydroponic gardens, we

Left, hydroponic unit using the author's new design under construction. Above, the $100 unit is finished and ready to be planted. Note submerged pump in the nutrient reservoir and the "spaghetti" feeder tubes.

now use an automated system almost exclusively. This system is comprised of an electric pump and a timer, which switches the pump on automatically two or three times a day for a period of one or two hours each time, moving the nutrient solution from the reservoir to the tank. Gravity then takes the solution back to the reservoir. This method works well with dishpan containers and with the larger tanks.

With the former, an external reservoir is required — again, a plastic gasoline or oil container, or, for more than five units, a plastic garbage can. On the reservoir, a spout is installed near the bottom on the side. This spout is connected by flexible tubing to the spouts of the dishpans, which must be placed higher than the reservoir, so that the solution will drain downhill into the reservoir.

For the pump, we use the submersible variety (the type which is sunk into the solution to be pumped) available at fountain, building or electrical suppliers. We use *Little Giant* submersibles, but there are several makes available and a supplier will recommend a suitable type and capacity. We would suggest a very corrosion-resistant pump because it will be immersed in a salt solution continuously — stainless steel, although expensive, is ideal for this purpose. To the pump we connect a piece of flexible tubing of the appropriate diameter. The best type of tubing we have used is *Tygon* and can be obtained from a fountain supplier. The opposite end of the *Tygon* tubing is sealed off with a clamp or may simply be heat-sealed using a soldering iron. Thus the *Tygon* tubing-plus-pump represents a closed system. The nutrient solution is delivered to the individual tanks through smaller diameter plastic spaghetti tubing (see photograph) which is attached to the *Tygon* tubing through brass fasteners. These fasteners look very much like rivets and can be purchased at hobby stores which specialize in leather working, as can the small pointed tool which is used to insert them into the *Tygon* tubing. The small diameter spaghetti tubing can be purchased in a variety of colours from electronics supply houses or as irrigation tubing from greenhouse suppliers. We prefer to use black, rather than transparent tubing, to keep down algal growth in the tubes. The usual outer diameter is 0.06 to 0.10 inches (60 to 100 mil). It is simply a matter of experimenting to find the size of tubing which will fit snugly inside the brass fasteners. If brass fasteners are unavailable, simply poke a small hole in the *Tygon* tubing using a sharp awl and push in the spaghetti tubing. This is a little more time-consuming but works just fine.

One of the advantages of using *Tygon* as the main tube is that it is slightly "sticky" and it will tend to grasp other types of tubing pushed into it. The spaghetti tubing should be whatever length is necessary, usually no more than two or three feet, to run to the individual tanks. We use two spaghetti feeder tubes per dishpan and, in order to weight them down and to prevent the jet of water from disturbing the aggregate, we attach a one-inch piece of *Tygon* tubing crosswise to the end of the spaghetti tubing in the same way as the tubing is attached to the main *Tygon* tube (using a brass fastener, if available). This end of the spaghetti tubing is buried just beneath the surface of the aggregate. This completes the automatic feeder system for dishpan containers. It can easily feed at least two dozen containers. All that is required to automate the system is a *three*-conductor timer to switch the pump on and off. (Because the pump is immersed in a water solution, it is dangerous to use simple two-conductor timers. Make sure the timer has that third ground connection.)

We have some advice concerning the dishpan system, either manual or automatic. First, the pans should be slightly inclined with the spout lower than the other end of the pan. This will facilitate drainage of the nutrient solution back to the reservoir. Second, with the automatic system, and only a few containers, it is necessary to place some type of flow regulator on the *Tygon* tubing to control the amount of solution delivered by the pump — otherwise the house may flood along with the tanks. Adjust the flow regulator, using a small clamp, so that the tanks do not overflow.

With the larger wooden containers, the automatic setup is virtually identical. However, this system has one great advantage over the dishpan containers — there is no necessity for an external reservoir because the reservoir is contained right in the tank, beneath the aggregate.

The pump is placed in the semicircular enclosure at the side of the tank, and sits on the bottom. It is connected to a four-and-one-half-foot length of *Tygon* tubing (for a four-foot-long tank), which is sealed at the end, as described for the dishpan tanks. At six to 12-inch intervals along the *Tygon* tubing, one-foot lengths of spaghetti tubing are inserted and their ends weighted with one-inch lengths of *Tygon* tubing, just as previously described. The four-and-one-half-foot length of tubing is laid down the middle of the tank on top of the aggregate, and the spaghetti tubes are inserted and oriented opposite each other so that one group of tubes covers one side of the tank and the other group covers the opposite side. Nutrient solution is pumped up from the reservoir, percolates through the aggregate and runs off the edges of the arborite platform.

TEMPERATURE AND LIGHT

The type of vegetable being grown will dictate temperature and light requirements. Warm temperature crops such as peppers, tomatoes and cucumbers require an ambient daytime temperature of at least 75 to 80 degrees F (23 to 26 degrees C) whereas cool weather crops such as lettuce and spinach prefer a daytime temperature of 65 to 70 degrees F (18 to 21 degrees C). In a typical house, it is fairly easy to find this range of temperatures, particularly as the lights will radiate a considerable amount of heat. Nighttime temperatures will be the most critical in houses that are not centrally heated.

We grow lettuce and spinach in an unfinished basement where the temperature stays around 65 degrees F, and grow our tomatoes, peppers and cucumbers in a small upstairs room close to a radiator. When the fluorescent lights are on, the temperature in the room reaches 85 degrees F (29 degrees C). For good fruit set and growth of tomatoes and peppers, it is important to provide plants with these higher temperatures.

Light requirements also vary, depending upon the crop. Tomatoes, peppers and cucumbers prefer high light intensities whereas lettuce, spinach and many herbs such as chervil and parsley can be grown at much lower light intensities. Clearly, plants which require higher temperatures also generally require the most light.

But almost all plants will require the installation of fluorescent fixtures, *even if the tank is located in a south-facing window*. Light from the sun is simply not enough, particularly during the winter. No matter what the circumstances, the plants should have 14 or 15 hours of light a day.

We provide light from *Cool-Lite* fluorescent tubes at the rate of eight 40-watt tubes (four-foot tubes) per eight-square-foot tank for our crops that require a lot of light, and four to six such tubes for lower light requirements. Light from windows will decrease the amount of artificial light needed, but it will always be necessary to provide such light from five to eight P.M. The importance of adequate light cannot be overemphasized. It is the single most important factor limiting the number of plants that can be grown in a unit. Watch the plants for spindly growth and poor fruit set — indicators of insufficient light.

Four-foot-long, four-tube fluorescent fixtures are the most convenient source of artificial illumination. We have mounted ours on chains or ropes so that their height can be adjusted as the plants grow. We usually locate the lights about one foot from the surface of the aggregate, and, as the plants grow, raise the lights. However, when the lights reach two and one-half to three feet above the aggregate it's time to

Sources

Books:

HYDRO-STORY
By C.E. Sherman and H. Brenizer
Nolo Press
Box 544
Occidental, California 95465
Recommended for beginners.

HYDROPONICS — GROWING PLANTS WITHOUT SOIL
By D. Harris
Sphere Books Limited
London, England
Distributed by:
Thomas Nelson & Sons (Canada) Ltd.
81 Curlew Drive
Don Mills, Ontario M3A 2R1
Recommended as an intermediate text.

GARDENING WITHOUT SOIL
By James S. Douglas
Key Book Publishing
Toronto, Ontario
Distributed by:
H.B. Fenn & Company Ltd.
2421 Drew Road
Mississauga, Ontario L5S 1A1
Recommended as an advanced text.

Equipment:

FUN WATER GARDENS
1134 Yonge Street
Toronto, Ontario M4W 2L8
Free literature. This is the leading manufacturer and retailer of home hydroponic systems in Canada. Source for complete units, as well as fluorescent light units, pumps, timers, plant food, growing medium and hydroponic literature.

CANADIAN HYDRO GARDENS LIMITED
411 Brook Road West
Ancaster, Ontario L9G 3L1
Pre-fab and do-it-yourself hydroponic growing kits for the home.

SPECIALTY GARDENS LIMITED
90 Earlton Road
Agincourt, Ontario M1T 2R6
Mail-order family business offering home systems, supplies and information on hydroponics.

APPLIED HYDROPONICS OF CANADA INC.
5322 Boulevard St. Laurent
Montreal, Quebec H2T 1S1
Manufacture and sell a small hydroponic nursery and a commercial-scale herb growing unit for restaurants.

EATON VALLEY AGRICULTURAL SERVICES
C.P. 25
Sawyerville, Quebec J0B 3A0
Seacrop liquid seaweed concentrate, blood meal and fish emulsion.

JENKINS HARDWARE AND SEEDS
P.O. Box 2424
London, Ontario N6A 4G3
Blood meal and *Alaska* fish fertilizer.

NATURALLY GREEN
322 Lindley
Bozeman, Montana 59715
Organic nutrient ingredients.

HOME HYDROCULTURE ASSOCIATION
Box 3250, Station D
Willowdale, Ontario M2R 3G6
This group offers a monthly newsletter as well as information on equipment, sources of nutrients, best plant varieties to grow and other help for hydroponic enthusiasts.

CITY GREEN HYDROPONICS LTD.
7515 Bren Road
Mississauga, Ontario L4T 3V4
Equipment including pumps, tubing and clamps.

ECO ENTERPRISES
2821 N.E. 55th Street
Seattle, Washington 98105
$1.00 catalogue includes an introductory sample of *Eco Grow* hydroponic plant nutrient.

---

start cutting back the plants rather than raising the lights further. Our lighting system is connected to a timer, so that daily maintenance of the units is minimized.

SEED VARIETIES

Plants that keep bumping into the lights, or threaten to turn the living room into the perfect setting for Martin Denny music are probably not the best varieties for hydroponic use. Ideal hydroponic plants will not grow too large, too fast; they will put their energy into fruiting. Seed catalogues are not geared to such varieties, and so it is often difficult to choose the right cultivars for one's particular needs,

and experimentation is the only way to find the answer.

We have been experimenting with suitable varieties for hydroponic culture for three years and can offer some advice on which ones seem to grow particularly well. For germinating tomato, pepper and herb seeds we use Jiffy Pots, which are placed in the aggregate after the seedlings sprout. Lettuce seed can be planted right on the surface of the aggregate, and pressed in slightly. Cucumber, bean and spinach seeds should be covered with a little aggregate.

The two varieties of tomatoes that we recommend most highly for growing and for eating are *Starshot* and *Stakeless*. These varieties are small, stocky and set lots of fruit — ideal for hydroponic culture. The small-fruited *Starshot* mature well before the larger-fruited *Stakeless,* and by regular planting of these two varieties, we have a continuous supply of tomatoes. One should have no difficulty getting 20 to 40 fruits per *Starshot* plant.

With sweet peppers, we recommend three varieties known as *Early Niagara Giant, Earliest Red Sweet* and *Sweet Hungarian.* Steve was told once that peppers don't do well in hydroponic culture, but he is enough of a pepper enthusiast not to be discouraged. Both of our pepper plants are now more than a year old and still producing at a fantastic rate, showing no signs of fatigue. To date, we have harvested more than 60 peppers from a single *Early Niagara Giant.* For hotter varieties, we have had good luck with *Hungarian Wax, Large Red Cherry Hot* and *Long Thick Red* peppers. Success with peppers depends upon a daytime temperature of 75 to 80 degrees F (23 to 26 degrees C). Tomatoes and peppers seem to grow well in the same tank.

For our cucumbers, we chose English varieties because they do not need to be pollinated. English cucumbers can be difficult to grow because of their unusual nitrogen requirements, but we have had success with two varieties, *Rocket* and *Toska 70. Rocket* seeds are, unfortunately, no longer available from any sources we checked, but Thompson & Morgan has just released *Fembaby,* a self-fruiting, all-female variety said to be ideal for indoor growing.

Both temperature and light are critical with English cucumbers, but even more important is the nutrient mix. Here is where experimentation comes in. Cucumbers require a considerably higher concentration of nutrients, especially nitrogen, than most other crops for good yield. If a single tank is devoted to cucumbers, there is no problem, but if cucumbers are grown with other crops, less nutrient must be used, or poor fruit set, excessive leaf growth and misshapen fruit will result on the other crops.

With the nutrient formulae provided earlier, cucumber growth and yield will be satisfactory, but certainly not spectacular, but the other crops should do well. This is a compromise and we have experimented by placing small amounts of nutrient directly around the cucumber plants when they begin to flower. Using this method, we have successfully grown cucumbers with tomatoes and, in fact, we have several cucumber plants which have been producing an average of two cucumbers each week per plant for more than a year. Commercial hydroponic growers, incidentally, not only use different nutrient solutions for different vegetables, but also use different formulae for various stages in the life of a single vegetable. For example, a young tomato seedling will receive one solution, whereas the same plant when flowering will have another. For simplicity's sake, the nutrients used by the home gardener must be something of a compromise.

David Stone

Most varieties of leaf lettuce grow well in hydroponic culture. A particular favourite of ours is *Buttercrunch,* a Boston variety. *Cos* lettuce also does well and is less prone to browning around the edge, probably because of its higher nitrogen requirements. If lettuce is grown in its own tank, we cut back on the nutrient solution (with the organic mixture, use less fish emulsion) since the nutrient requirements of lettuce are less than those of flowering plants.

The nitrogen requirements of spinach are higher than for most lettuce, but *Cos* lettuce and spinach grow well together. We like *Melody* spinach for hydroponic culture, but other varieties that we have tried have also produced well.

Most herb seeds are not sold as varieties and therefore there is no problem finding and growing them. We have successfully grown sweet basil, chervil, chives, sweet marjoram, parsley and sorrel. Other herbs would probably grow equally well — we simply haven't tried them yet.

Clearly, for us, hydroponic gardening is an ongoing process of experimentation and discovery. We usually find that people are quite skeptical about our claims — that yields are very high, that the fruit tastes sweet and delicious — and yet we have proved these things to our own satisfaction, as scientists, time and time again. The rewards of hydroponic gardening are tremendous. One of the nicest Christmas presents we know of is a vine-ripened pesticide-free tomato — it's guaranteed to take the chill from the worst weather that winter can bring.

Hydroponic Fodder

Seven pounds of feed from a pound of grain?
Just add water....

By David Ladd

Hydroponically-sprouted grain is a perfect example of a fine idea that never made it big in North American agriculture, primarily because of overzealous promotion a generation ago. Students of old farm magazines will recall seeing the advertisements for sprouting units that were claimed to produce an almost free ration that was nutritionally complete and — EVEN MORE — contained nature's magic ingredients.

Perhaps the advertising is understandable when one considers that sprouted grains — for both man and animal — are still considered to possess mystical powers in certain parts of the globe. Part of the magic relates simply to volume — five pounds of grain turns, in a matter of days, into 25 pounds of green grass. In Iran, and other countries, sprouted grains have been used for centuries to enhance the fertility of women and to speed their return to normal health after childbirth.

On an equally pragmatic level, animal husbandmen know that early spring grass is a powerful tonic, giving new vitality and vigour to animals emerging from a winter of dried feeds. Hydroponically-sprouted grain offers the same nutritional boost. Its effects are not at all magical, although there are a number of enzymes, hormones and "grass juice factors" involved that are still little understood.

What is known is that sprouted grain contains as much as double the protein of the original grain seed, the vitamin A content skyrockets and other vitamins and minerals increase. Farmers who supplement their animals' diets with sprouted grain report improved fertility, greater milk production and a faster recovery by animals that are sick or off their feed.

Dr. C. Murray Smith, a veterinarian practising near Lambeth, Ontario, was involved in sprouted grain research in the United States for 14 years. There, he says, blood tests and fertility counts indicated better fertility in stallions and higher conception rates in mares. According to Dr. Smith, statistics show that sows fed sprouted grains averaged more piglets per litter than those in control groups.

Smith emphasizes that the biggest merit of feeding sprouted grains is improved health — because the sprouts can only be used as a supplement, feed cost savings are secondary. Dr. Smith, who holds a patent on an automated sprouting system, says the merits may even be non-existent if the feeds are not balanced properly. (Livestock eating only this fresh, rich grass will react in the same way we would on a diet of nothing but fresh fruit.)

BURST OF GROWTH

Because grain sprouting seems to give something for nothing — fivefold increases in feed volume in just a week — it helps to understand what goes on within a seed as it sprouts.

In a dry grain seed the water content is about 11 per cent of the total weight, with the rest made up of shell, genetic material and a good food supply for the young seedling. After soaking in water for 24 hours, the moisture content has risen to 45 per cent or more of the total weight. The embryo — the living growth centre of the seed, now becomes active and produces a hormone called gibberellin, which travels to a layer of cells inside the seed coat called the aleurone layer.

This cell group then produces enzymes that break down the starches stored in the seed, in somewhat the same way that saliva breaks down starches into

BARLEY: BEFORE AND AFTER SPROUTING

	Nutrients Per 100 Grams of Dry Matter	
	Barley Grain	Barley Grass*
Protein	13g.	25g.
Ether Extract (fat)	2.1g.	4.2g.
Nitrogen Free Extract	76g.	46.2g.
Fibre	5.6g.	17g.
Ash	2.7g.	6.5g.
Calcium	.09g.	.12g.
Phosphorus	.47g.	.87g.
Vitamin A	0 I.U.	10,000 I.U.
Niacin	5.13mg.	39.85mg.
Riboflavin	4.95mg.	11.9mg.

Six days after sprouting. Fertilizer added to rinse water.

sugars for human digestion. With this food source now available, the seed enters into a period of rapid growth. Spurred on by various hormones that are activated in the germination sequence, the first leaf of the plant, the cotyledon, is formed.

It is at this stage that seedlings have used up much of their reserves to create — with the aid of water, heat and, possibly, light from the sun — a plant full of vitamins, protein and plant hormones. It is now that the plants are ripe for feeding as sprouts. After this point — about seven days after germination — the high quality nutrients are converted to cellulose and the feed loses its highly concentrated feed value. (See chart for comparison of dried grain to freshly sprouted grass.)

Interest in large-scale grain sprouting units is now increasing, but it is a relatively new idea in commercial agriculture. The minimum investment in a Canadian unit of this type is about $17,000, limiting it to those who want high quality feed and have the money to spare. (Arthur Godfrey feeds his horses sprouted grain.) For those of us who don't have a Secretariat stabled in the barn, much cheaper alternatives exist. In fact, anyone with a few animals or a flock of chickens or geese can, with little outlay of cash and a small amount of daily attention, grow "fresh, spring grass" all year-round.

To sprout grain at home, shallow trays of plastic, wood or metal are required. The commercial unit uses trays measuring about one foot by three feet, and four inches deep. Similar trays or garden flats can be purchased at some farm and garden supply stores or from some seed companies. The trays must allow drainage without allowing the grains to escape, and most plastic trays will have to be punctured with a nail or drilled on the bottom at one end to allow water to drain away, not sit and cause the seed to rot. Some sprouters choose to line their trays with a layer of edible paper (such as white newsprint) or a thin layer of soil to absorb excess water. Experimentation will determine the method best suited to the seed, the growing environment and the temperament of the individual sprouter.

Almost any seed can be sprouted for fodder, with the notable exception of corn. If kiln-dried, corn will not sprout at all, and otherwise is expensive, slow to germinate and may contain toxins. Wheat is difficult to sprout and moulds or becomes mushy easily, especially if pre-soaked. The best choices are alfalfa, barley, oats, buckwheat, beans or sunflower seeds — the latter are sprouted to feed the primates at the Metro Toronto Zoo. They need not be shelled before sprouting and are perfect for the sunflower gardener with a small flock of poultry. In fact, hard-shelled grains such as buckwheat and sunflowers are often ignored by fowl, but when sprouted they are eagerly consumed.

If you are purchasing grain, be very sure it is *untreated.* Grain dealers will, as a matter of course, sell you seed grain that is coated with fungicides unless you specify what you want. (Be prepared for a skeptical reception — sprouting grain is almost unheard-of in most areas.) Either buy untreated seed for planting, which may be relatively expensive, or feed grain, which will be much cheaper but may have a lower germination rate. The cheaper feed seed — provided it is not coming out of prolonged storage — will generally turn out to be more economical in the long run. Before hauling home 500 pounds of grain for sprouting, buy a sample pound or so and test it. Home-grown seed, of course, will be the cheapest available untreated seed and should germinate well if it has been stored properly.

PROCEDURES

Pour a quantity of seed into a bucket (the three-foot-square tray takes about five pounds), cover deeply with water and leave for 24 hours.

After this time, pour off the water and spread the seeds out in a tray about ¾-inch deep. The tray, at this point, can be placed in the dark or in light, but the room should be about 68 degrees F. Temperatures over 73 degrees create mould, while colder temperatures may also encourage mould and slow or stop sprouting. Light will not harm the seeds, but will be of no nutritional benefit until about the fourth day. Tilt the tray on a slight angle so that water can drain out through the holes in the bottom, and place a reservoir underneath to catch the water.

These seedlings should always be kept moist, and require watering three or four times a day. (A good routine is to water at breakfast, lunch, supper and before going to bed.) Obviously this method is not going to be feasible for the grower who is not at home during the day. He may want to try covering the sprouts lightly with newspaper or a thin layer of soil (they must breathe) to decrease evaporation. The same water or fertilizer solution can be used all week.

The addition of fertilizer is recommended to purchasers of new commercial sprouting units. This has been shown to give better results, but is not absolutely necessary. Barley sprouted with fertilized solution will show about 25 per cent protein, against 18 per cent in that sprouted with pure water. (Use a 20-20-20 fertilizer, two or three ounces in 10 gallons water.) We have never tried organic fertilizers, but manure teas should probably be avoided to prevent the transmission of parasites to animals ingesting the sprouted grain. Fish fertilizers that have been pasteurized would present no such problem, but might not be palatable to all animals.

Whatever your solution, the seeds must be given a good soaking each time they are watered. (In the commercial units, each spray cycle lasts 15 minutes, four times a day.) If the seeds start to smell or the roots start to turn dark, they are being over-watered or not drained properly. Ideally, if you pick up a clump of sprouts, only a small amount of water should drip through when the plants are shaken. Some mould may be present, but it should cause little concern unless it threatens to cover a large area of the tray.

By the seventh day, there should be a succulent crop of grass that is five to 10 inches tall with a mat of intertwined roots that will hold the plants together. In order to have a fresh feeding of greens each day, seven trays will be needed, so that a new batch may be started each day of the week. After each crop is harvested, it is a wise idea to rinse the tray with a mild solution of Javex (or Clorox) before reusing.

This seven-day schedule applies to barley, oats and alfalfa grown under ideal conditions. At home, sprouting time may lengthen somewhat (a *Harrowsmith* buckwheat trial took two weeks), while beans and sunflowers may be ready before a week is up. In all cases, the sprouts are ready for use when the first leaf is fully developed, whether that be after six or 14 days.

The complete mat of grass is now ready to be fed to your animals. Again, it must be stressed that this is *not* a complete feed. It must be balanced with other roughage — usually hay — and/or dried grain rations.

A dairy cow should receive about one to one and a half per cent of her body weight in sprouted grains per day — a 1,000-pound Holstein would thus receive from 10 to 15 pounds. Cut down or discontinue the supply when she has access to good outdoor pasture.

An adult sow's normal ration can be cut in half and replaced with seven to 10 pounds of sprouted grain daily. (As with all changes of ration, for all animals, the alteration is best done gradually. Some animals will take to the sprouts immediately, but others will take several days to become convinced that this new feed is good for them.)

For poultry, both the mat of greens and the regular scratch or layer feed should be supplied. The birds will choose the amount of each they want and the owner of a small flock will soon be able to calculate how often a new tray must be started. If the mat of roots is especially thick, chickens may just eat the grass and leave the roots, which, if still clean, can be fed to hogs or geese. Chicken and geese fed on the grass should have an increased rate of growth and will produce eggs that have the farm-fresh look of a nice, dark-yellow yolk.

Sprouted grain is both a good conditioning feed — for shiny coats and easier births — and a useful finishing feed for the cow, pig or fowl that will soon be slaughtered. In this latter case, sprout the grain until it is only about two inches high. At this stage, there is more starch left in the seedlings and this will help put weight on the animals.

Obviously, feeding sprouted grain involves more work than simply dumping a bag of Duck Chow into a feeder. It is labour intensive and therefore nicely suited to small farming operations or those growing their own feed and seeking the highest possible quality.

And, like the Persians, some might even want to try sprouts themselves. Alfalfa sprouts are already known as a delicious addition to the human salad or sandwich diet, and I have found sunflower sprouts to be quite tasty. Buckwheat sprouts are sweet when young and make a nutritious addition to winter salads. Hydroponically sprouted grains are, without doubt, a fine winter food for man and his beasts.

Boxing Tactics For High Latitude Horticulture

Notes from a green-thumbed Northerner

By Mickey Lammers

Even here in the Yukon, spring officially — if somewhat unconvincingly — begins on March 21st. The wind howls, the snow is everywhere and, despite the lengthening days, we still seem utterly trapped by the bleak grip of winter. I celebrate anyway, bringing small flats of frozen soil indoors to thaw beside the wood stove, marking with anticipation the first step in a new season of high-latitude horticulture.

Thirty miles south of Whitehorse, at an altitude of 2,400 feet, we have a very dry climate, officially semi-arid, and night frost is common. It can happen in May, June, July or August . . . not every year, but always a gloomy possibility. After 25 years in the Yukon, growing a garden almost every place we've settled, I decided the climate is one thing that cannot be changed, so why not live with it? It is possible for my family to grow all the vegetables we can eat during the summer — with leftovers for our chickens, rabbits and goat — and still have enough to pickle, store, can and dry for the entire winter. Gardening saves us a great deal of money year-round, as well as affording us considerable pleasure, because, over the years, I have devised a system that works dependably, economically, and with less work than one would imagine.

The backbone of our vegetable plot and the key to success with my "system" is a set of three growing boxes, which hold the northern climate at bay. The boxes are simply constructed of wood with removable plastic covers to help contain the sun's warmth and keep out the night frosts. A sort of mini-climate is established in each box, giving the plants a security almost unknown to outdoor gardens in this part of the world.

The boxes also provide a solution to the general lack of good soil here. There are many suitable localities in the North to build a house and live, but most have impoverished soil that makes growing a garden difficult. It can take years to raise the soil quality of a whole garden plot to a level that will produce healthy vegetables. My growing boxes require comparatively little earth, which can be gathered in short order and mixed with whatever humus-making and enriching material is available: old sawdust, rotted manure, composted kitchen garbage, peat moss, agricultural lime, wood ashes and bone meal. This soil becomes manageable and productive in a short time, and everything can be done with light tools — shovel, buckets and a wheelbarrow. Even on the most barren piece of land, a harvest is assured. One could even bring greenness to solid bedrock with a boxed-in growing system.

GREEN ARK

Although the growing boxes alone could provide a family with a continuous harvest of hardy vegetables from spring through fall, there is much more to my garden. In a fenced-in, 30-foot-square garden I grow all of the cabbage family, broccoli, kale and cauliflower as well as fava beans, peas, sugar peas and onions. A nearby field is planted with potatoes for us, winter rye, oats and field peas for our livestock. We have an eight-foot-square greenhouse, covered with a double layer of plastic, attached to the house and heated by the same wood stove that heats our quarters. The soil is local, mixed with a liberal amount of chicken and rabbit manure.

There is another 10-by-16-foot plastic-covered greenhouse, unheated, and using local soil fertilized with chicken and rabbit manure and wood ashes. This greenhouse is used for spinach, carrots, herbs,

William Lammers

green beans, parsnips, onions, lettuce and some flowers.

The garden, field and greenhouses require space, money, and considerable labour, at least initially. The boxes require less of all three, and have several advantages over greenhouses. For one thing, the frozen winter soil in the boxes kills most garden pests or insect eggs. I have never had a problem with insect pests in my growing boxes, although there are wireworms in my garden. Also, plastic is not cheap, and replacing it annually on a greenhouse is not only a chore but a nagging expense. Each growing box uses three plastic-covered sashes (one for each section). If these covers are left out all winter, the plastic will shatter as soon as the temperature dips to 40 degrees below zero Fahrenheit, but if I take the trouble to remove the plastic and store it indoors, the sashes will last three to four years.

Sun, rain and fresh air are free and the best medicine for all growing things. I have often wished I could remove the roof of my greenhouse while I stood watering, listening to the rain pitter-pattering against the plastic. In contrast, the removable covers on the growing boxes allow rain, sun and fresh air to reach the plants directly. I can take advantage of early spring rain, and then pull over the covers to keep out frost at night.

Each growing box is six by 12 feet, divided by two crossbeams into three six-by-four-foot sections. Each section has its own removable plastic sash cover. The boxes are three feet deep on the north side, sloping to 28 inches on the south. I half-fill mine with local soil, adding chicken manure and wood ashes annually. Because this leaves a foot and a half or less of growing space between soil surface and plastic cover, I do not plant tall vegetables, such as peas and beans, in the growing boxes. I also do not plant *Brassicas* (the cabbage family) here, because they require a lot of space. They could, however, be planted in a growing box if a gardener felt he could spare the space. (A cabbage plant will require at least eight inches of soil space in every direction.)

The boxes are set on logs that raise them a foot off the ground, enabling the spring air to circulate underneath, warming the soil. This spring defrosting is speeded up by installing the plastic covers in early May. Although the soil in the boxes will have frozen solid during the winter, it will be workable much sooner than the rest of the garden, and, of course, seeding can begin as soon as the soil can be worked. Where I live, that is May 10th, a full two weeks before I can begin seeding the garden.

In late March, I seed lettuce in a flat in the heated greenhouse for later transplanting to a growing box. By the second week of May, I seed all the growing boxes directly with radishes, carrots, Swiss chard, *Yellow Pe-Tsai Leaf* Chinese cabbage, beets, *Grand Rapids* and *Prizehead* leaf lettuce, onions, and *Bloomsdale* spinach. This is intensive gardening on good, well-fertilized soil, so the rows can be spaced only six inches apart. As soon as the seeds are in, I water them, cover the soil with old scraps of plastic, put the sashes on each box and forget about them for three or four days. One section is kept empty for *Butterhead* head lettuce, which is still in a flat in the hothouse and will be set out at the end of May. The plastic sashes will be used to cover the boxes at night, when necessary, until mid-June.

After just a few days of snow, clouds or sun, some seeds will have sprouted. (Radishes and Chinese cabbage are just the thing for impatient people.) As soon as I spot the telltale green, all scraps of plastic that were on the soil come off. Left too long, they will cause young plants to burn or mould. The sashes, however, are put back on. Like a greenhouse, the box might need air during the day; this is accomplished by propping up the sashes on sticks. If the air in the box gets too warm, over 85 degrees F, the plants will wilt easily and grow tall, spindly and weak.

My idea of vegetable gardening is to have fresh greens as soon as possible. By the first of June, we are able to start picking the odd leaf of lettuce for a sandwich, and by June 10th we have a salad each day — radishes, lettuce, spinach, cucumbers (thanks to the heated greenhouse) and Chinese cabbage. From then on, there is more produce than two people can handle, so the animals get a share. Thinning is important now. Radishes should have a space of one inch in the row; carrots, Chinese cabbage, beets and spinach need two inches; onions and Swiss chard, three inches.

Throughout their growth, but particularly in the early stages, the plants need to be watered faithfully. Growing boxes need more water than a garden because air circulates all around the box, evaporating moisture, and because the boxes are often closed, excluding precipitation. Our solution was to raise a 45-gallon tank on a wooden support higher than the boxes, allowing water to flow through an attached hose by gravity. We fill our tank with ice-cold well water, but in the tank it warms considerably, making it far better for the vegetables than a shower of cold water. Ideally, the tank could be set under a roof edge where it would fill automatically with rain overflow.

By the time the greens are big enough to form a solid mass in the box, providing their own shade, they require less water. In mid-June, I am able to remove the plastic shades and store them for use again in fall. From now on, it is a matter of allowing things to grow, harvesting, watering, and reseeding rows as they disappear. Spinach is the first to go to seed and that row is reseeded with purslane and *PeTsai*. Radishes disappear quickly, too. The Chinese cabbage section looks quite sad by mid-August. We harvest all of it for the chickens, who love it, and start again with another row of the same, or perhaps leaf lettuce. I always reseed when a row is harvested or goes to seed, and fresh produce continues to ripen until fall.

By the end of August, what is left of the beets can be harvested for storage and, somewhat later, the remaining carrots are gathered. Onions need all the time they can get. I never manage to grow them very large, but they make fine cooking onions for winter use. By the 15th of October, after many a night frost, we still have leaf lettuce and Swiss chard.

Once the plummeting temperature has clipped even these hardy workhorses, I remove the plastic from the sashes and store it for the winter. I add half a five-gallon bucket of chicken manure to each section of my boxes, over the frozen soil. Whenever the wood stove is cleaned out, each part gets a dose of sifted ashes. Then, as soon as possible the following May, I fork all this under to prepare my seedbed again.

William Lammers

The growing boxes are small garden plots designed to suit our climate and the *hardy* vegetables. Tender vegetables, the *Rocket* and *Starfire* tomatoes, and the *Hybrid Burpless* and *Mincu* cucumbers, grow in the heated greenhouse. Celery, corn, melons, pumpkins and squash are definitely warm weather plants and for all the space they would take up in the hothouse, I find it not worthwhile to grow them in any quantity. Many Northerners choose not to grow them at all. These plants are luxuries, tender southerners that require all the protection and coddling the gardener can spare.

But lettuce, carrots, cabbage, beets, onions, spinach — all the hardy root and leaf vegetables — (workhorses of the Northern gardener), can find space in the growing boxes, and will provide fresh, delicious vegetables from an otherwise barren backyard.

Master Plans, Horticulture Department

The perpetual companion planting scheme

By Robert G. White

"You can choose your companions," my grandmother used to say, "but your relatives are thrust upon you." While the old saw was meant to point out the human dilemma of co-existing with cousins, uncles and even siblings who roost uneasily in the same family tree, I've come to think of it whenever the annual garden is being planned.

In assembling a plot of vegetables, we previously gave no thought to the fact that the various species present were having their companions thrust upon them, often being put in situations which would never occur in nature. When my wife and I first read about the theories of companion planting — that vegetables can react in positive or negative ways to other nearby plants — we had serious reservations. But, being avid gardeners, we decided that we must prove or disprove — for ourselves — the claims that plants have "friends" and "enemies" among their foliose neighbours.

Our skepticism proved wrong and, in spite of our doubts, companion planting seemed to work. We found that by planting our vegetables with their recommended companions and with random plantings of herbs and flowers designed to act as repellents or trap plants for garden pests, the quantity of produce harvested from our garden seemed to increase. At the same time, we came to believe that the quality was also enhanced.

Working out a suitable vegetable plot, however, was not easy. None of the various articles and books to which we referred was specific enough in telling how we could take advantage of the inter-species relationships throughout the garden. Conflicts seemed to develop in every plan we drew. To complicate matters, we also wanted to continue to rotate our crops each year, meaning that the juggling and shuffling and planning of what was to go where would have to be dealt with each spring. Many diagrams went into the fire before we had one in which right companions were side by side and, out of this, we finally developed a chart that can be used *ad infinitum*.

Each year, we plot the garden starting at a different point on the schematic wheel (see chart on following pages). We have placed each variety of vegetable between the companion species with which it does best — tomatoes, for instance, would be placed between a row of onions and a row of peppers. These relationships are shown by the dark brown row indicators in the accompanying chart, while the rust coloured rows denote the optional vegetables, herbs or flowers that can be worked into the plan. Spinach, for example, could be interplanted with tomatoes and peppers.

We do not grow all of the plants shown in any single year, but we adhere to the basic framework of the plan and never place those vegetables with definite aversions to each other (tomatoes and potatoes do not mix, beans are retarded by the presence of onions) in close proximity. Separating the incompatibles is easily accomplished with rows of carrots, lettuce or radishes, all of which seem to be companions of the entire vegetable world.

Missing from the chart are those vegetables that, because of their size or space requirements, are isolated at the edges of the plot, but some consideration as to their placement was still undertaken. While corn, cucumbers and squash are all companions, corn and tomatoes should be separated, cucumbers should not grow next to potatoes or herbs, nor should squash and potatoes be side by side. Sunflowers are poor companions for virtually everything.

No doubt, many who read this will regard all of this as another attempt to inject complexity and mysticism where none is needed, or wanted. We like to think of ourselves as pragmatic gardeners, and we think the results are tangible enough to warrant the extra effort involved. There is only one recourse for the serious doubter — take hoe in hand and try it.

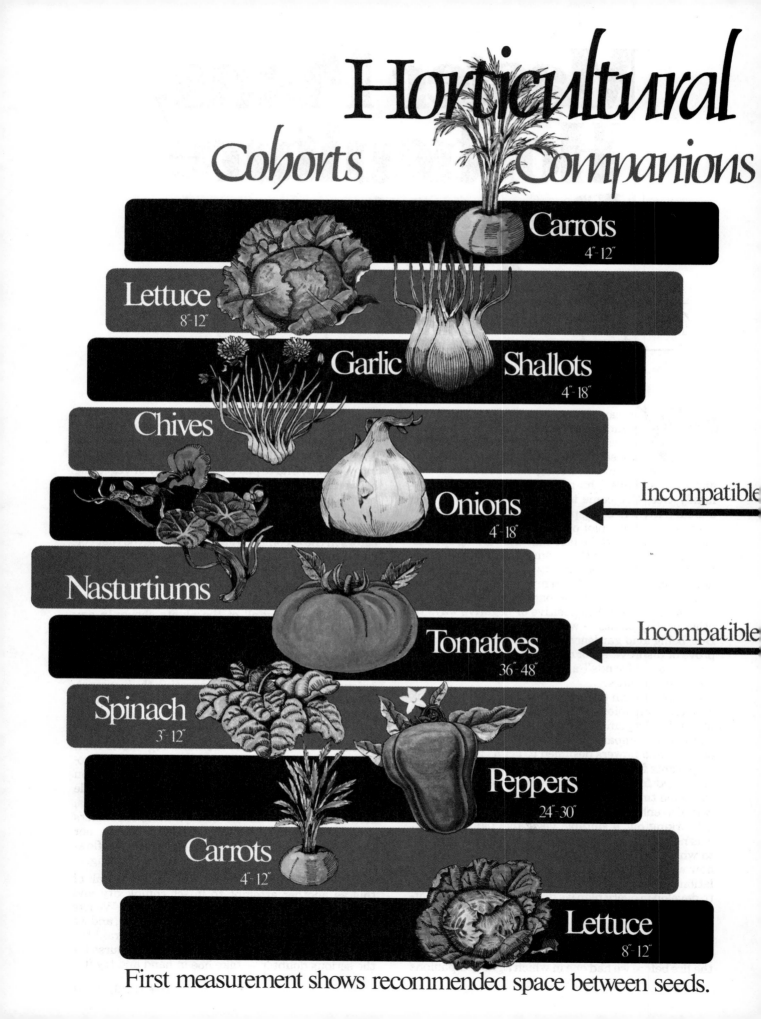

Horticultural

Cohorts

Companions

Carrots
4″-12″

Lettuce
8″-12″

Garlic **Shallots**
4″-18″

Chives

Onions
4″-18″

Incompatible

Nasturtiums

Tomatoes
36″-48″

Incompatible

Spinach
3″-12″

Peppers
24″-30″

Carrots
4″-12″

Lettuce
8″-12″

First measurement shows recommended space between seeds.

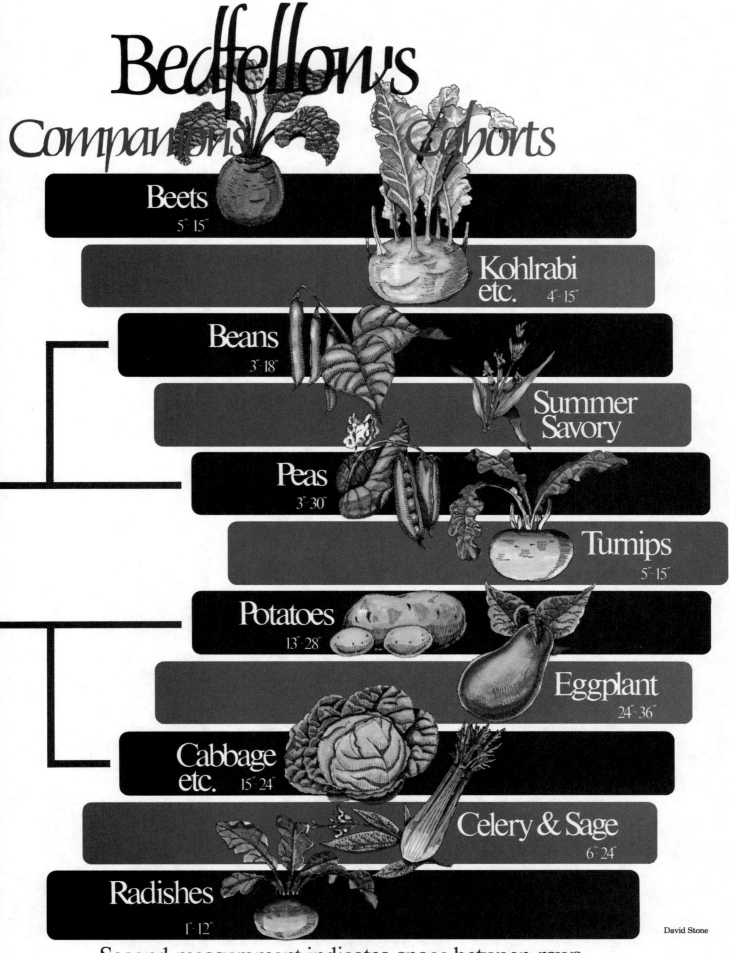

Bedfellows

Companions   Cohorts

Beets 5˝-15˝

Kohlrabi etc. 4˝-15˝

Beans 3˝-18˝

Summer Savory

Peas 3˝-30˝

Turnips 5˝-15˝

Potatoes 13˝-28˝

Eggplant 24˝-36˝

Cabbage etc. 15˝-24˝

Celery & Sage 6˝-24˝

Radishes 1˝-12˝

David Stone

Second measurement indicates space between rows.

The Family Plot

Starting a bed of asparagus where the devotees of Euell Gibbons do not stalk

By J. Peter Shinnick

Bill Milliken

When Benjamin Franklin, an American in Paris, picked up his asparagus spears and bit off the tops, the French thought him utterly *charmant.* How very New-Worldish! What Yankee flair! The bespectacled gent apparently brought as much *élan* to the dining table as he did to kite flying, living by a credo that advised: "Eat not to dullness, drink not to elevation."

Dullness has nothing to do with asparagus, a vegetable that had graced the tables of notables long before Franklin fingered it. A delicacy even for Pharaohs and kings, this elegant member of the lily family is one of Western man's oldest domesticated vegetables: Egyptian tomb paintings dating back to 3000 B.C. depict asparagus bunched, trimmed and tied for market.

Greeks and Romans of the ancient world are known to have dug roots of the wild asparagus from rich, riverbank beds and established them in home gardens. The plants grew lushly in the sandy alluvium of the Nile Delta, but they also proliferated by the mouths of rivers and in areas of sandy soil from the Mediterranean to Siberia. On the steppes of Russia, it is said, asparagus shoots are eaten like blades of grass by cattle and horses.

The Persians called the plant *asparag* meaning "sprout," and the Greeks modified this into asparagus — "to swell to be ripe" — although later generations would dub it "sparrow grass" or "sparagus." The vegetable retains its Greek name today, with the Latin term *officinalis* denoting the edible garden variety, as distinct from several other family members grown for their fernlike foliage.

Officinalis translates to "pharmaceutical" and the medical use of the plant actually overshadowed its culinary appreciation for centuries. In a long list of herbal attributes, Nicholas Culpeper claimed that asparagus "stirreth up the bodily lust in man or woman, whatever some have written to the contrary." Although Culpeper has never been accused of skepticism when it came to describing the medicinal value of plants, asparagus is universally regarded as something of an aphrodisiac.

No Roman garden was complete without a few asparagus plants — for "medicinal" purposes, of course. One can imagine a figure in his toga dashing down the Appian Way, orgy-bound, clutching a fresh bunch of asparagus in either hand. Rightly or wrongly, asparagus still rates number one among aphrodisiacs in the contemporary *Canadian Book of Lists*. We, of course, have not carried the asparagus cult as far as the lusty Romans, who managed to produce shoots weighing a third of a pound in the sandy marshes near Ravenna — a record that was only eclipsed 1,500 years later by French growers who showed up at market with spears that tipped the scale at two to the pound.

Athenaeus the Greek claimed asparagus to be a "remedy for every kind of internal disorder," and both the Romans and Culpeper's British followers believed it could cure everything from bee stings to toothaches. They also described it as a diuretic, and modern science says they were correct in this. Asparagus increases the secretion of urine and excites the urinary passages. It is the most vitamin potent of all garden vegetables, ranking near the top of the charts in niacin, riboflavin and thiamine, with respectably high levels of vitamins C and A.

GYPSY NATURE

King Louis XIV, *gourmet extraordinaire,* is credited with repopularizing asparagus as a vegetable. His largesse with the coveted spears extended even to certain members of the nobility imprisoned in the Bastille during his reign. A gastronomic history of the times reported one such meal, which included asparagus with mushrooms and truffles, along with such other dungeon fare as green pea soup, a joint of fowl, sliced roast beef, meat pie garnished with sweet breads, cocks' combs, sheep tongues *en ragout,* biscuits, fruits, a bottle of Burgundy and mocha coffee. (Imprisonment, where is thy sting?)

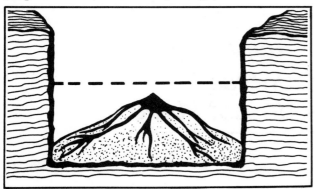

Once established, an asparagus bed will produce annually for 10 to 40 years, but it must be started correctly. A trench 12 inches deep and 12 inches wide is dug, and the bottom lined with rich, well-rotted manure or compost. Individual roots are placed in the trench at intervals of 18 inches and covered with good soil. The trench is gradually filled as the asparagus grows during its first season.

The English dined on asparagus with slightly less fanfare, but with equal enthusiasm. Samuel Pepys is said to have stirred up interest in asparagus' eating qualities among Britons. He noted in his diary: "We came to Gilford and there passed our time in the garden, cutting of sparagus for supper, the best that ever I eat in my life . . . . " (It is as true today as in Pepys' time that "sparagus" is at its succulent best when it comes straight from the garden. That which is called asparagus and which is sold canned or "fresh" — usually 10 days out of California — is nothing compared to the real thing plucked from the soil moments before it is eaten. There are no substitutes.)

By the 19th century, Isabella Beeton would claim the plant to be "a native of Great Britain," citing as evidence, "At Kynarth Cove, in Cornwall, there is an island called 'Asparagus Island' from the abundance in which it is there found."

Asparagus does tend to make itself indistinguishable from the native vegetation and what Ms. Beeton thought was indigenous was most probably a green relic of the Roman occupation of Britain. The plant has a gypsy nature that domestication has not curbed. Given only a short time in the garden, the progeny of asparagus can execute daring escapes that would be the envy of Papillon. The red berries that appear on the plants in August and September have a way of attracting birds and then being unceremoniously dropped in nearby fields and neighbouring gardens.

Being landless until recent years, I had come to depend on this wild — "feral" would be a more accurate description — asparagus. I still have a mental map of asparagus clumps growing beneath certain shrubs in Kelowna City Park and gardens throughout the downtown area. The only drawback to non-cultivated asparagus is that the pickings may be few and far between and, all too often, some other devotee of Euell Gibbons has stalked by ahead of you.

With each garden at a succession of rented homes during the past 10 years, I always swore secretly that I would plant asparagus when I had a home of my own. Perennials are a powerful bond to the land, and when my first three dozen asparagus crowns — dormant root clumps from which the plant is usually propagated — went into the ground, I felt I had become entrenched, less nomadic. I belonged.

In some ways asparagus is the most pleasant of gardening paradoxes, a vegetable delicate of flavour, high of price (if bought), yet extremely hardy and easily grown. Once established, a bed of asparagus will produce a crop every spring for at least 10 years and possibly for as long as 40.

My own patch started with 36 plants bought at a nursery, and I have since added about two dozen more that were found growing wild on my lot or choked by rocks alongside the highway. They grow anywhere, and seem to be forgiving of the anarchic gardener, such as myself, who often forgets to do the right things until it is too late.

TRENCH CULTURE

Asparagus develops a very robust root system, which must be encouraged so that it will be able to push forth a continuous supply of thick, healthy spears or shoots each spring. If planted shallowly, the root development will tend to push the crown too close to the soil surface where it may dry out and be damaged by even the lightest cultivation. Therefore, a classic method of planting asparagus has developed and it is highly advisable to follow it.

I dug a trench 12 inches deep and lined the bottom with a thin layer of rich topsoil and some treated sludge fertilizer (good compost or well-rotted manure works as well, or better) into which the young crowns were planted. Spring is the season to plant asparagus, and the trench is slowly filled with good soil, or compost and manure (or both) as the plants grow throughout the first summer. The secret is to bury most of the growing asparagus spears without covering the tips.

Having alluvial soil has helped me. The garden is part of a fertile delta built through a hundred thousand years of flooding and meandering by Mission Creek. (This was once the domain of the Salish Indians, until prospectors and missionaries settled the valley during one of the many pulsations of the British Columbia Gold Rush.)

Asparagus prefers a well-drained, rich soil (consider the Nile Delta). It likes full sun and lots of moisture as well. Those who are not blessed with the right growing medium, as I was, should add sand, limestone or wood ashes to increase the porosity of the soil. (Asparagus roots will rot if forced to endure long periods of waterlogged soil.) A good deal of well-rotted manure or compost should be dug into the asparagus bed initially, and added yearly thereafter.

Asparagus can be grown either from seed or crowns (roots); the former is a longer but far less expensive process. A 50-cent packet of seed should easily produce 100 roots — worth $15.00 or so from a local nursery or mail-order source. Grown from seed, however, plants cannot be harvested for at least three years; from crowns, for two years. As a rough estimate, figure on 10 to 30 crowns per person. Seven crowns will take 10 feet of row and should produce three or four pounds of greens by the third year.

To speed germination, soak seed in lukewarm water for 48 hours before late spring planting. Dig furrows four inches deep and 18 inches apart, and plant the seed one and one-half inches deep, one inch apart, in the furrows. After seedlings emerge, in about a month, thin them to four inches apart. The following year, the dormant roots can be dug and transplanted in the early spring. If the gardener is buying crowns he will start the cultivation process at this point.

In choosing a site for asparagus, keep in mind that the plant is a perennial and that its fronds grow chest-high and are capable of shading out lesser vegetables. Once established, a bed of asparagus will be difficult to cultivate and would be destroyed or seriously set back by the intrusion of a rototiller. Many gardeners choose to establish asparagus as a border planting, along a fence or as a backdrop on the north side of the garden. (Be sure, however, that in future years it will not come under heavy shade or have to compete with the roots of a nearby tree. Asparagus can be successfully grown with other perennials, such as rhubarb, flowers or in the herb garden. Keep in mind that its roots spread out laterally in a radius of about four feet and that the plants need a considerable amount of elbow room.)

The potential asparagus bed will benefit from deep tilling or turning over with a fork, a process that can be combined with the application of rotted manure or compost. All weeds and large stones must be cleared away, and sand added if the soil is very heavy with clay. The ideal soil pH for asparagus is 6.5.

For the first two seasons, the gardener cannot harvest. He waits, fussing with the less exalted annuals, always keeping an eye on the asparagus. An Italian gardener who stops by the house occasionally to tell me how to prune my grapes, calls the process of waiting "storing up power," and clenches his fist to illustrate. Photosynthesis gives the crowns the muscle to grow spears in the spring.

The urge to devour is strong, almost overpowering. We verge on becoming craving herbivores and we sometimes plunge back into some primordial past too distant to remember, overwhelmed by the urge to graze, to snap young spires off at the ground and eat them raw. More elaborate dreams are filled with moist images of steaming spears layered with hollandaise or butter.

It is good, for at least the first two years, to resist all but the occasional taste. The edible sprouts quickly develop into tall stalks, with distinctively delicate

Bill Milliken

A late season spear of asparagus emerges through a thick mulch of rotted manure, which many growers apply annually to satisfy the plant's heavy feeding habits.

branches (the true leaves are actually to be found at ground level and appear as triangular scales). Even the year harvesting begins, it is essential not to carry things too far. Depending on the age of the bed, the soil fertility, the weather and other factors, the cutting season may last from four to 12 weeks. It must draw to a close when the asparagus begins to shoot forth thin, leggy sprouts.

These will develop into the ferns and are best left untouched until well after the killing frosts of the fall have turned them brown. Asparagus thrives in cold climates, using the dormant winter months to rest in preparation for the coming spring. (Tony Horn of the University of Idaho even advocates that gardeners "leave the ferns all winter and remove them in spring just before new growth starts." This eliminates the risk of cutting away the foliage too soon, and may help the plant by trapping snow in a blanket above the crown.)

During the green months, resist the temptation to cut more than a few ferns to enliven summer bouquets.

These beautiful greens are indicative of the 150 or so varieties of asparagus known to botanists. Most of these are frilly affairs with an air of fragile domesticity and are grown as decorative plants.

WEEDS & WATER

Because the plants are perennial and because they grow in rich soil, weeds are apt to be a persistent problem. Many gardeners mulch with grass clippings or fallen leaves to help control weeds. Frequent light cultivation also helps in early spring before any shoots emerge. I have weeded my plants fairly diligently, but wild asparagus patches alongside Mission Creek and nearby roadways are doing nicely among couch grass, thistles, wild roses and barren rocks.

The wild plants, in fact, are sometimes subject to severe overpicking and yet seem to sustain themselves very well. My asparagus seems to grow not because of what I do to it or for it, but rather despite everything I forget. There is independence here. But, as I have said, my soil is the type that it prefers, and Okanagan Lake lies within shouting distance. Its water serves as a moderating influence bringing spring early to the shoreline — my first spears appeared in late March last year. Gardeners who are less favoured will have to be especially careful to weed the bed and water the plants sufficiently. Although the soil must drain well, asparagus is a heavy drinker.

Very few pests or diseases trouble asparagus. Rust has been virtually eliminated by the development of rust-resistant varieties, such as *Viking (Mary Washington Improved)* and *Waltham Washington.* It may, however, infest wild plants that have been introduced to the garden. Asparagus beetles, with either black or yellow spots, feed on plant stems and ferns occasionally, but they can easily be handpicked or dusted with rotenone. (Their black eggs can be seen attached to the stem at one embedded end.) Tansy planted between asparagus rows is said to deter cutworms.

As the plants develop, it will be obvious that some produce seeds and some do not. Asparagus is one of our few dioecious garden species: some plants are female (seed-bearing) and some are male. The seed-carrying berries, according to Isabella Beeton, are "capable of undergoing vinous fermentation and affording alcohol by distillation." That sounds a little more optimistic than does Culpeper's ambivalent description of the use of the seeds for a hot drink. Roasted and ground, he says, the seeds "have sometimes been used as a coffee substitute, but are often said to be poisonous."

My original plants have done so well that I've scouted the roadsides of the Okanagan for wild plants that had gone to seed. The berries were scattered in a number of beds between my herbs and they have germinated in great numbers, a thousand young plants at least. Never in my wildest fantasies had I expected asparagus in such abundance.

There is a great satisfaction in harvesting asparagus, but it must be done with care. Such high-technology items as knives can damage spears that are still below the surface of the soil, but most commercial asparagus growers do cut the stems an inch or so underground. This is somewhat akin to performing a vasectomy blindfolded: You might remove more than you had intended. The trick is to run the edge of the knife gently down along the spear, not cutting it, until the blade is an inch or so below the surface of the soil. Twist the blade carefully to cut only the spear being harvested.

Others choose to cut their asparagus off just at the soil surface, or to simply snap it off with their fingers. Whatever the method, asparagus should be cut when the shoot is four to eight inches tall and before the tip begins to open out into foliage. Spears will have to be cut every three days in cool weather and almost daily when the temperature is up. Be diligent. Left too long, the stems become woody.

French growers hill up rows of soil over the emerging spears, keeping them protected from the sun. This results in the elegant, blanched white asparagus so popular in some circles.

Most North Americans will prefer their asparagus green — a preference that assures more vitamins, less muted taste and much easier culture. Either way, asparagus is laced with vitamins and calcium, but low in calories and carbohydrates — only 20 calories in nine green, four-and-one-half-inch stalks.

But there is more to asparagus than vitamins and minerals. To the modern gardener, whatever a nutritionist or ancient Roman philanderer might add, asparagus is still a psychological curative, a little something for the soul. I can imagine an older world, without green things imported from California, at the end of a hard winter and endless meals of turnips and potatoes, when the first spears of asparagus appeared in the garden. Asparagus is the stuff of which spring tonic — or even spring itself for some of us — is made.

Heirloom Apples

Living antiques waiting to be collected from yesterday's orchards, farmyards and pastures

By Mike Poole

Anyone who was raised in the country must harbour somewhere in his or her memory a long-ago orchard where apples were already crisp and cool and tasted better than they have ever since.

The orchard of my boyhood was not much to look at — a scant acre of tall grass and a few dozen gnarled old trees, battered by the winds of a British Columbia coastal inlet. The orchard opened onto a salt marsh where an amber creek wandered to the sea. September brought coho salmon to the creek to spawn and with them came the cutthroat trout, quick and nickel-bright. We caught them with salmon eggs and cooked them like wieners over driftwood fires. Then, stuffed with singed, half-raw fish, we looked to the orchard for dessert.

I can't recall that any of us ever ate an entire apple there in the orchard; the idea was to sample as many kinds as possible before one's appetite surrendered. We scorned the windfalls and threw sticks to fell the best apples on the highest branches, catching them as they dropped and discovering, as often as not, that the crows had excavated the side we couldn't see. The *Gravensteins* were prized, of course, and the *Kings* were too hard and *Russets* too green, but we always tried them anyway. Most of the varieties were nameless to us; they were just apples, some bland or woody or both, others magnificent.

Twenty years later, an old man on one of British Columbia's Gulf Islands took me through an orchard that had been planted by his father with trees brought from Nova Scotia by sailing ship around Cape Horn. Here again were some fine old varieties and I began to wonder what had become of those long-gone apples of my youth. Why were there so few varieties in the stores? Where were the *Snow,* the *Seek-No-Further, St. Lawrence, Lady* and the dozens of others whose names I'd never known?

The answer, I was to discover, lies in the requirements of the modern commercial fruit industry. The ideal apple today has to roll down conveyor belts without bruising. It must be able to travel halfway around the world without deteriorating. And it must have the vivid colour and flawless skin that sells in the supermarkets. It must have a minimum diameter of 2.24 inches to achieve the desired Canada Extra Fancy or Fancy grades. Uniform in size and brilliant in colour, it may come to resemble a plastic ball glinting in the fluorescence of a fruit display aisle.

But apples are for eating as well as packing, shipping and merchandizing. Does flavour no longer count for anything among those who grow and sell food? Yes, to a certain extent, but other factors take precedence, as anyone who has eaten the physically stunning but insipid *Red Delicious* will know.

FORGOTTEN, BUT NOT GONE

Like it or not, this is the standard and it has cost us dearly. There were once perhaps 5,000 named apple varieties in North America; most stores today carry fewer than half a dozen, predominately *McIntosh, Delicious, Spy, Spartan* and *Cortland* in Canada. *Delicious* alone accounts for more than one-third of all apple sales in the United States. Some of the old varieties sank into an oblivion they richly deserved

State of New York Dept. of Agriculture/Apples of New York (1905)

Wolf River

REGISTERED 1879

because they were fit only for throwing or feeding to hogs. A few others, such as the *Newton Pippin*, which originated in a Huguenot settlement on Long Island, New York around 1730, have survived to become modern commercial varieties.

But what of all the others, the hundreds, perhaps thousands, of good varieties that couldn't meet the narrow requirements of the commercial market? They are still out there somewhere, blooming and bearing every year in derelict orchards and abandoned farmyards, in modern collections of old apples, on government experimental farms and in backyards all over North America.

These are genetic heirlooms and, unlike most valuable antiques, they can usually be had free for the asking and/or cutting and can be collected by anyone with the space in which to grow an apple tree. And, by using a bit of arboricultural sleight of hand, one can easily graft a full-sized old classic onto a modern dwarf apple rootstock to obtain a miniature tree that will bear standard-sized fruit.

Before picturing yourself wandering about with a rough cloth sack of apple pips slung over your shoulder, single-handedly bringing *Sops of Wine* back into the public eye, understand that apples seldom grow true to form from seed. Plant the seeds from a fine old *Baldwin* and you may grow a tree that bears *Baldwins* — but the odds are something like 1,000 to one against it. The tree is much more likely to produce something small, green and nasty.

Now if that seems to contradict all laws of nature and parenthood, remember that most fruit trees are extremely complex hybrids and even an abandoned old dooryard apple is constantly producing exotic hybrid seed each season, taking pollen from the four winds to create seeds of garbled ancestry. Only once in a very long while will such wild seed produce an apple superior to its parents. Thus, as a rule, nursery people no longer grow apples from seedlings; they propagate by grafting or budding, eliminating the guesswork and unpredictable results. At the same time they also eliminate the possibility of that rare and happy accident — a valuable new variety appearing from wild seed.

PIPPINS

At one time nearly all the orchards in North America were "wild" as opposed to grafted. The trees were all seedlings (sometimes called pippins) of unknown parentage, and the apples they produced were as different and varied as pebbles on a beach. They were called "natural," "seedling," or "common" apples and when you bought a barrel of them, you really didn't know what you were getting.

Except for crab apples, there were no native apples in North America. Immigrants brought seed from Europe and the introductions spread across the Continent along traditional Indian trade routes well ahead of white settlement. A U.S. military expedition against the Senecas and Cayugas in 1779 found heavily bearing apple and peach orchards near the Indian villages.

North America became, in effect, a vast natural research station where millions of seedlings were grown each year. Here and there the great varieties appeared — the first *McIntosh* tree at Dundela, Ontario; the *Spy* at East Bloomfield, New York; the *Wealthy* at St. Paul, Minnesota; the *Baldwin* at Lowell, Massachusetts and so on. By 1845 an American nursery catalogue could offer 350 varieties and those, it claimed, were only the best!

There were apples for eating fresh, apples for cooking, apples for baking whole, apples for preserving, apples for cider, apples for apple butter. There were apples that kept well in storage until April or May and others that ripened in August. And for the months between, there were apples to slice in quarters and hang on strings to dry in garlands around the kitchen stove.

A typical 19th-century farm grew three or four summer apples, perhaps half a dozen fall apples and six or eight winter apples, each for its own use. In "Fruits of Ontario," published in 1914, the Ontario Department of Agriculture recommended the following varieties:

Summer
Transparent, Primate,
Sweet Bough, Duchess
Fall
Chenango, Gravenstein, Wealthy,
McIntosh, Snow, Blenheim
Winter
King, Wagener, Swayzie,
Greening, Tolman Sweet, Spy

AMBROSIAL PRAISE

Compare this list with the current recommendations from the Ontario Ministry of Agriculture and Food ("Fruit Varieties," Publication 430), and we find that of the 34 varieties recommended to the modern grower, only four survive from the original list — *Transparent, Wealthy, McIntosh* and *Spy*. But do the new apples really taste better than the ones they replaced?

There are texts and descriptions of apples, old and new, which one can study, but the literature is quite limited and sometimes strays into the subjective. Consider this catalogue description of the modern English apple, *Merton Beauty*: "Ambrosial aroma symphony of floral, fruity and spicy elements. 'Chanel No. 5' of the apple world. Superbly integrated flavour culminates in ethereal suggestions of musky pear, cinnamon, rose and refined petunia."

Less voluptuous but more to the point are the *Poor-Fair-Good-Very Good-Excellent* rating systems used in one form or other by all the old books. The best of these is the two volume *The Apples of New York*, published by the New York State agriculture department in 1905, complete with superb colour photo-engravings. These books are out of print and hard to come by, but for apples introduced since 1920 (all 760 of them) there is a descriptive list in the readily available *Register of New Fruit and Nut Varieties* (see Sources).

No matter how lucid the descriptions, though, or how fine the photographs, books can never tell the reader what he really wants to know — how does an apple taste? For that one really has to go to the orchard and eat the apple fresh from the tree when it is at its best. And while poking around out there in

1. *Scion and rootstocks are split prior to grafting.*

2. *Scion and rootstock diameters should match.*

3. *Properly fitted whip graft ready for wrapping.*

4. *Elastic keeps graft tight and cambium aligned.*

5. *Grafting wax is essential to prevent drying.*

6. *Cleft graft is used to join stock of different size.*

7. *Bud grafting can join several varieties on one tree.*

8. *A properly cut apple bud ready for grafting.*

9. *Bud inserted in T-shaped split in host tree's bark.*

10. *Graft wrapped with elastic and ready for waxing.*

the orchards, one can pick up something else not available in books — local knowledge.

"HOG STRANGLERS"

Local people often can tell what varieties grow best in a particular soil type and climatic zone. Some apples from Ontario and Quebec — *McIntosh, Louise, Snow* and *Scarlet Pippin* — do poorly if moved too far south, while varieties such as *York Imperial* from Pennsylvania or *Grimes Golden* from West Virginia aren't at their best in Canada. Early-blooming summer varieties may not do well in an area of late spring frosts. There are winter-hardy varieties that will survive almost anywhere and many others too tender to withstand extreme cold.

Local people will know what apples to use for what purposes. I once asked an old apple farmer in Virginia why anyone would want to eat a *Ben Davis*, surely one of the worst apples ever grown. "Sonny," he chuckled, "we call *Ben Davis* hog stranglers. Hard as the back of God's head. They's for apple butter, not eatin'."

Local people will also know when best to pick apples and when to eat them. *Idared* for example, develops a much better flavour after a month or two in storage.

And only local knowledge can point out the best strains of any particular variety. Strains? Yes, apple trees are individuals and the fruit from one tree is never exactly like the fruit from another. Usually the differences are too slight to notice, but occasionally they are so conspicuous that the apple is given a name of its own. The Kentville, Nova Scotia, federal government research station has more than 40 strains each of *McIntosh* and *Red Delicious* and nearly 20 of *Gravenstein*.

Having whet one's appetite for one or more of the venerable apple varieties, there are a number of ways of going about growing them.

The easiest is to buy trees from a nursery — but finding a nursery which carries the variety you want may involve a long search with no guarantee of success. Few local nurseries have more than one or two antique varieties, and the nurserymen often cannot tell you very much about them because they've almost invariably been bought from someone else. These nurseries commonly sell "improved" varieties which are to be avoided if one is looking for the classic apple of that name. An *Improved Gravenstein*, for example, looks much more handsome than the old type, but the new taste is disappointing.

GRAFTING BASICS

Anyone serious about collecting old apples, however, should learn the basics of grafting. Grafting is a term that frightens off many people, even those with years of gardening experience, but there is no reason for this trepidation. The odds are overwhelmingly in your favour because the materials you are working with, if properly collected and handled, have a very strong will to survive.

Grafting simply means joining a cutting called a scion (pronounced *sy-on*) from one tree onto another. The object is to propagate the desired variety without having to grow it from seed.

Although a scion gathered from an heirloom apple can be grafted onto a mature tree of another variety, the beginner will find it much simpler to start with a new rootstock. Rootstocks are specially cultivated seedlings bred for disease resistance, winter hardiness and the ability to control the size of the mature tree that develops. The rootstock itself has been selected only for its role in grafting and its own fruits, if allowed to develop, would be inferior and similar to those of a poor crab apple.

An extensive range of rootstocks has been developed, from full dwarf Malling 26 (which produces a tree eight feet high at maturity) to stock that will result in standard trees of 15 feet or more. Generally, the smaller the tree, the earlier it will bear. And while this may count for little with a precocious variety such as *Idared*, which bears in three to six years, it may be important with one like the *Spy*, which takes 10 to 14 years to bear on a standard rootstock. Then again, one may prefer larger trees because they live longer and grow above the reach of livestock and deer.

Whip Grafting

The scions are best taken from the orchard in late winter or early spring, while the trees are still dormant. Now one must prevail upon that neighbour who shared his apple tree knowledge to spare a twig or two from his favourite tree. Government research stations can occasionally be prevailed upon to donate scions to the serious hobbyist. The scions should be about the thickness of a pencil, should have at least three buds each and must be cut from the previous year's growth. Wrap them in a damp sack or bury them in moist sand, sawdust or moss, and store them in a cool (34 to 36 degree F) place until spring, being sure they do not dry out.

To make the graft, cut both rootstock and scion on a smooth diagonal about two inches long, at a point where the two are the same thickness. (See photographs.) Split both scion and rootstock from about three-quarters of an inch below the tip of the cut down to about three-quarters of an inch above the base of the cut. Fit the two pieces together so that the tongue of one fits into the notch of the other, interlocking. Bring the cambium layer (that directly under the bark) of scion and stock into perfect contact on at least one side of the graft and wrap tightly with grafting elastic.

This procedure is called whip grafting and it can also be used to change the variety of an existing tree. Having collected a quantity of scions and kept them dormant in a cool place, one can graft them onto individual branches of another tree in the spring when the buds are beginning to swell or when they are just opening. Select only one-year-old wood to accept the scions and cut the branches off at the point where they are just the right thickness, again about the diameter of a pencil.

It is generally not recommended that the fruit characteristics of a tree be completely changed in one season. When converting a large tree, graft the topmost branches the first year, leaving the lower branches to help feed the scions but not in a position to shade them. These lower branches are then grafted the following spring. If the tree is large, however, it may be advisable to cut it back severely and follow the grafting procedure below.

Cleft Grafting

This method is also used in the spring when the buds on the established tree are swelling. Cut the branches back to the point where they are a maximum of two inches thick. Use a sharp, fine-toothed saw and do not loosen or tear the bark, making sure the end remaining is cut square and clean. Split the branch end (see photographs) just deeply enough to accept two wedge-cut scions, one on either side. (The cut may have to be held open with a knife blade while the scions are inserted.) Be sure to align the outside layer of cambium of each scion with the cambium of the branch, for this is where the actual graft takes place. Bind the graft with splicing tape and paint carefully with grafting wax to prevent drying.

There are probably as many grafting techniques as there are gardeners, certainly too many to go into here. Any comprehensive gardening book will explain them. But no matter what sort of graft you use, you should get at least 90 per cent success if you are scrupulous about three things: Be sure the scions are dormant, align the cambium layers exactly and wax thoroughly. Even a pin hole left unpainted can dry out the graft.

Budding

Many people find budding easier than grafting and you may prefer it. You simply cut a leaf bud from the tree you want to propagate, together with an inch-long piece of bark where the leaf joins the twig. The bud is slipped into a T-shaped slit on the bark of the rootstock or host tree and bound in place with grafting elastic. No grafting wax is needed. The rootstock or branch is cut off above the bud during the following winter, forcing the bud to grow.

The disadvantage of budding is that it has to be done in late summer when the bark will "slip" or

R.R. Sallows/The Ontario Ministry of Agriculture and Food

separate readily from the wood. You can't dig up the rootstocks at this time of year, so budding means stoop labour in the hot sun. (Winter or early spring grafting can be done comfortably at a bench because the rootstocks are dormant and can be moved.)

You may be tempted to graft or bud more than one variety onto a tree, especially if short of space. But this can create problems. The trick is to be sure you are combining varieties of roughly the same vigour. Otherwise, you will be forever pruning back the stronger grower to keep the tree in balance.

When choosing varieties, bear in mind that most apple trees are not self-pollinating. That is, they must have other varieties to pollinate them if they are to bear full crops. Pollination is almost entirely done by bees, not wind, so pollinators for your trees don't have to be immediately next to them. They may be your neighbour's trees, some distance off.

If there is to be pollination, however, the blooming period of different varieties must overlap. Suppose you have only one very early variety, such as *Red Astrachan*, and its bloom is over before any other nearby blossoms are open. Your *Astrachan* won't be pollinated and it won't bear.

Finally, some varieties such as *Spy* and *Transparent* will have a heavy crop one year and a light crop the next. This is because they are naturally biennial bearers, not due to any failure to pollinate. You can even cut the crops somewhat by thinning the budding fruit in the "on" years, but trees that are strongly biennial will remain so no matter what you do. *Baldwin*, once the most widely-grown apple in North America, fell from favour because it was incurably biennial.

By now you may be intimidated by all this talk of whips and clefts and budding and pollination. Don't be. It is all quite straightforward once you begin, and the land is thick with old apple buffs who are delighted to help anyone who shares their enthusiasm. You will find them the same way you find your apples — by just rambling around the country.

Finally, a warning: Tracking down old varieties can be habit forming. I speak as a victim hopelessly abandoned to its seductions. I started out to grow perhaps a half-dozen good eating varieties but today have nearly a hundred different apples growing in my orchard north of Vancouver. Having a large selection of heirloom apples from which to choose gives one a sense of wholesome wealth and, as the old cidermakers knew, the very best apple beverages result from the blending of different varieties. Still, I've tried to quit many times in the past and this year finally thought I had, but then I came across four dandy apples and, well . . . .

Sources

Rootstock:

Demand for rootstocks surpasses the supply in Canada, and they are rather difficult to purchase, especially in small quantities. Try local nurseries for a portion of their supply, although they may use all they can obtain for their own grafting programmes. The minimum order from a major supplier usually starts at 100. This will far exceed the needs of most beginning grafters, and the purchaser may want to split an order with friends and neighbours.

As a final resort, already-grafted trees of common varieties can be purchased from a local nursery. The tops of these trees can then be removed and the desired scion grafted on, or the old variety can be grafted onto part of the tree to create a two-variety tree.

GROEN'S NURSERY
R.R.4
Dundas, Ontario L9H 5E4
Standard and dwarf rootstock.

TRAAS NURSERIES
24355 - 48th Avenue
R.R.7
Langley, B.C. V3A 4R1
Dwarf and semi-dwarf rootstock.

Publications:

REGISTER OF NEW FRUIT
AND NUT VARIETIES
By Brooks & Olmo
University of California Press
2223 Fulton Street
Berkeley, California 94720

THE PRUNING MANUAL
Publication No. 1505
FRUIT TREE PROPAGATION
Publication No. 1289

Both available free of charge from:
Agriculture Canada
Information Division
Ottawa, Ontario K1A 0C7

ROOTSTOCKS FOR FRUIT TREES
Publication No. 334
Available free of charge from:
Ontario Ministry of Agriculture and Food
Information Branch
Legislature Buildings
Queen's Park
Toronto, Ontario M7A 1A5

Supplies:

WILLIAM DAM SEEDS
Highway No. 8
West Flamboro, Ontario L0R 2K0
Wilson's pruning paint.

T&T SEEDS LIMITED
Box 1710
Winnipeg, Manitoba R3C 3P6
Vinyl Ty Ribbon (stretches with plant growth).

Information:

NORTH AMERICAN FRUIT EXPLORERS
Henry Converse, Secretary
1848 Jennings Drive
Madisonville, Kentucky 42431
NAFEX lists many Canadians among its more than 1,000 hobby fruit growing members. Annual membership is $5.00, payable in U.S. funds, which includes a subscription to the quarterly *Pomona*, and access to the exchange of disease-free scions and budwood.

FRED JANSON
Highway 52
Rockton, Ontario L0R 1X0
Probably the finest private collection of old varieties in Canada. Will supply scions, trees or general information. Also runs Pomona Book Exchange and usually has *The Apples of New York* in stock. Extremely cooperative.

LAWSON'S NURSERY
Ball Ground, Georgia 30107
One of the largest collections of antique apple trees in the U.S. Send for free list.

Mission Improbable

Establishing a home vineyard : a primer for the bold and reckless

---

Staff Report

Given the choice, the typical wine connoisseur in Europe would most probably elect to drink from a decanter of Welch's Sweetened Grape Juice rather than defile his palate with a bottle of North American wine. He might have a vague impression of an upstart wine industry in California, but his inclination would be to sniff that the North American continent is a hostile environment for the grape. In short, he would regard a Canadian wine in much the same way a Québecois farmer might greet a tin of maple syrup produced on the Côte d'Azur.

Our wine snob would be blissfully ignorant of the fact that fully 70 per cent of all grape species known to man are native to North America and that fine varietal vines are now growing from British Columbia to New Hampshire, planted by bold and reckless souls who refuse to believe that northern climates must be off-limits to viticulture.

At least part of the popular belief that the better grapes will not grow here is based in fact. While explorers and early settlers found the wild fox grape — *Vitis labrusca* — growing in profusion, climbing huge trees with abandon and with no help from man, it was a grape ill-suited to fine wine making.

Heavy with pectin and laced with an aromatic component since identified as methyl anthranilate, the *labrusca* grape is best suited to making jelly or juice. Its heavy aroma and the flavour it imparts to wine is referred to by oenophiles as "foxy." It is the overpowering flavour one detects in the syrupy pop wines developed in Canada and the northern United States.

Nevertheless, the North American grapes proved intriguing to European vineyardists in the last century, who were impressed by their hardiness and resistance to mildew diseases. Returning to France with cuttings to use for plant breeding experiments and to enter in their botanical museum collections, they unwittingly carried with them a tiny stowaway which would touch off the worst plague in the history of grape culture.

This insect, the grape root louse, or phylloxera, is an aphid which is capable of killing vines, and it did just that in France. Outbreaks of the blight were first observed in 1860, but the phylloxera was not

Ted Streshinsky/The Image Bank of Canada

identified until 1868. Over the course of the next 20 years, nine out of 10 grape vines in France fell to the imported pestilence. Wine producing areas throughout Europe were caught in the spreading devastation, and millions of acres went out of production, never to be revived.

The vineyardists who endured were forced to replant — tearing out vines older than the men who uprooted them — using European varieties grafted onto phylloxera-resistant North American rootstocks or completely new grapes, produced by crossbreeding the European and North American types.

This latter procedure was not unlike crossing a Thoroughbred with a moose, but it proved successful in enough cases to bring new hope to decimated vineyards. One hundred years later, these hybrid vines are earning the fresh appreciation of North Americans who are intent on growing fine grapes where they have never grown before.

In contrast to the musky aroma of a Concord — generally regarded as the epitome of the *labrusca* grape — a classic wine grape is delicate, with subtle nuances of aroma and flavour. Before the great phylloxera outbreak, the fine wines were virtually all made from *Vitis vinifera,* the species that dominates the grape growing world outside North America.

Until very recently, it was widely believed that *vinifera* grapes could not be made to survive in most parts of this continent, and agricultural representatives will usually tell inquirers that attempts to grow these finicky vines are doomed to a frostbitten or mildewed failure.

Such was the conventional wisdom passed along to Casabello Wines in British Columbia 10 years ago. Ignoring the best advice of Agriculture Canada, the company planted *vinifera* grapes in the Okanagan Valley and were vindicated when the vines came through the first bad winter unscathed, while some neighbouring plantings of recommended varieties did not survive.

A willingness to attempt the impossible is almost essential for anyone who would grow wine grapes in Canada or the northern United States. The second prerequisite is facing the fact that these tender plants can never be left to cope on their own; they must be nurtured, protected and given great amounts of hand labour. Once established, their foothold in a foreign climate never becomes better than precarious.

Even after taking all the necessary precautions, the grower must remain philosophical and be prepared to accept a crop failure from time to time when a late spring frost creeps into the vineyard. (Early fall frosts are less threatening, as the wine making qualities of grapes are not ruined by a brush with freezing temperatures. Wine lovers, in fact, speak in hushed tones of the rare *Trockenbeeren-auslese,* a German white wine made with grapes that have been touched by frost.)

The home vineyardist is aided by the fact that he

side is a likely location, but some growers have abandoned the fields altogether to create an arbour on the sun-basked south side of their houses. (Such a structure, roofed in lush green grape leaves, can be highly attractive to humans on hot summer days, and in some cultures the grape arbour is used as a warm season living room.)

Frost protection is vital, as temperatures of 26 degrees F for several hours will kill all shoots, buds and open flower clusters. If the weather preceding a frost has been cool and cloudy, the vines can endure temperatures of 30 degrees for a short duration, but a sudden drop below 31 degrees in the spring will destroy succulent shoots and forming blossoms.

It is generally conceded that *vinifera* grapes grow

can lavish intensive care on his vines when the need arises. A drape of muslin or burlap can ward off an unseasonal frost, special winter mulches and coverings can prevent winter-kill, and labour-intensive pruning can help the vines take advantage of a short growing season. None of these tactics is available to large-scale commercial growers, which helps explain why more than half of all wine consumed in Canada is imported. Most of the rest is from the cold-resistant *labrusca* varieties — Concord, Catawba, Niagara and Agawam.

The secret to growing grapes in a northern climate lies in taking advantage of, or creating, a micro-climate — a place with maximum exposure to the sun and sheltered from cold winds. A south-facing hill-

best in the latitude belt from 49 degrees South to 34 degrees North, but some of the finest Rhine wines in Germany come from districts of 50 to 51 degrees North. (Consider that Winnipeg, Halifax, Vancouver, Ottawa and St. John's, Newfoundland all fall south of 51 degrees.) In the Rhine and Moselle Valleys, the vineyards resemble mountain goat country, being planted on precipitous hillsides facing south and west.

Frost always drains down and away from slopes, concentrating in lowlands, valleys and hollows — all of which should be avoided in selecting the site for a new vineyard.

In winter, ground level temperatures vary as much as 18 degrees F between the bottom of a hill and its summit, and that can be the margin of difference for a grape grower. Heavy frosts can kill the vines by freezing the fluids they contain, forming expanded ice crystals and doing irreparable damage.

Grapes love the sun. Even what seems a relatively short period of shade in the morning or evening will delay ripening, reduce vigour and result in lower yields. Vines should not be planted near large trees, which not only act as solar barriers but provide roosts for grape-loving birds.

Northern grape growers hope for a frost-free period lasting from mid-May when the buds pop out to early September, when the berries are ripe. The vines remain dormant until temperatures reach 45 to 50 degrees F and experience what is known as their "grand period of growth" in the early summer, with shoots pushing forward at a rate of an inch or more per day and blossoms forming when the mean daily temperature is near 68 degrees F.

Most Northerners will not have the luxury of choosing a site by its soil, and there is some comfort in knowing that grapes are much less demanding of soil than most garden vegetables. Boundless fertility is not necessary, and can be a detriment if high levels of nitrogen encourage vines to continue their heavy growth into the fall rather than slowing down and hardening off for winter.

Good drainage, however, is important, and heavy clay soils are to be avoided or broken up with sand or even gravel. (Gravelly soils are generally regarded as fine for grape culture. Moreover, the fine vineyards in Germany's cool white wine producing areas credit their flinty, shale-ridden soil with helping prevent erosion and with trapping the warmth of the sun.)

Poor water drainage is undesirable for two reasons. In terms of the quality of grapes harvested, excess water in the soil leads to excess water in the vines and, ultimately, in the berries. Of a more serious nature is the possibility of inviting an attack of mildew if water does not drain away from the root system quickly. In prime *vinifera* country in Europe, growers are pleased if there is no rain between the setting of the blooms and the harvest.

Depth of soil is a further consideration, and very shallow areas will work against the formation of healthy root systems. In reasonably loose, deep soil, grape roots will extend down six to 12 feet; in one instance, the roots of a single vine were followed down 40 feet. The bulk of the root system, however, is usually found between two and five feet below the surface of the soil.

In establishing a vineyard or small grape arbour, it may be advisable to mix well-rotted manure or compost, bone meal and lime into the soil to give the young vines a boost during their all-important first three formative years. After that, feeding is usually restricted with the *vinifera* and French hybrids, to encourage the formation of fruit rather than foliage. (For the American type grapes — Concord, Catawba, Elvira, Niagara — richer soils are required, as is generally the case for table grapes and those destined to become raisins.)

A final consideration in choosing a site involves the neighbours: grapes wither in the presence of most herbicides. Neighbours who use these chemicals should be aware of the presence of your new vineyard, and every effort should be made to keep the grapes well away from road crews who commonly defoliate roadside ditches and power line rights-of-way with 2,4-D, which is fast death to grape foliage.

PLOTTING

Rash is the best description of anyone who would plant an acre of grape vines before having learned the art firsthand and on a much smaller scale. Those who have visions of turning the hilly back forty into an expanse of *Gamay Beaujolais* should stop first and consider the work — and risk — involved.

In 1965, Professor A.J. Winkler of the University of California noted that a single family in the middle Moselle region of Germany could earn their livelihood with no more than 2 or 2.5 acres of grapes. In contrast, the average one-family vineyard in California had to cover 50 to 80 acres to provide a living. In the former case, almost all work was done by hand and it kept people busy. In California, much of the vineyard work is done with equipment, and, consequently, with a high financial overhead.

Under northern conditions, well-tended vines may yield from eight to 20 pounds of grapes each or — more to the point — one half to one and a half gallons of wine per plant. An acre should produce three to five tons of grapes, but this is dependent on a plethora of variables, including spacing within the vineyard.

Large commercial vineyards in Canada and the United States seldom leave less than eight feet between rows, and some are as much as 12 or 14 feet apart to facilitate the movement of heavy equipment through the field. This spacing between rows, however, can be manipulated, especially by the home grower, who will not be wheeling through his vineyard with a giant mechanical grape harvester.

Vines are normally planted eight feet apart within the row. It is known that the major competition for sun and growing space occurs within the row, so most authorities do not advocate crowding vines together. In a typical commercial planting, with eight feet between rows and nine feet between vines, there would be 565 plants per acre. In the Champagne region of France, the vine concentration can reach 3,000 per acre.

The following list shows the number of vines required to plant one acre of grapes at the indicated spacings (first dimension indicates distance between vines within the row):

SPACING	NUMBER OF VINES
8 x 14	= 350
8 x 12	= 410
9 x 8	= 565
8 x 8	= 645
8 x 6	= 850
6 x 4	= 1,820

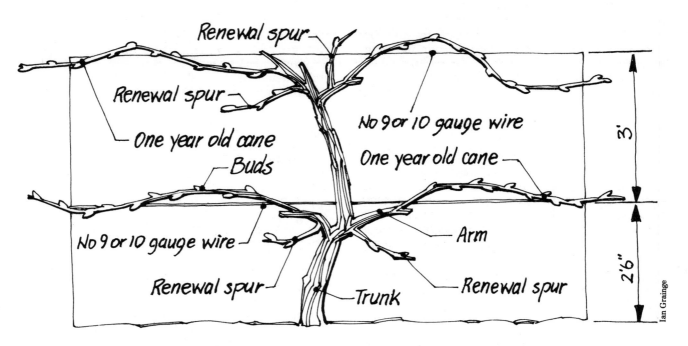

Renewal spur

Renewal spur

One year old cane

Buds

No 9 or 10 gauge wire

Renewal spur

No 9 or 10 gauge wire

One year old cane

Arm

Renewal spur

Trunk

3'

2'6"

Ian Grainge

The tighter spacings should be attractive to anyone wishing to make the best use of a small growing area; not only will yields be higher, but vines will be easier to cover in cold weather and the greater density of foliage will work to retain heat and encourage earlier ripening.

If planted on a slope, the rows should run across the hill to impede erosion. The Ontario Ministry of Agriculture recommends running the rows in a north-south orientation, "to get the maximum amount of sunlight on the vines." Other sources suggest an east-west orientation, which would be more in keeping with the solar dictum of facing due south in a northerly climate.

FORMATIVE YEARS

Three to four years will elapse between planting and the first useable harvest, but they are the most important in the life of a vineyard. The individual vines must be trained to form their main trunk or trunks and must be encouraged to develop a vigorous root system. In commercial grape production, 80 or 90 per cent of the plant's above-ground material is pruned away at the end of the growing season, and it is the strength of the roots that pushes forth the tremendous amount of new wood and leaves each spring and summer.

Although it is possible to start a vineyard with unrooted cuttings taken from another vineyard, the survival rate of such cuttings may be as low as 60 per cent and no higher than 85, resulting in a spotty stand of vines.

Newcomers to viticulture should seek out the very best one-year-old rooted cuttings or grafts they can find. Poorly grown, weak or dried out stock from mass market sources should be avoided, despite the price. The material should be certified free of viruses, and be able to meet stringent government standards, which means you should go to a grower who is set up to supply both small growers and the larger commercial vineyards. If you are planting grapes in soil where they've never grown before, the very last

thing you want to do is introduce a grape pest or disease.

A good nursery will keep their rootstocks stored at 95 per cent humidity and 34 degrees F temperature to prevent pre-season respiration which could cost a young plant the store of carbohydrates it sorely needs for its first season of growth. Because approximately half the price one pays for rootstocks goes toward proper packaging and shipping, they should arrive at the buyer's door in good shape. They should be stored briefly in a refrigerator or, preferably, planted immediately.

It is standard practice to sow a green manure crop prior to the planting of grape vines, both to add organic matter to the soil and to eliminate weeds. Manure and compost can be tilled in, and generous amounts will work to the advantage of the young vines. Deep cultivation prior to planting is important, and can be accomplished by ploughing, the use of a rear-end tiller or a hand spade. At least 10 inches of soil, and preferably 12 inches or more, should be worked into a loose condition. With a rototiller, this will require repeated trips over the same ground, but even so, most smaller models will not accomplish the task properly.

Commercial vineyards are often laid out with surveyor's tools — a crooked row being an embarrassment to a good farmer, and, with grapes, that crooked row will provide a lifetime of chagrin. Some growers erect their permanent supports or trellis systems before planting, while others mark each planting spot with a peg or stake. For the first year, a two-by-two cedar stake three feet high (with an additional foot and a half underground) will provide the needed support.

A furrow 10 or 12 inches deep or individual planting holes of the same depth should be made for each row. The rooted canes should measure 12 to 14 inches each, and only two inches should protrude once the furrows or holes are filled with topsoil. If more than two buds are exposed above ground on a cane, it should be pruned *after* planting. (If, on the other hand, a vine arrives with multiple canes, all but the best should be pruned off *before* planting.)

During the first summer, the vine should grow vigorously, and weeds must be kept in check to prevent any competition for available nutrients. This can be accomplished by hoeing, tilling between rows, or the use of a plastic mulch. Although heavy organic mulches will prove valuable in an established vineyard, their use in the first three years is not advocated, as they tend to keep the soil cool and encourage the roots to stay near the surface rather than to grow downward seeking water. Clear plastic mulch has an advantage over black in that it warms the soil more deeply.

The two buds should grow into healthy canes during the first season, but the vine must be pruned back to its original stub in the spring. This may seem drastic and counter-productive, but remember that, below ground, a full root system is developing. Young vines should not be pruned in the fall; older hardier ones can be pruned after all growth has stopped and they are dormant — never before the first hard frost.

Two buds should remain on the stub of the trunk, and each vine should be covered with a mound of soil or straw to prevent winter-kill.

The second season of growth will force the grower to decide how he wishes to train his vines, a dilemma for those who have no experience or grape-growing neighbours to rely on for advice. Reading the training and pruning sections of serious viticulture books can be a threatening experience. This is an art and science that dates to the beginning of the Christian era, and both Virgil and Pliny wrote of their modes of influencing the growth and fruiting habits of vines.

Their methods are still followed, but numerous other systems have been developed and the choice is difficult for newcomers. Two systems, however, are especially applicable for northern vineyards and will be discussed here. (Alternatives will be found in standard viticulture texts.)

The simpler of the two, sometimes referred to as the Russian system, is designed for vineyards in areas of extreme winter cold. To prevent the killing of aboveground trunk and canes, the vine is taken down from its trellis each fall and buried in four or five inches of soil or a heavy bed of straw or other protective material. Covered in this manner, the grapes can survive winter temperatures as low as 40 degrees below zero F.

With the arrival of spring, the vines are dug up and restored to their trellis positions before the buds get impatient and begin to develop under the soil. (If allowed to bloom underground, the buds may die from the shock of entering strong sunlight.)

In this system, the vine is not allowed to develop a strong, upright trunk. Rather, one or two trunks which arch out along the ground and then up to the trellis wires are encouraged. Such a trunk can easily be taken down in the fall and buried with little chance of cracking or breaking. Such an arch is formed by tying the second year cane to a stake placed some distance from the point where the trunk enters the soil. With vines that show an exceptionally strong desire to grow straight up — such as Seyval — U-shaped pieces of wire can be positioned over the cane and into the soil at intervals of several inches. (Imagine stapling an indoor vine to a window sill to train it.) The upper portion of the arched cane is tied to the trellis wire with strong wire.

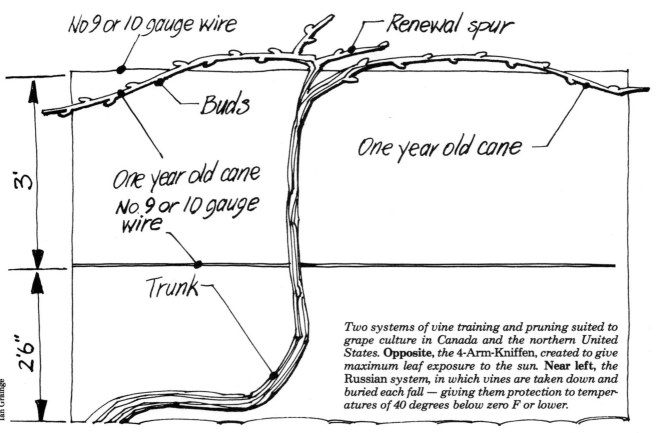

Ian Grainge

Two systems of vine training and pruning suited to grape culture in Canada and the northern United States. **Opposite,** *the* 4-Arm-Kniffen, *created to give maximum leaf exposure to the sun.* **Near left,** *the* Russian *system, in which vines are taken down and buried each fall — giving them protection to temperatures of 40 degrees below zero F or lower.*

If the trellis system was not put up in the first year, it must be constructed in the second season. The traditional trellis for either of the two systems described here consists of three-inch-diameter posts of cedar, tamarack or white oak spaced at 20-foot intervals. Heavy-duty end posts will serve to stabilize the network of wire and must be reinforced with a thrust brace or a guy wire.

The in-line posts should be driven two and a half to three feet into the ground and should stand five and a half to six feet high. (Treat the bottom end with creosote or other wood preservative.) Grapes in warmer climates are not always grown on such high trellis structures, but in short growing season areas the vines and leaves must be kept high off the ground and allowed to spread out to catch the sun. The Minnesota Grape Growers' Association, which recommends the winter-burial system, points out that, "On calm, clear nights during the spring, the temperature at ground level can be 10 to 15 degrees colder than at the six-foot level."

Commercial vineyards normally use cedar posts at the ends of rows, with steel fence posts in between. An occasional cedar post along the line can be added to give extra support to the metal posts, which have a tendency to bend when the vines are laden and strong winds are blowing.

Two lines of Number 9 galvanized wire are strung along the posts and stapled into the windward side so that strong gusts don't use the vine growth as a sail and pop the staples. To allow for occasional tightening of the wire, the staples are not driven in too deeply, and the end post is usually drilled to allow the wire to pass through and be tied off. The wire must be loosened each winter or it will contract with the cold and wreak havoc with the post system.

The bottom wire should be two and a half feet off the ground and the second wire three feet above that. (Some growers choose to use three wires instead, substituting lighter, cheaper Number 11 wire for the two bottom strands.)

KNIFFEN SYSTEM

Where the climate or the variety of grape allows, the ritual of burying vines can be dispensed with — although not without risk of some winter-kill or damage.

The classic system for northern growers is known as the 4-Arm Kniffen, designed to spread the foliage and thus take maximum advantage of the sun (the yield of grapes is in direct proportion to the amount of foliage that develops).

To train a vine for this approach, the strongest cane is selected during the second growing season and tied straight up to the top wire (once it reaches past the top wire it should be pruned off). By the end of the season, the four best canes nearest the two cross wires are chosen and tied down as "arms."

This is fruiting wood, from which will spring the grape clusters in the next season. In addition, one replacement cane is chosen for each arm, preferably the closest to the base of the arm. These canes are pruned back to leave two or three buds (compressed bumps which contain the dormant, undeveloped shoots). Also known as spurs, these stubs will be relied upon to furnish a replacement arm at the end

of the next season (in the 4-Arm Kniffen system the arms are constantly replaced).

All additional canes from the second year's growth are now removed, pruning them off close to the trunk. During the first two years, it is also important to remove any "suckers" or surface roots that appear at the base of the trunk. If caught in this early stage, further suckering should not be necessary later in the life of the vineyard.

In addition, the four arms must be reduced to prevent the formation of too many clusters of grapes. The grape has the entrenched desire to produce more fruit than is good for its own system. If too many clusters develop, none will be prime and so much effort will be put into ripening them that the vine will leave itself in a weakened state for the next winter.

Pruning is best learned at the elbow of an expert, and it requires experience to know just how much fruiting wood to leave each year. A rough guideline is to leave about 10 healthy buds on each of the four

arms. (Count out from the trunk and, after 10 buds, cut off the cane on the diagonal.)

The following year, the pruner must cut not only the old arms, but any unnecessary new growth, creating a new arm and being sure to leave a renewal spur near the trunk with two or three buds. The scientific approach to annual pruning after the second season is to leave a basic 20 buds per vine, *plus* 10 additional buds for each pound of year-old wood you removed. (Hence, the more vigorous and heavy the vine, the more buds that can be left and the greater the potential harvest next year.)

SAFETY VALVE

Although most pruning is done between the time the grape leaves fall and the next February, spring pruning is advocated for those in especially cold climates. Northern grape growers prefer to wait until the last expected frost before pruning their vines. However, it is important not to wait too long — pruning in May, when the buds have started their season's growth, will retard the vine's development by as much as two weeks.

Various garden writers have made the blanket statement that beginners are always afraid to prune as severely as is necessary. This is a mixed truth, for research has shown that unpruned grapes actually have the capacity of doubling the production of vines pruned correctly by conventional systems. *Vinifera* vines have been known to spread out to cover one half acre of ground and one Mission variety vine in California, trained onto an arbour and with a trunk circumference of nine feet, produced 16,000 pounds of grapes in the year 1893.

Commercial vineyards are unable to take advantage of minimum pruning systems, because it becomes difficult for pickers and field workers to deal with the vines. The key to minimum pruning lies in the removal of extra blossoms or immature berry clusters. This is known as cluster thinning and it is another art that must be learned with experience. (Thin too lightly and you end up with small clusters, small berries and low quality fruit. Thin too severely and you end up with healthy vines but fewer grapes than you deserve.) Too, heavy-duty permanent arbours or trellises must be constructed to carry the weight of vines and fruit that will develop.

Minimum pruning and cluster thinning mean that growth is directed to fruit and leaves at the trunk's expense. This results in a larger grape crop but a vine that is more vulnerable to winter-kill. Some gamblers may opt for minimum thinning but must depend on luck and extra winter insulation.

Winter-kill is not to be taken lightly, as a number of intrepid grape growers in Minnesota discovered in the winter of 1976-77. It was believed that cold would not harm the grape trunks, and the growers had adopted the practice of burying only the canes and buds, leaving the trunks arched and exposed above the snow. With several spells of minus 40 degree F weather, nearly 100 per cent of the exposed trunks were found dead the following spring.

ENEMIES LIST

Commercial grape growers often spray their crops up to 14 times per season, in a constant battle to control powdery mildew, downy mildew, grape mealy bug, grape berry moth and a host of other insects and diseases. The mildews, which can be lethal to the vines, are best fought by planting in an area that is not overly damp and that has good air circulation.

Where phylloxera is a problem, plant only those varieties that have been grafted onto resistant rootstocks. Various government booklets and other sources describe the common grape maladies, along with their chemical cures. Where insects are in-

Sources

Most nurseries offer table and juice grapes, mostly of the *labrusca* type, and these will prove satisfactory to many gardeners. Although more hardy and disease-resistant than their European cousins, these vines are not impervious to severe winter cold. Concord, the leading American variety, can be damaged at temperatures of minus 20 degrees F, and thus must receive protection in many areas. In general, the standard North American varieties require the same cultural care as the French hybrids and *viniferas* discussed, but are more charitable toward viticultural rookies.

The French hybrids, crosses between North American and European varieties, with taste and aroma approaching the subdued character of the pure *viniferas*, have been successfully grown on a small scale in many parts of this continent. Those recommended for their general hardiness and adaptability are:

Seyval (Healthy, adaptable to cold areas, makes a noteworthy white wine.)

Aurora (Excellent for eating, juice and white wine.)

Marechal Foch (Good disease resistance and the base for a fine dry, red wine.)

DeChaunac (Must be cluster-thinned, but robust and the precursor to a good red wine — from blue berries.)

Baco Noir (The choice for poorly drained, heavy soils but vulnerable to spring frosts. Makes a red wine.)

Those willing to attempt what has long been said to be impossible will find the following pure *vinifera* varieties to provide better odds than most:

Gamay Beaujolais (Native of France's famed Beaujolais region, this is a vigorous grape that can produce a superb red wine.)

Pinot Noir (This is the grape that makes the great burgundy wines of France. Not as productive as *Gamay Beaujolais*.)

Pinot Chardonnay (Classic white grape from which the white burgundies are made. Lush foliage, moderate production.)

Gewurztraminer (Adapted to cooler growing regions, this is an aromatic German white.)

White Riesling (The venerable white grape of the Rhine and Moselle valleys, with a distinctive varietal taste and bouquet.)

Small-Grower Suppliers:

ZIRALDO FARMS & NURSERIES
R.R.1,
Niagara-on-the-Lake, Ontario
Twenty-nine varieties (three *vinifera*, 17 French hybrids, nine *Labrusca*). Minimum order of 25 vines. Discounts for orders of over 100 and 1,000. Prices are F.O.B. — shipping and packaging extra.

McCONNELL NURSERIES
Port Burwell, Ontario N0J 1T0
Seven varieties available.

BOUNTIFUL RIDGE NURSERIES INC.
Princess Anne, Maryland 21853
Serving Canada and the U.S., Bountiful Ridge carries about 45 grape varieties.

TURKOVICS VINEYARD AND
GRAPE NURSERY
Glencoe Road
Westbank, British Columbia

JOHN PETRETTA GRAPE NURSERY
1340 Dilworth Crescent
Kelowna, British Columbia

BYLAND NURSERY
Box 222
West Bank, British Columbia
Located just outside Kelowna, Byland offers table grapes (seedless Himrod, Campbell) and three French hybrids (Foch, Riesling, Patricia).

volved, organic growers may be able to get by with rotenone and pyrethrum but otherwise must work to keep their vines vigorous and able to fend off disease. On the positive side, those who grow grapes far outside the commercial growing areas often report a minimum of disease and insect problems.

Birds are another matter, and they are especially fond of the thin-skinned French hybrids and *viniferas*. Grape clusters will ripen fully and colour properly even in the absence of light (unlike most fruit), and thus can be covered with bags on the vine to keep away the winged raiders. Special bird netting is also available and may prove a salvation to smaller vineyards.

Rabbits can be a problem, cleaning off young vines. They should be shot, kept back by the family hound or live-trapped and trucked far, far away. Mice can girdle vines that are mulched for the winter, and commercial growers sometimes place poison in the vineyards each fall.

Weeds, not unexpectedly, must be kept from overgrowing the vineyard. The space between the rows can be ploughed or tilled, and it is advisable to plant a green manure crop each year in this space. A grape hoe works well around the base of the trunks if mulch has not been used. Bindweed is one enemy which cannot be allowed to gain an upper hand. It will grow all over the vine, sapping nutrients from the soil and slowly choking the plant.

Having read this far, you should by now be aware of the fact that viticulture is not like growing radishes. After waiting through three growing seasons, fighting off endless numbers of birds, insects and mice, and nursing your vines through insidious attacks of mildew, you may find yourself with a harvest in which a person can, with justification, take great pride. On the other hand, you may end up with nothing but a profound respect for those growers in Canada and the northern United States who manage to make their living by the grape.

Grain Gardening

Bringing in the sheaves — no combine needed

By Jennifer Bennett

Never one to mince words, American expatriate novelist Henry Miller once remarked, "You can travel 50 thousand miles in America without once tasting a good piece of bread."

One might just as easily travel around the North American breadbasket without ever hearing the words *stock, sheaf, flail, winnow* or *reap* — at least not used in their original agricultural, Anglo-Saxon context. Grain, today, is something that comes from huge combines, million-dollar agribusinesses and farms that disappear over the horizon. But, of course, it was not always this way and still needn't be. Anyone with a spare quarter-acre of land (a plot measuring roughly 100 feet by 100 feet) is no more obligated to buy flour in white paper bags than to purchase peas in cans or fried chicken in waxed buckets.

Rye, buckwheat, oats, barley and wheat are not normally considered to be garden crops — a shame, because they can be cultivated with ease and their harvest must rank as one of the most satisfying of small-farming experiences.

FALL PLANTING

When North Americans think of grain, wheat comes immediately to mind. It is our most popular cereal and is possible, even easy, to grow on a small scale. Winter wheat can be planted in the fall in areas with mild winters where temperatures average higher than minus 7 degrees Celsius, but this rules out much of Canada and the northern United

States. Rye, however, is far hardier, and can be fall planted in almost all farming areas of Canada.

Rye is, in fact, the perfect beginner's grain, a fine choice for getting those hesitant, stubble-jumping feet wet. Like wheat, it is naked seeded and thus easy to prepare for grinding into flour. Oats, barley and buckwheat all have hulls and require an additional cleaning step to make them fit for bread making.

Planted this fall, a plot of rye will sprout and then remain dormant under the snow until early next spring, when it will resume growing and, happily, choke out most annual weeds that attempt to invade its territory. Rye is tall, easy to harvest and will make a delicious dark flour, a unique porridge, or can be sprouted as a fresh vegetable or fed to poultry and small livestock.

All home-grown grains demand a well-prepared bed for planting and it is best to use an area that has been cultivated and well-weeded for several years. Do not minimize, in your mind, the potential weed problem that will come of planting in a poorly prepared spot. Perennial weeds can cause serious troubles, as a broadcast-seeded area is impossible to weed without damaging the young grain crop. If you intend to plant grain next spring, now is not too soon to begin preparing the ground, assuring that it is well-tilled, weed-free and ready to be planted early in the growing season next year. Ideally, grains are rotated with legume crops (such as soybeans, peas or alfalfa, all of which fix nitrogen in the soil). Ploughing under one of these crops as a green manure will vastly improve a grain plot, furnishing the soil with nutrients and a good supply of humus. Well-rotted manure, compost and wood ashes can also be worked into the earth of a mini-grain field.

Some gardeners like to plant grain in rows, the method used in mainland China that makes cultivation and weed control easy. The moister the ground, the shallower it should be seeded, from two inches in dry, sandy soil, to one-half inch in heavy soil. Impossible to weed but an easier and more enjoyable way to plant is broadcasting the seed. Walk up and down the plot, scattering seed, and at the end, walk up and down in a direction at right angles to the first, scattering again. This is a wonderfully rhythmic, soothing process, sure to bring to mind thoughts of a ritual as old as the Bible:

"... Some fell by the way side and the fowls of the air came and devoured it up. And some fell on stony ground, where it had not much earth .... And other fell on good ground, and did yield fruit that sprang up and increased; and brought forth, some thirty, and some sixty, and some an hundred."

Mark 4: 4 — 8

Small broadcast seeders, unchanged in design for a century, are still available (see Sources). Once the grain is cast, rake the earth over it and roll the plot, if possible, to firm the earth evenly.

AGRICULTURAL ROULETTE

Rare is the seed catalogue that lists grains, and your seed grain is probably best sought out from local farmers or the *Farm Supplies* or *Feed Dealers* sections of your yellow pages. Prices vary from year to year, but expect to pay between five and 10 dollars for a bushel of seed. Some grain dealers will not sell less than a bushel — far more than most home grain patches require. If you try to avoid buying seed that has been treated with fungicides, the surplus can then be used for feeding livestock, milling or sprouting. Otherwise, excess seed can be shared with neighbours or stored for next year.

Do not buy wheat *grass* or rye *grass* — these crops are not grown for grain production. There are scores of grain varieties available, but most local seed dealers offer only one type of each cereal grain. If there is a choice, ask for the hardiest and, for hand-cutting, the tallest. When it comes time to swing the scythe, every extra inch of stalk will make the job easier.

Kodiak is one popular variety of rye, tall, very winter-hardy and resistant to snow mould — an excellent choice for the small plot. How much to plant depends on the space you have available and your ability to use up the grain produced. A full acre of winter rye will give an average yield of 25 bushels of grain, with each bushel weighing 50 to 60 pounds which, of course, will give you 50 to 60 pounds of whole grain flour. Rob Johnson, Jr., founder of Johnny's Selected Seeds, says that one-quarter acre is sufficient to supply all the grain needs of his young family.

Rye is sown at a rate of two bushels per acre, so it can easily be seen that a small plot, measuring 30 by 60 feet, is not going to need much seed — about five pounds — and should yield about a bushel of rye, more if you have fertilized well.

Actually, rye will grow in almost any soil, but, like other cereals, will do best in deep, rich earth. It requires less moisture than wheat and much less than oats. Winter rye should be planted at about the time of the first frost in fall and should be four to six inches (10 to 15 cm) tall when fall freeze-up shuts down its growth.

An error of two weeks or more in seeding time, especially with fall grains, can make a great difference in the eventual yield. As the weather becomes colder, some carbohydrates inside the plant change to sugar, which mixes with the sap in individual cells and lowers the freezing point, so the grain seedling hardens itself off. If the plants harden properly, they will stay dormant through the winter. One of the greatest hazards of fall seeding is an unseasonably early cold spell. Last year, a blizzard in early November killed half of the winter wheat in some areas of South Dakota.

The second major reason for winterkill is an unseasonably warm spell in very early spring. The plants come out of dormancy, begin to grow and are then vulnerable to freezing. Ice storms, too, can kill the seedlings. Nevertheless, winter rye can survive dips to minus 40 degrees Celsius.

No, grain growing is not without hazard, and there comes a certain point at which one must just sit back and be philosophical. You have graduated from the ranks of those who find radish growing a challenge. Grain does not require the constant tending that most vegetables demand, but it is vulnerable to the weather. Consider yourself part of a yearly agricultural roulette that has gone on for millennia.

In spring, all having gone well, the crop will come up quickly and should outstrip the growth of annual weeds. The rye should be ready to harvest in July or August, when the straw may be as tall as two metres (six feet) and the heads full and inviting. Check for readiness by trying to dent a kernel with a thumbnail . . . if it is very soft, the rye is not yet ripe. If it is possible just to dent the grain without excessive pressure, the rye is ready. If it is too hard to dent, the grain is already fully ripe and some will be lost in harvesting. (Very ripe grain loosens easily from the heads and much can be lost in hand gathering; grain to be harvested without a combine is ready for cutting a week sooner, so don't go by what the mechanized neighbours might be doing.)

CUTTING & FLAILING

The harvest requires, at minimum, a long, sharp knife or sickle. Cut as close to the ground as possible. Assuming you are right handed, hold the cutting blade in your right hand and grasp the straw to be cut with your left. Pull the sickle through the straw at an angle from left to right (inside to outside) and then lay down the resulting sheaf of straw and grain which is in your left hand. (Reverse the whole procedure if that is more comfortable.)

For larger patches of grain, a scythe with a grain cradle is highly desirable (but not easily come by these days). This is a very useful tool that allows the grain to be cut in nice neat piles.

It is convenient to have one person cutting, another tying the straw into sheaves. To do this, take a six-to-10-inch bundle of straw and tie it together

Buckwheat, distinguished from the other grains by its white or pink flowers, grows densely and can serve as a smother crop.

in the middle. (The old hands tie with straw, but baling twine is simpler for the novice.) Lean two sheaves together — heads up — and then lean another two against these; you should have a four-sided tepee. Fan out the bottoms so they will stand sturdily.

Now lean another eight or so sheaves around the first four and you have what is known as a shock. Grain will cure like this in the field in about 10 days, but it may be moved indoors if the last few days of the drying time are inclement.

Flailing is the next step. The traditional Spanish method was to spread the sheaves on a clean floor and have animals walk on it, knocking the grain out. The principle remains the same — though you will probably wish to replace goat power with gardener power.

The grain needs to be beaten loose from the straw and very energetic flailers might like to try battering the sheaves against the back of a chair. The grain tends to fly all over, and a sheet must be spread on the ground to catch it. Or spread the straw out on the sheet and then beat it with a broom or an easily made traditional flail. (Drill a hole in the end of two wooden sticks and connect them, series-fashion, with a leather thong.) When most of the kernels have been flailed loose, remove the straw, bring in fresh sheaves and begin again.

This completed, the grain must be winnowed. This

simply removes the grain from the chaff and it can best be accomplished on a windy day. The grain is poured out of one container from a sufficient height to allow the wind to whisk the chaff away as the grain falls into a second container. Repeat until the grain is as clean as possible. Some bits of chaff are destined to remain in the grain. Ignore them.

The leftover straw can be used as mulch in the garden, as bedding for livestock or litter for poultry, after which it can be composted and turned back to the soil.

Now the grain should be cured at least a month before grinding into flour. Green grain will gum up a flour mill and does not make the best bread. If the weather was wet while the straw was curing in the field (not unusual, unfortunately, in some areas), the grain should be dried further at this stage, by allowing air to circulate in it as much as possible. It can be poured into burlap sacks and the sacks inverted every couple of days on a slatted floor or it can be placed in a wire mesh box, screened on all sides. If the initial curing weather was dry, the grain can be left in any sort of container for the requisite month of curing.

The grain is now but a few hours away from being a hot loaf of home-grown bread.

This basic process of growing and harvesting winter rye can be followed for all of the following grains.

WHEAT

There are several types of wheat grown in Canada — *bread* wheats, usually spring sown and fall harvested, *utility* wheats, principally for livestock, *hard red winter*, which are the most commercially important in the United States, *soft white winter*, and *amber durham*, the hardest and most glutenous for pasta and semolina. All Canadian wheat is graded in comparison with *Marquis*, the landmark variety released in 1911. "Canada Western Red Spring" wheats are those equal to or better than *Marquis* in milling and baking quality. "Utility" grades are considered inferior to *Marquis* in one or more characteristics.

Soft wheats are generally hardier than hard wheats, but are not as glutenous, which means that bread made from soft wheat will be a bit denser and heavier than that from hard wheat (which allows easier incorporation of air into the dough). Hard wheat flour is used almost exclusively by commercial bakers, and results in the bread most of us are used to, but, in fact, bread made with soft wheat has more flour, and hence more nutrition, per loaf. It takes a bit of getting used to, but is often discovered to be preferable to the "spongier" hard wheat bread.

Winter wheat is sown at a rate of about one and one-half bushels per acre, at the same time as winter rye — when the first frost occurs, usually during the first two weeks of September in southernmost Canada.

Yields can vary from below 30 bushels an acre to over 60, but assuming the minimum, one could reap a bushel (about 60 pounds) from a plot 25 by 55 feet, which would require three or four pounds of seed. Fall sown, it will be ready for harvest by late July or August, just after rye. Among recommended varieties are *Sundance* for Alberta, *Westmount* for British Columbia, *Talbot* for Ontario and Quebec and *Lennox* for the Maritimes.

Wheat prefers a cool, moist growing season and a hot, dry ripening season. It is more discriminating about soil than rye, growing best on well-drained heavy loam or clay soil. Seeds should be planted at an average depth of one to one and one-half inches, perhaps a bit deeper in sandy soil.

Only rust-resistant spring wheats are sold in Canada, so there are few varieties to choose from, in spite of the fact that about 16,000 varieties of the cereal do exist. It should be planted as early as possible; that is, as soon as the ground can be worked in the spring, generally early May. It has been shown that every week's delay in planting, beyond the first date when soil conditions are favourable, results, in usual circumstances, in a 10 per cent reduction in total yield. Like winter wheat, spring wheat is sown about one and one-half bushels to the acre, and in about 10 days, the sown field should be alive with green shoots. Spring sown wheat is harvested in the fall in the same way as winter wheat and rye. *Glenlea* is a highly recommended hard, red, spring wheat.

The yield of spring wheat is generally much lower than that of winter wheat because it tillers less. Tillers are shoots that the wheat plants send up from the crown, just below the ground. Although each wheat plant will generally send up four or five tillers, under ideal conditions it can produce 40 or 50. Each tiller produces leaves on a stem and terminates in a head or spike, containing 40 to 50 grains of wheat. Winter wheat tillers more than spring, but any well-spaced wheat will tiller more than the same variety crowded.

BUCKWHEAT

Buckwheat, despite its name, is not related to wheat at all and is radically different in appearance from the other cereals. It is a herbaceous annual with white or pink flowers and dark green heart-shaped leaves. It has a profusely branched stem and may grow four or five feet high. The recommended varieties are *Tokyo* (buckwheat is very popular in Japan), *Tempest* and *Mancan*.

Insects are its main pollinating agents, so buckwheat profits from nearby beehives. And the beehives profit, too. (An acre of buckwheat can supply enough nectar for 100 to 150 pounds of honey.)

Buckwheat is very sensitive to frost and does not produce well in very hot, dry weather, preferring a cool, moist climate. However, it has a growing season of only 10 to 12 weeks and so can be planted in mid-June to avoid frost. It is generally sown at a rate of a bushel per acre, less than two inches deep. A bushel (48 pounds) can be expected from a plot about 20 by 100 feet. Buckwheat normally produces 15 to 20 bushels an acre, although yields of 40 have been recorded.

It has an indeterminate growth habit, which means that some of the seeds will be ripe when others are still green. When most of the grain, about three-quarters, is ripe, it is ready to harvest, but if an early frost occurs it should be harvested immediately to minimize damage. Rob Johnson prefers

Ontario Ministry of Agriculture and Food

Both wheat (left) and barley (right) require better soil than rye and prefer a cool, moist growing season.

to leave the harvest until after it has been killed by frost, finding that it is then easier to cure.

Cut the buckwheat in damp weather or before the morning dew has dried, harvesting the same way as wheat or rye, but instead of binding in sheaves, rake it into piles that will be turned daily until dry. The grain is then flailed, winnowed and cured like wheat. Buckwheat kernels are covered with hulls and the hulls are inedible. They will not grind easily and can be sifted out after the buckwheat is ground into flour. But buckwheat groats — hulled buckwheat — are much more difficult to produce at home and are best purchased.

Oats and barley are also hulled, and this remains their main disadvantage for the home flour miller, for their hulls are even more difficult to remove than those of buckwheat. Barley's hull even penetrates the grain at the crease; hence "pearled" barley is ground down sufficiently to remove this part of the hull. It is not impossible to remove most of both oat and barley hulls at home, though, and porridge-lovers should not exclude these grains from the garden.

OATS

Some naked seeded varieties of oats are available to the public, and they are worth seeking out: *Vicar* hull-less oats have been around for about 30 years. *Terra*, developed in Manitoba by Agriculture Canada, is the newest variety in Canada.

Oatmeal porridge is practically the national dish of Scotland, which says something about the climate oats prefer — cool and damp. (The Scots hull their oats in a small hand mill called a "quern" — unfor-

tunately unavailable in this country.) They are classified by the colour of their hulls; black, grey, red, yellow and, the most common in the north, white (actually pale yellow).

Oats are planted a week before the average date of the last spring frost, sown about two bushels per acre deeply enough to reach moist soil. A bushel, about 30 pounds, can be expected from a plot about 20 by 30 feet, which should take about two pounds of seed. They are ready to harvest in late August or early September, when the heads are yellow but about half the leaves are still green and when the kernel can be dented with the thumbnail but is not soft enough to squash between the fingers.

After cutting like wheat, the oats should be left to dry in rows like buckwheat for a month; they require more drying than other grains.

Oats have more protein than any of the other grains mentioned, and this may be why livestock will eat them so readily. Even oat straw is nutritious — good oat straw being better than poor hay. A cow or horse can be fed a sheaf a day all winter and will eat both the straw and the grain. Ground oats mixed with ground corn provide the standard cow ration used on most North American farms. Chickens, rabbits and pigs will eat unhulled oats, although they will prefer them ground or sprouted.

After flailing and winnowing, the hulls will still be present on the grain. To remove them, roast the kernels in the oven at 180 degrees F for an hour and a half. This makes the husks crisp and loose but as there is as yet no small-scale huller on the market, experimentation will lead to the best method for removing them. Any hard, striking action should work. Gene Logsden, author of *Small-Scale Grain Raising*, grinds the oats in his blender, and then sifts out most of the hulls.

BARLEY

Once the hulls are removed, barley will reward the persistent gardener with wonderfully hearty soups and stews, and maybe some home brew. There are many different types, some bearded and some, generally preferred for forage, beardless. The most common and the best for grain are known as six-row barleys. The other type, two-row barley, has fewer seeds on the head. In areas where winter wheat can be grown, winter barley can probably be grown as well. *Huron* is a recommended variety of *winter* barley for Canada, but can only be planted south of the 2700 heat unit line, in the mildest areas of Canada. Otherwise, plant barley early in spring and harvest it in August or September. It should yield about 25 bushels to the acre, so a bushel, 50 pounds, could be provided in a plot about 15 feet by 100 feet, seeded about two inches deep at a rate of two bushels to the acre, or about four pounds to the plot. Winter barley will be ready to harvest just 60 days after growth starts in the spring.

Like oats, leave the barley straw in piles, turning with a rake or pitchfork until dry. Threshing and winnowing are the same as for wheat.

STORAGE

Unlike the store-bought product that is treated with preservatives, home-milled flour and, for that matter, home-grown grains are subject to spoilage. They are also prime targets for vermin and insects. Grain should be stored in a cool, dry place. Metal drums or plastic garbage pails supported by bricks (in case of flooding) on the cellar floor are ideal. Small quantities may be kept in glass jars — light helps inhibit mould — that can be kept in the refrigerator. Some grain growers keep an old refrigerator in the basement, set at the warmest temperature, for grain and flour.

All the grains mentioned can be cooked and eaten as a sort of porridge, or they can be used in soups and stews, and of course in baking.

A neighbour of ours makes her own rye bread and wheat bread from home-grown grain, and finds that she may use slightly less flour than that recommended for commercial flour. If she wants a lighter loaf, she mixes in about 20 per cent commercial, unbleached white flour. But whole grain flour, she says, makes marvellous muffins, slightly heavier than usual but much tastier, and, if sifted, makes a good cake as well.

Bread made from home-grown wheat or rye is so different from the store-bought product that some wonder how the same word can encompass two so vastly different foodstuffs. Very simply, the bread made from home-grown and ground grain tastes like grain, a most remarkable flavour.

Sources

BISHOP FARM SEEDS LIMITED
Box 338
Belleville, Ontario K8N 5A5
(613) 968-5533
They will ship seed anywhere east of Sault Ste. Marie from the Belleville offices. A charge per bushel is added for small orders. Also handle vegetable seed in bulk, as well as broadcast seeders. Write or phone for a catalogue and prices.

BUCKERFIELD'S LIMITED
Box 7000
Vancouver, B.C.
(604) 294-3851
Twenty retail outlets throughout B.C.

JOHNNY'S SELECTED SEEDS
Albion, Maine 04910
Sells winter wheat, spring wheat, buckwheat and winter rye seed by the pound. Canadians must add 50 cents per pound plus 50 cents postage and handling. Write for catalogue. Also sells broadcast seeders and grain mills.

EARLY SEED & FEED LTD.
198 Idylwyld Drive South
Saskatoon, Sask. S7K 3S9
Sells seed grain and forage seeds by mail as well as vegetable seeds.

For United States customers, hull-less oats and barley are available by mail order from:

SELF-RELIANCE SEEDS
Box 44F
Guilderland, N.Y. 12084
Catalogue, $2.00

Grow Your Own (Green) Manure

Soil fertility without the 10-10-10

By Dr. Philip Warman and the Harrowsmith Staff

The skies above the Red River Valley, as the old-timers say, had opened right up, and Francis Anderson watched the sheets of autumn rain pelting his land, proving — he thought — that he must be doing something right. He had stopped using chemical fertilizers on his 320-acre grain farm two years earlier, had eliminated herbicides and pesticides the year before, and the organic conversion had hurt his productivity. Anderson persevered.

While the autumn rains poured, the Manitoba farmer watched his neighbour's soil grow muddy, dissolve and flow away in rivulets and gullies, thanks to the practice of "black summer fallow," leaving the soil exposed between crops and applications of fertilizer. Meanwhile, underfoot, Anderson's own soil continued to absorb the falling rain. Still spongy with decaying organic matter, the earth seemed full of life and evidence that Anderson's newly initiated practice of green manuring was beginning to work.

According to the Oxford English Dictionary, a manure is any substance, natural or artificial, used to increase soil fertility, but in common usage it is something shovelled out of the barn or henhouse. Green manure, in contrast, is succulent plant tissue incorporated into the soil to decompose and contribute to its fertility.

Not having made the tortuous journey through a cow or chicken, a green manure does not possess the concentrated richness of barnyard wastes, but it has distinct advantages to both the farmer and home gardener who wish to add organic matter to their soil. Animal manures can be scarce, are usually heavy, and may be difficult to spread uniformly without the proper equipment. A green manure, on the other hand, may start out as a 50-pound sack of buckwheat seed but, eight weeks later, will have burst forth into 10 tons of green matter and roots, waiting to be tilled into the soil.

With the price of commercial nitrogen fertilizers increasing by 10 to 20 per cent each year and a growing trend toward the use of organic fertilizers, green manuring is being looked at as an economical, practical and even aesthetically pleasing method of restoring productivity to idle or overworked land. It is even, occasionally, touted as the greatest new invention since sliced (whole grain) bread, but its origins are older than matzo. Centuries before 10-10-10 and Weedex appeared in the farmer's vocabulary, he had learned that the fertility of his soil could be maintained and weeds and erosion discouraged with a balanced programme of green manuring.

The ancient Greeks were turning under broad beans for this purpose in 300 B.C., and the planting of beans and lupines, both legumes, for soil improvement was a common practice in the early years of the Roman Empire. The Chinese, predictably, also wrote about the fertilizing value of weeds and grasses hundreds of years ago and early colonists in North America commonly used buckwheat, oats and rye to add tilth and richness to their soil. The practice never died out entirely, but the usage of green manures here peaked in the 1940s and has been in decline until just recently. There are faster routes to soil enrichment, and most farmers have been lured to the relative ease with which artificial fertility could be found — in bags. Just as man cannot thrive on a diet of liquid protein and vitamin pills, soil eventually loses its texture, tilth, friability and concentration of valuable soil microorganisms when fed only chemical fertilizers.

BUCKWHEAT REVIVAL

When Michael Webster moved to his 75 acres of marginal farmland near Verona, Ontario, the neighbours advised that he use buckwheat to revive fields that had turned, through years of neglect, into a hopeless tangle of weeds. He was unable to work the land that first fall, fearing that any bare soil would be flooded and eroded in the spring by a bordering stream.

Webster was on the land as soon as it could be worked the following spring, turning the weeds under, repeating this twice more, until, in early summer, he planted buckwheat. Able to thrive even in poor soil, the buckwheat grew thick and choked out most remaining weeds. Webster let the crop go to seed that fall and then, the following spring after it had sprouted again, he ploughed it under. A few weeks later he planted trefoil and timothy, a hay crop that has been producing abundantly and almost free of weeds, to the great amazement of local farmers who had never seen that field yield so well.

"The thing I like best about green manures," says Webster, "is that they will bring nutrients from the sub-soil with their roots, and the other thing is that most of them have multiple uses. Buckwheat helps eliminate weeds. Winter wheat and rye can be used for grazing. I can't imagine *not* doing it — it's equivalent to a cure for the common cold!"

If green manuring appears to be a panacea for farm and garden soil, it can — with planning and proper handling — be just that. But before covering your land with buckwheat or beautiful red clover, there are some negative aspects of green manuring and some soil science basics that should be understood. Ignoring them can render a green manuring plan useless or even of detriment to the land.

A green manure crop can add appreciable amounts of organic matter to a piece of land, with one or two tons of *dry* matter per acre a not unusual amount (the wet weight of the crop will be four or five times the dry weight). If this material is young and succulent when it is tilled under, it will encourage the microbial action of two important groups of soil microorganisms, whose functions are the key to soil health.

Heterotrophic (organic-matter-consuming) bacteria attack and break down the green manure into components that will be useable by the next crop grown. This process, especially in conditions of warmth and moisture, can be rapid, and it can liberate large quantities of carbon dioxide and weak acids from the plant residues. These acids are valuable in that they can react with insoluble soil minerals and release nutrients beneficial to plant growth. A good example of this effect is seen in high calcium soils which are green manured to increase the availability of phosphates.

Too, some green manure crops are better able to utilize some forms of phosphates and micronutrients than are the main crops to follow. Upon decomposition, furthermore, they may increase the availability of these soil components — a concept being tested with buckwheat at Macdonald College of McGill University.

For these decay bacteria to work, however, they must have nitrogen, which will be present in the soil and in the green manure crop in varying concentrations, depending on the species, the maturity of the crop and the growing conditions. If the green manure crop is high in nitrogen, the bacteria will feed on this source. If, however, the tilled-under material is low in nitrogen, the microbe population will be forced to tie up soil nitrogen to carry out their decay functions. They may actually deplete it to such an extent that the following crop, if planted too soon, will be nitrogen-starved.

To avert such a problem, it helps to understand that the ratio of carbon to nitrogen in plants changes from species to species and with the age of the plant. Usually referred to as the C:N ratio, this factor is shown graphically in the accompanying chart. The value of N is always one, and the value of carbon or carbohydrates varies from about 10, in the case of a young plant, to more than 90, in the case of old or dead non-leguminous plants. When C:N is greater than 30:1, the soil bacteria will draw on available soil nitrogen to survive. Hence, a nearly mature crop of rye, if ploughed under, will act as a detriment to the next crop if it follows too soon, while a legume, such as sweet clover, carries with it more than enough nitrogen for its own decay, and the excess becomes quickly available for the next crop.

As crucial as it is to plant growth, nitrogen is an abundant element, forming — in its gaseous state — 80 per cent of our atmosphere. Free-living soil organisms such as *Azotobacter* and *Clostridium* are able to "fix" this atmospheric nitrogen, converting it to soluble compounds such as ammonium, nitrate and nitrite which can be taken up by plants as masses of the microbes die.

Even more important to anyone considering green manures, are the *Rhizobium* genus of soil organisms, which work symbiotically with leguminous plants to fix atmospheric nitrogen. The legumes — alfalfa, clovers, peas and beans, lupines and others — often have root systems that are infected by this bacteria, which form small nodules visible to the naked eye.

The nitrogen-fixing bacteria in these nodules use energy from the plant's root system, but obtain their nitrogen from the air, creating soluble compounds for their own use. Optimally, some of the nitrogen is also used by the host plant. Legume plants can, therefore, be grown on soils low in nitrogen without the requirement of nitrogen fertilizers and can actually enhance the nitrogen content of the soil markedly. Throughout their life cycle, leguminous plants show a more attractive C:N ratio than do the grains and grasses.

Some legumes are better at accumulating nitrogen than others. The best is alfalfa, which in an average year might fix 200 to 250 pounds of nitrogen per acre. Other common legumes produce at the following rates: sweet clover, 150 to 175 pounds; soybeans, 80 to 100 pounds; beans, 50 to 60 pounds; peas, 40 to 50 pounds.

Without the proper bacteria, however, a leguminous plant cannot fix nitrogen and it is up to the grower to be sure they are present. *Rhizobium* bacteria are highly specialized single-celled organisms and each type teams up with a certain legume or group of legumes.

The following groups of legumes each host a different species of bacteria:
Alfalfa Group: alfalfa, yellow and white sweet clover
Clover Group: common clovers such as alsike, red and white
Pea Group: field, garden and sweet peas; hairy vetch, broad bean, lentil
Lupine Group: Blue and yellow lupine
Soybean Group: soybeans
Cowpea Group: cowpea, lima bean, peanut
Lotus Group: bird's foot trefoil and other lotus species

While these bacteria may be present in the soil, it is best to guarantee their presence by inoculating the seed you are about to plant with cultured bacteria. This bacteria is available in powdered form from better seed and horticultural sources. (Many garden seed houses offer a combination bean and pea inoculant powder, which is black and harmless to humans.)

This powder is easy to apply, and, in fact, the only problem you may find with inoculants is in locating a source. Many seed companies sell garden and field legumes, but neglect to carry the inoculum. Other seed dealers have the appropriate inoculum for the species, but they forget to mention it when you make your purchase. Some seed, however, is pre-inoculated and will be advertised as such.

Alternately, seed may be inoculated with soil in which the crop or a member of the same *Rhizobium* family has been successfully grown within the preceding year. This may be the ideal way to inoculate, as the bacteria will be fresh, and will be properly suited to one's climate. For instance, if a neighbour grew alfalfa last year, and inoculated his crop, your white clover seed can be dampened and mixed with some of his inoculated soil before seeding. If his crop was fixing nitrogen properly, nodules will have formed on the roots. Pink nodules are the assurance that nitrogen fixation is taking place. Dark or white nodules, or a lack of nodules altogether, means that nitrogen fixation is not taking place, usually due to a lack of the proper *Rhizobium*.

Keep in mind that seeds treated with fungicidal dusts containing copper or mercury compounds are *not* suitable for inoculation, because these chemicals are toxic to the bacteria. Also, some fertilizers cannot be mixed with inoculated seed, including superphosphate, ammonium sulphate, sodium nitrate, muriate of potash and potassium sulphate. Lime, superphosphate mixed with equal parts of lime, and rock phosphates are considered safe.

Anyone who neglects the inoculation step is sorely misguided, and will likely end up buying or hauling nitrogen-rich fertilizer to make up the deficiency later. (The inoculation itself involves dampening the seed with a solution of corn syrup and water (one tsp. syrup to one cup water), dusting the seed with the

Typical Green Manure Crops

Down-To-Earth Vegetable Gardening Know-How/Garden Way Publishing

Common Name	Legume	Soil Preference	Seeding Rate (lbs. per 1000 sq. ft.)	Depth to Cover Seed (inches)	When to Sow	When to Turn Under	Comments
ALFALFA	Yes	Loams	1/3		Spring	Summer or Fall	Prefers well-drained soils of high water holding capacity. Highest N fixation.
BARLEY	No	Loams	2½	¾	Spring	Summer	Not good on sandy or acid soils.
BEANS, Garden or Field	Yes	Loams	2½	1½	Spring	Summer	Warm weather crops. Do not sow until ground is warm and weather settled.
BROME GRASS	No	Widely Adaptable	1	½	Fall or Spring	Spring or Fall	Good winter cover. Easy to establish. Hardier than rye. More heat tolerant.
BUCKWHEAT	No	Widely Adaptable	1½	¾	Late Spring or Summer	Summer or Fall	Quick growing. Survives on the poorest soils. Plant only after ground is warm.
CLOVER, Alsike	Yes	Heavy Loams	1/8	½	Spring or Fall	Fall or Spring	Less sensitive to soil acidity and poorly drained soils than most clovers.
Ladino	Yes	Sandy Loams	¼	½	Spring	Fall	
Red	Yes	Loams	¼	½	Spring	Fall	
White Dutch	Yes	Heavy Loams	1/8	½	Spring or Late Summer	Fall	Good cover crop; long-lived, shallow-rooted.
CORN	No	Widely Adaptable	2½	1	Spring or Summer	Summer or Fall	Do not sow until ground is warm.
KALE, Scotch	No	Widely Adaptable	¼	½	Summer or Fall	Spring	Can be eaten after serving as winter cover. Interplant with winter rye for protection. Plant in summer for good growth before frost.
LUPINE, White and Yellow	Yes	Sandy Loams	2½	1	Spring or Fall	Summer or Spring	Difficult to establish. Seed costly.
MILLET	No	Loams	1	½	Late Spring or Summer	Summer or Fall	Requires warm ground. Fast growing.
MUSTARD, White	No	Loams	¼	¼	Spring	Summer	
OATS	No	Widely Adaptable	2½	1	Spring	Summer or Fall	Fast establishment, ease of availability.
PEA, Field	Yes	Heavy Loams	2½	1½	Early Spring	Summer	Distinctly a cool weather crop.
RAPE	No	Loams	¼	¼	Spring or Summer	Summer or Fall	
RYE, Spring	No	Widely Adaptable	2	¾	Spring	Summer	
RYE, Winter	No	Widely Adaptable	2	¾	Fall	Spring	One of the most important winter cover crops.
RYE-GRASS, Italian	No	Widely Adaptable	1	¾	Spring	Summer	
SUDAN GRASS	No	Widely Adaptable	1	¾	Late Spring or Summer	Summer or Fall	Rapid grower. Do not sow until ground is warm and weather settled.
SUNFLOWER	No	Widely Adaptable	¾	¾	Spring or Summer	Summer or Fall	Intolerant of acid soils.
SWEET CLOVER Common White	Yes	Heavy Loams	½	½			Quite winter hardy.
Annual (Hubam)	Yes	Loams	½	½			A true annual. Best results from spring sowings.
Yellow	Yes	Widely Adaptable	½	½			Stands dry conditions better than common white sweet clover.
VETCH, Hairy	Yes	Widely Adaptable	1½	¾	Spring or Fall	Fall or Spring	The hardiest winter vetch. Best sown in fall with winter rye or winter wheat.
WHEAT, Winter	No	Loams	2½	¾	Fall	Spring	

powder and planting immediately. The inoculant is a living material and must be treated as such.)

APPLICATIONS

If the theory of green manuring is intimidating to some, the actual practice shouldn't be. Most who use it find one or two crops that work well for them and their land, and simply fall into an annual routine of ploughing or tilling under the green manure.

"Alfalfa is best," says Francis Anderson, the Red River Valley grain farmer. "I have tried clover in a few fields, but I don't think it's as impressive, although it does come up faster." Having used conventional practices on his land since 1948, Anderson went organic 19 years later, and the conversion was not easy. Production fell at first but after 11 seasons he is now happy with his yields, which are supported solely by green manuring and the application of barnyard manure — of which he has little.

"We only have 100 hens and a few goats, so we can only fertilize one field a year with livestock manure," he says. His 12 fields are involved in a continuous crop rotation, and following the harvest of a main grain crop, a field will be planted with alfalfa, which grows for two or three years and supplies top quality hay crops while putting nitrogen into the soil. The alfalfa is finally ploughed down in the fall, left to decompose over the winter, then seeded the next spring with a crop that will use the accumulated nitrogen — wheat, oats, rye, field peas, sunflowers, millet, buckwheat or barley. These he will sell with an "organically-grown" label.

"Where we do things properly," says Anderson, "our yields are as good as an average crop anywhere else."

Quebec farmer Arthur Vandestar swears by red clover as a green manure. The owner of 140 acres near Ste. Marthe, Quebec, Vandestar has used plough-down crops and barnyard manure since 1970 and has had increased yields of vegetables, oats and wheat each year.

Intuition, says the Dutch-born farmer, plays an important part in the process. "The big thing is that you have to plough it in at the right time of year, not on a hit-or-miss basis. The soil has to be a bit wet or the material you plough in will just sit there and not do anything." Vandestar plants red clover with his grain crop, harvests the grain, cuts the clover hay once or twice as it appears, then ploughs under the field of clover the following spring.

The planting of green manures is normally done in the spring or fall, but 10 days to two weeks must be allocated between the ploughing down and planting of the next crop, to allow decomposition to take place. Weather and soil type will determine how effective the manuring has been, with prolonged cold slowing the process down and extended periods of heavy rain working to leach away the nutrients. In especially hot weather, with sandy soil conditions, appreciable amounts of the decomposing material can escape as gases into the atmosphere.

C.A. Mooers, in one Tennessee study, found that 6.2 tons of cowpeas (dry matter) per acre grown as an autumn catch crop in land devoted to continuous wheat production resulted in a decrease of .11 per cent in organic matter after 20 years. When animal

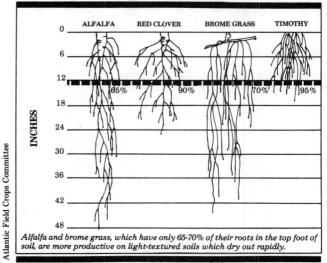

Rooting Depth in Soil

Alfalfa and brome grass, which have only 65-70% of their roots in the top foot of soil, are more productive on light-textured soils which dry out rapidly.

Atlantic Field Crops Committee

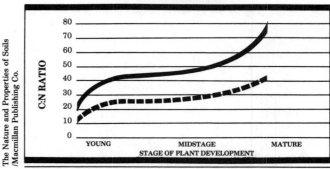

C:N Ratio

The Nature and Properties of Soils /Macmillan Publishing Co.

manure was substituted, organic matter increased .11 per cent under the same conditions and over the same time period.

On the other hand, and as is typical in "manure" research, C.J. Williard and E.E. Barnes in Ohio found that sweet clover, in a two-year rotation of corn followed by oats seeded with sweet clover, maintained the productivity of the soil and produced as high yields of corn as were obtained by ploughing under six tons per acre of manure or applying commercial nitrogen at rates up to as much as 100 pounds per acre.

The one thing that should be kept in mind is that a single species crop of green manure will either increase the humus content of the soil or supply additional nitrogen, but not both. Humus is increased by the addition of material which is fairly resistant to decompositon (e.g. old straw) and a high C:N ratio. Non-legumes are better at increasing humus, unless they are tilled in when still very young, succulent, rich with nitrogen and still have a low C:N ratio.

The criteria by which a green manure crop is chosen are simple, and the ideal choice should:
1) Be inexpensive to plant
2) Be easily established
3) Produce succulent tops and roots rapidly
4) Generate good ground cover rapidly
5) Be capable of growing on poor soils — sands and clays will benefit most.

Some growers choose to plant a mixture of species,

often a legume and a grass, and Bishop's Farm Seeds offers a mix called the Bearss Plowdown Mixture, with 60 per cent red clover, 20 per cent sweet yellow clover and 20 per cent ryegrass.

Other common combinations are oats and field peas or rye and vetch, in both cases a legume teamed with a non-legume. The grain crop in each instance offers some physical support for the legume, which in turn supplies them both with nitrogen. In such cases the perennial legume is planted more thinly than usual so that the annual "nurse-crop" — the grain — will not be choked out.

SCALING DOWN

Green manuring practices can be put to work in the home garden, although those with postage stamp-sized plots may find it easier to add several bushels of animal manure or well-rotted compost.

A rototiller is essential for working in the green manure on any scale at all, though someone with the will, a good spade and a strong back could conceivably manage to handle a small area.

Ideally one's garden should be divided into two or more sections. One part is dedicated to green manure while the other section grows vegetables, with the two alternating each year. It is also possible to put in a quick green manure crop in the early spring and have it tilled under in time for the planting of a later crop of vegetables. Peas, for example, can be planted very early and their green foliage turned in as soon as the crop is picked. If seed is coated with a fungicide such as Captan to help assure growth in cold, damp soil, it should not be dusted with inoculant, which is incompatible with the fungicide. The inoculant should be spread along the row where the seeds will grow, their roots eventually seeking out the inoculant.

Likewise, as soon as any vegetable has been harvested, the remaining plant material, while still green, should be turned into the soil to maximize nutrient gain. A very fast-maturing crop such as buckwheat can then be planted in that section of the garden. Buckwheat matures a lush foliage and goes to seed in only 10 to 12 weeks, so it can be planted throughout the season, if desired. Unless you want a healthy stand of buckwheat to appear the following spring, be sure to till the crop under before it does go to seed.

When the later harvest of tender vegetables such as tomatoes, peppers and beans is complete, their areas may be planted with a cover crop such as winter rye, wheat or brome grass, which will not be tilled or spaded into the garden until the following spring. Richard Raymond, author of *Improving Garden Soil with Green Manures,* recommends that home gardeners augment the green manures with compost, animal manures and wood ashes whenever possible. Most growers like green manuring because of the lack of backache.

In the final analysis, green manuring can increase both soil fertility and soil quality, helping to stabilize the soil structure, increase the water holding capacity and increase the infiltration of water into the soil and its percolation through the soil. It can serve an important protective function in covering fallow land and preventing erosion by water and wind. There are more convenient ways to add the three major fertilizing components, but people such as Francis Anderson have come to prefer green manuring as a permanent, affordable solution.

"I think a person gets to think differently after a while," he says, referring to his past use of chemical fertilizers. "Your values change. You try to think of new ways to get us out of this mess we're in."

Small is Bounteous

Improving one's lot in life

"The thing most generally raised on city land is taxes."

—*Charles Dudley Warner,*
My Summer in a Garden, 1871

By Dr. Stephen Tobe and Martha Tobe

Warner's observation still holds today, but standing at our kitchen window, surveying the tomato plants drooping under the weight of their own fruit, the pole beans coiling skyward around their stakes, cucumbers scaling the far fence and the white curds of cauliflower peering out from jade-green leaves, we are never moved to think of mill rates or school tax assessments. Throughout the summer our garden produces more than we can eat — a happy state of affairs for our non-gardening friends and neighbours — with substantial amounts to freeze, pickle and can for the winter. Mr. Warner might be cheered to know that all this comes from a hemmed-in downtown Toronto yard measuring but 20 by 30 feet, with an old garage standing in the middle.

Our garden, we think, is a refutation of the common belief that urban backyards can produce little more than the occasional salad or jug of fresh flowers. Serious food production in such surroundings may sound fanciful, but it is far from impossible. Through judicious use of the land, taking advantage of every square yard, and by employing such techniques as succession planting, terracing, block gardening and the appropriate selection of plant varieties, we've come up with a system by which every city gardener should be able to make the most of his lot.

TERRACING & SOIL PREPARATION

The soil in many urban — or even suburban — backyards often leaves much to be desired and may not be much better suited for vegetable cultivation than the pavement passing by the front of the house. It may be capable of supporting an apparently good crop of weeds, but this is no indication of how well it will satisfy the needs of heavy-feeding vegetables.

When we first seriously assessed the quality of our own garden soil five years ago, we discovered it to be almost pure clay — better suited to brickmaking than growing most vegetable varieties. We could have improved it gradually, by the addition of sand and great amounts of organic matter, but we decided that the most sensible route for us was to buy topsoil. Our source was the Holland Marsh, an area just north of the city and known for its black and extremely fertile soil.

To the appreciative eye and hand of a gardener, this type of soil — known to the commercial vegetable growers as "muck" — is a precious commodity, and we decided that it should be used as efficiently as possible. Rather than simply scattering it on top of our hardpan, we took a lesson from European gardeners and planned an area of terraces and raised soil beds.

Terracing has many advantages:
1. High quality top soil can be utilized, no matter what the fertility of the soil on which the terraces will be placed.
2. The terraces are off-limits to feet and wheels, preventing compaction of the soil, giving better drainage and aeration.
3. Provided the terraces are not built too wide, crops may be planted throughout the growing area, rather than in discrete rows, thus multiplying the yield.

4. Terracing is particularly compatible with trickle irrigation systems which are both more effective and less wasteful of water supplies.

Our terraces are constructed from standard concrete building blocks (16 inches long by eight inches deep and four inches high) but cedar planks or old railroad ties can also be used. (Avoid any freshly creosoted wood, or wood treated with Pentox, both of which are lethal to root systems.)

We chose concrete blocks because they are virtually self-supporting (no need for reinforcement, joining or carpentry skills). In addition, we use the blocks as pathways and never step into the beds, thus avoiding any soil compaction. In areas of the beds not dedicated to walkways, we have filled the open compartments in the blocks with soil and use these small spaces to grow onions, carrots, radishes and herbs.

A convenient width for each bed in a terrace system is two feet, although we have used widths of four feet successfully. Wider beds, unless they have access from both sides, tend to be more difficult to plant, weed, cultivate and harvest. We did not want to use mortar and confined our terraces to two or three tiers, but more ambitious builders might be inspired to more elaborate creations. Keep in mind, however, that higher terraces are more prone to damage from frost and earth movement in winter. The length of each terrace is entirely dependent on the geography of one's backyard and/or personal whim. Our beds measure from 10 to 16 feet long.

Before being caught in the spirit of pyramid building or terrace fervour, stop to consider how you might make the most efficient use of your sunlight. Ideally, the terraces should be oriented on an east-west axis — that is, with the highest tier to the north and thence sloping down to the south. This prevents the upper-level plants from shading the lower terraces; in our locale the sun always comes from a generally southerly direction.

Even if a terraced garden is not in your plans, it is extremely important that plant placement be done to match the individual vegetables with the various light levels found in most yards.

To assess scientifically the amount of direct sunlight various areas of your potential garden receive, draw a map of the yard and break it down into areas one or two yards square. On a sunny day early in the growing season, mark out the one or two yard sections on the ground and every hour note on the map if a particular section is receiving full sunlight. By the end of the day you will be able to draw a light contour map and will have identified offending structures and trees that cast sometimes surprising shadows.

With this knowledge, it will be a simple matter to match the available sunlight with the demands of various vegetable types. For example, tomatoes, peppers, corn, cucumbers, melons and squash all require as many hours of direct solar exposure as possible and will languish in the shade. Lettuce, radishes, parsley, chervil, watercress and certain other herbs thrive in much less direct sunlight. The better seed catalogues and gardening books all specify the

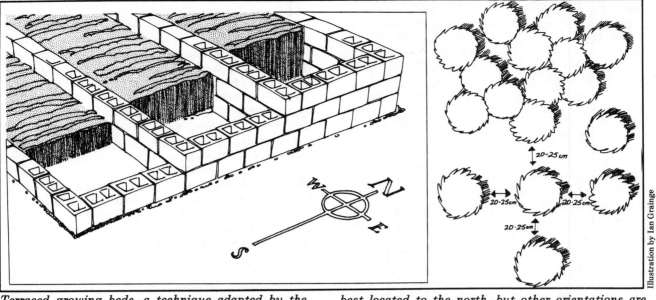

Illustration by Ian Grainge

Terraced growing beds, a technique adapted by the authors from traditional intensive European urban gardens, provide maximum growing room, with the block walls serving the double function of containing earth and providing a footpath. The topmost terrace is best located to the north, but other orientations are possible, as long as taller plants are always located at the north end of the beds. **Right,** *the authors broadcast their seed rather than planting in rows, then thin to assure that no space in the terrace is wasted.*

light requirements of different plants and will help the city gardener make best use of his limited space.

Having selected a site for one or more banks of terraces, the next step is to dig and break up the soil upon which the new garden will be built. It is most likely hard compacted earth that will prevent good drainage and aeration and also hinder the movement of useful organisms such as earthworms. Once this old soil is thoroughly loosened up, spread a one- or two-inch layer of gravel to provide a footing where you will be laying the blocks.

In four winters, the blocks in our yard have not undergone any significant movement and, accordingly, we have no regrets about not mortaring the low walls together. We did, of course, stagger the rows of blocks in bricklayer fashion for increased strength, making sure that the vertical seam between two blocks never connected directly with a vertical seam in the layer above (see illustration).

If winters are especially severe in your area, it might be wise to mortar the blocks or perhaps drive lengths of pipe or concrete rod through the inside holes in the blocks at occasional intervals. This reinforcement will also be necessary if the terrace extends much above three tiers. Once all blocks are in place, the tiers can be filled with soil and are ready for planting. (If a terrace construction project is undertaken in mid-summer or fall, in preparation for the following spring, the terraces could be filled with a mixture of soil, fresh manure and compost and allowed to mellow over the winter.)

Keep in mind that the soil in the terraces is *not* to be walked on — always use the concrete blocks for your footpath. The soil level in the beds will drop slightly during the first month or two, but the addition of mulch, compost or manure will restore things to normal.

The one direction in which any garden, however small, can expand easily is up, and we always take advantage of those vegetables which have a natural inclination to climb. Rather than plant bush-type snap beans and the stockier pea varieties, for example, we choose the leggy pole types and grow them on plastic netting in the back row (northernmost tier) or against a wall. Peas and beans grown in this manner are much easier to harvest and the pole varieties are often more prolific than their newer scaled-down counterparts.

Likewise, we never allow any of the cucurbit vine plants to grow freely on the ground — space is just too valuable — and these are trained up a wall of netting. All of our cucumbers, squash and melons grow this way, and they do very well for two main reasons: (1) The fruit is kept clean and off the soil, making attack by insects and fungal disease less likely. (2) The entire plant receives more sun and better aeration, further factors in reducing the likelihood of mildews and moulds getting a start.

The larger squash and melon will often need support for the developing fruit, which may break and fall because of their own weight. We use old nylons and panty hose tied to the netting to form a cradle which supports the fruit.

By covering border walls with garden netting and/or erecting support trellises and making the best use of vertical space, a diminutive garden can match or exceed the production of a much larger space.

With a new terrace or raised-bed garden ready for planting, it is time to abandon the traditional method of sowing seeds and setting out plants in rows. Because the block borders will be used for access, every square inch of available soil can be used as growing space. Rather than marching plants up and down the beds, we plant *throughout* the space, keeping in mind the minimum required spacing between plants as specified on the seed packets.

For example, if a terrace is being sown with lettuce, we simply scatter the seed lightly over the entire bed. Once the seedlings are two or three inches tall or when they begin to crowd each other, we thin them to the distance specifed by the seed company — usually seven to 10 inches. Thus, the distance between plants in any direction is seven to 10 inches. (The thinnings are never wasted, but go directly into the salad bowl.)

Using this intensive method of agriculture, the yields per unit of garden increase enormously. By experimentation, some gardeners have learned to break the spacing rules and plant even more thickly, but in any such system of concentrated production, it is important to maintain the soil with liberal applications of compost and manure to prevent the depletion of nutrients.

All larger plants, such as tomatoes and peppers, must go to the back row (or in terraces that run north-south, to the north end of the bed) and thus not shade the smaller vegetables, and when set out may be mulched with organic matter, such as leaves or grass clippings, or with the newer biodegradable brown or black plastic mulch. We have used both successfully, although the plastic is offensive to some people, and it is expensive. However, it does have the advantage of trapping the sun's heat and causing soil temperatures to increase more rapidly, so that plants can be set out or seeded earlier. Organic mulches, on the other hand, decompose as they prevent weeds and retain moisture, helping to fertilize the soil.

Succession planting is another tool for the urban or small space gardener and it is based on the rule that, as soon as one crop is harvested, its place is immediately taken by another. Alternatively, the harvesting of one crop provides the additional room needed by a second crop that is ready to expand. In the first instance, cool weather crops such as lettuce, radishes and spinach (which also happen to be fast growing) will either bolt or grow poorly in the hot summer weather and so it is advisable to harvest these crops well before the long and hot days. Lettuce which has been planted early in April will usually be ready for harvest by the beginning of June. However, it would be wasteful to leave this area fal-

low for the remainder of the season since it is only the beginning of the growing year for warm-weather crops. Accordingly, as soon as the lettuce has been removed, warm-weather seedlings should be ready and planted immediately. Melons, squash and cucumbers usually go in as soon as the lettuce is out, and beans replace the peas in our garden. Often it is not necessary to wait until the entire early crop has been harvested — rather, the warm-weather seeds can be planted as soon as the soil temperature is appropriate and as soon as space is available.

This brings us to the second type of succession planting and the radish-carrot and the pea-bean interaction provide good examples. Radishes and peas are cool-weather, rapidly growing crops. Beans and carrots are warm-weather crops and can usually be planted about the time of the last frost. We usually plant bean seeds right beside the pea plants and carrot seeds are interspersed among the radishes. By the time the peas and radishes have been completely harvested, the bean and carrot seeds will have germinated and you will be using your land efficiently. Remember — never let parts of the garden sit vacant. These techniques can be applied to a variety of other plants including spinach and cauliflower or other early crops followed by beans, cucurbits and tomatoes.

Companion planting can also be used by the city gardener to get the most from the land. Certain vegetables thrive in the presence of others in the bed — tomatoes and basil, carrots and radishes, squash and corn, etc. — but in addition, companion planting may encourage the planting of colourful flowers in your garden even though you may have assumed that limited space precluded the growing of decorative plants. The use of appropriate flowers can actually be of great value in the control of certain pests. For example, we usually plant marigolds with our tomatoes to control soil nematodes and plant nasturtiums with tomatoes, beans and eggplants to control whitefly and beetles. If you are using raised or terraced beds, you can simply plant your tomato and eggplant seedlings at the normal recommended spacing and set marigolds and nasturtiums between

them. The use of these two species has virtually eliminated our whitefly and nematode problems.

COMPACT PLANTS FOR SMALL SPACES

With limited space, it is important to grow vegetables which are both compact and high yielding. Many of the new hybrids available from the seed companies are very useful for city gardening and some of these include: *Stakeless* tomato, a beefsteak-type which usually will not exceed one and a half to two feet in height; *Starshot* tomato, a heavy producer that does not require staking, with fruit two or three ounces in weight; *Patio Pick* cucumber, a compact cucumber which can even be grown in containers; and *French Imperial* eggplant, a compact Japanese-type with long thin fruit. There are several other varieties which, although not as compact as the above plants, are very heavy yielders and are highly recommended for city gardening; *Sweet 100 Hybrid* tomato, a cherry variety which can literally produce hundreds of fruit per plant (if you like cherry tomatoes, this is the only variety to grow — the other cherry types are much less prolific); *Starfire* tomato, a fairly compact bush plant which produces large numbers of beefsteak-type fruit; *Salty* cucumber, a heavy yielding compact cuke which grows very well on garden netting, producing pickle-size fruit; *Samson Hybrid* cantaloupe, a variety which grows well on garden netting (be sure to support the fruit), producing the sweetest and most intensely flavoured melons we have ever had; and *Royal Burgundy* beans, a bush variety, which produces large numbers of purple-coloured pods over most of the growing season (the beans turn green after a minute or two of cooking).

Many of the varieties we have mentioned respond well to "suckering" or pruning. Suckers, in tomatoes, are the shoots that appear in the crotch formed by the main stem and main branches and which sap strength from the fruiting plant. Letting suckers develop fully results in a wildly bushy plant, but very poor tomato production. Most of the hybrid staking tomatoes, in fact, *must* be suckered.

In the case of cucumbers and melons, pruning helps to produce compact plants and better yields. Pinching off the main growing stem when the plant has developed six to eight leaves is said to force the plant to produce lateral stems and a better harvest. In fact, this type of lateral forcing is used by commercial growers and has usually worked well in our hands.

INSECT CONTROL

The city gardener often faces difficulties very different from those of rural gardeners. The most common pests of our own backyard include: whitefly on tomatoes; earwigs and sow bugs on lettuce, spinach, cauliflower and broccoli; green aphids on beans; onion maggots on the onions; red spider mites on beans, eggplant and cucumbers; and the familiar white "cabbage" butterfly and its green "looper" caterpillar larvae, which turn up on broccoli, cabbage, cauliflower and kohlrabi. Other city gardeners

Agriculture Canada recommends this plan, which could be improved by deepening each box to increase yields and prevent rapid drying of the soil.

Agriculture Canada

report problems with cutworms as pests of tomatoes, beans and the cucurbits, and squash bugs as a problem on the cucurbits, but we have had no trouble with either of these.

We do not bother to control earwigs and sow bugs because in small numbers they cause very little damage to crops. The other pests, however, must be controlled or crops may be seriously harmed. We prefer to use only manual (hand-picking) and "organic" methods of control; only in a dire emergency will we resort to pesticides and then only to the botanical rotenone or pyrethrum powder. For whitefly, we use companion planting of nasturtiums and marigolds and, in cases of heavy infestation, use a fine spray of water directed at the underside of the leaves of tomatoes. A spray made of ground hot pepper also seems to work. For white cabbage butterflies, the most effective method of control is the hand-picking technique — we simply watch for any signs of leaf damage caused by the caterpillars and as soon as these become apparent, carefully inspect the plant for the green larvae (they are difficult to see because they are so well camouflaged) and remove and destroy them. Onion maggots are very difficult to restrict and we have not found an effective control measure for them. Rather, we change the location of onions in the garden every year and try to harvest the plants before the maggots get well-established. In addition, the use of decoy plants such as chives can serve to concentrate the pests and the affected portion of the chive plant can be removed and destroyed.

Finally, there is the red spider mite. This is one of the most insidious and pervasive of arthropod pests (it is not an insect) and literally millions of dollars are spent each year by commercial growers in an attempt to control these organisms. They are very difficult to eliminate and we know of no effective methods of control, even with chemicals. About the best one can hope to do is restrict the mites by growing healthy plants that are well-supplied with nutrients. We have had limited success with spraying leaves with a dilute solution of soap several times each week. Spider mites will appear in virtually every garden and the gardener can only hope that conditions (they like hot, moist weather) will not be appropriate for the proliferation of the pests. Incidentally, the spider mite is practically unknown as a pest in rural areas except on indoor plants.

One final note on invaders — there are also four-legged mammals which can cause real difficulty to the city gardener. In Toronto there is a very large raccoon population living in the ravines of the city, and during the summer months these animals will often attack city gardens — in particular seeking out those which contain sweet corn. As any farmer knows, raccoons will ravage a plot of corn and we have found it just about impossible to grow enough to share with these beasts. If there are raccoons in the area, they somehow manage to appear just as the ears begin to ripen and in one or two nights will eat or ruin the entire crop.

We've given up on sweet corn but continue to accept the challenge and rewards of downtown horticulture. The old garage in the yard is being converted into a solar greenhouse and hydroponic growing area, lengthening our growing season and greatly increasing the food production potential of our land.

Standing in our backyard on a warm summer night, a star-filled sky overhead and ripening vegetables heavy with dew, we are doubly sure that a city lot, however handicapped, need not be relegated to bluegrass and croquet wickets.

Ted and Pat Michener

High~Rise Horticulture

Every twenty storeys, perhaps one good plot

By Jennifer Bennett

In a way, it is very much like *The Great Escape* in reverse. Where Allied prisoners of war, tunnelling to freedom, struggled to remove their bags of tell-tale earth without attracting the attention of Stalag guards, the balcony-bound gardener may find himself smuggling boxes of topsoil up the emergency stairway or feigning nonchalance while riding up the elevator with a bag of composted sheep manure.

Risking the wrath of a building supervisor may be enough to deter some apartment dwellers from turning their balconies into vegetable plots, but not Patricia Rogal, who gardens 18 storeys above Toronto. "I feel very strongly that I *pay* for that space out there. It's part of my home and I choose not to look out on concrete all summer. From here I can see hundreds, literally hundreds, of balconies that don't have a single green plant, and that appalls me."

Rogal has become accustomed to viewing the world in a frame of leafy growth, refusing to delegate her balcony to lawn furniture or bicycle storage. In the small Saskatchewan town where she grew up, her father annually "bought garden seed by the pound," and now she finds it difficult to understand why anyone would accept a view of sterile concrete when he could have a living screen of greenery and a daily salad of his own making. After six years of high-rise horticulture, Rogal can see the city only by peering over pots of tomatoes and herbs, around boxed flowers and foliage and beyond the tangle of climbing honeysuckle. This view, she insists, puts an entirely improved perspective on her city existence.

Fourteen storeys below and several miles away, Hellen Ostler sympathizes. Gifted with more than 200 square feet of rooftop growing space, Hellen and her husband have installed a lawn with a fountain, and, in large pots, planted two spruce trees, a pair of dwarf apples and two dwarf pears. A profusion of vegetables and flowers grows between the picnic table and the small garden shed. Like Rogal, the Ostlers have become old hands at urging greenery from elevated soil.

It has been estimated that there are hundreds of acres of unused flat rooftops in a city the size of Montreal, but covering them and the stacked hectares of balconies with productive gardens involves a stubborn spirit that even the most countrified gardener would have to admire.

Although the raccoons, groundhogs, two-footed vegetable poachers and most insects are left below, skyscraping gardens can be whipped by winds that tear leaves and vines, baked by Saharan temperatures and, because of the limitations of soil depth, desiccated in a matter of hours. Horticulture was surely the last thing an urban architect had in mind in designing a rooftop or balcony, and each green-thumbed high-riser must face a different challenge — be it too much shade or too little water.

"Everything seemed to be against me," says David Forgie, who has managed to grow tomatoes, cucumbers, salad greens, radishes, dill, various herbs and pole beans in a balcony plot above Toronto's Eglinton Avenue. "I didn't find the wind to be too bad, but things tend to dry out quickly. The biggest problem is water; the plants need to be watered a lot and city water is filled with chlorine and fluorine." (Although not lethal for most plants, these chemicals can be removed by allowing water to stand overnight in an open pail or other container.)

Forgie got around the problem of not being able to drive stakes into the ground by stringing his *Scarlet Runner* beans on cord tied from his own balcony railing to the railing above. Soil was acquired on an excursion to the northern outskirts of the city, carried back in plastic bags and used to fill an agglomeration of containers, including old aquariums and "anything that would hold soil." Despite the north-facing exposure, everything Forgie planted returned a harvest, owing partly to the extended growing season of a balcony — with the thermal mass of the building to retain warmth and the elevation to escape ground-hugging frosts.

HAZY ECONOMICS

Forgie freely admits that balcony gardening borders on the impractical and that it is not the key to independence from supermarket produce. Containerized vegetables have a way of costing as much, or more, than those from the market, especially when the grower buys soil, expensive pots, a watering system and fertilizers.

However hazy the economics of tight-quarter gardening, the less tangible rewards tend to override all else for many urban farmers. Witold Rybczynski, professor of architecture at McGill University, headed a rooftop vegetable growing project in Montreal in 1975. He and his colleagues undertook the project, thinking that it would save money for inner city families and make use of what they described as "rooftop wastelands." They were dismayed by the financial results.

"I think it costs more to grow vegetables in an urban situation, especially in containers, than to buy them," says Rybczynski. "We started with all the preconceptions. We wanted to use greenhouses to extend the season. We wanted to go into hydroponics, but people saw the tubes and white culture medium as being too technical, almost surreal. People wanted the feel and smell of soil and didn't want to get involved in anything technical. We had to change the direction of the project."

Nevertheless, Rybczynski feels strongly that the project was a success and says now that growing food to save money is not a major motivation for city gardeners. "There are other payoffs, in aesthetics, in recreation. We had a very, very strong reaction to the project." The Montreal rooftop growers are carrying on with the aerial gardens, having discovered the welcome change of pace of coming home from eight hours in an office or shop and digging in a grow-box or harvesting a salad's worth of lettuce and tomatoes before dinner.

While many of the participants were sufficiently satisfied with having turned a naked rooftop into a profusion of green, others have become "production oriented" according to Rybczynski, and continue to work with greenhouses and hydroponics experiments. (Occasionally a fanatic is born, as in the case of a young man known in certain Toronto gardening circles. Rejecting the confines of his balcony, he reportedly found a bedroom more to his liking and gardened happily and unnoticed until the tenant one floor below became alarmed at the stains spreading on his ceiling. Exactly what the building supervisor said when confronted by a layer of soil and crop of potatoes growing on the apartment floor is not known.)

CONTAINMENT

Containing one's earth and plants will be, for newcomers to balcony horticulture, one of the first challenges and one which must be met intelligently. To keep her costs under control, Torontonian Patricia Rogal is "a great believer in found-object containers." She recommends the square plastic carriers in which gallon jugs of milk are delivered to stores, styrofoam picnic coolers, wooden crates and fruit boxes.

"You have to use your imagination," says Rogal. "If you want a balcony to look *très élégante* then it will cost money, but I count on my plants to grow and cover their containers and they do so for most of the summer." Cedar tubs, half barrels and giant clay pots are available from hardware and import stores, as well as garden centres, but for all the expense, they do not guarantee any better harvests than "found objects."

The most important consideration in choosing a container is, of course, matching its size to that of the plant or plants it will house. A too-common error is to take the nearest coffee can, yogurt container or African violet pot and expect it to suffice. Except for starting seeds or temporarily holding transplants, such small vessels should be used only for the occasional pot of herbs. Because of the drying effects of wind and sun on a balcony or rooftop, more soil depth is necessary than might be used indoors or in a greenhouse.

The McGill project utilized wooden boxes, measuring about two feet by three feet and two feet deep. Good drainage was promoted by lining the bottoms with a half-inch layer of peat moss and vermiculite. The rooftop gardeners reported the best results when they planted just a single zucchini or broccoli to a box, two tomatoes or eggplants or three miniature cabbages, planted in a triangle. Such a box will accommodate three rows of peas and two of beans, or it can be broadcast seeded with carrots or lettuce (which are later thinned to leave two or three inches of space around each seedling).

Helga and William Olkowski, authors of *The City People's Book of Raising Food*, found that "with all the plants we tried, the larger the containers, the bigger the harvest. Tomatoes are particularly responsive to root depth. In our experience, the plant in the largest container will invariably live the longest and produce the most food." They decided that herbs and cherry tomatoes would tolerate a minimum of six inches of soil depth; radishes, lettuce and baby carrots could be planted in six inches but preferred eight; standard tomatoes, broccoli and cucumbers needed a bare minimum of one foot.

Whatever the container, proper drainage must be provided to avoid having water accumulate and initiate root decay. If a double pot system is used (a container with drainage holes or spaces inside a nonleaking container), the bottom of the larger container should be covered with peat moss or vermiculite so that the inner pot can drain into the space below.

The Best Veg

Vegetables	Balcony Requirements	Days From Planting to Harvest	Seeds or Transplants	Survive
Beans, bush	some sun	40-70	S	N
Beans, pole	some sun	60-90	S	N
Beets	some shade	45-65	S	Y
Cabbage	some shade	60-80	S or T	Y
Carrots	some shade	65-75	S	Y
Chard	some shade	45-60	S	Y
Cucumbers	some sun	55-70	S	N
Eggplant	some sun	65-80	T	N
Kale	some shade	60-70	S	Y
Lettuce	some shade	40-80	S or T	Y
Onions (Scallions)	some shade	20-75	S	Y
Peas	some shade	55-70	S	Y
Peppers	some sun	60-80	T	N
Radishes	some shade	20-50	S	Y
Spinach	some shade	40-50	S	Y
Squash, summer	some sun	50-60	S	N
Tomatoes	some sun	55-90	T	N

● **Stokes Seeds**
Box 10
St. Catharines, Ontario L2R 6R6
or
Box 548
Buffalo, New York 14240

...of Pot	Preferred Varieties	Comments
...diam., 8" deep for ...lant	*Topcrop* ●●● green *Honeygold* ● wax	Require warm weather. Limas, kidneys & navies are low producers.
..." diam., 8" deep for ...lant	Any	Higher production than bush varieties. Need about 8' vertical support.
...pends on variety. Space ...apart, 6"-12" deep.	Choose variety to suit container. Regular varieties in shallow soil, *Formanova* ● in deep.	Like cool weather, lots of water, loose, sandy soil. Greens are edible. Pick when young.
...diam. for 1 small ...nt, 12" deep	*Baby Head* ● *Midget Baby Head* ● *Dwarf Morden* ●	Like cool weather. Take a lot of space for little produce but miniature varieties maximize return.
...ace 2" apart, 8"-12" ...p depending on variety	Choose variety to suit container. *Planet* ● in shallow soil. Regular varieties in deep.	Like cool weather, good drainage. Prefer loose, sandy soil. Can be planted in alternate rows with lettuce.
...diam., 8" deep for ...lant	Any	Harvest outer leaves throughout season.
...diam. 12" deep for ...lant	*Victory* ●●● *Spacemaster* ●	Support vines. Need rich, well-drained soil, frequent feeding and watering. Hand pollinate.
..." diam., 12" deep ...1 plant	*Dusky,* ● *Long Tom Small Fruited* ●	
...diam., 8" deep for ...lant	Any	Like cool weather. A leafy member of the cabbage family with a delicate cabbage flavour, for use raw or cooked. Harvest outside leaves.
...diam. 8" deep for ...lant	Leaf varieties easier and earlier than head. Choose slow-bolting varieties.	Like cool weather. Try decorative varieties — red, etc.
...in to 2" apart, 6" deep	*Beltsville Bunching* ●	Prefer cool soil, good watering. Use in borders of other containers.
...' diam. for 3 plants, ...' deep	Edible-podded peas produce greater harvests - *Sugar Snap* ●●● *Dwarf Grey Sugar* ●● *Wando* ● is a heat-resistant regular pea.	Like cool weather, lots of water, support vines. Plant seeds in early spring or late summer. Pick often.
...diam., 1' deep for ...lant	*Canapé* ● *Earliest Red Sweet* ● *Park's Pot* ●	Water often, feed weekly after bloom. In windy areas, stake plants.
...ace 2" apart, 6"-12" ...p depending on variety	Grow variety to suit container. Small types can be grown around other plants.	Can be seeded and harvested all season, but taste best in cool weather.
...ace 6" apart, 6" deep	Choose slow-bolting varieties like *Melody* ●●●	Pick outer leaves. Harvest entire plant as soon as flower buds form. Like cool weather, loose, fertile soil.
...diam., 2' deep for ...lant	Any	Require heavy watering and fertilizing. Constant picking of small fruit prolongs harvest. Hand pollinate.
...diam., 6" deep for ...rries, 12" diam. 2' ...p for standard	*Tiny Tim* ●●● *Sweet 100* ●●● *Moira* ● *City Best* ●	Stake tall varieties. Keep watering and fertilizing programme consistent. Basil, parsley or oregano can be seeded in the box.

...ominion Seed House
...eorgetown, Ontario L7G 4A2

●**Burpee Seed Company**
  Warminster, Pennsylvania 18991

●**Geo. W. Park Seed Co. Inc.**
  Box 31
  Greenwood, South Carolina 29647

...he above seed companies will mail a free catalogue upon request.

Wooden crates, used alone, are often leaky enough to eliminate the need to drill drainage holes. (One Toronto high-rise gardener set a routine of watering in the very early morning so that the tenants downstairs wouldn't see water streaking from her balcony down their outside wall.)

If possible, the containers should be filled with a mix containing rich topsoil from a ground-level gardener or farmer. Potting soil from a supermarket can be good or it can be poor, but it is always expensive. If gathering soil on an excursion to the countryside, avoid the temptation to take any material from the side of a busy road. Such earth is inevitably contaminated with the heavy metals lead and cadmium and thus is unsafe for use in growing vegetables.

To help lighten the weight load — both for carrying and to avoid detaching balcony from building — soil is usually mixed with peat moss, perlite or vermiculite (expanded volcanic material and puffed mica, respectively). These substances also serve to improve the texture of the soil, which is unlikely to have the benefit of earthworms or decomposing organic matter to aerate the soil.

A full-fledged balcony garden could easily destroy the composure of most high-rise architects, and it is wise to keep in mind the fact that a cubic foot of soil weighs roughly 25 pounds, and most balconies are built to bear a maximum of 55 pounds per square foot. To avoid undue stress, place large containers against the wall and do not build rooftop grow-boxes without first investigating the strength of the roof supports.

Through trial and error, the Montreal group found that the ideal soil mix was seven parts topsoil and one part composed of equal portions of peat moss, vermiculite and perlite. The peat and vermiculite tend to hold moisture, the perlite promotes good drainage; all three lighten the load.

Pat Rogal is one person who has decided that she will have none of the staggering-under-a-bag-of-dirt routine. She gets potting soil from Simpsons, who deliver it right to her 18th-floor doorway, along with the vermiculite and peat moss. Each spring, she buys a bag of composted manure — "No Smell, No Burn" — and says that if she turns some of this into the top few inches of soil in each container, she needs to replace the soil only every three or four years. In fact, the firmly rooted apartment dweller may find that he never need replace his soil if he carries out a conscientious programme of fertilization, adding compost and manure each spring or fall, and using a fish emulsion fertilizer throughout the season.

Rybczynski's group discovered that plant growth and production was measurably improved with regular feedings of organic fertilizer every third week. Their combination included bone meal, granite dust, flaked seaweed, blood meal and liquid fish emulsion. A cheaper substitute would be a manure tea, made by soaking a cheesecloth bag filled with cow or horse manure, or perhaps a rich compost, in water overnight. The resulting fluid offers the plants an array of nutrients in a readily available form, and the remaining solid waste is mixed into the soil.

Large amounts of soil mix can be prepared en masse in the bathtub, in a garbage can dedicated to the purpose or in the individual containers themselves. Well-rotted manure or compost is a vital ingredient in any soil mix, especially if the base is commercial potting soil, which can be so thoroughly processed as to be nearly devoid of nutrients.

NATURAL RESTRICTIONS

Among the vegetables best suited to zero-elbow-room culture are peppers, tomatoes, eggplants, herbs, lettuce, green onions, snow peas, carrots and cucumbers. Others, such as potatoes, will produce but with such limited yield as to put them into the curiosity class. A single potato plant will turn out attractive foliage but may present the gardener with nothing more than a handful of small spuds by fall.

Some vegetables are simply out-of-bounds for even the most generous-sized balconies. Corn, for instance, must be planted in groups for pollination to occur. It will blow over easily, requires about 72 cubic feet of very rich soil for just one or two dozen harvestable ears and is on all counts a poor choice for a balcony plant. Likewise, a single pumpkin vine can blanket 50 square feet of garden with its huge leaves and massive fruit.

However, urban gardeners report success in growing the less rampant summer squash varieties — compact or bush types of zucchini or crookneck — which tend to become more manageable and less wildly over-productive in a container. Their attractive yellow flowers must, however, be hand pollinated because bees are rare guests of downtown, upper-floor gardens. Most other vegetables will be successfully pollinated by the high-rise winds.

By-passing the seed catalogue pages dedicated to corn, potatoes, squash, melons, Brussels sprouts and cauliflower, the apartment gardener can still find a vast array of likely fare for his little piece of the outdoors. Among beans, he may choose from both the pole and bush varieties.

Pole beans are ideal for a fairly sheltered balcony, one that is not attacked by vicious winds, and that gets some direct sunlight. Most pole beans are more prolific than their bush counterparts. The vines will wind around anything vertical that they touch, so the beans can be trained against strings, poles, or, if wind is a problem, a trellis against the wall. Their *raison d'être* will be as much decoration as sustenance. One is not likely to reap a bumper bean harvest from the number of plants that can be grown on a standard-sized balcony, but beans produce attractive flowers and foliage, as well as their fruit. Among the pole varieties, *Scarlet Runner* is very popular for its decorative clustered red blooms. The less attractive *Romano* produces a broader bean with better flavour than *Scarlet Runner,* and is the type that Hellen Ostler chooses. *Selma-Zebra* is a particularly early and short-vined bean (six feet maximum), better suited to balconies with limited sunshine and less vertical space for vines.

Like pole beans, peas take advantage of the space above the pots, clambering up vertical supports, but they require cooler early spring temperatures and demand heavy watering. The edible-podded varieties will give the best return per vine. Elizabeth Mobbs, who spent four years in an apartment above Toronto's Davisville area before moving down to

terra firma, liked *Dwarf Grey Sugar* snow peas, which require no staking. The new *Sugar Snap* peas, although they demand about six feet of vertical support, have plumper shells than the usual snow peas and should produce an even larger harvest. The McGill project found that *Little Sweetie* edible-podded peas outproduced all the other varieties they tried *(Sugar Snap* was not available at that time) and among conventional peas, they favoured the heat-resistant *Wando.*

Among cabbages, the Montreal participants discovered that miniature varieties, like *Morden Midget* were the most economical space users, but miniature varieties of root vegetables like *Parisien* carrots did not take full advantage of the depth of the McGill containers. The Montrealers settled on standard-sized carrots, although gardeners with shallow containers might want to plant short or round varieties.

Tomatoes are the staple crop of just about every garden, above or on the ground. Bush-type plants with small tomatoes, such as *Tiny Tim* cherry tomatoes, or climbing small-fruited varieties like *Sweet 100,* are ideal. Patricia Rogal figures that, because her balcony receives only four hours of sunshine daily in mid-summer, her *Tiny Tims* take longer to begin producing than the usual 45 days, but they still manage to develop ample fruit for salads during August and September. Larger tomatoes, although more difficult to grow, are tempting. Choose an early variety like *Moira,* a dwarf bush beefsteak, the first year, and see if conditions are favourable enough on your balcony to allow larger fruits to mature.

Peppers are popular and often successful on the balcony. Like tomatoes, they require at least several hours of sunshine daily. Well-tended, this is one vegetable that can actually make a difference in the grocery bill. Early, compact varieties like *Canape* should be chosen. Do not overlook yellow peppers,

Recycled boxes from Chinese groceries and insulated cold frames both worked well for Montreal community rooftop gardeners.

which are often easier to grow than the green varieties. (Peppers, incidentally are perennials. If the container is portable, simply bring the plant indoors when frost threatens. Water it all winter, and put it back on the balcony next spring. It may look a bit straggly after a winter indoors, but will quickly revive to produce very early peppers. Be sure to acclimatize it before it is to be put back outdoors, by moving it out for just a few hours the first day or two, and by shading it for its first week on the balcony.)

Cucumbers are another crop that takes advantage of vertical space, and does so admirably. The McGill students report: "Cucumbers, when strung, give prodigious yields. A hybrid gynoecious variety called *Victory* grew nine feet high in three months. The harvest was excellent. We did discover, however, that cucumbers require a soil depth of at least two and a half feet if they are to produce to potential."

Burpee Seeds has developed a *Spacemaster* cucumber especially for container growing, and recommends one plant to a six or seven inch (diameter) pot, or three plants to a 12 or 13 inch pot. These plants must be kept well-watered — once a day on most balconies — especially during hot, dry weather.

Leafy vegetables — lettuce, spinach and Swiss chard — can be quite successful if faithfully watered. Chard is especially hardy, and is a good substitute for spinach, which must be planted early as it goes to seed with July's high temperatures. Leaf lettuce varieties are less demanding than the heading types, and will also provide earlier salads. The McGill students liked *Buttercrunch.* Kohlrabi, broccoli and regular-sized cabbages will require big, deep pots, and will probably not pay for themselves, but again, smaller and earlier varieties are the best.

choice for the gardener who is nevertheless anxious to grow them.

Both annual and perennial herbs can be ideal balcony plants. Annuals, like basil and dill, which grow, go to seed and die in a single season, can be treated in much the same way as leafy vegetables. Parsley, a biennial, will produce nutritious greenery for two seasons before going to seed, and can be brought indoors to provide sprigs for winter dishes. Chives, likewise, can be brought indoors in winter or left on the balcony. Betty Mobbs used to plant chives, sage and wild marjoram, all perennials, in Styrofoam pots on her balcony. In winter, she would place another Styrofoam pot on top of the plant and wrap everything in a plastic bag. That way, she says, they wintered successfully. Patricia reports that her chives, planted in a packing crate two years ago and left on the balcony year-round, have reappeared to

This highly successful rooftop garden in Montreal included some 250 growing boxes, as well as greenhouses and a compost bin.

grace salads each spring. Thyme and mint should do the same. Tender perennials like rosemary and bay can be moved indoors in fall and wintered on a sunny window sill.

Watering, which commences as soon as the soil is mixed and continues, sometimes daily, until frost kills the most tender plants, is critical and even defeats some city high-risers. Mary Warkentin tried to grow tomatoes and herbs on her Toronto balcony one summer, but was discouraged after a weekend away from her apartment. "The plants were scorched," she says. "Having a garden is like having a cat or a dog. You have to be there all the time." Nevertheless, most apartment dwellers are able to coerce a friend into watering on the occasional weekend, and the gardener who finds he must neglect his plants for a few days can take precautions. Water in early morning or late evening — whenever the sun is not striking the plants — and then enclose the pot (but not the plant) in a plastic bag or sheets of plastic, covering as much of the soil as possible. Sheets or mats can be hung and secured on the sides of the balcony to reduce exposure to the sun and wind. Or, if the plants are not too large, they can be moved indoors for the gardener's holiday.

In the meantime, a special connection from the kitchen sink to the balcony will make watering easier. Watering must be very thorough, to assure that the soil is saturated enough for water to seep out of the bottom of the pot after each session. When the soil surface is dry, in the case of seeds or seedlings, or, for larger plants, when the top half-inch is dry, it is time to water. Use water that is at room temperature, particularly on sensitive seeds and seedlings.

When the produce is ready for the table, the city gardener should take care to wash all vegetables. He may have been scrupulous in not using sprays on his plants but, unfortunately, city air can be laden with chemicals of its own. Lead levels, especially, can be high in city-grown produce, especially if it is grown very close to a busy street, or in the path of polluted exhausts. If your balcony is receiving a regular coating of soot or other pollutants, you may want to follow the directions suggested by the Institute for Local Self-Reliance in Washington, D.C. which has been doing tests on its own city-grown vegetables. Fruiting crops such as tomatoes, peppers and cucumbers, they say, accumulate the least lead, with root crops and leafy crops attaining respectively more. As younger plants are the most contaminant free, plant and harvest frequently. Better soil quality also apparently helps the plant resist lead accumulation.

The most encouraging news comes from McGill University's Department of Renewable Resources, whose easily followed advice states, "Washing might be most beneficial in removing the contaminant." They also point out that there are positive aspects of city pollution: Plants thrive better in air that is enriched with carbon dioxide, and polluted air contains more carbon dioxide than unpolluted air. In addition, the plants produce oxygen, enriching the air where they grow.

Improved — albeit thin — air will be the least visible of the balcony gardener's contributions to his surroundings. Hundreds of tenants behind other, barren balconies will now be treated to the spectacle of a patch of green and the occasional tendings of the high-rise horticulturist. There are few gardens that can be enjoyed by so many people, including the gardener himself, who reaps a host of tangible and intangible rewards. Of her balcony garden, Patricia Rogal says simply, "It is a *joy.*"

Sources

ROOFTOP WASTELANDS
By the Minimum Cost Housing Group
School of Architecture
McGill University
3480 University Street
Montreal, Quebec H3A 2A7
Useful advice, gained through experience, for both balcony and rooftop gardeners. This study formed the basis of the government pamphlet "Container Gardening," publication 1653 available free from:
Information Services
Agriculture Canada
Ottawa, Ontario K1A 0C7

THE CITY PEOPLE'S BOOK
OF RAISING FOOD
By Helga and William Olkowski
Rodale Press, Inc.
Emmaus, Pennsylvania 18049
240 pages, paperback
Most of this book is dedicated to backyard, city gardens, but there is some information on container gardening.

GARDENING INDOORS
WITH HOUSE PLANTS
By Raymond Poincelot
Rodale Press, Inc.
Emmaus, Pennsylvania 18049
266 pages, paperback
Unique among the proliferation of house plant books, this illustrated guide offers detailed information on growing fruits, herbs, vegetables and ornamental house plants. Includes information on more than 200 species, including latest hybrids.

GREEN THINGS IN SMALL SPACES
By Marnie Collins
Methuen, Inc.
572 Fifth Ave.
New York, N.Y. 10036
154 pages, paperback
Geared to houseplants, but includes a few pages on balcony vegetables, hydroponic systems.

GARDENING IN CONTAINERS
By the Editors of Sunset Books
and Sunset Magazine
Lane Publishing Co.
Menlo Park, California 94025
80 pages, paperback
Large format, colourful book, more concerned with decorative than practical applications of container gardening.

The Tomato Ward

Contending with Blackheart, Catface, Leather-End and an array of other maladies that afflict our most popular garden crop

"If it rained, they stood apathetically about in the passages. Most of them, moreover, were suffering from malnutrition, because with the lapse of time they had contracted a distaste for the monotonous fare.... Many suffered, too, from the cold... weakened in body and soul, the slightest ailment meant a real illness which it was very hard to get at and treat correctly."

—*Albert Schweitzer,*
Out of My Life and Thought

This description of ailing prisoners may seem hauntingly familiar to gardeners whose tomato patches have begun to blossom with problems, becoming — in the worst years — a veritable rogues' gallery of strange foliage and strange fruit. Likening the modern garden tomato to a prisoner becomes much less far-fetched when one considers that man has captured the marble-sized wild *Lycopersicon* of South America, confined it, and bred it into the prodigious ultra-beefsteak-type fruits that we have come to covet.

In the past 40 years alone, horticulturists have managed to increase the commercial yield per acre of tomatoes by more than 400 per cent. The fruit that just 80 years ago was widely feared as poisonous — it is related to belladona, mandrake and other nightshades — now stands as the most important source of vitamins and minerals in the North American diet. Canadians consume an estimated 40 pounds each annually, and the per capita consumption in the United States exceeds 55 pounds; neither of these figures includes home-grown crops.

In making the tomato so fruitful and in extending its range virtually throughout the world, man has exposed this plant to an array of diseases and parasites. Hundreds of generations removed from their tough little South American ancestors, today's tomato plants with their huge, thin-skinned fruits have become easy marks for a host of wilts, blights, rots, spots and mosaics. North American varieties of *Lycopersicon esculentum* may be attacked by one or more of some 50 common afflictions, including such richly named horrors as Blackheart, Tobacco Etch, Catface, Buckeye Rot and Ghost Spot. Although many gardeners go years without a serious tomato problem, there are seasons when things seem to take a page out of Lewis Carroll and become "curiouser and curiouser."

The orthodox approach, still widely touted by radio columnists and mainstream garden writers, is to spray and dust the tomato patch regularly, whether it needs it or not. To these growers, tomato culture would not be complete without face mask, rubber gloves and sacks of Malathion, Maneb and Carbaryl. This, of course, is the California system in miniature; there, many growers routinely sterilize their fields, lay a plastic mulch and, at regularly scheduled intervals, dispense fungicides and pesticides until the fruit is picked, still green enough and hard enough to withstand anything short of a direct hit by a forklift tire. Much of this phrenetic and antiseptic activity is done for the benefit of the supermarket shopper; beauty in the celluloid tomato package is as deep as a clear, pale pink skin.

Fortunately, most gardeners are much more tolerant of imperfections. (As the old saying goes, "Every mother thinks her own geese are swans.") The organic gardener, especially, may be willing to accept the occasional blemish in return for a residue-free harvest of fully ripe, deep red tomatoes which have completed their flavour development. (Box-ripened commercial fruits suffer from contain-

Rudy Muller

ing too much starch, too little natural sugar and appreciably lower levels of vitamin C or ascorbic acid.)

EVASIVE ACTION

Flavour, in fact, is a factor that seldom enters into present-day commercial tomato production, in which sheer quantity and external appearance count for all. Crowding of plants, lack of crop rotation and the culture of a single variety — all conditions that encourage disease and serious pest damage — are almost endemic in commercial tomato farming, but are easily avoided in the home garden.

Disease management — minimizing the possibility of a disease starting or modifying its effects should it get a foothold — rather than ironclad control, the complete eradication of disease, should be the goal on the home front. It is now generally recognized that pesticide and fungicide use tends to lead to an ever-increasing need for pesticides and fungicides, and the backyard gardener is wise to avoid, or interrupt, such a cycle.

Fortunately for those of us who savour a truly garden fresh, juicy tomato, the factors that encourage high productivity and good flavour are intertwined with the non-chemical practices of disease management.

The organic garden health care plan for tomatoes is based on the proverbial "ounce of prevention" — from seed choice to tomato harvest and fall clean-up. The first step, of course, is to recognize the pestilence that has visited one's tomato rows and then begin a course of action to moderate its effects or evade its path next year.

SEED SELECTION

Having bred the natural broad-spectrum disease resistance out of the tomato, man is now industriously putting it back, malady by malady. "Resistance" as a descriptive term in the seed catalogues means virtual immunity to a particular disease and it is a factor well worth noting in selecting seed or buying transplants. The in-bred resistance is usually created by crossing domesticated tomato vari-

Dr. Arden Sherf and Agriculture Canada

Infectious or non-infectious, all tomato maladies are more easily avoided if the gardener is aware of the needs of tomatoes in general and his variety in particular. While Bacterial Leaf Spot, lower right, is caused by a disease organism that may infect plants in a close, humid greenhouse environment, both Blossom-End Rot, lower left, and Walnut Wilt, left, are caused by unsuitable outdoor growing conditions alone. Blossom-End Rot usually ruins the first fruit that develops during hot, dry summer weather. Tomato plants grown too close to a walnut tree will exhibit the symptoms of Walnut Wilt.

eties with wild relatives that have inborn resistance. The native South American *Lycopersicon hirsutum,* for instance, has a natural pest resistance and may lead to the development of future varieties that pests will shun. Such resistance can also be achieved, painstakingly, by grafting. Some varieties of nightshade are resistant to soil-borne wilt diseases; if a tomato is grafted onto such a rootstock, it will inherit the resistance. (Grafting research hit a temporary cul-de-sac when a tomato was grafted onto a nematode-resistant jimson weed root. The nematodes wisely steered clear of the plant, whose natural toxins suffused the roots, the vine and the fruit, making it inedible.) Genetic changes induced by certain chemicals or by radiation may also confer disease resistance upon a new tomato variety.

Plants that are resistant to Verticillium Wilt, one of the most common and destructive fungus diseases, are marked with the letter "V" or "VR" after the variety name. The letter "F" indicates resistance to Fusarium Wilt (rarely a problem in Canada), and "N" is added if the plant is resistant to attack by nematodes. For example, Stokes Seeds' catalogue describes *Ultra Boy VFN* thus: "*Ultra Boy*'s multi-tolerance to Verticillium, Fusarium and nematodes provides market gardeners and home gardeners with a good protection from troublesome wilts and blights. This disease tolerance lengthens the growing season and enables growers to pick amazing yields per plant — if properly cared for and fertilized." ("VF" is sufficiently important that some commercial varieties dispense entirely with more descriptive names. The most popular variety among commercial growers in California is the mundanely-labelled *VF 145.)*

Resistance to fruit cracking is often mentioned in the variety description. *Burpee's VF Hybrid,* while not resistant to nematodes, is described as having "amazing crack resistance."

Other varieties are "tolerant" to certain diseases — that is, they may be affected in an epidemic, but will probably not be killed. Tolerance is usually mentioned in the variety description. For instance, *Veemore* tomatoes, though they do not receive the "VF" label, are described by one seedsman as "tolerant to both Verticillium and Fusarium." Tolerance is ample protection in most home garden situations.

It is important to note that disease resistance is no guarantee of good flavour, and many organic gardeners decide to risk a disease outbreak in favour of a well-loved variety that is, as far as catalogue descriptions indicate, utterly defenceless. Many gardeners save, and swear by, seed of a favoured non-hybrid tomato whose offspring, unprotected by genetic armour, produce bountiful harvests every year. On the other hand, the variety *Floramerica VFN,* an All-America medal winner, may be resistant to "VFN" and tolerant to another dozen or so diseases, but its flavour has been found to be mediocre by some gardeners. Furthermore, "VFN" varieties may be just as vulnerable to unlisted ailments as are any other varieties. The *Beefeater Hybrid VFN* plants grown by one gardener of our acquaintance were initially set back

by Blossom End Rot and Blackheart, but eventually produced large, delicious fruit. A gardener will be wise to grow more than one variety each year if possible, to provide a measure of "health insurance," and to vary the harvest.

GOOD EARTH

Although the tomato plant is widely adapted to diverse environments, it thrives best under full sunlight and in a fertile, well-drained soil high in organic matter. Tomatoes grown in shady conditions have little chance of maturing fruit, while those grown in depleted soil will be scraggly and unproductive; in both cases, the plants are decidedly more vulnerable to disease and pest damage than healthy vines.

Old hands at tomato culture are aware of the value of rich soil, and most have fallen into a pattern of adding fresh manure to the space which will host their tomatoes the following spring or of working well-rotted manure or good compost into the soil two or three weeks before setting out the new transplants. Tomatoes are among the heaviest of garden feeders and fertile soil not only helps minimize disease problems, but prevents disorders related to deficiencies in soil nutrients. (A boron shortage, for instance, will produce misshapen tomatoes with scabby or corky patches on the skin.) In addition to animal manures and compost, tomato grounds benefit from the tilling in of wood ashes, which supply potassium, and bone meal, which is rich in phosphorous.

Tomatoes in most soils respond well to a booster dose of manure "tea" or other highly soluble fertilizer early in the growing season. By the time the first fruits are the size of a golf ball, the gardener should pour a bucket of manure tea or fertilizer solution around each plant. Manure tea is an unappetizing brew made by steeping several healthy handsful of fresh or rotten manure overnight in a pailful of water. The resulting liquid is infused with nutrients which easily soak in around the tomato roots to encourage adequate plant growth and good sizing of the fruit. Fish fertilizer emulsions and blood meal, which is highly soluble, will achieve the same results.

Too much fertilization, however, can encourage over-exuberant foliage growth to the detriment of fruit development. If overfed by fresh manure or by too heavy application of any nitrogen-rich fertilizer, blossoms may drop, rendering the vine useless but for its beauty as a green plant.

LOCATIONS

In setting tomato plants out, the rule of thumb is to leave three feet between rows and three feet between individual vines. Staked tomatoes — the so-called indeterminate varieties — may be planted somewhat closer, as may vines that will be trained up a wall or trellis.

To minimize the possibility of the spread of disease from one vegetable species to another, do not plant the tomato's garden relatives — eggplant, peppers, potatoes, or tobacco — near their red-fruited kin. Cucumbers and melons can also host tomato diseases. Leaf crops, onions, root crops, herbs, or *Brassicas* like cabbage, Brussels sprouts and broccoli are better bed mates for tomatoes. Nearby basil plants are rumoured to enhance tomato flavour, while marigolds, which can help ward off nematodes, are a particularly good companion crop. A chemical component of asparagus will also help prevent nematode infestation, and while it is hardly practical to plant tomatoes in the perennial asparagus bed, the organic gardener can take advantage of this valuable quality by pouring the water from cooked asparagus around his tomato seedlings.

Every year the tomato plants should be set in a different spot in the garden, so that any one spot is used no more frequently than once every three years. This helps soil fertility — different crops utilize, or even add, different nutrients — and also helps discourage diseases that live in decaying bits of tomato vegetation, or even in the soil where tomatoes were grown. In addition, tomatoes should not be planted where a botanical relative was sown the previous year.

One key to disease control is the elimination of any plant material which may harbour pathogenic organisms over the winter. Any diseased tomatoes or vines that appear should be collected and disposed of well away from the garden — not added to the compost pile or simply turned back into the soil. If a viral, fungal or bacterial outbreak occurs in an entire patch, all vegetation should be properly disposed of outside the confines of the garden once the season — or the plants — are finished. (The same holds true for diseased potatoes and potato vines, which can serve as a wintering ground for serious problems.)

MULCH & MOISTURE

Keeping the fruits from direct contact with the soil also helps prevent the loss of individual fruits to fungus, rot and certain insects. Staked tomatoes, of course, ride above many of these afflictions, but determinate — non-staking — varieties can be helped by a surrounding bed of mulch. Mulch also serves the important role of preventing sharp fluctuations of the moisture level in the soil. Mulching around plants helps to conserve moisture by discouraging evaporation from the soil, ensuring that mulched plants are more resistant to drought and certain drought-generated disorders than unmulched vines.

One caveat regarding mulch: It should not be applied too early. A heavy coating of mulch applied before the soil is warm will serve to set back transplants, which thrive on warmth. Once the plants are growing well and hot weather has set in, mulch may be laid down. (In permanent mulching systems, the covering layer can be drawn apart and the seedlings set in and allowed to establish themselves for several weeks before the blanket of mulch is tucked tight around them.) Plastic mulch, either black or clear, works well with tomatoes, but is expensive and adds nothing to soil fertility. Straw, old hay, grass clippings and leaves all work to conserve moisture, prevent weed growth and protect fruit from contact with soil-borne disease organisms while slowly adding to the health of the earth beneath.

Part and parcel of any disease control or prevention programme is the ability to recognize the different common tomato maladies, after which one can work to thwart them or at least lessen their ravages. The following problems are those most frequently encountered by gardeners in Canada and the northern United States.

FUNGAL DISEASES, include many different "blights" and "wilts," and are caused by microscopic parasitic plants that live on plants and on dead organic matter. Encouraged by damp, warm, overcrowded conditions, they produce spores which blow or are brushed or washed from plant to plant. Such spores often overwinter in rotting vegetation in the soil and erupt again when conditions are favourable. Anything that encourages good air circulation and good soil drainage and minimizes the handling of damp plants will help discourage fungal diseases.

Damping Off is caused by various fungi that live in the soil. It attacks young seedlings before or after they emerge from the soil, until they are about two weeks old. The affected stem shrivels and darkens at the soil line so that the young plant topples and dies.

When starting seeds indoors, garden soil should be sterilized before planting. Bake it in a shallow pan for an hour in a 200 degree F oven. As a further precaution, peat moss, which is slightly acidic and inhibits the fungus, can be mixed into the soil or sprinkled over it. Purchased sterilized potting soil or components such as peat moss, vermiculite or perlite need not be sterilized. Water the seed medium and seedlings only when almost dry. Excessive dampness favours fungal growth — hence the name, "damping off."

Early Blight is also known as "target spot" because of the circular dark brown or black spots of concentric rings that appear on affected leaves, which eventually die and drop off. When it attacks the stem with a black lesion, the disease is often called "collar rot." Although infection of the fruit itself is rare in the home garden, partial defoliation of the plant will nevertheless lower fruit size and quality.

Like damping off, Early Blight often attacks young seedlings. It too can be discouraged with a sterilized planting medium and by giving seedlings ample space in well-drained flats. If seedlings become infected before transplanting, discard them.

Septoria Leaf Spot flourishes in times of heavy rain and warm weather, first producing small, circular grey to tan-coloured spots on the lower leaves, stems and petioles (the small stems that support each leaf). In the centre of these spots, small black "pimples," the fruiting bodies of the fungus, may be seen with a hand lens or sometimes by the naked eye. Millions of spores produced in these pimples are splashed about by rain and irrigation and give rise to new infections in a few days. Infected leaves dry out and die from the base of the plant upwards. Although the fruits are rarely affected, fruit size and quality are lowered as the plant weakens from leaf loss. In addition, the remaining fruit is exposed to possible sunscald.

This fungus can overwinter on weeds or the remains of tomato plants. Be sure to plough in all remaining (healthy) tomato vegetation when the harvest is complete, or remove it to the compost pile. The remains of affected plants should be discarded away from the garden.

Late Blight erupts during the showery, cloudy days of late summer. It is not usually seen until a heavy foliage has developed and harvest has commenced. Although it is more commonly a disease of potatoes, Late Blight can be passed from infected potatoes to tomato plants (or vice versa) and will infest tomatoes severely. Greenish-black spots appear on the oldest leaves, enlarging rapidly. (The quickness of spread of crop diseases such as this led to the term "wild fire.") Bluish-grey fungus may appear under the leaves, virtually all of which will die. Infected, rotten fruits exude a musty, disagreeable odour.

Destroy affected tomato or potato plants, and all tubers. Potatoes and tomatoes should not be interplanted in the garden. If Late Blight has been a problem, choose a blight-resistant variety like *New Yorker* standard-sized tomatoes or *Nova* paste tomatoes the following year.

Anthracnose is a disease on ripe, red fruit. Spores of the fungus are spread by rain to green fruits where infection occurs, although it is not evident until the fruit ripens. Small, slightly sunken, circular spots appear and grow up to one-half inch in diameter, often merging to cover most of the fruit, particularly the lower side. The skin over these spots may crack, allowing other fungi to grow. Serious wastage results because the gardener must cut away blemished areas before eating or canning fruit.

This fungus persists through the winter on infected plant refuse. Remove all such vegetation after harvest and discard it away from the garden. Do not plant tomatoes or a relative in the affected spot in the garden for two or three years. Supporting the fruit above the ground will help prevent Anthracnose infection.

Verticillium Wilt is one of the most destructive of garden fungi, with strains attacking potatoes, peppers, melons and some berries and fruits as well as tomatoes. The fungus is capable of surviving several years in soil debris, then entering the roots and invading the water-conducting system of the plant. It is first evident as the wilting of one or two leaflets of a single, lower leaf. Leaves wilt and die progressively from the base to the top of the plant, some-

A.F. Sherf and C.D. McKeen

Prevention is the key to organic disease control. Once any of these diseases has infected a plant, the plant cannot be restored to health by natural methods. **Above,** *the fungal disease Verticillium Wilt affects many garden plants, but its infection of tomatoes can be prevented by purchasing resistant seed. Cucumber Mosaic,* **far right,** *is the result of a virus, and so is highly contagious. Bacterial Speck,* **right,** *like other bacteria-caused diseases, is seldom a problem in the garden, although it can trouble greenhouse gardeners.*

times on one side of the plant only. The plant itself may not die but will produce small fruit.

Choose resistant or tolerant varieties if Verticillium Wilt has been a problem.

VIRAL DISEASES, the "mosaics," are caused by organisms so miniscule that they can be seen only with an electron microscope. Often transmitted from host plants by insects like aphids or by the gardener himself, virus-caused diseases are best prevented by a conscientious programme of cleanliness.

Tomato Mosaic known commercially as "TMV" and **Cucumber Mosaic** cause light to dark green mottling of the leaves — a "mosaic" effect. Leaflets are usually distorted, puckered, and smaller than usual, sometimes assuming an indented "fern" shape. Plants will usually become pale green and spindly, and the harvest will be small and late.

Highly infectious, Mosaics are transmitted by leaf pruning and plant handling, and from such plants as petunias, snapdragons, peppers and tobacco. Do not grow tomatoes near these plants. It can also be present in smoking or chewing tobacco, so if the gardener uses tobacco he should wash his hands thoroughly with soap and water before handling tomato plants.

Cucumber Mosaic is often transmitted by aphids, especially when cucumbers or melons and tomatoes are interplanted.

BACTERIAL DISEASES are caused by single-celled organisms. Seldom a serious problem in the home garden, they may, however, present difficulties in a crowded, closed greenhouse environment (where virtually all types of diseases are likely to thrive).

In the greenhouse, use a sterilized medium for starting seedlings and for larger plants as well, if possible. Diseases like **Bacterial Canker, Bacterial Spot** and **Bacterial Wilt** can be discouraged by disinfecting pruning tools frequently, and washing one's hands often while working with tomato plants.

The first symptom of a bacterial disease is the wilting of leaflets. They become brown, dying from the margins toward the midribs. There may be a blackish speckling or spotting of fruit. Infected plants may die or they may survive in a wilted condition, bearing little fruit. Such plants must be removed and destroyed as soon as disease symptoms are noted. Any plants that have come in contact with the diseased plant should be destroyed also.

*Fruit Cracking, **near left,** is unsightly, but will not affect tomato flavour, provided the fruit is picked before skin breaks become infected. Cracks are caused by less-than-ideal growing conditions, and should cease when the weather improves. Fusarium Wilt, **far left,** is seldom a problem for northern gardens, and in any case, can be avoided with resistant seed varieties. Late Blight, **above,** is a fungal disease that may appear if the harvest season is especially damp and if plants are unhealthy or overcrowded.*

NON-PARASITIC DISEASES erupt when environmental conditions are less than ideal. They are not spread to or from other plants, but are temporary conditions that will pass when growing conditions improve.

Blossom-End Rot usually develops on the first fruits of a plant to ripen or on clusters of fruits formed during a prolonged hot, droughty period. A hard, sunken, dark area appears on the blossom (lower) end of the fruit, and spreads as the tomato ripens. The repulsive internal blackening called **Blackheart** is caused by the same conditions but may be present without the external symptoms appearing.

Blossom-End Rot and Blackheart may also be caused by a calcium deficiency in the soil. Calcium, which is required by rapidly growing plants, can be added to the soil in the form of finely ground limestone, gypsum or eggshells, before the plants are set out in the garden. Weekly, deep watering during droughts will help discourage the disorder. Mulch young plants in spring. If Blossom-End Rot is noticed, pick all damaged fruits and discard them, leaving the plant to put its strength into the healthy fruit.

Fruit Cracking is a response to radical changes in temperature and moisture, usually wet weather following hot, dry conditions. Concentric circular or radial, outward-pointing cracks develop at the stem end, and may provide entrance for fungi and other diseases.

Little can be done to prevent Fruit Cracking of susceptible varieties, although a consistent watering programme may help: Cracking, like Blossom-End Rot, can be reduced by mulching plants. It may be necessary to pick affected fruits before they are entirely ripe, allowing them to ripen indoors so that cracks will not become infected. Choose crack-resistant varieties.

Leather-End is a fruit condition characterized by bronzing and roughening of the skin at the *stem* end of the fruit. This affects only the appearance of the fruit and the texture of the affected skin, which becomes tough and leathery. The disorder develops late in the season, when the weather is cloudy and the long nights are cool. Gardeners who have persistent problems with Leather-End can pick the fruit while it is still green, and allow it to ripen indoors.

Sunscald may occur whenever green or ripening fruits are exposed to the hot sun for several days. A yellowish-white area of sunken tissue appears on the side of the fruit facing the sun. This may turn blistery and will flatten to a large, greyish-white spot with a very thin paper-like surface. Fungus infections often occur on such spots.

Defoliation, whether caused by excessive pruning or attack by disease, encourages Sunscald. Defoliated plants may require shading with cloth during the hottest part of the day. Verticillium Wilt-resistant varieties are also resistant to Sunscald.

Walnut Wilt is an example of a negative sort of companion planting. Walnut tree roots secrete *juglone*, a toxin that kills tomato plants. Do not plant tomatoes within 40 or 50 feet of a walnut tree, or on land from which a walnut tree has been removed within the last three years.

Catface is a distortion of the blossom end of the tomato fruit. Occurring most commonly on first fruits, it often causes protuberances, scabs and scaly dark green scar tissue in folds. Affected fruits are edible once the scarred portion has been removed.

This temporary condition is caused by an abnormal development of the pistil of the tomato blossom, and is aggravated by serious disturbances to growth, such as prolonged cool weather during blossoming.

Leaf Roll is common, temporary and not a cause for concern. The edges of the leaves roll upward and inward, overlapping in severe cases. However, the growth of the plant is not checked and a normal harvest of fruit is produced. Leaf roll can be caused by heavy rains or severe pruning.

Blossom Drop. If a tomato plant is under stress, blossoms may simply grow and fall off because fruit growth requires a great deal of plant energy. Conditions that cause Blossom Drop include extreme temperatures, either too hot or too cold, or sudden, drastic changes in temperature. It can also be caused by too little light (less than six hours daily), too much or too little water, or over-fertilization. Too, if blossoms are unfertilized they will fall off, but this is a problem only in the greenhouse, and can be solved by lightly shaking flowering plants or hand-pollinating flowers with a artist's brush.

Frost Damage occurs if fruit is frozen or exposed to frost. Exposed areas become dark and soft, appear water-soaked and will deteriorate rapidly. Cover plants when light frost is expected, and pick all fruit before a hard frost (temperature under 30 degrees F). If fruit is damaged, use as soon as possible.

"To most people, the Highlander is a long-horned, shaggy-coated, ferocious wild animal that can be dug out of a glacier after several years' immersion, to continue its mastication of heather, bracken, stones, fence posts and preferably people, utterly immune to all forces of nature, including earthquakes and volcanic eruptions."

Wildly exaggerated, of course, but the first time I laid eyes on a Highland cow, those words from the British *Highland Breeders' Journal* seemed quite apt. My husband and I were travelling on the Island of Mull in the Scottish Hebrides, and we had pulled off the road onto the unfenced moor for lunch. A group of these shaggy, long-horned beasts suddenly loomed out of the mist. Although somewhat taken aback, we couldn't help but be fascinated by their rugged, romantic appearance.

Now, several years later, I know that the writer did have a point. Although anything but "ferocious" — a Vancouver Island breeder of our acquaintance has a hard time fending off her "pets" as they vie for the sensuous pleasure of being scratched with her currycomb — the Highland's greatest asset is its hardiness, its vigour in cold temperatures and its ability to thrive on the roughest of range. While I can't say that I've seen a Highland beast dug out of a glacier, it probably wouldn't look very different from ours on a January morning.

That first impression in Scotland led to our having a growing interest in the prehistoric-looking creatures, and eventually to our own involvement in rais-

Yon Bonny, Canny Kine

By Donalda Badone

The Highlander — worthy of Gaelic praises and a serious look by northern farmsteaders

ing Highlands back home in Ontario. This was partly a "roots" thing, since my father had come from
Scotland, but perhaps, too, we were still a little under
the spell of the Hebridean Islands with their magical
landscape and their insular Gaelic culture surviving
in the lonely crofts and harbours.

As it happened, somebody knew somebody
who had Highland cattle. The result was that
two years ago, six cows with calves at side
spent four days and nights travelling from
Alberta to Ontario in a cattle truck.
When the ramp was finally lowered to
our field in Willowdale, the long-
travelled animals scarcely uttered a
moo before settling down to serious
grazing.

J.D. Wilson

Originally bred in the Highlands and the western islands of Scotland, an area well-known for severe winters, rugged terrain and winds that sweep in from the Atlantic Ocean, the Highland breed seems custom-made for our climate. Although unpopular with most commercial beef breeders because of their relatively small size and their only middling performance on good grasslands and in the feedlot, Highlands are in their element on poor land. There are registered herds in every province west of Quebec, as well as in Alaska and the Northwest and Yukon Territories. We recently visited the farm of Henry Carse, a breeder in the mountains of Vermont, who feels that Highlands may be the answer to a commercially viable beef industry on the restricted diet provided in those inhospitable hills.

As one might suspect, no significant change has occurred in the physical conformation of the Highlands for centuries. In fact, they closely resemble the *Bos longifrons* or Celtic shorthorn, one of the earliest known domestic races of cattle. While most cattle are believed descended from the Aurochs (primitive ox of central Europe), the Highland traces its remote ancestry to the Celtic ox, which was smaller than the Auroch and had the dished face that is characteristic of the Highland.

Domestic cattle had to be almost as hardy as the ancient ox to survive a Highland winter. Those needed for meat were butchered in the fall, but the rest were wintered over with so little feed that by spring they could scarcely stand in their "byres" — stalls that were often divided by only a partition from the family living quarters in the tiny, thatched stone cottages. Each crofter cultivated his own small plot of land and raised his Highland cattle for milk, meat and hides, and to pull his plough and wagon.

Agricultural practices improved, however, in the late 18th and 19th centuries, and cattle owners became interested in selectively breeding their livestock to upgrade the most valued characteristics. The Highland became known as a beef breed, rather than primarily as a milker. The Highland Cattle Society of Scotland was established in 1884. Its present patron is Queen Elizabeth, who has a herd on her Balmoral estate. Highlands are now established all over the world, especially in colder climates, and breeders' societies have been formed in the United States, Sweden and Canada, where the Canadian Highland Cattle Society was founded in 1964. Each spring and autumn the most important Highland show and sale is held at Oban, Scotland, drawing buyers from Denmark and Japan to vie with New Zealanders and Americans in paying top prices for the champions. The prize male in the most recent sale was Jock 20th of Leys, who sold for 1500 guineas, almost $4,000. The impetus behind most of this competition can be understood by a recent article on Highland cattle in Sweden that appeared in the *Highland Breeders' Journal.*

"The scope for a breed which can exist outside with minimal attention, having good mothering quality, good foraging ability, and which can provide a well-fleshed, fat-free carcass is tremendous, and these are all qualities that the Highland breed has in abundance. Those who presently have herds are enthusiastic and convinced after one of the worst winters experienced in Scandinavia for a long time. Calves were born and nursed in considerable depths of snow in extreme temperatures and survived. The herds were generally fed on pole-dried hay and given a little shelter where they could feed — usually open-fronted sheds — but with many herds this was not available."

Here in Canada, animal scientist John Lawson has done considerable research since 1956 with Highland cattle at the Agriculture Canada research farm at Manyberries, Alberta. "Highlands," he says, "are being used in areas of Canada where other breeds won't reproduce and in some cases won't even survive."

Lawson has studied the productivity of Highland and Hereford dams over a five year period at the Alberta station, and his resulting figures are based on herds of 100 cows kept under "short-grass prairie range" conditions. The purebred Highland cattle produced almost a ton more calves than did Herefords under the same conditions. Highland-Hereford cross dams were the best performers of all three. (See charts.)

The Highland's vigour was proved by a University of Alberta study comparing bison, yak and two breeds of domestic cattle, Hereford and Highland, for their ability to survive and reproduce in a northern environment. The traits examined included "ability to utilize forages of varying quality, metabolic response to cold, and behaviour." The lowest critical temperature was discovered, below which the animal has to divert energy away from growth and production in order to maintain body heat.

As could be expected, the bison were hardier than the domestic cattle, but the Highlands equalled the yaks and exceeded, in ability to withstand cold, the Hereford, the common "red white-face," the world's most popular breed of beef cattle.

Our Highlands stayed outside through all the snowy months without noticeable discomfort, only moving to the lee of the barn or the shelter of the woods when the cold wind blew from the north. Calving on the snow was accomplished without any trouble.

David and Nancy Pease of Ontario discovered the characteristic vigour of Highland cattle quite by accident. Like us, they were first introduced to the animals during a trip to Scotland, and bought two cows "as pets" when they returned home. Their Herefords, on the other hand, says Nancy, "were *serious* cattle. But the next spring the Highlands raised more calves than the Herefords and David said, 'Maybe there's a lesson to be learned here.'" So the Peases returned to Scotland and bought the grand champion Highland bull from the 1973 spring sale at Oban, Leodhas (pronounced Lewis) of Douneside, as well as seven cows and two bull calves. Two years later they imported six more females from England. In the meantime, they were discovering that, crossed with heavier beef bulls — Simmental, Welsh Black, Hereford or Tarentaise — the Highland or

Thriving on the author's farm near Toronto, this herd shows the typical long horns present in both sexes, as well as the good beef characteristics of this small breed.

Highland-Hereford cows would throw big calves and would produce enough milk to raise them well. To their advantage, the cows were themselves small animals, and so were economical to winter.

In addition, the Peases crossed a straightbred Jersey cow with Leodhas, to produce what Nancy describes as "the lazy man's Jersey," a cow that produces creamy milk in slightly less quantity than a Jersey but, from a health viewpoint, is more resilient than a Jersey and does not suffer from milk fever, an ailment common among heavy milk producers. "She has no problem with calving, either, and has been bred every year to a Hereford bull," says Nancy. "She's a small cow, about 900 pounds, Highland red, smooth-furred in summer with hair about three inches long in winter."

Good milk production is just one reason that Highlands are considered among the best of mothers. They also have a higher conception rate than most breeds. While a cross-country estimate of the ratio of "calves weaned to cows bred" is about 70 per cent, Lawson's figures from the Alberta research station indicate that the rate for both Highlands (79) and Highland crosses (82) exceeds the average. Added to this is a strong maternal instinct in the Highland strain. Abandoned calves are unknown, even for first-calf heifers. A cow is almost constantly by the side of her young, unlike other breeds which often allow their calves to forage at some distance. In a letter to the Scottish publication, *The Field*, a Hope Springs, British Columbia rancher wrote, "Highland cows are the best mothers I know in wolf and bear country. Their calves are always with them." Too, because of their small-headed, short-necked conformation, they seldom have difficulty in calving. Highland crosses share this advantage, as the breed is somewhat smaller than the beef cattle to which they are usually bred — Highland bulls weigh between 1,500 and 2,000 pounds, and a Charolais, about 3,000 pounds. The result is problem-free, unassisted births with a high survival rate.

Another advantage of the breed is its ability to convert practically any forage into meat, and first generation crosses seem to retain this ability. Scottish breeder Captain D.S. Bowser writes, "The cross Highlander has the inherent hardiness of the pure Highlander, plus hybrid vigour, together with the Highlander's foraging proclivity. Once they have cleaned up their daily feed, they scatter across the hill, picking up what they can, rather than standing about bawling for the next feed, and there is no doubt that they are able to make use of poor quality grazing and roughage." In short, Highland cattle will eat fodder that another breed would not touch.

LEAN QUALITIES

This does not mean, however, that a conscientious Highland owner will abandon his animals to the elements every fall, as the poor Scottish crofters once did. These animals appreciate the same care and feeding given any other breed, although they can be expected to use that care to greater advantage when the weather and pasture are poor.

The acreage required per head per year ranges all the way from one to 60 depending upon the quality of the pasture, the age and condition of the cattle, and

	Lower critical temperature °F (°C)		
	JAN.	**FEB.**	**MARCH**
Bison	—40 (—40)	—22 (—30)	—40 (—40)
Yak	3 (—16)	12 (—11)	1 (—17)
Highland	3 (—16)	—4 (—20)	7 (—14)
Hereford	10 (—12)	7 (—14)	27 (—3)

	Number of calves weaned in herd of 100	Average weaning weight	Total weight lbs.
Highland-Hereford	82	391 lbs.	32,062
Highland (purebred)	79	359	28,361
Hereford (straightbred)	71	374	26,554

whether a supplement is fed. About 20 pounds of grass-legume hay is recommended as a daily ration for wintering yearlings which will be pasture-finished the following summer. If the hay is comprised solely of grass, a protein supplement like corn will be needed. Our animals wintered well on half a bale of mixed hay a day each, plus a thrice-weekly oat supplement. Although they contentedly browsed our cedar brush between feedings, the thunder of the roller grinding their oats precipitated a general stampede to the feeding trough and much lowing if they weren't fed fast enough.

In a 1975 report by John Lawson entitled "Feedlot and Carcass Traits of Steers of the Highland and Hereford Breeds and their Reciprocal Crosses based on the Manyberries Project," Highlands were found to be about as efficient in converting feed into meat as were the other animals studied. But, primarily because of its small size, Lawson recorded, "The Highland was inferior to the other groups for most of the traits studied (final feedlot weight, average daily gain in the feedlot, cold carcass weight and dressing percentage.) It has a slower growth rate and poorer fattening tendencies in the feedlot and cannot be recommended as a pure breed in this environment. The reciprocal cross calves, on the other hand, were essentially equal to the Hereford in all respects, except for a trend to a lower percentage of choice and good grades."

The grades "good" and "choice" signified, among other things, a certain fat content in the meat, and it was the Highland's unusually lean beef that often disqualified it from these classifications. The ability of a carcass to take top designation, and therefore best price, is of great importance to the commercial beef producer, but Lawson states that the additional fat cover "does not necessarily bear a relationship to carcass quality." Highland beef is lean, a quality that is actually becoming increasingly popular.

Neil Hulbert, a California rancher who owns a meat processing plant, was having a problem with too much fat and waste. "Then," he says, "I bought a Highland bull, Wildemere Lochinvar." He bred him to Shorthorn cows and crossbred heifers and soon was producing leaner beef. "The doctors say the outside fat is what causes heart trouble," says Hulbert. "The Highland beef has a very fine marbled texture in the muscle, and very little fat outside."

Lawson points out that the leaner meat is a function of a slower growth rate. Both straightbred and crossbred steers in his study dressed out at close to the American average of 60 per cent of live weight, the purebred Highlands slightly below, the crossbreds slightly above. The percentages of the more valuable cuts were the same. One slight difference was that both Highland and Highland-Hereford steers produced more chuck and less plate-shank beef than the others.

VALUABLE COATS

We were sold on Highland beef when we attended the annual meeting of the Society at the Pease farm, and sampled the *pièce de résistance*, a joint of mouth-watering Highland beef. Tender, delicious and marbled with fat, it is a gourmet treat at exclusive restaurants like Simpsons-in-the-Strand in London, England. Perhaps Britons still feel as Daniel Defoe said they did in 1727, when large herds of Highland cattle were annually driven down to markets in southern England. "The beef is so delicious for taste," wrote Defoe, "that the inhabitants prefer 'em to the English cattle."

But delicious beef is only one product of the butchered Highland. Beautiful couch throws and rugs have been made from the luxurious hides of these long-haired beasts. Highlands owe their winter hardiness in part to this coat. The hair is long and naturally waved. It is produced in a double layer, a downy undercoat and a long outercoat, which is well oiled to shed rain and snow, and it may reach more than a foot in length. Much of the long hair is lost in the summer, so Highlands are most photogenic during the winter months. The hair itself, combed or collected from fences and posts where it is rubbed off in spring, is in demand for weaving. And the long, sweeping horns — usually upturned in the females, down in the bulls — are valued for wall decorations or in the production of horn merchandise. In Scotland, a thriving cottage industry turns out horn spoons, knife handles and other small implements.

Anyone living in the country with a small acreage can experience the many satisfactions of owning Highland cattle. One way, of course, is to buy a cow, borrow a bull or use AI (artificial insemination from a registered sire) and produce the beginnings of a crossbred herd or at least next year's beef. The Society (see Sources) is the best source of information on breeders and local herds. Prices of cattle fluctuate, naturally, but are comparable with those of other cattle, even though the Highland is rarer than many other beef breeds in North America. There are just 55 members in the Canadian Society, most of them in British Columbia and Ontario.

The Highland Cattle Society

In its native Scotland, the Highlander has evolved the ability to grow and reproduce under adverse conditions.

Perhaps the easiest way to raise a Highland is to put a steer on grass for the summer and butcher it in the fall. Even better is to have a succession of steers coming to maturity at two or even three years of age. This way, the first year's steer would be kept over until the fall of the second year, another yearling being purchased each spring.

The result will be a freezer full of remarkably lean beef. But there is another benefit; one, interestingly, of questionable merit. Aesthetically, Highlands are the most pleasing of cattle. Despite familiarity, each time we catch sight of one of these magnificent animals against the green of the fields, the dark of the bush or the white of the snow, we get a shock of pleasure. The sight of a herd of mixed colours, red, brindle, black, yellow, white and dun is simply breathtaking.

In fact, the Highland's beauty and its ability to conjure compelling memories or imaginings of the wild Scottish countryside sometimes urges the business instinct out of cattle owners. "People will keep a beast that would have been culled if it had been any other breed," says Nancy Pease. "There are a great many scruffy ones here (in North America), zoo types. A great many of our sales go to hobbyists, but we hope they will raise them as *cattle,* too. Some people keep Highlands for strictly sentimental reasons. I feel sentimental about them, too, but we select very carefully for commercial qualities, calving every year safely, and producing good calves."

The sentimental Highland owner can well be understood. Not only is the animal beautiful, even a scruffy one, but its owner taps into a wellspring of colourful tradition. Seemingly unpronounceable Gaelic words are woven throughout the lore of Highland raising.

Highland cattle yield both high quality marbled lean beef and luxuriant hides, even when raised on marginal bushland.

The journal of the Canadian Highland Cattle Society is called *The Kyloe Cry*. Highlands are often called "kyloes," a name which is believed to be derived from the Gaelic word for strait. On their journey to southern markets, the cattle would often have to swim across these straits or "*kyles*."

All pedigreed calves born in one year are assigned the same letter designation, and are often named accordingly. When it comes to naming Highlands, it's a help to know a little Gaelic. In 1979 the letter was "L." Loachag (Little Heroine) might have done for a heifer, or Lasgaire (Champion) for a bull calf.

There is no K in Gaelic, but 1978 was the K year. We very much wanted authentic names for our six calves but had to compromise a little. They have a Gaelic sound but not a Gaelic spelling. Our farm name is Cnoc Eilidh (Ellen Hill, pronounced Knock Elly) so we have four heifers called Knockbain (Fair-hill), Knocklea (Grey Hill), Knockangle (Hill of the Angels) and Knockantoul (Hill of the Barn) plus two bulls called Knockantarbh and Knocknacean, (Hill of the Bull and Hill of the Heads).

Gaelic terms are usually used for describing colours. *Ruadh* (roo-ah) is red; *buidhe* (boo-ey), yellow; *geal*, white; *riabhach* (ree-vak), brindle and *dubh* (doo), black. Fond owners might call a bull Prionnsa Dubh (Black Prince) or Gille Buidhe (Golden Boy). Of course, shirking romance, more than one breeder has reverted to the old familiar bovine names like Buttercup, Duchess and Bossie.

One of the most charming bits of Gaelic tradition surrounding the tending of Highland cattle is a benediction, which was sung in former times as the kilted Scottish cattleman sang to his herd while driving them to pasture in the morning.

Closed to you be every pit,
Smooth to you be every hill,
Snug to you be every bare spot,
Beside the cold mountains.
The sanctuary of Mary Mother be yours,
The sanctuary of Brigit the loved be yours,
The sanctuary of Michael victorious be yours,
Active and full be you gathered home.
The protection of shapely Cormac be yours,
The protection of Brendan of the ships be yours,
The protection of Maol Duinne the saint be yours,
In marshy ground and rocky ground.
The fellowship of Mary Mother be yours.
The fellowship of Brigit of Kine be yours.
The fellowship of Michael victorious be yours,
In nibbling, in chewing, in munching.

Sources

THE CANADIAN HIGHLAND CATTLE SOCIETY
Barbara Brotherston
Secretary-Treasurer
Box 509
Alix, Alberta T0C 0B0
Membership $10/year, includes quarterly journal *The Kyloe Cry* and the quarterly *Highland Breeders'*

Journal. Will send a membership list free upon request.

**AMERICAN SCOTCH HIGHLAND
BREEDERS' ASSOCIATION**
Gloria Allen, Secretary
Box 403
Kalkaska, Michigan 49646
Membership $25/year, includes quarterly journal.

HIGHLAND BREEDERS' JOURNAL
T.M.O. Lang
17 York Place
Perth, Scotland PH2 8EP
Sent free to members of the Canadian Highland Cattle Society.

A few of the North American Highland breeders:

TROSSACH FOLD
Marion Powling
R.R.1, Bench Road
Cowichan Station, B.C. V0R 1P0

ZETLAND FARMS
David & Marian E. Harbard
21431 - 24th Ave., R.R.2
Langley, B.C. V3A 4P5

BROTHERSTON ENTERPRISES LIMITED
George & Barbara Brotherston
Box 509
Alix, Alberta T0C 0B0

CNOC EILIDH
Lou and Donalda Badone
34 Avondale Avenue
Willowdale, Ont. M2N 2T9

Marian E. Harbard

Young cow and calf at Zetland Farms, near Langley, B.C., home of many grand champion Highland beef animals.

GLEN OSPREY FARM
David & Nancy Pease
R.R.6
Shelburne, Ontario L0N 1S0

ANDANA FARMS
John Mackenzie Anderson
P.O. Box 1953
Cincinnati, Ohio 45201

VERMONT FOLD
Henry H. Carse
Hinesburg, Vermont 05461
Note: One might expect to pay between $1,000 and $1,500 for a good quality, purebred Highland heifer in 1980, or from $300 up for a cow.

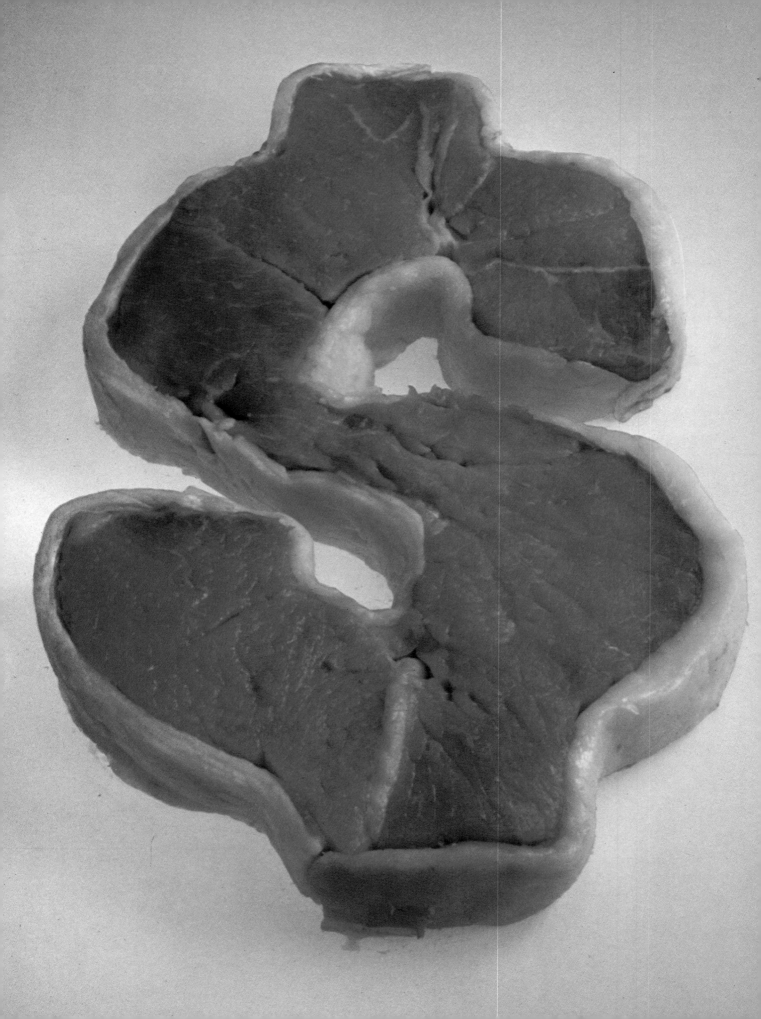

Boeuf
A la Farmstead

One sure way around the coming Great Beef Shortage

By Don Woodcock

Ernie Sparks

With the spectre of $3.00 a pound hamburger looming ever greater in the coming year, and with agricultural prognosticators talking of the worst prolonged North American beef shortage since the 1945-50 period, the neighbours' surplus calves will be drawing calculating looks for more and more of us.

While saving money — or just being able to afford red meat — is sufficient motivation for deciding to raise one's own beef, my own first two calves arrived simply because I wanted the pleasure of their company. I discovered that doing chores in the shadow-filled, fragrant, intimate sanctuary of the cow barn on a winter night worked a powerful, nearly mystical cure on a mind and body ravaged by 10 hours of city work and society.

One pair of the creatures was raised with much pleasure and little trouble and this led, naturally, to another pair, and another — for eight years, a pair of beeves each fall. The system of raising them evolved into a fairly reliable way of putting 400 pounds of free beef into the freezer, but even more important, our home-grown T-bones looked, smelled, cooked and tasted far better than any commercial feed-lot product ever offered on a supermarket counter for $4.00 a pound.

I had, as it happened, all the necessary ingredients for successful beef production already on the farm. I had eight acres of mediocre pasture land. I had fences — some good, some bad. I had a ramshackle, leaky, drafty old barn, and I had a well just a few steps from the barn door. I had too, as a heritage from my beginnings on a Manitoba farm, mouldy but well-rooted memories of how the game should be played.

I knew that raising two calves from near birth to the day they could be shoved out the barn door into the sunshine would be a straightforward task, but it would be a task. The animals would be dependent on me for feed, for their health and comfort. They would demand time. It would take time to clean that stall every day. It would take time to make sure the bedding was dry and fluffed up every night. A Saturday outing on the ski slopes would begin and end with a pitchfork in my hands. It wouldn't always be easy to come home late from the office and mix feed before mixing a cocktail. I knew that how dependable I proved to be as a mother to those calves would have a significant bearing on the success of my experiment. The children would, of course, become involved. In fact, as mine grew older, they took over most of the operation. But I knew that the kids could not be expected to shoulder the ultimate responsibility, nor could they be expected to do a perfect job every time, at every task.

Home-grown beef, I knew, would be a bargain bought with my own labour, day in and day out, warm weather and freezing weather. Occasionally my animals would have to wait several hours for morning or evening care, but of course it would always come. They would complain but they would not suffer, any more than I do when a meal is late.

I decided that for me, the pleasure of raising my own beef would vastly overshadow the difficulties.

There was only one nagging worry. Cattle, as I remembered things, had to be housed in a tight, warm barn during winter and barns were kept warm mainly because they were full of warm creatures. How, then, could I expect two baby calves to survive an Ottawa Valley winter in my huge, unheated derelict? Well, as ranchers all across the West have long

Don Woodcock

since proved, cattle can cope quite nicely with cold — provided they have a dry, draft-free shelter with plenty of food and water. Having established that fact through consultation with my local veterinarian and neighbouring farmers, I sallied forth to hand raise my own beef.

HOLSTEIN SOLUTION

I decided right away not to buy from a sales barn, for two reasons. I didn't believe that I had enough expertise in bovine matters to pick out a really good animal. I also knew that diseases are prevalent in stockyards and that buying such a calf would drastically reduce my chances of being able to keep it alive. Too often, young calves at a sales barn have been hauled there within hours of birth and are totally ill-prepared for what lies ahead. Canadian studies have shown that such sales barn calves have a 60 per cent mortality rate, unless given antibiotic injections.

As it happened, a commercial dairy farmer was one of my closest neighbours, and I knew from my association with farming and dairying that Holstein bull calves can make excellent beef animals — no matter what the Texan beef barons might say. My answer was evident.

The whole situation was, in fact, ideal. The stress involved in moving a calf from the place of purchase to one's own barn can take quite a toll. The shorter the travel distance the better, to the extent that a $90 calf from next door should be preferred over a $50 one from a sales barn 60 miles away. I used to fetch mine home in the back of a tiny station wagon. It took perhaps an hour to load them, drive the mile or so home, and deposit the calves in their new pen. In eight years, I had not a single loss and only one minor case of pneumonia which was quickly and cheaply cured by my local vet.

Buying from a good dairy herd also gives an indication of the health of the animal. Very healthy calves are, of course, of prime importance to any dairy farmer who wants to stay in business. Still, take a good look at the individual animal that is being offered. A manure-caked rump may mean scours

— diarrhea — the most common affliction of young calves. The animal should have a thick coat, bright eyes, perky ears and good posture. Its navel should not be swollen, nor its nostrils filled with mucus.

Ask the farmer if the calf has received colostrum, if you are considering an animal less than a week old. Colostrum, the first milk produced by the mother, is the substance that the calf receives for the first three days of its life and it contains components that immunize it from many diseases. Do not purchase a calf under three days old, nor one that has not or may not have received colostrum. (Sales barn calves sometimes arrive without having had any colostrum.)

Yes, I know dairy farmers don't breed Herefords, or Charolais, or any of the other fancy beef breeds. Most dairy farmers raise Holsteins or Jerseys. It happens that Holsteins or Frisians will grow just as big and just as fast as some beef breeds. The only difference is in "conformation." Holstein-Frisians are tall, leggy animals without those broad, flat haunches where fancy-looking roasts come from. No matter. The meat is leaner, of excellent quality, and the animals are more easily obtained at a reasonable price. Dairy farmers have no use for bull calves. Beef raisers want every calf to be a bull calf. It's that simple. However, the smaller dairy breeds, such as Jerseys, are not a good choice. They don't put on the beef that a Holstein does, and are more difficult to raise.

Too, beef calves are harder to come by, because they are more desirable to the commercial beef industry — a Holstein carcass cannot be graded "choice" simply because of its shape. A beef calf — if available — will cost a bit more than a dairy calf. There used to be a great price difference — only a few years ago, one could buy a dairy bull calf for $2.00 —but as Holstein calves are better appreciated, their value is increasing as, of course, is all beef.

I have paid from $35 to $95 for each calf. Other than a slightly higher initial cost, and their scarcity, there are no disadvantages to raising a beef breed, or a mixed dairy-beef calf, so buy one if one is available nearby.

With changes in dairy management in the past two decades, it is now possible to buy a calf at any time of the year, although they will be easier to come by from April to June and September to November. Many farmsteaders buy one in the spring, get it started in the barn, put it out to pasture for the summer and slaughter in the fall. Others bring the animal into the barn in the autumn to fatten it. Either way, the calf is indoors in the spring when it could be out on the pasture and the animal won't reach its optimum size — 700 to 1,000 pounds — by fall.

This is not necessarily a major drawback, especially if you feel any sense of urgency about getting beef into the freezer, but you should know that there is a higher proportion of bone to meat in baby beef. The beef of a younger animal is tender, but not as flavourful as that from an older animal, and tastes more like veal.

I always bought my calves in the late fall, as it had not taken long for me to develop a system that worked with astonishing success and condensed the critical, intensive-care period of the operation into a couple of months. There are two times when each animal must live in the barn: when it first arrives as a young calf, and when it is being fattened prior to slaughtering. I had it timed so that both of these periods occurred in the winter, so I could tend to all my animals, the calves and the yearlings, at the same time.

Each fall, when the pasture began to fail toward the end of October, I brought my two yearling steers into the barn, housed them in a divided stall erected in the driest and tightest corner of the old barn — a section that happened to have a good cement floor — and began the "finishing" process. At the same time, I drove over to my nearest neighbour, the dairy farmer, and bought two bull calves anywhere from two weeks to a month old. I accepted the first but preferred the latter — the older they are, the better their chances of survival. The babies were each allotted a small stall alongside their big relatives and immediately started on a diet of milk replacer (powdered milk from a feed store).

The stall into which the new calf is placed need not be very large. My stalls were about 12 feet square and four and a half feet high. They were divided by a couple of moveable two-by-sixes because I found the animals grow better when separated. To make certain there were no drafts, I surrounded the little guys' stalls with hay bales to a height of at least three feet for the first few weeks. They must have plenty of dry bedding and a constant supply of water. After ruining half a dozen buckets trying to knock ice out of them, I solved the water problem by installing a large galvanized wash tub in each stall, which was firmly anchored and offered easy access from both sides of the dividers. Each tub sat on a raised wooden frame into which I sank half an antifreeze can cut the long way. In the metal hollow formed by each split can I mounted a 100-watt light bulb, which kept the water from freezing on all but the very coldest nights.

Running water and individual self-serve water bowls would be grand, but there's no way to keep the system from freezing unless the barn is heated. I ran a length of one-and-a-half-inch flexible plastic pipe from the well up through the loft and down to the calf stalls. Provided the pipe is held in a smooth arc, with no low spots, it will drain both ways after use and never freeze. Well, almost never. For moving the water I got a wobble pump that also drained back after use. Housed in a tiny insulated shed with a heat lamp, it worked fine most of the time. For summer use, I installed a pressure-fed water bowl in the barnyard which eliminated any further fuss about water until freeze-up. Some bowls will freeze and burst at temperatures only a very few degrees below freezing, so buy a type that resists frost damage and has a convenient drain cock. Electrically heated bowls are also available.

Having installed the two wee beasts in their new quarters, one must now proceed to nurse them through the most critical period of their lives. Begin with a diet of milk replacer — one pound replacer dissolved in one gallon of warm water per calf per day. A coffee can makes a good measuring cup. Follow the instructions on the milk replacer bag carefully and begin very slowly, building up to the full ration

over a period of days. The quantity may be increased to one and a half gallons per day after three weeks.

The big danger at this point is scours, the most common cause of death in young calves. The mildest infections are known as "digestive scours," and can usually be cured by reducing the proportion of milk to water for two or three feedings. For more severe cases, in addition to reducing the milk allowance, replace one feeding entirely with a solution of one-half teaspoon of baking soda, two tablespoons of common salt, and one-half cup of corn syrup in one gallon of warm water.

More severe infections causing white, pasty feces are called "white scours" and, if blood is passed in the feces, "red scours." In these cases, or if the scours persist, call the vet. Learn how and when to administer scour tablets. After that you should be able to treat the problem yourself if necessary.

Understand that things can get a bit messy. With the hind end erupting in a Vesuvian manner, and the front end spitting scour tablets in all directions, it can be easy to lose control of the situation. After the first time I slipped and went sprawling in the muck with a bawling, kicking calf across me, I kept a special pair of overalls handy for scour treatment sessions.

Viral pneumonia is the other common ailment in young calves. Watch for a dry, harsh cough and laboured breathing. *Early* treatment by your vet is almost always successful.

It takes time to learn the idiosyncracies of each creature so that small changes in food intake or behaviour become early warning signals that something is not just right with your animal. The earliest possible treatment is always important. Be observant.

RATIONING

After two weeks (I always count the weeks from the time the calf arrives regardless of actual age), I offer a bit of good quality, dust- and mould-free hay each day. At four weeks, I offer "calf starter," a specially blended, granulated feed available from a farm supply dealer. I feed the starter "free-choice" — some in front of the calf all the time until he is consuming four or five pounds a day; then hold him at that level.

At six weeks, I begin weaning the calf, reducing the milk ration to zero by the eighth week. At eight weeks, the baby should be on a diet of starter, hay and water. At 12 weeks, I gradually switch from the starter mixture to a "calf grower" mixture and continue with the grower at the rate of four to six pounds per calf per day for another 12 weeks. After that I am home free — good hay twice a day, plenty of water, salt, mineral supplement, a clean stall and dry bedding are all the critter needs now. Don't be wasteful with the hay. I feed only what the animal will clean up — say a third of a bale a day at this stage.

Both calf starter and calf grower are available at feed stores, but they are fairly costly. Starter now costs up to $7.10 for 55 lbs. (25 kg.) and grower, up to $11.80 for 88 lbs. (40kg.). Although I buy prepared feeds, anyone with enough acreage can grow and mix his own.

Calf Starter

30 pounds crushed corn
10 pounds rolled or crushed oats
10 pounds crushed wheat
10 pounds ground soybeans
5 pounds bone meal
1 cup salt
4 ounces cod liver oil or vitamin A, D & E powder

Growing Ration

30 pounds crushed or coarsely ground corn
30 pounds rolled or ground oats
30 pounds rolled or ground wheat or barley
10 pounds ground soybeans
20 pounds dried skim milk or buttermilk
(If hay is not of good quality, add 4 ounces cod liver oil or vitamin A, D & E powder.)

After a dozen experimental failures, I finally evolved an efficient and cheap container for the feed mixtures. Fill a five-gallon pail half full of sand and cut a circle of three-quarter-inch plywood to fit in on top of the sand. Set the pail in a corner of the stall and secure it firmly. Presto — an excellent, stable and practically free feed bowl. Salt can be offered as a small block in the same container and the mineral substitute can also be added. The calf will eat its feed from the top and take what minerals it wants from the bottom where they always settle.

During these early weeks, two more tasks that I find particularly distasteful also have to be performed — castrating and dehorning. Both are done to protect the farmer from an animal that will become, after all, much larger than he, and should be considered if he intends to keep the calf for more than 10 months.

Castration is a matter of personal decision, but if it is going to be done, it must be accomplished before the animal is 10 months old, when it will become sexually mature. If the animal is not castrated, it will gain weight faster and produce leaner meat, but by one year of age it will become quite feisty.

Bulls are raised for meat because they grow faster than heifers, not because they have more pleasant personalities. I always had my animals castrated, and I had it done by a vet. However, those who wish to do it themselves will find it easiest to use an elastrator, a device that slips a round, rubber ring around the scrotum. This tightens and cuts off the blood supply, so that the testes wither and disappear. It causes a slight discomfort only for the first day if applied properly. The elastrator should be used when the calf is between two weeks and a month old. The elastrator, incidentally, can also be used for dehorning, but in this case the rubber ring cuts off the blood supply to the developing horns.

Dehorning is done at three weeks for the safety of the farmer, his children, and the animals themselves. A 500-pound calf swinging a head armed with two sharp spears is nothing to scoff at. Dehorning can be accomplished with an electric device that cuts the bud out, with an elastrator, or with a special caustic paste. This latter process has become the most common on small farms, and can be easily accomplished by the farmer himself. However, it is a good idea to let a veterinarian or other experienced hand do it the first time, as the caustic paste really burns and must

be applied correctly. I once tried using an electric dehorning device and I botched the job because I didn't hold the red-hot iron on the tiny knob of new horn long enough.

In about two months the little fellows should be eating calf starter and hay, while — under my system — the pair of yearlings are pleasantly filled out and ready for the table. The toughest part of the job is now behind you. All that remains is to provide routine care for the two young calves until green grass sprouts in the spring and they can be turned loose to fend for themselves.

How much pasture is needed per head of stock? This is essential data, but is impossible to provide in precise terms. Too many variables are involved. Rainfall, soil conditions, average temperatures, drainage, species of fodder sown, use of fertilizer — all these factors influence the amount of food produced by an acre of pasture. Phyllis Hobson, author of *Raising a Calf for Beef,* estimates that two acres of pasture are needed to raise one calf, using one acre at a time while the other grows. She also says that if one is mixing his own feeds, he will require one acre of hay and one of grain for each animal. The local agricultural representative can help analyze the situation on your farm. Even a tiny bit of pasture might be adequate if, for example, you are prepared to halter-break your calves and tether them along the road allowance each day.

BOVINE HOUDINIS

Once outdoors, a whole new side of the animals' personalities will emerge. Cattle are herd animals, and if there are more of them nearby — within a couple of miles, that is — those two lonely calves will do everything in their power to get to the rest. Young calves are absolute Houdinis when it comes to getting through fences. I've often wondered which is worse — tracking down a long gone runaway or facing the irate owner of a mangled garden plot (usually my wife). If there is sweet corn in the garden, count on cattle to sniff it out.

Later on that year, when the animals are back in the barn, it isn't at all easy to persuade the owner of that trampled garden to carry water from the house out to the beasts who did the mangling. One morning I went to do my chores only to discover that the well pump had frozen, and I was already 20 minutes late for work. My wife was used to my considerable, florid descriptions of the unpredictable temper of my city boss who simply refused to understand tardiness problems. Needless to say, it helps if one's partner is agreeable to the idea of raising home-grown beef.

In retrospect, I think these occasional little irritants were more than offset by the fun of the full-scale guerrilla war I waged with my children over the disposition of the end result of all that food we kept putting into the front end of the animals. It was a heart-warming thing to witness, at firsthand, the benefits of some old-fashioned "chores" in the raising of a family.

In any case, as long as the animals are on the pasture, there is little to be done and everyone involved in the beef raising project gets a bit of a holiday. But almost before the pitchfork callous has disappeared

Small-Scale Beef Production

Cost breakdown of raising two calves and selling one

ITEM	QUANTITY NEEDED	UNIT COST	TOTAL COST
Calves	2	$90.00	$180.00
Hay	170 bales	1.50/bale	255.00
Milk Replacer	100 lbs.	.55 lb.	55.00
Calf Starter	600 lbs.	.28 lb.	168.00
Calf Grower	900 lbs.	.13/lb.	117.00
Finisher (Feed)	2,100 lbs.	.09/lb.	189.00
Salt Block	1	3.50/block	3.50
Mineral Supplements	55 lbs.	11.55/bag	11.55
Veterinary Visits			30.00
Misc. Equipment			20.00
Slaughter Fee	1 steer	6.00	6.00
Butcher & Wrap	500 lbs.	.12/lb.	60.00

TOTAL 1,095.05

INCOME

Second steer sells on the hoof for 75 cents per pound.
Assuming live weight of 1,000 lbs. income is $750.00

YOUR BEEF COSTS $345.05

(Compare this to the current market price of "freezer beef" to determine savings. At $1.49 per pound, for example, a 500-lb. carcass after being cut, wrapped and frozen would cost $745.00. You save $399.95. If you sell one side of your butchered steer for $372.50 — the "freezer beef" price — your own beef will be free and leave a modest profit of $27.45.)

from the cattleman's index finger, summer will have slipped by, and he will be much wiser in the care of his animals than he was when he bought his first calf.

He will have discovered which calf is the traveller and which one has an addiction to garden produce. He may or may not have discovered the efficiency and versatility of a battery-operated electric fence unit coupled to a few hundred yards of easily moved fence wire. He will have discovered, I hope, that the critters need a spot that offers escape from the sun and the flies (trees, a shed, a lean-to), and where salt, water and mineral supplement are always available. He will have long since noted the astonishing differences in personality of the two charges. In fact, he might even have become quite fond of the beggars. Then, one late October morning, after a night's hard frost, he will realize it is time for the fattening stall. Now it is time to consider buying two new calves, and the work resumes on the two older calves brought in from the pasture.

The finishing process may take anywhere from 30 to 90 days depending on the animal, the farmer's preference in beef finish, and the amount of finishing mix he can afford. Too, if the animal comes off poor pasture in poor condition, it will obviously require a longer finishing period.

Custom mixes are available from feed stores, or the farmer can mix his own or just use one type of grain. Barley and oats are cheaper, cracked corn more expensive, and each type of grain adds a slightly different flavour and amount of fat to the meat. Experience will have to be the teacher.

I feed a commercial finishing mix at the rate of two pounds per 100 pounds of calf weight, or about 12 pounds a day after a gradual start. I increase this, as the calves grow, to nearly 20 pounds a day. A constant supply of water is absolutely essential when an animal is being fed that much grain.

The calf also needs hay for roughage. I learned this from one of my experienced neighbours who told me,

"I don't care what the book says. Those steers need some hay." Some specialists will say that hay is optional but my experience indicates that a fair proportion of hay — up to a bale each day — is needed for proper operation of the complex bovine stomach system. The animals I tried to raise on a grain-only diet simply did not prosper until I added hay, thanks to my neighbour's advice.

Farming neighbours, incidentally are one of the novice beef-raiser's best sources of information. Chances are they have a lifetime of experience and practical, down-to-earth advice free for the asking. A neighbour is the person who will quickly note that the pasture is being over-grazed, that the animals are doing poorly. He only has to be asked. My neighbour was the man who told me I was too soft-hearted to dehorn my animals properly and thereafter attended to the job himself.

The other useful sources of information are the "Ag Reps." These people are specialists, paid by the government to help with farming problems. Use them. The men I dealt with were knowledgeable and anxious to be of assistance. There are also booklets and pamphlets available from federal and provincial or state departments of agriculture. I used everything I could get my hands on.

Thanks to my farming background, I already knew that my hungry yearlings would continue to grow as long as they were fed, but my objective was not a 1,600-pound steer. What I was raising was "baby beef," by definition an animal 12 to 16 months old and weighing 700 to 1,000 pounds. After this point, the feed-to-meat conversion ratio drops, and

*Beef or mixed breed calves, **above**, will usually be more difficult to obtain and more expensive than Holsteins, which nevertheless yield lean, flavourful baby beef.*

the animal must be fed more and more grain to produce a pound of beef. It doesn't pay to prolong the process. I never fatten a steer for more than 70 days. The price of finishing ration and the amount of manure those darlings produce each day always quickly deflates my earlier feelings of fondness, to be replaced by visions of beef steaks — the sooner the better. Toward the end, I reduce the amount of grain and use more good hay to get excellent, lean beef that is tender, has good flavour and low shrinkage.

Once both animals are ready for the slaughterhouse, one is sold "on the hoof." I have no trouble finding customers — in fact, the same two families were waiting every year once they had sampled this delightful beef. They arranged for the slaughtering themselves, and each one took a side. An animal should dress out to 50 or 60 per cent of its live weight, so if one is dealing with 500 pounds of beef, he may find it easier to sell by the quarter than by the side. Current market prices for livestock are printed in the newspaper or can be obtained in Canada by calling the toll-free number (800) 267-8360. This gives the price per pound for steers and will give a good idea what to charge.

Depending on the market price of beef and what you decide to charge, the money you receive from the sale of one animal can cover all costs for both beeves. Keep in mind, of course, that if one or both of the calves dies or is killed, you can lose. That's farming.

Nevertheless, considering the price of retail meat

these days, you should be able to make the free beef system work. I did, except for 1974-75, when calf prices were high and finished beef prices were low. My costs were more than $500, while the steer I sold only brought in $350. That year, we decided to sell one-third of our own animal, as we had beef left over from the previous year, and by the time we'd done that, we had broken even again. Calf and beef prices fluctuate wildly, and grain and hay prices also rise and fall. If a farmer grows his own hay, as I did, he can save quite a bit, and most years my equipment and veterinary costs were negligible. Selling the meat cut and wrapped — rather than on the hoof — can bring a better price, if you wish to charge it, but in any case selling one animal will greatly reduce the cost of raising one's own.

Steers that are ready for the butcher can in no way fit into a small station wagon, so a local trucker can be enlisted to haul the animals to the slaughterhouse if you have no suitable vehicle of your own. Many slaughterhouses will kill the animal, and cut, wrap, label and freeze the meat on their own premises. In our case, the slaughterhouse would pass the carcass along to the local butcher for the finishing touches. The whole process is so painless and cheap that I have never considered trying to do the job myself.

Slaughtering and butchering an animal that big takes some experience and a decent place to work. Cutting up 800 pounds of steer on the kitchen table is likely to fray a few tempers before the mess is cleared away. Too, the carcass should be hung and aged a week or so at a controlled temperature and then frozen quickly. In our opinion, the basement is not an ideal ageing room, and the average home freezer will strain for a couple of days to freeze such a quantity of meat.

Once the meat is back from the butcher and in the freezer, there is nothing left to do but enjoy it, to think about how much money was saved — and to take care of next fall's set of calves. Again, there will be the irate garden owners, the broken fences, the guerrilla wars, the callouses and the frozen water lines. Unless you truly enjoy animals and the attendant chores, you may be better off paying the supermarket price.

Because we take pleasure in working with our calves, the rewards are both excellent meat — virtually free, but for the labour — and a satisfaction that cannot be measured.

Sources

RAISING A CALF FOR BEEF
By Phyllis Hobson
113 pages, Paperback
Garden Way Publishing
Charlotte, Vermont 05445

**MANAGEMENT & FEEDING
OF YOUNG DAIRY ANIMALS**
Agriculture Canada
Publication No. 1432

and
**BEEF PRODUCTION FROM
THE DAIRY HERD**
Agriculture Canada
Publication No. 1456

Available free of charge from:
Edifice Sir John Carling Building
930 Carling Avenue
Ottawa, Ontario K1A 0C7

Ted Grant/Image Bank

Equine Dollars & Simple Horse Sense

Don't know a windsucker from a cribber? Tread carefully when buying your first pleasure horse

By Helen Mason

I t was the perfect sales pitch for a 21-year-old city kid raised on *Black Beauty* and *My Friend Flicka:* "This is a good mare from out West," said the horse dealer, shaking his head sadly. "I'd hate to see her put down."

Not for nothing have horse traders acquired the wiliest of reputations and this one had made a sale simply by putting the power of life or death into my hands. I could no more have let him "put her down" than I could have pulled out a gun and shot her on the spot. I paid $150 cash for the gentle brown mare and had her trucked from the Toronto stockyards, where I'd found her, to my new country home.

Cinnamon was the daydreams of my lonely childhood come to life, the heroine of a hundred teenage novels about faithful fillies, their large brown eyes full of equine wisdom and loving concern for their youthful masters. A horse. The most noble of domestic animals. What prince, after all, would approach a princess on an Aberdeen Angus; however heated the battle, what king would ever offer his kingdom for a sow?

Joyfully, I groomed her and diligently mucked out her stall. What did it matter that she wouldn't let me tighten the girth when I saddled her? I rode bareback, climbing on from the top of a nearby fence. I didn't care that the insides of my thighs were raw from clinging to her shoulders. I was learning to ride.

Then reality began to close in. That December, during the first snowstorm of the season, the farmer friend, whose stall I had been using, was evicted and my mare abruptly lost her lodgings. Cinnamon and I walked for miles through the driving snow, looking for at least temporary accommodation, and we finally arrived at Dudley Oliver's riding stable. If Mr. Oliver was rendered speechless when a bedraggled horse and rider turned in off the road in the midst of the storm, his wife was not.

"My gaw-aw-awd, you could have been killed . . . ." Her voice followed us into the barn, where I quietly explained my predicament and asked if Cinnamon might be boarded there. Dudley Oliver consented, but a look of concern showed in his eyes when he examined the horse's feet. "I'd like the vet to take a look at her," he finally said. "There's something wrong with this mare."

The "something wrong" turned out to be founder or laminitis, a degenerative inflammation of the front hoof often caused by improper care of the animal sometime in its past. Cinnamon was a cripple in both forefeet — and in pain.

Hers was an advanced case and I was given the choice of ending her pain and her life or trying to keep her going on drugs which might, just might, alleviate the torture but never cure her. I chose the former.

Ten years later, I can look back and admit that I did everything wrong in buying my first mount, and my story is far from unique among horse tales.

I had learned, the hard way, the price of good — but ill-informed — intentions and a lesson best stated as: *Caveat emptor equi* — Let the horse buyer beware. The founder had been present for some time — certainly long before my visit to the stockyards — but I didn't know enough to spot it. An equine-wise friend brought along on my horse-buying mis-

However cute, a young animal is not a good choice for the first-time horse owner. This foal, photographed seconds after its birth, failed to survive its first year.

Bill Milliken

sion or a simple pre-purchase veterinary check would have stopped my naïve purchase and prevented a Christmas holiday spent weeping beside an empty stall.

I knew it would be months before I could afford to buy another horse, but I was lucky to be able to resurrect my dreams of horse ownership, with the help of Dudley and the others who were boarding their horses at his stable. They took pity and, over the months that followed, taught me not only to ride, but to apply the horseman's axiom: Never buy a horse in a hurry. It may take weeks, even months, of searching to find the right animal, but there is no shortage of riding horses in North America and the ideal mount for every rider can be found somewhere.

FIRST THOUGHTS

Before any idea of buying a horse becomes an obsession, one must seriously think about where he might park an expensive half-ton of horseflesh. Lacking a barn or proper stable, there are a number of other typical farm outbuildings which might be adapted to equine housing. Even a garage might do, but the recommended ceiling height is 10 feet, to allow clearance in the event that a horse rears up. (Repeated blows to the top of the head can lead to a fistulous condition known in horse jargon as "poll evil.")

The stall should measure at least 10 feet square, with 12 by 14 feet even better. The traditional horse barn is dry and free of serious drafts, but increasing numbers of casual horsemen are leaving their animals outdoors year-round, providing them with only a three-sided shelter, open at the front, which faces south. This inexpensive, easily constructed structure gives protection from wind and rain, and some veterinarians feel that horses housed in this way are more fit and in generally better health.

The drawbacks are mainly for the horse owner, who may find his animals harder to keep clean in inclement weather and may dislike the shaggy winter coat they develop. Those lured by the olfactory mystique of a warm barn will probably choose to keep their animals indoors. In addition to the stall itself, there must be room, under cover, for hay and bedding storage — about three and a half tons of hay per year per horse, plus additional grain and straw or wood shavings.

Clean water should be close at hand — a horse has a prodigious thirst and hauling water in buckets can be tedious. The stall door must be secure, and the wall supports bolted to the floor. More than one horse has escaped a homemade box stall by pushing the walls aside with its body. A horse is just smart enough to know how to use its considerable weight, and just dumb enough to use it in the wrong places.

A fenced-off paddock outside the barn is necessary. A round pen with a 20-foot diameter is ideal for longeing (pronounced lun-jing) — exercising or training the horse on a long lead. A larger pasture is also necessary, at least one acre of well-drained land

Grooming and feeding activities work to build the bond between horse and owner, a relationship important for both, and vital for the safety of the rider.

Whitney L. Lane/Image Bank

per horse in most areas, and preferably more. My inclination is for several fields of two or three acres apiece, which allows the horses to be rotated from pasture to pasture and gives the grass time to re-establish itself between grazings.

"Something there is," said Robert Frost, "that doesn't love a wall." One of those somethings is a horse, an animal that nature has perched permanently on its toes for fast flight and easy jumping. Prospective horse owners must think seriously about fencing before acquiring an animal — a horse that regularly goes wandering will be a cause of raging frustration and the perfect vehicle for creating "bad neighbours."

The pasture must be fenced securely, but horses and barbed wire do not mix. The animals may get tangled up in it, ripping shins and nostrils, pulling tufts from a well-groomed mane or tail. Electric fencing will not do as the only means of containment, although it can be useful as a back-up. (Pastured horses periodically check electric fencing: If the battery goes dead, if wet weather or grass grounds out the system, nothing will stand between a restless steed and freedom.)

The ideal fencing is both safe and strong. Board or post fencing is the most popular choice with horse

owners. White paint, although not essential, is more than a cosmetic covering for such a fence; horses are colour blind and apt to run against a dark fence at night.

ROOM & BOARD

Lacking suitable housing or fencing, the horse owner may be able to arrange stabling with a nearby farmer who is willing to rent or barter stall space and stable rights. Some horses like to have cattle for company, but others do not. Sometimes the bovine involved has other ideas entirely. A neighbour of mine bought a pony for his children, hoping to pasture it with his Jersey. The cow took one look at its new pasture mate and jumped the nearest fence, heading off for more congenial territory.

For the city-bound horse buyer, or the person who cannot devote the requisite hour or so of daily care to his horse, a boarding stable may be the answer. Such establishments take care of the animal's day-to-day needs, regular hay and grain feedings, stall cleaning, paddock exercise and provision of straw bedding. It is possible to arrange for boarding with riding lessons, boarding with training for the horse or a special boarding and breeding contract. Stables on the posh end of the scale will have an indoor riding arena for year-round use, but stabling and use of such facilities can run upwards of $250 per month. Less luxurious boarding can be had, away from major centres, for as little as $60 per month. In almost all cases, the horse owner will be expected to pay for veterinary bills, blacksmith calls and repairs to tack (riding equipment).

Financial considerations aside, there are very real advantages to caring for one's own horse, rather than leaving it to a stable hand. The horse learns to depend on whoever comes along with the daily hay, oats and pats on the neck. If, as is inevitable, the rider becomes "unseated," the two "part company," or some other euphemistic mishap occurs, the horse who knows he is carrying his meal ticket and friend will be much more likely to stand by until the rider has picked himself up and is ready to continue.

Caring for one's own horse means feeding two or three times a day, every day — no time out for good behaviour, or bad weather. It will mean — optimally — getting a seasoned horseman to help with the unpredictable questions and pitfalls. You may want him to check the horse every few weeks in the beginning. An improperly fed horse, for instance, can lose 100 pounds before it is even noticeable to the person with an untrained eye. With an older animal, such a weight loss could lead to prolonged or permanent health problems.

One of the best methods of finding out just how much work is involved in horse care is to "borrow" a livery stable mount during the months when it is not required by its owners. A summer camp, for instance, may use its animals only during July and August, and for the rest of the year, will often loan the horses and tack to responsible individuals. You provide the feed and maintenance.

Unfortunately, the pony purchased for children is often the worst victim of improper care. A starry-eyed child, even an over-eager adult, can quickly find himself tiring of the responsibility. Despite a child's insistence that he or she will care faithfully for little Midnight, the reality of horse care is beyond the abilities of most small children. The parent must be willing to take ultimate responsibility. Even pony riding is likely to lose its glamour after the young jockey has been thrown, bumped against a fence or had his head connect with a low branch.

Parents should be aware that a horse, even a small pony, can be a dangerous "toy" for an unsupervised child. Elementary safety procedures will be in order. Just as the intelligent parent shouldn't let his child play goalie without a face mask, he or she should also provide and insist upon the use of a riding helmet. Knowledge of such basic techniques as the "emergency dismount," taught by all reputable riding instructors, should be a preliminary to any youngster's involvement with horses.

My brother is experimenting with the lease of a 13-hand (one hand equals four inches) pony from a family whose children had outgrown it. His son is attempting to be responsible for the feeding and care of the animal, and the success or failure of this trial period will determine if the family is really ready for horse ownership.

ECONOMIC HORSE SENSE

Once the prospective buyer has assured himself that he has the time and space for a horse, there are several more mental steps to take before loosening the purse strings.

Forgetting the sight of the Cisco Kid on Diablo or Dale Evans galloping Buttermilk off into a cinemascopic sunset, what do you really want in a horse? A spirited, two-year-old Palomino stallion? Fine, provided you are well-heeled and an expert horseman. A horse is just big enough to be dangerous in the wrong hands, and the worst mistake a first-time horse buyer can make — other than dragging an equine basket case out of the Toronto stockyards — is to buy an animal he cannot handle with confidence.

Coat colour tends to preoccupy the minds of some novice horse buyers, and it shouldn't. Certain colours go in and out of fashion, as do breeds, but it is wise to remember the old horseman's saying that "a good horse can never be a bad colour." The type of horse required should be considered first. (A draft horse, for instance, would be unsuitable for show jumping.) The health, conformation and temperament should all be considered next, followed by breed and, last, colour.

What price a good first horse? Registered animals cost more than grades, and are probably no advantage to the beginner, unless he or she wants a mare to breed. In most parts of the country, expect to pay $500 to $800 for a reasonably trained grade horse or a mediocre registered animal. A horse with show prospects will cost more than $1,000.

Remember that the purchase price of a horse is but a fraction of the total financial outlay. The new owner must buy tack, which can easily come to $500; hay — unless he grows his own — at about $100 a year; straw or shavings, and grain. Just as surely as mares eat oats, the cost of concentrates may reach $150 per year for a medium-sized, active, mature horse. The cost of feed will vary, depending on the size of the animal, the amount of work the horse has

George Thomas

to do, and, in the case of a mare, if she is in foal or standing barren. Add the cost of boarding if you have no facilities of your own.

All of these figures will be much the same for the right horse that initially costs $800 as they are for the wrong horse with a price tag of $600. Penny pinching at the outset is simply a false economy.

The prospective buyer must consider — honestly — how well he can ride. If he has never fallen off, he's still a novice and needs a safe, gentle, sensible mount, one that can take him out on the trail and perhaps, as his ability and confidence increase, into the show ring.

Any horseman — or horse — can quickly spot a rider's lack of expertise. One of my own riding students claimed she was not afraid of horses, but under her my horse shied at things he never noticed with a different person in the saddle. There is no shame in being a beginner. We would all like to ride like Steve Cauthen, but it's better to be known as a realistic novice than an over-confident dreamer.

At the risk of creating another saying, I would caution the beginner not to buy any horse that knows less about horseback riding than he does. Many newcomers have fond ideas of buying and learning with a colt. Discard this notion at once. It is not only unfair to the rider, but unfair to the horse as well. The rider can always buy a new horse, but what

External Anatomy

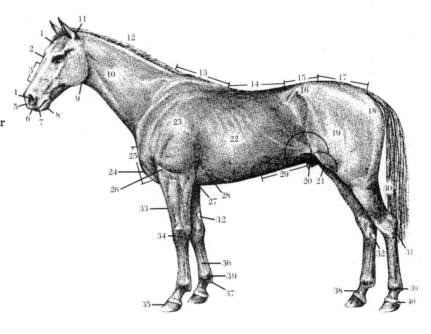

1 Forehead	21 Stifle
2 Face	22 Barrel
3 Bridge of nose	23 Shoulder
4 Nostril	24 Point
5 Muzzle	of shoulder
6 Upper lip	25 Chest
7 Lower lip	26 Arm
8 Under lip	27 Elbow
9 Throat latch	28 Girth
10 Neck	29 Abdomen
11 Poll	30 Gaskin
12 Crest	31 Hock
13 Withers	32 Chestnut
14 Back	33 Forearm
15 Loin	34 Knee
16 Point of hip	35 Hoof
17 Croup	36 Cannon
18 Buttock	37 Ergot
19 Thigh	38 Pastern
20 Flank	39 Fetlock
	40 Coronet

Illustration from THE HORSE/W.H.Freeman and Company

happens to the ill-trained animal that now has ingrained in him all the novice's bad habits?

In my opinion, the best mount for a beginning horseman is an experienced horse of at least six or seven years. Even a 12- or 13-year-old, well-schooled animal often has enough life left to challenge and teach the neophyte rider. Properly cared for, the horse can be ridden into his late teens in most cases.

George Saunders, author of *Your First Horse*, says, "I've seen many top performers on the polo team or in the hunting field who were almost old enough to vote." It won't take much equine know-how to tell a good older horse from what writer Monica Dickens calls "a comfortable, wise old cob, with feet like inverted buckets and a back like a fireside chair."

Reconsider, if necessary, any preconceptions you may have about the sex of your intended horse. A stallion may carry a romantic aura about it, and a rearing steed may look great under Zorro, but its natural qualities of feistiness, high energy and occasional unpredictability will not endear the stallion to a beginner. Even a stallion that has been gelded (castrated) late in life, rather than during the recommended period of birth to two years, may continue to "feel his oats" in some unfortunate situations.

The purchase of a mare offers the advantage of someday arranging for her to present you with a foal, perhaps when her riding usefulness is coming to an end. Keep in mind that a mare may be temperamental while she is in heat, and the most opportune breeding time is likely to occur every 21 to 23 days during some of the best spring and summer riding weather. Mares were traditionally used by Arab horsemen: They were preferred over stallions, and as the Arabs did not geld their horses, there was no third option.

A gelding is often the choice of the wise beginner. Without the strong hormonal drive of a stallion, he is likely to have the friendliest of personalities and the most predictable disposition, being less inclined to swings of mood or bouts of viciousness. However, bring an open mind along when picking a horse — the individual animal that attracts your interest may not conform to any of the sex roles described.

SENTIMENTALITY BE DAMNED

By the time one's horse sense has at last overtaken his romantic notions, it is time to take the plunge. As one horsewoman says, "Don't be sentimental when searching for a horse — there's plenty of time for that after the right animal has been found."

A friend or acquaintance with a good deal of equine experience can be invaluable in helping find one's *Equus primus*. In my own case, newfound friends at the stable helped steer me away from the sales barns.

Every week, in many areas, these outfits sell horses to the highest bidders. Often the winning bids are none too high, but then again the stock is usually none too good either — owners frequently use these facilities to unload spoiled or dangerous animals.

Unscrupulous dealers at such establishments may drug nervous or injured horses to camouflage their true condition. One of my friends, who had a job lead-

Conformation Defects

Ideal Base wide Toes out Base narrow, toes out Base narrow Bow-legged Knock-kneed Pigeon-toed

Ideal Stands wide Bow-legged Stands close Cow-hocked Ideal Camped under

Camped out Knee-sprung Calf-kneed Ideal Stands under Camped out Hind leg too straight

ing trail rides for a local livery, saw an all-too-familiar horse enter the sales barn ring one day. She knew him for his vicious nature and his tendency to run away with even the most experienced rider. That day, the temperamental animal appeared lamb-like in personality. The usual glint was gone from his eye and he quietly followed the orders of his rider. My friend imagined with horror the innocent buyer's predicament when the drugs had worn off. I'd hate to be in that saddle myself, or, worse, to put a child into it.

Trail horses or those from commercial establishments where they have been rented out at hourly rates are usually a bad buy as well. Too often, they have been ruined by the rough handling of weekend cowboys, and they are frequently "barn sour" (having a tendency to run back to the barn), dull-mouthed (having become insensitive from rough handling of the bit) or "stiff-sided" (from being exposed to constant heel-digging and incorrect turning signals, the horse now ignores all leg signals). A ride on one feels like a trip in a car with two flat tires and no shock absorbers.

Lesson horses, on the other hand, can be among the best choices. Sold by riding schools, they are often quiet, well-mannered and dependable mounts. I know of several that have been bought by green riders who later successfully rode them in local shows. Such a school horse may command a slightly higher price because of its background and because those offering it for sale know how to sell a horse.

Blacksmiths and trainers know where good horses can be found and, for a fee, will often agree to pick one for the new buyer. If not, they can frequently give some idea of an available animal's value and its mannerisms. Good leads can also be picked up at the local saddlery shop, the feed co-operative, pony clubs, breed associations and schools.

Newspaper ads and country store bulletin boards often advertise horses on the market, although their terms may be somewhat misleading. A "jumping" horse may be one that regularly clears the pasture fence to escape a bothersome dog, and wouldn't know a course of standards if it were dropped in the middle of the Grand National. Often "quiet" means that the owner has never asked the horse to do anything it wasn't about to do anyway — what Sigmund Freud described as "the less than ideal situation in which the rider is obliged to guide his horse in the direction in which the horse itself wants to go."

SNAKE OIL & STALLIONS

Then there are the horse dealers, who, as a class, have unfortunately attained a reputation second only to snake oil salesmen. In fact, they can be a valuable resource for the buyer. Local horse owners, stables and saddlery stores can recommend, or warn you about, individual dealers. Check with former customers. Although some dealers in the horse world are out to make the expedient buck, most are not and their advice can be valuable. One newly initiated teamster of my acquaintance decided he needed a driving team of his own and, refusing to listen to a horse dealer's advice, insisted on buying a young, barely trained stallion and an equally green mare. One set of broken harnesses and a crashed

Horse Buyer's Check List

		YES	NO
1.	Does he keep his ears forward and face you when you approach?	☐	☐
2.	Can you walk, trot, canter, stop and back him up?	☐	☐
3.	Is the horse short enough that you can bridle and mount him easily?	☐	☐
4.	Will he keep his head down and open his mouth for the bit?	☐	☐
5.	Will he allow you to groom and saddle him without resistance?	☐	☐
6.	Will he allow each of his four feet to be picked up and held for examination and cleaning? (DO NOT attempt this yourself with a strange horse. Accept the seller's demonstration or get an experienced friend or veterinarian to do it for you. Until a mutual trust has developed between owner and horse, there is much to be said against grabbing onto its most lethal parts.)	☐	☐
7.	Can you bring him down from a trot or canter to a walk without a Herculean battle?	☐	☐
8.	Will he move away from leg pressure? (To turn a horse to the left, the rider steers with the left rein and at the same time applies pressure to the horse's left side with his leg. If properly trained to respond to this signal, the horse will move his body to the right, in order to bring his rear end in line with his head.)	☐	☐
9.	Will he accept double riders?	☐	☐
10.	Will he pass a veterinary check?	☐	☐
11.	Can he be ridden bareback?	☐	☐
12.	Will he walk the margin of a busy road without flinching?	☐	☐

Answers

If you said "NO" to Number 1,2,4,5,6,7 or 10, forget the horse. A new rider shouldn't have to contend with these problems.

Does the horse fail in other areas? Think seriously about any question which received a "NO" answer:

Number 3. Do you want a horse which you will have to mount with a step ladder? What if you become unseated away from a fence or mounting block?

Number 8. A horse that won't move away from leg pressure may shy out in traffic on a busy road.

Number 9. You or your child may want to share the horse with a friend. Many teenagers ride double because one cannot afford a mount. Note, however, that the combined weight of the riders should not exceed roughly one-sixth the horse's weight.

Number 11. A marginal consideration, but for winter riding, it is nice to share the warmth rising from the horse's back.

Number 12. Do you want to spend all of your time in an exercise ring or pasture? Often the best trails can be reached only by travelling along a side road. You will want to be safe.

A good first horse should merit a "YES" response to all 12 questions.

manure spreader later, the teamster had learned his lesson and traded this frolicking twosome in on the dependable and well-used team of mares that the horse trader had recommended in the first place.

A breeding farm is the place to find a sound, purebred animal, registered or not. The breeder is trying to build a good reputation for his stock, and will try to steer the buyer correctly. He will, of course, exert his influence in promoting a particular breed of horse, and here is where the buyer must have done his reading homework to know the relative merits of different horses. He should know what type of work he intends to do and will avoid the mistake of choosing a dainty Arab when what he wants is an animal that can pull a log out of the bush when asked to.

Once you've found a likely prospect, take a long, critical look. The horse should be alert but not skittish. It should appear to be intelligent — a horse with droopy eyelids, dull eyes and a sullen or hangdog appearance is either sick, old or a genetic casualty. Check the colour of the lining of the nose and the eye membranes, which should be salmon pink. The coat should be smooth and glossy, the skin loose and supple. The horse should stand firmly on all four feet or rest one hind foot periodically. If it seems to be favouring a front foot or trying to take the pressure from it, move on to another horse. Check its manure, which should be regularly ball-shaped and flaky. The animal should be pleasantly filled out, neither too thin nor obese.

Try to arrive at the stable before the appointed time, so that you can catch the preparatory operations. It is often helpful to watch the horse being tacked up, which should not be an occasion for it to bite, kick, rear or resist in any way. If it co-operates with saddling and bridling, it will be ready for a ride.

"Make sure you ask the owner or one of his helpers to get on the horse first," one stable owner warned me. "No matter how quiet the horse is, you will want to see for yourself."

Next, the buyer should ride the horse himself, walking, trotting and cantering in both directions of the ring or pasture. The rider will soon be able to tell if the horse is a comfortable size for him. My five-foot-eight frame looks gawky on a 13-hand pony, and my legs are too long to administer any kind of effective leg control on such a mount. Similarly, a small child looks like a peanut on a raw-boned 16-hand hunter, and will find the horse almost impossible to saddle. (For a rough measure, the rider should be about one-sixth the weight of the horse. Feed companies and co-ops often will supply a free weight tape, with which anyone can gauge a horse's poundage to within 90 per cent accuracy.)

If the rider cannot walk, trot and canter the horse comfortably in both directions, either the rider needs more lessons or the horse is unsuitable. No one wants a phlegmatic beast, but a horse with too much spirit is likely to be more trouble than one that needs a bit of urging. Beginners too frequently destroy the mouths of restive horses by constantly pulling on the reins.

Take the horse for a ride, noting if it shies easily, and if it follows orders without complaint. Work the horse up to the point that will be expected of it in the future, noting whether it tires easily. Don't be fooled by sellers who claim that the horse is having an off day. Bear in mind, too, that the animal is going to be a long-term investment. It should be comfortable to ride.

Once the rider has dismounted, he should walk around the horse. The animal should appear calm, and should not make a dash for the barn the moment the reins are released. A cheerful mount, one that can be a pet as well as transportation, is the best choice.

Consider special needs as well. (See check list.) Will it be necessary to load and unload the horse from a trailer? Will the animal allow two riders to mount it? This may be important for children, who like to ride double. Will it be ridden bareback?

When the prospective buyer has found the horse he thinks he wants, he should still be wary. Sellers often ride down a hot horse before the purchaser arrives. Drop in unexpectedly for a second look, and bring an experienced friend. If the animal still looks good, arrange for a veterinary check. If the seller won't allow the horse to be examined, consider the horse a write-off. (It's your money; he can have no reasonable excuse for resisting.)

The veterinarian will observe the horse's general condition, inspect eyes, mouth, teeth, nostrils, glands, feet and legs. A hoof tester will be applied to his feet to check for the presence of founder or navicular disease, each a non-curable lameness in one or both of the front feet. If the veterinarian has any suspicion of a leg or foot problem, he may want to x-ray the horse, a procedure that is always worth the extra expense.

One of my friends fell in love with a school horse that she rode weekly. Deciding to buy the animal, she was pleased when he passed every one of her carefully plotted equine tests. Then she had him vetted.

"This horse is navicular," explained the veterinarian. "You will be able to ride him on the flat, but he will break down with any kind of hard riding." Regretfully, my friend decided not to buy the horse and spent three months tracking down an alternative, but finally found one that met all her requirements.

A veterinarian can also check the animal's heart and lungs, and advise the buyer on the necessity of floating (filing down) sharp teeth, worming or vaccinating. If the steed passes all tests, the owner will receive a Certificate of Soundness. The veterinary check may cost from $30 to $40, depending on locale.

Armed with this piece of paper, the rider and his new mount should be home free. The horse buyer who has remained patient — it isn't always easy — and cool-headed throughout this process can now relax and enjoy the horse, content in the knowledge that he hasn't wandered blindly into a rather expensive room in the school of hard knocks. Difficult lessons will remain, but starting with the "right" horse is no small advantage.

"Even after 20 years in the business," one former jockey told me, "I'm still learning every day."

George Thomas

In Praise Of Bigger Horses

Dobbin is beginning to pull his weight again

A Harrowsmith Report

In the years between 1920 and 1945 a fierce and, in retrospect, totally unnecessary battle raged across the rural heartland of North America: the fight between the tractor and the draft horse. It was a wasteful struggle, with the casualties all on one side, and the fact that it took place at all is attributable almost entirely to human greed. When it was over, the tractor had won. Most of its opponents, those great, gentle beasts descended from the medieval war-horse, whose partnership with mankind has continued for centuries, had been ingloriously ground up for dog food.

The contest was unfairly fought from the start. As Maurice Telleen notes in his introduction to *The Draft Horse Primer*, "the avowed purpose of these (tractor manufacturing) companies was to drive the horse into oblivion" and take over the entire agricultural market for themselves. Any means, fair or foul, to this end were adopted without hesitation. The corporations already had a massive advantage over local horse breeders in their ability to provide financing, permitting a farmer to buy a new tractor on time for a modest down payment where the local horseman wanted cash up front, in full.

But individual tractor dealers went their parent companies one better. They took draft horses in trade, as one would a used car, and promptly sent the already broken and well-trained teams off to the slaughterhouse. As the number of trained teams dwindled, the farmers' options narrowed.

The same people who made tractors also made most of the horse-drawn implements, from ploughs to spring harrows, and the replacement parts on which any farmer who clung to the old ways depended. Gradually, the manufacture of horse-drawn equipment was discontinued, leaving the farmers no choice but to switch to tractors. Along with these strategies, farmers were faced with an unending barrage of advertising geared to make the horse look outmoded and anyone who used a team appear as a quaint and rather ridiculous fool.

strategies, farmers were faced with an unending barrage of advertising geared to make the horse look outmoded and anyone who used a team appear as a quaint and rather ridiculous fool.

As a marketing offence, the campaign was an unqualified success. While in 1918 there had been 26.7 million draft horses in the United States alone, 60 years later there were only three million left. Unfortunately, common sense was also sacrificed. No one can deny that the tractor, like a chain saw, is a very useful tool, especially when large acreages are involved and time is at a premium. But urging all farmers totally to abandon horses for tractors was a bit like asking a cabinet maker to throw out his chisels because chain saws cut wood faster. In reality, both tractor and horse may have a place in modern agriculture, each doing the type of work it was designed for and where its unique qualities come into play. For the well-run small farm, the draft horse may be an important power source for the future when the harsh economics of petroleum begin to exact their toll.

DOBBIN'S REVIVAL

Fortunately, some farmers stubbornly refused to give up on Dobbin, believing — correctly at times — that their particular farms could best be held together without handing their souls to the local equipment dealer. These farmers, along with other draft horse enthusiasts, helped preserve the heavy breeds during the past half-century when the work horse was little more than a curiosity. Even in the boom years of agribusiness following the Second World War, they were evident at every county fair, showing their prize Percherons and Clydesdales and carrying off ribbons in pulling or ploughing contests. Even the most convinced "industrial farmer" had to admire the smartness and style of a matched team, ribbons in their mane, stepping 'round the show ring. Today, the ranks of the draft horse enthusiasts are swelling again, due partly to the aesthetic preferences of modern homesteaders and partly to simple economics.

The rising price of fossil fuels and chemical fertilizers and the increasingly rapid depreciation of machines built for planned obsolescence are making old Dobbin, who took 20 years to depreciate and who ate oats a farmer could grow himself, look like a budget-saver. Emission control is no problem — a horse recycles his own fuel, turning it into tons of rich manure to fertilize gardens and fields. Many owners of diversified farms and woodlots, unlike the agribusinessman chained to his mammoth, monocultural empire, have also begun to find tractors downright clumsy in the close, careful work their balanced operations require.

Figures compiled by various registry associations show that a renaissance of the draft horse may be at hand. While in 1970 only 670 Belgian horses were given new registration papers, in 1977 the number of new horses registered in a single year had risen to 2,133. In 1978, 2,416 Belgians were registered. Similar increases have been recorded for Percherons, Clydesdales and other working breeds.

Some small farmers, like Morley Pinsent of Breadalbane, Prince Edward Island, arrive at the decision to farm with horsepower via a process of elimination inspired by the realities of their bank accounts.

"Our search for a horse began soon after finding the perfect place to build a home and settle in, a 50-acre farm of woodland and field," says Pinsent. "We decided we had enough money for a good horse or a poor tractor, and a look at the used tractors available was enough to start us looking for a draft horse to suit our needs. A quick glance at tractor prices brings dreamers back to reality. Anything less than 15 years old is very expensive, complex and difficult to keep running without a lot of specialized skills. Anything older than 15 years is likely to need endless repair, parts searches and the kind of frustration we can do without.

"As for garden tillers," Pinsent continues, "they won't pull a log out of the woods, take the kids for a sleigh ride or mow a few acres of hay. Nor can they provide the simple joy and aesthetic pleasure that comes from sharing your work with a responsive animal in a quiet way. Your toil lightens when you can listen to the birds sing while you work."

Choosing a draft horse, however, is a task that should be undertaken with caution and patience. The same axiom that applies to selecting a saddle horse holds true in seeking an animal for harness work: Never buy a horse in a hurry.

MULE POWER

Drew Langsner, who uses two mules and a 1,500-pound Belgian draft horse named "Rosie" to work his hilly farm near Marshall, North Carolina, also points out that horses aren't the only animals that can pull a plough. On some smaller holdings where jobs are specialized, other beasts of burden may be preferable.

"At the light end of the scale come donkeys and ponies," says Langsner. "Mediterranean, Asiatic and African people have been using donkeys for farm work for centuries, while ponies were originally bred for work in mines and on small farms that couldn't support horses." Donkeys, he explains, are tough, hardy creatures, intelligent and able to forage on scrub growth that would starve horses. "Their bray is shrill and many folks find them unattractive, but donkeys are cheap. One very experienced ploughman we know prefers a hitch of five donkeys over a team of horses."

A good-sized pony, weighing 600 to 800 pounds, can be used for cart work, cultivating, laying out furrows, digging potatoes, sledding rocks and skidding firewood. A team of ponies, with harness and cart, can sometimes be bought for less than a middle-aged horse or mule. As for mules, which result from the cross between a horse and a donkey, they may be cantankerous but are nevertheless hard workers and known for their sure-footedness even on the roughest ground. They range in size from 650 to 1,500 pounds and can equal the working ability of a medium-weight horse team. The smaller "cotton mule"

Haying with horsepower on a Cape Breton farm, this Nova Scotia farmer resisted the temptations of the tractor industry. Part of the newer generation of horse owners, Louise Langsner, inset, harvests corn in a mule-drawn sled.

George Thomas

formed the backbone of agriculture in the southern United States for years.

The Morgan horse and the "farm chunk" are two other possible choices. The Morgan was originally bred as both a riding and harness horse, but its working characteristics have been ignored in recent years in favour of its riding qualities, and Morgans are expensive. The so-called chunk is generally a cross between a western horse and a larger draft breed, weighs between 1,200 and 1,500 pounds, is a good worker and can be obtained at a reasonable price.

Finally, there are the heavy breeds: the noble Belgians, Percherons, Clydesdales, Suffolks and Shires. These magnificent beasts weigh from 1,400 to 2,000 or more pounds, stand 17 or more hands tall and are massive reservoirs of raw power. "You can feel it through the traces when you're behind them," says Russell Gardiner, who farms 35 acres near Camden East, Ontario, with a pair of Belgian crosses. "It is truly astonishing to feel their strength when they lean into the collar." Yet these huge beasts are among the meekest and calmest of horses.

They are also, particularly if they are registered horses, among the most expensive to buy. A registered draft horse can easily cost $5,000 or more. They have hefty appetites as well, and generally should not be considered for very small-scale work.

SOUND PURCHASING

Experienced draft horse users advise beginners to buy locally whenever possible, and never at a horse auction. "The best bet is to buy from a local farmer,"

says Langsner. "Sometimes an older man gets too slow to follow the plough, or may have traded for younger stock when his older team is past doing a full, hard day's work. A local trader with a reputation for honesty can be useful, but he is in business for a profit and the same horse will cost more from him than from a farmer."

A novice buyer should take along a friend who is experienced with horses, and be willing to pay $25 to $35 for a veterinarian's "examination for soundness" before making a purchase.

Many potentially useful ponies, donkeys and riding horses have never been in harness and can be a good buy, but one will be taking more of a chance with these than with stock that is accustomed to a work role. They must also be broken gradually to harness, to prevent injury. A saddle horse will need time to build up the previously unused muscles needed in farm work and inflicting a sudden heavy load on him can strain him physically or break his spirit.

A good horse looks healthy. His body is "thrifty," neither fat nor lean, and his coat is sleek. His walk should be even, not stiff or limpy. Most horses won't come when called, but a healthy horse will show some curiosity. The eyes should be bright and alert, but not excited. Asking the owner to catch the horse will show whether it is willing or feisty. Many horses go through a small ritual of pretending resistance when approached, but a good one won't overdo it.

The veterinarian or experienced horseman should check the horse's teeth for general health and to

verify the owner's claim for age, and should also examine the animal's feet. The hooves should be free of cracks and not splayed out (opened like a spread lobster claw), and show no signs of disorders such as thrush or founder. Horseshoes are not necessary unless the animal will be worked on paved roads, rough gravel or ice, but hooves must be cleaned daily. A horse's hooves, like toenails, must also be trimmed periodically by a competent farrier. Ask the owner to lift each foot and demonstrate cleaning them — a horse that won't let his feet be handled can make life very unpleasant.

Most pulling type horses can be counted on to be useful to about 20 years of age, given adequate care and treatment. Unless a person is experienced in handling and training, it is best to get a horse well broken and gentle, but young enough to make it worth the investment. A draft horse of about five years of age is in its prime. If one is a complete novice with horses, an older animal is often the best choice, since it helps to have at least one member of the work force who knows what to do.

Prices for draft animals vary from region to region and according to seasons. They are lowest in late fall, as the horse will be doing relatively little work over the winter but will still be consuming hay and grain. In spring, when horses are needed again before the plough, prices go up. Bargain-priced ponies or donkeys sometimes go for as little as $25, but middle-aged mules, saddle horses and farm chunks are usually priced between $100 and $400. Large, well-broken mules and grade (non-registered) draft horses

A horse always starts on a cold morning, and the value of a good team is especially evident in winter weather.

might cost $500 or more. Registered, heavy breeds run from $1,000 to $5,000 or more.

The search for the right animal may take time and demand patience, but it should lead you to a number of old-time horsemen, auctions and farms — all of which can add to one's understanding of work horses. As time goes on you will find some wisdom in the words of 19th-century British horseman George Whyte-Melville, who said, "In the choice of a horse and a wife, a man must please himself, ignoring the opinion and advice of friends."

HAMES & TUGS

Some horses come with their harness, which can save a major expense. If an older man is selling, he probaby won't have further need for his harness. Try to get the harness worked into the price, and if there are ploughs, cultivators or a wagon around, consider striking a deal for the complete outfit.

A harness can be plain and simple, but it must be in fairly good condition. "New harness is pretty expensive, up to $500 for a team," says Russell Gardiner. "But a good used set can be had for $200 or less. A team will walk right out of their harness unless you have good stout stuff on them. Get into a corner with rotten harness and they're sure to break something." Gardiner also urges the novice to "make sure the owner shows you how to put the harness on before he leaves the yard."

A ploughman need not have a fancy rig, like those seen in parades and beer advertisements. Metal studs are purely decorative and even lead to rotten leather. Many of the chains and straps seen on show teams are also unnecessary for general farm needs. The most important item is the bridle, as it constitutes the point of control and command.

On old gear, see if the leather cracks when folded, or if it can be torn apart. If so, discard it — no amount of neat's-foot oil will help rotten leather. Stiff, dry and dirty leather, however, can often be renovated. Soak it in warm water. Once it softens take everything apart, noting very carefully what goes where. Scrub with saddle soap, then hang to dry. While the leather is still slightly damp, apply neat's-foot oil generously. (One harness maker suggests melting tallow into neat's-foot oil in even proportions.) Wait several hours, or overnight, before wiping off any excess oil that doesn't soak in. Reassemble carefully.

For driving lines use new five-eighths-inch hemp or Manila ropes with a simple knot tied at each end. Nylon ropes are comfortable to hold, but they stretch easily, resulting in a control lag when pulled. In use, never wind the ropes around one's hands. In case of a runaway, one could get caught and dragged off.

Next in importance is the collar. A horse actually pushes its load against its shoulders, so collars must fit. An oversized collar is worse than a small one, because it pulls up and against the throat, cutting off air. To size a collar, place it over the horse's head, then back against its shoulders. With a good fit one can easily slide a flattened hand between the horse's neck and the collar. If it's tight, one needs a larger size. If the fit is slightly loose, it may be possible to use a collar pad to fill in the space. Some horsemen like collar pads, while others prefer working without them.

Hames are S-shaped, wooden or metal fittings attached against the groove of the collar. These must be well fitted, and stout enough to hold up under a good strong pull. Trace chains or leather tugs are attached to the hames, and both types work well. A new pair of tugs, however, is almost impossible to find. For simple pulling work one only needs a simple harness with a single back band having hooks to hold the traces in place. This rig is excellent for cultivating, ploughing or any kind of direct pulling work. More elaborate harnesses are used for pulling wagons, logging or show.

Only a few horse-drawn implements are presently in production, mainly Amish wagons and a plough or two. Some old country hardware stores still stock plough points and common replacement parts. Single trees, sleds, harrows and drags can be made on the farm, while cultivators can be fabricated by a blacksmith or welding shop.

Mostly, one has to search for old, used gear. There is still a lot around. Once your eye is sensitized, useful items will show up almost anywhere. Older farmers will often part with a plough that's not going to be used again, even if they won't sell to antique collectors. Widows sometimes sell old equipment, but some are hesitant until they know that no kin is interested. In one case, Drew Langsner wanted to buy an old cultivator, but all 12 sons and daughters had an equal share in the "estate." The daughter to whom he spoke insisted that all had to consent before anything was sold off the place.

Farm dispersal auctions are sometimes good places to look. Equipment for sale is usually listed in the auction advertisements, but quality is not indicated. Horse-drawn implements are generally auctioned off last, as they draw the least interest. Bid very low, unless there are Amish or Mennonite farmers in the area, in which case there may be stiff competition for good equipment.

Horse-drawn gear can sometimes be obtained from used farm equipment dealers, especially implements that could be pulled with a small tractor. These would include small wagons, mowers, rakes and manure spreaders. Be sure to check machinery carefully. Have a good idea of how a mower works before buying one. Parts are hard to find, and expensive to fabricate.

EQUINE ESP

It is also possible to adapt some of the old, smaller, pull-type tractor equipment for use with a team of medium-sized or larger horses. Often all that's needed is a "fore cart," a wheeled rig that supports the implement's weight, with a tongue out front to hitch the team to, and an old tractor seat over the axle. One can also advertise for wanted equipment. Be very specific in wording an ad, and try to find out exact details before driving a long distance to look something over.

As for learning to drive a team, the basics are, in Gardiner's words, "fairly simple, like riding a bike," but they boil down mainly to communication. "You must have self-confidence and patience with animals," says Langsner. "The secret is repetition, doing the same thing over and over until it becomes a habit for the horse. There is a great deal of what I call ESP involved. This sense will develop naturally if one concentrates solely on the task at hand. Don't chat with a friend while driving, for example. This will only confuse the horse."

Gardiner notes that it is best to start with an already-trained team or, if one of your animals is green, to begin working him in tandem with an older, experienced horse. Asking a neighbour familiar with draft horses to observe while you learn can also be helpful, as the old-timer passes on tips and hints gleaned from the school of hard knocks.

Remember that a horse is a naturally wary animal who needs to be assured that there is no enemy, obstruction or unsure ground ahead. A horse must develop confidence in its master before it will go comfortably in strange places. It is always a good idea to begin work with a new animal in an open area, free of clutter, debris, tangled wire or sharp obstructions. An uncomfortable horse can even be spooked by a change in wind direction.

Once in harness, the horse will probably keep its ears turned back, listening for commands or signals. There is never any need to yell, or raise one's voice.

Learning the art of handling draft animals on the Langsner farmstead, **inset,** *a novice crew nevertheless manages to plough a large garden. Logging in rough terrain,* **background,** *is a special forte of the draft horse.*

George Thomas, Drew Langsner (Inset)

Equines have very good hearing. Remember also that horses have "ramped vision"; they can only focus along a rather narrow horizontal band at one time. This is caused by their flattened eyeball, which results in separate bands of focus due to the variable distance from the lens to the retina. A horse without blinders can also divide its visual attention; one eye can focus straight, while the other scans off to the side.

Finally, treat a horse like a friend. It's very unnatural for him to wear a harness and to plough in straight lines. Getting such ideas across takes time and real dedication.

A PLACE TO ROLL

A working farm horse is performing much heavier labour than a saddle horse used only for occasional hacking, and consequently has higher energy-replacement needs. Telleen notes in *The Draft Horse Primer* that a good rule of thumb is to "feed daily one pound of (alfalfa) hay for each 100 pounds of live weight" of the horse. Hay rations should be supplemented with grain, such as oats or corn, with minerals, a salt lick and plenty of clean, fresh water. Horses should never be heavily watered just prior to working, although a moderate drink is permissible.

Five or six acres of good pasture will provide the bulk of a medium-sized team's rations over the summer months, replacing the hay portion of their diet. It will also provide a place for the horses to roll, play and unwind from their day's labours. Horses, like people, need recreation to keep them fit and mentally alert.

A well-matched team of draft horses is a power source to be reckoned with, as a visit to any of the numerous "horse pulls" in rural North America will aptly reveal. But, on many modest-sized farmsteads, a single horse can supply nearly all the draft power required for the job. The cost of one horse is relatively small, and hitching, handling and care simpler than in caring for a team.

Undoubtedly, the occasional chore will come up where more than a single horse is needed. That is the time for the owner of a single horse to rent, borrow or trade. Remember, with a good horse in the barn you have a specialized source of power to swap. The neighbour's 90-horsepower tractor may be surprisingly available after the horseman has spent a morning skidding select logs out of that "hard to get at spot" in his woodlot for him, or after a horse and sleigh helped clean out a barn when the stable cleaner broke down and the snow was too deep for anything else in the country to move.

A single draft horse in good condition can plough half an acre a day with a single-furrow, walking plough. Depending on the type of soil and degree of tilth required, a horse should also easily handle harrowing or "fitting up" half an acre to an acre per day. Spreading fertilizer, lime or manure is also a straightforward pulling chore and just the kind of thing for the draft horse.

*Albert LeBlanc of Cape Breton ploughs and fits his land above the Margaree River with horse-drawn implements, including the spring harrow shown, **inset**.*

George Thomas

Ploughing with a horse and walking plough is a job requiring considerable practice. Morley Pinsent's first attempt with "horse, plough and ploughman all novices resulted in a plot that looked like a mole convention gone amok, a sweating horse, a cursing ploughman and a tearful wife looking at what was to have been the garden. Some perseverance, a lot of practice and a few refinements gleaned from old-timers resulted in a passable job and a good feeling of accomplishment."

A single horse is essentially limited to spring tooth, pin or chain harrows. Disc harrows require the power of a team.

The planting of field crops can be handled with either a team or a single horse and broadcast seeder. Broadcast seeders look like seed drills, but instead of putting seed into the ground they lay it evenly on top. A trip over the field afterward with light harrows will cover the seed.

Once row crops are planted and growing, a draft horse becomes a really able helper with weeding and hilling. The manoeuvrability and precise power of a well-trained horse make these chores not only bearable, but enjoyable. Hitch the horse into a scuffler (cultivator) and, if the garden layout is carefully planned, an acre-sized garden can be cultivated and weed-free in an hour or two.

The fruits of a farmstead harvest take many forms, including hay, garden produce, grain, maple sugar and wood. If you have only a few acres of hay to put up, a single horse and some manpower can easily handle the task. Single-horse mowers are common in many parts of Europe, but unfortunately tend to be scarce in North America.

A single horse can handle a mower with about a four-foot cut. The power required to drive the cutter bar limits the size of mower a horse can handle for any sustained length of time. The old-fashioned dump rake was traditionally used with a single horse and any place with a history of draft horse farming abounds with these simple, effective devices. Loading, hauling and storing the bulky crop is the biggest part of haying. It can be as simple as a pitchfork, horse and cart or as complex as imagination and a truly staggering assortment of machinery from yesteryear will allow. In general, strive for the simplest arrangement that will get the job done.

Grain harvesting, unless the crop is small, has become a job for the high-powered tractor set, although some Iowa farmers with two-ton draft horse teams will swear by horsepower. For the small holder, the custom man with his combine is the easiest way to get this crop off. Even the old horse-drawn binders needed three animals to pull them.

THE EXTRA HAND

Small-scale row crop, garden and maple sugar harvests are, with few exceptions, done by hand. Horses, hitched to a wagon, cart or sleigh, provide the power for moving the harvest to storage or processing. Cartage jobs of this kind are where the horse excels. A well-trained animal can move to voice commands and, once the routine of a task is learned, needs very limited direction, saves a lot of steps, and is almost like having an extra hand in the field.

Of all the places that horses can assist on a farmstead, it is perhaps in the woods where they are at their best. A well-disciplined and quiet horse in the bush is equal to a tractor and an extra person. In fact, a horse that has seen several years of woodland work can make a man and tractor look completely helpless in the woodlot. Man, saw and horse work as a skilled team, usually with the horse responding to voice signals from the horseman. Some farm woodlot work in Eastern Canada is still carried out with the aid of a horse, and even the tall timber country of Oregon and Washington still has a place for the woods horse. Commercial thinning of Douglas fir stands is often done with horses, since little or no damage is done to the standing timber or forest floor.

Any sensitive woods husbandman cannot help but notice the difference in an area logged with horses and one logged with the aid of machinery. The only evidence of logging in the horses' part of the woods is a bit of a path with the surface inch or less of ground scratched and a few stumps and brush piles visible. The manoeuvrability of a "skid horse" allows the logger to be very selective, while avoiding the necessity of making a road or trail to the felled logs for

In its heyday, the draft horse powered North American agriculture, providing a reliable source of power when given proper care and handling by patient husbandmen.

tractor and pickup to pass through. Horses operate even better in the bush during winter than in summer or fall, allowing this work to be done during a relatively slack time of year.

Most jobs that make a small holding go 'round usually involve moving something from one place to another. An endless supply of rocks pop up in pasture and field to be moved to the rock wall or pothole; the manure accumulated in the barn has to be moved to the field to compost, then moved again to be spread; brush has to be hauled from fence lines; supplies from building to building, and a sow to a neighbour's for breeding. All these and the endless variety of other moving tasks can be accomplished, summer or winter, with horses, truck, wagon and sleigh. Road maintenance can be done with horses pulling a fresnel or a log-drag. The logging harness and chain can be used to drag heavy loads over short distances. Imagination is the only limit to the everyday usefulness of a well-trained draft horse.

"Our house lies a snowy one-third of a mile from the nearest road throughout the winter," says Morley Pinsent. "A horse and sleigh make that distance insignificant. Although we have shelter for the horse at the road, we often find it faster, simpler and more enjoyable to trot past the snow and ice covered car, bells a-jangle, and carry on to our destination by 'one-horse open.' As one gets accustomed to hitching the horse, it becomes easier, faster and more pleasant than starting a car for a short winter run — especially considering the shovelling, scraping and pushing that seem to be part of car life in rural Canadian winters. This joy of horse-drawn travel tends to carry through into summer as short trips become more horse-powered and less petroleum-fuelled."

Working with horses tends to push a person into ever greater "self-sufficiency," since the simple nature of it all makes one anxious to mend, repair, manufacture and maintain for himself. It even helps spark latent interests in leatherwork, woodwork and blacksmithing.

Slow down, "get a horse" and create a pleasant spectacle, as Pinsent does, rumbling across the meadow with draft horse and brightly-painted dump cart, singing to all who will listen, the horseman's cry from Jethro Tull's *Heavy Horses:*

"Bring me a wheel of oaken wood,
and a rein of polished leather,
a Heavy Horse and a tumbling sky,
Brewing heavy weather."

Sources

Magazines:

THE DRAFT HORSE JOURNAL
Edited by Maurice & Jeannine Telleen
808 Des Moines Street
Webster City, Iowa 50595
Published quarterly.

THE EVENER
Edited by Elizabeth Jones
Putney, Vermont 05346
Published 11 times per year.

CANADIAN PERCHERON BROADCASTER
Bruce Roy
Box 9
Cremona, Alberta T0M 0R0
Published annually.

Books:

THE DRAFT HORSE PRIMER
By Maurice Telleen
386 pages
Rodale Press
Emmaus, Pennsylvania 18049
The complete book of draft horse handling, care and farming.

GENTLE GIANTS
By Ralph Whitlock
176 pages
Lutterworth Press
Distributed by:
G.R. Welch Co. Ltd.
310 Judson Street
Toronto, Ontario M8Z 1J9.

THE HORSE IN THE FURROW
By George Ewart Evans
292 pages
Faber and Faber Limited
Distributed by:
Oxford University Press
70 Wynford Drive
Don Mills, Ontario M3C 1J9.

Associations:

CANADIAN CLYDESDALE ASSOCIATION
J. Douglas Charles, Secretary
1501 Arlington Avenue
Saskatoon, Saskatchewan S7H 2Y3

CANADIAN BELGIAN HORSE ASSOCIATION
Paul Lindquist, Secretary
R.R.1
Cameron, Ontario K0M 1G0

CANADIAN PERCHERON ASSOCIATION
Bruce Roy, Secretary
Box 9
Cremona, Alberta T0M 0R0

Great Eggspectations

Whipped in a soufflé or dropped from a helicopter, the egg is one of nature's most perfect designs

By Jennifer Bennett

Bob Anderson/The Image Bank of Canada

"**A** hen," quipped Samuel Butler, "is but an egg's way of making another egg."

Clearly an "Egg-Firster," Butler is but one of many to exalt the mystery and uniquely aesthetic quality of the egg. Throughout history, eggs have been, in turn, feared, worshipped, sacrificed, used as charms and talismans, touted as aphrodisiacs and, at times, relied on to divine the future.

The "Cosmic Egg" turns up in the folklore of many cultures and their attempts to explain man's relationship to the universe. An ancient Hindu sacred work, *Chandogya Upanisad,* says the world "turned into an egg. It lay for the period of a year. It was split asunder. One of the two eggshell parts became silver, one gold . . . . What was the inner membrane is cloud and mist. What were the veins are the rivers. What was the fluid within is the ocean. Now, what was born therefrom is the sun."

The Maoris of New Zealand tell of the egg dropped by a bird into the primeval sea. It burst to free a man, a woman, a boy, a girl, a pig, a dog, and — conveniently enough — a canoe to hold them all. Similarly, among the Finnish legends is the tale of a teal's egg that fell and broke, the fragments forming earth, sky, sun, moon and clouds. Folklorists believe that early Britons went into their fields and tossed eggs into the air with a twist that hopefully would assure their landing intact — a ritual supposed to bring fertility to the land.

EGGS AWEIGH

Along similar, if less bucolic, lines of thought, Colonel J.N. Shipster scattered eggs to the wind at Fort McClennan, Alabama in 1970. Perhaps the ultimate test of what has been called nature's most perfect design, Shipster took a dozen fresh eggs aloft in a helicopter and dropped them onto a grassy field from a height of 185 feet. The egg dropper was moving at a speed of 20 knots and the U.S. Army obligingly provided radio communication between chopper and the impact zone. Nine of the 12 eggs were recovered in perfect condition. Shipster concluded that, as the eggs would have reached their terminal velocity at about 200 feet, he had proved their ability to withstand drops from any height.

(It may be worthy of note that adult chickens fare less well in Canadian tests conducted by the Aeronautics Division of the National Research Council, developers of the great poultry cannon. The device was designed about 10 years ago to test the ability of airplane windshields to resist impact with birds. According to Tony Bosik of the NRC, the cannon still receives regular use, fed with four-pound Leghorns bought from a local farmer. The chicken gun is capable of firing the birds at velocities of from 100 miles per hour up to the speed of sound. The Leghorns are used either freshly killed or frozen-then-thawed, and must be put in special bags for higher speed tests so that they will hit the windshield reasonably intact. The testers reckon that the complete, unplucked birds offer the same threat to a windshield as most ducks or geese that planes are likely to encounter when flying.)

Such indignities aside, egg layers have been working contentedly for man since their domestication some 5,000 years ago. While egg consumption here is dropping slightly each year, North Americans consume an average of about 230 eggs each annually. The typical Leghorn hen in a commercial egg factory produces about 240 eggs in her 12 months of laying, hence the rough equation of one chicken for each man, woman and child on the continent. (If all the eggs laid in the United States in the month of March were placed end-to-end, they would easily stretch the 240,000 miles to the moon.)

Any discussion of eggs seems to encourage a *Guiness Book of World Records* mentality, and it must be noted that the world mark for egg production belongs to a Black Orpington that laid 361 eggs in New Zealand in 1930. Also, an incredibly prolific English Rhode Island Red hen, named Penny, laid 20 in a week and an astounding seven in a single day on September 11, 1971.

FULL-TILT LEGHORNS

An egg a day is the best most poultry owners can expect from a chicken at the peak of its production, but this accepted limitation of nature may eventually fall to the poultry geneticists. A century ago, for example, the average Leghorn produced only 100 eggs a year and by 1960, through selective breeding, this figure had risen to 207.

Today's average commercial Leghorn starts laying at five months of age and will continue full tilt for 12 months, after which she is dispatched down the road, most often into the cauldrons of the potpie and chicken noodle soup industry. During her short

life, this Leghorn eats 95 pounds of feed, yields 21 dozen eggs, eliminates about 50 pounds of high-nitrogen fertilizer and, at the end of it all, will supply about four and one-half pounds of meat, as well as feathers and offal for fertilizer and pet food.

All of this takes place in huge sheds where the floor area is often measured in acres, with tens of thousands of young pullets banked into wire cages. The five-month-old female Leghorn is placed in a two-cubic-foot all-wire box with three other pullets of the same age (who are perhaps sisters). The four quickly establish a pecking order within their standing-room-only quarters, and in this artificially-lit, mini-society are largely oblivious to time or the seasons.

The wire cage floor is sloped so that the eggs roll onto a constantly moving conveyor belt which carries them through an automatic "car wash" type device that cleans them and then applies a coat of mineral oil to extend their shelf life.

Commercial egg production is kept artificially high by maintaining light in the shed 16 hours a day — hens do not lay in the dark. And so, quite spent a year later, the birds are shipped out en masse to be replaced by truckloads of fresh hens. It is the stuff of nature lovers' nightmares: birds whose beaks are severely clipped so they won't harm each other, birds that never see the light of day, never scratch in real earth for worms or seeds, birds that never raise chicks and, in fact, are as virginal as the day they were hatched, when they finally make their way — hanging by their feet — down that last assembly line.

Anyone who has taken pity on such birds and bought a few with intentions of liberating them in a lush barnyard will be aware of just how helpless these worn-out egg machines are. They can barely eat, have great difficulty in walking and very often die within days of having their environment changed.

Little wonder then that the commercial supermarket egg produced by such chickens is the subject of such suspicion among those who seek natural foods. Having been convinced that white sugar and white bread have been leached of all their goodness, it is easy to look askance on those lily-white Leghorn shells. But while they *may* contain nutritionally inferior, not-so-fresh yolks and whites, the chalk-coloured Leghorn shells are no real indication of an egg's merit.

Brown eggshells are produced by an inherited factor carried by certain breeds of chickens, with the shell picking up its pigment from the blood of the hen. Shell colour, however pleasing, is not affected by diet nor is it in any way indicative of a superior egg. Nonetheless, hens that produce brown eggs tend to do so less efficiently than the highly tuned Leghorn, so the consumer may be able to convince himself that he will be getting a less "mass-produced" egg if he buys a brown one.

The way to be certain, of course, is to raise your own flock of hens and collect your own eggs. Six to 12 birds will keep most families well-stocked, with occasional surpluses.

If you feed the birds exclusively on commercial laying mash and keep them tightly confined, there is little likelihood that the eggs produced will be any better tasting than those from the market. The advantages begin to come into play when the birds have access to sunlight, when they are allowed to run and are fed a varied diet, including table scraps and green roughage.

The resulting fresh eggs will have deep-orange yolks that stand up proudly when cracked into a flat pan and will have whites that spread no farther from the yolk than its diameter. In contrast, not-so-fresh eggs have runny, watery whites and yolks that flatten out immediately. At the very least, the "farm fresh" egg is higher in Vitamin A (as indicated by its yolk colour) and there is no shortage of praise for its superior taste.

The Leghorn may or may not be included in a barnyard flock, but there can be no question of its ability to convert feed into eggs efficiently. With a diet of concentrates alone, a Leghorn will eat about four and one-half pounds of feed to produce a pound of eggs. A meat-type bird, in contrast, will lay big, lovely eggs but will consume eight pounds of grain to create a pound of them.

Broodiness, the mothering tendency of some chickens to sit on and hatch the eggs they or other birds lay, will lower a hen's productivity. On the other hand, it will supply you with a feathered incubator and the cheapest, least bothersome and most fascinating method of filling the ranks of your flocks.

Most birds that lay white-shelled eggs are not known for their broodiness, and it has been scrupulously bred out of the Leghorn for generations. These birds are flighty little things that probably now feel no sorrow at seeing their just-wrought eggs zipped away on a conveyor belt, and the whole business of broodiness is quite beneath them. Likewise, the heavy meat-type birds spawned by the broiler industry have very little inclination to reproduce themselves.

The compromise is a dual-purpose breed that will work quite diligently at egg laying and also be meaty enough for the table. Some of the most popular of these are the Plymouth Rocks, Rhode Island Reds and New Hampshires, all of which lay brown eggs.

The Araucana, a South American chicken which lays blue-shelled eggs, is a lean bird like the Leghorn, and not worth raising for its meat. In this same class are the California Gray, the Minorca and Ancona, all of which produce white-shelled eggs in good quantity. Bantams, on the other hand, are broodiness personified, and will raise the young of anything that lays eggs.

The state of the chicken in North America is perhaps best indicated by the fact that 85 per cent of all birds alive today are crossbreeds. Pure Leghorns and White Rocks account for another 12 per cent, with all other breeds combined totalling but two and one-half per cent. The backyard chicken flock appears to be the last stronghold of many formerly popular chicken breeds.

EGG BIOLOGY

Whatever the type of bird doing the laying, the basic process is the same. A just-hatched female chick has 3,600 to 4,000 minute ova packed in her ovaries and between five and six months later, depending on breed and environment, these will begin appearing as pullet eggs.

Unlike game birds, the chicken is an indeterminate layer; that is, it will continue to lay no matter how many eggs have been produced, as long as they are removed each day. (Determinate birds have a built-in trigger mechanism that tells them to start sitting once a set number — 12 to 24 — of eggs has been laid.)

Once the yolk has been released from the ovary, it enters the oviduct where it *may* be fertilized, but, if not, it will continue on its merry way just as if it had been, but *sans* embryo. In the oviduct are glands which secrete albumen (egg white) to cover the yolk, and lower in the route other glands add two shell membranes. In the final stretch are glands which secrete calcium carbonate to form the hard outer shell. This last step takes up 21 of the 24 hours that it normally takes to make an egg. As soon as the shell is complete, the egg is laid. Within 30 minutes the next yolk is released to begin its journey.

If two or more egg cells happen to mature at the same time, they may be enveloped by the same albumen and shell, producing double or triple-yolked eggs. In fact, a five-yolked egg was once laid by a Black Minorca in England in 1896. The monstrous product was more than a foot around the long axis. Occasionally a more mysterious phenomenon occurs. A very large egg appears, about the size of a pear, and inside is — not five yolks, nor one huge yolk — but a layer of albumen surrounding another perfect egg inside a perfect shell. Such oddities are most common in older hens, while the first pullet eggs are known for their multiple yolks and imperfect shells.

Nothing has yet been said here about the rooster. His Nibs is not required to be present simply for the production of eggs. If fertile eggs are desired, one rooster should be added for each 10 to 15 hens of the dual-purpose breeds. (One male for each 15 to 20 hens of the light breeds is recommended, while heavy breeds need a rooster for each eight to 12 females.)

A single mating produces male sperm that are viable in the hen's reproductive system for two to three weeks. The first fertile egg should appear 24 hours after the first mating.

If the resulting eggs are destined to be hatched in an incubator or under someone else's broody hen, they should be gathered at least three times each day, or every hour in very hot or cold weather. It is most convenient to have eggs hatching in batches, so the required number is gathered and then all started on the same day. Fertile eggs can be held in cool (50 to 60 degrees Fahrenheit), dark conditions, preferably 70 to 80 per cent humidity, for up to 10 days before the incubation is initiated.

As the egg is laid, the embryo is in the process of forming (as indicated by a small blood spot), but this development ceases once the temperature of the egg drops below 80 degrees. When raised to optimal hatching temperature — about 100 degrees — the chick's development resumes. Eggs not gathered and cooled promptly have a low viability as the embryo will have been growing but under less than proper conditions.

Fertile eggs destined for hatching must be stored small-end down. The large end of the egg contains an air sac, and if stored incorrectly this may dislodge and move to the small end of the egg. Eggs are hatched commercially with the large-end up, for the head of the chicken will form there and it will need the air sac in the hours just before pipping out of the shell. Chicks which develop with the head crowded into the pointed end of the egg are often deformed and do not survive hatching. If fertile eggs are held more than five days before hatching they should be turned twice a day to prevent the yolk from attaching to the shell. During the incubation period broody hens instinctively turn their eggs several times an hour, and home hatchers should turn their eggs gently three times each day from the second to the eighteenth day. (When hatched flat on their sides — the most common home method — eggs are usually marked with an "X" on one side to assure that none are missed when a batch is turned.) If all has gone well, the chicks emerge on the twenty-first day.

PERFECT NUTRITION

A small flock of laying hens is surprisingly easy to care for, requiring less than five minutes a day to check feeder and waterer, refill if necessary, and to gather the eggs — a most satisfying task. Keeping the bedding in nest boxes clean will usually assure clean eggs, but any dirt or adhering litter can be brushed or washed off. Some poultry keepers are staunchly opposed to washing the egg, pointing out, correctly, that it decreases its storage life. Most farm or backyard eggs are used so quickly, however, that washing is of minimal effect. (Be sure to wash in warm water — the shell has 6,000 to 8,000 micropores, and if cold water causes the inside of the egg to contract, water, perhaps contaminated with bacteria, will be drawn into the egg.)

Unlike their caged cousins, small flock hens need not be replaced each year. They will lay at a gratifying rate for a good three years, taking a pause once each year to moult.

With even a small producing flock, you will soon become clever at discovering the ways and means of using eggs. For one thing, a dozen farm-fresh eggs makes an excellent gift or barter item, and one which — if your hens help feed themselves by foraging or if part of their diet is home-grown — has cost considerably less than commercial eggs.

Very shortly you will be expert in the ways of omelettes, egg salads, sandwiches, soufflés, quiches, sauces, meringues, cakes and a host of custards and desserts too rich to mention. You may even rival French gastronome Grimod de la Reyniere, who once sat down and counted 685 known ways to serve eggs. Fortunately, an egg is a perfectly balanced formula, a nutritionally complete blend of protein, minerals and vitamins.

The high protein content makes them useful not only as a meat substitute but also as a thickener; the protein will shrink and solidify in cooking, making eggs ideal for sauces and puddings. This very quality should encourage wariness in cooking eggs over high heat, unless you like them rubbery. Medium heat will give tender, flavourful dishes.

Don't use an egg less than three days old for hard-boiling, beating or baking. Really fresh eggs will turn greenish when hard-boiled, will be difficult to peel and will not beat to much of a volume. Eggs are at their best between three days and two weeks, after which it is all downhill.

If you find yourself with a true glut of eggs, you may be tempted to set a record of your own. There's the U.S. colonel's egg drop feat, but it might be easier to attempt the long-distance throwing record — now standing at 316 feet between thrower and catcher — without breaking the egg. Or there's egg shelling, for which two blind Englishmen hold the unenviable mark for shelling 1,050 dozen hard-boiled eggs in just over seven hours in 1971.

And, just to test the ingenious engineering that makes an egg, you can try the old Charles Atlas arm-breaker. Weave your fingers together and place a raw egg between, so that the points are in the centre of each palm. Now try to break the egg by pressing your hands together. Don't worry — you can't do it.

In the end, the egg retains its mystery and its timeless value to our diet. Those who know the returns and rewards of keeping a flock of chickens will easily appreciate the old vaudeville gag which states:

"The chicken must be the most useful animal . . . ."

"Yes, you can eat it before it's born and after it's dead."

Beginnings In Poultry

Chicken without the Colonel, eggs without the McMuffin

By Jennifer Bennett

There is nothing quite so vulnerable as that first boxful of day-old chicks and nothing that says so clearly you've arrived in the country — or at least a small town (urban poultrying being restricted to midnight skulkers and those with tolerant neighbours).

Our own experiences with domestic fowl had never gone much further than reading *Chicken Little* as children and it was pure adventure picking up our first 50 White Plymouth Rocks and 15 Leghorn/California Gray crossbreeds from the hatchery.

"Ohh, ah," was all we could say. How could we ever eat them, these cute, yellow golf-ball sized fluffs? Before they even made a dent in the first 50-pound bag of feed, however, the two breeds exhibited their differences — and their purpose in life. The White Rocks, bred strictly for meat production, were docile, big and quiet. The Leghorns would just about jump out of their skins if we so much as said, "Here chick." And they were always like that. The White Rocks got so big they almost tipped over. Putting on quantities of white meat, they were as top-heavy as topless dancers and would sometimes land on their noses when they

Bill Milliken

Its numbers are decreasing as hybrids overtake older standard poultry breeds, but the New Hampshire's big brown eggs and meaty carcass still win it a devoted following.

jumped from the ramp that led to their run. The Leghorns, on the other hand, were like little ballerinas, alert, taut and high-strung.

We did manage to butcher our White Rocks at 14 weeks — all except one we called "Spot" who had flown over the dividing fence into the Leghorn run just the day before. She was the only one of the Rocks who ever made it over (the Leghorns navigated the fence with frustrating ease). Spot's departure time seemed so auspicious that we gave her away to a friend, where apparently she is still laying big brown eggs.

The butchering turned out not to be the unpleasant experience we had first imagined. It was, after all, the reason we had raised the birds. I was surprised by my lack of city-bred squeamishness. It seemed the sort of job best done well and respectfully.

On summing up the expenses, we discovered that the White Rocks cost us only slightly less per pound than the cheapest grocery store chicken, but included in the tally were all the starting costs such as fencing and waterers that could be used for later flocks.

The Leghorns, two years later, are still laying well, and have paid for themselves over and over. They consume about one-quarter of a pound of feed each per day, giving, at this point, a return of two very large eggs per pound of feed, which means the eggs cost about 60 cents per dozen, and less when

the weather is warm and we can supplement their diet with garden thinnings, grass clippings and other free food.

Having started with chickens, I doubt that we will ever be without them. They are among the least demanding of farm animals to keep, they make use of feed that would otherwise be wasted and the rewards are constant — among them the pleasure of simply watching the birds as they go about their daily business. Chickens are funny, poignant, clever, silly and endearing. They will turn their heads to the side when they can't figure out what is going on, and that is often. For though we hear that the modern chicken has a bigger brain than its reptilian ancestors, it's not about to help you write your thesis. Your fowl will depend on you for their survival, but will repay the favour with a constant display of strutting, preening, crazy-legged running and periodic shows of barnyard romance.

SHELTER

Perhaps the leading consideration for first-time poultry raisers should be housing. Day-old chicks in quantities of 25 to 50 will fit nicely in an extra-large cardboard box or other indoor makeshift enclosure, fenced off with cardboard, bales of straw or boards. You will have several weeks grace while the chicks keep warm under their brooder lamp, but you should have a pretty settled idea of where they will go from there.

The basic necessities are: a power source (to keep water unfrozen in winter), a dry floor, nest boxes (one box to every four hens), roosts (about eight to 10 inches per bird), a door big enough for you to get in, an opening for the chickens to enter and leave, partial shade and tight joints all around (weasels, skunks, rats, raccoons and cats must be excluded for fowl tranquillity).

A shed or section of a barn can easily be adapted to raising chickens or a new coop can be built with only the most rudimentary of carpentry skills. There must be allowance for ventilation in warm weather and a certain amount of insulation in areas with cold winters (extreme cold cuts egg production drastically). The average small flock will fit nicely into a space of about five-by-seven or six-by-eight feet, with a sloped roof six and one-half feet at the front and four and one-half at the rear. Adult birds will require about two square feet per bird. Roosts can consist of two-by-two lumber in a grid that keeps 14 inches between parallel roosts.

Baby chicks require a space of about five feet in diameter for 50 birds or less, nine feet for 100. One of the greatest dangers is suffocation, caused by their piling up for warmth. This can be avoided by rounding all corners with cardboard, straw or cloth, so that you have made a sort of nest. A brooder bulb is the cheapest reliable method of providing heat, and costs just a few dollars at most hardware stores. It should be hung in the centre of the pen so that the temperature is about 90 degrees F directly beneath. The bulb is raised each week, causing the temperature to decrease by about five degrees.

Actually no thermometer is necessary, as the chicks will quickly let you know if conditions aren't right. If it is too cold, they will pile up directly under the lamp and if the lamp is hanging too low, they will crowd to the edges of the enclosure, climbing all over each other to escape the heat. When things are just right they'll move freely about the space, sleeping in a neat little ring around the focus of the lamp. If the weather is warm, they will be able to venture outdoors in about two weeks, by which time they will have begun to feather out.

Chickens must never be out of feed and clean water for more than a few hours at a time, especially young chicks. (The rate of digestion in chickens is amazing — just two and one-half hours from beak to cloaca in a laying hen — and any disruption will interfere with growth or egg production.)

Baby chicks can be fed out of shallow plates and simple waterers, but their in-born ability to waste feed and fill water with litter will soon become maddeningly apparent. Jar waterers make good sense, and hanging feeders can be put in place after a week or 10 days to make best use of the feed.

New chicks require a balanced, high protein diet that is not easily formulated at home. Hence, most small flock owners rely on "starter mash" to get chicks off to a healthy start. Starter rations are usually "medicated," mainly to prevent coccidiosis, a discouraging malady that shows up as diarrhea and results in dead chicks.

By six weeks of age the chicks will have become not-very-attractive teenagers and should be *gradually* converted to "growing mash" which contains less protein, fat and vitamins than the starter ration. (Abrupt changes in feed can kill a young bird.) If you are raising pullets to be egg layers, convert them to "laying mash" at 18 to 20 weeks of age.

It is possible to formulate your own rations, especially for older birds, but follow an established recipe (see Sources). Many backyard poultry raisers use commercial rations and augment them with their own grain and with supplemental feedings of meat and fish scraps, stale bread, sprouts or cultivated greens (comfrey or *Pe-Tsai*, Chinese celery cabbage, both of which are fast-growing and can be harvested repeatedly). Because you are probably not interested in the all-out growth rate desired by big-time poultrymen, growing rations can be extended by mixing in cheaper grains or "hen scratch."

Always include grit in the diet of any chickens receiving whole grain. If they are allowed free range, they'll do fine for themselves, but otherwise you must provide them with fine gravel. Even tiny chicks who are not eating grain will appreciate some coarse sand. Grit is used in the bird's gizzard, where it grinds the grain into a form that can be easily digested. It has been found that considerable force is generated by the kneading walls of the gizzard. (A turkey, for instance, can grind 24 walnuts in the shell in its gizzard in four hours.)

THE STOCK

By far the most popular method of establishing a flock is to buy day-old chicks in the spring and early summer, to take advantage of the warm growing season. Almost everyone in the country knows a source for baby chicks; you need only ask around.

Bill Milliken

Of Asiatic origin, the Cochin is now raised primarily for show, although its feathered shanks, protection from cold weather, make it a barnyard conversation piece as well.

Be discriminating. Egg birds simply are not built to give tender, ample quantities of meat (though they will tastily grace a soup or stewpot when their laying days come to an end). Meat birds kept around for their eggs are eating heavily, mainly to support their body weight, and thus are hard to justify. Picking a suitable breed can mean the difference between having an economically sensible flock or a group of pets.

(In ordering, it helps to know at least the most basic chicken terms of reference. A *cockerel* is a male bird that hasn't reached roosterhood. A *pullet* is a young female chicken. A *capon* is a castrated male, a *poulard* (only rarely seen) a neutered female. "*Straight-run*" is the cheapest way to buy chicks — they haven't been sorted by sex, and you will get roughly half pullets and half cockerels.)

There are, for the record, more than 350 types of chickens in the world. According to the Standard of Perfection, set by the American Poultry Association, they are divided initially into classes, usually referring to the bird's place of origin: American, Asiatic, Continental, English, French, Mediterranean, Oriental and Polish. Most of these are represented only at poultry shows, but birds from the American, Asiatic, English and Mediterranean classes especially may be found in the home flock. The American birds are generally dual-purpose and layers of brown-shelled eggs. They include the Dominique, Araucana (notable for its pastel-coloured eggshells), Java, Jersey, Black, Lamona, New Hampshire, Ply-

bred for increased vigour), and there are many birds today that carry brand names. Among the highly bred meat bird types used by commercial broiler producers are the Hubbard, Shaver and Pilch. If you want a specific type of chicken, you will probably have to search for it. The poultry journals are a good place to start (see Sources).

When buying locally the choice is simplified, as most hatcheries that sell to the general public offer a pragmatic selection: one meat variety, one egg variety and, hopefully, a dual-purpose breed. The latter make the most sense for many farmsteaders, allowing the flock to perpetuate itself with its own chicks. Most easily found of the dual-purpose breeds are the Rhode Island Red (with deep red plumage), and the New Hampshire (descended from the Rhode Island, but with less intense colouration), the Barred Plymouth Rock and the Wyandotte. All lay brown eggs, and all are good choices for a beginner.

Fancy birds are mainly for show, although many an adventurous small flock owner has bought one or two to see what sort of "barnies" — barnyard chicks — develop. Fancies include Silkies, Sumatras, Yokohamas and Sultans. Bantams are also a fancy type. Most of them are not a distinct breed but are selectively-developed smaller versions of the normal-sized varieties, and are about half the regular size. There are Bantam Rhode Island Reds, New Hampshire, Plymouth Rocks and such. The Banty, known for its ear-piercing crow and compact, pleasing appearance, will lay eggs that are a surprising size for such a small bird, and is an excellent brooder, pleased to hatch even goose eggs. Most Bantam owners figure on using three Bantam eggs for two regular ones in cooking.

RUNNING FREE?

Perhaps the most perplexing question facing new poultry owners is whether or not to let the birds have totally free range. Those hemmed in by neighbours or traffic will probably opt for providing their fowl with a run, as will those with fine flower gardens (don't count on training a chicken to do anything). Likewise, they can quickly bring disaster to a young vegetable garden, scratching up neatly planted seeds and plucking tender seedlings.

If given a small pasture or barnyard of their own, chickens will be reasonably content to stay put. They do not normally stray far and you needn't worry about eggs being laid hither and yon or your birds getting lost at night. Their house is very much their home, and at the first sign of dusk, they will troop dependably back into the henhouse. (In fact, they will do the same during an eclipse of the sun.)

Where predators are a serious problem, a run may be essential — to be completely safe from hawks, cats and things that crawl fences in the night, the top of the run may also be covered with mesh or netting.

Crowding, especially when birds are confined indoors, can lead to cannibalism, the unhappy habit some birds display of pecking each other, sometimes to death. Some breeds are more prone to this

mouth Rock, Rhode Island Red and Wyandotte. Another is the Chantecler, the only breed in the Standard that was developed in Canada, and is practically nonexistent here today. The White Chantecler was developed in Quebec from Wyandotte, Rhode Island Red, Cornish, Leghorn and Plymouth Rock stock, and entered the Standard in 1921. According to Douglas Gill, an Ontario breeder who has a small flock of Chanteclers, the bird was bred specifically for the Canadian climate and lays all winter through the coldest weather.

The Asiatic birds have large bodies, feathered shanks, heavy bones and generally lay brown eggs. Major breeds are the Brahma, Cochin and Langshan.

The English class of birds is usually best suited to meat production, although they produce eggs fairly well. They include the Australorp, Cornish, Dorking, Orpington and Sussex. They usually have white skin (the notable exception is the Cornish, whose yellow skin has greatly enhanced its popularity in North America) and lay brown eggs.

The Mediterranean birds are small and usually kept for egg production. They all lay white-shelled eggs, and include the Ancona, Blue Andalusian, Buttercut, Leghorn (originally from Italy), Minorca and Spanish.

All of these are purebreds, and may be scarce or even nonexistent in many parts of the country. Most commercial hatcheries sell hybrids or strain crosses (e.g. two distinct strains of Leghorn cross-

than others. One solution is to hang a piece of beef fat in the house with the hope that the birds will peck at this instead, another is to curtain windows, or you may want to try adding a teaspoon of salt to each gallon of drinking water.

Egg eating by the hens is also sometimes a problem. It may signal a poor diet, boredom, or simply bad luck — perhaps a thin-shelled egg has broken in a nest, and a bird has acquired a liking for her own produce. Frequent collection of eggs will help, and in fact, two collections a day are always advisable. You could resort to leaving a "plant" — an egg you've blown out and filled with hot pepper — to discourage the habit.

Laying hens need a great deal of calcium for eggshell formation. This is partly taken care of in the laying mash, but if you are frequently gathering thin-shelled eggs, feed the shells, ground-up, back to your layers. (Wash them first, so the birds don't acquire a taste for eggs.) As this alone will probably not give them enough calcium, you may want to add oyster shells, which are available from feed stores.

Some hens simply never lay well and you should be prepared to "cull them" — a euphemism meaning preparation for the fricassee. There seems to be something uncomfortably reminiscent of the chicken factory in getting rid of non-producers, but unless you intend to run a shelter (and this will quickly get out of hand with poultry), a non-layer must be weeded out. Often, this bird will be at the bottom of the pecking order and its sexual characteristics will be poorly developed — it may have a pale, small comb and dull eyes; its pubic bones will be close together; its vent small and dry. If you have any doubts, separate it from the other hens for a week or two. If no eggs appear you have a candidate for the kitchen.

Once the young flock is laying and any initial culling done, things will likely remain constant for at least two years. There may be the occasional bird found to be living on a free lunch, but don't get rid of any poor hen who's just moulting. This feather changing takes about eight weeks every year, and during it there will be no eggs.

During the second year, your flock will deliver larger eggs, and in the third the eggs will still be large but possibly thin-shelled. Keeping the birds for more than three years is a doubtful practice.

If you've been allowing one or two birds to sit on some eggs, then you'll have established a continuing source of meat and eggs, but things will get a bit complicated. You may want to band or mark your hens so you'll know who is three years old and who is two.

The barnyard flock is a wonderful place for experimentation. If you buy, say, an Araucana rooster, a Leghorn hen, a New Hampshire hen, an Araucana hen and a Banty, each hen will be able to raise chicks that lay eggs of a different colour and size.

The coloured egg gene (of the Araucana "Easter egg" bird) is dominant. Half the offspring of an Araucana and a brown-shell bird will produce dusky green shells; if an Araucana is mated with a white-egg bird, half will produce light blue shells. Purebred Araucanas produce eggs in the purple to pink range. If you buy a Cornish, any bird crossed with it will produce acceptable meat-type chicks. (Cornish hens are somewhat infertile, but a Cornish rooster will do fine.) Add a few really fancy breeds to the flock, and the possibilities are endless. Mendel would be in a geneticist's heaven.

Sources

Mail-Order Chicks:

FREY'S HATCHERY
70 Northside Drive
St. Jacobs, Ontario N0B 2N0
Serving small farms and small hatcheries, Frey's is a family-run business that ships chicks to all parts of Canada, including the Far North. Offers 16 varieties, mostly dual-purpose. Highly recommended source. Write for catalogue.

MURRAY McMURRAY HATCHERY
Webster City, Iowa 50595
U.S. source of mail-order chicks — good variety, informative catalogue and friendly service.

Periodicals:

FEATHER FANCIER
Box 239
Erin, Ontario N0B 1T0
Monthly newspaper filled with news and classified advertising for poultry, pigeons, rabbits and cavies. $7.50 per year, sample copy 75 cents.

Books:

THE HOMESTEADER'S HANDBOOK TO RAISING SMALL LIVESTOCK
By Jerome Belanger
246 pages, Paperback
Rodale Press
Emmaus, Pennsylvania

CHICKENS IN YOUR BACKYARD
By Gail and Rick Luttman
172 pages, Paperback
Rodale Press
Emmaus, Pennsylvania

The Gobbler's Challenge

Turkey husbandry: Coping with the meaty dodo of domestic birddom

---

By Jennifer Bennett

Pity the turkey. Early settlers and native peoples may have known his wild forebears as a sly and wily quarry, and Benjamin Franklin may have pronounced him "more respectable" than the Bald Eagle, but times have changed.

The ponderous modern version of the Pilgrim's favourite bird seems to have had the nobility bred right out of him and earned him a new reputation for stupidity surpassed only by the long-extinct dodo. He has become disease-prone, cannibalistic and a bad lover, to boot. His physical form, once as beautifully functional as "the mast of a ship," in the words of poultry expert Arnold Morphet, has become "pretty near square — that's what the housewife likes and that's what sells the meat." Genetically beefed up by hundreds of generations of artificial selection, today's 30-pound turkey males may fill a platter admirably, but they are often too awkward to breed with the smaller females.

While most poultry breeders take little or no time to look at life from their Christmas dinner's point of view, Arnold Morphet has, and it is distinctly grim.

There was the time, for instance, when Morphet, one of Ontario's best-known turkey experts and then employed by the University of Guelph, was called by a worried university caretaker to look at a flock of "sick" hen turkeys on the range.

"I said to him as we got into the car, 'Wouldn't it be comical if we drove all the way out there because they're lovesick?' I knew he didn't have a male bird in the bunch," recalls Morphet.

"So I went, and there they were and this fellow said, 'See? See what I mean?'" The hens were sitting everywhere, not moving, just waiting for old Tom to come along and do them a good service.

Alas, they waited in vain. The best that most modern female turkeys can expect is artificial insemination, while those that are given the opportunity to encounter a male must be strapped into an "apron" or "saddle" to protect their backs from being shredded by the spurs of His Immenseness.

All commercially produced turkey eggs are then hatched in an incubator, and the resulting deprived young, with no hen to guide them, "almost seem to lack the instinct to eat," according to small-time turkey farmer Hubert Earl.

Those who would raise a few birds for the family table must face these facts, and those who have already had luck in keeping chickens, ducks or geese must put their self-confidence aside when attempting to rear *Meleagris gallopava* for the first time. One must make allowances for the birds' bred-in idiosyncratic nature, but success with homegrown turkeys, especially those allowed to range freely, will yield many memorable meals — meat distinctly superior to the inspected, injected, poly-wrapped bundles from the supermarket.

PLAGUES & OUTBREAKS

"Turkeys take a lot of care. You really have to be cautious raising turkeys," says Hubert Earl, who began raising his own on a small scale 23 years ago near Addison, Ontario. That first year he learned the hard way that domestic turkeys are not as hardy as chicks. Given a pair of young poults by a friend, he took them home and raised them in a cardboard box until they were about a month old. Then he put them

Al Satterwhite/The Image Bank of Canada

in an old chicken coop — and they lasted only 10 days.

"Chickens carry a lot of diseases and turkeys are very susceptible to disease. Both developed blackhead (named for the grayish colour of affected birds' heads, a condition caused by poor circulation of the blood). It's probably the one disease that plagues us most with turkeys."

The young poults require scrupulously clean quarters. Earl, who raises turkeys, geese and chickens on his mixed farm, says: "I wouldn't advocate that anyone, whether they think they've had disease or not, take an old poultry building, particularly if chickens were in it, and try and raise turkeys there." Chickens not only carry blackhead, but coccidiosis as well, both of which can be lethal to turkeys. Any building, even if it has not held poultry before, should be disinfected before the poults arrive.

Arnold Morphet tells of a building he was asked to inspect for an owner who wanted to put turkeys on the third floor. "It was spotlessly clean, and the lad said, 'I want to put turkeys in that top floor. Do you think there is any danger of having blackhead?'

" 'Well,' I said, 'there shouldn't be much danger, but anything can happen.' I don't think they'd been in there more than three weeks and they had the blamedest outbreak of blackhead I'd ever seen. Was it pigeons? Was it sparrows that got in there? I don't know."

Every spring, before the poults arrive, Earl scrubs his turkey house down with a solution of Creolin, a tar-scented disinfectant used frequently in horse barns. The building is then aired out so it will be perfectly dry, and litter — Earl uses shavings, but straw or sand will do — is spread over the floor. The litter, too, should be clean and dry. Newspaper is not suitable, as young birds cannot get a good footing on it, and are apt to become spraddle-legged.

Turkey poults require much warmer quarters than baby chicks when they first arrive, starting at temperatures between 95 and 100 degrees Fahrenheit, and gradually cooling five degrees each week.

"Sometimes we got them in May or June, when it was hotter inside than outside, and they were getting along just fine. But you could hardly stand to go in there," says Earl. Warmth is best provided by heat lamps. The red bulbs have an added advantage in that they provide little light. If the poults find it difficult to see each other, they will also be hard-pressed to peck each other to death, a habit to which they are unfortunately disposed. "I learned something from a fellow who raised pheasants, because they, too, are terribly cannibalistic," says Earl. "We used red heat lamps for the first six weeks, darkened all the windows, and the red lamps were hung over the feed trough and over the waterer. We never lost one to cannibalism, so that was something in itself, because generally, in a hundred, two or three will get pecked at rather badly."

For the farmer who only wants to raise five or 10 turkeys, cannibalism may not be a problem because crowding is one of its chief causes. Minimally, poults require a square foot of space each when they are a day old, with an additional square foot of space needed each month until they are five months old.

Five square feet per bird should be enough, after five months, to last until maturity.

A turkey house must have all its corners rounded so that poults crowding away from the heat lamp, if they feel too warm, will not pile up in a corner and suffocate. Arnold Morphet recommends that a piece of plywood with an 18-inch base, tapered to a triangle shape, be nailed in each corner. With this system, poults cannot fly over a barrier into the corner, where they can die from the cold. Hubert Earl simply uses a cardboard guard that skirts the house in a circle. If the heat lamps are placed adequately, poults will distribute themselves evenly around the heat. Conversely, if they feel cold, they will huddle directly under the lamp and again run the danger of smothering each other. Turkeys are notorious for crowding and piling up. "I've seen two of us in a pen," says Morphet, "just working as hard as we could, throwing them apart, and the top ones just coming on and the bottom ones just sitting there. When those things start to pile up you can't pull them apart fast enough, they'll smother on you."

Before the poults arrive, check with a thermometer to see that the temperature is fairly uniform at floor level throughout the rounded-off area they will inhabit.

EARLY MASH

Also, before they arrive, check with the local feed supplier to find out if turkey feeds are available. Unless there is a commercial farm nearby, turkey feed will not likely be stocked, and the company will have to be given a few weeks' notice to supply you. Medicated pre-starter will feed the poults from the day they arrive until they are 10 days to two weeks old, and during that time each bird will eat about two pounds. From two to seven weeks of age, they will consume turkey starter, followed by turkey grower ration supplemented with range feed and home-grown grains. Each feed change should be introduced gradually by mixing the rations. An abrupt feed change is a shock to the delicate system of a poult.

Commercial turkey feeds have a very high protein content, which forces the young birds into fast growth, particularly at the early stages when the most economical gains take place. Pre-starter mash, fed only for the first 10 days to two weeks, has a protein content of about 29 per cent, compared with chick starter, with 18 to 22 per cent protein. Turkey starter contains about 25 per cent protein, and growing mash about 20. High protein levels enable the birds, which have been especially bred for fast weight gain, to develop to their full potential.

Water, of course, must be constantly available. It must be very clean, and if the waterer or feed trough has been used before, it should be washed with disinfectant and then thoroughly rinsed. It is a good idea to have a cover on both the feeder and waterer, allowing the young birds access through the sides, but keeping their droppings out of the food and preventing them from becoming entrapped in the feeder or drowned in the waterer.

As anyone who has had to climb a tree after an errant bird will know, turkeys love to roost. They should be provided with simple roost structures, not

more than four inches off the floor for newly arrived poults. If they learn to roost at an early age, crowding problems will be lessened, and the birds will stay cleaner and healthier. Eventually the roosts should be raised to about one foot from the ground.

BREED CHOICES

There is, technically, only one breed of turkeys, but there are important differences between the varieties most commonly seen today. The commercial market is dominated by the Large White Hybrid, which accounts for almost 90 per cent of all turkeys raised. These are descended from the Holland White and the Broad Breasted Bronze, with the latter's highly desirable chest span, but without the dark pinfeathers that processors like to avoid. Large White males mature at 30 pounds or more, with the females achieving a weight of 18 to 20 pounds.

Although relatively scarce — less than three per

Turkeys of the Large White breed, in which males may reach 33 pounds.

cent of the North American turkey population — the Broad Breasted Bronze is still favoured by some who raise roasting birds. There are a number of strains of Bronze turkeys, and some exceed even the Large Whites in size — with toms weighing in at 36 pounds and hens at 20.

Those whose ovens can't accommodate one of these hulks may prefer the small, "broiler" type variety usually called the Small White or Beltsville Small White, after the Maryland breeding station where it was developed. In appearance they are merely scaled-down versions of the Large White Hybrid, with males maturing at 21 pounds and females topping out at only 11.

Sources of turkey poults are few and far between, and some small-scale raisers annually drive some

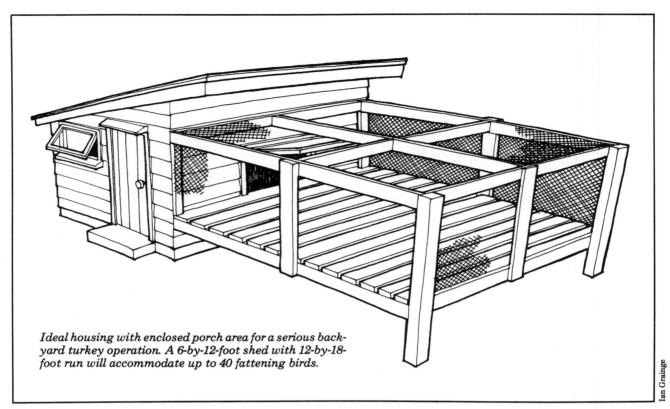

Ideal housing with enclosed porch area for a serious back-yard turkey operation. A 6-by-12-foot shed with 12-by-18-foot run will accommodate up to 40 fattening birds.

Ian Grainge

distance to pick up their day-old birds. Those fortunate enough to live near a backyard turkey breeder may be able to coax a few poults from him, but most will have to order stock through a supplier of baby chicks. The young turkey poults will have been hatched at one of the relatively few large commercial turkey hatcheries in North America and flown or trucked to distribution points.

That, says Arnold Morphet, is where the trouble can begin. If newly-hatched poults are shown food and water, they have no trouble comprehending what to do — but they forget quickly. Day-olds shipped from commercial establishments will not have seen food or water and, in breaking the fast, you must show them how to eat and drink.

Grit, hard-boiled egg yolk or chopped green onion will attract the birds' attention to the feed tray. Once they start to peck, nature usually takes over. Hubert Earl dips the beak of each bird in water then in feed, repeating this until each gets the idea.

"I still have my bag of marbles," he says. "In fact, that's what we used to use them for, putting marbles in the feed for the day-old poults." Seeing the bright, colourful bits of glass, the birds would peck at them and inadvertently pick up some feed.

VITAL GRIT

Grit — insoluble fine gravel — should also be provided in its own dish from the day the poults arrive. Young turkeys have an almost insatiable appetite for roughage. Clean, small-grained gravel can be used, but commercial chick grit, available at feed stores, is cheap and reliable.

The birds' need for roughage has added to their reputation for stupidity, and quite unfairly. Arnold Morphet says: "I've seen a poultryman put a whole flock of turkeys out on a field of alfalfa that had been seeded down in oats the year before, and oat stubble was still showing. Those turkeys went out there and they didn't eat that green feed; they ate old oat stubble and it just came through their intestines and gizzards like a bunch of darning needles! Sometimes you'd say they were stupid, going out there and eating that fibre instead of that green feed, but the grower had been stupid in his way of feeding them! He hadn't fed any amount of grit before he turned his turkeys out on the range, and he gave them no whole grain."

Turkey starter feed, like pre-starter, is medicated to help prevent outbreaks of blackhead (entero-hepatitis) and coccidiosis. Although organically-inclined farmers, such as Hubert Earl, usually skip the medication in grower rations, leaving the feed unmedicated from day one is very risky. Blackhead, as any turkey raiser will confirm, can quickly wipe out a whole flock, and at $1.50 a poult that can be a sizable investment lost. Still, for those who wish to try it, Morphet offers a starter mix he remembers from his early turkey-raising days: boiled eggs, the curds from sour milk, corn meal and bone meal. "That was basically our starter for young turkeys. And don't ask me why, but when it was really cold we used to have the idea to put some red pepper out there. They'd eat that stuff just like nobody's business!"

If a bird seems listless, off its feed and segregating itself from the flock, there is a good chance it has blackhead. The bird must be instantly removed from the flock and isolated. "It has gone too far if you see yellow droppings," says Earl. "If you spot yellow droppings on the floor, try to scoop it up and get it out of there because the others will peck at this and they'll eat it." Earl uses Nitrofurazone or "NF-180" to treat the rest of the flock — one tablespoon in a pail of feed each day for three days — and wets a piece of bread, coats it in the medication and forces it

Jack Chiang/Kingston Whig Standard

down the throat of the sick bird. He keeps that poult isolated until it has completely recovered, repeating the treatment as necessary. "Once the epidemic starts, it can virtually wipe you out in a matter of days."

Litter must be kept dry and clean, and the turkey house must be free of draft. "I remember," says Earl, "one year we had 25 Bronze turkeys, and we had gone to the bother of making a nice little turkey pen that was all open-wired. We moved the turkeys out there when they were a month old, and we lost them — all but two."

Turkeys, especially when they are young, are exceedingly vulnerable to dampness and drafts.

By the time they are full-feathered, however, they can begin to venture outdoors. Old-timers would say they were ready "when they shot the red," says Morphet. This is when the red begins to show on their necks, "getting close to eight weeks, maybe a little younger the way we feed them today. Basically, what we're talking about is when one wing overlaps the other on their backs, so that rain doesn't hit the bare back."

An intermediate environment can be provided at this point, in the form of a sun porch enclosed with chicken wire. This is attached to the turkey house, has a slatted, above-ground floor covered with wire netting so the droppings fall through, and allows the turkeys to go outside while still keeping them confined. Then, "on an exceptionally hot day," when they are eight to 10 weeks old, says Earl, the birds can be let out. If their range is open, however, the young birds, bewildered by their new surroundings, may just keep walking in one direction — over the county line. Keep a close eye on them the first time out. Whenever a heavy rain threatens they should be herded back under cover.

On the range, turkeys must still have access to their mash. At this stage, they will be eating grower or half-and-half grower and grain. Hubert Earl gives his birds one pail of growing mash and one of grain, and lets them eat whichever they choose. Wheat is especially popular, oats, barley and corn less so until the weather gets cold. Then corn and barley, fattening feeds, are eagerly consumed by the birds, and will add a good finish to the carcass.

Turkeys can be moved from area to area of the range, with waterers, feeders and a portable shelter. Unlike chickens, they will choose to roost outdoors, and will station themselves on fences or on the ground. If a large field can be dedicated to the turkeys, their shelter should be started at the lowest point of ground and gradually move uphill, so that the bird's droppings are carried downhill and away from the turkeys in heavy rain. Turkey droppings are an extremely rich fertilizer, and if managed properly, a flock can actually improve the fertility of a field. The key is to rotate the turkeys, rather than letting them overgraze and concentrate their waste in one area.

In a small lot, they are likely to range over the entire space, which should be fenced to contain them. They may have to be brought inside at night, as a roosting turkey is a plump and easy prize for a marauding fox or dog. Turkeys are easily herded, which makes moving them into the turkey house at night, or when inclement weather threatens, a fairly simple chore.

Outdoors they will discover the thickets, their natural habitat, and the garden. "They don't come alone," says Earl. "They bring a whole army of troops with them and they can make short work of a cabbage patch. You have to watch because they know where to go, where you can't see them until

Broad Breasted Bronze turkeys now account for less than three per cent of commercial flocks, but some smaller producers prefer their looks and large size.

they are right in the garden, and when my wife or I go to the door they'll just tear back to where they were before.''

Out on the range, turkey behaviour seems bizarre and full of quirks, but the birds are nevertheless in their element. Frightened by the shadows of clouds passing over the moon, roosting unaffected on fences in winter while minus 60-degree F winds whistle underneath them, heading off in a straight column, marching for a quarter mile without stopping, guarding the gates, displaying their feathers for passing visitors, turkeys outdoors are turkeys at home. Once they have passed the critical age of three months, the danger of disease is largely over, and if maintenance is reasonably careful, the flock should survive.

Turkeys are generally ready to be butchered when they are from 22 to 30 weeks old, depending on the size of carcass desired. Arnold Morphet, who has been involved in turkey research for 30 years, says when he first came to Guelph "we didn't think a turkey was in condition to kill until it was 28 to 30 weeks old. We'd say it took us about 125 pounds of feed to turn out turkeys, on the average. Today, we say the hens have got to go by 22 weeks and the toms by 24 weeks, and we expect to average 20-pound turkeys ready for the oven on 70 pounds of feed. That's a far cry from 125.''

Pet turkeys on the farm, especially Hybrid Whites, may reach 50 to 60 pounds if kept too long. This is a little hard on the pocketbook, and also strains the freezer when Tom finally arrives there. For Christmas turkeys, the poults should not be bought much earlier than June.

Butchering turkeys is a bit more difficult than doing chickens, because the birds are so large. Before, and even after, decapitation (the easiest method of killing) a bird can flap so strongly that it will take two people to hold it down. The bird should then be dunked in a large pot of near-boiling water for about a minute, suspended and plucked. Plucking and cleaning a turkey is no more difficult than preparing a chicken, except, again, that the larger size

stretches the job out. In comparison, however, the time invested is worthwhile. A 30-pound turkey takes only slightly longer to prepare than a six-pound chicken, and far less time than five 6-pound chickens. If this is done a day or two before Christmas or Thanksgiving, then a truly delightful feast, fresh turkey, is in the works. Frozen, the flavour is slightly reduced, but the result will still be far superior to anything raised commercially, and particularly to the automatic, self-butter-baste turkeys that command very high prices on the market.

When late fall arrives, the farmer may decide he would like to keep a few hens over to produce eggs, perhaps to raise his own poults. Although this is expensive, (turkeys have voracious appetites) and an unreliable procedure, it can be done, and Hubert Earl has had some success. Hybrid White toms, he cautions, should not be kept for breeding, but males of smaller breeds can be, and females of any breed will do. One tom will serve 15 females. The indecorous affair called a turkey apron, or turkey saddle, may be necessary for breeding. Large toms can easily tear the soft flesh of a female in mating, and this protective apron provides a shield against the male's long toenails. Turkey aprons are occasionally required for birds in confinement, when no breeding is planned, because the hens will sometimes lie on the ground waiting for a male, like those reported by the alarmed Guelph employee. If space is limited, the other turkeys will blithely walk right over them.

"You know when the females are ready to mate," says Earl, "because they'll squat in the yard right in front of you and you practically have to kick them out of the way.

"In the breeding season, hens look for very secluded places like fence lines, in dense brush, and they really hide their nests. You have to watch to see where they go and know where their nests are, because skunks and foxes will have their eggs as fast as they can lay them.''

"When they do hatch," he says, "the young poults are vulnerable again. Despite their fiercely protective mothers, who will fly at an intruder, they are easily lost in the long grass and brush. They are not as apt to peep an alarm as chicks are and the hen can simply lose them. You will do well to raise half of what they hatch out.''

Indoors, trap nests are used by some commercial hatcheries to keep eggs and birds from "going all over." A similar system is advocated by Hubert Earl, but he advises that conditions as close as possible to nature be met, using a layer of damp litter or sand under the nest for added humidity, and plenty of nest material to keep the eggs together. He uses old rubber tires for turkey nests. Plenty of padding underneath is necessary, because turkeys have the odd habit of occasionally laying their eggs while standing up. When he was at Guelph, Arnold Morphet says, the most frustrating thing he had to contend with was the problem of broken eggs, courtesy of standing mothers. The solution, he finally discovered, was a layer of foam rubber under each nest.

Regular-sized chickens and, better still, banty hens can be used to incubate the speckled, goose-egg sized turkey eggs, although the turkeys themselves can do an admirable job. A banty, which can sit on four eggs, is a fiercely protective mother who will gladly wait out the 28 days until the eggs hatch. After this, the poults must be removed from the chicken, who is not really suited to raising such big, unruly babies. Once a foster mother hen has had her comb yanked by the beak of a young poult, Morphet says, she is likely to spend the rest of her days afraid of turkeys. Comb and wattle pulling is normally practised by turkeys, especially toms engaged in courting battles.

It is possible to have one's turkey raising go full circle, from poult to egg to Christmas dinner. It is possible, too, that if the farmer is careful and his operation clean, the whole process can be painless, even enjoyable. For one thing, it will introduce him to the ranks of those who can debate firsthand whether or not turkeys are really as stupid as they seem.

"Stupid?" Hubert Earl laughs. "Last year, the turkeys were closest to the barn, so I fed them first, and then I'd go down and feed the White Rocks and the turkeys would be happy. They'd be eating away, and I wouldn't be in the barn five minutes when I could hear those s.o.b's down there pecking the White Rocks out of the way to get their feed, but there would never be one of them down there until I was out of the way. And when I came out, they'd just run. I dare say they are stupid like a fox."

Sources

Turkey poults are fragile creatures. Carefully consider the time required and the stress involved in shipping from the source you choose.

MODERN HATCHERIES LTD.
14 Memorial Blvd.
Dauphin, Manitoba R7N 2A4
Broad Breasted Bronze and Nicholas White (a larger breed) available. Write for free catalogue and price list.

HYBRID TURKEYS LTD.
9 Centennial Drive
Kitchener, Ontario N2B 3E9
(519) 578-2740
Will ship poults by air (freight charges extra).

CHINOOKBELT HATCHERIES
1414 - 9th Avenue S.E.
Calgary, Alberta T2G 0T5

(403) 264-4795
Will ship poults according to buyer's instructions.

SUSSEX POULTRY LTD.
Box 609
Sussex, New Brunswick E0E 1P0
(506) 433-2268
Pick-up sales only.

HAMBLY HATCHERIES
2649 Commercial Street, Box 21
Abbotsford, B.C. V2N 4N7
Pre-order basis.

COUVOIR DORVAL INC.
2941 Boul. des Sources
Dorval 700, Quebec H9R 4N3
Pick-up sales only.

COUNTRY HATCHERY
Wewoka, Oklahoma 74884
Poultry of many kinds including turkeys, geese, pheasants, pea fowl. Send 50 cents for illustrated brochure.

The Essential Ploughman

An introduction to one of agriculture's most vital — and rewarding — rituals

By Thomas Pawlick

The trees along the fence row are festooned with mobs of red-winged blackbirds, starlings and grackles newly returned from the south — hundreds of bird voices shrieking, rasping and muttering at once.

Abruptly, at the sound of a tractor engine moving up the laneway, their chatter stops. A second's hesitation, then a fluttering cloud of birds launches in alarm, arcing away in unison through the air to the opposite side of the field.

They settle again, in the safety of distant branches, and watch as a battered red International Harvester tractor rolls through the gate into the field of recently grazed, fall-planted rye, a two-bottom mounted plough swinging from the hitch behind the old machine, like a dog's tail wagging. The tractor bumps to the south end of the rectangular field, to a point halfway across the field's width, and turns north.

The birds wait, eyes focussed on the driver as he sights on a stump midway across the north end, downshifts into first gear and, as the tractor starts forward, smoothly drops the hydraulic lift. The tips of the descending ploughshares brush through the green stubble, skim the soil surface, bite in. The coulters straighten, revolving, the blades lift and turn the earth — and the warm clay soil, with a rich, sensuous "swissssshhhhhhhhhh," begins to fold.

The birds' fear vanishes. One by one, they sweep down behind the plough, into the furrows, hopping back and forth, darting and pecking at the fresh-turned ground where a spring banquet of grubs and worms is spread.

Constantly trailed by the birds, the ploughman lays down furrow after furrow, each straight and true, each contributing to a welling sense of contentment. Whether done in spring or fall, with a tractor or a horse, ploughing is always hard but always intensely satisfying work. It is the basic creative act at the heart of agriculture and stirs deep feelings of communion with the natural world in those who till the soil.

But ploughing involves much more than emotions. It is an art, but a highly technical one, part of the overall science of tillage, whose secrets must be mastered by anyone who wants to raise a healthy crop on a healthy piece of land. Until a grower has become a thorough ploughman — technically as well as emotionally — his stewardship and cooperative place in nature remain incomplete.

Indeed, soil scientists, who previously assumed that North Americans had learned the necessity of soil conservation after witnessing the ravages of the great prairie Dust Bowl of the 1930s, have been alarmed to see a gradual return in some regions to the kind of careless attitudes that caused that epic disaster. Both inexperienced city families migrating back to a land they really do not understand and "industrial farmers" intent on forcing ever higher, ever faster returns from high-yield, "hurry-up" crops pose a threat to that most basic of natural resources, the land.

"Soil is an inheritance which provides the foundation for our life and civilization," writes K.M. King, chairman of the Department of Land Resource Science at the University of Guelph. "Man obtains

Andris Leimanis

most of his food, clothing and shelter from the products of the soil, and the manner in which the soil is managed determines our present and future welfare." King's position is, if anything, understated. Survival itself depends on the land, and an understanding of the basics of tillage is indispensable in any soil management plan.

No one who assumes responsibility for a country property, whether he rents it out or cultivates it himself, should be ignorant of the subject

ESSENTIAL TOOL

Farmers plough for several reasons, some very obvious and some less so. Basically, they are: 1) to create a favourable seedbed by improving soil "tilth," namely its physical granularity; 2) to add fertility to the soil by burying crop residues and manure which will break down and become humus; 3) to remove or prevent the growth of weeds; 4) to destroy insect pests and disease organisms; 5) to promote the circulation of air and water through the soil.

For the past 300 years, the instrument most frequently used to perform this multitude of functions has been the mouldboard plough, the essential tool of North American agriculture.

It is a beautiful, streamlined implement, as graceful as any sculpture. Raised for transport, the flowing curve of its blades makes them look like wings, but they are far from fragile. For example, a two-furrow, 14-inch plough working at an average depth of six inches in soil with a resistance of nine pounds per square inch will be pulling against 1,512 pounds of force. In soil with an average density of 60 pounds per cubic foot, a plough working at six inches depth will move 1,306,800 pounds of soil — 653.4 tons — per acre. This is hardly a delicate tool.

There are three types of mouldboard ploughs: *fully-mounted,* or integral ploughs, *semi-mounted* or semi-integral ploughs, and *pull-type* ploughs, also called trailer or drawn ploughs. The fully-mounted plough, as its name implies, is supported entirely by the three-point hitch of the tractor on which it is mounted. This system of mounting, also known as the "Ferguson system" after its inventor, Harry G. Ferguson, was introduced in the 1930s and is by far the most manoeuvrable. A fully-mounted plough can be raised by the hydraulic lift and backed into tight corners, making it ideal for work on small homesteads or for market garden operations too large to be handled efficiently by a rototiller.

The semi-mounted plough, which sports a wheel at one end and hitches directly to the tractor at the other, is less manoeuvrable, but allows the tractor greater stability and provides a more uniform width and depth of cut than a fully-mounted plough. Trailer or pull-type ploughs are completely self-contained units supported by their own two- or three-wheel suspension systems and attached to the tractor only by its drawbar. They produce near-perfect depth control and tractor stability, but are difficult to manoeuvre.

Both semi-mounted and pull-type ploughs can support more blades than fully-mounted ploughs and are the preferred tool on large commercial farms where multi-furrow implements with as many as eight ploughblades, or *bottoms,* are often seen.

Edi Klopfenstein

A mouldboard plough bottom consists of a central metal base plate, called the *frog,* to which is attached the *ploughshare,* or horizontal cutting edge which slices into and lifts the soil; the *shin,* or vertical cutting edge; the *mouldboard,* which turns and inverts the slice of earth, and the *landslide,* which steadies the plough and counteracts the forces which tend to push the implement sideways. The frog, in turn, is bolted to the plough *beam.*

Most modern ploughs are also equipped with *coulters,* round steel discs mounted immediately in front of the plough bottom, which revolve and cut through plant debris on the surface, making it easier for the plough to cover up stubble and sod.

Ploughshares and mouldboards may be made of soft-centre steel (SC), carburized steel (CARB), solid steel (SOLID), chilled cast iron (CHILLED) or plain cast iron (CAST), and must be marked with the abbreviation indicating the material used. The longest-wearing and most expensive ploughs are made of soft-centre or carburized steel, the cheapest and least abrasion-resistant of plain cast iron. Solid steel and

Ploughing on the contour is a difficult art to master, but it prevents erosion on hilly land. Two-way ploughs with reversible bottoms are used for the job.

operate with reasonable efficiency in almost any kind of soil.

Coulter types include plain, notched or rippled styles. The latter two types are best for use in areas with heavy surface plant debris, or "trash." Plain coulters are the most frequently used.

In selecting a plough, the principal things to keep in mind are the amount of work to be done, the kind of soil in which the plough must do it and the size of the tractor. Obviously, it would be absurd to hitch a tiny, one-furrow mounted plough to the back of a monstrous 350-horsepower, four-wheel-drive prairie pounder; an eight-furrow trailer plough dragging behind a little 12-horsepower lawnmower special would be equally out of place.

For the small holder, with a property ranging from perhaps 10 to a maximum of 50 acres, a two-bottom, 14-inch, fully-mounted plough with a general purpose mouldboard is usually regarded as the most efficient primary tillage implement. Mounted on a smaller tractor, in the 25 to 35 horsepower class, such a plough will do perfectly adequate work in most clay or sandy loam soils.

Brand-new, a two-bottom mounted plough may cost $1,000 or more, plus freight. Used, one can be found for as little as $250, perhaps even less at a country auction on a rainy day, when crowds are thin. A new three-bottom plough may list at $1,700, while a used one might sell for $750.

ABUNDANT VARIABLES

Choosing the right plough for the work is a fairly straightforward task, but the variables involved in learning how and when to use this "primary tillage" instrument are abundant enough to occupy a lifetime of study. Most farmers have, in fact, spent their lives studying the question of tillage and most will admit that it is one subject they will never exhaust.

The first thing the ploughman must learn is how to adjust his equipment.

"It's a good idea to go ahead and run a short furrow, then come around and drive the tractor into it so the rear wheel is actually in the furrow as it would be during tillage," says agricultural engineering specialist Don Gordon, of the University of Guelph. "Each adjustment affects all of the others, so they should be carried out in the proper sequence, namely depth, pitch, level and width of cut. It's easier to remember the order if you abbreviate it as D-P-L-W."

The depth controls for three-point hitches vary from manufacturer to manufacturer, but most small tractors equipped with a hydraulic lift feature a spring-loaded depth control stop, usually operated by a small hand wheel located just below the driver's seat on the right-hand side. Ploughing depth is set by lowering the hydraulic lift until the plough bottom is at the desired level, then tightening the hand wheel at that position to maintain the setting. The operator's manual for the tractor will provide details of each manufacturer's particular system.

The pitch of a plough — its horizontal angle from front to back — should be parallel with the soil surface. If a plough sits too far back "on its haunches" with the shares pointing upward, it will not penetrate adequately. If it sits too far forward "on its

chilled cast-iron shares fall between the extremes of price and durability. In general, soft-centre steel mouldboards are considered the best all-purpose type under average field conditions.

Mouldboards and shares come in various shapes and sizes, each designed to do a different job in different circumstances. The size of a plough is its width in inches, measured from the "wing" or rear corner of the share across to the landside. Common sizes are 10, 12, 14, 16 and 18 inches, with the 14-inch being most popular.

Mouldboard designs range from the long, narrow Scotch bottom, designed to run in exceptionally heavy clay or sod, to the slatted bottom, intended for use in waxy or sticky soils, to the stubble bottom, abruptly curved so as to turn over tall stubble. The best all-purpose style, however, is appropriately called the general purpose bottom, and is designed to

The ploughman's work begins with the back furrow, running down the centre of the field. If the back furrow is not straight, all others will be off-kilter.

Harold Clark

frame to which the two lower links of a three-point hitch are attached. By repositioning the bolts laterally, according to instructions in the plough operator's manual, the width of the cut can be altered. Instead of these bolts, some types of mounted ploughs may feature a lever or crank which rotates a cross shaft to alter the width of the cut. Whichever mechanism is used, the object in setting the width is to assure that all of the bottoms on a plough are cutting uniformly.

The check-chains — attached to each of the hitch's two lower links — should also be adjusted prior to work to be sure they are loose enough to allow the plough free play, but not so loose that the swaying links will foul the tractor's rear tires during operation. These adjustments complete, the novice sodbuster is ready to go to work.

Most ploughing, particularly with a small tractor, is done in first or second gear — the workhorse gears which develop power — although third or even fourth gear may be used from time to time in very light, well-worked soils. In general, the heavier the soil, the lower the gear. Turning the tractor around between furrows, with the plough hitch raised, a higher gear is used than when the share is actually in the ground.

Unlike books, fields to be ploughed are started in the middle, that is, halfway across the width of the field and about 15 feet in from one end (see diagram). This 15-foot space, where the tractor can turn around, is called a *headland.* The first furrow should run straight down the centre of the field, ending at a point roughly 15 feet short of the opposite end. Here the plough is lifted free of the soil, the tractor turned around, and a second furrow, parallel to the first but running in the opposite direction, is begun.

A mouldboard plough always turns the soil it slices toward the right, so these first two adjacent furrows, going in contrary directions, will flop up against each other, forming a ridge down the centre of the field. Because of its resemblance to a spine or backbone, this ridge is called the *back furrow.* It should be as near to the exact centre of the field as possible and as straight as the hand of the ploughman on the steering wheel can make it, otherwise all of the other furrows will be thrown out of line. An error of a foot or so in aligning the back furrow can translate into a misalignment, by several feet, of the finished field.

Some farmers are practiced enough that they can align their back furrow by eye alone, casually sighting on some landmark at the end of the field. Others pace off the distance and set markers, a rock or a wooden stake, at either end of the field as guides. There are even a few perfectionists who will go to the extreme of stringing a line the length of the field, as they would string a line for putting up fence. All have the same goal: keeping their furrows straight. It is as much a matter of pride as of practicality, as the tone of Orville McCormick's voice betrays when he recalls: "When my Dad got done ploughing a field, you could shoot a rifle straight down his furrows!"

After the back furrow has been cut, the ploughman continues making furrows of the same length

nose," it will penetrate too deeply, causing excessive draft (resistance to forward motion) and the resulting furrow walls will be broken.

The top link on a standard three-point hitch attaches to the plough saddle and regulates pitch. Tighten it to tip the plough bottom forward, loosen it to tip the bottom back.

The level, or tilt, of a plough is its horizontal angle from side to side and is controlled by the right-hand lower link of a three-point hitch — the link with a small hand crank sticking out of it. To level the plough, simply turn the crank until the desired angle is achieved. It is considered permissible for the plough level to tilt slightly to the right, toward the furrows.

The width of cut of a plough is limited, of course, by the size of the bottom and shape of its share. Within these limits, however, the width of a fully-mounted plough can be varied slightly by adjusting the pivot and lock pin bolts along the plough's draft bar — the horizontal bar at the front of the plough

Top, *properly ploughed field, showing pattern of work and drainage furrow in bottom right corner. Years of correct ploughing technique will result in a desired crowning effect on a field's topography,* **below.**

parallel to it, raising the plough out of the ground at the end of each cut to turn around and always *turning to the right*, so that each furrow slice will fall toward the centre of the field.

When the total area of ploughed ground extends to within 15 feet of the edge of the field on all four sides, the up-and-down phase of the job is complete. Still required are four or five passes around the circumference of the field, again turning always to the right, and the work is done. A final drainage furrow, leading from the low point of the field to the nearest drainage ditch bordering it, will provide the finishing touch.

A field ploughed consistently in this pattern, with furrow slices falling toward the centre, will gradually assume a gentle "crown top" shape, with the high point in the middle and a slope leading down to the sides. This promotes good drainage and prevents the formation of puddles, avoiding both drown-out and winterkill. Turning the furrow slices toward the centre will also help prevent topsoil from being washed away by rain runoff. Ploughing the opposite way, turning to the left and pushing the furrow slices out toward the edges of the field, would eventually create a concave, pan-shaped field with a depression in the centre.

An area of ground to be ploughed is referred to as a *land*. Very large fields may be broken up into several rectangular lands, each of which is ploughed as if it were a separate field. Farmers' opinions differ over the ideal size of a land, some asserting the correct width should be 150 yards, others opting for lands as narrow as 12 paces across.

Narrower lands help reduce compaction of the soil because the tractor has to travel less frequently across the headlands of a narrow strip en route to each new furrow. Narrow lands also permit farmers to make several *dead furrows* in a field. A dead furrow — created when two furrows are ploughed adjacent to each other, but with the slices falling outward in opposite directions — makes an efficient drainage ditch. Such furrows are automatically produced at the juncture of two ploughed lands, both of whose furrows are turned toward their respective centres.

Unless a ploughless or "zero tillage" system is in use, fields in hilly areas, where the danger of erosion by water running downhill is ever-present, should be ploughed on the contour. Contour ploughing is somewhat difficult for beginners to master, and the advice of a more experienced neighbour or an agricultural engineer should be sought prior to laying out the basic contour lines to be used as guides.

In general, the system involves establishing one or more contour lines on a slope and using these as back furrows for each land. All furrows should be turned uphill wherever possible, as an anti-erosion precaution. (Special two-way ploughs with rotating, reversible blades have been designed to make this easier.) Complete coverage of surface plant stubble or debris is not recommended on hilly terrain, as the presence of some trash helps prevent erosion.

Laying out contour lines is a two-person task, in which one person sights along a carpenter's level mounted on a stick while the other person acts as a sight target and drives in marker stakes at the appropriate places. Although time-consuming, taking the trouble to lay out such a system is far preferable to allowing runoff or gully erosion to wash away a hilly homestead's most productive soil. Even a single wet season can play havoc with fields on which the principles of contour farming have been ignored.

TRASH AND TILTH

Whether or not a furrow slice should completely cover all stubble and surface plant debris after it has been turned over has been debated ever since 1943, when Edward Hubert Faulkner published his controversial book *Plowman's Folly*. Traditionally, farmers had aimed for total coverage of trash by the furrow slice and considered any bits of stem still showing after a plough had gone through a field as evidence of sloppy work. Judges at country fair ploughing matches still subtract points from a contestant's score if they can spot a blade of grass after the plough has gone through the ground. "You've got to cover that grass, to keep it all out of sight, if you want to get those points," says champion competition ploughman Turner Hunter of Barnston West, Quebec.

Among other things, however, Faulkner held that completely burying plant material slowed or prevented its decomposition into humus by cutting off the bacteria involved in the process from their atmospheric source of oxygen. Soil scientists today, though they disagree with some of Faulkner's ideas, agree that perfect coverage is not always desirable.

"What some farmers would call untidy ploughing can be all right under certain conditions," says soil specialist Dr. J.W. Ketcheson of the University of Guelph. "When ploughing in fall, particularly in clay loam soils, you want to leave some trash showing, perhaps two or three inches. This improves water infiltration and promotes better mixing of trash throughout the plough depth, thus improving the tilth of the whole plough layer. It also helps reduce erosion by wind and water." In general, a "wick" of organic matter between furrow slices promotes faster decomposition of plant residues, increased soil porosity and protects against the loss of topsoil through erosion.

Despite these advantages, partial coverage still has serious drawbacks, especially in regions where weeds or an earlier cover crop such as clover may be established.

"If you are ploughing down clover in the spring, you have to cover it completely or it will all grow in again and crowd the following crop," says Ketcheson. "The same is true of weeds. In the spring, you want to cover the surface trash totally — especially if green growth is showing — to keep the weeds down." The failure of Faulkner's *Plowman's Folly* thesis to adequately address the problem of weed control is probably its "most serious weakness," he adds. Farmers following zero-tillage practice tend to rely too heavily on chemical herbicides.

Weeds are not a problem in fall ploughing for the obvious reason that they will not grow over the winter.

Whether trash should be covered is not the only

question influenced by the season when ploughing is done. Soil structure, compaction, moisture content and the protection of topsoil from erosion are all affected by the weather and time of year when a field is tilled. Also a factor is the type of soil involved.

"An ideal seedbed will be composed of fairly loose soil particles or aggregates ranging from one-half millimetre (one-hundredth of an inch) to three millimetres (0.11 inch) to one and a half centimetres (one-half inch) in size," says Ketcheson. "About 60 per cent of the aggregates should be in the 3 mm size, 20 per cent ½ mm and another 20 per cent one and a half cm. The soil moisture content should be somewhere between the usual wilting point (10 to 15 per cent moisture) and average field moisture capacity (30 to 40 per cent moisture)." Moisture capacity is the maximum amount of moisture a soil will hold below the saturation point. The wilting point is the level at which plants growing in a soil wilt for lack of moisture.

Fine-textured clay and clay loam soils are made up of microscopic particles which bond together easily when wet to form large, sticky clods. Dry, these clods can be as hard as a block of Portland cement. Because ploughing such soil, particularly when wet, encourages the formation of these clods, it is best to plough clay soil fields in the fall, thus permitting frost action over the subsequent winter to break the clods down naturally. A few passes over such a field with a disc harrow and cultivator the following spring — operations referred to as "secondary tillage" — will produce a good, loose seedbed.

Ploughing such soil in the spring and trying to break down the resulting clods without benefit of prior frost action would be wasteful of both time and fuel. The extra number of trips a tractor would be forced to make over the damp spring soil to break the clods up would also increase the danger of soil compaction. As the authors of *Tillage Practices for Field Crops in Ontario* put it: "The combination of fall mouldboard ploughing and spring secondary tillage has given the highest yields on finer-textured soils. Spring primary tillage must be avoided where possible (on such soils)."

Medium-textured loam or silt-loam soils, on the other hand, should be ploughed in the spring. As the same authors explain: "Erosion can be a serious problem on silt soils, if the surface is left unprotected in a finely aggregated state. When soils high in silt content are mouldboard ploughed in the fall, the combination of frost action over winter and heavy rains in early spring may pulverize and puddle surface soil excessively, leaving it highly vulnerable to water erosion. Spring mouldboard ploughing is frequently desirable on these soils."

Spring ploughing is also preferable in hilly, sloping regions where water erosion over the winter could result from fall ploughing. In general, level, clay or clay-loam soils should be fall ploughed; hilly, loam or silt-loam soils should ploughed in spring.

Coarse-textured sand, gravelly-loam or loamy-sand soils are porous enough that they may not need any ploughing at all. Even secondary tillage on such soils may be reduced to the minimum necessary to control weeds and incorporate crop residues. Tilth takes care of itself.

· Al Sugerman

Ploughing, or "primary tillage," is only the first of a series of operations aimed at producing the best possible seedbed for agricultural crops.

Questions of crop rotation and the use of winter cover crops to prevent erosion also come into play in deciding whether to fall plough or reserve primary tillage until spring. Fall rye planted as a cover crop over the winter may be ploughed under as green manure in the spring, followed by a crop of oats. The same process may be followed with a hay field due for rotation into grain. On the other hand, a grower may prefer to plough a hay field under in the fall, to gain the advantage of a better seedbed and earlier spring planting. The decision whether to fall or spring plough is sometimes wholly subjective.

Soil moisture is another crucial factor in deciding when to plough. As mentioned earlier, the moisture content of the ideal seedbed should be somewhere between the usual wilting point and field moisture capacity. This is also the best time to plough. Ploughing when the ground is too wet will increase soil compaction and clodding — if the ploughman is lucky enough not to bury the tractor's wheels hub-deep in mud. Even tile-drained fields, though they dry earlier in the spring, cannot be worked too soon. "A good rule of thumb is: If it sticks to your boots, stay out of it," says Ketcheson. Ploughing when the soil is too dry will prove extremely heavy going in clay — if the plough can cut through at all — and will increase the danger of wind erosion in silt soils.

The act of ploughing itself also tends to dry out the soil, by increasing evaporation from the upper soil layers. "You can't plough too close to planting," Ketcheson says. "If you plough and try to plant next day, it won't work because the top few inches of seed-bed will be too dry to permit germination. You need to wait two or three days, for the soil to re-firm and re-establish moisture contact with the underlying soil before seeding."

The ideal depth to which a field should be ploughed has also been disputed. In the past, farmers regarded depths of six to eight inches as normal and frequently advocated "subsoiling" — ploughing as deeply as 12 to 20 inches in order to bring up the comparatively non-organic subsoil and mix it with organic matter at the surface. Soil scientists today, partly influenced by the "zero-tillage" theories of men like Faulkner, but backed up by field plot research, recommend much shallower ploughing.

"Ploughing between 10 and 15 centimetres deep (four to six inches) is about ideal," says Ketcheson. "Every time you add an inch to your ploughing depth, you increase your draft (resistance to forward movement) by more than one-quarter. If you go from two inches to four inches deep, for example, you will more than double your draft." Shallow ploughing, then, saves fuel by creating less of a load on the tractor pulling the plough. It also decreases the tendency toward over-tillage — working the ground to such a fine tilth that aggregates needed to maintain soil structure disappear and the soil becomes virtual powder — the kind of powder that blew away in the great Dust Bowl of the 1930s.

Deep ploughing and subsoiling can still be practised periodically. Occasionally turning a field over to a depth greater than six inches helps eliminate "plough pans," also called "plough soles," which tend to form when soil is constantly worked to the same depth. If furrows are always, say, five inches deep, the soil below five inches will be untouched by the plough. This deeper soil will be affected by the weight of the tractor passing over it, however, and may gradually compact into a layer less pervious to air and water. Such traffic pans can create serious drainage and rooting problems and should be broken up by deeper ploughing from time to time.

The ease with which certain soils compact under the weight of a tractor or turn to powder with constant working is another reason why soil scientists now recommend minimum tillage — that is, working the soil only as much as necessary to achieve good tilth and weed control.

"Farmers with big equipment, massive four-wheel-drive tractors, are tempted to flog the soil, going over it too fast and attempting to beat it into submission. This breaks down its structure and increases compaction," says Ketcheson. "But a small tractor going over the ground too many times can create as many problems as a large one going fewer times. We stress minimum tillage."

The rule, "work the soil, don't overwork it," applies to secondary tillage as well as ploughing.

SECONDARY TILLAGE

Any tools used to further break down or condition the soil after a plough has gone through it are referred to as secondary tillage implements. These include disc harrows, spring-tooth cultivators, spike-tooth harrows, rollers and various other instruments which are attached to the tractor drawbar and towed through a field. These implements may be used one at a time, or hitched together and pulled in tandem to reduce the number of tractor passes.

Sources

FUNDAMENTALS OF MACHINE OPERATION (FMO) — TILLAGE
John Deere Service Publications
Department F
John Deere Road
Moline, Illinois 61265 USA
Part of a series of manuals on farm equipment, this is an excellent, well-organized introduction to the use of tillage equipment and modern tillage practice, profusely illustrated with photos and diagrams.

FARM MACHINERY AND EQUIPMENT
By Harris Pearson Smith
McGraw-Hill Publications
Toronto, Ontario
A thorough discussion, in textbook form, of the operation and maintenance of farm implements, with excellent chapters on tillage equipment.

ONTARIO SOILS
L.R. Webber, Editor
Publication 492
Ontario Ministry of Agriculture and Food
Parliament Buildings
Toronto, Ontario
A good, general introduction to soil science for the layman, particularly as pertains to tillage.

TILLAGE PRACTICES FOR FIELD CROPS IN ONTARIO
By T.J. Vyn, T.B. Daynard and J.W. Ketcheson
Ontario Ministry of Agriculture and Food
Parliament Buildings
Toronto, Ontario
Though it deals with Ontario soils, this excellent, detailed discussion is valid for tillage on most Canadian farms.

APPROVED PRACTICES IN SOIL CONSERVATION
By Albert B. Foster
Interstate Printers & Publishers Inc.
Danville, Illinois
Contains valuable chapters on zero tillage and contour ploughing, with clear diagrams.

The disc harrow breaks up clods and chops surface trash into shorter lengths. Cultivators also break clods, but pull up the roots of persistent weeds like quack grass, or "twitch," as well. The spike-tooth harrow distributes or shifts loose surface soil, while rollers pack it together.

The usual tillage sequence in clay or clay loam soils is to fall plough and follow through with secondary tillage in spring. Normally, the latter involves two passes with the disc harrow and two or more with a cultivator. The field is then sown and gone over once with a spike-tooth harrow to cover the seed. Finally, a roller may be used to pack down the soil, assuring good contact between the seed and the surrounding soil particles which conduct moisture.

In loam or silt-loam soils, spring ploughing may be followed by two passes with a cultivator, followed by seeding and covering with a spike-tooth harrow. In some cases, if the soil is dry enough, a harrow or packer pulled behind the plough can produce a decent seedbed in one pass.

Sand or sandy-loam soils may be worked in spring with a cultivator alone, followed by seeding and rolling to prevent excessive dehydration of the soil surface layer.

Some farmers make use of secondary implements in the early fall. For example, a disc harrow may be used immediately after fall harvest — prior to fall ploughing — to break up trash and stubble and scatter or bury any weed seeds present in the field. Two or three weeks are then allowed to elapse, during which the weed seeds will germinate. Fall ploughing after such a preliminary operation will succeed in destroying the resultant weed seedlings, rather than simply burying weed seeds which might be brought to the surface again in later tillage operations.

Just as certain patterns are followed in ploughing, so are they employed in secondary tillage. In working a field with a disc harrow or cultivator, the operator may use a grid pattern, first travelling lengthwise, then across the width of a field. He may also reverse the direction of travel, turning first to the right, and on a second pass to the left, in an effort to vary the coverage. In this way ridges and gulleys are avoided. The tiller must be careful to keep the number of trips over the field to the minimum needed to produce correct tilth. Too many trips will compact the soil levels beneath the top layers where the disc or cultivator blades reach.

All of these operations, of course, presuppose that the equipment being used is in good condition, that plough blades are not rusted and scour well, that ploughshares are sharp and that implements, particularly disc harrows, are well-greased.

A plough is said to *scour* when the soil being turned sheds clean from the mouldboard and leaves a polished surface. A bottom pitted by rust will not scour well and will wear out faster as layers of metal are removed in the oxidation process. The advice of agricultural engineer W.K. Bilanski in this respect is worth heeding: "Before the plough is put away for storage, be sure that all mud, grass and other dirt are removed because rust is likely to form under such layers. After the plough has been cleaned it should be touched up with paint wherever necessary. Each part that is likely to be affected by rust should be sprayed with a light, waxy coating using one of the modern 'rust preventives' now available." In lieu of such commercial chemical compounds, liberal painting of the share and mouldboard with old crankcase oil, the blacker and thicker the better, will also protect the metal from corrosion. Shares and other parts of modern ploughs are replaceable, but there is no reason for them to wear out before their time.

Moving parts on ploughs, disc harrows and other implements usually have grease nipples located at various points, where grease should be applied at least twice per season. Equipment should also be checked regularly for loose bolts or screws, which could cause friction and excess wear if not tightened.

None of these details is present in the conscious mind, however, as the old red tractor, its driver weary and dry in the throat, makes its last pass around the five-acre field of rye, now ploughed under and ready for discing. Morning has turned to late afternoon. The blackbirds, their appetites long since satisfied, have gone elsewhere and only a few killdeer still search the furrows for grubs. Their shrill piping pierces the air above the newly upturned soil.

The ploughman steers his machine toward the gate, hydraulic lift raised once again, but pauses and puts the tractor in neutral when another man comes walking across the furrows. It is his neighbour, a dairy farmer 20 years older and 20 years wiser than the ploughman himself, a man whose advice is always appreciated. This time, however, no advice is forthcoming, just a smile of kinship. The neighbour has cultivated his own wheat field today, finishing only 10 minutes earlier. The two drivers have watched each other moving slowly up and down their respective fields all day.

"All done, eh?" asks the older man, his eyes scanning the furrows silently. "Could your whistle stand a wetting?"

The younger man dismounts from his tractor and the pair clump away across the furrows. The work has been approved. A rite as old as agriculture itself has been performed.

Ulrich Kretschmar

Of Chicots, Lodgers & Widowmakers

Chain saw mayhem — and how to avoid it

By Wayne Lennox

An unnoticed root snagged his Greb hiking boot, causing him to stagger and nearly fall; the unfamiliar burden in his left hand was a definite hindrance to keeping his balance. The new chain saw felt very heavy, and his arm had already begun to ache. He smiled slightly to himself when he considered that this was only a lightweight model — purchased somewhat reluctantly after resisting the temptation of the more powerful professional-size saw he had admired.

By now he had walked the 200 yards from his old pickup to the stand of timber designated by the government as fuel wood, free for the cutting, and he was relieved to put the machine down for a moment to catch his breath. Somehow, he had always imagined a chain saw to be an easily manoeuvred tool, an extension of one's arms and certainly not this cumbersome brute he had acquired.

Leaning against an old birch, he reflected on the importance of the chain saw in his newly started self-sufficiency campaign, how fall was showing clear signs of arrival and how his reawakening in-stincts — and the neighbours — told him it was time to get in the firewood. The new Franklin he had installed in the parlour was waiting, and his wife wanted to fire up the old range — left behind by the farmer who had sold them the house — for the end of the canning season.

The salesman at the hardware store had convinced him that this saw would enable him to procure the six to eight cords of wood he had been told would be necessary to carry them over until next spring. The old fellow had even been generous enough to explain all about felling trees; he felt confident that he would be able to do it himself with little trouble. After all, there wasn't a great deal to it: Simply cut a notch and then make a felling cut. The sketch of this procedure was still fresh in his mind.

Drawing a handkerchief from his rear pocket, he lifted the ratty baseball cap from his balding head and mopped his brow. He had regained his physical composure and he figured he was ready to get down to the business at hand. Looking the stand of trees over carefully, he felt a momentary loss of confidence.

"Where the devil do the lumberjacks start?" he wondered.

Finally he mentally selected his first tree; though he was somewhat unsure of his choice, he knew he had to start somewhere. Remembering to check the saw before beginning, he examined the chain's tension and then glanced at the cutting teeth. He really didn't know exactly what he should be looking for, but the fellow in town had guaranteed that the saw would cut through wood like a "hot knife through cold butter." That platitude was assurance enough for him, though he had brought along a round file all the same, sold to him with the saw. He had received several other small tools at that time, and these he removed from his other pocket rather self-consciously — if the bloody saw stopped running, he wasn't at all sure if he would be the one to fix it.

The saw had been filled with gas and chain oil back at the truck; he planned to return later to pick up the containers and his lunch — the chain saw had been enough for the first trip. Running through a mental check, he felt — hoped — that everything was ready. He bent over and braced the saw with a hand on the handle, flipped the switch, grasped the starter cord firmly in his other hand and tugged hard. Nothing happened. He repeated this procedure several times, with the same result. Puzzlement furrowed his brow. Then it dawned on him: He had forgotten the choke.

The next pull on the cord yielded a hesitant cough from the saw. He shoved the choke back in, and on the next pull the morning stillness vanished as the saw roared to life with a clamorous din and a cloud of bluish smoke. He revved the saw several times until the motor was warm enough for work.

Then he approached the big maple he had decided would be his first victim. It was an awesome old giant with a very heavy lean. Clumsily he brought the saw into position and cut a notch of sorts. Sweat was already running profusely and spreading in stains across his shirt. Not only was this hard work, but the smoke from the exhaust caused him to wince and cough.

Moving into position directly opposite the notch, he began his felling cut. A certain excitement was beginning to build within him — he felt like David felling a leafy Goliath. He had cut only about a third of the way through the trunk when a horrendous cracking, rending sound shattered his self-possession and instantly transformed his excitement to fear. Instinctively he perceived that something was wrong, very wrong. Suddenly, with blinding speed, the maple split vertically from the felling cut to a point about 30 feet up, as if it had been struck a blow by some gargantuan logger's axe.

The tree began to fall, and slowly the butt, hinged on the stump slab, swung higher and higher into the air. He was frozen with terror, unable to move, his mind unable to cope with what was happening. In what seemed like an eternity, the top of the maple struck the ground causing the trunk to bounce off of its precarious perch and begin its fall, toward him. His whole body had been immobilized but now his legs began moving him back, stumblingly, almost of their own volition. This bit of movement brought him back to reality at last, and the extreme danger of his predicament filled his consciousness. At the last second, he dropped the saw and turned to run, instead of attempting to dodge sideways as an experienced logger would have done.

The baseball cap afforded him absolutely no protection as the edge of the maple butt hit him a glancing blow on the back of the head, stunning him; a split-second later, it struck him on the shoulder, crushing it instantly. He and the tree finished the fall as one, and as the maple came to rest, his left leg was pinned beneath it. Pain and shock coloured the world in reddish hues; in a daze he realized the situation and the realization brought a new resurgence of fear — at 34 he was too young to die.

Just as the crashing sounds of the felled tree had been absorbed by the forest, the increasingly feeble calls for help were greeted with silence by the darkening woods.

MENACING SCENARIO

If back-to-the-land magazines ever took to printing the "This Happened to Me" tales so familiar in the hunting and fishing magazines, real-life chain saw mishaps along the lines of this fictitious scenario might become less commonplace. The spectre of increasing numbers of such accidents does, in fact, loom greater today, as literally tens of thousands of inexperienced people head for the forests and hedgerows to cut fuel wood to fuel tens of thousands of new and rediscovered wood stoves. Unfortunately, many of these individuals do not appreciate the danger that a chain saw, improperly handled, or a tree, improperly cut, can present.

After six years' experience as a lumberjack, I still have a very healthy respect for the chain saw. It can be a vicious maimer — the cutting teeth are designed to draw themselves into *anything* they touch — and every tree being felled carries with it a potential, occasionally formidable, danger.

It should be obvious that the threat of injury and the possibility of death are facts with which anyone, professional lumberjack or weekend logger, who cranks up a saw and introduces whirring chain to bark must be prepared to contend. There is no shortage of people working in northern woods who could show the scars that came about when they dropped their mental guard while operating a chain saw.

This is not to say that cutting firewood is the equivalent of handling deadly reptiles, but, as rural activities go, it is one that strongly demands adherence to basic rules of safety. Because the falling tree presents a greater danger to one's health than the saw itself, it is important first to know the proper techniques for felling.

HUMBOLDT NOTCH

The standard felling technique consists of cutting a notch into a tree slightly above root level and then cutting toward the notch from the opposite side until the tree separates from the stump and begins to fall. This is an oversimplification; safety comes in knowing the refinements.

Before cutting a notch, you first have to determine where the tree will fall. Although the notch allows the tree to fall by providing a collapsing space, certain factors will determine the final direction of fall,

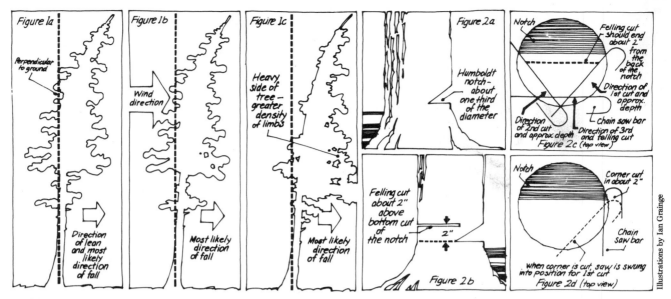

Figure 1a — Perpendicular to ground / Direction of lean and most likely direction of fall

Figure 1b — Wind direction / Most likely direction of fall

Figure 1c — Heavy side of tree — greater density of limbs / Most likely direction of fall

Figure 2a — Humboldt notch — about one third of the diameter

Figure 2b — Felling cut about 2" above bottom cut of the notch / 2"

Figure 2c (top view) — Notch / Felling cut should end about 2" from the back of the notch / Direction of 1st cut and approx. depth / Chain saw bar / Direction of 3rd cut and felling cut / Direction of 2nd cut and approx. depth

Figure 2d (top view) — Notch / Corner cut in about 2" / Chain saw bar / when corner is cut, saw is swung into position for 1st cut

Illustrations by Ian Grainge

and hence determine the placement of the notch. In other words, the notch cannot be cut just anywhere, but must be cut with regard to certain elements that affect fall. These include:

(A) The tree's lean — technically speaking, the vertical deviation from the perpendicular.

(B) The prevailing wind direction.

(C) The balance of the tree — a greater density of limbs or branches on one side of a tree will tend to pull the tree in the direction of the heavy side. (See figures 1a, 1b, 1c.)

Failing to take these three factors into account will lead, if not sooner, then later, to a dangerous situation for the wood cutter.

Once the direction of fall has been determined, as accurately as you can estimate, then you begin to cut the notch. The most common notch is known as the "Humboldt," which looks like a horizontal "V." It should be about one-third of the way through the trunk (see figure 2a). After the notch has been cut, the felling cut should be started about two inches above the bottom cut of the notch (see figure 2b). For proper control, the felling cut should be executed in a three stage or triangular fashion, rather than just straight in from the back (see figure 2c).

As most fuel wood is hardwood — birch, maple, beech, oak — one of the most prevalent hardwood felling dangers is the "barberchair" — to be described later. To avoid this possibility, you should always remember to "cut the corners" in about two inches first (see figure 2d).

For your own safety, remember never to overcut the felling cut, or to cut completely through to the notch. This is known in logging vernacular as "shaving the stump." The properly felled tree remains hinged to the stump by a "snipe" to prevent "kickback" — also to be described later. The snipe is a strip of wood fibre about two or three inches wide that remains affixed to the trunk of the falling tree and acts as a hinge on the stump. The snipe provides a great deal of control over the tree's fall and direction of descent and also prevents the tree from jumping back or slipping off the stump. Thus when making the felling cut, stop about two inches short of the back of the notch (see figures 3a and 3b).

Finally, there is the technique known as "holding the corner" which allows one to determine the path of the falling tree. Professional loggers have developed other methods of "drawing" or "placing" a tree, but the following is, in my opinion, the safest (see figure 4a).

From the sketch we can see that the snipe has been cut in a wedge so that at point A there is more wood fibre than at point B. Consequently, when the tree begins to fall, it is "drawn" or pulled to one side of its normal path of fall, i.e. to the side with the greater density of fibre (see figure 4b). The benefits of drawing and placing a tree will become more apparent in the following section on felling dangers. It is possible to draw a tree, by holding the corner, as much as 10 to 15 feet to one side of its normal path of fall. However, you must remember not to overcut the snipe.

FELLING DANGERS

Having examined basic felling techniques, we can move on to a description of the hazards to be alert for when you consider cutting down a tree.

I have only logged in Northern Ontario and, consequently, have picked the felling terminology of that area. The jargon most certainly varies in different parts of the continent, but I'm sure that wherever loggers work they have evolved a descriptive term for every conceivable threatening situation in felling trees. Lumberjacks have, to a certain degree, romanticized the danger of their profession, and this tendency finds its expression in their parlance. It is a language peppered with chicots, lodgers and widowmakers, and it helps set loggers apart from the rest of society.

This romanticization seems, in part, to be rooted in the way lumberjacks think about trees. It appears to me that in the feller's imagination a tree can almost assume the dimensions of deliberate, conscious foe who has certain tricks to be reckoned with. A tree is a worthy adversary who puts up a good fight and therefore merits, if not admiration, then certainly respect. Consequently, lumberjacks have bestowed a special name upon each of the most outstanding weapons in the trees' destructive arsenal.

(It is interesting to note that this attitude towards

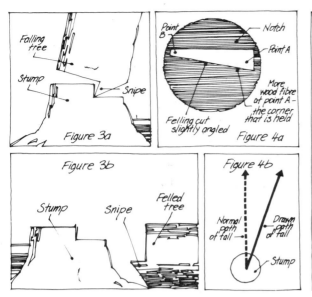

Figure 3a

Falling tree

Stump

Snipe

Figure 4a

Point B — Notch

— Point A

More wood fibre at point A — the corner that is held

Felling cut slightly angled

Figure 3b

Stump   Snipe   Felled tree

Figure 4b

Normal path of fall

Drawn path of fall

Stump

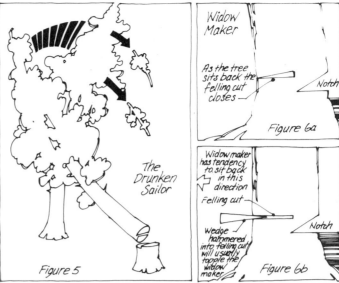

Figure 5

The Drunken Sailor

Widow Maker

As the tree sits back the felling cut closes —

Notch

Figure 6a

Widow maker has tendency to sit back in this direction

Felling cut

Wedge hammered into felling cut will usually topple the widow maker

Notch

Figure 6b

trees does not seem to carry over into any like consideration for chain saws. Chain saws are simply tools, dumb machines, possessing no living cells, and though treacherous enough in their own way, they have not inspired the same flowering of romanticism. I suppose that a chain saw is perceived as the logger's ally in this symbolic battle, and thus there is something sinister about an ally that attacks and injures a worker; saws are simply not deserving of a lumberjack's imaginative creativity.)

Logging philosophy aside, the jargon does have a purpose, and the following terms are worth knowing, even for a once-a-year logger.

The Drunken Sailor: In an analogy to the legendary behaviour among sailors, this term is used to describe a fairly common felling occurrence and a dangerous one. When a tree is cut, especially in rather dense stands, quite often on its way down it will brush by a standing tree or trees causing them to sway to and fro in a drunken fashion. This in itself is not dangerous, but if limbs are broken from the felled tree and become lodged in the standing tree, the "drunken sailor" can, on the rebound, hurl these projectiles towards the woodsman with what seems like unerring accuracy (see figure 5).

This phenomenon is particularly characteristic of softwoods, because they tend to have greater flexibility, though it can and does happen with hardwoods. Upon occasion, the whole top section of a tree will be broken off and whipped at the feller, whose chances of escape are somewhat small.

In effect, there isn't really very much you can do about this hazard. It is one of those things that will happen in spite of good felling techniques. An awareness of the possibility that this can occur is probably the best protection. It is also important, however, to look for an opening in the timber, to cut the notch carefully and accurately, and try to place the tree into an area where it will avoid contact with other trees as much as possible.

Furthermore — and this is one of the most important points to remember about felling in general — when the tree first begins to fall, step back three or four paces and keep a sharp eye on the sky (it is advisable in dense brush to cut yourself an escape

path before beginning felling). Most danger — not just flying limbs from the "drunken sailor" — will be likely to come first from above. When you are quite sure that nothing is falling upon you, then survey the situation in general.

On practically no occasion, when confronted with danger, should you turn and run from it; it is far better to face what is happening and be able to dodge it rather than to turn your back on it.

The Widowmaker: Widowmakers are possibly the most serious threat to professional lumberjacks, and their danger must not be underestimated by anyone felling trees.

It is not uncommon to misjudge a tree's direction of fall, especially when there is no wind and the tree is rather straight. When you attempt to fell the tree, it does not fall in the planned direction, but instead "sits back" on the stump, closing the felling cut. The tree remains standing, but its vertical stance is, of course, very precarious, and it can come crashing down at any time (see figure 6a).

In most cases, it is possible to recognize what is happening and to withdraw the saw bar from the cut before it is pinched; otherwise you will have to deal with the problem directly. If the tree is not small enough to shove down by hand, you will be faced with a number of temptations. There is often the thought of waiting for nature to take its course — to leave the widowmaker and to go on to another tree, trying to keep an eye on the treacherous killer while waiting for it to fall.

The chain saw's noise virtually eliminates any chance of hearing those ominous cracking sounds — the falling tree's warning — and it is impossible to be alert at all times. Preoccupied with the work at hand, you can all too easily forget about the widowmaker, as many loggers have, much to their danger.

On the other hand, you may be tempted to cut the tree right off the stump, or to hack away at the notch — commonly called "cutting the throat" in the logging trade (one of those not so commendable techniques mentioned earlier). This is definitely not advisable, and though it may seem to be expedient, this action can also complicate the situation by creating another hazard, the "kickback."

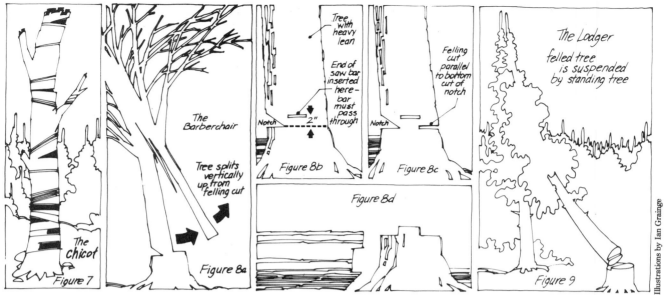

The Barberchair

Tree splits vertically up from felling cut

The Chicot

Figure 7

Figure 8a

Tree with heavy lean

End of saw bar inserted here — bar must pass through

Notch

2"

Figure 8b

Felling cut parallel to bottom cut of notch

Notch

Figure 8c

Figure 8d

The Lodger

felled tree is suspended by standing tree

Figure 9

Illustrations by Ian Grainge

The best way to prevent becoming a victim of a widowmaker is to dispense with it immediately. You will not likely have the services of a skidder, the lumberjack's most usual means of dealing with the widowmaker, and you will likely have to resort to the use of a wedge. Though they are a bit of a nuisance to carry around, a wedge and a small axe are essential in dealing with widowmakers. The tapered end of the wedge is introduced into the felling cut, and, using the butt end of the axe, hammer the wedge into the cut until the tree totters and begins to fall (see figure 6b).

If you suspect that a tree you are felling may sit back, then you can employ a little preventative medicine; after beginning the felling cut, you can insert the wedge, and keep forcing it deeper into the felling cut as the saw advances.

A wedge is also useful for "placing" a tree. Provided that the lean is not too great, the wind is not overly strong, or that the density of limbs is not overpowering, then you can notch your tree against these factors and wedge it down in the direction you desire.

The Chicot: A constant menace in the forest, the chicot is a standing dead tree which is either very brittle or so flimsy that often the mere surface vibrations created by a tree felled nearby can cause it to collapse. The worst chicots are birch; in many cases the only thing that keeps the birch chicot standing is the bark casing — inside there is nothing but very heavy, rotten wood (see figure 7).

The Forest Products Accident Prevention Association, the safety enforcement agency for professional loggers, decrees that loggers should fell every chicot in the area in which they are working, *prior* to actual productive felling. This also is probably the best precaution for you as well.

The Barberchair: The imaginary accident depicted at the beginning of this article was based on a phenomenon known as a barberchair, and the possibility of this taking place is always present when one is felling hardwood. The possibilities are vastly increased, however, if you do not cut the notch deeply enough or if you fail to "cut the corners." Moreover, a birch or a maple with a heavy lean can barberchair

even if the proper precautions are observed (the greater the lean, the greater the stress on the wood fibre).

As you make the felling cut, the strain created by the heavy lean, or an inadequate notch and uncut corners, causes the tree to split vertically up from the cut. The falling tree is hinged on this huge upright slab, and as the tree falls the butt is swung high into the air. When the top strikes the ground, the butt is often bounced off its perch to come crashing down. On occasion, however, the butt will remain hung up but ready to slip off without warning (see figure 8a).

By observing the proper felling techniques, most barberchair incidents will be prevented, but trees with a very heavy lean deserve some special attention. There is a special technique, though not widely practised — as far as I know — for felling hardwoods that present a very definite risk of a barberchair.

The notch is cut as usual, but here the similarity to standard procedure ends. Next, the end of the chain saw bar is pushed straight into the tree parallel to the intended direction of the felling cut (if the tree is large, you may have to cut in towards the centre from both sides as the bar may not be long enough to pass completely through). There is no question that cutting with the end of the bar is a bit chancy at any time, but I believe that it is the lesser of two evils. The saw must of course be held *very* securely, because it will have a tendency to jump around somewhat.

Finally, the felling cut is made opposite the notch and *parallel* to the bottom cut of the notch, thus about two or three inches *below* the centre cut. When the felling cut coincides with the back of the centre cut, the tree will separate from the stump, probably very quickly, and begin to fall. The butt of the tree cut in this manner will look something like an obese and squarish "U" (see figures 8b, 8c and 8d).

The Lodger: Lodgers are felled trees that don't quite make it to the ground, but instead get hung up in one or more standing trees as they fall (see figure 9).

The obvious — but wrong — solution to this predicament would be to fell the tree or trees in which

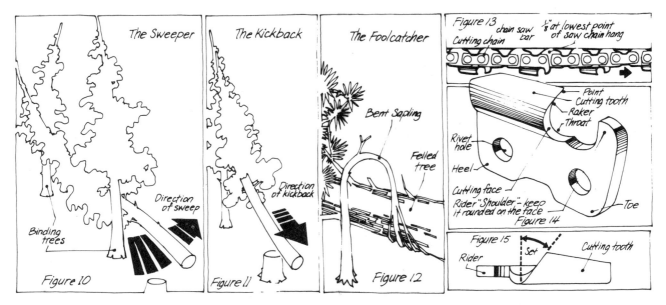

The Sweeper — Figure 10
Binding trees
Direction of sweep

The Kickback — Figure 11
Direction of kickback

The Foolcatcher — Figure 12
Bent Sapling
Felled tree

Figure 13
Cutting chain
chain saw bar
⅛" at lowest point of saw chain hang

Point
Cutting tooth
Raker
Throat
Rivet hole
Heel
Cutting face
Rider "Shoulder" - keep it rounded on the face
Figure 14
Toe

Figure 15
Rider
Set
Cutting tooth

the lodger is hung up. The reasons for not doing this are threefold: first of all, the lodger can become dislodged at any time, and, because you have to position yourself practically under the lodger, you are taking a risk best avoided; secondly, the weight or stress that the lodger brings to bear upon the standing tree or trees can cause them to barberchair when cut; finally, when the supporting tree or trees are cut you must scramble madly for safety, and a slip or trip can mean disaster.

Since, again, you don't have the benefit of a skidder at hand, which can simply pull the lodger down, you will probably just have to cut it down in pieces. In other words, move up the suspended trunk of the lodger about two to four feet and cut a section off (always make a small cut *down* into the trunk first, and then make your main cut *up* towards this downcut. If you attempt to cut all of the way down through, the bar will be pinched as the cut closes). Continue this procedure of cutting off two to four-foot sections until the lodger is practically vertical, and then cut the tree in which it is caught. The danger is greatly reduced in this manner.

Sweeper: A falling tree can become a sweeper if it happens to slide down between two standing trees that cause the trunk to bend. Naturally any bent body, be it a fishing rod or a tree, has a tendency to spring back to its original shape — provided the breaking point has not been reached — when released. As the tree falls further down between the standing trees, the bind increases. When the butt eventually disengages from the stump, the tree has been released and the butt 'sweeps' violently sideways as it seeks to achieve its straight shape. Only another large tree will not be mowed down by the sweeper (see figure 10). Sweepers can usually be avoided if you are careful, since recognizing the potential situation is the key to prevention.

Kickback: Kickbacks most commonly occur when a cutter is not paying attention to his task, and inadvertently shaves the stump, eliminating the snipe and leaving the falling tree without a hinge. With nothing to restrain its backward motion, the falling tree can become a launched battering ram. This will invariably happen if the top of the felled

tree strikes a standing tree. The falling tree will naturally follow the path of least resistance, and with the snipe gone, that is straight back off the stump. The butt can be driven back with the speed and momentum of a train as the top slides down the trunk of the standing tree. At times you must be nimble indeed to dodge a kickback (see figure 11).

The only way I know to prevent such a peril is to exercise a little prudence while felling. The urge to hurry the job or a lack of attention can be your biggest enemies, and you must guard against them.

The Foolcatcher: Though rarely fatal, foolcatchers can be quite injurious at times. They are usually dangerous by-products of felling, in that they are traps set by the felled tree for the unwary.

Generally a falling tree crushes most of the smaller trees in its path. However, small hardwood saplings, maples in particular, possess an incredible flexibility; sometimes they can be bent completely over, creating a tremendous force just waiting to be released (see figure 12).

It is easy to visualize oneself moving up the felled tree, cutting limbs from the trunk and mistaking the bent sapling for a branch among the limbs and leaves. When the sapling is cut, the unfortunate fool who happens to be in the path of the sprung sapling can suffer cuts, bruises, a broken nose, a loss of teeth or a blackened eye.

These are the most common felling dangers you may encounter, but there are other hazards to be sure. It must be kept in mind that quite often two or more of these phenomena can occur at the same time. For example, a tree can barberchair and kickback almost simultaneously; I knew more than one lumberjack victimized by such deadly combinations.

Remember: A tree may be lovely to behold, and its warming fires may be comforting, but it can be a most redoubtable adversary when you want to cut it down. Accord a tree the respect it deserves, in every way.

SHARP MENACE

Having accepted the fact that the falling tree is the primary threat to chain saw users, we can now talk about the tool itself, which is no mean menace.

When motionless, the working part of a chain saw appears innocuous enough, a not-so-very-sharp relative of a bicycle chain. When moving, however, it is an instrument to be reckoned with, the sum of its trim cutting edges making it capable of inflicting serious injury before a person's pain reflexes cause him to react.

In normal operation, the saw is held firmly with two hands and kept a healthy distance from the body. Contact with the moving chain, however, can occur in one of several ways:

1. The operator can fall onto the moving chain.
2. The chain can break and fly back at the operator.
3. The operator can cut down through a branch or trunk carelessly, allowing the cutting bar to touch his legs or feet.
4. The saw itself can kick back, hitting the user.

While the first three instances are obvious enough, and preventable by careful use of the machine and attention to the condition of the chain, "kickback" — not to be mistaken for a tree kickback — deserves further explanation.

A cutting chain, moving at high speed and striking a small branch or some other obstruction, has the tendency to kick the saw out of your hands, and possibly back against your face, arms or chest. The possibility of kickback can be aggravated by such conditions as a saw that is idling too fast — the chain is thus in constant motion — or by gloves that are wet or greasy, therefore providing for a poor grip on the chain saw's handle, and lastly, by poorly filed cutting teeth.

Kickback can be initiated by the top of the cutting bar, especially the upper half of the rounded nose, coming into contact with wood or other material. Virtually all cutting should be started with the main body of the bar. It is also important that the chain be brought up to cutting speed before starting to make any cut.

PROPER DRESS

Scandinavian lumbermen have a much better safety record than their North American counterparts — a fact partly attributable to the protective clothing they wear, including hard hats, face protectors and leggings with built-in metal mesh to stop — momentarily at least — the progress of a misguided chain.

The weekend logger may not want to equip himself so fully, but parts of this garb make very good sense. Safety glasses or goggles are necessary, unless you wish to spend the day picking sawdust and splinters out of your eyes.

Non-slip safety boots with guard toes are a wise investment, especially if you will be splitting quantities of stove wood later. Protective gloves are also available, backed up with ballistic nylon, although any heavy-duty work gloves will do. Close-fitting clothes should be worn and long hair tucked under a cap whenever you are working with a chain saw.

If you value your hearing, a pair of inexpensive ear plugs or sound mufflers will prevent damage from the noise of the high-speed engine.

Never carry a saw very far with the motor running. I personally nearly lost an arm because I once

Bill Milliken

Having made both his Humboldt notch and his felling cut too shallow, this weekend woodcutter works to topple the tree with wedges.

failed to take this simple precaution. I was in a hurry, moving from tree to tree with the motor running; in my haste I tripped on a snag, and as I fell a twig jammed itself against the accelerator trigger. I was very fortunate to fall to one side of a saw which was going at full speed. If you have to walk more than 10 or 15 feet with a saw, shut it off and start it up once you have carried it to your immediate destination.

Even when the saw is stopped, its cutting teeth are very sharp; falling on them could result in a serious laceration. The proper way to carry a saw is with the bar or blade and chain pointing back (the saw is always carried by the handle), and the exhaust pointing away from the body. If you fall, then you will not be falling onto the cutting chain.

IDLE

A chain saw's clutch is of the centrifugal variety. That is, when the motor is revved up, the clutch is engaged. If the saw is idling properly, the chain will not be moving until you squeeze the accelerator trigger.

At times a chain saw will have a mechanical mind of its own. If it happens to be an idling problem, there seems to be an inclination among professional loggers — and I see no reason to doubt that this inclination would not be present with others — to simply increase the idling speed to circumvent the problem. This, however, also keeps the chain moving continuously, even when your finger is not on the accelerator trigger. The danger inherent in this is readily apparent. Keep your saw maintained and in good running condition.

THE CHAIN

Inattention to the chain itself is a major factor both in unsafe use of the saw and in poor cutting performance. Chain tension is extremely important, and a too-slack chain will eventually jump off the bar with possible unhappy results. A chain that is forced into a situation where it breaks can be a lethal, uncontrolled object.

Fortunately, it is relatively easy to gauge the proper tension of a cutting chain. Ideally, when the saw is stopped, the chain should sag about one-eighth of an inch from the bottom of the guide bar at the chain's lowest point. Looser than that and the chain will have a tendency to jump its track; tighter and the chain links will become prematurely worn. The chains of sprocket or roller-nose bars, however, should not have any sag.

Every saw features a tension adjustment screw for increasing or decreasing tautness of the chain. To effect a change, you must first loosen the nuts that hold the bar to the saw. Next slacken or tighten the screw until the desired tension is achieved. Tighten the nuts and you are ready to cut.

The most likely cause of a chain break is a cracked link or links. Cracks can occur in old chains, poorly filed chains or in chains that have overheated as a result of too great a tension or a lack of oil. It is essential to examine the chain regularly for evidence of cracks, and to replace the chain or the broken links, as the occasion demands. I once heard of a lumberjack who was killed when a chain broke and then whipped around his neck, cutting his jugular. Beware the damaged chain.

FILING

Filing is almost an art, and in most cases an amateur is best to entrust it to someone who knows how. One should, however, be able to recognize a suitable job, if for no other reason than to ascertain whether or not the fellow being paid to file the saw is up to snuff.

Furthermore, if you decide to attempt filing yourself, then it is important to have high standards. Today there are many gadgets on the market that will permit you to file a saw with more than an acceptable level of competence — although nothing compares to the ability to file well freehand (a skill that comes only with a great deal of practice).

I should first point out that there are two separate and distinct parts to the cutting link: the cutting tooth itself and the rider (see figure 14). Most lumberjacks use a rider gauge, and you shouldn't be without one. These are inexpensive, yet almost indispensable. Placed over the cutting link, the rider gauge exposes the rider, which is then filed down with a common flat file to the level determined by the rider gauge. Some rider gauges feature an adjustable component that can be dialed to the proper height for the type of wood you are cutting; others consist simply of two standard heights. Generally, for hardwoods, the rider should be between 20 to 30 thousandths of an inch lower than the top of the cutting tooth; for softwoods the rider can be cut a bit lower: to between 30 to 40 thousandths of an inch (there is more leniency with softwoods).

The rider simply determines to what depth the cutting tooth will sink into the wood. Riders that are too high will not allow the teeth to cut efficiently. You can usually tell when this condition is prevalent, because you will find yourself trying to push the saw through the cut. (A saw should pull itself through the cut, and forcing it indicates high riders or poorly filed cutting teeth.) The opposite condition — riders that are cut too low — can present some danger. In effect, you are forcing the tooth to cut more wood than it is supposed to. You will be aware of this when the saw seems to be bouncing in the cut and the chain wants to grab and jam. The possibility of chain breakage increases dramatically if the riders are cut too low; consequently the risk of injury increases as well. Keep the rider gauge handy at all times.

A good point to remember when filing riders is to finish off the job with a few strokes of the file to the shoulder of the rider (see figure 14). This is a minor technique, but one that helps make cutting smoother.

The cutting tooth is considerably more complex, and, when filing it, you are actually shaping it to cut at its optimum capacity, and this also means safely.

The set of the tooth must also be considered. (Set refers to the angle relative to the axis of the chain when it is on the bar.) The set determines the width of the cut; a greater angle means a wider cut and a lesser angle means a narrower cut. For hardwoods the set should be around 20 degrees, while for softwoods 30 to 35 degrees is acceptable. Because hardwood is just that, hard, a lesser set is significant, as you don't want the saw to work any harder than it has to. Furthermore, hardwoods are denser and will not tend to bind the saw in a narrow cut, but the less dense softwoods require a wide set to avert binding (see figure 15).

It is important to cut the throat adequately — the shaving cut by the tooth is cleared through the throat. Use care not to overcut the throat, however, because this will render the points too pronounced. In this case, the cutting teeth will tend to hook too sharply into the wood, and this can result in chain breakage or kickback. The points should be cut as depicted in the diagram in figure 14.

To conclude, the two most important points to remember when filing are not to give the cutting tooth too much set, and not to overfile the throat, thereby giving the tooth too much point.

In contrast to the precise art of chain sharpening is the final aspect of safe chain saw use: mental attitude. Cutting firewood or felling trees is decidedly not an activity to be shared with Jack and The Boys and a case of beer. (Save the beer for the end of the day.) Neither is it something to be done in haste or when you are tired or groggy. Your motions should be careful and deliberate. To repeat, the lumber camps of Canada are filled with stories about unfortunate men who lost their concentration or did not accord this tool the respect it deserves.

Back to the Sauna

North Americans, it appears, are ready to take the heat

By Aili Förbom Brown

"*Lämmitetäänkö sauna?*"
Though the phrase will stymie the best of non-Scandinavian tongues, it is one of the most vital in all of Finland, a query that can be prompted by the opening of a business conference, a broken love affair, the end of a long journey or the beginning of a marriage. Although these diverse events seem to have little or nothing in common, to a Finn they call for the traditional invitation: "Shall we heat the sauna?"

To the uninitiated, sitting in a small, wooden room on Spartan benches with the temperature soaring up to 220 degrees Fahrenheit may sound like nothing less than torture. To sauna addicts, it is the most cleansing, relaxing experience known — one of life's simplest pleasures and one that can restore body, mind and, often, strained relationships.

It is almost certain that the sauna (pronounced *sow*-oo-nah) originated in Finland, where there is said to be one for every eight people in the country. When new areas of the Finnish countryside were settled in times past, the sauna was usually the first building to go up, serving double duty as the family home until the house was up.

An old folk adage states that, "If spirits, tar or the sauna don't cure you, you're finished," and the Finn firmly believes it, taking a sauna cure for everything from mosquito bites and bruises to rheumatism. Finnish mental hospitals use the "hot sauna to cold lake" routine as part of their treatment programme. Researchers in that country have also shown that sauna devotees tend to have healthier circulatory systems than those who avoid the heat. A Boston physician, Dr. D. Donald Snyder, believes that the sauna technique could reduce the number of treatments needed by patients on artificial kidney machines because the induced sweating brings out body wastes.

Emigrating Finns have long worked to spread the gospel throughout the world, but many today are bemused by the current excited reaction among North Americans who have newly discovered the habit. A sauna to a Finn is as basic as the food he eats or the air he breathes; he can only smile when new enthusiasts assume they have found the very latest eco-status symbol.

Fortunately, the simplicity of the ancient saunas of Finland cannot be much improved upon. The pleasure comes from intense, dry heat taken in an unpretentious wooden room. Early saunas were made of logs, and it is highly unlikely that any synthetic substance will replace unpainted, untreated wood as the material of choice for the interior of a sauna.

Wood has the ability to absorb hot water vapours and thus acts to maintain the dry heat that is so essential. (Skeptics often refuse to believe that human beings can sit in temperatures of 170 to 220 degrees Fahrenheit and survive, let alone profess to enjoy themselves. After all, everyone knows that water boils at 212 degrees. Generations of healthy Scandinavians are proof that terrific temperatures — as long as the humidity is kept low — are not only bearable but stimulating.)

THE RITUAL

Most saunas consist of two rooms. One is for dressing and, in Finland, often doubles as a spare sleeping area for guests. Typically it is very simply furnished, with benches along the walls, wooden pegs on which to hang clothes and a supply of coarse towels, usually linen, because they dry so much more thoroughly than soft terry cloth. Even when electricity is available, many prefer the subdued glow of an oil lamp, lantern or even a candle. Frequently, a small window is built into the wall dividing the dressing room from the steam room, and the light is placed on a shelf or stand there, making the dressing room light and the sauna room mystically dark.

The steam room itself is also extremely simple — stark in fact. The *kiuas* (*kee*-oo-us) or heating unit on one side, the *lauteet* (*lau*-teet) or tier of benches on the other. On the wall is a thermometer, and the only

Water is thrown on the hot stones sparingly, about a cupful at a time, so as not to create a roomful of steam.

There is a great deal of ritual involved in this custom. The Finns consider the sauna sacred, and loud talking, singing and other unseemly behaviour is frowned upon. In fact, it is thought that anyone who breaks these rules will be punished in some way later.

Most take the sauna in three stages. First, several minutes of steaming followed by a rinse, a swim or a roll in the snow, depending on the weather and the inclinations of the individual. The second step is more steam, followed by a shampoo and another cooling off break and finally a third round of steam, the washing of the body with a coarse brush, *loofa* or sponge and a final rinse.

The true sauna addict adds another dimension to this ritual. This is the stimulation of his skin and circulation by literally "spanking" himself all over with a *vihta*, a switch made of birch branches. These are gathered early in the summer when the foliage is out in full leaf and at its prime. Several short branches are tied together and, in the hands of an expert *vihta* maker, these bouquets become works of art. They are tied in pairs and hung over a rafter to dry. Although the leaves become so dry that they crumble at a touch, they have the strange ability to reconstitute themselves, and can be used twice.

Prior to use, the *vihta* is placed in a pail of lukewarm water and, after soaking, is transferred atop the hot *kiuas* stones. There it is turned constantly and in a matter of moments the leaves' original resilience is restored. During the process a most heavenly smell has permeated every corner of the sauna. It is to retain this natural and earthy tang of smoke and birch leaves that most people avoid the use of highly perfumed shampoo and soap in the sauna. The birch odour is, in fact, so distinctive and desirable that one distributor is marketing toiletry products called simply "Sauna."

During the summer months, a fresh *vihta* is made for each use, but those made for midwinter bathing are handled with care. Some freezer owners have discovered that a *vihta* placed in a plastic bag and frozen can be used immediately upon thawing, without the reconstitution step.

Those taken aback by the whole idea of self-flagellation will be pleased to learn that a great many Finns do not fancy the *vihta* habit.

Unfortunately, too many people are put off the sauna habit itself by an unpleasant first experience, usually because they have tried to take too much heat, too quickly. A properly built sauna has benches in tiers, like bleachers in a stadium, and it is well for the beginner to start on the first level, where it is coolest, and gradually work up to the third bench. The hottest part of the room is near the ceiling and the head naturally gets the most steam, so many prefer to lie on the top bench with their feet elevated — a fine position for getting blood to the brain.

One first-timer vowed that if she ever escaped from the paralyzing heat, the whipping and the scrubbing with a brush that made her kitchen broom seem velvety by comparison, she would never venture into a sauna again. After a shower and a short

Owner-built sauna in rural Quebec provides a place to cleanse body and mind.

William Nunnelley

other accessories are those necessary to the sauna bath: containers for water, and a ladle of some kind with which to throw water on the *kiuas*.

The *kiuas* itself is infinitely variable (each sauna owner thinks his is by far the best), but it often takes the form of a box-like affair made of bricks and cement with a firebox inside. The stove is completely mounded with clean stones which absorb heat from the firebox and maintain the temperature of the room. Pipes from the firebox lead to a container or tank to supply hot water. A tub elsewhere in the room contains cold water — often carried in pails from the lake.

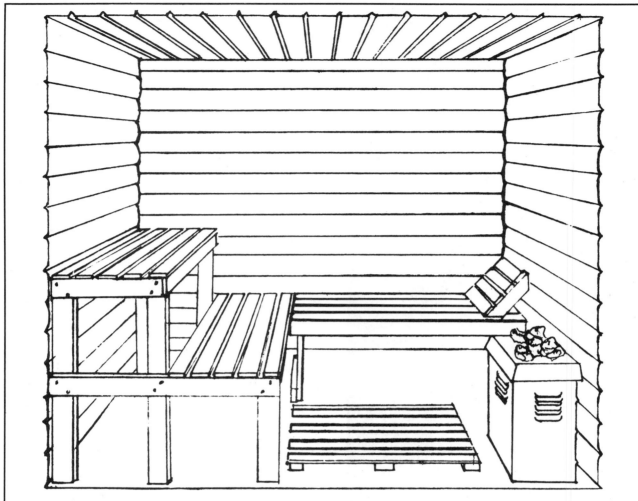

Little evolved from the primitive Finnish designs, the modern sauna remains simple. The benches at different levels allow bathers to seek their own heat zones.

nap, however, she felt "a profound sense of well-being; strong, weightless, clean beyond description and as refreshed as though the gods had rubbed me with a magic elixir." Such are the sensations that tie people to the sauna.

There is no set formula for how a sauna must look or be constructed. The size can vary greatly and it can be an independent structure or nothing more than a small room tucked into the corner of a basement. One might spend a small fortune on a custom-built redwood sauna with automated heat controls, but the fact is that a totally acceptable model can be made with little or no expense.

A source of heat will be the first consideration for most sauna builders, but it should not prove a vexatious problem. A variety of electric *kiuas* — neat, compact and controlled instantly by a switch — are now available. They are mandatory where wood cannot be burned, but they are not cheap.

On the opposite end of the spectrum is the original, old-fashioned *savu* or smoke sauna that is seen only rarely in this country. In these the fire is started early in the day and, since there is no chimney, the smoke rises through the stones, fills the room completely and escapes through a *rappana*, a small opening high on one wall, and through the door if it is left ajar.

The heat radiating from the rocks brings the room temperature to the sizzling point. The difference in heat is impossible to explain — it's a typical case of, "If you know, you know, if you don't know, it simply can't be described." Through the years the smoke in a *savu* sauna blackens the walls and the delicious aroma of smoke lingers in the building at all times. When an older Finn reminisces about "the good old days," it is as often as not the *savu* sauna which evokes the greatest feeling of nostalgia.

The compromise, of course, is a wood-heated sauna with a proper chimney. Those adept at masonry may elect to build in a *kiuas*, using a small oil drum placed on its side as the nucleus. The drum is enclosed on each side, below and at the back in a box of bricks or sheets of steel. A chimney vents smoke outdoors and a hinged door (which can be made with the original drum lid) is added at the front of the firebox.

Simpler still, one can install a woodburning stove and, if it has a large surface, cover the top with stones, or even build it into a brick box in the manner described above. A shallow metal box or tray, set on the stove top, can also serve to contain the hot rocks. Almost any type of wood stove will provide the necessary heat, and one needn't go looking for an expensive new airtight just to heat the sauna.

FLOOR PLANS

The most common failing in saunas designed by amateurs is a ceiling built so high that the lower levels of the room are left too cool as the heat rises. In a properly planned sauna, the ceiling will be only 12 inches from the top of the uppermost bench (eight feet high will work in most family-type saunas).

Ideally, the sauna should be lined with cedar, which resists decay, has a fine aroma and easily absorbs moisture. Other woods commonly used are pine and spruce; solid planks are most aesthetically pleasing, but plywood can be used. Nothing in the sauna should be painted, as the high temperatures will bring forth unpleasant vapours. Ideally, varnish and wood preservatives should also be shunned — for similar reasons — but some builders prefer to use "marine" plywood to prolong the life of the building.

A small window is considered desirable to let in light and allow the sauna to air after use. Many saunas, however, have only a small vent opening near the ceiling on one wall to help regulate the temperature. This *rappana* (about 6 by 18 inches) has a sliding door in grooves and can be opened when ventilation is needed.

Size of the floor area will depend on how many people are intended to fit into the room at one time, as well as on other constraints. Six feet by seven feet is probably the minimum practical size. To make the sauna practical for year-round use and to conserve energy, insulation is highly recommended. The floor may be wood or cement, preferably with a slight slope running to a drain. If the heat source is not built-in, care should be taken to assure that nearby wooden surfaces are protected from the heat — either with brick, stone or aluminum sheeting.

To heat water, an ordinary new galvanized garbage can may be set beside the stove, placed on a simple stand to raise it off the floor. A copper tube can be connected between stove and water container, leading from the bottom of the garbage can into a coil in the heat box and back to the upper level of the water can. Water will circulate freely when the stove is hot and copious amounts will be produced in a single sauna session. (In rural areas of Finland the women always made use of this water for laundry washing once the weekly sauna bathing was done.)

Sauna initiates are often aghast after their first hour — the minimum total bath time for noticeable results — in the sauna. First-timers find the "dirt" seems literally to roll off one's body. Most of this, of course, is not dirt at all, but dead skin.

In addition to cleansing the pores, a sitting in the sauna gives the heart and circulatory system a moderate workout (bathers' pulse rates rise to about the same level measured at a brisk walk). Most medical authorities who have gone on record about the health aspects of sauna bathing believe it is beneficial — most importantly in relieving tension. However, anyone with heart problems, diabetes, or high blood pressure may have to forego the sauna; individuals with these or other major health problems should talk to their doctors first.

For maximum enjoyment, the sauna should be entered with an empty stomach. The sweating out process eliminates both water and salt from the body and leaves the sauna bather with a definite craving for something salty as well as a refreshing drink.

A sausage is often eaten at the end of the ritual, cooked in a pan on the *kiuas* stones (nothing but water and the *vihta* are ever placed directly on the stones) or in the dressing room. (The more elaborate saunas now have a fireplace in the dressing room, and many like to spear the sauna sausage on a stick and cook it over the open flame.)

A traditional after-sauna drink is *simaa*, a type of mead. There are as many recipes for this mildly alcoholic drink as there are designs for *kiuas*, but in the wake of the intensive heat it is always refreshing and a fine way to end a sauna with friends. (See recipe below.)

Hospitality, in most parts of the world, revolves around an invitation to a meal. When a Finn wishes to extend his friendship, he is very likely to invite you into his sauna. It is an invitation that should never be turned down. Sauna diplomacy, in the words of a former member of the Finnish Parliament, is very simple:

"Problems that seemed insoluble solve themselves after we all have had a sauna. I wish they would introduce steam baths at United Nations meetings and other international conferences. The people of the world would understand and respect each other better if they once sat together in the solemn but relaxing atmosphere of our native bathhouse."

Regardless of whether your sauna is ready-built of fine cedar or an old shed converted to a better use, I predict you'll soon find yourself to be a serious sauna addict — and that is the very best addict of all.

"Lämmitetään sauna!" (Let's heat the sauna!)

SIMAA

(After-Sauna Mead)

This is the traditional Finnish beverage to refresh drained tissues after a sauna. The recipe varies from family to family and some use honey, rather than sugar.

Bring to a boil in a large kettle, 6 qts. water.
Remove from heat and dissolve in it immediately:
2 cups white sugar
2 cups *dark* brown sugar
juice and rind of one large lemon
Stir until sugar is dissolved.
Allow to stand until lukewarm and then add:
1 tsp. dry winemaker's yeast
1 cup of hops (home-grown or obtained from a drug or health food store)
After the yeast has dissolved, stir again very thoroughly. Allow to stand at room temperature for 24 hours stirring occasionally. Strain and bottle.

To each qt. add 1 tsp. white sugar and 1 or 2 raisins. Leave again at room temperature. When the raisins rise to the top, the bottles should be put in a cold cellar or the refrigerator. If left out at this stage, it will continue "working" and become sour and alcoholic.

(Warning: Do not cap or cork tightly or bottles may explode. Better yet, use a winemaker's airlock to allow carbonation to escape while keeping dust and flies from the *simaa.)*

Pond Culture

Fresh trout for breakfast, water for the
asparagus and a cool place to swim:
Enter the era of the backyard lake

By Tim Matson

Conceived by a 15-ton Caterpillar one warm June morning, the new pond grew slowly through the summer drought, swelling with the juice of invisible springs. Luck was with me. All around, the Green Mountains were turning brown and the corn stood still. By July, my well, like most others nearby, had dried up. From the hill I watched folks drive to the village with jugs for water. When the wind blew, their gardens grew dust.

In the early mornings, all through the drought, I skimmed off clear bucketfuls of water for the day's cooking and washing. Then I dove in, stirring up clouds of mud — which bothered me not at all. After my mineral bath, I lay in the sunrise to dry while the young pond steamed like a giant brown cappuccino. Still later, after irrigating the garden, I brewed a coffee for myself. Same water. It was a good year to have dug a pond.

This summer the pond is a year old, and in celebration I ponder the delights and risks of its creation. Instinct led me to water. Life in these hills is incomplete and impractical without access to a brook or pond. My shallow spring supplied me well, but my spirit was tinder. I could build a cabin with a chain saw and thrive without electricity or plumbing, but dryness impoverished me. So did the oily outboards in the nearest lake. In the early spring, two years ago, I began planning the pond.

A likely site lay a stone's throw downhill from my cabin, an acre of alder swamp bubbling with underground springs and fed by an overland vein of mountain water. To be sure, I called on the free counsel of the local conservation agent who came out and bored into the muck with his auger and pulled out an encouraging amount of watertight clay. In the fall I hired a backhoe cowboy to dig a well that later ran dry, but while he was here I asked him to scoop out two test holes at the site where I envisioned the pond. These pockets filled fast and held water. The spot began to look like a good gamble, so when the sun rolled around again in the spring, I started to clear the land.

So far my pond investment had come to about 10 dollars in backhoe time and 50 cents in telephone calls. Clearing the swamp added little to the list of expenses. But it turned into the toughest effort of the whole endeavour. Armed with a smoking McCullough 10-10 chain saw, I slogged through a steaming jungle of thick alder, puncturing my boots on glistening stumps and sinking up to my knees in muck. Gradually I discovered a peculiar rhythm in swamp clearing. Plunging deep in mud from tree to tree sapped my strength, but then cutting didn't require much effort. Having sunk down to nearly eye level with the base of the tree, I could saw it off at the roots without even bending over. And, despite a full dressing of spring foliage, the alder was light enough to wing over my shoulder into the brush heaps ringed around the site. No dragging heavy timber through the muck.

A neighbour had warned me that bulldozing the debris under is a poor strategy, at best. Rotting organic matter can unplug the best-planned pond.

"She'll leak," he said.

To avoid leaving pockets of brush which would rot, collapse and lead to the downfall of the pond, I gathered the dead branches and waste wood into piles. These were kept small so they would dry more quickly and burn safely.

And so the pond clearing bloomed in tune with the undulations of backwoods inspiration. My pond muse relaxed her grip on me temporarily during heat waves and deer fly season, and in the wake of moonlit roadhouse rambling. And good country manners brought me out of the marsh to welcome wandering wood nymphs. In other words, I took my time. And in that spirit I cleared the swamp by Hallowe'en.

AQUACULTURAL REVOLUTION

Winter. A white tide swept into the mountains and the cabin seemed to be afloat in an ocean of snow. At night, by the light of a glowing kerosene lamp, I primed myself on pond culture.

If my own pond clearing was leisurely, the evolution of North American aquaculture has been, until very recently, downright sluggish. Fish farming, for a myriad of reasons, has been the forgotten cousin of agriculture, despite the fact that, practised on a small-scale, it returns a greater net profit per unit than any but a few intensively produced specialty crops.

In Japan, the government's five-year plan adopted in 1976 officially called for increased fish farming and a de-emphasis on deep-sea fishing with its declining catches and the possibility of international hostilities.

In China, nearly every commune has its series of ponds, converting feed and fuel to fish at a rate five to 10 times more efficient than that achieved by our western beef producers. In the United States, aquaculture is just catching on: American trout farmers have doubled their output in the past four years; catfish farms which harvested 13,500 tons in 1968, exceeded 84,000 tons in 1975.

Canada has no statistics on aquacultural production, according to Dr. Ian Pritchard, associate director of fisheries research in Ottawa. "Aquaculture in Canada is still very much in the cottage industry stage," he says, "but is on the increase."

"In the future, fish farming will become a major source of animal protein as our wild fish resources become more and more depleted as a result of contamination and pollution of lakes and rivers," says Herbert Blum of the Ontario Ministry of Agriculture and Food. "Trout was once a luxury, but with increasing beef prices it is becoming competitive with meats and therefore may become more of a staple food." A quiet revolution in food production is definitely under way.

Pond culture is on the rise for a number of reasons, not all of them directly related to fish rearing. Country landowners are looking for simple recreation with a reasonable price tag. Swimming pools can cost as much as a house; they punch holes in the environment, drain resources and are often a nuisance to maintain. A pond, on the other hand, can be constructed for as little as the price of a used car. It carries none of the stigma of a swimming

Don McCallum

Farm ponds can provide beauty as well as low-cost irrigation water and increased fire protection.

pool in a conserver society and serves a multitude of purposes that are not the least frivolous.

A pond offers immediate home and barn fire protection in remote territory, and in some instances can lower insurance premiums.

Real estate value is enhanced when a marsh or eroding slope is transformed into a pond. Figures in this county indicate that the value of a new pond is at least three times its construction cost.

We are living in an era of unprecedented home gardening, coupled with shrinking water resources. Meteorologists predict that summers in North America will continue to get hotter and drier — premature predictions of an imminent Ice Age to the contrary. A pond can supply low cost water for irrigation and reassuring protection from drought.

Ponds can be designed to power milling equipment or one of the new, small-scale hydroelectric generators (see *The Harrowsmith Sourcebook*).

The proliferation of sophisticated earth-moving equipment throughout the countryside, combined with free government consultation and design services in most provinces and states, makes pond building easier than at any time in history.

Spring. Traditionally the season to do anything but build a pond. Bulldozers tend to disappear in the mire. The traction is poor both for excavation and for the fine dressing of embankments. Yet early in June the unseasonably dry weather was on my side. I wanted to try it.

CALCULATED GAMBLE

I called back the agent who had taken the clay tests and asked him to check the site again. He came, eyed the sparkling water holes and guessed it was fit. Of course, it was just a guess. If I wanted their "official" collaboration, their office would evaluate contour maps of the watershed above the pond site and blueprint an excavation and piping plan. All this free, but in exchange I would pay construction costs and agree to follow the government's directions explicitly. "No shortcuts," the conservation officer said.

I began to look around for a man with a bulldozer and good grades in pond construction. Down the valley lived a friend who had recently put in an elegant pond. Swimming there a year before, I'd marvelled at the clear water, bright green banks, and throngs of rubbery tadpoles flourishing in a pond less than a year old. I telephoned him and got the name of his pond builder.

"Uh, by the way," he blurted. "The pond dried up. It's a goner." He filled me in. Built in the fall, the pond rose, froze and topped off perfectly the next spring. In June it was pristine, as I had seen.

Then, in July, the pond started to leak. In a few weeks it was down badly. Desperate, my friend poured in a batch of chemical sealant. This served only to pollute what remained — a crater-sized mud puddle not even suitable for ducks.

"Did you use the Soil Conservation Service?" I asked.

"Nope."

I hung up with a sinking feeling. Building ponds was for gamblers, I saw. My friend had picked up a bad hand: not enough clay in the subsoil, not enough water, not enough savvy. And I had heard of other losses. But I calculated that I had one very strong card — a reliable, steadily flowing spring. Still, I grew wary. Imagine a defoliated crater in your meadow, proof of an aquatic bomb.

I felt squeezed between the tyranny of expertise and faith in my home-grown instincts. I called over my friend's pond builder. He arrived one bright May day, and we tramped all over the pond site. He didn't say much, except that he had four ponds in his own backyard. We trucked down into the valley so he could look back up at the mountain watershed. It reminded him of the place where he had built a six-acre giant that finally blew its dam and washed out the neighbours. I took a deep breath and asked him to estimate the price of my pond.

"Three thousand dollars."

He must have seen me wince.

"Or put your pond closer to the cabin, that's what I'd do. Smaller, for just two thousand."

It looked to me like a pond close to the house would go dry, another waterless crater. Or float me away some dark and stormy night.

The pond builder itemized vast amounts of dirt, dams, trucking and piping. On top of it all, he wanted to rebuild my driveway. It added up to much more money than I had imagined. Whatever became of the old-time farm pond, I wondered, as he drove off in his truck.

A couple of days later I visited my neighbours

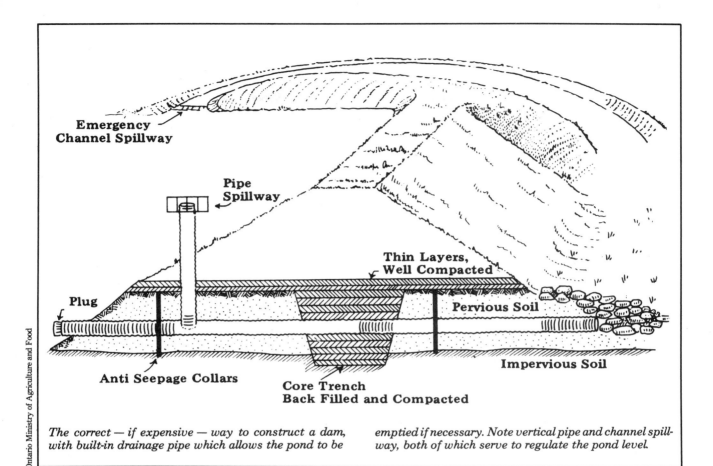

Emergency Channel Spillway

Pipe Spillway

Plug

Thin Layers, Well Compacted

Pervious Soil

Anti Seepage Collars

Core Trench Back Filled and Compacted

Impervious Soil

The correct — if expensive — way to construct a dam, with built-in drainage pipe which allows the pond to be emptied if necessary. Note vertical pipe and channel spillway, both of which serve to regulate the pond level.

across the road. A storybook north-country couple who have built their own barn, they operate a 1,000-bucket maple sugarbush and stock a cellar full of rich preserves. They cultivate two immense gardens, with their own family cemetery between. In times past they had owned my land. Holding only 60 acres now, they had white hair and a flawless homestead, including a sparkling pond. I told the old man about my encounter with the pond builder. He laughed and said that he had hired a dozer and driver to dig his pond for only $200.

"Course, that was a few years back." He said that he knew of the small marsh where I planned to dig; he'd watched it through scores of seasons. "Should make a great pond," he nodded. "Thought of it myself." Best of all, he recommended a good neighbourhood contractor.

Walking home, my hesitations flew. I felt charmed. A spatter of rain began, and I sensed a safe afternoon for torching brush. Walking around the marsh, I saw a nest containing the shells of woodcock eggs that had hatched, the chicks run. Good omens. So the brush piles flared. A fireball lifted into the June shower, scorched a yellow birch tree 50 feet away and sent crimson rainbows shooting through the air. When the smoke cleared, the pond was ready for excavation.

I phoned the neighbourhood contractor, and a few days later he drove up in a shiny new Cadillac. While we walked over the blackened earth discussing ponds, his wife sat in the car. I've seen that before — the fancy auto with the dutiful spouse waiting inside. It's a syndrome of the sensible,

reliable Yankee builder. I trusted him. No one who's really made a living driving rough riding machines goes around in a truck.

The contractor wanted to begin straight off while the dry weather held. He estimated one or two days of primary digging, as long as the D-6 didn't sink in the swamp. Later, once the excavated earth had dried, a smaller dozer would dress the embankments. At $35 an hour, he figured on bringing in my pond for less than $900.

The pond would be roughly oval in shape, with excavated earth used to strengthen the embankment or dam on the downhill side. No piping would be needed, we agreed. I wanted to try a natural overground spillway, eliminating the need for expensive pond plumbing to carry away excess water. It would be up to me to line the spillway with rock to prevent erosion. Later, if the overflow began to cut away at the dam, a concrete trench could be built. He cautioned against using a pipe set at the high-water level to carry away the overflow.

"Water sneaks under there, winter comes along, and it freezes and lifts up the pipe. Then you're right back where you started," he said. A bottom drain — allowing complete draining of the pond — would not be necessary in this case, he felt. At a cost of an additional $500, I thought it was uneconomical, to boot.

A roaring bulldozer woke me the next day. Clanking off its trailer and thundering up the hill, the yellow Caterpillar arrived like an earthquake, pumping shock waves through the ground and adrenaline into my veins. Driving the machine was a member of the contractor's dozer team. He trailed a double track of mutilated earth wherever he moved. After manoeuvring the Cat into position on the uphill side of the swamp, he paused.

I greeted him, shouting over the roar of the diesel. His name was Sonny. He jumped down and tested his footing on the site, then climbed back into the seat, looked at his watch and started. Later, he told me that when he stepped onto that mushy ground, he was sure the dozer would bury itself.

As it turned out, Sonny dug a beautiful 60-foot-diameter pond, eight feet deep in the middle, with no holdups. At one point we saw that the pond wanted to sidetrack into the woods. My McCullough was sharp and well-behaved. This was fortunate, because water was filling in fast and Sonny had hit the point of no return. He didn't hesitate a second, smashing through the swamp, brushing past me as I dropped a slew of balsams, trimmed the branches and cut logs light enough to throw clear. Here was real, living sculpture, complete with a dash of dangerous improvisation: the art of building a backwoods pond.

SEETHING WITH LIFE

The fast transformation from swamp to pond has been astounding. After the initial excavation, the pond filled slowly and the banks dried. Two weeks later Sonny was back for a day with a small dozer to tidy up the shoreline. Afterward I raked stones out of the earth and piled them near the spillway trench. Then I seeded the ground with perennial ryegrass, and it grew courageously despite the lack of topsoil. Except for minimal mulching, I've let the grass fight for itself. Any fertilizer would run off into the pond and create an algae bloom, and green water is not at all conducive to a trout's spawning instincts.

At about a month of age the pond was five feet deep and quit filling because of the summer drought. My well was dry, but the pond kept me solvent. Then September rains brought new life to the pond. The water began to rise. Late in the month, less than four months after the excavation, a northeaster blew the leaves off the trees and filled the pond. I had been waiting to find the precise path the spillway would take before laying in the stone. Now, with the pond gushing over, I stood in the drenching rain and watched the water cut the trench. I let out a cheer. I didn't quit singing until the last rock was heaved into the spillway and it was done.

That was less than a year ago. Today the pond seethes with life. Trout stocked in early May leap for flies, glinting in the sun. In the shallows, water scorpions scull over gelatinous clouds of frogs' eggs. In one spot, mulch hay rots and leeches down the bank, feeding a small growth of emerald green algae. Back when the ice broke, that bloom was the first green of spring. At sunset the frogs sing.

Everything is in motion, yet there are no moving parts. The pond takes care of its own. For the trout, it creates shelter, food and fencing. I throw in an occasional supplement of home-grown worms to fatten the fish without the expense of commercial "Trout Chow." For people, it is a lush panacea sure to rouse a morning swimmer quicker than coffee, or douse a case of midnight insomnia faster than warm milk and whisky. And a midday jump in the pond is the best way I know to keep haying through a heat wave.

Henry David Thoreau, it can be recalled, jumped into Walden Pond "to bring back the heroic ages." Each morning he bathed according to the conceit of an ancient Chinese king: *Renew thyself completely each day; do it again, and forever again.* Of course, Thoreau did not have to build his own pond, nor would he approve of the notion of modern aquaculture. He was intoxicated by the naturally fertile soil and easy angling in virgin waters. Thoreau belittled organized husbandry, preaching the farmers back into the trees. Partly because of his writings, the country pond has conjured up images of wilderness fishing and infrequent, leisurely use. The advent of widespread backyard aquaculture will change all that, giving the pond a serious role in family food production — without detracting from the invigorating effects of a leap into cool waters.

A couple of days ago, thinking about my pond and looking through the local newspaper ads, I saw a 1971 Saab listed for $850. "Good condition, no engine." I laughed. Eight hundred and fifty dollars is just what my pond cost. No engine.

J.D. Wilson

How to Buy
A Used Pickup Truck

"Start at 1966 and count backwards"

By Gerry Kopelow

The old farmer must have walked away from the truck in some kind of rage, slamming the door and vowing never to return. The first time I saw the pickup, a 1955 Dodge half-ton, its homemade box was still filled with barn manure that was supposed to be delivered, cross-country, out to the fields; the chickens had begun to camouflage the paint job; the scratches showed through to three generations of coatings, blue, green and gray now giving way to streaky guano white. In another few years the truck would be a rusted-out hulk but at the time I stumbled upon it the exile had only just begun.

The problem was minor — a two-dollar rotor that had split — but when the truck refused to start the prairie farmer figured he had had his money's worth in 22 years of farm and city driving and he wasn't about to spend any more cash on what he considered an ancient wreck. When I showed up in the barnyard on the advice of a mutual acquaintance, he choked back his surprise that anyone would want to buy it and asked $125. We bargained down to $85 and after about an hour of tinkering I drove the truck home. The brakes gave out on the way, but after fixing those and pumping $500 into the machine, I had a truck to be proud of: cheap transportation and more.

In the past few years of steady driving it has demanded only one major repair.

Agree with it or not, back in the late fifties and early sixties the men who worked on the assembly lines of Oshawa and Detroit were still craftsmen. They took pride in their work and so did the motor companies. Materials were inexpensive and oil was abundant. It was an era that won't be by this way again. Times have changed and so have the standards of craftsmanship.

The rapid multiplication of small industries and the new prosperity on the farm created a need for a tough, sturdy service vehicle that was not only reliable but that was easily stripped down when things went wrong. The pickup truck filled the bill; it was strong, it was versatile, and, most of all, it was eminently repairable.

Today, many of the mechanical assemblies that go into a vehicle are meant to be discarded when they fail in service. They are encased in pressed metal shells with no provision for lubrication. If dirt gets past a seal and the unit breaks down, the whole thing must be replaced, usually at a hefty tariff. This was not the case with the older vehicles. Heavy castings and strong, accessible parts allowed the owner of a 1950 vintage half-ton to put 20 years and 150,000 miles on his truck, given a prudent maintenance programme.

HOT ROD PSYCHE

It is also true that before the days of antipollution devices and oil shortages, engines and their owners could breathe easier. This is not to say, however, that an old-style truck is a worse environmental offender than its modern descendant.

About 15 years ago the auto makers, to satisfy some fundamentally warped aspect of the North American psyche, substituted power for strength in engine design. What this means is that the common low revving, low compression six-cylinder was almost universally replaced by a high revving, high compression eight-cylinder engine in both cars and trucks. The heavy, slow-power units incorporated in vehicles before the big freeways were built could pull and pull hard, but they simply could not accelerate fast enough for modern tastes.

The irrational need for super acceleration plus the introduction of the energy-inefficient automatic transmission created a fuel-wasting monster of a motor. At high acceleration and under high compression, these engines burn gasoline incompletely and spew forth toxic unburned hydrocarbons and other noxious elements in the exhaust stream. A great deal of air pollution plumbing is required to civilize these waste products.

The big-piston slow-moving sixes of the early days were different. At low RPMs and at low compression, the fuel mixture burns more completely so that less unburned gas escapes in the exhaust. The engines have more than adequate power at sane speeds, and at fewer revolutions per minute, service life is extended dramatically.

The 1966 GMC panel was more expensive but still well worth the price. It appeared one morning in the farmyard across the road but sat there untended all that winter. In the spring I finally asked about it.

My neighbour's brother had purchased it for $350 from an insurance company which inherited it following a low speed head-on collision. The damage was not great but the company believed the truck was old and useless to start with. The new owner, a welder, fixed the front end, repainted the interior and exterior, reupholstered the seats, put on new 17-inch grip tires, repaired the radiator damage and rebuilt the brakes. Even the engine had been worked on. The truck drove beautifully, but the first time his wife tried to park it she found the steering too difficult and thereafter refused to drive or even ride in the thing. The poor man was happy to sell it for $750. He even threw in a spare tire and a new battery. In the three years I've driven this vehicle I've had to make a few minor electrical repairs and replace one seal on the rear axle.

COUNTRY GEMS

These stories are typical and with a little know-how you, too, can buy a mechanical gem of lasting value. First, you require some basic pickup knowledge.

Country trucks do even better than their city kin, so if you get the chance, buy in the country. There are two good mechanical reasons for this suggestion. First, a city truck has probably seen hard use during short trips through stop-and-go traffic. This means that its engine has had to function in conditions of maximum wear below its designed operating temperature. This, of course, means a reduced service life. Secondly, because of the intensity of traffic in the city, roads must be kept clear in winter and, consequently, heavy doses of salt and sand are applied. This combination means corrosion and rust for the body and undercarriage parts of any vehicle. In rural areas, salt is not so casually used and a 20-year-old truck often needs little or no bodywork. The vehicles are usually run over forgiving highway miles and, when in service around the farm, motors are more than likely left on long enough, and kept hot enough, to keep engine oil fluid for good lubrication.

There are also social reasons for buying in the country that deserve consideration. The farm truck will probably be sold by its original owner, rather than a used car dealer. What this means is that the machine in question was purchased with cash in 1958, say, and then well-maintained for the next 15 years or so. The truck was an integral part of the economy of that particular farm and treated accordingly. When the farmer aged a bit and turned over some work to his son or a neighbour, his truck became less important. The old man figured that when the next repair came along, he'd just sell the old clunker and get himself a modern pickup truck (with softer seats) or even a new car. If you approach such a fellow at just such a moment, likely he'll be quite pleased and let you have it for anywhere from $50 to $200.

Along with the truck you might get a cup of coffee and a piece of homemade pie and, if you've had the presence of mind to bring along a pencil and paper, you'll get yourself a list of that vehicle's strengths and weaknesses, as well as its mechanical history from day one. If the man likes your manner, he'll tell you in detail what needs fixing and what doesn't, to-

J.D. Wilson

gether with tips on how to start the damn thing in all kinds of weather.

A truck can be visualized as four major systems interlocked into a mutually dependent whole: the engine and power train; a conglomerate of related systems including suspension, steering and brakes; the electrical system which embraces the starter, generator or alternator, ignition, lights and accessories; and the body of the vehicle.

Evaluating an engine in a short period of time requires skill that is quickly available only from a mechanically knowledgeable friend or through a check-up at a reliable garage. Even so, knowing a few simple guidelines will enable the novice mechanic to weed out the really useless performers. Bear in mind that even a major overhaul in a six-cylinder engine should cost no more than $500 (depending on who does the work) and is not a bad investment. Whatever one human being has put together another human being can take apart and repair: don't be too intimidated as you enter the automotive world.

What you want to know about an engine is whether or not pistons, valves and bearings fit together within reasonable tolerances so that the motor can work efficiently. Clouds of blue smoke indicate that the pistons and their sealing rings are too close to the cylinder walls or that the valves are loose in their guides. Both conditions cause lubricating oil to enter the combustion chamber: hence the blue smoke. A good quality compression gauge, about $20 at automotive supply stores, will give the whole story about the pistons and valves. The instructions with the gauge should give a short course on engine testing, and will enable you to pin down the problems. Poor valves mean about $200 work at a good shop, poor piston rings mean a major rebuild, usually $400 to $500.

Returning a sense of solidity and character for the devotion of a mechanically-minded owner, an old pickup can be a bargain in a time of rapidly escalating new truck prices.

Oil pressure is the indicator of bearing condition. The lubricant in an engine is pumped from the crankcase through small interior channels to various critical points. If the main bearings are worn, for example, the oil will meet little resistance as it flows through the space between bearing and crankshaft so that oil pressure will read low. The old vehicles had no use for idiot lights but were always equipped with oil pressure gauges. Oil pressure at fast idle for a cold engine in fair condition should be 40 to 60 pounds per square inch. Anything below 20 pounds on a hot engine at normal operating speeds means new bearings and possibly a new or reground crankshaft will be required. This work can cost anywhere from $200 to $300 at a garage. If bearings, piston rings and valves all meet minimum standards you can generally assume at least 20,000 miles of basically trouble-free service from the motor in question.

Most other problems will be external to the main engine functions and can be dealt with by an ardent beginner with sufficient patience. Remember that a well-cared-for engine, properly run, will last up to 150,000 miles. You'll find that the average farm truck has seen less than half of that figure. Encouraging, isn't it?

ETERNAL SIXES

I would suggest you disregard the various V-8 engines you encounter in favour of an in-line six-cylinder power plant. My Dodge has what is called a flat head engine; it was the Chrysler standard for many years. The valves are in the block with the pistons rather than in the cylinder head which makes the engine a very reliable performer. These engines are still being made today, but not for vehicles. They are used as stationary industrial engines and as the power source for mobile cement mixers and air compressors. They won't go fast but they go practically forever.

My one-ton is pulled by the dependable, standard, GM overhead valve, straight six-cylinder engine. Here the valves are mounted in a separate cylinder head rather than in the block as is the case for the Chrysler. The GM engine has been built for years and years and although improvements in material and design have been made, parts from all models are still interchangeable.

The rest of the drive train consists of transmission, universal joints, drive shaft and differential.

The job of the transmission is to match the most efficient engine speed to any given road speed of the vehicle. Choose a four-speed transmission if you can: it will allow hard pulling at low speeds and will probably outlast the truck. Choose a floor shift rather than a column shift: this will eliminate at least half-a-dozen unnecessary linkages and give hassle-free service. Make sure the transmission has no obnoxious noises when in use. It will cost about $150 for a rebuilt three-speed and about $300 for a rebuilt four-speed unit.

U-joints give the drive shaft "flex" and allow the power from the output shaft of the transmission to reach the rear axle despite displacement of the rear end on bumps and uneven road surfaces. U-joints are cheap and easy to replace, but bad U-joints sometimes indicate trouble with transmission or differential bearings.

The differential is a configuration of heavy gears in the back axle through which power flows from drive shaft to rear wheels. The differential allows the rear wheels to turn at different speeds so that in cornering the outer wheel can turn faster than the inner.

A simple check on this essential mechanism may be carried out as follows. With the engine off, transmission in neutral, and wheels blocked, get under the truck and turn the drive shaft back and forth. More than a quarter turn free play means work is needed on the differential, but the truck will likely be driveable. Excessive play in the differential causes extra wear for the rest of the drive train, including the engine.

HEAVIER METAL

Assuming the ignition, steering and brakes all work sufficiently well to get your truck home you should have, at this point, gathered enough information to make a decision about whether the truck is a good buy. You must realize of course that the electrical, steering and braking systems will all need attention after you own the vehicle. This kind of work is labour-intensive and not extremely expensive to undertake. Similarly, you can expect to do some bodywork, but it is really surprising how well the heavy sheet metal of the earlier models will have survived over the years.

I can say confidently from experience that any used truck may be completely rebuilt for under $2,000 by anyone willing to put in the effort. This means new engine, rear end, transmission, brakes,

J.D Wilson

Rugged, elegantly simple and inexpensive transportation in the form of a 1949 Ford.

steering box, bodywork, suspension work, new major electrical components and even money left over for paint. Not bad, especially when you figure that a new truck can cost $9,000 these days, and that no used vehicle will need everything done to it at once. The most important consideration, however, is that anyone who repairs his own vehicle becomes, in the process, independent from the financially and psychologically crippling dependence on garages, mechanics and service managers.

There are two basic requirements that I advise you to satisfy before beginning work on your new/old machine. First, it would be beneficial to purchase one or two unserviceable clunkers of the same vintage as the truck you have determined to rebuild. Such wrecks may be obtained for $10 to $50 depending on their condition and the disposition of the owner. Trucks, like people, tend to age differently, and many useable spare parts can be salvaged from a seemingly useless old hulk.

After collecting these spares you should somehow obtain a factory service manual for the make, model and year of your particular truck. These invaluable texts are complete in every detail and offer instruction, understandable to the persistent would-be mechanic, on all aspects of repair and maintenance on the vehicle. Some service operations are best left to trained personnel with special equipment, but for the majority of repairs, you will find clear directions requiring only a normal set of tools.

The service manuals may often be bought from a dealer or manufacturer for $10 or $20. In the case of very old models the appropriate book may be out of print and consequently unavailable through direct sources. Do not fear. There is an underground network of old truck freaks, and an ad in the classified section of the newspaper will often turn up a service manual.

Failing even this approach, it is still possible to

force a soft-hearted truck dealer to let you into that back storage cupboard where he keeps all his manuals from 20 years ago. Technical vocational high schools, too, have libraries for their automotive shops and the faithful searcher will likely be able to borrow the necessary documents for photocopying.

Whatever the effort you must expend, don't give up the search for your vehicle's service text. It will guide you through the basic operations necessary to keep your truck in good running order and it will explain those inexplicable idiosyncracies that each and every machine has built into it. You will find, through constant consultation with your trusty manual, that gradually all the mechanical knowledge you'll ever need will be implanted in your mind.

ESSENTIALS

A word now about safety. Even a partially functional engine, transmission and rear end will get your truck moving. You must have, however, completely reliable brakes and steering at all times, or you risk severe injury to yourself, of course, and others.

The steering box changes the rotational motion of the steering wheel into the directional shifting action of the front wheels. It should be checked and immediately repaired if necessary. Most old trucks could do with a rebuilt one, which will cost about $60 or $75 and is well worth it. The various ball joints, the flexible links in the steering chain, are cheap and require only muscle to install. Any work on the steering requires a wheel alignment, about $95 at a shop, and, for a little extra cash, you might get the experts to check out your work. It's well worth it in peace of mind.

Most brake work can be done cheaply and well by an amateur, but I strongly advise consultation with a reliable mechanic *before* and *after* you do any work on this essential system. All wheel cylinders, the master brake cylinder and all brake shoes should be replaced, but carefully. Remember, your life depends on these crucial bits of steel and rubber. Take your time. One hundred dollars will likely buy all the parts you'll need.

(The powdered asbestos from worn brake shoes is dangerous to your health so a protective mask should be worn when cleaning out the debris in and around brake parts.)

There is one major change I suggest be made to older vehicles in order to guarantee better performance. I recommend that the old-fashioned six-volt electrical system be changed over to a more modern 12-volt system. This switch will give more reliable starting, better ignition, and, because it is more commonly used, will make your truck easier to work on when far from home. The changeover means that all electrical components such as lights, starter motor and battery must be replaced with 12-volt equipment. A modern alternator with a built-in regulator can be bought used, but fully guaranteed, from an auto wrecker for $25 to $50. A rebuilt starter will probably be required during the course of your truck's overhaul, so exchanging a 12-volt unit for the old six-volt one isn't much trouble. The fuel gauge will be almost impossible to replace, so you'll simply have to get good at estimating when you need fuel.

If you have an extra $25 or $50 at this point, a very good investment would be an add-on capacitor discharge (C.D.) ignition system. This classy device will relieve the points of their heavy work load and prolong the life of these critical parts almost indefinitely. At the same time, the C.D. ignition will produce a stronger spark, resulting in much better starting and improved all-around performance.

Any machinery in constant use requires regular attention and ongoing repairs. There is no reason you can't provide them to keep your truck running for a long, long time. But then, of course, there is the unexpected. When it comes, don't be shy; ask for advice from those who know, and, perhaps, even from those whom you think don't know. Help with seemingly impossible problems may appear from the most unlikely source. One mid-winter crisis involving my old Dodge illustrates this point. I had been using the truck for a few months and had logged about 2,000 miles after the first engine rebuilding I'd ever undertaken. To tell the truth, I was quite pleased with my achievement.

At one in the morning I was driving home from a late job in the city, and suddenly the motor began making terrible noises and pumping out the strangest-smelling white smoke. I coasted over to the shoulder (by this time the engine had stalled), and examined my vehicle. There was liquid dripping from the tailpipe. Antifreeze!

I figured at that point the engine was blown completely. If antifreeze had somehow gotten into the lubrication system, then the whole thing would have to be stripped down and cleaned. Depression struck. A few days later, after the truck had been towed home, I was getting some milk at the dairy down the road. I told my story to the sympathetic farmer and he just cracked up at my long face.

What Bob told me was that, when he was younger, most trucks were powered by engines similar to the flat head six in my Dodge. He said that once in a while the cylinder head of such an engine would warp slightly, causing the head gasket to leak. The result would be the symptoms I'd experienced. He could remember that his father kept spare gaskets in the truck, and if the malfunction occurred in the field, would make the repair on the spot.

"How about all the antifreeze in the crankcase?" I asked.

"Simple," was the reply. "What you do is drain the contaminated lubricant and then refill the crankcase to a normal level with diesel fuel. If you run the engine at fast idle for a few minutes, the fuel oil, which is a light lubricant but still a mild solvent, will wash the inside of the engine. Do it twice or more and drain it each time until the fuel oil comes out clean. Then you fill it up with regular oil, and the truck is back on the road."

Well, I couldn't find that particular technique in the manual, but I did everything I was told, and my Dodge has run like clockwork ever since.

The Primal Knead

An illustrated introduction to the yeasty arts

By Patricia Mestern and Elizabeth A. Long with photography by Ernie Sparks

Bread baking is a little like riding a horse — the novitiate sometimes suspects that the ingredients sense his lack of confidence and rebel accordingly. The yeast refuses to bubble, batter sticks accusingly to the baker's fingers, loaves mysteriously wilt and flatten, the resulting bread passes for hardtack, and, all in all, the baker is dumped unceremoniously on his culinary backside. We have several acquaintances who failed the first time and have not tried baking bread again. They commonly believe they just don't have "the knack."

There is, indeed, a knack to bread making, but no mystery is involved, just a bit of knowledge and practice. Cooks accustomed to precise recipes may feel uneasy when faced with directions to "add about five or six cups of flour" or "bake 30 to 45 minutes or until done" but, in fact, this latitude in bread recipes makes it harder to have an utter disaster. Bread making, outside the kleenex-loaf factories, is more craft than science, such a variable and subjective experience that some flexibility is mandatory in a recipe, but it is a craft whose principles are easily mastered, and whose mastery is endlessly satisfying.

Following the accompanying illustrated directions and making a few batches of "basic bread," any cook should feel confident enough to begin altering ingredients and varying shapes on his own. Once accustomed to the feel and temperament of dough, he'll have the skill to make any yeasted product from bread sticks, bagels, pizza dough and hamburger buns to croissants, filled and braided holiday rings and Danish pastries. All are variations of a simple, basic procedure.

THE INGREDIENTS

Every bread recipe calls for flour, liquid and yeast (or starter, in the case of sourdough). These are the essentials. Everything else is optional. The ingredients in any bread recipe are a casual mingling that produces a distinctive taste and texture — heavy or light, dark or white, hearty or sweet, plain or exotic — each fragrant and impossible to resist.

Yeast

Yeast is the single most important ingredient in bread making, a living fungus that must be treated with a little understanding. There are 3,200 billion yeast cells per pound, not one exactly like any other. In its granular, dried form it may not look alive but it is (you hope) merely dormant, waiting to begin to grow in the presence of moisture. Actually, even in the dormant state it reacts with the moisture in the air and slowly deteriorates. The freshest yeast is therefore the best. Active dry yeast, bought in bulk from a natural food store for about $1.60 a pound (there are approximately 48 tablespoons to a pound) is the most economic bet, unless the baker can buy a professional brand of yeast such as Fermipan dry or Engedura active dry from a natural food store or bakery. Small foil packets are an extremely expensive way to obtain yeast — each packet, containing a tablespoon's worth, retails for about 21 cents, making it one of the costliest components of homemade bread. Yeast cakes are also not recommended, as they have a short shelf life (about three weeks), require refrigeration and contain a chemical antioxidant. But active, dry yeast purchased in bulk, and stored in a plastic bag or jar in the refrigerator or in a cannister on the shelf should ensure a supply of vigorous leaven for whenever the mood to bake strikes.

Aside from its freshness — really old yeast, or yeast that has been improperly stored, may be useless — temperature is the most critical factor in yeast's viability, and is therefore one of the more important aspects of making bread. Because yeast is a living organism, it requires warmth to work best. It is generally activated by warm liquid (human body temperature or slightly higher) then kept within the most favourable temperature range — between 75 and 95 degrees Fahrenheit. Below that, its action slows, stopping at about 35 degrees, although action will begin again when the dough is reheated. Bread dough can, therefore, be refrigerated for about 12 hours or frozen for a couple of days. Manufacturers of frozen loaves triple the usual amount of yeast to insure that their produce will still rise after two or three months in the freezer. Chilled or frozen dough must be restored to room temperature before it is baked. Above 95 degrees, the yeast action accelerates, but the bread quality suffers. If subjected to temperatures above 140 degrees, the yeast will die. This is supposed to happen in baking, but may occur prematurely if the yeast comes in contact with very hot ingredients, or if the rising dough is left in too warm a place.

There is a great variation in the amount of yeast called for in bread recipes, although the standard is about one tablespoon to two cups of liquid. Simply put, quantity is not a critical factor. A small amount of yeast will simply take longer to raise dough than a larger amount of the same yeast. If the baker is in a hurry or is using a heavy flour, he may choose to double the listed amount of yeast. This will make the bread more nutritious (and more expensive) but will not give the bread a yeasty taste (over-rising does).

To activate the yeast, the baker adds it to a small amount of warm liquid. If this liquid feels barely warm when dribbled on the inside of the wrist, it is the correct temperature. Activated yeast requires a carbohydrate, which it ferments, to continue to function. Honey or a bit of sugar is usually dissolved in the liquid before the yeast is added, and, as the other ingredients are mixed in, the fungus will make equally good use of such sugars as glucose, fructose and, eventually, maltose. The warm liquid/sugar/yeast mixture is set aside for about 10 minutes while the yeast begins to multiply, creating a foamy layer over the liquid. This is called "proofing," possibly because the quality of the yeast is proved in the process. If the liquid is warm but the yeast does not foam within 10 minutes, discard the mixture and look for a source of fresher yeast before trying again. There is no sense at all in trying to make bread with dead yeast. If, on the other hand, the yeast foams, the baker is already well on his way to producing bread that will at least be palatable. With a few more successes along the way, it has every reason to be excellent.

In the presence of warmth, moisture and sugar or starch, yeast converts the carbohydrates into ethanol and carbon dioxide. This gas rises in bubbles, producing a foamy layer over the water and also creating the bubbles that make bread rise.

Flour

These bubbles can be retained in the dough only if the flour contains gluten (composed chiefly of the proteins gliadin and glutenin) which forms an elastic network that traps the gas and expands with it. All leavened breads therefore contain mainly wheat or, to a lesser extent, rye flours, which have the ability to form a gluten network. Barley, rice, buckwheat, oat and corn flour make fine flat breads, but must be mixed with wheat flour to produce a porous loaf.

Wheat has the highest gluten content of all the grains, and flour made from protein-rich hard wheat (bread flour) has the most of all. Soft wheat contains less gluten, and is used in pastry flour, to make a smaller, heavier final product. All-purpose flour will give a satisfactory loaf, but not the superior loaf that hard, red spring wheat will produce. Rye is the only other cereal with the gluten content necessary to raise dough, but as it lacks elasticity, rye flour is often blended with wheat flour.

Whole grain flours are heavy, and do not tend to rise as well as white or sifted flours — the forming gas bubbles are simply weighed down by the flour. In addition, the bran present in whole grain flours tends to cut the gluten strands, producing a more crumbly loaf. Careful treatment of whole grain dough is therefore preferred to enhance the gluten development as much as possible. Allowing bran or cracked grains to soak a half hour before adding them to the recipe will soften the gluten-cutting edges. Whole grain dough is folded gently, rather than stirred like white dough.

Some natural food stores sell gluten flour, a hard wheat flour with the carbohydrates removed. It still contains the protein, however, and is useful in diabetic diets, specialized high-protein breads, or in combination with the low-gluten flours like buckwheat.

For best results, the beginning baker should adhere to the following flour guidelines, at least until he has discovered his preference in flavour and texture. Flours low or lacking in gluten may be substituted for up to one-quarter of the hard wheat flour measurement — that is, no more than two cups of corn meal, buckwheat flour, triticale flour, barley flour, potato flour, oat flour, rice flour or soy flour in the following basic recipe for two loaves. Oat flour or soy flour, incidentally, will add to the keeping quality of the bread, although, as the taste of soy flour takes some getting used to, you will want to use it sparingly. Rice flour is sweet and will tend to make a moist, dense, smooth loaf, while barley flour is especially good if toasted before being added to the dough, imparting a sweet, cake-like quality.

This rule of thumb is also useful for the coarser additions, which are stirred in after the first addition of flour. Cooked whole grains add a moist, chewy character, while cracked wheat, seven-grain cereal, corn, rye or barley contribute an interesting variation to the texture with small, chewy bits. Bran and rolled oats not only improve the fibre content of the bread but give loaves a unique flavour and texture. (Oatmeal bread for cucumber and mayonnaise sandwiches is a delicacy that is hard to surpass.)

The fineness of the grind and the type or combination of grains used will have a greater influence on the final texture and flavour of the bread than will any other ingredient. Be warned, however, that the lower the proportion of wheat flour used, the closer you come to duplicating ancient flat breads.

Good bread recipes always give vague flour measurements because the amount of flour that will be absorbed by a batch of dough depends on the quality of the flour (its dryness and hardness), altitude, humidity and the temperature in the kitchen. The idea in producing a moist, tender loaf is to work in just as much flour as it takes to make the dough workable, so that it does not stick like warm bubble gum to the baker's hands but feels fairly smooth and springy to work with. This is, of course, a subjective matter, one that will be learned by the second or third batch. Rye and whole grain flours will always produce a slightly stickier loaf than white, as will the use of honey, molasses or syrup. If, with these grains, extra flour is added until the dough is not at all sticky, the loaves may turn out heavier than desirable. All of this is a matter of experience, and certainly not cause for trepidation. No dough should be outright gooey, but even if it is, the resulting loaves should not fail. They will just be lighter, more porous and crumbly than otherwise. Too much flour will make the loaves rather dry and heavy, and will also produce a dough that "remembers" all your attempts to fold it into its pans, unfolding again before your eyes. But while these characteristics may disqualify loaves from the blue ribbon competition at the County Fair, they will not prevent them from tasting just as delicious as those with the ribbons. Bread is a very forgiving teacher.

Liquids

The most frequently used liquids are water, milk or a combination of both. Milk helps to brown the crust and makes a nutritious, tender bread that will keep longer, while water breads retain the pleasant taste of the grain. Liquids may be substituted freely, and dry milk powder can be added to any recipe for extra nutrition. Old recipes often directed the cook to scald milk before adding it to the yeast. This precaution stems from the days when most bakers used raw milk, which contains enzymes that counteract the yeast action. The high temperature of scalding killed these enzymes and rendered the milk suitable for bread making.

Pasteurized milk does not have to be scalded, although it does have to be warmed before it comes into contact with the yeast. To save using a pot, simply mix hot water with cold milk to produce a suitably lukewarm liquid. Some bakers argue that scalded milk improves bread's texture. If milk is scalded, it is most important that the baker cool it to lukewarm before adding it to the recipe, remembering always to keep the yeast's environment cozy — not too hot, not too cool.

Besides milk and water, almost any liquid can be used in a bread recipe; water saved from cooking vegetables (potato water gives bread extra body), fruit or vegetable juices, yogurt, sour cream, sour milk, buttermilk, beer, meat stock.

Fats

Some form of fat or shortening is optional in bread, although most recipes call for it, as it adds to the flavour, moistness and keeping qualities. While European breads are usually made with only yeast, salt, flour and water, most North Americans prefer a loaf containing fat. Butter will give a delicate, tender crumb, and is used particularly in sweet, dessert-type breads or rolls. Margarine is often substituted for butter, as a matter of economy. Vegetable oil is probably the most common fat ingredient in bread and has the advantage of already being liquid, but lard and shortening are also popular. Try bacon drippings in hamburger buns, or chicken fat in herbed rolls.

Fats may be substituted at will. When using a solid fat, such as butter or lard, melt it in the hot liquid, and let both cool to lukewarm before they come in contact with the yeast. As fat retards the action of yeast, it is generally kept to a minimum (two or three tablespoons for a two-loaf batch) and is not added until after the yeast is proofed.

Sweeteners

Sweeteners are also optional, but again are favoured, even in sandwich loaves, by most North Americans. All sugars help to produce a brown crust. The choice of the individual sweetener will affect colour, flavour and texture, especially as some are liquid and some dry. Liquid sugars such as honey, molasses and syrups — maple, malt, carob and corn — contribute not only flavour, but extra moistness. Honey will also help keep bread products fresh longer, a bonus if the baker chooses to make a large batch and freeze part. White sugar and brown sugar are the most commonly used dry sweeteners. Again, all may be substituted freely, although if a liquid sweetener is called for and a dry used, or vice versa, a slightly different quantity of flour will be needed to compensate for the change in moistness.

Eggs

Eggs, another optional ingredient, are usually called for in dessert breads and extra-light bread and rolls, but any recipe can take the addition of an egg or two, particularly breads that are heavy on whole grains. They should be lightly beaten and added with the other liquids. Doughs containing several eggs rise more slowly, but after baking the only evidence of the eggs will be a slightly yellow, rich loaf.

Salt

Salt is almost mandatory for good flavour, although it can be omitted for salt-free dieters. As salt inhibits the action of the yeast, it is not added until after the yeast has been proofed and is usually dissolved in the liquid ingredients rather than sprinkled directly on the foamy yeast.

Supplements

Nutritional fortifiers may be added as well. Eggs and milk powder will improve a bread's nutritional quality, as will wheat germ, soy flour, and brewer's yeast, which got its name from its origins, centuries ago, on the bottoms of the vats in which beer was made. Today, special non-bitter cultures are grown for eating. Sold now as food yeast, torula or brewer's yeast, it is a dead fungus that cannot be used to raise bread, but it is the baker's best source of B vitamins and is also an excellent source of iron. It does have a distinctive flavour, however, and should be used frugally at first.

Epicurean Extras

Seasonings are limited only by the baker's imagination and budget. Try cheese and herbs in savoury breads, spices, dried fruits and nuts in sweet breads. Seeds, whole or ground, add textural interest as well as flavour. Vegetables can also give a unique character to bread. For two loaves of bread, try adding two or three finely minced raw or sautéed onions, or up to a cup of sprouted grains, a cup

The Bettman Archive

of mashed potatoes (especially good with rye flour), or a cup of mashed yams or sweet potatoes. This latter ingredient sweetens bread and may even be used as the sole sweetener. Up to one cup of grated, raw carrot, parsnip or zucchini, or the same amount of diced tomatoes, green peppers or celery also bestows not only nutrients but an individual character on homemade loaves.

Add moist ingredients with the liquid and oil, and bulky ingredients such as raisins, nuts, or diced celery by kneading them into the dough just before it is shaped into loaves (so as not to interfere with the gluten development).

Finishing Touches

Certainly one of the charms of baking bread has to do with shaping the loaves. The beginner may choose to bake his first loaves in pans, as they do constitute a yardstick to judge size for the second rising. However, adapting unusual and inventive moulds or modelling free-form loaves on buttered cookie sheets is, in itself, a great satisfaction. Bread dough baked in a greased coffee can makes an impressive, mushroom-shaped loaf that is born to be sliced into big sandwiches. Some bakers also like to use clay flower pots or soufflé and casserole dishes.

But bread dough does not need to be restrained — it will expand, of course, during the second ris-

John McClure, one of a growing number of men being drawn to the satisfying art of bread making, here displays his locally famous French loaves in Chester, Vermont.

Ellen Johnson, "Garden Way Bread Book," Garden Way Publishing

ing, but will retain whatever shape you pat, twist, braid or roll it into.

Dough can be rolled out flat, spread with a filling, then rolled up and shaped into a log or a ring, or sliced into pinwheels and arranged side by side. For instance, a sweet dough rich in butter and eggs might be spread with butter, honey, cinnamon, nuts and raisins, whereas a rye dough could well be spread with sour cream and sautéed mushrooms and onions. Then again, a dark dough and a light dough could be pressed out and rolled up together to create a marbled loaf.

Any basic bread dough recipe can be doctored to become rolls instead — rolls as humble as hotdog buns or classic crescents, bow knots or swirls — baked on buttered trays, round cake pans or muffin pans. (Remember to reduce the baking time.)

Loaves with diagonal slashes — traditional for crusty French bread — or crosses or floral designs are marked by decisive movements with a razor blade, just before sliding the bread into the oven.

Glazes, endowing loaves with a professional look, require no particular skill. Investigate the effects of glazing with plain water, milk, egg white beaten with water, beaten whole egg, melted butter or oil. A glaze should be brushed on *gently* (heavy pressure will cause the loaves to fall) just before the bread is placed in the oven. If the baker intends to garnish the top of the loaves or rolls with seeds (poppy, sesame, caraway, flax or anise) or nuts, he will first need to apply an egg, or an egg white, glaze to help the seeds cling.

Sweet breads are often glazed after baking with simple mixtures such as icing sugar mixed with a few drops of water, milk or fruit juice.

Equipment

You will need a big bowl for bread making. Large pottery bowls work well and conserve heat. Enamel-coated metal dish pans are big and inexpensive, although the enamel does tend to chip off after a few years. You will also need cookie sheets or bread pans. Pans that can be seasoned, such as Ekcoloy, are ideal. Bread pans should never be washed. Grease or oil them lightly before each use, release the loaves, let them cool and then store them, stacked. Don't use them for meat loaves or anything sticky that will necessitate their being washed. Properly seasoned bread pans are a joy to work with, and will last a lifetime.

For kneading you will require a sturdy table or counter that is a comfortable height, about the level of your downstretched wrists; you will want to bear down with a fair amount of pressure using the muscles in your upper arms and shoulders. (You will tire easily if your working area is too high.) If you use a bread board, which should be large, at least two feet square, place a wet towel between the board and the table to keep it from slipping.

THE METHOD

Following is a method for making any bread. The italicized amounts refer to the recipe for "basic bread," but, once this recipe has been mastered, the baker can ignore measurements and use this method with substitute or additional ingredients of his choice.

Basic Bread

(makes 2 big loaves)
1 Tbsp. active dry yeast
 (or 1 package)
½ cup warm water
1 tsp. honey
2½ cups warm milk or water
2 Tbsp. oil or melted butter
2 Tbsp. honey
1 Tbsp. salt
7 or 8 cups hard wheat flour. This may be all whole wheat or all unbleached white, or a combination of both. We used half white and half whole wheat for the dough in the accompanying photos.

1 If using dry active yeast, the first step is to proof the yeast. Using a cup or small bowl, mix a moderate amount of warm liquid *(½ cup water)* and a pinch of sweetener *(1 tsp. honey)*, then sprinkle the yeast *(1 Tbsp. yeast)* on top. Leave it for about 10 minutes, until it has started to multiply and has puffed above the surface of the liquid.

While the yeast is proofing, using the large bread bowl, combine the remaining liquid ingredients *(2½ cups warm milk or warm water)*, the sweetener *(2 Tbsp. honey)*, the salt *(1 Tbsp. salt)*, and the fat *(2 Tbsp. oil or melted butter)*. These may be heated together to melt the shortening and to aid the salt and sweetener in dissolving while scalding the milk at the same time. The liquid mixture must, however, be lukewarm when it comes in contact with the yeast.

2 When the yeast has proofed and the liquid ingredients are lukewarm, pour the yeast mixture into the liquids in the bread bowl, and stir to blend. At this point, beaten eggs or mashed or grated vegetables may be added if desired. Now, add part of the flour *(3 cups)*. It is usual to add the flour measurement in two stages, approximately a half at a time. The first addition is the flour with the highest gluten content — thus, you would add white flour before whole wheat, and whole wheat before, say, buckwheat — which is then beaten hard, about 100 strokes, with a wooden spoon to develop the gluten strands. Don't worry if the mixture remains somewhat lumpy; the kneading will smooth it out. Now,

stir in the rest of the flour, a little at a time *(about 3 or 4 cups)*, until the dough begins to leave the sides of the bowl. It will be barely past the runny stage. (You will not have used the full flour measurement yet, as more will be incorporated during kneading.)

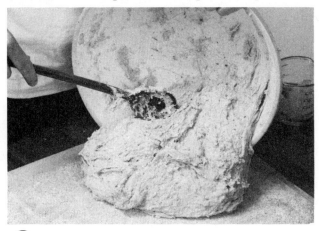

3 You now have dough. Spread about a half-cup of flour on the table or breadboard and turn the dough out onto this flour, scraping the bowl and adding any straggling bits to the top of the dough.

At this point, if you cover the dough with the inverted bread bowl and allow it to rest for 10 or 15 minutes, it will be considerably more manageable when you come back to it. (Some recipes call for mixing a "sponge" with a portion of the flour and allowing this mixture to rise before adding in the remaining flour. This accomplishes much the same goal — gluten development — as the beating and resting steps above.)

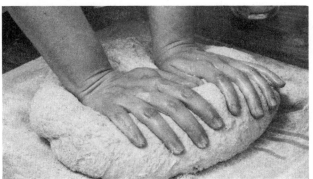

4 You are ready to knead. You can use bread hooks on a food processor if you like, but you will miss the essence of bread making, and unless your hands are in the dough, you won't know whether or not you have just the right amount of flour. Kneading is easy and comes naturally, although many books outline extremely complicated directions — equivalent to the Arthur Murray School of Bread Baking. Relax and enjoy the process of kneading. All you want to do is further develop the gluten strands while keeping the dough in a lump. At first the dough is going to be quite wet, so in the beginning just turn the lump and push at it a bit with the heels of your hands, spreading more flour on the board and the dough whenever a sticky area of dough appears. As flour is incorporated, the dough will become easier to work with.

5 Take the far edge of the dough and fold it towards yourself. Press the seam down with the heels of your hands and give the lump about a quarter turn so that you have a fresh edge to fold. Continue to fold, press and turn again, doing whatever feels most comfortable. You will probably notice that you are developing a rocking motion; when you fold the dough, you tend to pull it towards yourself, when you press the seam, you instinctively push it away. This is the aspect of bread making that erases the blackest of moods and is conducive to strong feelings of legitimate self-satisfaction.

Use plenty of elbow grease and pause now and again to flour the board and your hands or to turn the dough over whenever it begins to stick. Gradually, the dough will change under your hands, becoming springy and elastic, until finally it will seem to have a life of its own, no longer merely yielding, but bouncing back. Usually, after about 10 minutes of steady kneading, the dough will spring back when you poke your thumb into it, signalling that it is ready to be put to rise. Dough made with white flour will also blister when folded. Whole wheat dough or dough made with a liquid sweetener may still feel tacky, but will pass the poke test.

6 Grease or oil the bowl you mixed the ingredients in, greasing right over the encrustment that may remain in the bowl. Butter is best, as oil tends to be absorbed into the rising dough causing it to adhere to the bowl, but as this is easily reclaimed it is a small matter. Place the ball of dough in the bowl, turning the dough to grease all surfaces. This prevents the dough sticking to the bowl and developing a dry crust. Drape a clean, dampened tea towel over the bowl. Don't cover it tightly. The dough needs room to rise and, if it meets resistance, may fall back on itself. Place the bowl in a spot without drafts that may cause it to rise unevenly. The yeast will continue to work at any warmish temperature, but the warmer the spot (remember that yeast dies at 140 degrees F) the faster the rise and the cooler the spot, the slower and more evenly textured the rise. Choose a spot to suit your needs. If you will be busy all afternoon, put the bread in a cool place, perhaps even the refrigerator, so that it will not be risen until you are ready for it.

There may, in fact, be times in your life when you run out of bread and time all at once. You just do not have three or four straight hours at home to put a batch of bread through all the necessary processes. This is the time to try the cold dough, or cool-rise method. It only takes about half an hour to prepare and knead the dough, which is then refrigerated for up to 24 hours. We find it particularly handy to whip up a batch of bread in the evening, slip it into the refrigerator overnight, and bake fresh bread the following morning. It's a farmstead marvel for guests. If you are ready to work with it and it has not quite doubled, bring it out of the refrigerator to continue rising. Either or both risings may be done in the fridge, but the bread must be allowed to sit for about 20 minutes at room temperature before baking. A slow rising not only gives the baker breathing room, it also makes for a fine, homogeneously textured bread.

As most bakers like their bread to rise in an hour or two, they choose a warm location — a sunny window sill or an electric oven with the light turned on. The warmth from the bulb is ideal for rising bread, as is the heat from the pilot light of a gas oven. Or use the warming section of a wood stove, set the bowl in a sink of warm water, or, if the oven has been on, put the bowl in the oven with the door ajar. In any case, whole grain breads will take longer to rise than will white breads.

7 Leave the dough until it has risen to about double its original size. This is an approximate measure, but you will be able to tell roughly just by looking at it. If you aren't sure, try poking the dough with a finger. If the indentation remains, it is ready to punch down. Over-rising is not desirable, as the dough will take on a yeasty taste and will eventually fall.

8 When the dough has doubled in bulk, it is ready to be punched down to collapse the large carbon dioxide bubbles and expose the yeast to fresh maltose. Clench your fist and thrust it into the centre of the dough. It will heave a sigh and collapse around your hand. You may punch it all over, or turn it out of the bowl and knead it a couple of times, or both. (If the baker feels moved to slap the dough or smack it against the table top a few times, it can only improve the texture.) This is the time to knead in raisins, nuts, diced cheese, sprouts or whatever other bulky ingredients are desired. This is performed without further flour, incidentally. Flour will not be absorbed and will dry out the loaf.

Some recipes call for only one rising, and others call for as many as four or five. Each time the dough will rise a little faster, and the bread's texture will be finer. Any recipe can be given an extra rising and punching down, but you can't go on indefinitely as the yeast will eventually exhaust itself. Most recipes, like our basic bread, call for two risings — one in the bowl and one in the pans.

9 Now, using a knife, (because cutting is not as destructive to gluten strands as tearing is) divide the punched-down dough equally into the number of loaves you are baking. One method for shaping loaves is to take each lump of dough in turn and roll it out with a rolling pin into a rectangle about one-half-inch thick. The rectangle need be only approximate. As you roll, you will notice air bubbles being pushed to the edges and bursting. That is the desired effect. The more bubbles you expel at this point, the better textured the bread will be.

10 When you have a flat rectangle or reasonable facsimile, start from the long side to roll the dough up like a jelly roll, pushing the ends in if the loaf is a little too long for the pans. Roll the dough tightly so that you do not incorporate more air as you go. Finish rolling the dough up, pinch the seam together, and place the loaf in the buttered pan with its seam down. Another method is to roll out an approximate triangle and begin to furl the dough at the apex.

Other bread makers prefer to just shape their loaves with their hands into loaf-shaped pieces. This may allow large tunnels and bubbles to survive in the loaves, however, the kind that allow jam to dribble out onto your hands.

The loaves should fill the pans no more than one-half to two-thirds full. If you have too much dough, cut off the excess and make it into rolls, by shaping golf-ball-sized pieces and placing them about an inch apart in a greased baking pan. If you have too little dough, it is nothing to worry about. The loaves will just be slightly flatter than you may be used to. Butter is superior for greasing the pans, as it stays where you smear it. Oil tends to run down the sides, often necessitating a certain amount of prying to remove the finished loaves from their containers.

11 Now, to further insure that the big bubbles have been removed, take each pan and drop it from a height of about three inches onto the table a few times. Set the filled pans aside, covered again with a damp tea towel, once more choosing a spot that best fits your schedule. (If this rising is to take place in the refrigerator, grease the tops of the loaves, as the dough will dry out more quickly there.) The rising will take less time now, only about 30 minutes if the loaves are in a draft-free, warm spot. This time, check for doubling just by looking. When they are almost ready, begin preheating the oven to the baking temperature (375 degrees F). The loaves should be just slightly above the top of the pan. Do not poke them, as the evidence will remain.

12 If you err on the side of under-rising, fine. The loaves will rise a bit in the oven before the yeast dies, and the bread will just be a little denser than otherwise, a quality some bakers prefer. Allowing the loaves to rise too far, however, can be disastrous. They may dribble out of the pans, or fall back on themselves. If this happens, remove the dough from the pans, punch it down again, reform into loaves, and let them rise again. (This time, they will rise even faster than last time, so be ready.)

Just before placing the loaves in the preheated oven is the time to glaze and garnish them. If you want a really crisp, French-style crust, brush the loaves with cold water, place a pan of boiling water in the oven with the baking loaves, and mist the tops with cold water periodically (use a plant mister) during baking.

Always leave space around each loaf in the oven for air to circulate — otherwise the bottoms may burn. Incidentally, loaves may be taken from the oven halfway through baking and kept in the refrigerator for two to three weeks. Then, when you have need of fast, fresh-baked bread, return to the oven to finish baking. (This is the principle of "brown and serve" rolls.) When the loaves are almost done, the kitchen will smell of baked bread, the crusts should appear golden brown and the bread will draw away from the sides of the pans. Just before baking time is up *(about 35 minutes)* tap the top of the nearest loaf. It should sound hollow. If it does, remove it and turn it out of its pan. It should be medium-brown all over and should also sound hollow when rapped on the bottom. If it is not done, just return it to its pan and continue baking.

If it is, test the other loaves for doneness and turn them out on their sides immediately onto a rack. They should drop right out of their pans, but if they do not, work around the edge of the pan with a knife and try tapping them upside down. If the loaves are left in the pans to cool, the steam, having nowhere to escape, will make the loaves soggy.

If your loaves brown unevenly, it could be the result of a hot spot in the oven. Try rearranging the loaves about halfway through future bakings.

If you like soft crusts, butter the cooling loaves or cover them loosely with a tea towel, or both.

Perfectly baked bread will look ragged and doughy if it is sliced while still warm, and should be completely cool in two or three hours. At this point it can be placed in plastic bags and frozen for future use, or placed in the bread box.

It is, of course, the bread maker's right — and privilege — to cut into the bread before it is properly cooled. Still-hot, home baked bread slathered with creamery buttery is one of life's more satisfying delights — and one that is unwisely resisted.

Bill Milliken

Homestead Chutzpah

The organic brunch: whole wheat bagels and homemade herbed cheese

By Catharine Reed

My introduction to homemade Boursin-type cheese came unexpectedly and in the least likely of places — the hills of Central Mexico. All morning we had been clambering up steep, rocky paths carved through the brush by centuries of use by little burros laden with firewood and twigs. I struggled to keep up with our leader, a vigorous and youthful white-haired lady of 72, who possessed not only an inexhaustible fund of energy but also an endless supply of information on these Mexican hills and villages. But that was not all.

When we finally paused for lunch, she proudly announced that one of her many projects was making what she called "Boursin" cheese, and from her lunch bag produced large samples of creamy cheese laced with savoury home-grown herbs. Boursin is actually a brand name for a delectable French cheese, which like Rondelé, Tartare and several other brands, are all Gournay-type cheeses mixed with various herbs and, usually, garlic. I have long had an affinity for these cheeses, and the white-haired woman's version was at least as delicious as the expensive little packages one buys in delicatessens and enlightened supermarkets. Later I was treated to a tour of her herb garden in the small town of

Jocotepec, and to a lesson in making this delicate, buttery cheese.

On our hiking trip we had sampled the herbed Gournay with homemade five-grain bread and home-grown avocados, but on arriving back in British Columbia I decided that the cheese would go very well with homemade bagels. Bagels and cream cheese is a classic, so why not whole wheat bagels and creamy, herbed cheese?

This recipe makes about 12 ounces of cheese and calls for fresh herbs, which make the cheese especially memorable. At this time of year it may be necessary to substitute dried herbs, using ⅓ teaspoon of the dried product in place of one tablespoon of fresh herbs.

There are two ways to make this cheese, one calling for the use of rennet to curdle the cream, and a simpler recipe that uses fresh cultured buttermilk instead. Rennet will produce a consistency more like the commercial Boursin — rich and slightly crumbly. Buttermilk yields a cheese more like a cream cheese. Both are delicious.

Rene Tunney

Herbed Cream Cheese

2 quarts cream (for a less rich cheese substitute part or all milk)

¼ tsp. commercial liquid rennet or dissolve ¼ rennet tablet in 1 oz. cool water

4 medium garlic cloves

¾ tsp. salt

1 tsp. freshly ground black pepper

2 Tbsp. dry white wine

All or some of the following herbs:

  1 Tbsp. fresh basil

  1 Tbsp. fresh rosemary

  1 Tbsp. fresh thyme

  1 Tbsp. fresh sage

  1 Tbsp. or more fresh parsley

  2 tsp. fresh tarragon

Catharine Reed

Step One: Peel and crush the garlic cloves and tie them in a cheesecloth bag. Pour cream into a large stainless steel or enamel pot, drop in the garlic and heat it gradually to 90 to 100 degrees F, using a dairy or candy thermometer to read the temperature. Stir in the rennet, cover the pot, wrap it in a terrycloth towel and set it in a warm place until the cream has set (about ½ hour).

Step Two: Line a colander with three or four layers of cheesecloth or a tea towel. (The latter is more economical, as it can be washed and re-used.) The cloth should have been wrung out in cold water, so that it is damp. Place the cloth-lined colander in a bowl and pour the curds and whey into the colander. Remove the garlic and set the whey aside. (Do any of your animals like garlic?) Enclose the colander and bowl in a large plastic bag and put this in the refrigerator, letting the cheese drain for three or four hours.

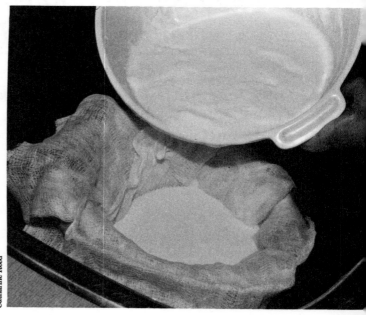

Catharine Reed

*Top, this delicately flavoured cheese can be made with few ingredients and simple equipment. When rennet is not handy, buttermilk can be used as a starter culture. **Middle**, a small cheesecloth bag filled with crushed garlic is dropped into the cream and starter, and left there until the cream has clabbered. **Bottom**, the curds and whey are poured into a cloth-lined colander to drain. A longer draining time renders a less sticky final product.*

Step Three: Spoon the curd into a clean bowl. Add salt, pepper, wine and herbs. All herbs should be chopped very fine. Mix thoroughly with a fork, shape into four rounds, wrap them tightly in plastic wrap and refrigerate. Gournay is a cheese that should be enjoyed young: it is at its best when it is up to a week old. It will be moist and fluffy, slightly crumbly but spreadable, white to off-white with flecks of green. When made entirely with cream, it is surpassingly rich, yet mild.

To make this recipe using buttermilk as a starter culture, rather than rennet, just substitute 1½ cups of buttermilk for the rennet. (Be sure to read the label of the buttermilk container; it should list Buttermilk Bacterial Culture as an ingredient. Some buttermilks today are cultured with citric acid and will not serve to make cheese.) The buttermilk method takes from 24 to 28 hours to set, or the process can be speeded up by gradually heating the cream and buttermilk mixture to 170 degrees F and holding it there for about 30 minutes.

Incidentally, if only salt is added to flavour the cheese, it can be used in desserts or any other appropriate cream cheese recipe. (This cheese can also be frozen. To use, allow it to thaw completely, then beat with an egg beater until smooth.)

Whole Wheat Bagels

Bagels are a traditional Jewish bread, once only a Sunday-brunch delicacy. Now these doughnut-shaped buns are so popular all week that some large cities sport bagel restaurants, like pizzerias. Here, bagels may be bought by the dozen to take out or they may be eaten on the spot — plain bagels, onion bagels, garlic, sesame seed, cinnamon, and raisin and poppy seed bagels. They are eaten as is, fresh from the oven, or cut open and spread with any favourite filling, like a sandwich. Cream cheese is a popular and traditional accompaniment, as is smoked salmon (lox).

The first bagel, the story goes, was made by the Polish owner of a Viennese coffee house in the 17th-century. Here, he served individual half-moon breads called "kipfel." Later, inspired by the shape of the Polish king's stirrup, he changed the name of his creation to "beugel," pronounced boy-gel, the German word for stirrup. Somewhere along its evolutionary path, the bagel became circular and its name became Anglicized.

Present-day European bagel makers consider their baked goods a creative enterprise, like a *boulanger* with his *croissants*. Soft water, they say, is absolutely critical to a high quality bagel. Each bagel uses three and one-half ounces of dough, and must have the proper-sized hole, about the size of a quarter, although each is handmade.

Commercially, the dough is made from high gluten flour, so that the resulting product has a distinctive chewy consistency. As whole wheat flour interferes with normal gluten development, this recipe will make a slightly less "chewy" bagel, but the higher nutrition of these bagels compensates for any small loss in texture. Using all white flour will produce a more traditional bagel.

½ Tbsp. (½ package) dry yeast
1 tsp. sugar
3 eggs
½ cup vegetable oil
½ Tbsp. salt
1 cup warm water
3 Tbsp. sugar or honey
3 cups unbleached white flour
3 to 4 cups whole wheat flour
1 egg, well beaten
sesame seeds, poppy seeds, or dried onion flakes
  (optional)

In a small bowl, dissolve the sugar in ½ cup of warm, not hot, water. Sprinkle yeast over, and let stand in a warm spot (about 80 degrees F). Meanwhile, in a large bowl, beat 3 eggs. Add oil, salt, water and sugar or honey. When yeast looks foamy on top, stir yeast solution into egg mixture. Stir in 3 cups unbleached white flour. Beat until smooth. Add whole wheat flour a cup at a time, working it in, until the mixture is a soft dough. Knead 5 minutes on a floured board, continuing to work flour in until the dough is no longer sticky. Grease bowl, replace dough, cover with a clean, damp tea towel and let rise in a warm place for about 50 minutes, or until the dough has risen to about one and one-half times its original size. Punch down and remove dough from bowl. Divide dough into thirds, placing two of the thirds in plastic bags in the refrigerator to keep moist while the first section is being prepared. For large bagels, divide dough into 8 pieces. Roll each piece out in a tube about 8 inches long, and connect the ends to form a doughnut shape. Bagel experts do this by looping the dough around their fingers, but I find that it is most easily managed with the dough flat on a table. Make sure that the ends are pressed together securely.

Drop each ring into rapidly boiling water, leave for 10 seconds, and then remove with a slotted spoon. Place the rings on a greased cookie sheet, or one that has been liberally sprinkled with corn meal. Using a pastry brush, wash each bagel with well-beaten egg, and then sprinkle on poppy seeds. Bake at 425 degrees F for 20 minutes, or until golden brown. Prepare the rest of the dough the same way. (Makes 2 dozen large bagels.)

Bagels may be frozen for future use, or kept in the bread box for a week or so. They are good with anything — the traditional lox, homemade herbed cream cheese, pastrami and bean sprouts or with avocado and tomatoes — and they are delicious when hot.

The Loaves Of Tutankhamun

In praise of sourdough, the most ancient of leavened breads

By J. Peter Shinnick

They came in almost as many variations of shape and colour as did the gods of their bakers — sesame, poppy seed and camphor; round, domed, conical, braided or fashioned into the form of a bird, a fish, a pyramid or even the sacred cow, Hathor. These were the loaves of ancient Egypt, the hearthstone of civilized bread making.

Archaeologists speculate that the elaboration of the leavening arts came about after an unknown baker, somewhere in the distant, eastern parts, left his Nile-water-and-meal dough in the sun too long. Exposed to wild yeasts, the mixture began to ferment but the Egyptian baker decided to bake the seemingly spoiled loaf over a bed of coals. A wonderful, magical thing happened. As the bread baked, it grew in size, became light, airy and far more palatable than earlier, unleavened heavy loaves had been. When cut open, this new bread revealed a network of holes and tunnels. The Egyptians, ever fascinated by secret passages, compared this mysterious process to the growth of a baby within a womb — coining the 6,000-year-old phrase "a bun in the oven." (This analogy continued strong even in Greece and Rome, where parallels were symbolically drawn between the domed shape of ancient outdoor ovens and the form of an expectant mother.)

Leavened bread, the Egyptians soon discovered, required a partially closed chamber to rise to its full potential, and they are credited with the invention of the first ovens — conical affairs made of clay bricks and fired by wood — which gradually evolved and spread throughout the Mediterranean. The Egyptians went on to more sophisticated forms of bread making, isolating and propagating different yeast cultures, and the loaves they produced became so important that they were used as a medium of exchange, as wages for workers and as fitting gifts for the gods.

Tutankhamun's 14th-century B.C. tomb contained, among the treasure trove, a hand grain mill, which discoverer Howard Carter believed to have been placed there for use by Tut's *shawabtys*, small statues placed in the tomb to act as servants for the dead king. Also found was a miniature granary with 16 compartments filled to the brim with grain and seeds. Some tombs also contained finished loaves of bread intended to satisfy the post-mortem royal appetites. The basic ingredients of all these breads were leavening starter, stone ground wheat flour, salt and water.

The bread itself was sourdough and, all the modern packaged yeasts and recipes aside, it remains the finest of breads, rich both in flavour and local culture. It is also a bread that appeals to one's sense of personal economics — I have not bought a package of yeast for three years, baking one and perhaps two large batches of bread each month.

Rather than baker's dried yeast, the starter culture is the essence of sourdough bread, and it resulted from the Egyptian discovery that it was not necessary to allow every batch of bread to ferment before baking, but if a small amount of fermented bread dough were kept and added to the following batch, that later bread would also rise. As long as the baker always set a bit of dough aside, he would have his leavening for the future.

The starter is usually a mixture of flour, water and perhaps milk, yogurt, potato water or commercial yeast — the latter is quite unnecessary, I believe. This mixture ferments as yeasts in the starter components or in the air react with the flour, and bubbles of carbon dioxide are released. If the mixture is stored in a cool place, the yeasts will become dormant, although they will still be alive and so must occasionally be fed with additional milk and flour. When the starter reaches room temperature, it again bubbles and ferments. Incor-

Terry Shoffner

porated into dough, its fermentation enables the bread to rise.

EQUINE MIXERS

The Greeks improved on Egyptian thinking in the areas of philosophy and science, but did little to advance the art of the Egyptian bread makers. The Romans, too, carried on the basic Egyptian procedures, but were the first to have professional bakers who were regarded as artists, then elevated to the ruling class of public officials.

At first, however, baking was a domestic skill and Pliny the Elder (Gaius Plinius Secundus, to those who knew him) noted that there were no commercial bakers in Rome until the latter part of the second century B.C. Only when wealth began to accrue to Rome, when the women, formerly the wives of warrior peasants, took to wearing rouge and make-up and adopting other habits of the Roman-conquered East and began to see baking as beneath them, did a professional class of bakers appear. Roman ovens were shaped like beehives and bread was baked either on a spit (*panis artopticius*) or in earthen pots (*panis testuatis*).

The bakers themselves were often freed slaves, and one of these, Marcus Virgilius Euryasaces, invented the first mechanical dough mixer, which consisted of a large stone pot with wooden paddles or stirrers. A horse or donkey supplied the power to these first mass-production dough machines, setting in motion a string of events that seems to have culminated in today's automated bread factories. (In ascending the social and political order, the bakers who finally held important powers in the government are blamed for creating some of the conditions that led to the fall of the Empire.)

Politics notwithstanding, the Roman loaf, like its predecessor from the shadows of the pyramids, was sourdough. Because one loaf begets the next, due to the reproductive qualities of the starter, this ubiquitous bread has travelled with mariners and explorers, prospectors and trappers to the most remote points on earth.

YEAST REVEALED

Sourdough bread was almost as important to the North American pioneer as it was to an Egyptian priest, although by then the magical process had been somewhat demystified. Once the Dutch scientist Anton van Leeuwenhoek saw yeast cells under his microscope in the 17th century, man began to understand how bread rises. By the time the immigrant North Americans were jealously guarding their little jars of sourdough starters, scientists knew that free-floating, wild yeast cells in the air would feed on natural sugars in flour, literally changing their eating habits as they used up one type of sugar and moved on to the next. Diastatic enzymes working on the starch in the flour produce maltose to feed the yeast, if the temperature is kept warm.

This is not simply a chemical process, like that undertaken by moistened and heated baking powder. Yeast is a living substance that has an innate resistance to doing anything. German philosopher Arthur Schopenhauer once said that wakefulness is a constant struggle against the more natural state of sleep, just as walking is a constantly averted falling. Yeast seems to be the living proof of this observation. It much prefers to sleep in a dormant state at the back of the refrigerator between baking sessions than to be disturbed and forced to reproduce. The baker must beguile it into doing his bidding.

Once activated, yeast ferments glucose, fructose, maltose and sucrose (various types of sugar), producing carbon dioxide bubbles and ethanol, an alcohol which evaporates in baking, exuding the familiar bakery fragrance. Because the ethanol dissipates in baking, one's homemade bread is not about to take the place of his favourite brew. Its formation, however, does emphasize the intimate links between the baker and the brewer, both of whom profit by the activity of yeast and the properties of grain. The liquid that rises to the top of the starter was, in fact, called "hooch," and gratefully consumed by the "sourdoughs" of the the north — gold diggers who assumed a distinctive, malty odour from carrying their precious caches of sourdough starter in jars suspended around their necks.

Incidentally, these pioneers recommended that if the starter turned green it be tossed out, but if it turned orange it was still fine. Fortunately, modern refrigeration has made such crude distinctions unnecessary. If the starter does turn colour, any colour, throw it out.

SLOW STARTS

As the bread bakes, the carbon dioxide bubbles, evidence of the yeast's brief reproductive orgy, will expand with the heat. The process is best complemented by a flour that is high in gluten, preferably hard wheat flour. (Soft wheat flour and rye flour can also be used, but the bread will not rise as high.) The protein in the flour changes as it is heated by a process called denaturation, forming stiffened walls around the bubbles, so that the bread does not collapse upon cooling.

These processes are common to all breads, but sourdough differs from the rest. I think sourdough bread is about as close to perfection as man has ever come. We have put men on the moon, but improving on the basic sourdough recipe used by Tut's bakers escapes us. It is a deliberate, slow-rising creation that demands patience. My first loaf took about a week.

Unlike regular yeast breads, practically everyone's sourdough bread is different, especially if each uses a different starter. The flavour of the starter, and of the resultant bread, will depend in part upon the wild yeasts that happened to float past the day the starter was made. More uniform, but less adventurous starters can be bought in some health food stores.

Sourdough bread is so distinctive that some bakers have gone to great lengths to hold onto a particular batch of starter or a special recipe.

About 10 years ago I read the story of a Parisian

Right, *the author's sourdough bread in progress, and* **above,** *an exuberant creator of sourdough French bread displays a long, proud loaf.*

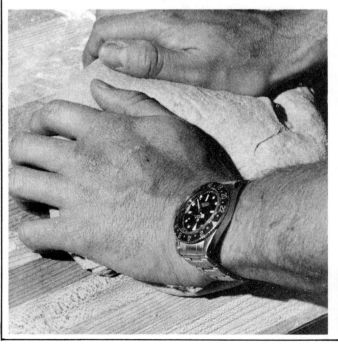

J. Peter Shinnick

baker who stubbornly continued to bake sourdough bread by methods passed down to him by his father and grandfather, and many generations before him. The *baguette,* made of white flour and shaped like an oversized cigar, this baker argued, was a modern invention lacking in texture and taste. (The French and the ancient Egyptians have often been considered the world's best bread makers.)

In Europe there are still professional bakers who use nothing more than flour, water, salt and sourdough starter in their bread. The good ones are fanatic when it comes to buying their wheat, and they still work with whole grain flour ground by stone. More than one film star has been known to include a clause in his or her contract requiring daily air shipments of sourdough whole wheat bread from Paris to remote tropical locations.

Intrigued by the simplicity of the ingredients and teased by the possible flavour of such a bread, while floored by the possibility of ever air shipping imported bread for my toast some morning, I began to experiment. Having made my first loaf of bread when I was five or six years old, I am accustomed to turning out the most unspeakable failures when I experiment. During my years in Gabon, Equatorial Africa, I often made bread in an overturned oil drum insulated with nothing more than dirt. (Ovens are probably the only aspect of bread making that has improved through the centuries. Nothing seems to work as well as a modern range — be it electric, oil, natural gas, or wood-fired — when it comes to baking bread.) There were failures by the score, but when the successes began to emerge from

the oven a couple of years ago, they made up for all the effort.

My recipe here calls for nothing but the basic four ingredients used by Tutankhamun's bakers. One may add just about anything to make a bread more suited to individual tastes, but remember that sourdough has a distinctly un-sweet taste, and it is this flavour that you must work with when you add ingredients. The aroma of sourdough bread rising is far removed from the smell of working wine. Butter, oil, or lard will tend to neutralize that flavour a bit, as will sugar or other sweeteners. Molasses will mask the sourness somewhat, and sunflower seeds and nuts seem to harmonize nicely. Make the basic recipe, though, before doing any experimentation, because every homemade starter is different, and some are so mild that the loaves are almost indistinguishable from regular, yeast-risen breads.

Hard water can retard the action of sourdough starter, keeping the bread from rising properly. On the other hand, if the water is too soft, the dough will be unmanageably sticky. The best water has a neutral pH or is slightly acidic. Chlorine or fluorine additives to an urban water system, contrary to what one's keenly honed sense of suspicion may indicate, seem to have no measurable effect on the action of sourdough starter. One's first batch of bread will be experimental. If it is not satisfactory, try adding a teaspoon of vinegar to the recipe.

Because yeast cells add protein and vitamins to a finished loaf, and because sourdough is so distinctive, so wild and unpredictable, no chemically leavened bread will ever have the quality of a sourdough loaf made from good flour in a warm kitchen by someone who cares about the finished product. Wine may gladden the heart, but it is good bread that makes us strong.

THE STARTER

1 cup unflavoured yogurt
½ cup powdered skim milk
1 cup hard whole wheat flour
  (or hard white flour, if preferred)
1 cup lukewarm water

Test the water. You should not feel it at all, or just feel a slight warmth, when it is dripped on the inside of the wrist. Mix all the ingredients in a bowl (glass, plastic or enamel), cover with a tea towel and allow the mixture to sit in a warm, draft-free spot. The back of the stove or near a heat outlet is a good place. Ideally, the temperature of the ingredients will remain lukewarm or slightly warmer. (Temperatures over 95 degrees F are lethal.) If all goes well, bubbles will form on the surface in three or four days, indicating that the starter is "working." (If, after seven days, nothing at all has happened, and if the starter begins to smell foul or look mouldy, throw it out and try again.) At this bubbling stage it is ready to be used or stored. Most recipes call for one cup of starter, so in any case you will probably be storing a portion of it.

Before storing the new starter, refresh it from its past days of activity by adding a tablespoon of powdered milk, a tablespoon of warm water and a half cup of flour. Place it in a glass, plastic or enamel container — never metal. The container should be loosely capped. Do not cover it tightly as the starter can expand in storage and may burst the container.

It is particularly important if you are not baking regularly (and therefore the starter is not taking nourishment from a portion of the sponge), to restore the starter with flour and a little milk powder — about a tablespoon of each — every week or so. If it begins to look dry after a few months, add enough lukewarm water so that it again acquires the consistency of batter.

Whenever a sponge is mixed in preparation for baking, replenish the remaining starter with some of the sponge just before baking commences. If one cup of starter was removed, it should be replaced with a cup of the sponge the following morning. If you have a particularly good starter, one whose flavour is especially pleasant, take good care of it. When I last made bread — I make sourdough once a month — I forgot to return part of the sponge to my three-year-old starter, and the culture expired. I am now starting again from scratch. Starter can provide years, even generations of use, if properly attended.

If, by chance, the starter does go mouldy or begin to smell, throw it out and start again. It is normal for liquid to rise to the top (the hooch). This needs only to be stirred into the starter before the sponge is made.

THE J. PETER SHINNICK EXTRAPOLATED RECIPE FOR ANCIENT SOURDOUGH BREAD

1 cup starter
16 to 20 cups whole wheat flour
6 cups lukewarm water
1 Tbsp. salt

Mix water, starter and 6 cups of flour. Let the sponge rise overnight (8 to 12 hours) in a warm, draft-free place, the bowl covered with a tea towel (the sponge may rise slightly, so use a fairly large bowl).

The longer the sponge sits, the stronger the resultant bread will taste. The next morning, replace one cup of the sponge in the starter supply in the refrigerator. Into the remaining sponge, fold in salt and enough flour to make the dough damp without being wet. Folding is important for proper gluten development of whole wheat flour. My results with this flour had never been satisfactory until I read the virtues of gentle handling and careful folding in the *Tassajara Bread Book*. Do not stir, but try to keep the dough in a single piece from this point onward.

Continue folding in flour until the dough can be turned out onto a board without sticking to the bowl or spoon. Dusting occasionally with flour, knead the dough until it is firm and elastic, about 10 minutes. Place the dough in a greased bowl, turn to grease all over, cover with a tea towel and set in a warm place to rise for five or six hours, by which time it should have doubled in size. Knead again, cut into four pieces and shape these in greased pans. Again set in a warm spot, cover with a tea towel, and let rise until doubled in size (about two hours). Bake for 45 minutes at 375 degrees F. The loaves will be golden brown on top, and should sound hollow if tapped on the bottom. Remove from the pans and allow to cool on a rack.

At Home with The Rolling Stones

An introduction to home mills and milling

By Marlene Anne Bumgarner

Ownership of a portable grain mill is one of life's small, rare pleasures and, unbeknownst to most of today's home millers, it is a satisfaction that harks back to 12th-century England when one ground his own grain only surreptitiously and in bold defiance of the law.

Beginning in about 1150, the first so-called laws of "Milling Soke" were passed, granting a prior exclusive rights to grind the grain of a particular district or "soken." Thus empowered, the favoured landlord then bought or destroyed the small hand mills that would have afforded the peasantry a clear measure of independence. Until the 14th century, such laws continued to be enacted, forcing the small farmers to carry or cart their grains to central mills, whose services, naturally enough, were performed only for a price.

The miller himself, in addition to being in league with the local landlord, often added to his own unpopularity by dishonest manipulation of weights, measures and payments. The result was a general mistrust of millers throughout the Middle Ages.

First is the miller with his dusty head,
He sells you the flour to make into bread
Mixes whitening, bone dust, and other bad things
And I'm sure of all rogues he must be the king.
　　　　　　　　　　　　　　—J. Catnach,
　　　　　　　　　　　　　　New Chapter of Cheats

When the laws were finally repealed, hand mills again came into frequent use, and new designs were created and sold for the grinding of "corn," as wheat was called in England. A late 18th-century writer recorded in *London Magazine* that, "There seems a great inclination in people to buying their own corn, and grinding it with these new invented hand mills, lest they should be poisoned or cheated."

With hand mills regaining popularity today, kitchen hand millers are taking their places at the end of a long historical chain of those who have ground grain to make flour, a process that traces its roots to the dawn of civilization when man rolled one stone back and forth against another to grind his grain. Mechanization brought first the slave or animal-driven mill, then the Roman water mill of the 4th century, and, about 1,000 years later, the windmill. Throughout, with the canniness of those 12th-century landowners, the powerful continued to try to grind a profit from their fellow man's desire for bread. A Dutch count of the 14th century extracted a yearly tax from windmill owners in his area for the use of the wind that blew across his land.

Tide-driven mills followed, but nothing changed the course of milling as drastically as the invention, in the 19th century, of the steel roller mill which crushed grain instead of grinding it. Within two decades, most of the North American water and windmills were left to biodegrade quietly into the landscape, and the era of big business grain milling had really begun.

Still, the use of hand mills persisted in a small way. William Coles French wrote in *Life in Rural England* in 1929: "Within living memory (if not now), the 'quern' or hand grinding stones were in frequent use in the Hebrides. The crofter's little store of grain from the poor stoney field of his croft could by this ancient method be converted into a flour more consistent with the teaching of up-to-date science than the ordinary white flour, which is over-refined."

My husband and I, like those Scottish crofters,

Ernie Sparks

also grind our own flour. Our electric Mil-Rite may be a far cry from a stone quern, but it affords at least as many advantages as that rugged piece of equipment did for its poor owner. Not only does our mill ensure us a supply of absolutely fresh, whole grain flour, but it has also expanded the variety of grains in our diet. Rice flour, for instance, if available commercially at all, is often three months old by the time it is purchased. I can grind a fine flour or a coarse one, crack grains for breakfast foods or bulgur and can even mill livestock feeds in small quantities. Because whole grains can be bought in bulk for half the cost of the corresponding flour, all of these staples became much more economical once we assumed the role of home millers.

The spot in the kitchen occupied by the Mil-Rite did not always support an electric mill. When John and I first decided to grind our own flour in 1972, we had no electricity, so we needed either a hand or bicycle-powered mill. Because space was limited, we chose to buy a hand-powered model.

The second choice we had to make was between steel grinding burrs and stones. A stone mill is a miniature grist mill, the same type that our ancestors utilized. Although now modernized with a steel housing, the stones work on the same principle as the old water and windmills of the past. One stone is usually stationary, while the other revolves against it, crushing the grain which is fed into the space between the stones. Grooves in the stones allow the flour to spill out the sides. If the space between the stones is even in all areas, the flour will be of uniform grind. Millers of the past would constantly rub the flour between thumb and forefinger as it passed out of the stones, to ensure that the texture remained homogeneous. This repetitive action gradually gave them the characteristic large, flat "miller's thumb." Usually, the space between the stones can be altered to vary the coarseness of the flour.

Steel burr mills are at once more rugged, less precise, and more versatile than stone mills. Two steel plates rub against each other to crush or pulverize the grain or legume. Such mills are sometimes sturdy enough to grind dried bones or shells for the barnyard.

Stones give the finest-textured flour in one pass through the mill, and are generally preferred by those who primarily want to grind flour. Grain must often be put through a steel burr mill several times before it equals the fineness of flour that has passed once through a stone mill. Set the steel blades some distance apart at first, crack the grain, then adjust the blades more closely together as the grits are processed again for flour. Metal burrs, however, should do a very good job with legumes — peas, beans or nuts.

Stones gum up if legumes are put through the mill — I can attest to that. These vegetable seeds have a higher oil content than true grains such as wheat or rye, so the stones quickly glaze and heat up when grinding them. If a stone mill does become clogged with legumes or wet grain, the stones can often be cleaned if the miller puts through a hard grain such as rice or popping corn.

The traditional bias against steel mills results from the fact that they are usually run faster than

stone mills — stones will simply break if they are run too fast — and the faster the mill runs, the hotter the grain and flour become. This isn't a problem if the flour is used right away, but if it goes into storage after milling, the high temperatures will result in reduced vitamin content and hasten rancidity. With a hand mill, however, this is hardly a factor, because the mill runs only as quickly as the miller can turn the crank, a snail's pace by modern milling standards.

CHOICE AT HAND

The hand mill business can be a bit flighty; some models appear and disappear within a few months. There are, we found, quite a few reputable models to choose from (see chart) but in our search we could find only one that could be adapted to either steel burrs or millstones. This seemed to be the best of all possible worlds. With the stones in place, we could grind a fine flour in one operation; with the steel burrs, we could handle split peas, corn meal, soy flour and peanut butter. This mill was a Corona steel burr mill, which sold at that time for slightly over $20. For an additional $26 we purchased a stone conversion kit which, with a little hole drilling to make the stones line up properly, worked well. All three arrangements — stone, steel or combination — are still available from the Retsel Corporation, although the prices are now somewhat higher. Another convertible stone/steel mill is now available — the Danish Diamant from In-Tec equipment. This mill has another advantage in that it is also convertible from hand to a one-half or one horsepower electric motor.

The Corona mills, incidentally, are imported from Colombia, and the stone burrs manufactured and fitted by the Retsel corporation. Elmo Stoll, who operates Pioneer Place in Ontario, says that his brother found the Coronas omnipresent during his nine-year stay in the Honduras. "The natives use these mills every morning to grind corn for tortilla making," says Elmo. "However, they do not grind the dry grain. Instead, they soak the corn in a lye-water solution overnight, then wash it vigorously the next morning, removing most of the skins from the grains of corn, which have swollen to several times their original size. Then the wet corn is put through the mill several times."

Other hand-operated mills from several manufacturers, using either stones or steel, but not both, are available in the price range of about $25 to more than $90.00. If I had to choose again, I would still prefer the Corona convertible. The conversion worked admirably, and we ran into none of the problems that some of our friends encountered with other mills — one that we heard of had the habit of breaking off where the clamp met the mill.

A clamp is attached to most hand mills, although others, like the Bell No. 2, have a base suitable for bolting to the counter. This arrangement is really better. My first mill was clamped to a wobbly kitchen table for several months, and we can still see the marks on the linoleum made by the table feet dancing about as we ground our grain each week. We found that it is worthwhile to take a little time and effort to attach the mill permanently to the counter, or to drill a hole in the counter so that the mill can be

anchored securely when in use. This helps prevent scars made by the mill's movement on a good table top, and saves time that will otherwise be spent retightening the clamp every few minutes during grinding.

JOGGING SUBSTITUTE

We lived with that Corona for several years, all the way through recipe testing for *The Book of Whole Grains*. John and I ground many hundreds of cups of flour and we never needed to go out jogging for exercise. Grinding enough flour for a batch of bread is *hard work*. Each of us had our own technique, but mine was usually two-handed. It is important to choose an installation spot where the miller's arms can swing freely while grinding.

Anyone interested in baking with a variety of whole grains should consider purchasing a hand mill, but it can be tedious to prepare all one's flour for baking that way — it takes 30 to 40 minutes of hard grinding to produce eight cups of whole wheat flour, enough for about two loaves of bread. Some of my friends have found it best to purchase whole wheat flour in 10 or 20 pound bags, whole wheat pastry flour in five pound bags, and two to three pounds each of several whole grains such as corn, barley, brown rice and rye.

Then, when they need them, my friends grind variety flours by hand a cup at a time. This gives them relatively fresh wheat flours without the work of grinding for hours and hours, and also gives them variety flours that would be old or expensive, if available at all, commercially. One cup of rice or barley flour takes only about five minutes to grind.

A few mills can be converted to bicycle power (see chart). While the resulting installation may not be particularly aesthetically pleasing, and will take up quite a bit of room, such a mill makes the best use of human power for grinding.

We use a great deal of whole grain flour, and had come to appreciate the flavour of freshly ground grains so much that we decided to invest in an electric grain mill. We purchased our Mil-Rite two years ago, and soon wished we had put in electricity years earlier.

There are basically three types of power grain mills: box-type mills, freestanding mills, and mixer or juicer attachments. The main problem with the box-type is that they are usually difficult to clean and tend to trap the steam released by the heated grain, encouraging the growth of mould and attracting insects to the flour. Two box mills which attack the cleaning problem are the Uni-Mill and the Excalibur, which have easily removable stones and good accessibility to the interior of the machines.

Mills which attach to food processing machines include the Bosch grain mill, the Kitchen Aid, and the Champion Juicer mill. These have some disadvantages, too. They are expensive to purchase unless the buyer already owns the food processor, and because they are an add-on piece of equipment the mechanics are sometimes difficult. They do not, however, have the steam problem of the box mills.

In the freestanding group are mills such as Retsel's electric line (Mil-Maid, Mil-Rite, and Mil-Master), Vitamix, All-Grain, and the Lee mills. There are others, too, available in different areas.

Most electric mills share one problem — speed. Since in all but one case (Retsel) the stones or steel burrs are mounted directly on the motor, most grinding wheels turn extremely fast, about 1700 rpm. Depending upon the mill, the flour arrives in the collection box at a temperature between 110 and 160 degrees F. The hottest flour we experienced came

Comparing The Small-Scale Grain Mills

Please note: Prices given here are approximate, as they vary between areas of the country, from year to year, and will be higher if transportation costs are involved for Canadian customers. As of January, 1980, however, all motorized flour mills may be imported duty-free. The duty status of hand-operated flour mills is unclear. Write for complete information.

NAME OF COMPANY	NAME OF MILL	TYPE OF MILL	PRICE
All-Grain Stone Ground Mills Horizon Marketing Division P.O. Box 15783 Salt Lake City, Utah 84115 (801) 487-4625	All-Grain H-10 A-22 A-44	Hand mill Freestanding power mill Freestanding power mill	$60 $300 $400
C.S. Bell Company Box 291 Tiffin, Ohio 44883 (419) 448-0791	Model No. 2 Model No. 60	Hand mill Freestanding power mill	$60 $90
Bosch Kitchen Products 235 W. 200 South Salt Lake City, Utah 84101 (801) 322-1668	Bosch mixer & grain mill Magic Mill II	Mixer attachment power mill Freestanding power mill	Mixer $240 Mill $150 $280
Garden Way Catalog Charlotte, Vermont 05445 (802) 425-2121	Garden Way Grain Mill Kit	Box power mill	$170
The Grover Company 2111 S. Industrial Park Avenue Tempe, Arizona 85282 (800) 528-1406	Marathon Uni-Mill	Box power mill	Mixer $290 Mill $295; can be purchased separately
In-Tec Equipment Company Box 123, D.V. Station Dayton, Ohio 45406 (513) 276-4077	Atlas No. 1 Diamant Gaubert	Hand mill Freestanding hand or power mills	$210 $275 $115
Kitchen Aid c/o Hobart Corporation Troy, Ohio 45374 (513) 335-7171	Kitchen Aid mixer	Mixer attachment power mill	Mixer $180 Mill $50
Lee Engineering Company 2023 W. Wisconsin Avenue, Box 652 Milwaukee, Wisconsin 53201 (414) 933-2100	Lee Model 500 600 S-500 S-600	Freestanding power mill Freestanding power mill Freestanding power mill Freestanding power mill	$110 $140 $160 $185
Mill & Mix Co. Inc. P.O. Box 697 Brigham City, Utah 84302 (801) 723-6250	Mill & Mix All-American	Box power mill Box power mill	Mixer $290 Mill $170; can be bought separately

MOTOR HP	SPEED (LBS./HR.)	REMARKS
1/3 3/4	10 to 12 14 to 16	Stone burrs Bicycle conversion accessory (about $75) available for A-22 and A-44. Both have stone burrs.
		Steel burrs. A very sturdy cast-iron assembly with a long handle for easy grinding. Flour requires 3 passes through the mill.
1 or 2	100 to 300	Hand crank option, suitable for home or farm use. Steel burrs. Purchase motor separately. C.S. Bell also offers a selection of heavy-duty farm and commercial-capacity mills.
1/2	30	Slow, even coarse or fine grind. Must detach mixer repeatedly to check flour level.
5/8 to 1-3/4		No cracked grain. Loud, but self-cleaning and lightweight.
1/2		Stone mill manufactured by Grover exclusively for Garden Way. Garden Way sells several mill models from other manufacturers.
1/2	60	Sold with Blakeslee mixer from England, or separately. Steel cutting edges on stones. Convertible to hand or bicycle power. In Canada, a metal-burred grain mill attachment (approx $100) is available for the Blakeslee mixer. The Grover Co. also sells whole grains by mail order to U.S. customers.
	15 to 20	In-Tec imports European flywheel mills. Atlas has interchangeable steel flour and feed burrs.
1/2-1	40 to 110 with power	Interchangeable stone or steel burrs. The most versatile mill.
1/3-3/4	30 to 90 with power	Steel burrs. Flour may need sifting.
		Metal burrs. Grinds wheat flour coarsely but softer grains more finely.
1/6 1/6 1/4 1/4	3 to 5 3 to 5 6 to 10 6 to 10	Bag to catch flour. Metal impeller with stone burrs on all models, which are designed to grind flour only. Cannot grind wet grain, beans or peas.
3/4	60	Stone burrs. Many optional accessories, such as juicer, food chopper.
1/3	20	

NAME OF COMPANY	NAME OF MILL	TYPE OF MILL	PRICE
Plastaket Manufacturing Co. Inc. 6220 E. Hwy 12 Lodi, California 95240 (209) 369-2154	Champion Juicer mill	Mixer attachment power mill	Juicer $210 Mill $90
Retsel Corporation Box 47 McCammon, Idaho 83250 (208) 254-3325	The following mills are imported from Landers & Cia., Medellin, Colombia: Corona No. 1CT Corona No. 2CT Corona No. 3CT Corona No. 1CT-R The following mills are manufactured by Retsel: Little Ark Mil-Maid Mil-Rite Mil-Master	 Hand mill Hand mill Hand mill Hand mill Hand mill Freestanding power mill Freestanding power mill Freestanding power mill	 $30 $30 $55 $37 $48 $180 $228 $278
Sunset Marketing 8549 Sunset Avenue Fair Oaks, California 95628 (916) 961-2896	Hi-Life No. GF1 GF2 GF3 GF4	Box power mill Box power mill Hand mill Box power mill kit	$200 $240 $70 $70
Victor Manufacturing and Sales 8141 - 7th Avenue S.W., Dept. F Seattle, Washington 98106 (206) 763-0428	Victor	Freestanding power mill	$73
Vitamix Corporation 8615 Usher Road Cleveland, Ohio 44138 (216) 235-4840	Vitamix	Freestanding power juicer/mill	$300

from the Vitamix juicer, which uses metal cutting blades like a blender. The coolest came from the Retsel mills, the result of a gear-down arrangement that has the grinding shaft revolving much more slowly than the motor. This was one reason we chose the Mil-Rite.

Another problem common to electric mills is the difficulty in grinding wet grains or legumes. Most will gum up if the miller tries to do very fine corn meal or split peas. Some manufacturers skirt this issue, suggesting that the miller combine, for instance, soy beans and rice in the grinder together rather than trying soybeans alone. This works for some things, but not all. Three exceptions to the wet grain problem are the Uni-Mill, which has steel blades mounted on the stones to cut the grain before grinding it, the All-Grain, and the Kitchen Aid grinder attachment, which uses metal burrs rather than stones.

FLOUR POWER

Some of the electric mills can be used without power; several makers sell hand cranks, and a few sell bicycle conversion kits. All but the Retsel and Bell, however, are arranged so that the miller must first turn on the motor in order to turn the stones. In Retsel mills, a gear can be removed so that turning the crank moves the stones, and the mill can be operated at full normal speed with the extra-long, sturdy handle offered. The Bell power grist mill can be disconnected from its motor, and a handle attached directly to the grinding wheel shaft.

One approach to the sustained-power-outage problem is to own a hand mill as well as an electric mill. This system has a double advantage (although it is expensive and space-consuming). As almost all electric mills use stones, a small steel-burred hand mill can be used, even when power is plentiful, to grind grains for which the stones are not suited.

One distributor is downplaying the need for hand conversion, passing out recipes for sprouted wheat foods instead. This is Magic Mill Company, the distributor of the Magic Mill box-type grinder (now discontinued), the Bosch mixer and grinder attachment, and now the new Magic Mill II.

Rather than a stone or a pair of metal burrs, the Magic Mill II uses a vacuum-cleaner type motor to power a set of metal "fingers" which move rapidly, resulting in cut, rather than ground, flour. The Magic Mill produces excellent fine or coarse flour, but cannot be used to make bulgur, soy grits, or polenta — coarsely cut wheat, soy beans and corn respectively; its coarsest final product, produced by pulsing the motor, is no coarser than Malt-o-Meal or Ovaltine. However, for those who desire only flour, the Magic Mill has the advantage of grinding at a low temperature, being lightweight, processing either dry or wet grain, and being extremely easy to clean.

After each use of any mill, it should be thoroughly cleaned. Flour particles left there can become rancid and spoil the flavour of any later effort. I use a vegetable brush to clean all surfaces after dismantling the mill. Although it is seldom necessary to use

MOTOR HP	SPEED (LBS./HR.)	REMARKS
1/3	25 to 30	Steel burrs. Heats flour, small hopper.
		Steel burrs, small hopper
		Steel burrs, high hopper
		Interchangeable stone or steel burrs. Retsel stone assembly.
		Steel burrs, but modified to grind fine flour in one operation.
		Stone mill. Power conversion kit available.
1/6	5 to 7	
1/4	10 to 15	All 3 power mills have stone burrs and geared transmission. Gear removed for manual operation. Handle accessory available.
1/2	15 to 20	
1/2	40 for fine flour,	GF1 and GF2 both have stone burrs and optional bicycle adaptor. GF2's only advantage is its appearance. GF3 has stone burrs. Bicycle or motor conversion kit with ball-bearing shaft available. Box power mill kit does not include motor or cabinet, but produces GF1 when complete.
1/2	60 for coarse flour, all power mills	
	10	Stone burrs. Cast aluminum body. Bag for flour.
	2 cups in 2 minutes	Milling feature is built into juicer. Grinds and prepares only one loaf at a time.

water, any parts of the mill that are washed should be dried thoroughly so that the metal will not rust. Avoid washing the grinding stones if possible. Metal burrs may be washed, but again must be thoroughly dried before the mill is re-assembled.

The choice of an appropriate mill is, in a sense, as important as the selection of a new car. After all, most mills should last a lifetime, so the choice need be made only once. Comparisons can be difficult, however, because many mills are sold only by mail, and retailers who do sell mills often handle only one make. Any purchaser lucky enough to find a store that sells several brands can have the salesperson demonstrate all of them, using a variety of grains and legumes. What happens if there's a small stone in with those beans? I worried about that with mills like the Vitamix and the Magic Mill II, but I didn't toss one in to find out while it was being demonstrated. Perhaps another shopper would have.

One of the best ways to learn about different mills is to talk to people who have them at home. In this way, the prospective mill owner can also discover the characteristics of freshly-ground grains, and the ways in which various home millers adapt themselves to using this food. Usually homemakers who have explored whole grain products are those who care about nutrition, but having made the switch from white flour to fresh whole wheat flour, they discover several things that are a little dismaying. Whole wheat flour is coarser and heavier than white; baked products made from trusted recipes often turn out hard, flat and dry until the baker has done some experimentation with the ingredients. Also, whole grain flour (if it is really "whole") and cracked grains tend to become infested with bugs even if they are kept in the same canister in the cupboard where the all-purpose flour stayed white and unblemished for years. And they become rancid. Whole wheat flour which is several months old tastes bitter and sharp to the tongue.

TEXTURAL CONCERNS

The texture of whole wheat flour is coarser than white flour because the latter contains a higher percentage of soft, starchy material than whole wheat, and contains none of the fibrous bran or the oily germ. It is lighter, but also less nutritious. Most of the vitamins and minerals which are found in a germ of wheat have been removed during milling, and only a select few are replaced — enriched flour in Canada must contain thiamine, riboflavin, niacin and iron.

Since whole wheat flour has more protein than white flour made from a comparable grain, it has more gluten, which is the substance that forms the cellular structure of bread and contains the expanding gas bubbles produced by the growing yeast. Gluten is great for bread, but it creates an undesirable texture in cakes, muffins and pastry.

I solve this problem by keeping some soft pastry wheat along with the hard bread wheat in my storage cupboard. The pastry wheat (usually a spring variety) has less protein and slightly more starch, yet still has the high vitamin and mineral content of a whole grain product, as well as the fibre and the nutty taste. By grinding soft wheat just before baking, and by being careful not to beat the mixture too much, which develops the gluten, I can create tender, flaky pie crusts, muffins or cakes with whole wheat flour.

Rye flour produces a slightly smaller loaf than hard wheat, but still contains an adequate amount of gluten for most needs. One problem that can be found in all grains but is most commonly associated with rye is ergot, a fungus disease caused by *Claviceps purpurea*. Ergot in flour causes St. Anthony's Fire, a scourge that periodically swept through villages in the Middle Ages, causing symptoms of burning (hence the name), hallucinations — LSD is contained in ergot — and, in the worst cases, circula-tory failures, gangrene and death. Dark purple or black specks in the grain are signs of ergot, usually caused by damp weather before harvesting. Hand-pick any affected rye to remove all of the ergot bodies.

Pests do not infest white flour because it is "dead" — bugs are not without their own taste standards. Whole wheat flour is a living product, and, having the vitamin E-rich germ blended through it, becomes rancid quickly, exuding a mild smell attractive to insect pests. The high temperatures of commercial milling, and some home mills, hasten this rancidity and vitamin loss through oxidation, so the longer flour sits after milling, the less useful it will be.

Sources

AGRI RESOURCES
R.R. 3
Napanee, Ontario K7R 3K8
(613) 354-4694
Sells a German hand-powered stone mill, the OH. Unusual design with two steel supports, replaces the BH they previously sold.

ANDERSON'S ORGANIC GRAINS
Box 186
Lowe Farm, Manitoba R0G 1E0
(204) 746-8887
As well as organically-grown whole grains and flours, they sell the All-Grain mills. Enquire about prices.

BERRY HILL LTD.
75 Burwell Road
St. Thomas, Ontario N5P 3R5
(519) 631-0480
Sells all models of C.S. Bell mills, and an electric dough maker, postpaid anywhere in Canada. Enquire about prices, as they depend upon whether or not the customer has a federal sales tax exemption.

G.S. BLAKESLEE & CO. OF CANADA LTD.
66 Crockford Blvd.
Scarborough, Ontario M1R 3C3
(416) 751-2625
Distributors of the Blakeslee mixer (imported from England) and a steel-burred grain mill attachment. Write for address of nearest distributor.

COLE CREEK FARMSTEADING PRODUCTS
R.R. 1
Verona, Ontario K0H 2W0
Only Canadian source for the Diamant. This convertible hand-to-power mill was recommended by *Organic Gardening* magazine as the best mill they tested.

ENERGY ALTERNATIVES
2 Croft Street, Box 671
Amherst, Nova Scotia B4H 4B8
(902) 667-2790
Suppliers of Corona hand mills, and the Mil-Maid and Mil-Master from Retsel.

GOURMET-BAZAAR
805-10th Avenue
Lachine, Quebec H8S 3G3
Sell the Vita-Mix Juicer/Mill.

HARMONY'S CONSUMER CORP. LTD.
168 Gladstone St.
Ottawa, Ontario K2P 0Y3
(613) 238-6191
Retail (not mail order) and wholesale distributors of the Champion Juicer and the grain mill attachment. Write or call for the nearest retailer.

HEALTH EQUIPMENT SUPPLIES
9342-118 Ave.
Edmonton, Alberta T5G 0N4
(403) 477-1328
Sell the Mill & Mix together, or the mill alone.

McFAYDEN SEED CO. LTD.
P.O. Box 1600, 30-9th St.
Brandon, Manitoba R7A 6A6
Sell the Corona King convertible mill (stone or steel burrs) with a one-quart aluminum hopper.

NEW-WAY HOME PRODUCTS
Box 3000
Morden, Manitoba
Steel-burr Corona mill, and a hand-crank bread maker.

PIONEER PLACE
Route 4
Aylmer, Ontario N5H 2R3
The best Canadian source of Corona mills and accessories. They also sold the SFINX 150 in 1979, a Czechoslovakian steel-burred hand mill which is "for all practical purposes identical" to the Corona #1CT. They expect to list only one of these in their next catalogue. Pioneer Place also sells a hand-crank bread maker and the C.S. Bell corn sheller. Write for catalogue, $2.00 postpaid.

KEEP IT COOL

I mill my own flour at a low temperature just before using it, and store any excess in a moisture-tight container in the refrigerator or freezer for a constant supply of sweet, nutritious flour, and no insect problems.

Any whole, unbroken grain product can be kept longer than the cracked or ground grain, because the oil-rich germ is intact. It is the spreading of this oil throughout the flour that leads to rapid deterioration in quality. Grains are naturally designed to stay dormant if stored whole in a cool, well-ventilated place; they are, after all, seeds that are waiting to be sown in spring. If the grain is kept dry (to prevent mould or sprouting) and cool (to prevent hatching of any insect eggs which might have accompanied the grain from the field) we find that whole wheat grains can be kept over a year without any problem. We put wheat into large plastic garbage bags first and fasten them securely, and then put these bags into galvanized garbage cans, which are placed in a cool part of our garage or barn. A basement or pantry would be most suitable where winters are severe.

Grains which we use less, such as barley, brown rice, rye, millet and buckwheat, we keep in five-gallon plastic buckets, with lids, in the same area. As long as the lids are secured firmly to keep out rodents, our grain keeps well.

The choice of a mill may take several months or even a year. All of the mill manufacturers have literature available, which the consumer can peruse at home. A local hardware store will often order the particular mill that a customer desires. When looking at a mill's features, consider the following: Does the mill take up so much room that it has to be put away after each use, or can it be kept bolted to the counter? Is it attractive — and is that important? Is it merely a showpiece that doesn't do the job? What grains and how much of them do you hope to be able to grind? Will the company that sells the mill be able to supply parts if needed? Metal burrs may have to be replaced every few years, while stones, if properly treated, should last for decades. If the company is a fly-by-night outfit, the purchaser may find it difficult to buy replacement burrs or stones when needed. Will the mill ultimately save money? If you buy an expensive mill, grow none of your own grain, and end up grinding little, it may be a costly venture.

With the proper mill — the one best suited to the home miller's requirements — cooking with fresh flour and whole grains should be a pleasant experience, and perhaps provide some insight into the private joys of Isaac Bickerstaff's famous recluse:

There was a jolly miller once
Lived on the River Dee;
He worked and sang from morn till night
No lark more blithe than he.
And this the burden of his song
Forever used to be —
I care for nobody, no not I
If nobody cares for me.

Rally 'Round the Cookstove

At once primitive and futuristic, the woodburning range presents a challenge to the microwave generation

---

By Merilyn Mohr

Does your beechwood sizzle but your sausage snoozle? The first soul-cheering crackle of wood in the firebox of a newly installed cookstove will soon ring hollow when the oven temperature balks at an insipid warm and the water refuses to boil.

Judging by the number of such stoves that end up acting as little more than impressively funky fern stands, fledgling wood stove cooks today are suffering from an informational generation gap. The skill of starting and keeping a fire in an old kitchen queen was, in the past, handed down from mother to daughter and rarely written down. It passed into virtual extinction with the changeover to gas and electricity. Barring the friendly advice of an octogenarian, one is faced with the time-consuming frustration of the "practice makes perfect" school of woodburning knowledge. All too many fail to make the best use of their stoves, while others give up on the woodburning kitchen range as being primitive, unmanageable and agonizingly slow.

To the microwave generation, a stove fuelled by wood may seem like nothing more than another curious antique, but it is worth remembering that the old range now being sold at a farm auction was once the very hub of country life. Coming in out of the cold, family and strangers alike would quickly sidle up to the stove to warm hands and chilled posteriors and accept the inevitable cup of tea, coffee, hot chocolate or perhaps a steaming bowl of broth from the stock pot simmering at the back.

A platter of biscuits or a slice of leftover apple pie could likely be found in the warming oven — along with the salt box (kept there where it wouldn't cake up) and a plate of eggshells (drying to be crushed and fed to the laying hens). Hot wash water came out of the built-in reservoir and the Saturday night bath took place directly in front of the stove, with the oven door open to keep bathers comfortable. Wet mittens, socks and odd bits of laundry found their way to the stove for drying, and the occasional sick puppy or orphaned lamb would find itself being nursed back to health in a box placed near or behind the big stove.

With no plugs, buttons or timers, the kitchen wood range served as a furnace, clothes dryer, humidifier, toaster, broiler, food dehydrator, yogurt maker and water heater. Although the fact wasn't appreciated in its heyday, this stove was perfectly insulated from the rate hikes in electricity and gas that today make the kitchen stove one of the most expensive-to-run appliances in the house.

MORNING RITUALS

Fundamental to efficient wood stove cookery is good wood. While the worth of a wife was once judged by her ability to keep a fire, the worth of a husband was measured in the woodpile he provided. Both quality and quantity scored points — with far-sightedness playing a crucial role. The rule a generation ago was that wood destined for the kitchen stove should be no less than two years off the stump — cut, split, stacked under cover and bone dry.

This was more than a role-playing game between the sexes — not even the best of wood stove cooks can turn out a meal or even keep the kitchen warm with a pile of green elm. Perhaps the most common complaint about woodburning ranges is that they take so long to heat up, that the kettle literally never seems to boil. With the right wood, however, the morning ritual of laying the fire is its own reward, particularly on those I-can-see-my-breath-in-here mornings. An experienced hand with a stock of the right wood can get a cold stove crackling with warmth and have the water boiling in 10 minutes — the tea should be ready in the time it takes to set the table.

The first step in lighting the fire is to be sure the

Photograph circa 1909, courtesy of the Library of Congress Collection

grates are clear and that a good flow of air will be able to pass through the kindling. Most mornings, a quick shake or shovelling will knock the ashes into the ash bin; any unburned wood or clinkers (if you have been burning coal) should also be removed at this time.

This is also the time to be well aware of the anatomy of your particular stove. Although great variations exist — we are talking about models manufactured over a span of 100 years — most have three moving parts that must be manipulated when starting a fire. The first is a draft control at the base of, or under, the firebox; it should be fully opened to start a fast fire.

Most stoves have a flue damper — a butterfly-type valve in the stove pipe at the back of the unit — and this, too, must be opened when starting a fire to allow the maximum draft.

The third setting may be marked "Bake-Kindle" or it may be a simple, too-easily ignored lever or sliding mechanism that controls the flow of smoke and heat in the stove. This is the oven damper control and when open it allows the draft to go immediately up the chimney and thus promotes a rapid burn in the firebox. Closed (or on the "Bake" setting), it forces the hot air to flow around the jacket that surrounds the oven before exiting.

With everything open, the fire is ready to be lit. Some people burn a few wads of newspaper first on especially cold mornings to heat the pipes and start a good draft. Then a fresh layer of crumpled newspaper goes into the firebox, followed by dry kindling that will spark into flame quickly. This wood should be finely split — no bigger than the thickness of a broom handle was the old-timer's rule of thumb — and of a light, fast burning species.

The softwoods are preferred here because they throw a great deal of heat in rapid order — especially the coniferous woods containing resins that spit, spark and, in general, get things moving quickly. Pine, spruce, fir and balsam are very good, while other kindling woods of choice are poplar, cedar, aspen, sumac or cottonwood.

Once the kindling is roaring along, bigger pieces of wood should be added — preferably split and no more than two and one-half inches in diameter. This is *bisquit wood* — well-split and also a fast burning wood that will produce the temperatures necessary to bake soda bread or boil the first pot of water in the morning. Any of the kindling woods will do, as well as white, black or yellow birch, all of which produce quick, hot flames.

Rather than wait for the entire body and top of the stove to heat up, lift one or more of the inner metal plates off and set the pot on the open ring directly over the firebox. This will cause the bottom of the pot to blacken, but this is all part of cooking with wood.

With the fire going well, the oven damper can be closed and the other dampers as well. If no baking is planned immediately, open the oven door to throw more heat into the room.

DIALLESS COOKERY

On a wood stove, the temperature of the heating surface is controlled not by manipulating the heat with the twist of a dial, but by moving pots and pans to different parts of the stovetop. Low-Medium-Hot are all there, and it doesn't take long to discover just where. A pot of stew bubbles furiously when set directly over the firebox, yet simmers gently when slid to the back or far end of the stove.

Judging oven temperature at first may seem formidable when one has been accustomed to the thermostatic certainty of electricity. Although some models boast thermometers or even thermostats on the oven door, they give only a broad idea of the heat within. Many do not work at all or are wildly inaccurate. It is wise to purchase a small moveable oven thermometer from the hardware store and thus be able to measure accurately the temperature in various parts of the oven.

Cooks of the past relied on various other tests to determine exactly when the muffins or Yorkshire pudding could go into the oven. The "feel test" involves holding your hand in the oven until it becomes uncomfortable. If you can't bear the heat, your bread will thrive. If you can hold steady for a few seconds, the oven is ready to receive cakes and roasts.

The Domestic Cookbook of 1888 provided this slightly more accurate test:

"To ascertain the right heat of the oven, put a piece of writing paper into it, and if it is a chocolate brown in five minutes it is the right heat for biscuits, muffins and small pastry. It is called a quick oven. If the paper is dark yellow it is the right heat for bread, pound cake, puddings and puff paste pies. When the paper is light yellow it is right for sponge cake."

Another time-honoured trick predicts that an oven that takes five minutes to brown a teaspoon of flour in a piece of crockery will be right for baking bread.

Each stove has its own quirks, and you will soon learn that there are definite hot spots that can be taken advantage of for some baking and that must be avoided for others. Generally, the upper third of the oven will be very hot, as will the side wall nearest the firebox. For slow baking, some cooks take the oven racks out and set the roasting pan directly on the floor of the oven or on bricks placed in the oven. To brown roasts or baked goods, put them on the uppermost rack and feed the fire with small splits of wood, keeping the draft open. Flames should lick across the top of the oven jacket and will give the desired top heat — but food must be watched carefully at this stage or singeing will occur.

For a good, steady heat during long baking jobs, dry hardwood serves best, with ash, hard or soft maple, beech, hickory, oak, cherry and applewood at the top of the list. This is a good opportunity to use unsplit pieces from branches (three to four inches in diameter) or culled small trees. If well-seasoned wood is unavailable, certain species can be counted on to burn reasonably well even if green. Ash is very good in this regard, as are yellow birch, black birch, sumac and beech. (To assure a stock of well-dried kindling for the next morning, some stove owners place a quantity of wood in the oven before retiring. The fire, of course, should be damped down for the night and the oven door left open to prevent the wood from getting too hot and igniting.)

If your oven doesn't get hot enough to bake, either

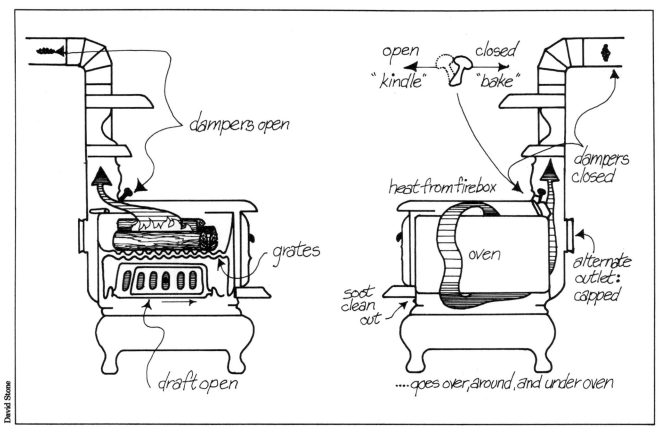

the wood is too wet, the dampers are open and allowing all the heat to escape up the flue, or the warm air is being insulated from the oven by the build up of fly ash (or a combination of the three). The top of the oven just below the cooking surface and the cleanout under the oven (often just a small door) should be scraped periodically to ensure maximum oven efficiency. Some expert bakers, however, choose to leave a light layer of ash over the top of the oven to act as a slight heat buffer which helps prevent singeing.

CAST IRON & SOAPSTONE

Proper cookware will take best advantage of that heat. Just as stainless steel is well-suited to electric cooking, cast-iron pots do most justice to a wood cookstove. Besides holding the heat evenly and browning food deliciously, they are easiest to care for and are virtually indestructible. As they blacken with age, the firebox plates can be removed with impunity. Let your pot call your kettle black!

If an auction or attic yields hand-me-downs in good condition, so much the better. The market price and quality range of new cast-iron ware is considerable: $25 will buy a four-piece cheaply-made set or a single quality frypan. The best cast-iron pots come from Canada and the United States, with the latter enjoying the price edge. Unseasoned ware is the most practical. It has a thin wax coating (to prevent rusting in transit) which washes off with soap and water.

New or used, cast iron must be seasoned before its debut and regularly thereafter, by rubbing with unsalted shortening and heating in a low (225 degree F) oven for a few hours. The pot should be wiped clean of excess oil and allowed to cool gradually. Once sea-soned, a rinse under the tap will keep it clean and rust-free, and food won't stick.

Soapstone, a talc rock with a characteristic greasy feel, is a traditional material used in the manufacture of wood stove skillets and pancake griddles. The soapstone absorbs and holds heat very well, and many old-timers claim that the very best hotcakes come from the perfect, even heat of a soapstone griddle. These utensils are still being made by the Vermont Soapstone Company, Perkinsville, Vermont 05151, which will supply current prices on request.

Caring for your cookstove entails more than the semi-annual blitz on an electric range. Aside from keeping the stove free of ashes, it must be washed and seasoned like the pots. For daily cleaning, hot water and soda will remove spillage. Towel drying is imperative since iron will rust when air-dried. If the stove surface is rough-cast, season by rubbing periodically with a piece of fat or shortening, then build a low fire, taking care to wipe away excess oil, which will smoke. If the cooking surface is polished iron or steel, rub with a heavy flannel cloth and a paraffin wax instead of seasoning it.

Although connoisseurs maintain that it has degenerated in quality over the past half-century, stove polish is still the best way to restore a stove's ebony gleam. Available at hardware stores in both liquid and paste form, the paste proves more economical and effective while less noxious. Daub it on with a flat 1" paintbrush (they used to sell daubers specifically for blacking) and polish with newspaper, which can be burned. A 1910 publication of "Mother's Remedies" suggests that before blacking the stove, allow soap to dry on your hands. After the job is done, both blacking stains and soap wash off easily.

Despite the added work — call it involvement if you wish — rewards are measured daily. Not only does the slow, even heat of the woodburning range produce superior culinary fare, deeply-browned and flavour-rich, but the heat is ubiquitous, accommodating a five-course meal as easily and economically as a single cup of tea.

Just as electric and gas ranges are godsends to meals-in-minutes devotees, the wood cookstove engenders its own style of cookery. Soups, stews and tomato sauces can simmer for hours or even days, gathering flavour with no pain to anyone's energy conscience. The oven, always warm, begs for hot breads and muffins. Stir-frying is easily accomplished on a wood stove, with an open cooking ring serving as a steady base for the bottom of a *wok*.

The warming oven has a myriad of uses and is the place for dough to rise, yogurt to culture, herbs to dry and dehydrated fruits to reconstitute themselves slowly in a pan of water.

At the acme of cookstove popularity, recipes were not the precise combination of proportions they are today. Most cooks kept their favourites at their fingertips, with variations and substitutions made possible by an understanding of each ingredient's function in the final fare. Included here are a selection of specialties from households long reliant on wood for heat as well as hearty meals.

MIRACLE MUFFINS

Muffins are the stand-by of wood stove cooks. This basic recipe is easily adapted to a main course bread, sweet finale or anytime snack.

Mix together 2 cups of whole wheat flour, 4 teaspoons of baking powder, 1 teaspoon of salt and ¼ cup of sugar. In another bowl, combine 1 egg, 1 cup of milk and ¼ cup of oil. Add the wet ingredients to the dry and stir until just combined. Spoon into greased muffin tins and bake in a very hot (450 degrees F) oven for about 15 minutes. For a dinner muffin, reduce the sugar and add bacon bits, grated cheese or herbs. For dessert, add spices and chopped apple, fresh berries or drained fruit. Nuts, soy grits, dried fruit, sunflower or sesame seeds all give crunch and added nutrution. One cup of the flour can be replaced with one cup of cornmeal, oatmeal, bran or a combination of grains. Keeping basic proportions in mind, experiment to invent your own favourites.

DUTCH PANCAKES

Nothing cooks pancakes like a cast-iron skillet on a cast-iron stove. A good hot fire makes the skillet spit back when a few drops of water are sprinkled on it.

Stir together 2 cups of whole wheat flour, ¼ cup of cornmeal, 4 teaspoons of baking powder, 1 teaspoon of salt and ¼ cup of sugar. In another bowl, combine 2 cups of milk, ¼ cup of oil, melted shortening or drippings and 2 eggs. Whisk the wet ingredients into the dry until no longer lumpy. Ladle onto a hot, oiled griddle and cook until bubbles appear on one side. Flip and cook until done. Serve with applesauce, yogurt, sweet syrups, cinnamon or jams. These pancakes are good plain, but become a meal when you add chopped apple, broken bacon bits, cracklings or cheese. Try combinations such as cinnamon-apple, bacon-cheese, orange rind and cottage cheese.

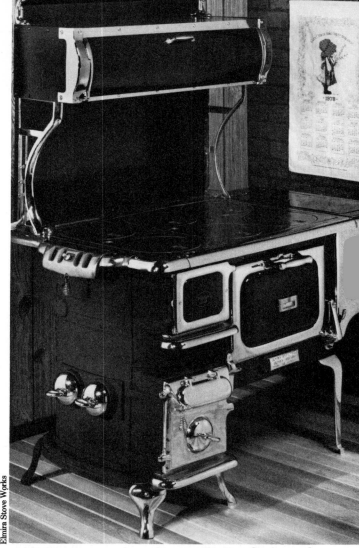

Elmira Stove Works

Airtight ranges, such as this new Findlay Oval, are the next logical step as the back-to-wood movement continues.

OMA'S POTATO SOUP

Meat trimmings and bones, vegetable "liquor" and leftovers find their way into the kettle of stock simmering at the back of the stove, to combine their flavours in a true *pot-au-feu*. A winter favourite is this hearty *potage*.

Prepare beef stock by simmering at least 3 pounds of meaty bones with about 6 cups of water and a bay leaf. When the meat falls off the bones, remove bones and bay leaf, adding 1 chopped carrot, 1 diced celery stalk, 2 chopped onions, 4 large potatoes, peeled and diced, and 1 pound of sliced green beans. Add salt, pepper and Worcestershire sauce to taste. Simmer until the vegetables are tender and the soup is quite thick. Sprinkle with chopped parsley, rounds of smoked sausage or croutons.

Note: You can make your own croutons by cubing stale bread and mixing thoroughly with a combination of melted butter or oil, grated onion, garlic salt, celery seed, paprika and Worcestershire sauce. Toast in a low oven until crispy and golden brown.

GOOD BAKED BEANS

Baked beans are a natural for wood stoves. With the home fire burning all day to warm the winter kitchen, the long cooking time is no extravagance, but an efficient use of energy.

Soak 4 cups of dried white beans in cold water overnight. Drain, cover with water and simmer until the skins burst when blown upon. Drain. Add 1 cup of brown sugar, 2 chopped onions, 3 teaspoons of dry mustard, 4 teaspoons of salt, 1 teaspoon of pepper, 1 cup of ketchup and 1 cup of chopped bacon or salt pork. Add enough boiling water to cover the beans and bake in a covered casserole in a low oven until tender (all day). Add water or tomato juice as necessary and uncover for the last hour to brown the beans.

MARY'S FAVOURITE BISCUITS

This sweet hotbread comes from a 91-year-old neighbour of stout pioneer stock who lives alone in her wood-heated farmhouse. She says simply, "Friends seem to like these best."

Mix together 2 cups of flour (one can be whole wheat), ½ teaspoon of salt, 3 teaspoons of baking powder and ½ cup of sugar. This makes a very sweet treat, so feel free to reduce the sugar. Cut in ½ cup of shortening until fine. Make a hole in the centre and add about ¾ cup of sweet milk, stirring with a fork to make a soft dough. Put out on a pastry board and knead 10 times. Roll to a half-inch thickness and cut with a round cutter. Place on a baking sheet, prick with a fork, and bake in a very hot oven until golden (450 degrees F for about 15 minutes).

CRISP COOKIES

Oatmeal cookies are standard fare where there are children. This recipe is reprinted as it was related by an elderly woman who stored her favourite "receipts" where they were handiest: in her head.

Take half as much flour and sugar as oatmeal, and mix with half as much shortening as flour. Add salt to taste and a teaspoon of soda for every cup of flour. Thicken with sour milk to the desired consistency. A soft dough can be dropped by the spoonful onto a greased cookie sheet for a cake-like cookie, or a stiffer dough can be rolled and cut with a cookie cutter, formed into a ball and pressed with a glass or the tines of a fork. Bake in a moderate oven (350 degrees F) until brown. This recipe works well in the following ratio: 3 cups oats, 1½ cups flour, 1½ cups sugar, ¾ cup shortening, 1 teaspoon salt, 1½ teaspoons soda and a scant ½ cup of sour milk.

RYE BREAD (BAUERBRÖT)

Finally comes the staff of life: bread. One local woman who generally uses her electric stove still keeps the wood stove for baking bread. Nothing can surpass the even brownness and slightly woodsy taste of a fresh-baked loaf from a cookstove oven.

For the starter, dissolve 1¼ teaspoons of dry granulated yeast in ⅓ cup of lukewarm water. When softened, beat in 1½ cups of lukewarm water and 2 cups of white flour. Let rise until it doubles, then sinks (about 3 hours). You can either use it now or refrigerate it overnight. Let it come to room temperature again before using.

For the final dough, soften 1¼ teaspoons of dry granulated yeast in ⅓ cup of lukewarm water. When dissolved, beat into starter, along with 1¼ cups of lukewarm water, 1½ teaspoons of salt and 4 cups of dark rye flour. Beat hard. Continue to beat, adding whole wheat flour until stiff. Let rest 10 minutes, then knead, adding flour until dough is smooth and elastic (about 2 cups of whole wheat flour altogether). Let rise until doubled in size, punch down, turn and let rise until doubled again. Punch down and form into a long, oval loaf, just less than the length of a cookie sheet. Place in a clean linen towel and suspend in a sling from a closed drawer. This will force the dough to rise up and not flatten with its weight. Let rise until tripled, then roll quickly but gently from the towel onto a greased cookie sheet sprinkled with cornmeal. Slash the top diagonally with a sharp knife and brush with water. Set immediately in a very hot oven (450 degrees F) and brush with water every 5 minutes until a crust has formed (3 times). Bake 20 minutes at high heat, then 20 minutes at moderate heat (350 degrees F). The frequent door-opening at high heat will have effectively lowered the temperature to the required degree but, if not, leave the door ajar for an additional few minutes. After baking, allow the loaf to cool gradually for 20 minutes more in the oven with the door open.

MRS. TOPPS' TEA BREAD

A company cake is always in the larder for unexpected guests. This tea cake is delicious plain or sliced and buttered.

Cream 2 tablespoons of butter with ¾ cup of sugar. Beat in 1 egg. In another bowl, mix together 1 cup of whole wheat flour, 1 cup of white flour, 1 cup of bran, 4 teaspoons of baking powder and ½ teaspoon of salt. Add the dry ingredients to the creamed mixture alternately with 1¼ cups of sweet milk, beating after each addition. Fold in 1½ cups of chopped glazed cherries, dates or nuts (mixed). Bake in a loaf tin for about 1 hour at a moderate temperature (350 degrees F). This cake improves with age.

Tastes Like Chicken

La nouvelle cuisine rustique

By Stephen Pitt

GOOD GROUNDHOG...

Party Bucket

Graham Pilsworth

Five-thirty on a brand new summer morning. The sun is up and peering over the horizon with one bleary red eye. A few insects are astir already, and somewhere a couple of crows are kick-starting. The air is thick and dew-clammy, laden with the sweet smell of wild flowers, wet grass, and almost-ripe grain. It's that time of morn when the whole world seems on the verge of going back to sleep again, except at the edge of Farmer Brown's favourite grain field where comes the sound of furious industry.

Sharp incisors on tender stalks. Not-yet-golden grain disappearing down a furry brown gullet. It is a groundhog bringing in some of Farmer Brown's sheaves. He swallows the grain directly, not bothering to fill his cheek pouches, then runs for home. The woodchuck has no reason to fear that any harm may come to him; he's been working this field for two summers without incident.

Two summers of easy living have made the chuck large and chubby. Now, with his belly almost full of fresh grain, and the security of the burrow barely 30 feet from where he crouches, the little brown beast cannot but feel at one with this big beautiful world. He sits up to enjoy the full warmth of the sun as it rises out of the east.

Mercifully, as Audie Murphy once wrote, you never hear the one that gets you.

The groundhog slumps to the ground, dead almost before the report of the .22 rifle reaches his ears. Now Farmer Brown also rises from the east, brushing the dirt from his elbows. Tired of the woodchuck's thieving ways, and also afraid for his prime steers who have displayed a talent for stumbling in groundhog holes, Farmer Brown has finally gotten around to getting himself out of bed 40 minutes early to deal with this pest once and for all.

Farmer Brown looks at the rodent that has been polishing off $25.00 worth of grain a year. Disgustedly he picks it up by the tail and drapes the meaty brown carcass over a nearby rail fence for the crows to pick at. He also hopes the forlorn little body will stand as a warning to all other chucks in the vicinity to keep out of the grain field. (Don't scoff. It wasn't too long ago that the same philosophy was applied to people. Although the deterrent factor seemed to have questionable effects on the human race, it appears some people still have faith in the groundhog.)

His morning vendetta complete, Farmer Brown returns to the house for breakfast. Mrs. Farmer Brown has it on the table. As her husband sits down she comments on the outrageous price of bacon. He murmurs agreement (this is a beef farm), not stopping to think that 10 minutes ago he left six pounds of fresh grain-fed meat lying on a cedar rail. Two years at $25.00 a season, it is costing him over $8.00 a pound for crow bait. One of his prime steers would be cheaper in the long run, but why should the crows get anything?

Why not eat the groundhog? He once was a very acceptable part of the North American larder. Pioneers knew the virtues of a good groundhog stew, and I'll wager that few crows that lived during the Depression (the last one) managed to grow fat on fresh-shot groundhog meat.

It is only in the last couple of decades, when hunting has become a "sport," not a necessity, and when even the farmer's wife picks her vegetables out of a supermarket freezer section, that the groundhog has become a culinary *persona non grata*.

I repeat: Why not eat the groundhog? A woodchuck's credentials put most accepted barnyard "eaters" to shame.

KNOWN QUANTITIES

First of all, your average groundhog is raised on the very same diet that makes Farmer Brown's prime steers rate $2.00 a pound and up at the meat counter. Chucks like oats, barley and wheat. Or if they live in the poorer neighbourhoods, chucks eat clover, grass and wild flowers. The occasional chuck does make a meal out of skunk cabbage or worse, but that is the advantage of eating groundhog meat. Chucks dine in the vicinity of their burrows. A quick survey of the foliage around the hole will tell you exactly what your groundhog has been raised on. Can you claim to know as much about the last roast you bought?

Second: Groundhogs are lazy. They eat. They sleep. They sunbathe whenever the coast is clear. The only work they do is when they are young and have to scrape out a burrow for themselves. From then on they live the life of leisure, breaking training only to mate (once a year at best) and to widen the sides of the burrow to accommodate their ever-fattening bodies. All this adds up to some exceptionally tender eating. Compare it to the woodchuck's acceptable first cousin, the rabbit, who runs himself stringy all day. And people pay gourmet prices for rabbit meat.

Which brings us to point three: Groundhog meat is free; sort of. If you own farmland in eastern mainland North America, then you have groundhogs (if you live west, you've got marmots — chucks with racing stripes). And if you have groundhogs, you have raised them as surely as if you had taken them into your barn, set them up in a stall, and got up at dawn every morning to shovel grain into their troughs. At the rate woodchucks eat you won't get all your money back, but it's better than nothing. Think of it in the light of a tax return. Here's how to do it.

To begin, first you shoot the groundhog. Aim for a head shot because this kills the chuck instantly and does not spoil the meat. If you cannot get close enough for a head shot, or if you cannot shoot well enough to guarantee an instant kill, go home and have a peanut butter sandwich. It will save a lot of bother.

Groundhogs, in spite of the easy life they lead, possess an amazingly strong will to survive. If wounded, they will crawl down their burrows and take up to a week to die. The only humane thing to do is dig it out and kill it, and you have no idea how deep a woodchuck burrow is until you have to dig one out. (I had to once, because I made the mistake of stalking a groundhog with a weekend nimrod who also happened to be a certifiable idiot. He shot the chuck from 40 yards with a shotgun. This riddled the beast but did not kill it. I dug the chuck out, killed it with my rifle, then I killed the hunter, too. It did little

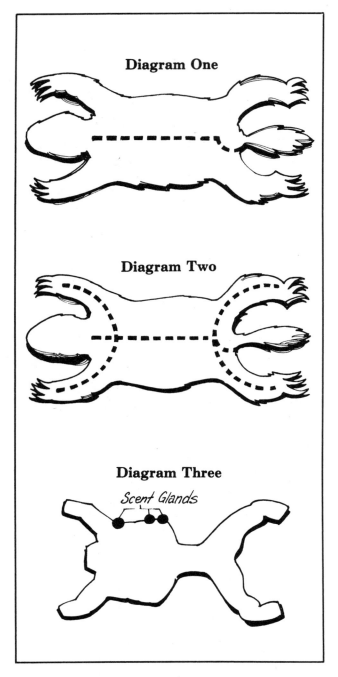

Diagram One

Diagram Two

Diagram Three

Scent Glands

After the blood has stopped flowing freely (half an hour should do it) take the carcass down and lay it flat on its back. If you have not already slit open the groundhog's belly, now is the time to do it. Use a very sharp knife for the neatest results. Make the incision from the throat to the anus. (If the chuck was a male, pass the genitalia close on one side or the other, Diagram One). Next make horizontal cuts up the underside of each leg, connecting with the main incision (Diagram Two).

Now, carefully peel back the skin in all directions, trying to use the knife sparingly or you will blemish the meat underneath. The skin should peel away quite easily, coming off the head like a sweater. Try not to let the hair touch the meat, as it adds nothing to the flavour and it has probably been some time since that groundhog had a bath. (What's the use when you are living in a hole?)

Once the skin has been stripped off, take a meat cleaver or hatchet and remove the head, tail and all four feet. Take out the intestines, heart, lungs, liver and all other assorted organs and deposit them in a bag marked "Offal." You will also have to strip away a fair amount of fat from the body, but under that is tender, dark, fine-grained meat. Unlike yourself, the chuck is now almost dressed for dinner but there is one more thing to keep in mind.

Scent glands. Groundhogs and certain other small game animals have scent glands (or "kernels" as they are known in the more genteel dissection circles) and they are located under the front armpits and along the back. They are used for personal identification and once-a-year mating purposes, and while they may smell like Hai-Karate to other groundhogs, they will turn your dinner into something reminiscent of a groundhog locker room. Locate these kernels (they look like little grey bumps) and cut them out (Diagram Three). You are now ready for the next move.

The next move is ageing the meat. This is another optional step. Ageing is a process that has fallen out of practice except in the finest of meat circles. Ageing the meat, that is hanging it up in a cool and shady place at 35 to 40 degrees F for a few days, gives the natural enzymes in the meat a chance to break the flesh down and tenderize it. All the best restaurants age their meat, not only their prime groundhog but beef filets and other lesser cuts, too. I recommend hanging the carcass for at least 24 hours. Whether it helps the meat or not is debatable, but you may need this breather to get your appetite back.

MARINADES

Finally comes the marinade. All groundhog meat should be marinated prior to cooking. It removes the last traces of what some people refer to as "that outdoorsy taste." There are two marinades I can suggest.

The first is for the gourmet cooking snob. Mix one quart of dry red wine with one quart of cool water (bottled Perrier if you are really jet set). Add half a dozen cracked peppercorns, half a tablespoon of salt and just a dash or two of powdered basil. Soak the meat for six hours, turning the carcass every now

to relieve my feelings about a completely wasted groundhog, but it did help fill in that hole.)

One other thing to consider is that a groundhog that is not killed instantly makes for some pretty terrible eating. The agony seems to sink right into the meat, and George Harrison's old brown shoe is tender by comparison. Make it a head shot or nothing.

PROCEDURES

Once you have shot your groundhog, immediately hang it upside down in a shady spot to bleed. Bleeding makes the later cleaning steps a little less messy, and it is also essential to the good taste of the meat. Slitting the jugular veins in the throat will help speed up the process, and some people also prefer to slit open the belly at this point and remove the intestines and such to help the meat cool off. I find that this is not really necessary on a small game animal like a groundhog, but it doesn't hurt.

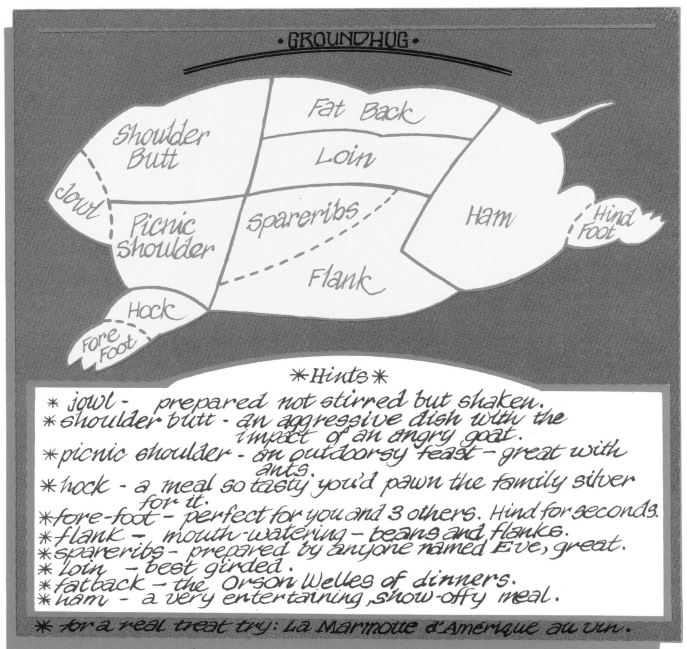

· GROUNDHOG ·

Shoulder Butt

Fat Back

Loin

Jowl

Picnic Shoulder

Spareribs

Ham

Hind Foot

Flank

Hock

Fore Foot

Graham Pilsworth

Hints

* jowl - prepared not stirred but shaken.
* shoulder butt - an aggressive dish with the impact of an angry goat.
* picnic shoulder - an outdoorsy feast - great with ants
* hock - a meal so tasty you'd pawn the family silver for it.
* fore-foot - perfect for you and 3 others. Hind for seconds.
* flank - mouth-watering - beans and flanks.
* spareribs - prepared by anyone named Eve, great.
* loin - best girded.
* fatback - the Orson Welles of dinners.
* ham - a very entertaining, show-offy meal.

* for a real treat try: La Marmotte d'Amerique au vin.

and then. Wipe the meat dry before cooking or it will not sear properly. That's Marinade Number One.

For Marinade Number Two, take two quarts of cool water and add two tablespoons of salt. Soak for six hours and wipe dry. This marinade is for the backwoods he-man snob. Now we are ready for the final step: the cooking. Select one of the following recipes.

ROAST CHUCK A L'ORANGE

groundhog
2 oranges
butter
flour
basil
parsley
pepper
salt

Slice the oranges into rounds, then cut them in half. Stuff the groundhog's chest cavity with the orange slices and place the meat in a medium-deep pan. Place additional slices around the chuck and between the legs which should be tied together with string to help keep the juices in.

Preheat the oven to 325 degrees F. Allow about 35 minutes for every pound of chuck to be cooked. When he's done he should be golden brown; knowing the groundhog's predilection to sunbathing this is the way he would have wanted to go, with a full belly and a brown skin.

The pan drippings can be converted into an interesting gravy. Take the meat out, put it in another pan and then back in the oven at a low heat to keep warm. Add about a cup of water to the pan's brownings, bring to a boil and stir to dissolve the scrapings on the bottom. Lower the heat to medium, then take a small jar or cup and mix 2 or 3 tablespoons of flour with ¾ cup of water. Stir it into the pan a little at a time until the gravy reaches the desired consistency, then add salt, pepper, basil and parsley to taste. As I said, this gravy is quite interesting, particularly with the orange slices floating around in it.

Put new potatoes and greens on the side and you're all set for Sunday dinner.

GONGCHOW CRANBERRY SURPRISE (COUNTRY STYLE SHAKE-N-BAKE)
groundhog
bread crumbs
eggs
flour
oil
garlic powder
cranberry jelly (chuck berries)

With a name like Gongchow Cranberry Surprise, some readers might expect this dish's taste to be questionable. It's actually quite nice, and not at all hard to make.

Take a small bowl, add 2 eggs, 2 tablespoons of water and a dash of salt, pepper and garlic powder. Beat lightly until mixed. Now take 2 pie tins and put half a cup of flour in one, and ¾ cup of bread crumbs in the other.

Take your groundhog meat, having cut it up in serving size pieces ahead of time, and dip it first into the egg mix, then into the flour, back into the egg mix, then into the bread crumbs. Put all the pieces on a tray, add a little more salt, pepper and garlic powder if you like, then put them in the refrigerator to set. Covering them with tin foil keeps the meat moist.

After the crumb coating has set, remove the meat from the refrigerator and let it warm to room temperature. Take a frying pan and fill it ¼ inch deep with cooking oil. Heat the oil and brown the meat evenly on both sides.

Now add half a cup of water to the pan, a bit at a time, and beware of the spattering fat. Cover with a lid and let it cook over low heat for half an hour. Then remove the lid to allow the breading to become crispy.

Serve with cranberry jelly. Surprise.

GROUNDHOG FRICASSEE
groundhog
flour
bacon grease
1 cup chopped onion
1 cup boiling water
salt
sage
cayenne
1 crushed bay leaf
pepper

Cut meat into serving sizes. Mix 5 tablespoons flour and ¼ teaspoon of pepper, and rub it into the meat. Heat the bacon grease in a deep frying pan and put the meat in to brown. Once this is accomplished, add the chopped onion and let it brown, too.

Now add 1 cup boiling water, scrape the sides and

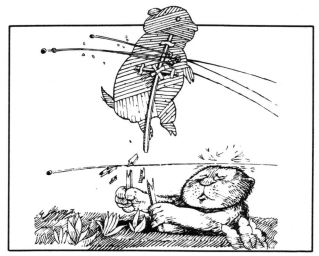

Graham Pilsworth

bottom of the pan and stir up the juices. Pour a little more water over the meat to moisten it, then sprinkle on the powdered bay leaf, a pinch of powdered sage and 1 tablespoon salt.

Cover the pan and let it simmer for 45 minutes (longer if the groundhog was a big one). Do not add more water unless the pan gets very dry. When finished you should have some lovely looking brown groundhog meat swimming in a thick gravy-like sauce. Guaranteed to change your mind about groundhogs if anything will.

As for what kind of wine you should serve with groundhog, ask the man at the liquor store for his recommendation.

SHISH KECHUCK
groundhog
peppers, sweet variety
mushrooms
onions, small size
tomatoes, small
lemons
garlic
olive oil
Sauternes

Cut the meat into 2-inch squares. Mix half a cup of Sauternes with an equal measure of olive oil, add 1 tablespoon of freshly squeezed lemon juice, a little salt, a dash or two of pepper and 1 crushed clove of garlic. Throw in the meat cubes and let them soak overnight in a cool, dark place (the refrigerator).

Next day, stoke up the barbecue. Slice the onions in halves and cut the peppers into 2-inch squares. Now skewer the ingredients on long thin sticks. (You can get metal skewers at the supermarket, but wooden ones are preferred if available.) Skewer the ingredients in whatever order pleases you. Make sure the coals are hot, then broil until the meat is dark and crisp and the vegetables are slightly black around the edges and sizzling in the middle. Leftover sauce can be dripped over the food at 5-minute intervals. They should be ready in 20 minutes.

You can either eat Shish KeChuck on the stick, or forego the possible self-inflicted skewer wounds and just wrap a piece of soft pita bread around the meat and vegetables and pull the skewer out. Now you have **Groundhog Souflaki**. Enough to make a Spartan's mouth water.

Arctic Sugar

Syrup making without the maple — Yukon style

By Mickey Lammers

We begin on the first day of May. In what has become a ritual, we head out to the trees in the early afternoon, loaded down with spiles, jars and a small collection of tools. The weather is usually lovely, bright but snappy enough that our coats come off only after the work starts. Up the hill we tramp to a grove of trees where there are still traces of snow on the ground. Gunnar drills a hole in the first tree, bangs in a spout, bangs in a nail above the spout, and I hang a jar in position. The procedure is repeated 50 times in all — a familiar rite of spring in any maple sugarbush. But here in the Yukon we are thousands of miles northwest of the nearest sugar maple tree, and so we turn to the birch.

In Scandinavia and Scotland, in Russia and Canada, wherever the maples are replaced by forests of birch trees, this process has become a spring event. Birch sap was so popular in Russia in the last century that apparently whole forests of the trees were obliterated by overzealous tree tappers. A recent Russian study states that "Evidently the healing properties of birch sap were of such help that even in ancient times the sap was gathered early in the spring and used in its raw state as a natural drink." Bartholomew, an English herbalist of the Middle Ages, says of birches, "And men useth therfore in spryngynge tyme and in harvest to slyt the ryndes and to gader ye humour that comyth oute thereof and drynkyth in stede of wyn. And such drynke quencheth thurste. But it fedyth not nother nourryssheth not, nor maketh men dronke."

The Huron Indians are known to have sucked sap directly from birch trees when they were thirsty, while a Canadian Chippewa who lived north of maple tree country said that his people would tap white birch trees and boil the sap into syrup, noting that the run of sap did not last as long as that for maples.

Unfortunately, we were not aware of all this when we read *The Maple Sugar Book* by Helen and Scott Nearing several years ago. Having finished the book, we felt we knew quite a bit about sugaring — maples, that is — and only one sentence from the Nearings gave us any hope of making syrup in the Yukon: "Sugar lies in watery solution in the sap of palms, birch trees, walnuts, hickories . . . ." Birch trees we have, and we decided to give it a try. That was 1975. Tapping the birches has now become a yearly event, something we anticipate as the start of a busy outdoor season.

SAPPING BUG

The first step in this venture was to gather the paraphernalia needed to collect and transport the sap. Because the stand of birch we tap is some distance from the house, and our bush road is never in the best of shape in the early spring, our handy friend Gunnar transformed a junked VW Beetle into the Sapping Bug. Consisting of the car frame and engine, some creative metalwork, a seat, roll bar, box to hold the sap container and balloon tires, the reincarnated Beetle provides unorthodox but reliable access to the birch grove.

Located on a hillside about two miles from home, the clump of birch contains about 50 good-sized trees, just enough for our needs. One large tree,

I DON'T KNOW FRANK, MAYBE
THE TREE'S SICK...

according to Grieve's *Modern Herbal*, should produce from 16 to 18 gallons of sap (per season) "and a moderate tapping does no harm."

A moderate tapping of birches usually amounts to one spout per tree, or none if the tree is under nine inches in diameter. Those eager Russians who wiped out entire forests set a poor, but all too easily imitated, example. All varieties of birches, incidentally, may be tapped. The sugar content varies from variety to variety, year to year, and, like maples, from tree to tree, but none produces a harmful sap.

We made our own spouts of plastic pipe — they should be about a half-inch in diameter, or the correct size to fit the hole drilled in the tree. We bought a breast drill and bit, and gathered a hammer and large nails. To catch the sap we used recycled half-gallon jars, to which we attached wire around the necks, leaving a wire loop to hang on the nail. The inventory was completed with four sturdy plastic buckets to carry the sap from the trees to the Bug, and a 25-gallon plastic container with a tight-fitting lid, that would sit on the Bug waiting to transport the syrup to the outdoor fire back at home.

To boil the sap down, we had decided to make a barrel stove using an old oil drum set in a horizontal position slightly depressed into the ground, with a door in one end, a collar for the stovepipe on top at the other, and a large enough hole to fit a round washtub in the middle. We placed two metal rods over the central hole so that the washtub could rest on these, over the flames, and so that it would be fairly easy to remove when the syrup was done.

Fortunately, my husband Bill and I run a sawmill, and have a ready supply of fuel. We cut a mighty heap of two-foot slabs, a waste product with lots of bark and pitch, just right for our purpose. The first year we underestimated our fuel requirements and had to cut again halfway through our 10-day sapping. Each gallon of maple syrup is estimated to require about one-twentieth of a cord of wood, but most birch trees have a less concentrated sugar content than most maples, so boiling down birch sap requires even more wood; a cord may be burned in producing only 10 to 15 gallons of syrup. We had hoped that the ratio of sap to syrup would be about the same for birch as it is for maple, about 40:1, and though that was not the case, we did manage to achieve the respectable ratio of 50:1 by boiling the sap down to a much lighter syrup than the heavier commercial types.

LATE BLOOMERS

Being neophytes, we had to try to determine when we should start tapping. No one in the area could give us any information, so we just experimented with a handy test tree near the house. Much to our surprise, the sap did not begin to flow until May first that year. We now know that birch trees are normally tapped later than maples, generally in April in the southern parts of Canada and the northern United States. In the Soviet Union, according to a government report, "The Use of Birch Syrup in the Food Industry," birch sap is gathered "in the early spring with the first intensive melting of the snow." In 1976 we again started on May first, but the following year we climbed the hill to start sapping April 27th. The early start lasted only three days, and then all the spouts froze up and the sap stopped running. For two days the jars hung empty. I guess May first is the right day to start here, the time when the first Yellow-Shafted Flicker appears, and the spring noises of the water birds in the Yukon River can again be heard.

Once having tapped the trees, we go to the birches every evening and empty the jars into the plastic buckets which we carry down the hill to the container on the Bug. The next morning we empty our booty through a strainer into the tub on the barrel stove, and when the tub is full we start a roaring fire which will burn two hours before the sap comes to a rolling boil. The trick now is to keep it boiling, and that means a steady job of stoking the fire until three or four o'clock in the afternoon, when a thin brown layer of syrup has finally appeared in the tub. To prevent this from scorching, I transfer that small amount to a pan and boil it down to two quarts of light-bodied syrup on the propane stove. I fill two sterile jars and seal them to prevent fermentation.

LIVESTOCK TONIC

The first three days of gathering are 10-gallon days, but then the sap runs stronger and each evening our 25-gallon container is full. At the best of times, our 50 spouts may produce more sap than we can use. One year we had a pig. Why not, we wondered, feed him those extra two or three buckets? We filled his bucket with sap. The pig never hesitated. His snout went in and he didn't lift his head until the bucket was empty. I think he even smacked his lips. The reaction of the chickens was much the same. They crowded around the waterer, pushing and fighting to get at the sap. It seemed quite amazing, but then birch sap has long been considered a real "spring tonic" and perhaps the animals knew what was good for them. The Russian researchers stated in 1974, "In our opinion, the main direction for the use of birch sap in the food industry should be in accordance with the possibilities of the sap in its raw state, since the living elements of the organic cells, the important components of the sap, appear to be to a significant degree unstable. Only in this case can the value of the natural sap be preserved in a drink with a pleasant, smooth and natural taste.

"A whole range of macro- and microelements (potassium, sodium, magnesium, iron, copper and others) appear to be the important components of natural birch sap which predetermine its large physiological role."

Birch sap is a diuretic, and, according to the 17th-century herbalist Nicholas Culpeper, "is available to break the stone in the kidneys and bladder, and is good also to wash sore mouths." Some of the sap's health-enhancing properties may be due to its unusual carbohydrate composition. In analyzing the carbohydrates of birch sap, Dr. Mariafranca Morselli, a University of Vermont botanist, found an average of 49 per cent fructose, 35 per cent glucose and 15 per cent sucrose in four samples, while maple syrup contains about 99 per cent sucrose and one per cent glucose.

By May 11th, the sap runs with less enthusiasm and becomes slightly milky, so we know the end is in sight. On the 14th we remove the spouts, plug the holes with tight-fitting sticks or whittled pieces of wood, and carry the jars home for the last time. By now we have 19 or 20 quarts of syrup.

I find the syrup very nice to sip, as is, in a small quantity. The colour is brown, the taste somewhat like mild molasses. A quart of syrup can be boiled down to a pint of a thicker consistency to be used on pancakes, or it can be further cooked to sugar, considered a treat by early Scots and Scandinavians. But above all it is an unmatched secret ingredient in whole wheat bread, not only imparting a lovely colour to the bread, but also improving the flavour and making the use of sugar or honey unnecessary.

Those with prodigious old maples may scoff at the notion of tapping a birch, but with the range of the sugar maple confined to eastern Ontario, Quebec, parts of the Maritimes and the northeastern United States, many of us count ourselves fortunate to have access to a birch woods. If the effort is at times disproportionate to the amount of syrup produced, one needs only take into account the feeling of working outdoors again after a long winter, sharing the spring sun with the returning songbirds and taking that first taste of fresh, sweet sap.

Sources

COLE CREEK HOMESTEADING EQUIP.
R.R.1
Verona, Ontario K0H 2W0
(613) 374-2936

Cast-iron door and pipe collar to fit 45-gallon drum. Write for new price list. Cole Creek also markets a "homestead-size" syrup evaporator system, suitable for boiling down and finishing syrup outdoors. It is a convenient size for those who wish to prepare up to 20 gallons of syrup a season.

DOMINION & GRIMM, INC.
8250 - 3rd Avenue
Ville d'Anjou
Montreal, Quebec H1J 1X5
(514) 351-3000

Canada's largest supplier of maple syrup making equipment, with catalogues in either French or English.

COOMB'S MAPLE PRODUCTS, INC.
Jacksonville, Vermont 05342
(802) 368-2345

Homemade evaporators designed for backyard syrup makers (evaporating pan atop barrel stove).

The Great Canadian Wine

It's only a naïve little domestic white with very little breeding, but we think you'll be amused by its presumption

By Elizabeth A. Long

We discovered the Great Canadian Wine by mistake. After our first long, cold winter confined in a small log cabin with two energetic preschoolers, we greeted the arrival of spring with the enthusiasm universally reserved for this season by most early religious cults. Any excuse to get out and be active was welcomed by the entire family. Maple syruping was an obvious solution. Luckily, we had planned our spring activity the previous summer by identifying and marking the best and most easily accessible sugar maples on our property.

During that winter, while I had been busy tracking down new recipes for homemade, country wines — the hedgerow variety whose ingredients are easily available and free — I discovered an old recipe for Birch Sap Wine, a great delicacy of Baltic origin. The recipe was said to produce a light, white table wine. I was consumed with enthusiasm. However, our cabin was consistently too cold during the winter to conduct a fermentation, so all wine making had to wait until the arrival of spring. And so it was that while

we tapped our sugar maples for syrup, we also tapped a couple of white birch trees for wine.

Life became exceedingly hectic for a few weeks, as our method for converting maple sap to syrup was primitive and slow. In later years, the whole operation was conducted outside, but that first spring we endeavoured to boil down the sap in a cauldron suspended in our large stone fireplace. The sticky steam rose up the chimney and, I suspect, coated it with sooty sugar — not to be recommended. However, we were one step ahead of one city-bound syrup maker of whom we had heard; she enthusiastically boiled down her sap on the top of her unvented kitchen stove in a basement apartment. She did get her syrup, but caramelized the entire apartment in the process.

Since our cauldron was fairly small and the sap run was rapid, we started to stockpile sap in our tin bathtub beside the hearth. After the second child had been fished out of the sap-filled tub, and all the balls, boats and rubber toys had been dried off and confiscated, we began to question this method of syrup making. Finally nature took a decisive hand in the matter when we discovered tiny bubbles appearing in the waiting maple sap — it was beginning to ferment, and had to be used quickly.

"Why not use it to make wine?" I queried. "If you can use birch sap, why not maple sap?" And so the Great Canadian Wine was born. I had already put down two experimental gallons of birch sap wine and merely repeated the process, substituting maple sap for birch sap in the recipe. We then sat back and waited.

RAVE REVIEWS

It was almost a year later that we were able to sample our new wines. The birch sap wine was good, but the maple was great, receiving rave reviews from all who sampled it. Over the years I have experimented and modified the original recipe, omitting the raisins and substituting maple syrup for the sugar. It has become one of our favourites, truly a native Canadian wine. Many skeptics have assumed that it must be sickly sweet, but as with any wine it can be as dry or sweet as the wine maker's palate dictates. The yeast, being a living organism, requires food to stay alive and to reproduce. Any form of sugar is an ideal food and in return the yeast will produce alcohol. If we provide the yeast with more sugar than it can consume, the excess will remain in the wine, sweetening the flavour. Too little sugar will produce a weak wine, low in alcohol content and with poor keeping qualities. I personally like a dry wine, and so strive to have just enough sugar to produce a good, full-bodied wine in which all of the sugar has been used in the conversion to alcohol. A general rule of thumb is to use two and one-half pounds of sugar per gallon for a dry wine, three pounds for medium, three and one-half pounds for sweet. For the birch and maple sap wines, I reduced the sugar to two and one-quarter pounds per gallon as both the saps contain a fair quantity of natural sugar. A good book on wine making is always a help for the novice.

A word of warning. Many books that have come out in recent years advocate the use of chemicals, turning the art of wine making into a science. Chemicals are not necessary, and I feel that they are undesirable in country wines. Some may be downright dangerous; I have seen asbestos pulp recommended for clearing wine. I would advise against it — any wine properly prepared and left long enough should clear naturally. Campden tablets, to kill natural yeasts in the initial must (mixture of ingredients) or to prevent late fermentation occurring in the bottles, are often listed in modern recipes, but Campden has been linked to miscarriages when consumed by pregnant women.

Natural yeasts may sometimes be undesirable, except in grape wines, but they can easily be eradicated if the wine maker brings the ingredients to the boiling point before wine making begins. Remember to let it cool, covered, before adding the wine yeast or the high temperature will kill that yeast, too. Special cultures of wine yeasts are available from wine supply stores and some specialty grocery shops. Each imparts a distinctive, subtle flavour. If the wine is made from a fruit pulp or flowers to which one must

David Stone/Horst Wolfe

add water and let it steep, the water should be brought to a boil before it is added to the must. Bottling the wine at the correct time — not too early, fermentation must have ceased completely — in corked wine bottles and storing them at the right temperature, ideally 50 to 55 degrees F, will eliminate the need for adding Campden tablets.

The recipes for Birch Sap Wine and the Great Canadian Wine follow, but first I would like to give a few words to the wise concerning tree tapping — nobody wants to obliterate forests or even a few trees for lack of a little common sense. Birch and maple may be tapped in the same manner. *Never* tap a tree less than nine inches in diameter. Whereas large, mature trees can support two or even three taps, smaller trees (and the birch usually fall into this category) should have only one tap. Tap only during the early spring sap run. The night temperature should be 32 degrees F or lower, but the daytime temperature must rise above freezing. Here in the Ottawa Valley the run generally lasts two or three weeks, starting in late March, but time and duration vary in different areas and from year to year. The drilled hole should be at an angle of about 30 degrees and bored just deeply enough to hold the tap (just beyond the inside of the bark). If the drill penetrates too far it will extend into the heartwood and will miss the sap. Remember also, if the snowbanks are high when the tapping is done, the taps should be placed quite low on the trunk. Otherwise, as the snow melts, it will become increasingly difficult to reach the buckets. When the buds on the trees start to swell and burst into leaf, it's time to stop. Be sure to plug the tree with a wooden plug when sap taking is over.

Maple wine is an obvious choice for maple syrup makers, who already have the basic ingredients on hand, but it is equally good for the city or suburban dweller who has a single good-sized maple shade tree in the front yard. Bigleaf, silver, red, black and sugar maples and box elder trees will all give a suitable sap. There might not be enough sap for syrup making, but there should be plenty for wine. It should also be noted that unadulterated maple sap makes a delicious, refreshing spring drink. We generally keep a container of it in the refrigerator during sap gathering times (it can also be frozen and used at a later date). The Indians used maple sap as a spring tonic; it contains sugar for energy and a bountiful supply of trace elements that the body craves after months of stored winter food.

EQUIPMENT

Before the would-be wine maker embarks upon his first project, he should buy or find a few pieces of equipment that will make the process easier and more foolproof. Both of the following recipes make a bit more than a gallon of wine, so the wine maker will need a clean crock or a new plastic garbage pail, which will be reserved for wine making only, large enough to comfortably hold one gallon of liquid. A five-gallon size is convenient and allows the wine maker to increase his later ventures. This container must have a cover that will keep out dust and fruit flies, but loose enough to allow the gases produced in fermentation to escape — an airtight container would probably cause an explosion. A towel secured with a large elastic band or a shower cap will work well. For straining the must, a jelly bag, colander or sieve lined with cheesecloth will be necessary. From the big container, the wine is strained into a big bowl or canning kettle and then siphoned into a clean, glass carboy which will be fitted with a fermentation lock. Recycled gallon wine bottles work fine, but special jars made for this purpose can be bought in wine supply stores, where the fermentation lock, a plastic device that allows gas to escape but prevents the entry of air, can also be found. If the wine maker cannot find a fermentation lock, he may try lightly corking or loosely screw-capping the carboy. This will, however, allow some air to enter, and during

this period of gentle fermentation the wine is vulnerable to airborne yeasts which can cause it to turn to vinegar.

A length of clean siphoning hose, about three feet long, will be needed when the wine is racked (siphoned off the bottom sediment, often called the lees).

The inventory is made complete with a few clean, sterilized wine bottles, preferably tinted, and corks — a gallon of wine will fill about five bottles. A corker costs about $20 and can fit the standard, straight-sided corks into wine bottles, a good investment, but the wine maker may choose to buy tapered corks, which can be pushed in fairly adequately by hand. A less aesthetic but cheaper alternative is to use recycled screw-top bottles.

TRADITIONAL BIRCH SAP WINE

1 gal. birch sap
2 lemons
1 sweet orange
1 Seville orange (if available)
1 pkg. yeast (preferably a white wine yeast, but
  failing that, 1 tsp. baker's yeast can be used)
1 lb. raisins, chopped
2¼ lbs. sugar for dry wine (2½ lbs. to 2¾ lbs.
  for medium and 3 lbs. for sweet
  — honey may be substituted for sugar)
yeast nutrient (if available)

THE GREAT CANADIAN WINE

1 gal. maple sap
2 lemons
2 oranges
30 to 32 fl. ozs. maple syrup for dry wine
33 to 36 fl. ozs. maple syrup for medium wine
38 to 42 fl. ozs. maple syrup for sweet wine
yeast and nutrient as above
These are approximate measurements as homemade maple syrup varies. Experiment. (If you do not have maple syrup to spare, use the birch sap recipe and substitute maple sap.)

Quantities listed will produce 1 gallon of wine — to increase quantities, just increase all ingredients proportionally. It is actually easier to succeed with large quantities of wine than with small, as a 5 or 10 gallon fermentation vessel will maintain a more even temperature. However, most people like to experiment with 1 or 2 gallons first to see if they like the finished product before embarking on mass production.

METHOD

The day before you start your wine, activate the yeast. If you buy a wine yeast it will probably have directions on the package. If not, or if you are trying to make do with household baking yeast, proceed as follows: Heat 1¼ cups of sap (any fruit juice may be substituted) to the boiling point. Add 2 Tbsp. of sugar, honey or maple syrup. Cool to body temperature (lukewarm) and add yeast. Leave 24 hours in a clean, thin-necked bottle or jar plugged with cotton.

The next day, peel fruit, being careful to discard as

Peter Hutchinson

much white pith as possible. Squeeze the juice from the fruit and set it aside. Boil the peel with the remaining sap for 20 minutes. Add enough water to restore to its original volume, then pour into a clean crock or new plastic garbage pail containing the sugar or honey or maple syrup and the raisins (if they are to be used). Stir to dissolve the sweetener. When the mixture has cooled to lukewarm, about 70 degrees F, add the juice squeezed from the fruit, the activated yeast and, if desired, the nutrient. Cover the crock with a secured towel or shower cap and place it in a warm spot, preferably about 60 to 75 degrees F. Stir daily. When the initial rapid fermenta-

tion has quieted down in about a week, strain into a clean glass carboy and screw on a fermentation lock. Leave for several weeks. When the wine is clear, rack it into a clean carboy and refit the fermentation lock. Be patient. Leave it until all signs of fermentation cease. If it throws a deposit, rack it again. You may want to do this several times. Bottle and try to keep it six months before sampling. A year is supposed to be better, but we have seldom managed it. It can be drunk within three months, for the desperate, but definitely improves with ageing. The filled wine bottles should be stored in a cool, dark place, on a slight angle, so that the wine just touches the cork.

Sources

SYRUP TREES
By Bruce Thompson
Walnut Press
P.O. Box 17210
Fountain Hills, Arizona 85268
164 pages—Paperback

Many Canadian cities have wine-making supply shops that are either self-contained or within large department stores. For those without access to such shops, mail-order sources, such as the following, should be able to provide any specialty items:

WINE ART
E.G. Arthurs & Sons Limited
2046 Avenue Road
Toronto, Ontario M5M 4A6

WINE-ART SALES LIMITED
3429 West Broadway
Vancouver, B.C. V6R 2B4

THE WINE WORKS
392 Waterloo Street
London, Ontario N6B 2N8

THE VINTAGE SHOP LIMITED
5766 Fraser Street
Vancouver, B.C. V5W 2Z5

The Underground Brewmaster

---

*Modern North American beer
is mostly brewed (and priced) by accountants
— but there is an alternative*

By Frank Appleton

On the grey, overcast, depressing days that are Vancouver's hallmark, I would find myself walking through the modern, efficient plant — all stainless steel vessels, sparkling tile walls and well-scrubbed floors — and I would wonder about its future and my own. I had worked in this brewery through most of the sixties and, in the beginning, no doubts ever entered my mind. As the quality control supervisor, I was part of a very small team that produced 7,500 gallons of O'Keefe beer each day.

This technologically marvelous plant with all of the newest equipment allowed the brewhouse, where the brew cycled through the mash tub, the lauter tub and the brew-kettles, to be controlled by one man — and he did little more than stand and watch the dials. Another man oversaw the fermentation cellar and another the storage cellar.

Despite the computerized brewing cycles, these were key men in maintaining a high standard of cleanliness, and in keeping foreign organisms out of the beer. I could tell from the results showing in my petri dishes back in the laboratory just how well these men were doing their jobs, and a good working relationship existed in the plant. It was a satisfying feeling, and, although it wasn't much, it seemed important to the few of us that at least we were responsible for what we made.

One such morning I was walking past the brewmaster's office when he called me in to look at a pile of new labels, information handouts and ad campaign literature on his desk.

"Want to take a look at our new product?" he asked.

I was slightly bewildered. I should surely have heard about plans for our making a new beer months ago. My pride was insulted — I should have been among the first to know — but the brewmaster looked at me with a sour smile and said, "This is the first *I* heard about it, too. We go into production next month. All the specs are here — everything. All of this done for us by the marketing department in head office. Isn't that nice of them?"

As he spoke I absent-mindedly riffled through the new material from Toronto and then came upon a particularly glowing description of the new beer. I pushed it across the desk and pointed to the signature.

"Yes, I know," the brewmaster said, shaking his head. "It's my signature. An endorsement of a beer I haven't even tasted yet."

His signature had been transferred to the ad literature to lend an air of authenticity, but he had never been consulted. In times past, the brewmaster was an all-powerful figure. This man — after 10 years' training in the art and science of brewing — now held down a job that consisted only of filling out endless forms and preparing tedious budgets for the head office in Toronto.

My own training had been as a microbiologist, but when, a few days later, I received a letter from Toronto outlining my role in bringing out the new beer, I discovered that my functions would include a mass of routine checks to make sure that the labels were

printed correctly and that they were square on the bottles. I knew that the time had come to clear my desk and head for that piece of land I had acquired in the West Kootenays. It was time to become a home brewer.

NO ACCOUNTING FOR TASTE

Before setting out to learn the art of making beer at home, it helps to know what you are leaving behind. First, of course, is the increasingly exorbitant price of commercial beers. Fully three-fifths of the purchase price goes to taxes in one form or another. Another fifth runs the brewery's advertising and marketing departments, pays distribution costs and provides profits for the stockholders. The single remaining fifth is what it costs to make the beer, including all ingredients, wages and equipment.

It doesn't take a great deal of calculating to realize that you can make beer for a lot less than you pay at the store. The beer I'm currently making costs about 10 cents per 12-ounce serving, as compared to more than 40 cents at the Brewers' Retail.

More aggravating than the cost of the stuff, to my mind, is the lack of any alternative to the blandness of present-day beers. The drive for super-efficiency has wreaked havoc among North American breweries. Every brewery has the same computerized equipment. Every brewery makes its beer from a mix of ground malt and an "adjunct" of corn meal or ground rice, which makes the product lighter in body and colour, not to mention cheaper than using all malt.

The stage has been reached where all the big breweries are making virtually the same product, with different names and labels. Accompanying this trend is a shift in power from the hands of the brewmaster to the marketing, accounting and advertising men.

The small breweries that produced the unique brands and flavours that once gave this country an international reputation have been swallowed in the past 30 years by three giants: Canadian Breweries, Molson's and Labatt's. Ninety per cent of the beer consumed in Canada is produced by these conglomerates, and, fervid TV commercials to the contrary, what is found inside their bottles is essentially the same product.

Like tasteless white bread and the universal cardboard hamburger, the new beer is produced for the tasteless common denominator. It must not offend anyone, anywhere. Corporate beer is not too heavy, not too bitter, not too alcoholic, not too malty, not too yeasty and not too gassy. In other words, corporate beer reduces every characteristic that makes beer beer.

A deluge of light lager has gradually washed away the distinctive old brands, while the differences in beers have come to be determined by new labels, carton designs and massive advertising campaigns. And, to pay the stunning cost of these promotions, the mass market breweries are always seeking ever cheaper ingredients and techniques.

So — if you want a brew that really has a taste and character and that you can afford to drink, you have to make your own. It's rewarding. It's simpler than you probably suspect. And you don't have to be a reformed O'Keefe employee to carry it off.

A BRAU FOR ALL SEASONS

The home Bräumeister can originate his own flavours and alter his recipes to match the seasons. Light lagers or *weissbier,* for the summer, malty ales and porters for the winter. Home-brewed beer reflects, in full measure, the talent and imagination of the person who makes it.

Beer is made by fermenting a sugary solution of malt extract (called wort) with yeast. Malt comes in many forms. It is barley which has been allowed to germinate slightly and is then roasted. The wort is often flavoured with hops.

After fermenting, the beer is decanted off the yeast and placed in a secondary fermentor to finish off and to clear. In a simpler method, the beer is run directly into bottles to complete the secondary fermentation.

Although this same basic procedure is used in all beer making, lagers, ales, pilsners, porters and stouts are all vastly different brews. The variations come about by changing the ingredients, the fermentation times and temperatures. For instance, lagers call for malt that is light in colour and flavour, while a heavier ale would start with a dark and heavy malt. Porters and stouts need malt that has been roasted to a dark brown to give characteristic colour and taste. (Some choose to cheat a bit and darken their brew by adding caramel.)

Lagers are fermented with a "bottom yeast" which settles to the bottom of the fermentor when spent, and which is called *Saccharomyces carlsbergensis* in deference to you-know-whom, the discoverer. Ales are fermented with the vastly different *Saccharomyces cerevisiae,* the common wine and baker's yeast.

You can buy malt extract already flavoured with hops, for convenience, or, if you want to add a distinctive touch, you can add Brambling or Fuggles hops to lagers, Kent or Golding hops to ales and stouts. The variations are endless. Fortunately, the equipment is more basic.

A plastic garbage pail, six feet of clear, three-quarter-inch plastic tubing, a wooden spoon, coloured glass bottles, caps and a capper will do the job.

The principal utility, a plastic garbage pail which can hold 15 gallons, is ideal for beer making. Whatever you use should have 50 per cent more capacity than the liquids you intend to put in, to allow for foaming. I always make 10-gallon batches and consider that any volume less than five is not worth the trouble.

Guard the pail *religiously* for this purpose only. Some reactionaries I know swear by their earthenware crocks, and they do have the advantage that the thick walls reduce quick changes in air temperature. Their big drawback is that a tiny crack in the glaze can go undetected, and the porous clay beneath is a great breeding ground for spoilage bacteria. Also, they're *heavy.*

If you decide to try cellaring or secondary fermentation before bottling, you must put the beer into a carboy with a tight airlock. Glass ones are best, for you can see what fermentation or clearing has taken place. But they are breakable and you don't want to leave a full one opposite the kitchen window: Light has a negative effect on all but the darkest beers, enhancing something called a *redox reaction,* about which all you really need to know is that the end result is a stale tasting brew.

For the same reason, the final bottles you use should be amber tinted. The beer store will sell you all the empties you need at the standard five cents per bottle, but count on having to scour out cigarette butts and strange forms of life.

If you have a choice, take the quart bottles over the small 12-ounce size, otherwise you end up dealing with a mountain of containers. Since you always lose the bottom half-inch in the bottle to the yeast sediment, you're further ahead losing it to a quart rather than a pint. Domestic champagne bottles are worthy of consideration too. They are strong, capacious and take a regular cap.

Other equipment I would want to have: a liquid thermometer for taking the temperature of your wort; a hydrometer for taking specific gravity readings that determine alcohol content and the progression of the fermentation; a gravy baster to draw samples of the wort and beer; kitchen scales for weighing out whole malt and sugar; a small funnel to help when you add sugar to your bottles and, of course, a capper. It's worthwhile paying a little more for a good capper (about 14 dollars) because many of the cheap ones break.

The techniques of the home brewer differ from those of the commercial brewery in two important respects: Breweries start with whole malt; most home brewers use malt extract, which comes in nice, convenient cans. Breweries are able, by using sophisticated equipment, to store the carbon dioxide from the first fermentation, filter all traces of yeast from the beer, then put the carbon dioxide back again. The home brewer must always have yeast present in his beer, if he is to have carbonation and a good "head." Ensuring a yeast-free, drinkable, clear product is a matter of careful storage of your bottles — and patience. But this is getting a little ahead of ourselves. First let's go through a typical preparation.

1. Make up your wort. If you are using malt extract, it is as simple as emptying the can of thick syrup into warm water.

If you are using whole malt, it first has to be ground, using a large hand coffee grinder (set to "coarse"), a grain mill (also on coarse grind) or a meat grinder with its smallest rings in. Then the ground malt is weighed and put into the specified amount of hot water. To get the greatest amount of saccharification (conversion of the starch in the malt to sugars, such as maltose, by the enzymes formed by malting) the "mash" must be held at 145 to 155 degrees F for two hours.

If malt extract is used, there is no starch to be converted, and sugar must be added as regular white sugar (sucrose). DON'T turn up your nose at adding white sugar — the yeast doesn't have the same problems metabolizing it that humans do, and it all makes alcohol. Whole malt users will now have to strain the brew, to remove the insoluble matter from the grain, and by now they are beginning to mull over the merits of using straight extract. From this point on, the wort is treated the same, no matter what starting materials were used.

2. To Boil or Not To Boil? The boiling brew-kettle is one of the symbols of the brewing art. It is also one of the more pungent-smelling of inventions, as anyone who lives close to a brewery would vouch. That smell is a mixture of the delicate aromatic ingredients of the wort being driven up the stack and lost to the outside world. I never quite understood the theory behind boiling off some of your most valued constituents. However, this is an obligatory practice in modern breweries, because in order to get the last bit of fermentables out of the spent mash left behind on the filter or lauter tub, the mash is sprayed with hot water ("sparged") and the resultant weak solution run with the rest into the brew-kettle.

This results in having too weak a wort for good beer, so the excess water is evaporated by boiling the hell out of the brew for two or three hours. You, of course, being your own brewmaster, don't have to indulge in this sort of nonsense. If you *have* started with ground malt and have spent grains to deal with, sparge them very slightly and feed them to the chickens — they'll love them and you won't have lost a thing. And if you *do* end up with a wort a little weaker than you want (check by testing with a hydrometer; specific gravity of 1.030 for a light lager, 1.045 for a heavier ale) then you can dissolve some sugar in the brew instead of boiling off excess water.

You will read elsewhere that the wort must be boiled to sterilize it and to extract the resins of the hops but, in fact, both ends are attained by temperatures well below simmer. Wort held at 160 to 180 degrees F for 30 minutes will be completely pasteurized. A full hour at that temperature will effectively remove 90 per cent of the resins of the hops. If you don't believe me and *insist* on boiling your brew just bring it to a low boil and add the hops for no more than half an hour.

Since you are not likely to find a container that can go onto the stove with 10 or even five gallons inside, don't even try. Heat as much as you can — two or three gallons will go into a standard preserving kettle — along with the malt extract and hops, then simply add the balance in hot water after the wort has been transferred to the primary fermentor.

Good fresh hops, which you are not likely to obtain in any beer supply store, should be sticky with a yellow resin that smells like the Garden of Eden and that tastes like someone hit the bitter button at the back of your tongue with a sledge hammer.

Hop oil is a volatile compound, and will waft aromatically into the air if the hops are kept unsealed and warm, making the store smell very good, but doing nothing for your beer. So don't bother buying those dried-up remnants purveyed in unlined cardboard boxes — they're not worth the money.

There are some sealed aluminum packages of imported hops available at some pretty fancy prices, but the best solution, for those who can't grow their own, is hop extract which is now appearing at some outlets.

The extract is merely added to the mix, but fresh or dried hops are wrapped in cheesecloth and allowed to float on the surface. Dunk the bag into the wort occasionally whenever you stir the brew. After the heating and after the bag of hops has cooled, wring it out before discarding.

The entire hot batch of wort, with one slight exception, is siphoned off from your kettle or pot into the primary fermentor, your familiar, *sterile*, plastic garbage pail. You remove a quart so that while the main batch cools you can busy yourself making a home for your yeast.

3. Prepare Your Yeast Starter. Adding the yeast, the only temperamental ingredient, is the most critical step in the entire operation. Yeast is a mass of living organisms, and has to be nurtured for best results.

Two tablespoons of powdered yeast dropped abruptly into 10 gallons of cooled, sugared wort will be like the first lonely French settlers dropped off at Hochelaga to do or die. Hochelaga became Montreal, but if the hostile natives get the upper hand in your wort, your brew will become vinegar. So the idea is to get a fermentation happening within a few hours, which can be done with a starter. Disregard the instructions on the packages of ale and lager yeast which say they can be added, cold turkey, to the cooled wort.

Isolate a quart of the sweet wort in a jar of at least twice that size to allow for foaming, cool to 70 or 80 degrees F and add the yeast. On this limited terrain the yeast will quickly take hold and will foam and bubble away within the hour. The population has exploded. When the starter is added to the wort (which has been cooled to 60 or 70 degrees F) it is like adding several hundred tablespoons of the original dried yeast.

4. Fermentation—Some Stirring Thoughts. Fermentation is conducted in a closed container, such as a plastic garbage can, with a removable lid so you can stir your brew. It must be carried on at an *even* temperature of 50 to 70 degrees F (lower for lagers, higher for ales). Great variations in air temperature around your fermentors will cause your yeast to "set back" or slow up its fermentation, and it may not restart again. So if your wood stove goes out at night in the winter and the temperature in your kitchen drops to 30 degrees F, don't be surprised if you get an odd-tasting batch.

Now, here's a tip you won't find in the home-brewer books: When you add the starter, stir it so energetically that you *beat in some air*, causing the wort to foam. Do this a couple of times on the first day and once on the second day. Quietly stir without foaming on the third and fourth days, and not at all on the fifth or succeeding days. (Most fermentations should take five to seven days. Check to see that there are no more bubbles coming off, and that the specific gravity has fallen to 1.000 or thereabouts. If this hasn't happened in seven days, your temperature has been too low or too changeable, or your starter wasn't powerful enough.)

Most knowledgeable home brewers react with astonishment when I tell them to beat air into the brew at the beginning of fermentation, and sputter, "But alcohol is only produced in the absence of air. And what about contaminating the brew with *acetobacter?*" (*Acetobacter* is the chief villain of the wine and beer brewer — the main organism responsible for creating vinegar, but it can work only if air is present.) The prevailing wisdom is to keep the air out — period. This is excellent advice — for any brew past the second day of fermentation. You see, *acetobacter* also needs alcohol for the production of acetic acid, and early in the fermentation there is not enough there to give it a chance. Also, the beer yeast is undergoing such a rapid growth at the beginning — if you've done everything right — there is not much chance of a foreign organism taking over.

Which brings us back to the real reason for beating air into the brew at all — it causes an extra "rush" of growth in the yeast population. Yeast *will* grow well without oxygen — in fact this is the condition necessary at mid and latter stages of fermentation, for the production of alcohol. But it grows *fastest* when there is some air present. To give it that early boost, commercial breweries blast a quantity of sterilized air into the wort as it enters the fermentors. The equivalent home-brew technique is to create a good froth with your wooden spoon on the first and second days. But remember — no such disruptive activity after that.

5. Secondary Fermentation — Carboy or Bottle?
When fermentation has ceased the beer is siphoned into a secondary fermentor, *or* directly into the bottle. In the commercial brewery, this stage is the cellaring or "lagering" of beer, and has two steps, *Ruh Storage* and *Cold Storage*. These are essentially settling, clearing and ageing stages, with a filtration between each stage, so the finished beer emerges sparkling clear and ready for the 12-pack.

With home brew, since you must get a small fermentation going in the bottle to give you your final carbonation, and this inevitably gives rise to a suspension of yeast, I don't personally see what value secondary fermentation has. True, the nice clean yeast deposit you get out of your carboy, if you do a secondary fermentation stage, can be used to seed your next batch. Too, use of a secondary fermentor will reduce the amount of yeast deposit in the bottle. But to me, these are small considerations beside the need for an extra vessel. (A secondary fermentor can't be another plastic garbage can, but must be a narrow-necked carboy-type of vessel into which you install an airlock. The liquid is just left to sit and settle, like wine.)

The other negative considerations are the need for extra cleaning, and one additional transfer of the brew, which may give rise to contamination. The only reason I can think of to use a secondary fermentor is if you are trying to produce a batch of very strong beer, with a high alcohol content. Such a fermentation may run 10 to 15 days, and there is just too much danger of contamination from the air if the brew is left in something like a plastic tub for that long. So, it should be transferred to a carboy with an airlock.

6. Bottling.
Just as you once encouraged air to mix with your wort, now you avoid it like the plague. When transferring beer from the primary or secondary fermentor to the bottles use a flexible plastic siphon — not just because it's the easiest way to do it, but because the siphon moves the brew gently without causing agitation. The hard part is to heft your crock or plastic tub onto a table or high bench without stirring up the liquid. Get someone to help and allow the beer to sit and settle for an hour or so, so

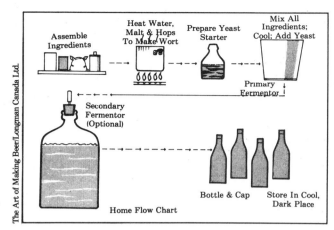

The Art of Making Beer/Longman Canada Ltd.

Assemble Ingredients · Heat Water, Malt & Hops To Make Wort · Prepare Yeast Starter · Mix All Ingredients; Cool; Add Yeast · Primary Fermentor · Secondary Fermentor (Optional) · Bottle & Cap · Store In Cool, Dark Place · Home Flow Chart

that as little sediment as possible is transferred to the bottles. You will have no trouble filling in the time by preparing your bottles.

Cleanliness is a must right through the brewing process. The simplest way to achieve it is by rinsing everything frequently with clean, cold water. If this cold water treatment had been applied to the bottles accumulated from the commercial brews you downed, as they were emptied, the following step would be unnecessary. If not then you will now need a strong cleaning agent, such as Javex which contains chlorine, bottle brushes and scalding hot water to rid your bottles of the mouldy deposits on the bottom and to eliminate all traces of microbiotic life. Any traces of chlorine left in the bottles will ruin your beer so the bottles must be thoroughly rinsed.

It's to be hoped that the weight lifter you commandeered into helping lift the crock hasn't escaped, because he can now be given an easier job. As you fill the bottles (all the while licking your lips and watching that wonderful amber liquid rise in each bottle), your companion takes them out of your hands, slips a cap on the head and crimps it tightly with the capper. (Be sure to fill them right up, to within an inch of the top.)

7. Ageing.
All you need now is patience and a cool, dark place, preferably with a temperature of 40 to 45 degrees F. If it's colder than that, the secondary fermentation you need to produce carbon dioxide won't happen. If warmer, the yeast will stay in suspension and the beer will refuse to clear. How long do you leave it? Well, you *can* drink week-old beer, if you're a great admirer of that yeasty flavour. Two weeks minimum is my rule of thumb. Four weeks is even better, but the slight improvement thereafter is not really worth waiting for. Beer is not like wine, which can steadily improve over months and even years. Laboratory tests show beer is at its optimum when aged for six to eight weeks.

FINESSE
A word about water. Beer is 95 per cent water. If your water has an odd taste, so will your beer. The lighter the beer, the more noticeable this will be. Good, clean, aerated water makes good beer. Fortunately, most places in Canada have excellent water. In cities, chlorinated water supplies are often the rule. Simple boiling of the water will drive this off. If you are in the country and have a choice between well water and water from a mountain stream,

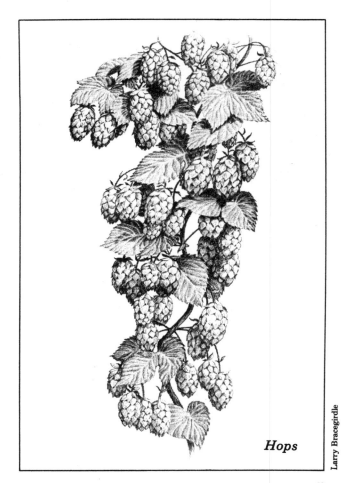

Hops

Larry Bracegirdle

tion. Oxalic acid in quantity produces gout. But unless you're drinking a gallon of brew a day, don't worry. Potassium metabisulphite or KMS is a nasty, sulphitic-smelling compound (Campden tablets are the same thing) which you'll wonder about adding to your prize brew. And rightly so. KMS is an anti-oxidant and antibacterial agent which should not be needed at all if you transfer your beer quietly through a siphon (never *pour* it) and have kept your standards of cleanliness high. Sodium alginate and similar substances are called "heading compounds," and are added strictly to give a good head on the finished product. Keeping your containers clean and detergent-free will eliminate your need for this. Gelatin is a "fining agent" used to clear stubbornly cloudy beer. It won't do anything that patience won't do. If your beer remains cloudy after months in the bottle, probably your bottle-storage area is too warm. Or your beer wasn't completely fermented when bottled.

If you've done things correctly, however, the yeast will drop to the bottom of the bottle leaving a completely clear liquid. That being the case, pop the cap and carefully decant the beer into a pitcher or mug and — *Ein Prosit!*

Here's wishing you and your brews lots of parched, appreciative throats. Once you've found out how easy it is, you won't be short of friends, and you'll find it hard to down a pint of that factory-made ferment. Maybe you'll be one of the few innovators who goes on to bigger and better brews. Which reminds me, I just discovered a dandy 40-gallon fermentor, cost: absolutely nothing. It is a commercial fibre-board drum with a heavy plastic liner such as is used to ship many food additives. In fact these are the very drums big breweries receive alginate and KMS in. They throw them out all the time. Why don't you try the side door at your local Big Three brewery? Just don't tell them what you want it for — or who sent you.

LAZY MAN'S BREW

2 - 2 lb. cans of hop-flavoured malt extract (light or dark to choice)
5 lbs. white sugar
4 Tbsp. baker's yeast
10 gals. hot water

Have your tub marked inside at 10 gallons. Run in the hot water. (I usually run mine directly from the hot water tank (150 degrees F) through the shower-head. This aerates the water nicely and makes it convenient to rinse out the extract cans.) Mix in the extract and the sugar. When completely dissolved, fill the empty extract cans half-full with wort, cool to 70 to 80 degrees and add your yeast to the cans. While this starter is working, the tub of wort is cooling. When it gets down to 70 to 80 degrees too, the two cans of starter will be bubbling away. Stir the starter in vigorously and ferment for 6 to 7 days at 60 degrees. Bottle and age for a month.

LIGHT LAGER

2 - 2 lb. cans of light malt extract
6 lbs. white sugar

choose the latter. If the choice is between the well and a creek that meanders through farmland, use the well. I've heard some home brewers make a big fuss about rain water as the *sine qua non* of their operation, but in my experience, the pure, super-aerated state of rain water is often diminished by having it sit for weeks in a slimy water butt.

"*Hopfen, Wasser und Malz, Gott erhalt,*" goes the old German proverb. (Hops, water and malt are maintained by God.) Well they left out the yeast, but apart from that, the proverb covers all you need to make fine beer. Now in all modern books on home brewing, you will find also listed in the recipes citric acid, ascorbic acid, gelatin, gypsum, potassium metabisulphite, sodium alginate and other compounds. If you are bewildered by this, take note that *none* of these things is necessary for the production of a perfectly good brew. If one of the reasons you are making your own beer is because you don't like to drink mass-produced, "chemical" beer, then also note that the chemicals used by the big breweries are these same things. None of these compounds is considered toxic, but the point is that none is really essential.

Citric and ascorbic acids are used to increase the acidity of the wort, so it is at a suitable level for good yeast growth. If you suspect your water is alkaline, buy a pH test kit and check the pH of your wort. If it is between four and six you're fine. If it is higher, you can lower it with a few drops of lemon juice. Gypsum is used to artificially "harden" the brewing water. The excess of calcium then acts to neutralize the small amount of oxalic acid produced in fermenta-

4 oz. Hallertauer hops (if you can get them, or Bram-
ling or Fuggles if you can't)
4 Tbsp. lager yeast
10 gals. hot water

Into a metal container, run your water and mix in
the extract and sugar. Take some of the sweet wort
and make the starter, as in Lazy Man's Brew. Heat
the wort to simmering point and put in the hops,
wrapped in cheesecloth. Stir for an hour. Run the
brew to your fermentor and add the starter when
cool. Ferment for 7 days at 55 degrees F. Run to
secondary fermentor and store for 2 weeks at 45
degrees before bottling.

MEDIUM ALE

4 lbs. whole malt
1 lb. corn meal
4 lbs. brown sugar
3 oz. Kent or Golding hops
2 Tbsp. baker's yeast
5 gals. water

Grind the malt. Heat 2 gallons of the water to 150
degrees F in an over-large container and add the
ground malt and corn. Hold at 150 degrees for 3
hours, stirring often — an electric blanket will stabilize the temperature. Allow to cool overnight.
Strain the wort into a canning kettle adding as much
water as possible leaving several inches for foaming.
Add the sugar while the water heats until simmer-

ing. After half an hour remove a quart of the wort,
cool to 70 to 80 degrees and add the yeast. Meanwhile add hops to the kettle, simmer for an hour.
Siphon to the fermentor and add the leftover water,
if any. When the wort cools to 70 degrees add the
starter solution which will have foamed up in the
meantime. Ferment for 9 to 10 days or to a specific
gravity of 1.010. Bottle and allow to age 1 month.

OATMEAL STOUT

1 lb. whole malt
½ lb. roasted barley or black malt
½ lb. oatmeal
4 lbs. brown sugar
2 oz. Kent or Golding hops
2 Tbsp. baker's yeast
5 gals. water

Grind the malt and prepare the mash as for ale,
above, adding both malts, the oatmeal and as much
water as possible to the brew-kettle. Add the sugar
and hops and simmer for 40 minutes. Remove the
wort to the primary fermentor adding the balance of
water. While the wort cools prepare the yeast starter. When it foams add the starter to the wort. Colour-
ing can be adjusted at this time by adding one or
more teaspoons of caramel which darkens the beer.
Start light and experiment. You can add more in the
next batch. Ferment for 10 days or to a gravity of
1.010.

Green Cuisine

Home-grown or gathered in the wild, watercress is nature's delectable spring tonic

By Catharine Reed

There is no shortage of North American woodsmen who believe — strongly enough to bet their Sierra Club drinking cups — that watercress is a native plant. Growing wild in every province and state, its lush profusion of green foliage carpets the shores of shallow streams and boggy places from inner city parks to alpine meadows.

Actually one of the more successful feral plants introduced to this continent, watercress is believed to have arrived here with the early explorers — who knew it to be a cure for scurvy — and settlers who brought cress to be cultivated in their gardens or the nearest bit of fresh water. But it was so successful in escaping, that wild food stalker Euell Gibbons reported having collected untamed watercress throughout the continent as far north as Ketchikan, Alaska and even from stream sides in Hawaii. Its distribution to remote areas of Canada has been aided and abetted — sometimes unwittingly — by birds, animals, prospectors and trappers. Coming upon a cress-lined stream in a wilderness area can lead to speculation about its origins: Was it brought there on the muddy hoof of a deer, discarded by some mountain man who stopped for lunch or planted by a watercress-loving wanderer?

The peppery taste of *Nasturtium officinale* has been a favourite of man for at least 5,000 years. Watercress was fed to the children of ancient Persia to improve their growth (not a bad choice as the leaves are vitamin-rich and high in calcium). The plant is believed to have originated in Asia Minor or the Mediterranean and the Romans used it as a salad green. The Greeks, and others, treasured it as an herb, using it to treat, among other things, anemia, nervousness, rheumatism and insanity. Greek warriors ate watercress with bread in prodigious portions in the belief that it made them strong, decisive and quick-witted.

Cooks today know it as a refreshing addition to soups, salads, omelettes and other dishes — a stimulant for the appetite and a clean-tasting green that seems, like parsley, capable of aiding digestion.

I happen to be blessed with a very prolific patch of cress in a nearby creek and have come to rely on it as a near-constant source of greens for the kitchen. Usually one must range farther afield to locate a supply of watercress, and the places to look are along shallow streams, ponds, drainage ditches and road culverts.

Watercress prefers cool, running water, but it will grow in polluted streams. If there is any doubt as to the source of the water, the cress should be washed and soaked for 30 minutes in a pot with clean water and a water-purifying (Halazone) tablet. Steaming or boiling will also destroy any bacterial contaminants. You should, however, take no chances with watercress which may have come in contact with chemical wastes, as these can accumulate in the plant tissues.

Cress, which is a member of the mustard or Cruciferae family (including turnips and cabbage), is easily recognized by its hollow stems which float, and glossy vivid green leaves, with the terminal leaf being the largest (up to about an inch across) on a stem which may be six inches long. The plants grow white flowers and show white rootlets springing from nodes along the stems (avoid the root-covered lower end of the stem, as it is bitter). Cress can be collected throughout the year, except of course when the ground is frozen or covered by snow.

CULTIVATION

Cress is easily established at the edges of bodies of fresh water, either by tucking bunches of harvested stems into the mud or by scattering the small seeds in likely places. (The downstream side of a pond dam near the water outflow is an excellent spot.) Many seed houses offer watercress seed in packets and these can be sown in flower pots, hydroponic units, damp spots in a greenhouse or shady, wet areas of a garden or yard. (Be sure not to order garden cress, which is not an aquatic plant and has a totally different appearance and taste.)

Watercress prefers running water, but it will grow to harvestable size in about 50 days when kept moist in good garden soil. The plants thrive on limestone soils, and if an artificial growing medium is being created, mix good garden soil with an equal portion of peat or wood humus and a handful of ground limestone.

Planted in pots or non-aquatic sites, watercress

will produce a crop, but will not become a permanent source of greens, as will a planting in a nearby stream or pond.

My own cress supply is so abundant that I've come up with a repertoire of recipes — some variations of classic watercress dishes, some improvised — which anyone in need of a tangy, unusual spring tonic may find of interest.

CHINESE WATERCRESS

Watercress is a favourite ingredient for cooks in China, and one simple dish involves stir-frying a pound of cress, upper stems and all, in a pan with 2 tablespoons of oil, and 1 tablespoon of grated ginger root.

Three to 4 minutes of stir-frying will wilt the leaves and coat them with oil, after which they are removed from the heat, tossed with soy sauce and served immediately.

GREEK WATERCRESS SALAD

6 handsful watercress, chopped
1 seeded and sliced cucumber
3 to 4 oz. crumbled feta cheese
Dressing:
(Mix and let stand 1 hour in the refrigerator)
½ cup olive oil
2 Tbsp. wine vinegar
juice of ½ lemon
1 Tbsp. fresh mint leaves, finely chopped
1 Tbsp. fresh oregano (or ¼ tsp. dried)
1 tsp. honey or sugar
pinch of cinnamon
salt
freshly ground pepper

WATERCRESS DRESSING

This dressing is delicious on green salads, tomato salads, and on seafood, such as cold salmon, shrimp or crab.
Combine:
½ cup olive oil or salad oil
juice of 2 limes (or 1 lemon)
1 Tbsp. fresh tarragon (or ¼ tsp. dried)
1 tsp. salt
freshly ground black pepper
3 handsful watercress, finely chopped
Chill well before using.

SALAD DELUXE

6 handsful watercress, chopped
½ lb. nitrite-free bacon, fried and crumbled
2 cups mushrooms, either raw or sauteed in butter
½ cup pine nuts
Dressing:
(Mix and let stand for 1 hour in the refrigerator)
½ cup olive or salad oil
2 Tbsp. wine vinegar
1 clove garlic, crushed
1 tsp. honey or sugar
salt
freshly ground pepper
pinch of dry mustard and nutmeg

Note: If watercress is bitter, which is sometimes the case with larger leaves or late in the season, add more honey or sugar to the dressing, and it will completely take away the bitterness.

WATERCRESS CHINESE SALAD

4 handsful watercress, chopped
1 cup bean sprouts
8 canned water chestnuts, sliced thinly
Dressing:
(Mix and let stand 1 hour in the refrigerator)
2 tsp. soy sauce
2 tsp. sesame seed oil
1 tsp. honey
salt
few drops of lemon juice

CREAM OF WATERCRESS SOUP

Simmer 10 minutes:
6 handsful chopped watercress
4 cups chicken stock
Purée in blender; set aside.
Melt 3 Tbsp. butter; add 2 Tbsp. flour and cook 5 minutes. Add a little of the hot soup; stir. Add this mixture to the rest of the hot soup and bring to a boil. Reduce heat and add:
1 to 2 cups of cream
¼ tsp. nutmeg
pinch of paprika
freshly ground pepper
salt

CLEAR SOUP

Heat 5 cups chicken stock. Add 2 cups watercress, finely chopped. Add salt and pepper and a little paprika. Cook about 5 minutes. (Overcooking causes watercress to lose its colour.)

CHINESE CLEAR SOUP

To 5 cups cold water, add 2 cups watercress, finely chopped. When water boils, add ¾ lb. finely sliced pork or beef tenderloin. Let boil 5 minutes. Add salt, pepper, 3 slices of fresh ginger and simmer 5 minutes more.

CREAMED WATERCRESS

Melt 3 Tbsp. butter. Add ¼ cup finely chopped onion. Cook 10 minutes. Add 2 cups watercress, finely chopped. Cook 3 minutes. Sprinkle with 1 Tbsp. flour; stir. Add ½ cup cream; cook 5 minutes. Season with salt, pepper, nutmeg and a pinch of sugar. Garnish with chopped sautéed almonds or roasted sesame seeds.

SANDWICHES

Watercress enlivens almost any sandwich and is especially good with avocados, sprouts, tomatoes, cream cheese and mayonnaise. Try a sprig with smoked salmon, or smoked salmon and cream cheese.

Index

Personal
Subscription
Order Form

Please start a *Harrowsmith* subscription in my name.

☐ One year (8 issues) for $12.00 ☐ Payment enclosed.
☐ Two years (16 issues) for $22.00 ☐ Please bill me.

Name

Street/Rural Route

Town

Province/State   Postal Code

Payment must be made in Canadian or U.S. funds. All subscriptions outside North America, $16.00 per year Surface Mail; $28.00 per year Air Mail.

Gift Subscription
Order Form

Please enter a Gift Subscription in the name of the person listed below.

☐ One year (8 issues) for $12.00 ☐ Payment enclosed.
☐ Two years (16 issues) for $22.00 ☐ Please bill me.

Gift Name

Street/Rural Route

Town

Province/State   Postal Code

Your Name

Street/Rural Route

Town

Province/State   Postal Code

A tasteful gift card will be sent to you for personalization and forwarding to the gift subscription recipient. Should the recipient of this gift already be a *Harrowsmith* subscriber, his or her subscription will be extended by the number of issues ordered.

Gift Subscription
Order Form

Please enter a Gift Subscription in the name of the person listed below.

☐ One year (8 issues) for $12.00 ☐ Payment enclosed.
☐ Two years (16 issues) for $22.00 ☐ Please bill me.

Gift Name

Street/Rural Route

Town

Province/State   Postal Code

Your Name

Street/Rural Route

Town

Province/State   Postal Code

A tasteful gift card will be sent to you for personalization and forwarding to the gift subscription recipient. Should the recipient of this gift already be a *Harrowsmith* subscriber, his or her subscription will be extended by the number of issues ordered.

BUSINESS REPLY MAIL
No postage stamp necessary
if mailed in Canada

POSTAGE WILL BE PAID BY

MAGAZINE
CAMDEN EAST, ONTARIO
CANADA K0K 1J0

BUSINESS REPLY MAIL
No postage stamp necessary
if mailed in Canada

POSTAGE WILL BE PAID BY

MAGAZINE
CAMDEN EAST, ONTARIO
CANADA K0K 1J0

BUSINESS REPLY MAIL
No postage stamp necessary
if mailed in Canada

POSTAGE WILL BE PAID BY

MAGAZINE
CAMDEN EAST, ONTARIO
CANADA K0K 1J0